SECOND EDITION

BLACK HISTORY

MONTH

RESOURCE

BOOK

SECOND EDITION

BLACK HISTORY

MONTH
RESOURCE
BOOK

MARY ELLEN SNODGRASS, EDITOR

Foreword by RITA C. ORGAN

Curator of Exhibitions at the
Museum of African-American History

GALE

DETROIT • NEW YORK • LONDON

Mary Ellen Snodgrass, *Editor*

Gale Research Inc. Staff

Melissa Walsh Doig, *Editor*
Dawn R. Barry, Ashyia Henderson, *Associate Editors*
Catherine Donaldson, Allison McClintic Marion, Rebecca Parks, *Assistant Editors*
Linda S. Hubbard, *Managing Editor*

Deborah Milliken, *Production Assistant*
Mary Beth Trimper, *Production Director*
Evi Seoud, *Assistant Production Manager*

Cynthia Baldwin, *Product Design Manager*
Barbara Yarrow, *Graphic Services Manager*

Theresa Rocklin, *Manager, Technical Support Services*
Jeffrey Muhr, *Technical Support*

ISBN 0-7876-1775-X
Printed in the United States of America

Library of Congress Cataloging-in-Publication Data

Black history month resource book / Mary Ellen Snodgrass, editor —
    2nd ed. / foreword by Rita C. Organ.
        p.   cm.
    Includes bibliographical references and index.
    ISBN 0-7876-1775-X (alk. paper)
      1. Afro-Americans—Study and teaching—Activity programs.
I. Snodgrass, Mary Ellen.
E184.7.B53   1998
973'.0496073'007—dc21   98-4380
[B]   CIP

To the civic leaders, educators, and librarians
who teach us the importance of black heritage

Contents

Business and Advertising

Cooking and Nutrition

Dance

Genealogy

Geography

History

Journalism

Language

Literature

Math

Music

Religion and Ethics

Science

Sewing and Fashion

Sociology

Speech, Debate, & Drama

A Mosaic of Culture

By Rita C. Organ
Curator of Exhibitions at the Museum of African-American History in Detroit, Michigan

 African Americans—one of the larger pieces of the mosaic.

It brings me great pleasure to author the foreword to the second edition of the *Black History Month Resource Book*. This resource has contributed significantly to the programming and school outreach I have conducted in the last several years. It also provides information for teachers so they can offer a more comprehensive view of American History to their students.

In the museum profession, we are afforded the opportunity to educate and entertain our visitors in an informal learning environment. Much of what we do is provide exhibits and programs which can supplement curriculum for teachers. Over thirty years ago, at the advent of the African American Museums Movement, I was just a child growing up in Omaha, Nebraska. Someone whom I have admired from afar was a trailblazer and champion for increasing education and knowledge about African Americans. We share a hometown and a passion for spreading this erudition. Bertha Calloway, Director of the Great Plains Black Museum, noted in the foreword of this book's previous edition the commonality in the lack of education being taught in the Denver and Omaha school systems. As a product of the latter environment, I agree with her. In my schooling, I do not recall teachings by, for, or about African American contributions to this society outside the mention and minimal analysis of slavery, emancipation, and the Civil Rights Movement. It was not until my senior year of high school that I was able to define for myself a desire to seek out more so I could stand on solid ground knowing who I am as an African American and from where my ancestors came.

Subsequently, I have resided in cities with significant African American populations, studied African American heritage and the heritage of my regional surroundings, and held positions in my field designed to uplift African Americans. Life has compelled me to take advantage of the history and folklore of the areas in which I have lived—the politics of Oakland, Berkeley, and Washington, D.C., the Southern and sometimes Northern ways and lore of Louisville and Indianapolis, and Michigan's contributions to the Underground Railroad and the automotive industry. This coast-to-coast exposure confirms that African Americans are diverse culturally, spiritually, and politically and that there is no one African American voice. Our common bond is, however, the enslavement of our people, our fellowship, and our community beliefs.

In teaching African American history in the schools, it is critical not to fall into a unilateral approach to instruction. Educating about African American history requires thought and examination of the subject matter. I challenge teachers to reveal the obscure person, invention, event, or movement in addition to teaching about the more famous Dr. Martin Luther King, Jr., Harriet Tubman, and Malcolm X. Who people are, where they live, and what they eat or wear are important factors in a culture's existence. In an examination of why they eat certain foods or wear particular items, we may find a direct relation to the crops they are able to grow or the climate in which they live.

Information on Africa is the foundation for a good beginning. Acknowledge Africa, its ancient origins, and African American connections to a culturally and geographically diverse continent which has made significant contributions to the world. For according to Jack E. White, "Africa is not so much a lost continent as an imagined one." African American history did not begin with slavery, and there is a vast richness of African heritage just waiting to be discovered by young minds. The cinematic interpretation of the *Amistad* Revolt has helped in revitalizing the many truths about African heritage and has provided youngsters with a means of looking at slavery through a different set of lenses.

The biggest challenge is inclusiveness. Featuring isolated units on cultural groups during certain months out of the year is good because it forces recognition. In time, however, it should become second nature to include African American and other cultural histories throughout the fabric of what is taught. This kind of approach builds self-esteem and worth among students as opposed to being acknowledged or validated once a year and forgotten thereafter. It allows students to view each other on equal grounds, instead of imposing the one-time-a-year rule. Many school systems have incorporated African American history into their existing American history courses. African American history is a valid subject for research and discussion inside of classrooms and out. Today's educators must ensure that regular courses in American history continue to include problems of racism and African American contributions to America.

It is important to present material that is fresh. The obscure can assist in finding hidden dimensions to our nation's history. Additional learning materials like video and audio tapes, CD-ROMs, and maps are great ways to enhance the subject matter and also appeal to different learning styles as opposed to just emphasizing reading and writing during Black History Month. Encourage students to seek out alternative ways to self-educate. Local programs, educational television, and museums offer many opportunities for self-education. Activities can include classroom and hallway displays created by the students, guest speakers, field trips to museums and historical societies, auditorium and classroom programs, dramatic readings, competitions, and yes, even quizzes!

According to historian Darlene Clark Hine, there are three challenges we face in full integration of African American subject matter into American history: treatment of African Americans outside of the topics of enslavement and civil rights, opportunities for those youngsters who will be the next generation of scholars and professors, and lastly, innovative and creative ways of disseminating the information. As educators, it is our responsibility to foster a relationship between scholarly and non-scholarly approaches as well as to encourage life-learning from our surroundings and those important figures in our own family histories.

Delve deeper into this resource book and others to find a broader, more integrated approach to teaching African American history. There are so many disciplines to which African Americans have made contributions and equally as many reasons to bring to light obscure stories deserving of acknowledgment. Search for the little known facts about African American history in categories which may have been overlooked in the past! The *Black History Month Resource Book* will provide materials and ideas which will encourage teachers, engage young people, and tap into a reservoir of curiosity to kindle imagination.

For hundreds of years African American talents have been neither encouraged nor recognized by professional or artistic institutions. It is still difficult for artists to gain recognition, and in light of budget cuts in this area, fostering talent is equally difficult. However, young people need encouragement. Art history can be incorporated into instruction via other subject matter. For example, when teaching about the enslavement, consider Dave the slave who was a prolific potter in South Carolina during the ante-bellum period. He wrote rhyming couplets on his vessels during a time when it was illegal for slaves to read or write. Aviation is another area that fascinates most youngsters. For this, the achievements of Bessie Coleman, the first black woman to receive a pilot's license and become a circus stunt pilot, are notable.

African Americans have served in the military since the Civil War—in segregated units until the 1950s when units were desegregated. There are some outstanding military figures in African American history, those who served and were highly decorated and those who have fallen. Crispus Attucks was the first black to die in the American Revolution. "Chappie" James was recognized as a flying ace while a Tuskegee Airman, and in 1975 was the highest ranking military officer and the first African American four-star general. The highest military honor given is the Congressional Medal of Honor, instituted during the Civil War. Approximately 46 black servicemen received this honor. Sergeant William H. Carney was the first to receive the medal in 1863 during the Battle of Fort Wagner.

There is an African proverb which says, "Come into my home, sit at my table; then you will know me." African American cooking is largely Southern in origin and is influenced by methods and foodstuffs from the African continent. There is something special about African American cooking—something called "soul", a distinctive food category on its own. There are canning and bottling procedures common to older African American women and preparing and seasoning of foods that have been passed through the generations. The sharing of a meal is an important social occasion in many cultures. Traditionally, certain etiquette is observed. Eating only occurs by using the right hand, elders eat first and the choicest morsels were reserved for guests or important people. Students might enjoy investigating the customs surrounding eating both in African American culture and their own, trying to learn the origin and meaning of particular habits. A beautiful way to build solidarity and respect among young people for each other is to share a meal, for it is also said in Africa, "These are my friends; we have eaten together."

What about the oral tradition and storytelling techniques indigenous to African Americans? This is one of my favorite areas of examination. For African Americans, stories are the artifacts of our lives. The oral tradition is the means by which we have passed down our history and heritage via stories through the generations. It is important to help students of all backgrounds understand and appreciate the role of storytelling in the African American community as well as in their own. Stories will encourage students to identify themes and lessons in their lives and promote positive traits and behaviors. In Africa, the griot is the keeper of the history of the village. During the enslavement, the preacher took on that role, sharing history and biblical verses with the slaves. In contemporary times, grandmothers are largely keepers of the culture. There is nothing like sitting on the "stoop" while grandmothers and aunts spin a couple of good yarns. Storytelling is a universal concept that can appeal to all students.

Instead of viewing America as a "melting pot," I prefer to see it as a mosaic. In a mosaic, the pieces are different shapes, colors, and sizes. African Americans represent one of the larger pieces to the mosaic, comprising the largest ethnic minority in America with a rich, significant history that is constantly evolving. The *Black History Month Resource Book* will aid you in revealing the legacy, contributions, and gifts by African Americans to the world. The scholarship in this guide will allow teachers to provide accuracy and meaning to the achievements of African Americans and to help students stretch beyond the normal limits of instruction.

Preface

In the five years since the publication of *Black History Month Resource Book,* a nationwide emphasis on the contributions of all humankind has redirected the American sense of self-worth. For the good of all, schools, libraries, civic organizations, communities, churches, and the media are acknowledging and celebrating black achievements—from films and books about Joseph Cinqué and his fellow African mutineers aboard the *Amistad* to the inclusion of stories of Anansi the trickster and the *Epic of Sundiata* to world literature and the joyous singing of "N'Kosi sikelel' i Afrika," South Africa's energetic, uplifting national anthem. To accommodate the explosion of these and other topics and materials, the month dedicated to honoring black presence has expanded into a serious year-round study of all strands, forming a complex national and world history. In anticipation of continued advancement in human relations, the second edition of this resource book challenges users to broaden their awareness of the importance of African, Caribbean, and African American culture to daily life.

Despite a growing egalitarian spirit, there is no reason to retire into self-congratulation; racism is still a viable force. Fueled by ignorance, examples of bigotry crop up daily. Against heady strides toward a united citizenry, pockets of elitism, extremism, and violence continue to limit opportunity and threaten local harmony. The antidote to snobbery, exclusion, denigration, name-calling, bomb threats, church burnings, and more insidious forms of hate crime is a generous outpouring of understanding and acceptance. Above all, educators, librarians, civic and religious leaders, and news gatherers must remind themselves that there is no justification for complacency. For ministers and rabbis, church school and classroom teachers, mayors, museum directors, docents, retirement home program leaders, music and historical societies, book clubs, and scout leaders, the challenge to improve humanistic knowledge and awareness is ongoing.

Content

The second edition of *Black History Month Resource Book* addresses the future concerns and needs of an ever-changing society. The text contains 390 activities and features 57 new entries along with updated source lists and indexes. The body consists of 22 chapters covering varied interests: art, architecture, and photography; arts and crafts; biography; business and advertising; cooking and nutrition; dance; genealogy; geography; history; journalism; language; literature; math; music; religion and ethics; science; sewing and fashion; sociology; speech, debate, and drama; sports; storytelling; and writing. Under these headings appear suggestions and models for menus, musical compositions, personal grooming, maps, games, nature lore, displays, contests, bulletin boards and web sites, culture fairs, and individualized reading and study. Each entry contains a descriptive heading and the name of the originator if the concept came from an outside source. The format lists specific age/grade levels or audiences, such as classes, clubs, or gatherings that might benefit most from the activities. A general description of each topic precedes a detailed procedure, budget, and source list. For maximum benefit to organizers, I have included alternative applications that suit the material to specific needs.

To assist the reader in locating items most appropriate to a particular group, *Black History Month Resource Book* concludes with four indexes: the first lists entries in alphabetical order with page numbers; the second lists age/grade level; the third addresses budgets with costs ranging from under $25 to more than $100; the fourth is a general subject index. Appended to the text is a list of resources, including anthologies, current books, electronic publications, films and videos, internet sources, miscellaneous sources, periodicals, philanthropic foundations and charities, publishers, resource centers, and video distributors that I have used in compiling this work.

Acknowledgments

The researching of myriad details for *Black History Month Resource Book* sent me to a number of reference librarians, advisers, and suppliers. I am most grateful to Mark Schumacher, reference librarian of the Jackson Clinton Library at the University of North Carolina-Greensboro; Corki Miller and Beth Bradshaw at the Elbert Ivey Library in Hickory, North Carolina; Lynne Bolick Reid and Wanda Rozzelle at the Catawba County Library in Newton, North Carolina; Burl McCuiston at the Lenoir-Rhyne College Library in Hickory, North Carolina; ballet master Louis Nunnery; Rich Haunton, manager of Waldenbooks; and my sister, Frances Hilton, owner of Chapter One Books. For daily sanity, I thank my secretary, Andrea Pittman, who is never dismayed by office chaos.

I am particularly indebted to Chris Nasso, Vice President, New Markets, at Gale Research; Linda Hubbard, managing editor; Melissa Walsh Doig, editor; Dawn Barry, associate editor, Marco Di Vita, typesetter. Just as books require the cooperative effort of many people, race relations require some muscle and grunt work. I commend all who put the second edition of *Black History Month Resource Book* on paper and into the hands of the reader. There is much to learn. On with the job!

M. E. S.
December 1, 1997

Art, Architecture, and Photography

LIVE | **African American Plaza**

Age/Grade Level or Audience: Civic groups.

Description: Plan an African American commemorative plaza.

Procedure: Locate community planners, architects, sculptors, landscapers, and artists who can coordinate plans for a local plaza, sculpture garden, park, welcome sign, mural, geodesic dome, or boulevard dedicated to the accomplishments of African Americans.

Budget: $100 or above

Sources:
A field trip to centers of African American pride, such as New Orleans, Detroit, Charleston, Harlem, Atlanta, Louisville, Watts, Africatown in Montgomery, or other Afrocentric areas might stimulate ideas for a local tribute to black contributions.
"African American Civil War Memorial," http//www.npca.com/div/aacw.html.
Cantor, George, *Historic Landmarks of Black America*, Gale, 1991.
Discovering Multicultural America (database), Galenet, 1997.

Alternative Applications: Set aside a section of a local museum or civic hall to honor the accomplishments of black citizens. Consider the following suggestions:

- ♦ Collect local paintings, documents, maps, photographs, sculpture, basketry, masks, and framed awards to arrange in a display.
- ♦ Offer videotapes of singing groups, theatrical organizations, storytellers, dance troupes, and other performers.

♦ Display handicrafts, for example: stained glass, ironwork, basketry, needle-work, homemade dolls, carvings, taxidermy, and publications, such as recipe collections, chapbooks, and poetry albums. Provide plaques to explain the role of each in community life.

♦ Honor black veterans of all wars by listing names, dates of service, and awards.

♦ Stress the accomplishment of youth groups, such as the Junior Police, Big Brothers, Big Sisters, Scouts, and 4-H clubs.

African American Sculpture

Age/Grade Level or Audience: High school or college art class; civic center or museum display, art league.

Description: Study of the work of Ed Hamilton, Cincinnati-born sculptor.

Procedure: Present the artistic works of Ed Hamilton on slides, magazine pictures, photographs, or posters. Discuss his most famous works *Joe Louis, Booker T. Washington, Bush Warrior, Sun Goddess, Juju Man, Confinement Emerging, In Memory of Joseph Cinque,* and *Nile Mother.* Invite volunteers to present historical background in the form of handouts, brochures, oral commentary, or overhead projection.

Budget: $50-$75

Sources:
"African American Civil War Memorial," http//www.npca.com/div/aacw.html.
"Diaspora Art," http//www.diaspora.com/art.html.
Naylor, Colin, ed., *Contemporary Artists*, 4th edition, St. James Press, 1996.
Mabunda, L. Mpho, ed., *The African American Almanac*, 7th edition, Gale, 1997.
Saccardi, Marianne, *Art in Story Teaching Art History to Elementary School Children*, Linnet Books, 1997.
St. James Guide to Black Artists, Gale, 1997.
"University of Texas at Austin Center for African and African American Studies," http//www.utexas.edu/depts/caaas/.
Willis, Judy Marie, "Ed Hamilton Molding History," *Upscale*, June/July 1992, 54-55.

Alternative Applications: Invite art students to emulate Hamilton's search for an understanding of African influences by molding models of significant figures from black history or by sketching designs for memorials, monuments, coins, bas-reliefs, or plaques. Encourage the inclusion of persons of both sexes and all disciplines, such as Shaka Khan, Sheba, Mae Jemison, Charles Drew, Mari Evans, York,

Pearl Bailey, Toussaint L'Ouverture, Nikki Giovanni, Lionel Hampton, Tiger Woods, Morgan Freeman, Zora Neale Hurston, Matthew Henson, or Judith Jamison.

African Archeology

Age/Grade Level or Audience: Middle school or high school history classes.

Description: Create a time line of events from ancient African cultures.

Procedure: Introduce early African civilizations and have groups of students gather facts about such African achievements and civilizations as these:

Abu Simbel	Axumites	Bachwezi
Benin	Berbers	Carthage
Changamire	Cheops' pyramid	Darfur
Ewe	Great Zimbabwe	Kanem-Bornu
Kilwa	Kongo	Kush
Library of Alexandria	Lozi	Luba
Lunda	Mali	Monomotapa
Nok	Oyo	Sheba
Songhay	Sphinx of Gizeh	Wadai

Place their findings chronologically alongside these worldwide artistic and architectural accomplishments:

Anasazi pueblos	Angkor Wat	Appian Way
Caernarvon	Camelot	Chichen Itza
Colossus of Rhodes	Easter Island	Eiffel Tower
Great Buddha	Great Wall of China	Hanging Gardens, Babylon
American Indian mounds	Leptis Magna	Mount Rushmore
Nintoku mounds	Notre Dame Cathedral	Olduvai Gorge
Palace of Knossos	Parthenon	Point Hope, Alaska
Roman Colosseum	Rosetta Stone	Sancta Sophia
Stonehenge	Suez Canal	Taj Mahal
Temple at Jerusalem	Tintagel	Troy
Washington Monument	World Trade Center	

Budget: Under $25

Sources:
"African Diaspora," http://www.pitt.edu/~cedst10/.

"African Documents," http//'www.halcyon.com/FWDP/africa.html.

"Africa Online," http//africaonline.com.

Elleh, Nnamdi, *African Architecture Evolution and Transformation*, McGraw-Hill, 1996.

Gaines, Ernest J., *Timetables of History*, Random House, 1996.

Harley, Sharon, *Timetables of African-American History A Chronology of the Most Important People and Events in African-American History*, Simon & Schuster, 1996.

Jackson, John G., *Introduction to African Civilizations*, Citadel Press, 1994.

Saccardi, Marianne, *Art in Story Teaching Art History to Elementary School Children*, Linnet Books, 1997.

Trager, James, *The People's Chronology*, revised edition, Henry Holt, 1996.

Viney, Graham, *Historic Houses of South Africa*, Abbeville Press, 1997.

Alternative Applications: Have students create a hall display by placing dated information on a long horizontal scroll and illustrating these and other architectural designs:

- ◆ beehive style
- ◆ cone-topped buildings
- ◆ fortress-temple
- ◆ Moorish
- ◆ mosque
- ◆ mound
- ◆ post and lintel
- ◆ pueblo
- ◆ pyramid
- ◆ ziggurat

African Art and Architecture

Age/Grade Level or Audience: General audiences; museums, art leagues.

Description: Study uniquely African art forms.

Procedure: Present a multimedia showing of African art forms, emphasizing these:

- ◆ Ashanti brass castings
- ◆ Congolese bronze work
- ◆ Ibo beadwork
- ◆ Nigerian stone carvings
- ◆ Nok terra cotta masks

♦ Poro masks and headdresses
♦ Subsaharan sculpture, panels, screens, and woodcarvings
♦ Sudanese jewelry
♦ Yoruba funeral art and shrine objects
♦ Zimbabwean stone buildings

Also include these utilitarian objects baskets, wooden utensils and trays, woven fiber rugs and mats, ivory carvings, mud architecture, fetishes, pottery, ornamental swords, combs, mirrors, pipes, staffs, ornate musical instruments, leather goods, ironwork, petroglyphs, and pyroengravings.

Budget: $50-$75

Sources:

Abusabib, Muhamed A., *African Art An Aesthetic Inquiry*, Coronet Books, 1995.

"African Architecture," http//www.global.org/bfreed/archeol/af-arch.html.

Clarke, Duncan, *African Art*, Random House Value, 1995.

Coleman, A. D., "Celebrating Survival," *Art News*, February 1997, 102-105.

Elleh, Nnamdi, *African Architecture Evolution and Transformation*, McGraw-Hill, 1996.

Leuzinger, Elsy, *The Art of Black Africa*, Rizzoli, 1997.

Saccardi, Marianne, *Art in Story Teaching Art HIstory to Elementary School Children*, Linnet Books, 1997.

Viney, Graham, *Historic Houses of South Africa*, Abbeville Press, 1997.

Alternative Applications: Invite an art expert to present a lecture, workshop, or slide program connecting African art with art of Europeans, such as Henri Matisse, Rosa Bonheur, Georges Braque, Mary Cassatt, Amadeo Modigliani, Claudine Claudel, and Pablo Picasso, many of whom studied African styles and techniques. Conclude the presentation with comments and questions from the audience about where each artist came in contact with African models or how and why they traveled to Africa.

African Homes

Age/Grade Level or Audience: Kindergarten and elementary school art classes; church, or school groups; 4-H and Scout troops.

Description: Create a gallery of African homes.

Procedure: Have students work in groups to sketch various types of African houses, particularly these:

- Asante steep thatched, wood-frame houses joined in a circle and linked by mud walls
- Bemileke cluster houses with tall cone roofs made of grass
- Caribbean balcony houses that imitate African flair
- Egyptian brickwork
- Malian village compounds, including round-top houses for the extended family, granaries, and walls
- Mousgoum mud cone houses molded of mud and stones and marked with vertical lines to channel the rain
- Nuba linked houses, which feature red clay walls, pointed cone roofs, and pig and goat houses
- Somolo multistory mud roofs and central granary and grinding room
- Yoruba courtyard houses with carved posts, thatched roofs around the outer rooms, and open central court
- Zulu semi-spherical framework houses covered with grass mats and arranged in a ring protected by a woven twig fence

Have students draw people in the houses. Encourage the use of crayons, washable paints, and markers available in multicultural skin tones of sepia, burnt sienna, mahogany, tan, peach, olive, bronze, terra cotta, tawny, and beige.

Budget: $50-$75

Sources:

Ancient Egyptian Construction and Architecture, Dover 1997.

Coleman, A. D., "Celebrating Survival," *Art News*, February 1997, 102-105.

Elleh, Nnamdi, *African Architecture Evolution and Transformation*, McGraw-Hill, 1996.

Viney, Graham, *Historic Houses of South Africa*, Abbeville Press, 1997.

Alternative Applications: Have volunteers pantomime a day in the life of the residents of these homes. Decide who performs these chores:

- tending animals
- collecting firewood
- cooking, preserving food, gathering herbs, fruits, and berries
- entertaining children, protecting the family, babysitting, teaching young children
- gardening
- grooming hair and nails
- hunting for fresh meat
- making baskets and utensils
- sewing, washing clothes, weaving, making clothes

Ask volunteers to describe how idle time is spent, such as in singing, drumming, or playing a flute, making pottery or jewelry, or storytelling.

Black Art

Originator: Charles L. Blockson, Ed.

Age/Grade Level or Audience: Middle school, high school art or humanities class; civic clubs.

Description: Analyze and discuss works by major black artists from all parts of the world, particularly Africa and the Caribbean.

Procedure: Display slides, books, prints, and films of black art and architecture, featuring the work of these:

- ♦ architects Paul R. Williams, Vertner Woodson Tandy, John Anderson Lankfor, and Norma Merrick Sklarek
- ♦ art satirists Palmer Hayden and Archibald Motley
- ♦ collagist Romare Bearden
- ♦ illustrator Brian Pinkney
- ♦ landscape artists Adele Chilton Gaillard and Lois Mailou Jones
- ♦ lithographers Ugo Mochi, Elizabeth Catlett, Grafton T. Brown, Camille Billops, and James Wells
- ♦ muralists Jacob Lawrence, Robert S. Duncanson, and Charles Alston
- ♦ painters William E. Scott, Charles White, Alma Woodsey Thomas, Emilio Cruz, Malvin Gray Johnson, Phoebe Beasley, Georg Olden, Sam Gilliam, Claude Clark, Charles Searles, Cheri Zamba, David Butler, Minnie Evans, Clementine Hunter, Tshibumba Kanda-Matulu, Gwendolyn Knight, Alma Thomas, Allan Rohan Crite, Edward Mitchell Bannister, Elazier Corter, William Henry Johnson, Frederick Brown, Bob Thompson, and Henry Ossawa Tanner
- ♦ photographers Gordon Parks, James VanDerZee, Lorna Simpson, and John W. Mosley
- ♦ portrait artists Thomas Blackshear, Higgins Bond, Jerry Pinkney, Hyppolite, Philomé Obin, Rigaud Benoit, Joshua Johnston, and Castera Brazile
- ♦ sculptors Geraldine McCullough, Meta Warrick Fuller, Richard Barthé, Sokari Douglas Camp, S. J. Akpan, Kane Kwei, Selma Hortense Burke, Eddie Dixon, Marion Perkins, Elizabeth Catlett, Barbara Chase-Riboud, Mae Howard Jackson, Elizabeth Prophet, and Richard Hunt

Highlight the works of a few notable black artists, particularly

- ♦ Augusta Savage, New York sculptor whose *Lift Every Voice and Sing* was exhibited at the 1939 New York World's Fair

◆ Jacob Lawrence, creator of series on Frederick Douglass and Harriet Tubman
◆ Henry O. Tanner, creator of *Raising of Lazarus*
◆ William H. Johnson, a Paris expatriate who gained fame two decades after his death, a creator of vigorous, primitive paintings.
◆ Edmonia Lewis, creator of "Death of Cleopatra" and the bust of Henry Wadsworth Longfellow that stands in the Harvard University Library.

Determine themes and techniques which separate black art from works by members of other races, as is evident in Savage's use of the Negro National Anthem for a title.

Budget: $75-$100

Sources:
"African American Artists," http//www.libraries.uc.edu/libinfo/aaa3.html.
"African Ebony Carvings and Statues," http//www.natashascafe.com/html/ebony. html.
Brown, Christie, "Look at the Eyes! They Evoke a Serpent," *Forbes*, September 14, 1992, 512-524.
"Caribbean Cultural Center," http//www.nando.net/prof/caribe/Caribbean_Cultural_ Center.html.
"Haiti," http//lanic.utexas.edu/la/ca/haiti.
Hughes, Robert Hughes, "Return from Alienation," *Time*, August 31, 1992, 65-66.
Discovering Multicultural America (database), Galenet, 1997.
Mabunda, L. Mpho, ed., *The African American Almanac*, 7th edition, Gale, 1997.
St. James Guide to Black Artists, Gale, 1997.

Alternative Applications: Set up a children's workshop to encourage imitation of black art styles and media. Consider the following outlets for youth art:

◆ sidewalk chalk drawing contest
◆ group mural or frieze
◆ experiments in mosaic made from confetti, colored sand, or aquarium rock
◆ papier mache masks
◆ weaving and macrame workshops
◆ clay reproductions of ceremonial pottery
◆ snapshot and video autobiographies

Black Builders

Originator: Marjorie Roberts, teacher, Scottsdale, Arizona.

Age/Grade Level or Audience: Elementary and middle school history classes.

Description: Create an awareness of the black role in building America's historic monuments.

Procedure: Present drawings, pamphlets, travel guides, and other examples of historic residences, gardens, orchards, walks, wells, piers, barns, granaries, businesses, churches, graveyards, and monuments that were built by slave labor. Include these:

- ◆ Thomas Jefferson's Monticello
- ◆ Andrew Jackson's Hermitage
- ◆ Louisville's Farmington Mansion
- ◆ Charleston Slave Market
- ◆ Tryon Palace in Tryon, North Carolina
- ◆ George Washington's Mount Vernon
- ◆ historic sections of levees along the Mississippi River
- ◆ antebellum mansions of Louisiana, Mississippi, Georgia, and South Carolina, such as Drayton Hall, Middleton Place, Boone Plantation, Kinsley Plantation, and Fairvue Farm
- ◆ Caribbean mansions and sugar mills, including Sweet Bottom, Sally's Fancy, Bonne Esperance, and Parasol on St. Croix

Budget: $50-$75

Sources:

Travel guides from the American Automobile Association (AAA) or state travel bureaus, such as "A Closer Look Louisville's African American Historic and Cultural Guide" from the Louisville Convention and Visitors Bureau.

Cantor, George, *Historic Landmarks of Black America*, Gale, 1991.

Discovering Multicultural America (database), Galenet, 1997.

Howarth, Sarah, *Colonial Places*, Millbrook Press, 1994.

Kalman, Bobbie, *Colonial Town Williamsburg*, Crabtree Publishing Co., 1992.

Mabunda, L. Mpho, ed., *The African American Almanac*, 7th edition, Gale, 1997.

Alternative Applications: Give a talk on the labor-intensive job of brickmaking, which was done by hand by African slaves, particularly women, the elderly and handicapped, and children. Ask a volunteer to read about the job in an encyclopedia or from an Internet source and describe the process for the class. Stress the demands brickmaking placed on workers as they built and paved whole cities, courtyards, and harbors. Present variations in the process as reflected in raw materials of a given area, such as red clay of the Southern Piedmont and gray clay and clam and mussel shells along the eastern U. S. shore. Note that today, slave-made bricks and cobbles are collectors' items, some of which still bear laborers' fingerprints and trademarks.

Black Landmarks

Age/Grade Level or Audience: High school or college art, architecture, or African American studies class; travel clubs; museums.

Description: Organize a display featuring buildings and monuments significant to black history in the United States.

Procedure: Using Internet sources, models, posters, postcards, art prints, drawings, photographs, and other media, create a display of architectural sites that highlight black history, such as these:

- Slave Market, Middleton Plantation, Drayton Hall, and Catfish Row in Charleston, South Carolina
- black regimental headquarters, Fort Huachuca, Arizona
- home of Frederick Douglass, Cedar Hill, Washington D.C.
- Augustus St. Gaudens's sculpture of black soldiers who fought in the Civil War, Washington, D.C.
- Dexter Avenue Baptist Church, Montgomery, Alabama
- a reconstructed plantation at Stone Mountain, Georgia
- home of Louis Armstrong, Long Island, New York
- Charles L. Blockson Afro-American Collection, Temple University, Philadelphia, Pennsylvania
- depot of the Underground Railroad, Levi Coffin House, Fountain City, Indiana
- African Meeting House, Boston
- Scott Joplin's home, St. Louis, Missouri
- Boley Historic District, Boley, Oklahoma
- Fairvue-Isaac Franklin Plantation, Sumner County, Tennessee
- Tallman House, an Underground Railroad station in Janesville, Wisconsin
- Jackson Square, New Orleans
- Cotton Club in Harlem, New York
- Gettysburg National Cemetery in Gettysburg, Pennsylvania
- Ford Theater, Washington, D.C.
- Jamestown, Appomattox Courthouse, Williamsburg, and Harpers Ferry, Virginia
- Underground Railroad Museum, Nebraska City, Nebraska
- Africatown, Mobile, Alabama
- Afro-American Historical and Cultural Museum, Philadelphia, Pennsylvania
- National Museum of African Art, Smithsonian Institute, Washington, D.C.
- Museum of National Center for Afro-American Artists, Roxbury, Massachusetts
- Schomburg Center for Research in Black Culture, New York Public Library, New York City.

Budget: $75-$100

Sources:
Reference works, including encyclopedias, art histories, travel guides.
"African American Civil War Memorial," http//www.npca.com/div/ aacw.html.
Cantor, George, *Historic Landmarks of Black America*, Gale, 1991.
Discovering Multicultural America (database), Galenet, 1997.

Alternative Applications: Using Internet sources, models, slides, posters, postcards, art books, and other media, demonstrate the purpose and meaning of the Watts Towers to the black community in Los Angeles. Explain how Simon Rodia (1875-1965) built the spires from crushed glass, rock, and other found materials. Lead a discussion of the significance of art created by ordinary people. List artistic components, particularly bits of found materials suitable for cementing into a wall, corner marker, monument, archway, or welcome sign:

- ◆ quartz, mica, shells, and creek stones
- ◆ aluminum cans, wrought iron, and sections of abandoned railways
- ◆ driftwood and cross-sections of logs
- ◆ metal signs and markers
- ◆ concrete sidewalks, marble headstones, and steps
- ◆ copper tubing, doorknobs, hardware, and other recycled construction materials.

Present your suggestions to a civic or garden club, Chamber of Commerce, or city council as a community beautification project similar to the Watts Towers.

Blacks in the Saddle

Age/Grade Level or Audience: Elementary school art classes or art museum workshop.

Description: Create a cartoon storyboard for a comic book, children's magazine feature, one-hour television video, or docudrama on a black Western hero.

Procedure: Have students sketch in cartoon style the adventures and achievements of frontiersman Jim Beckwourth, Bulldogger Bill Pickett, or Nat Love, King of the Black Cowboys. Stress the excitement of hunting, trapping, sharpshooting, learning the cowboy's trade, moving herds to Midwestern markets, training for rodeos, and demonstrating trick riding and roping for an audience. Draw actions shots against natural backdrops of mountains, plains, rivers, deserts, and trails.

Budget: Under $25

Sources:

Black Cowboys: Legends of the West, Chelsea House 1996.

Discovering Multicultural America (database), Galenet, 1997.

Katz, William Loren, *Black Indians A Hidden Heritage,* Atheneum, 1986.

———, *The Black West,* 3rd edition, Open Hand Publishers, 1987.

Knill, Harry, *Black Cowboy,* Bellerophon Books, 1993.

Love, Nat. *The Life and Adventures of Nat Love.* Black Classic Press, 1988.

Mabunda, L. Mpho, ed., *The African American Almanac,* 7th edition, Gale, 1997.

Stewart, Paul W., and Wallace Y. Ponce, *Black Cowboys,* Phillips Publishers, 1986.

Alternative Applications: Apply the storyboard concept to the lives of black explorers and scientists, for example, Matthew Henson, Mae Jemison, Booker T. Washington, Guion Bluford, or York, the black servant who accompanied the Lewis and Clark expedition up the Missouri and Columbia rivers to the Pacific Ocean and back.

 A Caribbean Garden

Age/Grade Level or Audience: Kindergarten and elementary art classes.

Description: Have students work in groups to design a garden.

Procedure: Have students study pictures of these and other native Caribbean plants:

allspice	anthurium	bamboo
banana tree	bay tree	bird of paradise
bougainvillea	breadfruit	casuarina tree
dusty miller	flamingo flower	frangipani
ginger	guava	hibiscus
jade vine	lily	lime tree
mahogany	oleander	orchid
passion fruit	pineapple	royal palm
sea grape	tuberose	vanilla
whitewood		

Have participants draw a scene from a park, walkway, courtyard, or garden depicting the colors and shapes of Caribbean flora. Ask a separate group to sketch in colorful native birds, particularly pelicans, herons, parrots, and parakeets.

Budget: Under $25

Sources:

"Caribbean Cultural Center," http//www.nando.net/prof/caribe/Caribbean_Cultural_ Center.html.

Fitzsimmons, Cecilia, *Fruit*, Silver burdett Press, 1996.

"Fruit Facts," http//www.crfg.org/pubs/frtfacts.html.

Jones, David L., *Palms Throughout the World*, Smithsonian, 1995.

"Palm Trees," http//miavx1.muoh9o.edu/~dragonfly/itb/palm_tree.htmlx.

Wilsher, Jane, *Spices*, Garrett Education Corp., 1995.

Alternative Applications: Bring to class some of the most fragrant substances harvested and traded in the Caribbean. Blindfold volunteers and have them identify the aromas and textures of coffee bean, bay leaf, banana, vanilla, cinnamon, ginger, lime, allspice, coconut, nutmeg, mango, pepper, paprika, and pineapple.

Designer Mural

Age/Grade Level or Audience: Civic, church, community, or school groups; 4-H clubs and Scout troops; garden clubs and neighborhood beautification committees.

Description: Organize a designer mural to brighten a neighborhood.

Procedure: Have volunteers lay out a design featuring accomplishments of African Americans from the arrival of the first slaves to the present. Arrange scenarios in chronological order, for example:

- ◆ first slaves from ships at Jamestown habor
- ◆ Emancipation Proclamation
- ◆ Harlem Renaissance
- ◆ civil rights sit-ins and marches of the 1950s and 1960s
- ◆ Million Man and Million Woman marches

Use bright colors to emphasize diversity and creativity.

Budget: $75-$100

Sources:

Discovering Multicultural America (database), Galenet, 1997.

Gaines, Ernest J., *Timetables of History*, Random House, 1996.

Harley, Sharon, *Timetables of African-American History: A Chronology of the Most Important People and Events in African-American History*, Simon & Schuster, 1996.

Hornsby, Alton, *Chronology of African-American History*, 2nd edition, Gale, 1997.

Mabunda, L. Mpho, ed., *The African American Almanac*, 7th edition, Gale, 1997.

Alternative Applications: Select a volunteer each day to draw in a segment of the mural until its completion. Suggest that each volunteer pick one person or event to portray a single aspect of black history, such as these:

- ◆ achievements in film, television, publishing, dance, or stage
- ◆ black Olympic medalists or popular athletes
- ◆ encouragement of voting rights
- ◆ famous speeches and demonstrations
- ◆ founding of influential black colleges or universities
- ◆ Harlem Renaissance
- ◆ return of war heroes
- ◆ women's rights

Designing a Winner

Age/Grade Level or Audience: High school or college computer art or drafting classes.

Description: Collect ideas for a series of Afrocentric toys, computer games, and board games.

Procedure: Have participants submit three-dimensional proposals for educational toys, board games, and computer games that stress African American themes, locations in Africa or the Caribbean, Afrocentric styles and colors, or words and events derived from black history. For example, design a hand-held computer game that matches pictures and names of African animals, such as the gnu or gibbon.

Budget: Under $25

Sources:
Computer drawing and drafting software.
Adams, W. M., *The Physical Geography of Africa*, Oxford University Press, 1996.
"Africa Online," http//www.africaonline.com.
Binns, Tony, *The People and Environment in Africa*, John Wiley and Sons, 1995.
Mabunda, L. Mpho, ed., *The African American Almanac*, 7th edition, Gale, 1997.

Alternative Applications: Create catalogs, billboards, or websites introducing Afrocentric toys and games to individuals, families, teachers, librarians, day-care centers, camp counselors, and merchants. Include advice on how to select appropriate Afrocentric entertainment for children of all ages.

Moorish Architecture

Age/Grade Level or Audience: College art and architecture students; adult travel clubs.

Description: Present an overview of the world's most famous Moorish architecture.

Procedure: Organize a slide show, series of drawings, photographs, or other depictions of Moorish art and architecture, which spread through southern Europe from 711 to 1400 A. D. Point out details that set it apart from other styles. Feature such buildings as Spain's Alhambra and Venetian palaces.

Budget: $75-$100

Sources:

"Architecture and Design," http//physserv/physics.wisc.edu/~shalizi/notebooks/ arch.des.

De Angelis, Michele, and Thomas W. Lentz, *Muslim Architecture of the Iberian Peninsula: Eastern and Western Sources for Hispano-Islamic Building Arts,* Locust Hill Press, 1987.

Kunjufu, Jawanza, *Lessons from History: A Celebration in Blackness,* African American Images, 1987.

Alternative Applications: Have students draft details from Moorish architecture alongside the delineations of Egyptian, Celtic, Mayan, Aztec, Greek, Ionic, Doric, Corinthian, Polynesian, Gothic, Romanesque, post and lintel, ziggurat, and modern buildings.

 ## Photo Map

Age/Grade Level or Audience: All ages.

Description: Organize a photo history of African American life in a city, county, or state.

Procedure: Highlight an oversized map with detailed views of architecture or historical landmarks significant to African American history. Have volunteers provide pictures to document community growth in homes, churches, factories, historical streets, auditoriums, cemeteries, monuments, theaters, and sports centers. Feature teams, singing groups, dancers, sculptors, artists, inventors, civil rights leaders, educators, and other memorable people.

Budget: $75-$100

Sources:
Local historical societies, public libraries.
Cantor, George, *Historic Landmarks of Black America*, Gale, 1991.
Discovering Multicultural America (database), Galenet, 1997.
Katz, William Loren, *The Black West*, 3rd edition, Open Hand Publishers, 1987.
Ki-Zerbo, Joseph, "Oral Tradition as a Historical Source," *UNESCO Courier*, April 1990, 43-46.
Magnin, André, *Seydou Keïta*, Scalo, 1997.
Myers, Walter Dean, *Brown Angels: An Album of Pictures and Verse*, Harper Trophy, 1993.
————, *Glorious Angels: A Celebration of Children*, Harper Trophy, 1995.
————, *One More River to Cross: An African American Photograph Album*, Harcourt Brace, 1995.
Parks, Gordon, *Half Past Autumn A Retrospective*, Bulfinch Press, 1997.
Windham, Kathryn, *Encounters*, Black Belt Press 1997.

Alternative Applications: Videotape a tour of an area, detailing the achievements of African Americans. Capture profiles, still shots, processions, religious celebrations, holidays, and other significant events. Provide voice-over and background music to complete the montage. Display at museums, street fairs, libraries, schools, or public meetings. Offer the videos for sale. Collect similar creative efforts from other areas.

Photo Tableaux of History

Age/Grade Level or Audience: Photography classes and clubs; drama classes, civic gatherings, church or school ethnic fairs or Black History Month celebrations.

Description: Organize a series of reenactments of history to photograph or videotape.

Procedure: Create scenes from African American history using a variety of participants, settings, costumes, and props. Photograph the tableaux as a lasting record of the group's effort. Place finished photos in an album alongside explanations of the events. Consider these important historical moments:

◆ The arrival of 20 black on an unnamed ship to Jamestown, Virginia

◆ In November 1786, black worshippers led by Richard Allen and Absalom Jones boycotted Philadelphia's St. George's Methodist Episcopal Church rather than be segregated in a separate gallery.

◆ On August 21, 1831, Nat Turner led seventy confederates on a rampage which terrified slave owners with the dangers of a general revolt of all slaves.

◆ The summer of 1865 brought Jubilee, the freeing of the slaves, which spread gradually across the United States.

◆ Booker T. Washington delivered his "Atlanta Compromise" speech in Atlanta on September 18, 1895, to encourage social accommodation of free blacks.

◆ In 1906, W. E. B. Du Bois organized the Niagara Movement at Harpers Ferry, Virginia, a drive which evolved into the National Association for Colored People.

◆ The black migrations from Southern plantations to Northern industry, beginning in 1910 and continuing into the 1940s.

◆ On May 17, 1954, Chief Justice of the Supreme Court Earl Warren announced to Thurgood Marshall, adviser to the NAACP, and all of America that the court voted unanimously to end the policy of "separate but equal" in public schools.

◆ From the courage of one dissenting seamstress, Rosa Parks, on December 1, 1955, black bus patrons in Montgomery, Alabama, launched a 381-day boycott, giving rise to a new leader, Martin Luther King, Jr.

◆ On September 25, 1957, 1,000 troops entered Little Rock, Arkansas, to enforce the federal order to integrate schools by escorting nine black teenagers into Central High School.

◆ On April 4, 1968, the nation mourned the assassination of Martin Luther King, Jr., at the Lorraine Motel in Memphis, Tennessee. Five days later, 200,000 mourners accompanied a mule-drawn wagon bearing the coffin through Atlanta to King's grave.

Budget: $75-$100

Sources:

Bennett, Lerone, "10 Most Dramatic Events in African-American History," *Ebony*, February 1992, 107-116.

Discovering Multicultural America (database), Galenet, 1997.

Myers, Walter Dean, *Brown Angels: An Album of Pictures and Verse*, Harper Trophy, 1993.

———, *Glorious Angels: A Celebration of Children*, Harper Trophy, 1995.

———, *One More River to Cross: An African American Photograph Album*, Harcourt Brace, 1995.

Parks, Gordon, *Half Past Autumn: A Retrospective*, Bulfinch Press, 1997.

Windham, Kathryn, *Encounters*, Black Belt Press 1997.

Alternative Applications: Collect candid shots of these workers:

artisans	carpenters	cooks
crafters	farmers	fishers
iron workers	migrants	performers
sewers	street workers	vendors
weavers		

Also, feature families, mothers and babies, worshippers, funerals, weddings, graduations, and festivals. Use photos or videotape in a gallery display or as studies for sculptors, muralists, painters, or commercial artists.

The Shotgun House

Age/Grade Level or Audience: All ages.

Description: Present a floorplan and description of the shotgun house.

Procedure: Using floor plans, drawings, posters, or overhead projection, detail the architectural style of the shotgun house, symbolic of Black Southern lifestyle. Depict the typical arrangement of three rooms in a row, a door at each end, and the gable end facing the street. Discuss the expedience of its arrangement, especially as it applies to heating and cooling. Explain why these buildings are common to the Caribbean, New Orleans, and Charleston.

Budget: $50-$75

Sources:
"Shelia Collectibles," http//www.erinet.com/granio/key03.html.
"Houses of Key West," http//www.netreaction.com/hlaw.
"Project Row Houses," http//www.neosoft.com/~prh/.
Vlach, John Michael. *The Afro-American Tradition in Decorative Arts*, University of Georgia Press 1990.
Wilson, Reagan, and William Ferris, eds. *Encyclopedia of Southern Culture*, University of North Carolina Press, 1989.

Alternative Applications: Using the shotgun floorplan, create a mural, triptych, or frieze of black family life on a tobacco or truck farm, fishing village, or indigo, rice, rubber, or sugar plantation. Indicate daily activities, especially cooking, dining, relaxation, play, handicrafts, gardening, and sleep.

Arts and Crafts

African Animal Fair

Age/Grade Level or Audience: Kindergarten and elementary craft classes; religious schools; summer reading programs; classes for handicapped children.

Description: Organize a clay animal fair.

Procedure: Read aloud from storybooks about African animals or look up pictures on the Internet. Have students choose animals to model. Provide commercial clay or one of the following homemade dough recipes:

Simple Dough

4 c. flour
1 c. salt
1 ½ c. cold water
vegetable dye

Cooked Clay

¾ c. salt
½ c. plain or shaker flour
2 tsps. alum
¾ c. water
2 tbs. oil
vegetable dye or paint

Stir first three ingredients in a pot over medium heat until thickened. Blend in oil. Cool; then color with drops of food coloring or tempera paint. Demonstrate how to roll, knead, shape, and paint African animals, such as the giraffe, crocodile, gnu, gorilla, lion, tiger, dik-dik, rhinoceros, gazelle, emu, elephant, cobra, python, or wildebeest. Bake figures made from simple dough on a cookie sheet for one hour at 350°.

Use clay to make oversized animal heads. Emphasize the variety of pelts and skins by using vivid colors, such as black and white stripes for the zebra, brown with buff spots for the giraffe, a hairy tan ruff for the lion, slick green skin for the python, and a pointed white tusk for the rhinoceros or elephant. Attach an arrow-shaped fastener to the finished heads. Bake; then use heads as pot pets by securing the arrow over the rim and into the soil of a potted plant.

Budget: $50-$75

Sources:

The videos *Animals of Africa* (1987) and *Animals Are Beautiful People* (1994).

Arnold, Caroline, *African Animals*, Morrow Junior Books, 1997.

Burgess, Anna, *Do-It-Yourself Project Book*, Troll Associates, 1994.

Butterfield, Moira, *Fun with Paint*, Random Books, 1993.

Dahlstrom, Lorraine M., *Doing the Days: A Year's Worth of Creative Journaling, Drawing, Listening, Reading, Thinking, Arts and Crafts Activities for Children*, Free Spirit Publications 1994.

Diakité, Baba Wagué, *The Hunterman and the Crocodile*, Scholastic Books,1997.

Hamilton, Robyn, ed, *Africa Activity Book Arts, Crafts, Cooking and Historical Aids*, Edupress, 1996.

Hamilton, Virginia, "The Animals Share," *Scholastic Storyworks*, October 1997, 20-23.

Hopcraft, Xan, "What I Learned from a Cheetah," *Scholastic Storyworks*, September 1997, 6-13.

O'Halloran, Kate, *Hands-on Culture of Ancient Egypt*, Walch, 1997.

———, *Hands-on Culture of West Africa*, Walch, 1997.

Pinter, Helmut. *African Grey Parrots . . . as a Hobby*, T. F. H. Publications 1995.

Sattler, Helen Roney. *Recipes for Art and Craft Materials*, Lothrop, Lee & Shepard, 1987.

Theroux, Paul, "Down the Zambezi," *National Geographic*, October 1997, 2-31.

Williams, Wendy, "Of Elephants and Men," *Animals*, November/December 1997, 24-30.

Alternative Applications: As an alternate method of shaping animals, use papier maché

Papier Maché

> wet paper strips
> glue
> wire

Form with wire a simple animal shape of head, backbone, legs, and tail. Soak paper in water. Squeeze dry. Shape mass around wire structure. Complete with a coating of glue and a layer of dry paper strips. Dry and paint. Decorate with yarn, felt, cloth, toothpicks, popsicle sticks, buttons, dry beans and pasta, and fake fur.

African Cards

Age/Grade Level or Audience: Elementary or middle school art classes.

Description: Redesign a deck of playing cards on African or African American themes.

Procedure: Discuss with students the medieval European history of ordinary playing cards. Divide them into groups to replace the joker, ace, king, queen, jack, spade, heart, diamond, club, and numbers with African motifs found on Maasai, Egyptian, Zulu, Berber, Moorish, Yoruba, or Ethiopian pottery, screens, jewelry, architecture, artifacts, face painting, body tattoos, headdresses, and costumes. Select a special group to redesign the card backs for the entire pack. Suggest a map, musical instrument, profile, or flag as a unifying motif. Use the colors of Africa red, green, yellow, black, and white.

Budget: Under $25

Sources:
Beckvermit, John J., *African Art Playing Card Deck*, 3rd edition, U. S. Games, 1995.
Dacey, Donna, "Crafts of Many Cultures: Three Seasonal Art Projects with Global Appeal," *Instructor*, November-December 1991, 30-33.
Mabunda, L. Mpho, ed., *The African American Almanac*, 7th edition, Gale, 1997.
Müller, Claudia, *The Costume Timeline: 5000 Years of Fashion History*, Thames and Hudson, 1993.
Sanders, Marlita, "Dollmaking: The Celebration of a Culture," *School Arts*, January 1992, 27.
"Tanzania," http//www.africa.com/~venture/wildfron/wildanz.htm.
"Uganda," http//imul.com/uganda/
"Zimbabwe," http//www.mother.com/~zimweb/History.html.

Alternative Applications: Have students extend the project to redesign these and other cultural symbols arising from sources other than Africa:

Bayeux Tapestry	Caribbean batik	coins
family crest	I Ching cards	Mayan calendar
royal coat of arms	stamps	state seal
tapestries	Tarot cards	

Stress important moments in black history, such as the arrival of the first slave ship to New World shores, first Juneteenth celebration, Emancipation Proclamation, or creation of the Freedman's Bureau.

African Ornaments

Age/Grade Level or Audience: Kindergarten or elementary crafts classes; religious schools; classes for the handicapped.

Description: Create African ornaments for decorating trees, windows, doorways, wreaths, and packages.

Procedure: Have handicrafters cross two thin 6-inch dowels or bamboo garden sticks and secure in place with a pipe cleaner or twist-tie. Using red, green, yellow, and black yarn, wind a single thread around each rod and on to the next rod. Alternate colors to create variations in the pattern. For an unusual effect, twine two colored strands at a time, such as green and red or yellow and black. Tie the last thread into a knot. Complete the ends of the ornament with yarn pompoms, paper stars, buttons, foil, or ribbon streamers.

Budget: $50-$75

Sources:

The video "Kwanzaa" (Schlessinger Media), Syracuse Cultural Workers Catalog, phone: 315–474–1132.

Ajmera, Maya, and Anna Rhesa Versola, *Children from Australia to Zimbabwe*, Charlesbridge, 1997.

Copage, Eric V., *Kwanzaa: An African-American Celebration of Culture and Cooking*, Morrow, 1993.

Corwin, Judith H., *Kwanzaa Crafts*, Watts, 1995.

Deshpande, Chris, and Iain Macleod-Brudenell, *Festival Crafts*, Gareth Stevens, 1996.

Drake, Jane, and Ann Love, *The Kids' Summer Handbook*, Ticknor and Fields Books, 1994.

Easy-to-Make Whirligigs, Dover 1997.

Kallen, Stuart A., *Eco-Arts and Crafts*, Abdo & Daughters, 1993.

Lohf, Sabine, *Things I Can Make*, Chronicle Books, 1994.

Mason, Kate, *Make Your Own Cool Crafts*, Troll Associates, 1994.

Oni, Sauda, *What Kwanzaa Means to Me*, DARE Books, 1996.

Robartson, Linda, *The Complete Kwanzaa Celebration Book*, Creative Acrylic, 1993.

Ross, Kathy, *Crafts for Kwanzaa*, Millbrook Press, 1994.

St. James, Synthia, *The Gifts of Kwanzaa*, A Whitman, 1994.

Zweifel, Frances, *The Make-Something Club Fun with Crafts, Food, and Gifts*, Viking Child Books, 1994.

Alternative Applications: Make oversized ornaments to serve as Kwanzaa door or mailbox decorations or celebrations of Juneteenth or Black History Month. Sprinkle with glitter. Use the ends of the dowels as spokes on which to hang smaller ornaments, feathers, stones, and found objects.

All-Occasion Cards

Age/Grade Level or Audience: All ages: civic clubs; crafts clinic; church school.

Description: Create a mass-produced card factory.

Procedure: Assemble tools and art supplies to fashion a selection of all-occasions cards for birthdays, anniversaries, graduation, sympathy, get well wishes, and holidays, such as these:

Bar Mitzvah	Christmas	Easter
Hanukkah	Kwanzaa	New Year's
Ramadan	Rosh Hashanah	Thanksgiving
Valentine's Day	Winter Solstice	

Select the best designs for a particular occasion. For example, choose fold-out memory books for birthdays or Grandparent's Day or pop-up cards for Valentine's Day. Make multiple copies of each using desktop publishing software, photocopies, tracings, stenciling, or block prints. Collate the finished cards into stacks, match with colored or white envelopes, and assemble in boxes. Take orders or sell the card selections in a hospital or museum gift shop, retirement home, street fair, craft show, or door to door.

Budget: $50-$75

Sources:

The video "Kwanzaa" (Schlessinger Media); Syracuse Cultural Workers catalog, phone 315-474-1132.

Copage, Eric V., *Kwanzaa: An African-American Celebration of Culture and Cooking*, William Morrow & Co., 1993.

Gaylord, Susan Kapuscinski, "Festive Gift Books Memory Book," *Instructor*, November/December 1997, 63, 73.

MacDonald, Margaret Read, *Folklore of World Holidays*, Gale, 1992.

Oni, Sauda, *What Kwanzaa Means to Me*, DARE Books, 1996.

Robartson, Linda, *The Complete Kwanzaa Celebration Book*, Creative Acrylic, 1993.

Ross, Kathy, *Crafts for Kwanzaa*, Millbrook Press, 1994.

Ruelle, Karen G., *Seventy-Five Fun Things to Make and Do by Yourself*, Sterling, 1993.

St. James, Synthia, *The Gifts of Kwanzaa*, A Whitman, 1994.

Techniques for Marbleizing Paper and *Lacy Cut-Paper Designs*, Dover, 1997.

Alternative Applications: Create a postcard series featuring landmarks in Africa, the Caribbean, or black America, such as scenes of the Limpopo River, Mount Kilimanjaro, and Lake Chad in Africa, Ocho Rios or Kingston Harbor in Jamaica; the marketplace of Antigua, Jamaica, Barbados, or St. Kitts; or Catfish Row in Charleston, the Apollo Theater in Harlem, or Motown's Hitsville in Detroit.

Animal Movies

Age/Grade Level or Audience: Elementary or middle school art classes; religious schools; scout troops; 4-H clubs; classes for the handicapped.

Description: Organize a movie-making workshop.

Procedure: Have participants follow these suggestions:

- ♦ Study the movements and habits of an African animal, such as the swift gazelle, slithering mamba, flapping flamingo, bounding leopard, delicate dik-dik, or awkward, lumbering hippopotamus.
- ♦ Select an animal to draw on twenty index cards.
- ♦ Depict the animal moving from one side to another or from the ground into the air through twenty small increments.
- ♦ Arrange the twenty pictures in time order.
- ♦ Fasten the left edge of the card stack with staples or brads.
- ♦ Flip the right edge rapidly or slowly to make the animal move.

Budget: $25-$50

Sources:

Arnold, Caroline, *African Animals*, Morrow Junior Books, 1997.

Diakité, Baba Wagué, *The Hunterman and the Crocodile*, Scholastic Books, 1997.

Hamilton, Virginia, "The Animals Share," *Scholastic Storyworks*, October 1997, 20-23.

Hartmann, Wendy, *One Sun Rises: An African Wildlife Counting Book*, Dutton Child Books, 1994.

Hopcraft, Xan, "What I Learned from a Cheetah," *Scholastic Storyworks*, September 1997, 6-13.

Kingdon, Jonathan, *Island Africa: The Evolution of Africa's Rare Animals and Plants*, Princeton University Press, 1992.

Pinter, Helmut. *African Grey Parrots . . . as a Hobby*, T. F. H. Publications, 1995.

Theroux, Paul, "Down the Zambezi," *National Geographic*, October 1997, 2-31.

Williams, Wendy, "Of Elephants and Men," *Animals*, November/December 1997, 24-30.

Alternative Applications: Create similar index card movies featuring one of the following scenes:

- ◆ Caribbean limbo line
- ◆ jazz street performer
- ◆ Kwanzaa feast
- ◆ practicing shaman or native healer
- ◆ steel drum band

- ◆ Carnaval dancers
- ◆ Kenyan marching band
- ◆ Mardi Gras float
- ◆ South American carnival
- ◆ Zulu dancer

Batiking

Age/Grade Level or Audience: Kindergarten or elementary art classes; religious schools; Scout troops; 4-H clubs.

Description: Organize a batiking workshop.

Procedure: Have students decorate flags, banners, handkerchiefs, T-shirts, table mats and napkins, or pillowcases with crayon stenciling and iron-on designs of drawings of African or Caribbean designs. Cover their work with newspaper or brown wrapping paper and iron lightly on a solid surface. After repeated ironings, the wax crayon will soak into the paper, leaving the color in the fabric. Display finished batik designs on a bulletin board, clothesline, or library showcase.

Budget: $50-$75

Sources:

Dahlstrom, Lorraine M., *Doing the Days: A Year's Worth of Creative Journaling, Drawing, Listening, Reading, Thinking, Arts and Crafts Activities for Children*, Free Spirit Publications 1994.

Duckitt, Hildagonda, *Traditional South African Cookery*, Hippocrene Books, 1996.

Favorite Birds Iron-On Transfer Patterns, Dover.

Fischer, Alexandra E., *A to Z Animals Around the World*, Putnam Publishing Group, 1994.

Hamilton, Robyn, ed, *Africa Activity Book Arts, Crafts, Cooking and Historical Aids*, Edupress, 1996.

Hartmann, Wendy, *One Sun Rises: An African Wildlife Counting Book*, Dutton Child Books, 1994.

Isadora, Rachel. *Over the Green Hills*, Greenwillow Books, 1992.

Kaaza, Keiko. *A Mother for Choco*, Putnam, 1992.

Müller, Claudia, *The Costume Timeline 5000 Years of Fashion History*, Thames and Hudson, 1993.

Alternative Applications: For older handicrafters, have participants paint fabric with melted paraffin to block coloration, then dip into pots of vegetable dye to color unwaxed surfaces. Conclude by ironing fabric between layers of newspaper or brown wrapping paper until wax is absorbed. Display batiked fabrics in a hallway parade, visit to a retirement home, arts fair, or PTA program.

Black History Desk Calendar

Age/Grade Level or Audience: Middle school or high school art classes.

Description: Have twelve students provide artwork to accompany a twelve-month calendar.

Procedure: Encourage students to create contrasting, thought-provoking artwork to accompany a twelve-month calendar. Stress events that fall in a particular month, such as these:

- ◆ Martin Luther King's birthday and the Emancipation Proclamation in January
- ◆ Black History Month in February
- ◆ Malcolm X Day and African Liberation Day in May
- ◆ Juneteenth in June
- ◆ Marcus Garvey's birthday in August
- ◆ Umoja Karamu in November
- ◆ Kwanzaa in December

Use photography, collage, or other media to highlight calendars. Reproduce in black and white and distribute as gifts or sell as a sorority, art, or civic club project.

Budget: $25-$50

Sources:

Gaines, Ernest J., *Timetables of History*, Random House, 1996.

Harley, Sharon, *Timetables of African-American History: A Chronology of the Most Important People and Events in African-American History*, Simon & Schuster, 1996.

Jackson, John G., *Introduction to African Civilizations*, Citadel Press, 1994.

MacDonald, Margaret Read, *Folklore of World Holidays*, Gale, 1992.

Trager, James, *The People's Chronology*, revised edition, Henry Holt, 1996.

Alternative Applications: Post a monthly calendar board in a school, museum, library, post office, mall, or civic building. Hang colored markers, crayons, and pencils on strings and encourage participants to enter such important dates in black history as birthdays of heroes and sports stars, Nelson Mandela's release from prison, and the speeches of Barbara Jordan, Frederick Douglass, and Reverend Jesse Jackson.

Bookmarks

Originator: Gary Carey, teacher, editor, and writer, Lincoln, Nebraska.

Age/Grade Level or Audience: Elementary school students.

Description: Create a variety of hand-lettered bookmarks featuring quotations by Nelson Mandela, Mary Carter Smith, Dr. Martin Luther King, Jr., Maya Angelou, Frederick Douglass, Marion Wright Edelman, Reverend Jesse Jackson, Joycelyn Elders, Wole Soyinka, Barbara Jordan, Sammy Davis, Jr., Fannie Lou Hamer, Faye Wattleton, Andrew Young, Pearl Bailey, Booker T. Washington, Marcia Gillespie, Frederick Douglass, Sojourner Truth, Toni Cade Bambara, Ernest J. Gaines, Ida Wells-Barnett, or other black notables.

Procedure: Have students use yardsticks to mark large sheets of tagboard or construction paper in 1" X 5" rectangles and inscribe short, memorable quotations on each. Suggested lines include these by Dr. Martin Luther King, Jr.:

- ◆ Injustice anywhere is a threat to justice everywhere.
- ◆ I believe that unarmed truth and unconditional love will have the final word in reality.
- ◆ Nonviolence is the answer to the crucial political and moral questions of our time.
- ◆ He who accepts evil without protesting against it is really cooperating with it.
- ◆ Our destiny is tied up with the destiny of America.
- ◆ Now is the time to make real the promises of democracy.
- ◆ One day we've got to sit down together at the table of brotherhood.
- ◆ We are inevitably our brother's keeper because we are our brother's brother.

◆ The time is always ripe to do right.

After decorating the tagboard with drawings, stickers, or pictures cut from magazines, have students coat the poster with sheets of clear stick-on plastic or laminate by machine. Cut the final page with scissors or paper cutter. Use bookmarks as banquet favors or rewards for reading or class attendance, as gifts to handicapped children, or retirement home projects.

Budget: $25-$50

Sources:

Delamotte, Eugenia, Natania Meeker, and Jean O'Barr, eds. *Women Imagine Change: A Global Anthology of Women's Resistance, 600 B. C. E. to Present*, Routledge, 1997.

Diggs, Anita Doren, ed., *Talking Drums: An African-American Quote Collection*, St. Martin's, 1995.

Maggio, Rosalie, *The New Beacon Book of Quotations by Women*, Beacon Press, 1996.

"Mother Wit Words of Wisdom from Black Women," *Ebony*, March 1997, 60.

Mullane, Deirdre, *Words to Make My Dream Children Live: A Book of African American Quotations,* Anchor Books, 1995.

Riley, Dorothy Winbush, *My Soul Looks Back, 'Less I Forget': A Collection of Quotations by People of Color*, Harper Perennial, 1993.

Alternative Applications: Assemble finished markers on a classroom clothesline made of twine and attach with paperclips, or adorn with tassel ties through a hole punched in one end and distribute as tray markers in hospitals, cafeterias, or restaurants.

 **Box Zoo**

Age/Grade Level or Audience: Kindergarten and elementary crafts classes; religious schools; scout troops; 4-H clubs; classes for the handicapped.

Description: Create an African zoo.

Procedure: Have students collect grocery boxes and cartons. Spray paint with a neutral color. Have students use colored pencils, chalk, crayons, colored markers, acrylics, or tempera paint to depict a different African animal on each box, for instance the gorilla, rhinoceros, leopard, ocelot, emu, hippopotamus, ostrich, elephant, giraffe, lion, tiger, gnu, wildebeest, dik-dik, orangutans, crocodile, mamba, and cobra. Arrange the finished boxes in a window display or create a pyramid or wall for a hall display.

Budget: $50-$75

Sources:

Connor, Nikki, *Creative Crafts from Cardboard Boxes*, Copper Beech Books, 1996.

Diakité, Baba Wagué, *The Hunterman and the Crocodile*, Scholastic Books, 1997.

Fischer, Alexandra E., *A to Z Animals Around the World*, Putnam Publishing Group, 1994.

Hamilton, Robyn, ed, *Africa Activity Book: Arts, Crafts, Cooking and Historical Aids*, Edupress, 1996.

Hartmann, Wendy, *One Sun Rises, An African Wildlife Counting Book*, Dutton Child Books, 1994.

Ruelle, Karen G., *Seventy-Five Fun Things to Make and Do by Yourself*, Sterling, 1993.

Tabor, Nancy M., *Fifty on the Zebra*, Charlesbridge, 1994.

Theroux, Paul, "Down the Zambezi," *National Geographic*, October 1997, 2-31.

Williams, Wendy, "Of Elephants and Men," *Animals*, November/December 1997, 24-30.

Alternative Applications: Use a box zoo as a stage setting for a PTA program on African wildlife or endangered species. Have each participant carry a box to center stage and explain the pictured animal's habits, diet, colors, shape, movements, and natural habitat. For an added treat, have students organize their words into poems, stories, or songs.

Camp Africa

Originator: Kim Jolly, Director, International House, 322 Hawthorne Lane, Charlotte, NC 28204 (704-333-8099).

Age/Grade Level or Audience: Elementary and middle school children.

Description: Create an in-house camp.

Procedure: On successive Saturdays, after school, or in the evenings, introduce campers to a different African culture at each session by telling stories, playing or singing native music, organizing map drawing, introducing students to Kwanzaa rituals, showing videotapes such as *Sarafina!* and *The Power of One*, or developing craft tables where young artisans can choose among cloth or mask painting, batiking, cooking, jewelry, calligraphy, puppetry, rock painting, or flag and banner making. A useful craft focus is the creation of a Kwanzaa table setting:

◆ Have students saw 1" x 12" boards into one foot platter lengths and sand the ends smooth.

◆ Organize a grass, vine, rushes, or straw weaving shop to create covered baskets to hold bread and fruit or decorations, such as native flowers, ferns, or feathers.

◆ Include mat weaving to provide the table with a single runner, place mats, hot pads for casseroles, or mats for seating. Stress geometric designs in typical African variations of red, green, black, and yellow.

◆ Form bowls, serving spoons, and ladles out of gourds and clay. Paint each with non-toxic materials to match mats.

◆ Create decorative jewelry out of different pasta shapes, buttons, and beads strung on elastic thread. Paint the finished pieces the colors of Africa.

◆ Use acrylic paints or colored markers to decorate smooth stones to resemble African frogs, toads, locusts, butterflies, fish, birds, snakes, or alligators.

◆ Paint faces with festive designs—leaves, animals, ritual symbols, and letters.

◆ Make spice balls from 12-inch circles of cheesecloth filled with whole spices and tied with raffia, yarn, or ribbon.

Conclude Camp Africa with a public display of student work alongside candid shots and videos of participants at work, dancing, singing, telling riddles, or listening to stories.

Budget: $50-$75

Sources:

"The Complete Kwanzaa Celebration Basket," http//lainet3.lainet.com/~joejones/kwanzaa/htm.

Cooke, Andy. *Bear's Art School Face Painting Kit*, Barrons Juveniles, 1996.

Copage, Eric V., *Kwanzaa: An African-American Celebration of Culture and Cooking*, Morrow, 1993.

Cut and Make African Masks, Dover Publications.

Duckitt, Hildagonda, *Traditional South African Cookery*, Hippocrene Books, 1996.

Favorite Birds Iron-On Transfer Patterns, Dover.

Ford, Juwanda, *K Is for Kwanzaa,* Scholastic Books, 1997.

Frank, Vivien, *Making Masks,* Book Sales Inc., 1992.

Hamilton, Robyn, ed, *Africa Activity Book: Arts, Crafts, Cooking and Historical Aids*, Edupress, 1996.

Kallen, Stuart A., *Eco-Arts and Crafts*, Abdo & Daughters, 1993.

"Kwanzaa," http//www.dca.net/~areid/kwanzaa.htm.

"Kwanzaa Bazaar," http//shops.net/shops/Kwanzaa/item-5.html.

"Kwanzaa Links," http//new.melanet.com/kwanzaa/links.html.

Lohf, Sabine, *Things I Can Make*, Chronicle Books, 1994.

Merson, Annette, *African Cookery*, Winston-Derek, 1987.

Oni, Sauda, *What Kwanzaa Means to Me*, DARE Books, 1996.

Robartson, Linda, *The Complete Kwanzaa Celebration Book*, Creative Acrylic, 1993.

Ross, Kathy, *Crafts for Kwanzaa*, Millbrook Press, 1994.

St. James, Synthia, *The Gifts of Kwanzaa*, Albert Whitman & Co., 1994.

Alternative Applications: Organize a city-wide system of Afrocentric day camps for children, families, scouts, church and civic groups, and handicapped or elderly people. Distribute Afrocentric workshop ideas and methods to day-care workers, educators, 4-H and scout leaders, PTA committees, settlement workers, and religious leaders for application to other settings, such as church school, camporees, classrooms, sheltered workshops, and community fairs. Publish instructions for cooking, crafts, and games at a civic or educational website or by e-mail to schools and clubs.

Clasped Hands

Originator: Susan E. Koricki, elementary school teacher, Germantown, Maryland.

Age/Grade Level or Audience: Elementary and middle school art classes; church schools; Scout troops; 4-H clubs; retirement homes.

Description: Create a sign-in board celebrating black history week.

Procedure: Have a volunteer create two model hands, one dark and one light. Place hands at the center of a bulletin board that features a quotation urging racial harmony, such as the Reverend Al Sharpton's declaration "No justice. No peace." and Rodney King's plea, "Can't we just get along?" Suspend a pencil by a long string so that students, parents, staff, and visitors can make personal replies to the quotation.

Budget: $25-$50

Sources:
Delamotte, Eugenia, Natania Meeker, and Jean O'Barr, eds. *Women Imagine Change: A Global Anthology of Women's Resistance, 600 B. C. E. to Present*, Routledge, 1997.
Diggs, Anita Doren, ed., *Talking Drums: An African-American Quote Collection*, St. Martin's, 1995.
Maggio, Rosalie, *The New Beacon Book of Quotations by Women*, Beacon Press, 1996.
"Mother Wit Words of Wisdom from Black Women," *Ebony*, March 1997, 60.
Mullane, Deirdre, *Words to Make My Dream Children Live: A Book of African American Quotations,* Anchor Books, 1995.
Riley, Dorothy Winbush, *My Soul Looks Back, 'Less I Forget': A Collection of Quotations by People of Color*, Harper Perennial, 1993.

Alternative Applications: Distribute dark and light paper so that students can draw two hands and interlock them. Have students inscribe their opinions of how racial harmony can be achieved. Post hands on the walls and bulletin boards of a school, mall, restaurant, museum, library, airport, bus station, retirement home, and hospital. Center the display with an original caption, for example, "Give Fellowship a Hand."

Crafts Clinic

Originators: Obakunle and Tejuola Akinlana, storytellers, teachers, and artisans.

Age/Grade Level or Audience: All ages.

Description: Locate artisans to staff a crafts workshop.

Procedure: Invite black artists and crafts specialists to demonstrate the fundamentals of these skills:

basketry	batiking	carpentry
carving	ironwork	jewelry
leathercrafting	mask making	needlecraft
pottery	sand sculpture	screen printing
stained glass	tanning	weaving

For instance, offer a class in gourd decoration. Demonstrate how to weave twine and beads over a globular gourd to create a shekere, a rhythm instrument common to the Yoruba and to African American storytellers. Provide the workshop free or at reduced cost to indigent community members. Include craft demonstrations as part of a street or crafts fair, library workshop, museum display, or community Afro-festival. Invite participants to sell their wares.

Budget: $50-$75

Sources:
Craft items from SELFHELP Crafts U.S. and International, 704 Main Street, P.O. Box 500, Akron, PA 17501-0500 (717-859-4971).
For information about the shekere, contact Obakunle and Tejuola Akinlana, Midland, North Carolina (704-888-6302).
Conner, Nikki, *Creative Crafts from Cardboard Boxes*, Copper Beech Books, 1996.
Cooke, Andy. *Bear's Art School Face Painting Kit*, Barrons Juveniles, 1996.

Donna Dacey's "Crafts of Many Cultures Three Seasonal Art Projects with Global Appeal," *Instructor*, November-December 1991, 30-33.

Dubuc, Suzanne, *Make Up Funny Masks*, Adams Inc., 1993.

Frank, Vivien, *Making Masks*, Book Sales Inc., 1992.

Gibbons, Gail, *Catch the Wind: All About Kites*, Little, Brown, 1989.

Hamilton, Robyn, ed., *Africa Activity Book: Arts, Crafts, Cooking and Historical Aids*, Edupress, 1996.

"Handicrafts, Handicrafts, Handicrafts," http//www.interking.com/be/a/Handicrafts.html.

Kallen, Stuart A., *Eco-Arts and Crafts*, Abdo & Daughters, 1993.

Lohf, Sabine, *Things I Can Make*, Chronicle Books, 1994.

Mabunda, L. Mpho, ed., *The African American Almanac*, 7th edition, Gale, 1997.

Sanders, Marlita, "Dollmaking: The Celebration of a Culture," *School Arts*, January 1992, 27.

Ruelle, Karen G., *Seventy-Five Fun Things to Make and Do by Yourself*, Sterling, 1993.

Alternative Applications: Create a database of craft ideas, such as making a shekere, thumb piano, or other African musical instrument or producing masks, screens, shell jewelry, batiking, pottery, weaving, sculpting, body painting, and other handicrafts of Africa, the Caribbean, or the sea islands of Georgia and South Carolina. Share your information via e-mail, at a local library or school website, or on IRIS, Prodigy, or other information services.

Crocheting a Bit of Africa

Age/Grade Level or Audience: Elementary and middle school art classes; church schools; scout troops, 4-H clubs; classes for the handicapped; sheltered workshops; retirement homes.

Description: Incorporate the colors of Africa in crochet.

Procedure: Teach a small group to crochet simple chain stitches in a straight line or circle. Use yarns of varying materials and weights in Africa's traditional colors—red, green, yellow, and black. Have students shape their crocheted chains into friendship bracelets, table mats, runners, afghans, and lap robes. For more advanced handicrafters, suggest patterns for round caps, mittens, and vests. Groups of crocheters may join chains to create couch throws, bedspreads, floor and sofa coverings, and testers.

Budget: $50-$75

Sources:

Gryski, Camilla, *Friendship Bracelets*, Morrow, 1993.

Hamilton, Robyn, ed., *Africa Activity Book: Arts, Crafts, Cooking and Historical Aids*, Edupress, 1996.

"Janet's Crochet," http//www.rahab.net/janets_crochet/

"Learn to Crochet the Mile a Minute Way," http//www.schoolroom.com/videos/v2. 63.htm.

Mountford, Debra, *The Harmony Guide to Crocheting Techniques and Stitches*, Crown Publishing Group, 1993.

O'Reilly, Susie, *Knitting and Crochet*, Thomson Learning, 1994.

Alternative Applications: Organize a similar workshop to teach knitting. Concentrate on the garter stitch, which is a simple maneuver for beginners. Repeat to create shawls, afghans, baby blankets, wall hangings, and other items in the colors of Africa.

 ## Crocodile Trains

Age/Grade Level or Audience: Kindergarten craft classes; day care projects; religious schools; classes for handicapped children.

Description: Create crocodile train pull toys.

Procedure: Have students tie together two egg cartons, bottom sides up, with strings, twist ties, or pipe cleaners. Attach a whole egg carton, top side up, to the front for a head/engine and halt a bottom portion, split lengthwise, for a tail. Separate the upper and lower segment of the head/engine to resemble open jaws. Paint the outer body/train green to resemble a crocodile. Glue on buttons or paint eyes on the front portion. Glue cardboard teeth to the inside of the mouth, which should be colored red. Attach bright-colored cardboard or plastic wheels to the outer edges with brads. Tie a pull string to the front.

Budget: $25-$50

Sources:

Diakité, Baba Wagué, *The Hunterman and the Crocodile*, Scholastic Books, 1997.

Hamilton, Robyn, ed, *Africa Activity Book: Arts, Crafts, Cooking and Historical Aids*, Edupress, 1996.

Kallen, Stuart A., *Eco-Arts and Crafts*, Abdo & Daughters, 1993.

Lohf, Sabine, *Things I Can Make*, Chronicle Books, 1994.

Stone, Lynn, *Crocodiles*, Rourke Corp., 1990.

Storms, John, *Cory the Crocodile*, Heian International, 1993.

Alternative Applications: Make a crocodile from burlap or muslin bags painted green. Cut out arm and neck holes. Place a bag on each child. Have participants hold to the waist of the child ahead in line. Select a leader to choose the pace and direction as participants emulate wobbly crocodile movements around the room or playground. Provide music for the crocodile to dance to, such as "See You Later Alligator," "Never Smile at a Crocodile," "I Went to the Animal Fair," or "The Hokey-Pokey."

Design America

Age/Grade Level or Audience: All ages.

Description: Hold a black history design contest.

Procedure: Have entrants redesign or describe a common American symbol to include the contributions of non-white people. For example, present one of these from the black perspective:

- Air Force One
- American flag
- Arlington Cemetery
- FDR Memorial
- Golden Gate Bridge

- Justice Department statue
- Madonna of the Trail
- Mayflower
- Mount Rushmore
- Oregon Trail
- Pentagon
- Smithsonian Institution
- Statue of Liberty
- Suffragette Statue in the Rotunda Capitol
- *U. S. S. Constitution*
- Uncle Sam
- Vietnam Women's Memorial
- White House

- American Eagle
- Apollo 13
- Capitol
- Friendship 7
- golden spike on the transcontinental railroad
- Liberty Bell
- Marine Corps War Memorial
- Minuteman
- national seal
- paper currency or a coin
- Santa Fe Trail
- Spirit of St. Louis
- Stone Mountain
- Tomb of the Unknown of the Soldier
- U.S. Marine insignia
- Vietnam War Memorial
- Walking Liberty Dollar

Publish results in a local newspaper, arts newsletter, television interview, or traveling show.

Budget: $50-$75

Sources:

Travel guides from state travel bureaus, brochures from the American Automobile Association, and Internet travel websites.

"Great American Monuments," http//www.mmnewsstand.com/static/products/5173/index.html.

Nishiura, Elizabeth, ed., *American Battle Monuments: A Guide to Battlefields and Cemeteries of the United States Armed Forces*, Omnigraphics, Inc., 1996.

O'Halloran, Kate, *Hands-on Culture of Ancient Egypt*, Walch, 1997.

———, *Hands-on Culture of West Africa*, Walch, 1997.

"Patriotic," http//www.findphoto.com/Patriotic.htm.

"Tourmobile," http//www.tourmobile.com/sites.stops/washmon.html.

Young, Donald, *Natural Monuments of America*, Random House, 1990.

Zinsser, William K, *American Places: A Writer's Pilgrimage to Fifteen of This Country's Most Visited and Cherished Sites*, HarperCollins, 1993.

Alternative Applications: Propose the creation of a new insignia, park, performance center, building, monument, or other commemoration of American multiculturalism. Have a technical art or drafting class choose a place, style, purpose, and inscription for the memorial, such as a permanent Smithsonian exhibit honoring all Olympic athletes, a bas-relief on the U.S. Capitol featuring the diversity of races and their contributions to America, tribute to victims of slavery or civil rights demonstrations, or national children's theme park honoring all races.

 Desktop Puzzles

Age/Grade Level or Audience: High school computer or desktop publishing class.

Description: Create children's puzzles for Black History Month.

Procedure: Have participants choose information to include on a variety of puzzles, including these:

crossword puzzles	dot-to-dot puzzles	geometric puzzles
hidden pictures	mazes	rebuses
scrambled words	seek-and-find grids	spirals

For example, make a starburst of numbered lines for children to fill in with letters of a black hero's name. Use familiar names, such as baseball great Jackie Robinson, comic Bill Cosby, or singer Whitney Houston. Assemble finished puzzles and word activities in a booklet. Reproduce copies for a summer reading program, after-school project, church school, or home-bound resource. Provide group leaders with answer sheets.

Budget: $25-$50

Sources:

"African American History," http//www.msstate.edu/Archives/History/USA/Afro-Amer/ afro.html.

African American History in the Press, 1851-1899, Gale, 1996.

Asante, Molefi K., *Historical and Cultural Atlas of African Americans*, Macmillan, 1991.

"Black History," http//www.slip.net/~rigged/history.html.

"Black History Month Let's Get Started," http//www.netnoir.com/spotlight/bhm/ jbhm.html.

Corbin, Raymond M., *1,999 Facts about Blacks A Sourcebook of African-American Achievement*, 2nd edition, Madison Books, 1997.

"The Faces of Science African Americans in the Sciences," http//www. lib.lsu.edu/lib/chem/display/faces.html.

Hine, Darlene Clark, Elsa Barkley Brown, and Rosalyn Terborg-Penn, *Black Women in America: An Historical Encyclopedia,* Carlson Publishing, 1993.

Nelson, Rebecca, and Marie J. MacNee, eds., *The Olympic Factbook: A Spectator's Guide to the Summer Games*, Visible Ink Press, 1996.

Saari, Peggy, and Daniel B. Baker, *Explorers and Discoverers: From Alexander the Great to Sally Ride*, U•X•L/Gale, 1995.

"This Person in Black History Thurgood Marshall," http//www.ai.mit.edu/~isbell/ Hfh/black/events_and_people/001.thurgood_marshall.

Trager, James, *The People's Chronology*, revised edition, Henry Holt, 1996.

Alternative Applications: Post models of types of black hero puzzles in a handbook of desktop publishing art. Use the handbook as a text for future computer classes.

Doll Displays

Originator: Leatrice Pearson, teacher, Lenoir, North Carolina.

Age/Grade Level or Audience: All ages.

Description: Have participants dress dolls in period costumes and arrange them in scenarios to represent events in black history.

Procedure: Invite local civic clubs, literary guilds, sororities, fraternities, and other public-spirited organizations to dramatize a significant moment in African American history by dressing small plastic dolls and placing them in shadow-box settings or displays. Feature events such as the bravery of couriers for the underground railroad, the exploits of Buffalo Soldiers, the Montgomery bus boycotts organized by Dr. Martin Luther King, Jr., Mae Jemison's space flight, the first black fighter pilots in the United States military, or the activism of Sojourner Truth, Fannie Lou Hamer, Faye Wattleton, and other abolitionists and women's rights leaders. Accompany each entry with a short summary of the event, its date, and the outcome. For example, a depiction of the underground railroad might tell how and where it was started, its duration, and the approximate number of people who used it to escape slavery. Plastic dolls are available in handicraft supply stores. For inexpensive substitutes, use wooden clothespins or dowels with styrofoam or papier maché heads.

Budget: $25-$50

Sources:
"Handicrafts, Handicrafts, Handicrafts," http//www.interking.com/be/a/Handicrafts. html.

Kallen, Stuart A., *Eco-Arts and Crafts*, Abdo & Daughters, 1993.

Lohf, Sabine, *Things I Can Make*, Chronicle Books, 1994.

McDiarmid, Hugh, "Dolls Revive Black History for Students," *Detroit Free Press*, January 21, 1997, 1B, 4B

Ruelle, Karen G., *Seventy-Five Fun Things to Make and Do by Yourself*, Sterling, 1993.

Sanders, Marlita, "Dollmaking: The Celebration of a Culture," *School Arts*, January 1992, 27.

Alternative Applications: Organize an annual competition, especially in areas where there are numerous clubs. Include a multiracial panel drawn from newspaper staffs, school and college faculty, libraries, city and county offices, and art councils.

The Door to Awareness

Age/Grade Level or Audience: Middle school or high school classes; shopping mall; office building; civic center; or hospital.

Description: Sponsor a door decorating contest.

Procedure: Have participants use found objects, collage, watercolor, pencil sketches, or African designs as decorations for doors. Give prizes for the most original, the most artistic, or the most historically accurate. Emphasize the following motifs:

- ◆ African animals in their natural settings
- ◆ Caribbean carnival costumes and floats
- ◆ Kwanzaa table settings
- ◆ maps, seals, coins, coats of arms, and crests
- ◆ native hairstyles, jewelry, and headdresses
- ◆ natural foodstuffs and spices from Africa and the Caribbean
- ◆ symbols and flags

Budget: $25-$50

Sources:

Magazines such as *Ebony, Essence, Jet,* and *Emerge.* Craft items from SELFHELP Crafts U.S. and International, 704 Main Street, P.O. Box 500, Akron, PA 17501-0500 (717-859-4971).

Copage, Eric V., *Kwanzaa: An African-American Celebration of Culture and Cooking,* Morrow, 1993.

Dahlstrom, Lorraine M., *Doing the Days: A Year's Worth of Creative Journaling, Drawing, Listening, Reading, Thinking, Arts and Crafts Activities for Children,* Free Spirit Publications 1994.

Hamilton, Robyn, ed, *Africa Activity Book: Arts, Crafts, Cooking and Historical Aids,* Edupress, 1996.

Mabunda, L. Mpho, ed., *The African American Almanac,* 7th edition, Gale, 1997.

Stevich, Ute, *Haitian Celebration: Art and Culture,* Milwaukee Art Museum, 1992.

Alternative Applications: Have students decorate a series of cardboard or wooden panels with African or Caribbean scenes, such as these:

- ◆ basket weaving
- ◆ family games
- ◆ gardening and harvesting
- ◆ native festival
- ◆ religious rite
- ◆ cooking and preserving food
- ◆ fishing expedition
- ◆ market day
- ◆ picking and preparing fruit
- ◆ travel

Locate the panels in an auditorium or mall and have visitors vote for the winners in each category.

Dual Art Contest

Age/Grade Level or Audience: All ages.

Description: Offer a two-stage art contest to celebrate Black History Month.

Procedure: Assist the Friends of the Library, PTA, or civic group in proposing an adult contest. Have participants select a scene from black history to draw or sketch. Reproduce the winning entry as a coloring or paint-by-number contest for children.

Budget: $50-$75

Sources:

African American History in the Press, 1851-1899, Gale, 1996.

Asante, Molefi K., *Historical and Cultural Atlas of African Americans,* Macmillan, 1991.

"Black History," http//www.slip.net/~rigged/history.html.

"Black History Month Let's Get Started," http//www.netnoir.com/spotlight/bhm/ jbhm. html.

Corbin, Raymond M., *1,999 Facts about Blacks: A Sourcebook of African-American Achievement,* 2nd edition, Madison Books, 1997.

Hine, Darlene Clark, Elsa Barkley Brown, and Rosalyn Terborg-Penn, *Black Women in America: An Historical Encyclopedia,* Carlson Publishing, 1993.

Mabunda, L. Mpho, ed., *The African American Almanac,* 7th edition, Gale, 1997.

Nelson, Rebecca, and Marie J. MacNee, eds., *The Olympic Factbook: A Spectator's Guide to the Summer Games,* Visible Ink Press, 1996.

Saari, Peggy, and Daniel B. Baker, *Explorers and Discoverers: From Alexander the Great to Sally Ride,* U•X•L/Gale, 1995.

Shapiro, William E., ed., *The Kingfisher Young People's Encyclopedia of the United States.,* Larousse Kingfisher Chambers, 1994.

Alternative Applications: Offer books on black history as prizes for the best colored page or the most appropriate captions.

 Floor Art Festival

Age/Grade Level or Audience: K-3 classes; day care; church school; after-school projects.

Description: Create floor art in African colors.

Procedure: Cover a porch or gym floor or a mural with a design that features African colors, which are red, green, yellow, white, and black. Use chalk, tempera paint, or colored markers to design a hot air balloon, carousel ride, or carnival scene in which people of all races have fun together.

Budget: $25-$50

Sources:

Ajmera, Maya, and Anna Rhesa Versola, *Children from Australia to Zimbabwe*, Charlesbridge, 1997.

Kallen, Stuart A., *Eco-Arts and Crafts*, Abdo & Daughters, 1993.

Lohf, Sabine, *Things I Can Make*, Chronicle Books, 1994.

Zweifel, Frances, *The Make-Something Club Fun with Crafts, Food, and Gifts*, Viking Child Books, 1994.

Alternative Applications: Have participants sit in a ring around colorful floor art and discuss what the colors of Africa represent. Conclude by having each participant imagine taking a ride on the carousel or balloon and having fun with others.

Freedom Stamps

Age/Grade Level or Audience: Middle school and high school art classes; church schools; scout troops; 4-H clubs; retirement homes.

Description: Design stamps for the United States, Caribbean, or African postal systems.

Procedure: Instruct students to use oils, pastels, water color, acrylic, charcoal, or pen and ink to create designs commemorating important people and events in black history. Consider these as models:

- ◆ Alex Haley's creation of a family tree
- ◆ Duke Ellington's performance at Carnegie Hall
- ◆ emancipation of Haitian slaves
- ◆ Hatshepsut's architectural achievements
- ◆ Judith Jamison dancing "Cry!"
- ◆ Mae Jemison's first space flight
- ◆ Matthew Henson's arrival at the North Pole
- ◆ Ossie Davis's contributions to entertainment
- ◆ Phillis Wheatley's poems
- ◆ Salem Poor's role in the Revolutionary War
- ◆ Shaka's rise to the throne
- ◆ Sojourner Truth's feminist speeches
- ◆ Solomon's introduction to the Queen of Sheba
- ◆ Spike Lee's depiction of young American blacks in movies
- ◆ Tiger Woods at the 1997 Masters Championship Golf Match

Budget: $25-$50

Sources:

Carvell, T., "Spike Lee: Madison Avenue's Gotta Have Him," *Fortune*, April 14, 1997, 84-86.

Corbin, Raymond M. Corbin's *1,999 Facts about Blacks*, Madison Books, 1997.

Gaines, Ernest J., *Timetables of History*, Random House, 1996.

Harley, Sharon, *Timetables of African-American History: A Chronology of the Most Important People and Events in African-American History*, Simon & Schuster, 1996.

Hine, Darlene Clark, Elsa Barkley Brown, and Rosalyn Terborg-Penn, eds., *Black Women in America: An Historical Encyclopedia*, Carlson, 1993.

Alternative Applications: Divide participants into small groups to design other advertising media:

billboards	book jackets	cereal boxes
magazine ads	milk cartons	packaging
snack foods	sportswear	street markers
television ads	travel brochures	websites
welcome signs		

Determine concepts that deserve emphasis, such as family unity, education, good health practices, and active participation in government.

Gourdheads

Age/Grade Level or Audience: Elementary and middle school art classes; church schools; scout troops; 4-H clubs; retirement homes.

Description: Create a gourd painting workshop.

Procedure: Have students depict famous black people in gourd paintings. Supply acrylic paints and dried gourds that resemble heads. Glue on hair, ears, noses, and other features cut from styrofoam, packing materials, cardboard egg cartons, clay, or papier maché. Fill a gallery with a group of famous gourdheads, such as athletes, inventors, civil rights and feminist role models, religious leaders, writers, artists, actors, musicians, entrepreneurs, explorers, and military heroes.

Budget: $50-$75

Sources:

Cosby, High Noon Books, 1997.

Jordan, High Noon Books, 1997.

Lanker, Brian, *I Dream a World: Portraits of Black Women Who Changed America,* Stewart, Tabori & Chang, 1989.

Shaq, High Noon Books, 1997.

Smith, Jessie Carney, *Notable Black American Women,* Gale, 1992.

Whitney, High Noon Books, 1997.

Alternative Applications: Make gourdheads of a variety of racial groups. Decorate with headdresses, veils, hats, mustaches, glasses, elaborate wig styles, pipes, cigarette holders, fans, and earrings. Feature famous musical groups, such as the Supremes, Harlem Boys Choir, Platters, Inkspots, Pointer Sisters, Jackson Five, Sunsplash, and rap and hip-hop groups. Assemble and mark with a banner or caption featuring their greatest achievements, such as platinum albums, movies, Grammys, Emmys, or appearances at the White House.

Heritage Jubilee

Age/Grade Level or Audience: All ages.

Description: Organize a heritage jubilee, a crafts fair featuring talent of all types, from cooking to poetry and posters to dance.

Procedure: Have participants send in a written proposal of craft or talent to be displayed at a local community center, church, library, museum, or school. Arrange booths to accommodate the following crafts:

basketry	batiking	carvings
fashion design	hatmaking	jewelry
leathercrafting	macramé	masks
painting	photography	posters
sewing	stained glass	statuary
tole painting	weaving	

Provide a stage for dance, singing, recitation, and skits; a children's section for hand and face painting, storytelling, puppetry, sand art, and cornrowing; and a kitchen area for the sampling of foods and beverages and distribution of recipes.

Budget: $50-$75

Sources:
Cooke, Andy. *Bear's Art School Face Painting Kit,* Barrons Juveniles, 1996.

Dacey, Donna, "Crafts of Many Cultures Three Seasonal Art Projects with Global Appeal," *Instructor*, November-December 1991, 30-33.

"Handicrafts, Handicrafts, Handicrafts," http//www.interking.com/be/a/Handicrafts. html.

Kallen, Stuart A., *Eco-Arts and Crafts*, Abdo & Daughters, 1993.

Lohf, Sabine, *Things I Can Make*, Chronicle Books, 1994.

Ross, Kathy, *Crafts for Kwanzaa*, MIllbrook Press, 1994.

Sanders, Marlita, "Dollmaking The Celebration of a Culture," *School Arts*, January 1992, 27.

St. James, Synthia, *The Gifts of Kwanzaa*, A Whitman, 1994.

Zweifel, Frances, *The Make-Something Club Fun with Crafts, Food, and Gifts*, Viking Child Books, 1994.

Alternative Applications: Introduce youngsters to African instruments, such as the water drum, thumb piano, shekere, or panpipes. Hold a performance of ensembles at the jubilee.

 Jointed Dolls

Age/Grade Level or Audience: Middle school or high school; scout troops; church school; 4-H clubs.

Description: Have students assemble oversized paper dolls with jointed limbs; then dress them in the style of a particular tribe, such as the Maasai, Ibo, Berber, Zulu, Kikuyu, Pygmy, or Yoruba.

Procedure: Using themselves as models, have students work in pairs to accomplish the following:

- ◆ Lie down on heavy wrapping paper or cardboard and let a partner draw a human pattern.
- ◆ Cut the shape into moveable upper arms, lower arms, hands, thighs, lower legs, feet, upper and lower torso, and head.
- ◆ After connecting the pieces with brads or cord, have participants tack their models to the wall.
- ◆ Using colored markers, tempera or acrylic paints, cloth and leather scraps, yarn, buttons, and other found materials, color or dress each model in the style of a young or adult man or woman from a particular African tribe.

Budget: $25-$50

Sources:

Ajmera, Maya, and Anna Rhesa Versola, *Children from Australia to Zimbabwe*, Charlesbridge, 1997.

Hamilton, Robyn, ed, *Africa Activity Book: Arts, Crafts, Cooking and Historical Aids*, Edupress, 1996.

Müller, Claudia, *The Costume Timeline: 5000 Years of Fashion History*, Thames and Hudson, 1993.

Puppets, Jumping Jacks and Other Paper People, Dover.

Sanders, Marlita, "Dollmaking The Celebration of a Culture," *School Arts*, January 1992, 27.

Alternative Applications: Have students group paper dolls into families and include children and infants as well as older adults involved in normal activities, such as these:

- ♦ planting and harvesting
- ♦ worshipping or celebrating a military victory or national holiday
- ♦ cooking, preserving food, and eating
- ♦ entertaining guests from other tribes or nations
- ♦ playing tag and other games
- ♦ dancing and singing
- ♦ asking riddles and playing charades
- ♦ carrying out important ceremonies or rituals, such as coming of age, marriage, burials, or hunting and fishing parties.

To increase doll motion, have students attach twine or wire to the upper edge of the arms or legs. By pulling downward on the cords, the puppeteer can make the doll move.

Maasai Pendants

Age/Grade Level or Audience: Kindergarten through elementary school; Brownie or Cub Scouts; classes for the handicapped, religious schools.

Description: Create an individualized pendant from found materials or common kitchen items.

Procedure: Have students cut a five-inch circle from cardboard or styrofoam, punch a hole through the edge, then insert a thirty-inch cord or lanyard through the hole. Supply dried beans or peas, aquarium gravel, bits of colored tile, acorns, seeds, popcorn, and other small particles to be arranged in concentric circles and glued into place. Apply a layer of hairspray or polyurethane spray to strengthen each design.

Budget: $25-$50

Sources:

Bentsen, Cheryl, *Maasai Days*, Doubleday, 1991.

Hamilton, Robyn, ed, *Africa Activity Book: Arts, Crafts, Cooking and Historical Aids*, Edupress, 1996.

Margolies, Barbara A., *Olbalbal: A Day in Maasailand*, Macmillan Children's Group, 1994.

Turle, Gillies, *Art of the Maasai*, Knopf, 1992.

Alternative Applications: Have students complete a Maasai wardrobe of jewelry and clothing, including upper-arm bands, earrings, torques, waist chains, anklets, head wrap, headdress, sarong, and toe and finger rings or have them work as a team to dress a single mannikin, papier-maché model, or small doll.

 Mankala

Age/Grade Level or Audience: All ages.

Description: Teach interested participants to make and play their own game of mankala, an amusement enjoyed throughout Africa.

Procedure: Using an egg carton, twelve small bowls, or saucers scooped out in sand, have players place four beans, seeds, or other colored markers in each cup.

- ◆ The first player empties one cup and sows the markers into each of the next four cups.
- ◆ The player then empties the fifth cup and drops the five markers in the next five cups. The player continues sowing seeds until reaching an empty cup to contain the last seed.
- ◆ The second player begins at any cup and duplicates the sowing system.
- ◆ Scoring awards a point for any player whose last seed falls in a cup containing three seeds. The player receives all four seeds.
- ◆ When only eight seeds remain, the next player claims them.
- ◆ The player with the most seeds wins.

Budget: Under $25

Sources:

"The Arcade," *Homefront*, Winter 1997, 19.

"Games," http//touchstonegames.com/mankala.cgi.

"Mankala," http//www.elf.org/Mankala.html.
"Mankala Version 1," http//www.funet.fi/pub/languages/tcl/alcatel/code/mankala/
  README.

Alternative Applications: Using desktop publishing software, create an illustrated guide to mankala. Begin with a storyboard and draw in each panel the steps to setting up a board and playing the game. Complete the project with a drawing of a game in progress on the cover. Bind finished introductions to mankala to distribute as giveaways at summer reading programs, religious camps, children's birthday parties, and events with door prizes.

New Games for Old

Age/Grade Level or Audience: Middle school and high school art students.

Description: Redesign familiar games from a black perspective.

Procedure: Have students select a game to redesign, such as Monopoly, Clue, Scrabble, Pictionary, darts, Parcheesi, Chutes and Ladders, Uncle Wiggily, or Pin the Tail on the Donkey. Replace old gameboard and game paraphernalia with information gleaned from black history and experience. For example try these alterations:

- ◆ For Monopoly, replace Park Place with Bourbon Street and the Reading Railroad with the Underground Railroad. Use play money copied from African or Caribbean currency.
- ◆ For Clue, exchange Colonel Mustard with Bill Pickett. Substitute a lasso for the candlestick.
- ◆ For Scrabble, make a special list of words that count extra points, such as Zulu, Yoruba, gnu, emu, ostrich, Zaire, Benin, Egypt, Congo, Niger, or Limpopo.
- ◆ For Pictionary, limit choices to objects, games, people, or animals from Africa or the Caribbean, such as the emu, rhinoceros, or flying fish.
- ◆ For Pin the Tail on the Donkey, create large color pictures of African animals, such as a giraffe, elephant, gnu, wildebeest, gorilla, dik-dik, gazelle, baboon, hyena, or water buffalo. Offer a variety of tails to suit the animals. Have blindfolded students pin the tail on the animal it belongs to.
- ◆ Make paper javelins or dart guns from soda straws. Post a large map of Africa and vary the targets, for instance the Niger River, Lake Chad, Victoria Falls, or the Seychelles Islands. Assign values to each goal, depending on size, for example a single point for the Sahara Desert, three points for

South Africa or Algeria, or five points for the Ivory Coast or Mount Kilimanjaro.

Budget: $25-$50

Sources:

Cantor, George, *Historic Landmarks of Black America*, Gale, 1991.

Fischer, Alexandra E., *A to Z Animals Around the World*, Putnam Publishing Group, 1994.

Ginsberg, J., "Family Ties," *National Geographic World*, August 1997, 21-23.

Hamilton, Robyn, ed, *Africa Activity Book: Arts, Crafts, Cooking and Historical Aids*, Edupress, 1996.

Hartmann, Wendy, *One Sun Rises: An African Wildlife Counting Book*, Dutton Child Books, 1994.

O'Halloran, Kate, *Hands-on Culture of Ancient Egypt*, Walch, 1997.

————, *Hands-on Culture of West Africa*, Walch, 1997.

Alternative Applications: Create a new board game by having students draw a large map of Africa and develop rules for a safari.

- Make game pieces representing various ways of traveling, such as canoe, raft, camel, donkey, elephant, bicycle, ox cart, pedal cart, bush plane, ferry, tram, or all-terrain vehicle.
- Turn natural and social barriers into lost turns, such as poachers in Kenya, Victoria Falls, a termite hill, the Sahara Desert, the Nile River, animal stampedes, grass fires on the savannah, dry water holes in Somalia, sandstorms in Tunisia, passport check south of the Aswan Dam, rebel juntas, or Apartheid laws.
- Have players advance on the roll of the dice, the selection of a card from a deck, or the spin of the arrow toward a number.
- Give extra turns to players who roll doubles, land on a capital city, or pass two borders in one turn.
- Reward the player who completes the circuit.

Origami Animals

Age/Grade Level or Audience: Elementary and middle school art classes; church schools; scout troops; 4-H clubs; retirement homes.

Description: Have students fashion African animals with origami.

Procedure: Distribute tissue, typing paper, onion skin, or rice paper along with patterns for making African animals out of folded paper. Assign groups to create a menagerie of African animals, including gorilla, lion, elephant, crocodile, emu, rhinoceros, mamba, gazelle, flamingo, python, dik-dik, cobra, wildebeest, and others. Group animals into a shelf or window ledge display.

Budget: $25-$50

Sources:

Biddle, Steve, and Megumi Biddle, *Origami Safari*, Morrow, 1994.

Diakité, Baba Wagué, *The Hunterman and the Crocodile*, Scholastic Books, 1997.

The Encyclopedia of Origami and Papercraft Techniques, Simon and Schuster, 1997.

Fischer, Alexandra E., *A to Z Animals Around the World*, Putnam Publishing Group, 1994.

Fun with Animal Origami and *Fun with Easy Origami*, Dover.

Ginsberg, J., "Family Ties," *National Geographic World*, August 1997, 21-23.

Hamilton, Robyn, ed, *Africa Activity Book Arts, Crafts, Cooking and Historical Aids*, Edupress, 1996.

Hartmann, Wendy, *One Sun Rises An African Wildlife Counting Book*, Dutton Child Books, 1994.

Isadora, Rachel, *Over the Green Hills*, Greenwillow Books 1992.

Montroll, John, *African Animals in Origami,* Antroll Publications, 1993.

"Safari," http//www.odsnet.com/blackmambahomepage/safari.html.

"Serengeti," http//www.cyberatl.net/~young/

Thomas, Meredith, *Paper Shapes*, School Group, 1994.

Urton, Andrea, *Fifty Nifty Origami Crafts*, Lowell House, 1993.

Alternative Applications: Suspend origami animals on strings from lights or paddle fans or create mobiles by tying finished figures to crossed dowels, a drying rack, latter, window frame, or series of interconnected bamboo sticks. Vary colors, weights, and shapes.

Pieces of Africa

Age/Grade Level or Audience: Middle school and high school art classes; church schools; scout troops; 4-H clubs; retirement homes.

Description: Organize a mosaic workshop to honor Black History Month.

Procedure: Demonstrate how mosaics are made with the following steps:

> ◆ Have mosaic makers select an African theme to recreate, such as a native costume or colorful animal, for example a giraffe, snake lizard, butterfly, or moth, or a famous landmark in Africa, particularly Mount Kilimanjaro, Lake

Chad, Niger River, the Seychelles beaches, the Bight of Benin, or Victoria Falls.

◆ Draw a simple outline on cardboard, glass, tagboard, or wood.
◆ Assemble colored bits of construction paper, shredded magazine pages, broken pottery, aquarium rock, glass beads, sand, creek stones, pasta, dried peas, powdered cleanser or detergent, shells, spices, or seeds.
◆ Match strength of glue with weight of pieces.
◆ Fill in one color section with glue.
◆ Sprinkle on pieces in that color.
◆ Continue gluing and filling on one color at a time.
◆ Spray the finished work with polyurethane fixative or hair spray or cover with protective glass or clear glue-on plastic sheet.

Budget: $50-$75

Sources:

Dacey, Donna, "Crafts of Many Cultures Three Seasonal Art Projects with Global Appeal," *Instructor*, November-December 1991, 30-33.

"Making Mosaics," http//www.larkbooks.com/catalog/forhom/ makmosaics.html.

Müller, Claudia, *The Costume Timeline: 5000 Years of Fashion History*, Thames and Hudson, 1993.

O'Halloran, Kate, *Hands-on Culture of Ancient Egypt*, Walch, 1997.

———, *Hands-on Culture of West Africa*, Walch, 1997.

Alternative Applications: Have advanced mosaic makers embellish and texturize their drawings or turn them into 3-dimensional views by altering smaller and larger pieces, such as driftwood, shells, twigs, leaves, grass, and other found objects. Suggest that some mosaics may be pressed into clay pots, pots, dishes, trays, wall hangings, or hot pads. Display horizontally on tables and in showcases rather than vertically on walls to protect mosaics from disintegration.

 Puppet Show

Age/Grade Level or Audience: Elementary school students; Cub or Brownie Scouts or 4-H clubs.

Description: Organize a puppet show on black heroes of the Old West.

Procedure: Have participants make brown paper bag or thin cardboard puppets attached to wooden spoons, dowels, or paint stirrers to act out the lives of Nat Love, Bill "Bull-Dogger" Pickett, Britton Johnson, Arthur L. Walker, Jessie Stahl, Matthew Bones Hooks, Jim Taylor, "Stagecoach Mary" Fields, Charlie Glass, George Mourse, William Robinson, Jim Beckwourth, and other famous settlers, black drovers and cowboys, stagecoach drivers, broncobusters, pony express riders, and rodeo stars. Present the finished show for a banquet, camporee, parents' night, P.T.A., shopping mall or retirement home demonstration, program for handicapped children, county fair exhibit, or civic presentation.

After research is completed, divide participants into small groups. Have one group write the words of the rodeo announcer, sheriff, or trail boss, who will tell the backgrounds of the main characters and announce their ranch, stage driving, and rodeo feats. Have a second group use colored pencils or markers, crayons, chalk, or watercolors to draw the characters on the backs of brown paper, cardboard, cartons, wooden spoons, or clothespins. To make the figures more realistic, have children attach moveable paper arms and legs with brads and glue on felt, cloth, or string for hair, eyebrows, jeans, boots, hats, and western shirts and glue or staple the additions to the wooden spoons, dowels, or paint stirrers. Have the last group follow a similar procedure to create paper puppet horses and steers and stagecoaches.

Present the puppet show behind a draped table, counter, or puppet theater with curtain and puppeteers' bench. Have the narrator stand at the side and read the script as other troop members manipulate the puppets to illustrate the text.

Budget: $25-$50

Sources:
Black Cowboys Legends of the West, Chelsea House 1996.
Buchwald, Claire, *The Puppet Book: How to Make and Operate Puppets and Stage a Puppet-Play*, Plays, 1990.
Duch, Mabel, *Easy-to-Make Puppets: Step-by-Step Instructions*, Plays, 1993.
"Folkmanis Puppets," http//www.idis.com/puppets/
"Handilinks to Puppets," http//www.ahandyguide.com/cat1/p/p100.htm.
Katz, William Loren, *Black Indians A Hidden Heritage,* Atheneum, 1986.
———, *The Black West*, 3rd edition, Open Hand Publishers, 1987.
Knill, Harry, *Black Cowboy*, Bellerophon Books, 1993.
Janes, Susan Niner, *Puppet Theater Funstation*, Price Stern Sloan, 1996.
Love, Nat. *The Life and Adventures of Nat Love.* Black Classic Press, 1988.
Mabunda, L. Mpho, ed., *The African American Almanac*, 7th edition, Gale, 1997.
Preston, D., "Fossils and the Folsom Cowboy," *Natural History*, February 1997, 16-18.
Sierra, Judy, *Fantastic Theater Puppets and Plays for Young Performers and Young Audiences*, H. W. Wilson, 1991.

Alternative Applications: Organize a traveling wild west show for visits to other neighborhoods, schools, churches, clubs, or libraries. Use the black western puppet show for other groups as well, such as church school studies, neighborhood and police clubs, and library summer reading groups. If there are large numbers of participants involved, have other participants make posters announcing the show or create scenery, such as fencing, trees, ranch buildings, audiences, passengers, animals, stagecoaches, or arenas.

Stained Glass Animals

Age/Grade Level or Audience: Elementary art classes; church schools; scout troops; 4-H clubs; retirement homes.

Description: Create a window display of stained glass animals.

Procedure: Have students color African animals on onion skin or other translucent paper. Assign groups to create a window display of African animals, including the hippopotamus, rhinoceros, African elephant, gorilla, tiger, zebra, camel, crocodile, mamba, emu, and others. Make a lighted display by placing stained glass animals on a lightboard, window, or sheet in front of a spot light. Use the backdrop as part of a skit or presentation on African wildlife or endangered species.

Budget: $25-$50

Sources:
"Clip Art Connection," http//www.ist.net/clipart/themespc.html.
"Clip Art Sites," http//www.aoa.dhhs.gov/aoa/pages/clipsite.html.
Cymerman, John Emil, *Zoo Animals: Punch-Out Stencils*, Dover.
Dover Deskgallery: Animals and Plants, Dover.
Favorite Birds: Laser-Cut Plastic Stencils and *Animals: Laser-Cut Plastic Stencils*, Dover.
Green, John, *Wild Animals Coloring Book*, Dover.
Hamilton, Robyn, ed, *Africa Activity Book: Arts, Crafts, Cooking and Historical Aids*, Edupress, 1996.
Wild Animals Stained Glass Coloring Book, Dover.

Alternative Applications: Stencil animal shapes onto banners, poster paper, T-shirts, tablecloths, and other blank surfaces or color wild animals and display the finished pages on a bulletin board. Contrast African animals with animals from other countries, such as the American bison, llama, koala, yak, dingo, wombat, and kangaroo.

 Sweets to the Sweet

Age/Grade Level or Audience: Kindergarten or elementary art classes; church schools, scout troops, 4-H clubs, classes for the handicapped, retirement homes.

Description: Create valentines acknowledging the contributions of great black Americans.

Procedure: Have students cut out large valentines and decorate each with a name of a great black American and a symbol of that person's contribution. For example:

- ◆ Matthew Henson–dogsled
- ◆ Judith Jamison–ballet slippers
- ◆ Frederick Douglass–liberty bell
- ◆ Dr. Mae Jemison–spaceship
- ◆ Louis Armstrong–trumpet
- ◆ Scott Joplin–piano
- ◆ Maggie Lena Walker–penny
- ◆ Nat Love–lasso
- ◆ Whoopi Goldberg–purple flower
- ◆ Thurgood Marshall–gavel
- ◆ Hattie McDaniel–Oscar
- ◆ Alex Haley–map of Africa
- ◆ Dominique Dawes–trapeze
- ◆ Tiger Woods–putter
- ◆ Michael Jackson–glove
- ◆ Harry Belafonte–bongo drums
- ◆ Diana Ross–microphone
- ◆ Gregory Hines–tap shoes
- ◆ Faye Wattleton–family
- ◆ Jackie Robinson–baseball bat
- ◆ Maya Angelou–caged bird
- ◆ Arthur Ashe–tennis racket
- ◆ Madame C. J. Walker–curling iron
- ◆ Jean Du Sable–map of Chicago
- ◆ Morgan Freeman–movie reel

Vary valentines with suncatchers, 3-dimensionsl hearts, pop-up hearts, or crowns formed of hearts.

Post valentines on a bulletin board, lunchroom banner, hallway, door, or ceiling. Send a bundle of valentine mementos to a local library, museum, civic center, retirement home, legislator, or school for handicapped children. Vary the shapes of the cutouts to represent the symbols of each person's contribution. Hang the cutouts on a tree or bare branch, from a mobile or railing, or taped to window panes. Stress the colors of Africa green for nature, yellow for the sun, black for black people, and red for the blood of all humankind, which had its beginnings on the continent of Africa.

Budget: $25-$50

Sources:

Corbin, Raymond M. Corbin's *1,999 Facts about Blacks*, Madison Books, 1997.

Corwin, Judith H., *Valentine Crafts*, Watts, 1994.

Hine, Darlene Clark, Elsa Barkley Brown, and Rosalyn Terborg-Penn, eds., *Black Women in America: An Historical Encyclopedia,* Carlson, 1993.

Hornsby, Alton, *Chronology of African-American History*, 2nd edition, Gale, 1997.

Lanker, Brian, *I Dream a World: Portraits of Black Women Who Changed America*, Stewart, Tabori & Chang, 1989.

Smith, Jessie Carney, *Notable Black American Women*, Gale, 1992.

Alternative Applications: Share biographical valentines with other classes via letter and e-mail and on websites and Internet service, such as IRIS or Prodigy. For more information, consult Sandra Oehring's "Teaching with Technology," *Instructor*, November/December, 1992, 60.

'Toon Time'

Age/Grade Level or Audience: All ages.

Description: Hold a cartooning contest.

Procedure: Help the Friends of the Library, a local newspaper, journalism class, civic club, or arts league organize a contest featuring political or humorous cartoons illustrating a moment in black history. Develop guidelines such as these:

- ♦ one entry per person
- ♦ drawings must be on white 11" X 14" paper
- ♦ drawings must be done in black ink, charcoal, or pencil
- ♦ captions must be produced in 10- or 12-point type

Divide the contest by age. Award prizes for children's, teens', and adults' divisions. Post entries in a store window, mall, civic center, art museum, sidewalk display, or other centralized location. Have visitors to the exhibit vote on the best work in each category. Reproduce the best efforts for sale or distribution or print a brochure of the top cartoons.

Budget: $50-$75

Sources:

Asante, Molefi K., *Historical and Cultural Atlas of African Americans*, Macmillan, 1991.

Blitz, Brice, *Cartoon Drawing Kit*, W. Foster Publications, 1995.

Edwards, Don, *Cartooning*, Airbrush Act, 1993.

Jones, Marty, *Cartoon Workshop Kit*, Hunt Manufacturing, 1997.
Lightfoot, Marge, *Cartooning for Kids*, Firefly Books Ltd., 1993.
Snodgrass, Mary Ellen, *Contests for Students*, Gale, 1991.

Alternative Applications: Use black themes, events, or heroes in a cartooning workshop. Clip examples by noted cartoonists, especially these:

- ◆ Elmer Simms Campbell's cartoons for *Esquire*
- ◆ Ray Billingsley's "Curtis"
- ◆ Robin Harris and Bruce Smith's animated "Bebe's Kids"
- ◆ "Where I'm Coming From," drawn by Barbara Brandon
- ◆ humor of Walt Carr and Gerald Dyes in *Ebony*
- ◆ Ron Bryant's political cartoons in *Emerge*

Have participants isolate unique elements in each, such as profiles, caricatures, dialect, and satire.

T-Shirt Factory

Age/Grade Level or Audience: All ages.

Description: Organize a T-shirt factory to celebrate Black History Month.

Procedure: Have participants apply, embroider, paint, or stencil appropriate symbols, words, messages, patterns, or figures on T-shirts to be worn during Black History Month. Suggest the following decorations:

- ◆ messages of peace and healing
- ◆ tributes to civil rights leaders, particularly Mark Mathebane, Martin Luther King, Jr., Sojourner Truth, Abraham Lincoln, Rosa Parks, Fannie Lou Hamer, and Nelson Mandela
- ◆ symbols of African pride, such as flags, family scenes, or portrait busts of leaders
- ◆ abstract designs surrounding single words, such as "Peace," "Unity," "Friends," or "Brotherhood"
- ◆ short African aphorisms, such as these:
    "He who learns, teaches."
    "Poverty is slavery."
    "A brother is like one's shoulder."
    "The teeth are smiling, but is the heart?"
    "Love is like a baby; it needs to be treated tenderly."
    "There is no medicine to cure hatred."
    "To try and to fail is not laziness."

◆ quotations from white leaders, such as Lincoln's famous comments:

"As I would not be a slave, so I would not be a master."

"A house divided against itself cannot stand."

"Might makes right."

"A just and lasting peace among ourselves."

"With malice toward none, with charity for all."

Budget: $50-$75

Sources:

"Clip Art Connection," http//www.ist.net/clipart/themespc.html.

"Clip Art Sites," http//www.aoa.dhhs.gov/aoa/pages/clipsite.html.

Delamotte, Eugenia, Natania Meeker, and Jean O'Barr, eds. *Women Imagine Change: A Global Anthology of Women's Resistance, 600 B. C. E. to Present*, Routledge, 1997.

Diggs, Anita Doren, ed., *Talking Drums: An African-American Quote Collection*, St. Martin's, 1995.

Maggio, Rosalie, *The New Beacon Book of Quotations by Women*, Beacon Press, 1996.

"Mother Wit Words of Wisdom from Black Women," *Ebony*, March 1997, 60.

Mullane, Deirdre, *Words to Make My Dream Children Live: A Book of African American Quotations,* Anchor Books, 1995.

Riley, Dorothy Winbush, *My Soul Looks Back, 'Less I Forget': A Collection of Quotations by People of Color*, Harper Perennial, 1993.

Watts, Lynda, *Making Your Own Cards: Creative Designs for Special Occasions*, Sterling, 1995.

Alternative Applications: Sell stenciled or screen printed T-shirts, tote bags, posters, calendars, placemats and napkins, note paper, caps, playing cards, and other items by mail or at libraries, museums, school homecoming, street fairs, or civic celebrations. Set a community goal and use the money to build a day-care center, shelter for the homeless or AIDS victims, halfway house for alcoholics, mental patients, abused women, or the mentally handicapped, or road marker or other monument to black pride.

Biography

African and Caribbean Leaders

Age/Grade Level or Audience: Middle school and high school history classes; historical societies; civic clubs.

Description: Narrate capsule biographies of great African and Caribbean leaders.

Procedure: Describe in short biographies the contributions of founders, philosophers, rulers, prime ministers, counselors, and freedom fighters of black nations. Include these:

Affonso I	Ahmadu	Akhenaton
Banda	Ibn Battuta	Steven Biko
Barthelemy Boganda	Amilcar Cabral	Mary Eugenia Charles
Joseph Cinque	Jeanne Martin Cissé	Cleopatra
Elizabeth Domitien	Felix Eboué	King Ezana
Usman Dan Fodio	Frene Ginwala	Gudit
Hannibal	Felix Houphouet-Boigny	Imhotep
Jugurtha	Hastings Kamuzu	Modibo Keita
Jomo Kenyatta	Chief Khama	Sir Seretse Khama
Osai Tutu Kwamina	King Lobengula	the Mahdi
Nelson Mandela	Quett Masire	Mayotte
King Menelik II	Michel Micombero	Mobutu
Moshesh	King Mswati	Mansa Musa
Frederick Mutesa II	Nefertiti	Charity Kaluki Ngilu
Ngouabi	Macias Nguema	Kwame Nkrumah
Julius Nyerere	Queen N'Zinga	Milton Obote

Ruth Perry	Ramses	Queen Ranavalona III
Haile Selassie	Leopold Senghor	Shaka
Sobhuza I	Tarik	Theodore
Sekou Touré	Ertha Pascal Trouillot	King Tut
Bishop Desmond Tutu	Osei Tutu	

Budget: Under $25

Sources:

The films *Zulu* (1964), *Mandela* (1987), and *Khartoum* (1966).

"Africa," *Current History*, May 1997, 192-236.

Almanac of Famous People, Gale, 1997.

Buttenwieser, Susan, "Time Flies When You're Changing the World," *Ms.*, November/ December, 1997, 46-51.

Gevisser, M., "Africa after Mobutu," *Nation*, June 2, 1997, 6-7.

Goldberg, J., "Our Africa," *New York Times Magazine*, March 2, 1997, 32-39.

Jackson, John G., *Introduction to African Civilizations*, Citadel Press, 1994.

"Nelson Rolihlahla Mandela," http//www.anc.org.za/people/mandela.html.

"Nzinga Warrior Queen," http//www.netins.net80/showcase/alurir/ nzinga.html.

Ogot, Bethwell A., ed., *General History of Africa from the Sixteenth to the Eighteenth Century*, University of California Press, 1992.

Peretz, M., "When They Were Kings," *New Republic*, June 17, 1997, 46.

Squitieri, Tom, "Despite Democracy, Hope's on Hold in Haiti," *USA Today*, October 15, 1997, 1-2A.

Useem, Andrea, "Kenya's First Woman President?," *Ms.*, November/ December, 1997, 23.

Welsing, Frances Cress, *The Isis Papers*, Third World Press, 1991.

Alternative Applications: Have students make an illustrated timeline of great African leaders from the list above. Key major items to a map that places individuals in their homelands or kingdoms, such as Axum, Songhay, Shoa, Congo, Ngola, Ashanti, Zulu, Basuto, Edo, Ewe, Somalia, or Ethiopia.

Bessie Smith

Age/Grade Level or Audience: School music groups; music clubs; civic groups.

Description: Present a profile of a black person who overcame prejudice.

Procedure: Emphasize the life of a resilient survivor, such as Bessie Smith, a singer who refused to allow discrimination to eclipse her career. Create a bulletin board, handout sheet, or oral report on these details:

◆ born to a large, poverty-stricken family on April 15, 1894, in the black quarter of Chattanooga, Tennessee
◆ discovered by Gertrude Rainey at thirteen
◆ hired as a dancer by Moses Stokes's traveling minstrel show in 1912
◆ sang at Charles Bailey's 80 Theatre in Atlanta in 1913 for $10 a week
◆ married Earl Love in 1922
◆ discovered by the head of Columbia Records in 1923
◆ recorded "Down Hearted Blues" and "Gulf Coast Blues"
◆ established her style with "Tain't Nobody's Busines, If I Do" and "Weary Blues"
◆ concentrated on the blues of prisoners, day laborers, and the poor and homeless
◆ became the highest paid black entertainer of her day and introduced the blues to mainstream American music
◆ achieved fame for "Nobody Knows You When You're Down and Out"
◆ recording career ended in 1933 after styles changed to swing
◆ died in Mississippi in 1937 as the result of a car accident

Budget: Under $25

Sources:

"Bessie Smith," http//home/gte.net/deltakit/bessiesmith.htm.

"Bessie Smith Hall," http//www.chattanooga.net/chamber/bessie.html.

Buttenwieser, Susan, "Time Flies When You're Changing the World," *Ms.*, November/ December, 1997, 46-51.

Hine, Darlene Clark, Elsa Barkley Brown, and Rosalyn Terborg-Penn, eds., *Black Women in America: An Historical Encyclopedia,* Carlson, 1993.

Smith, Jessie Carney, *Notable Black American Women,* Gale, 1992.

"This Week in Black History," *Jet*, September 28, 1992, 29.

Weatherford, Doris, *American Women's History*, Prentice Hall, 1994.

Alternative Applications: Initiate a bulletin board honor roll featuring other survivors who overcame prejudice, for example Anita Hill, Mark Mathabane, Marian Anderson, Phillis Wheatley, Jackie Robinson, Harriet Jacobs, Tiger Woods, Ida Wells-Barnett, Wilma Rudolph, Josephine Baker, Joe Louis, Arthur Ashe, Lynette Woodard, and Charles Drew. Write terms that capture the uniqueness of each—sports champion, colonial poet, former slave, crusading journalist, Olympic star, or breaker of the color barrier. Award each a symbolic gold star, ribbon, medal, or title.

Bio-Flash

Originator: Leatrice Pearson, teacher, Lenoir, North Carolina.

Age/Grade Level or Audience: Elementary and middle school history or language classes.

Description: Generate a series of biographical flashcards to teach students about the accomplishments of black people.

Procedure: Inscribe the front of a 4" X 12" card with a few details about a famous person's life, for example:

- ♦ first black female chief of police of Atlanta
- ♦ co-discoverer of the North Pole
- ♦ child-care worker who established homes for AIDS and crack babies
- ♦ first black justice on the United States Supreme Court
- ♦ playwright in ancient Rome
- ♦ first black female astronaut in space
- ♦ Greek slave who wrote animal fables
- ♦ singer invited by Eleanor Roosevelt to perform in Washington, D.C.
- ♦ author of *The Count of Monte Cristo*
- ♦ founder of Chicago
- ♦ talk show host and actress who starred in *The Color Purple* and *Sarafina*
- ♦ highest rated black TV comedian
- ♦ sister singer of a top pop vocal family

On the back, print the answers in large block letters Beverly Harvard, Matthew Henson, Clara Hale, Thurgood Marshall, Terence, Mae Jemison, Aesop, Marian Anderson, Alexandre Dumas, Jean Baptiste Pointe Du Sable, Whoopi Goldberg, Bill Cosby, and Janet Jackson. Drill students on the names until the class is familiar with at least twenty-five famous blacks.

Budget: Under $25

Sources:
African American Profiles, Visible Ink Press, 1997.

Almanac of Famous People, Gale, 1997.

"Bill Cosby," *Jet*, February 3, 1997, 62-65.

Chambers, Veronica, "Nouveau Soul Sister," *Newsweek*, November 24, 1997, 64-65.

Corbin, Raymond M., *1,999 Facts About Blacks*, Madison Books, 1997.

Cunningham, Ann Marie, "Loving the Unloved Children," *Ladies Home Journal*, November 1997, 206-208, 297.

Enda, Jodi, "Little Rock Welcomes Its Heroes," *The Oregonian*, September 26, 1997, A1, A23.

Graham, Jefferson, "Cosby's Comedic Coming of Age," *USA Today*, November 10, 1997, 3D.

Halberstam, David, "And Now, Live from Little Rock," *Newsweek*, September 29, 1997, 59.

Haskin, Jim, *One More River to Cross The Stories of Twelve Black Americans*, Scholastic, Inc., 1992.

Henry, Tamara, "Role Models in the Making," *USA Today*, September 20, 1997, D1, D2.

Jones, Steve, "Janet Digs Deep," *USA Today*, October 7, 1997, 1D, 2D.

Myers, Walter Dean, *One More River to Cross: An African American Photograph Album*, Harcourt Brace, 1995.

Phelps, Shirelle, ed., *Contemporary Black Biography*, Gale, 1998.

Plowden, Martha, *Famous Firsts of Black Women*, Pelican, 1993.

"The Poetry of Rita Dove," *Scholastic Scope*, September 1997, 21-23.

Severson, Molly, ed., *Performing Artists.*, U•X•L/Gale, 1995.

Skow, John, "The Joy of Being Whoopi," *Time*, September 21, 1992, 58-60.

Williams, Paige, "A Light in the Dark 'From Slavery to Freedom' at 50," *Charlotte Observer*, 1G, 4G.

Alternative Applications: Play this game in reverse, with students identifying names by mentioning details of famous lives. For example:

♦ Rita Dove—youngest and first black Poet Laureate of the United States
♦ Alice Walker—Humanist of the Year 1997
♦ Eddie Robinson—football coach for Grambling State University
♦ Shirley Chisholm—first black woman to run for U.S. President
♦ William Lloyd Garrison—editor of the abolitionist newspaper *The Liberator*
♦ Josephine Baker—exotic dancer and member of the French Resistance
♦ William H. Johnson—painter
♦ Toni Morrison—Nobel Prize winner for the novel *Beloved*
♦ Denzel Washington—star of the films *The Preacher's Wife* and *Malcolm X*
♦ Ron Brown—member of President Bill Clinton's cabinet
♦ David Satcher-director of the Centers for Disease Control

Follow up with student-made search-and-find puzzles, rebuses, cloze activities, and other word games that require the student to match name with accomplishment. Publish word games via desktop publishing, databases, e-mail, school website site, or Internet services such as IRIS or Prodigy. Share students' work with other classes or sister schools.

Black Autobiography and Biography

Originator: Leatrice Pearson, retired English teacher, Lenoir, North Carolina.

Age/Grade Level or Audience: High school or college language, history, or African American studies class; adult book club or literary society.

Description: Organize a roundtable to read and discuss black biography and autobiography, which are major contributions to literature by black writers.

Procedure: Introduce readers to a variety of black narratives, particularly these:

- Anne Moody, *Coming of Age in Mississippi*
- James W. C. Pennington, *The Fugitive Blacksmith*
- Dick Gregory, *Nigger*
- Frederick Douglass, *Narratives of the Life of Frederick Douglass*
- Lorraine Hansberry, *To Be Young, Gifted and Black*
- Harriet Jacobs, *Incidents in the Life of a Slave Girl*
- Richard Wright, *Black Boy*
- Eldridge Cleaver, *Soul on Ice*
- Malcolm X and Alex Haley, *The Autobiography of Malcolm X*
- Claude Brown, *Manchild in the Promised Land*
- Pearl Bailey, *Raw Pearl*
- Billie Holiday, *Lady Sings the Blues*
- Mary C. Terrell, *A Colored Woman in a White World*
- Ethel Water, *His Eye Is on the Sparrow*
- Nina Simone, *I Put a Spell on You*
- Tina Turner, *I, Tina*
- Jamaica Kincaid, *My Brother* and *Annie John*
- Wally Amos, *The Famous Amos Story*
- Sam Davis, Jr., *Yes I Can*
- Melton A. McLaurin, *Celia: A Slave*
- Darryl Strawberry, *Darryl*
- Winnie Mandela, *Part of My Heart Went with Him*
- Langston Hughes, *I Wonder As I Wander*
- Charlayne Hunter-Gault, *In My Place*
- Chester Himes, *The Quality of Hurt* and *My Life As Absurdity*
- Susie King Taylor, *A Black Woman's Civil War Memoirs*
- Gustavus Vassa, *The Interesting Narrative of the Life of Olaudah Equiano, or Gustavus Vassa, the African; by Himself*

Include the life stories of Leontyne Price, Steven Biko, Kathleen Battle, Jessye Norman, Muhammed Ali, Rosa Parks, Zora Neale Hurston, Michael Jordan, Bill Cosby, Mike Tyson, Muhammed Ali, Josiah Henson, Prince, Marva Collins, Adam Clayton Powell, Huddie "Leadbelly" Ledbetter, Thurgood Marshall, Paul Robeson, Jackie Robinson, Tituba, Robert Mugabe, Haile Selassie, Florence Griffith Joyner, Bessie Smith, Marian Anderson, Jackie Joyner Kersee, Tiger Woods, Wilma Rudolph, Nelson Mandela, Mark Mathabane, and Harriet Tubman. Invite participants to read aloud from significant passages and discuss personal strengths that made these survivors overcome racism and despair.

Budget: $25-$50

Sources:

"African Writers," http//www.africaonline.com/AfricaOnline/griotstalk/writers/
 series.html.

Baker, Henry, *The Colored Inventor*, Arno Press, 1969.

Black Writers, Gale, 1998.

Corbin, Raymond M., *1,999 Facts About Blacks*, Madison Books, 1997.

Discovering Multicultural America (database), Gale Research, 1997.

Edwards, Barbara Audrey and Dr. Craig K. Polite, *Children of the Dream: The
 Psychology of Black Success*, Doubleday, 1990.

Hine, Darlene Clark, Elsa Barkley Brown, and Rosalyn Terborg-Penn, eds., *Black
 Women in America: An Historical Encyclopedia,* Carlson, 1993.

Smith, Jessie Carney, *Notable Black American Women,* Gale, 1992.

Alternative Applications: Using Maya Angelou's skillful approach as a
model, discuss autobiography as a multicultural art form. Contrast her personal narratives, especially *I Know Why the Caged Bird Sings* or *The Heart of a Woman,* with
these works:

- ◆ Mark Mathabane, *Kaffir Boy*
- ◆ Amy Tan, *The Joy Luck Club* or *The Kitchen God's Wife*
- ◆ Zlata Filipovich, *Zlata's Diary*
- ◆ Yoko Kawashima Watkins, *So Far from the Bamboo Grove*
- ◆ Mark Twain, *Life on the Mississippi*
- ◆ Joy Adamson, *Born Free*
- ◆ James Joyce, *Portrait of the Artist as a Young Man*
- ◆ George Orwell, "Shooting an Elephant"
- ◆ Maxine Hong Kingston, *Woman Warrior*
- ◆ Jung Chang, *Wild Swans: Three Daughters of China*
- ◆ N. Scott Momaday, *The Way to Rainy Mountain*
- ◆ Elie Wiesel, *Night* and *All Rivers Run to the Sea*
- ◆ Corrie ten Boom, *The Hiding Place*
- ◆ *The Diary of Anne Frank*
- ◆ *Black Elk Speaks*

Black Award Winners

Age/Grade Level or Audience: Middle school and high school history and journalism classes; civic groups; museums; and libraries.

Description: Honor black people who have received prestigious awards.

Procedure: Make a bulletin board display listing important honors and awards
given to black achievers such as these:

♦ Susan Taylor—recognition by the Women in Communications Matrix Award

♦ Ralph Ellison—Harold Washington Award

♦ Gwendolyn Brooks—Guggenheim Fellowship

♦ Ernie Davis—Heisman Trophy

♦ Lorna Simpson—solo photographic exhibition at New York's Museum of Modern Art

♦ Henry Johnson and Needham Roberts—Croix de Guerre during World War I

♦ Hattie McDaniel—Academy Award for best supporting actress in *Gone with the Wind*

♦ Bill Cosby—election to the Television Hall of Fame

♦ Gwendolyn Brooks—appointment as Illinois's poet laureate

♦ Martin Luther King, Bishop Desmond Tutu, and Ralph Bunche—Nobel Peace Prize

♦ Alice Childress, Walter Dean Myers, and Leontyne Price—Coretta Scott King Awards for young adult literature

♦ Walter Dean Myers—Newberry Award

♦ Al Jarreau—Grammy for pop-jazz music

♦ Katherine Dunham—Albert Schweitzer Music Award

♦ Alain Locke—Rhodes Scholarship

♦ Lorraine Hansberry, Lena Horne, and Ruth Brown—Tony Award

♦ Vanessa Williams and Suzette Charles—Miss America title

♦ Gale Sayers—Jim Thorpe Award

♦ Tiger Woods—Masters championship

♦ Chanda Rubin and Althea Gibson—Wimbledon championship

♦ Alice Coachman, Florence Griffith Joyner, and Wilma Rudolph—Olympic Gold Medal

♦ Paul Robeson—Donaldson Award for his 1944 performance in Shakespeare's *Othello*.

♦ Phyllis Tucker Vinson—NAACP Medgar Evers Community Service Award

♦ Clara Hale—Truman Award

♦ Duke Ellington and Marian Anderson—Presidential Medal of Freedom

♦ Maya Angelou and Judith Jamison—Candace Award

♦ Charles Gordone, Scott Joplin, Toni Morrison, and Maya Angelou—Pulitzer Prize

♦ Augusta Savage—commission for a sculpture for the 1939 New York World's Fair

♦ Gwendolyn Brooks, Toni Morrison, and W. E. B. DuBois—membership in the National Institute of Arts and Letters

♦ Toni Morrison and Derek Walcott—Nobel Prize for Literature

♦ Architect Paul R. Williams—Beaux Arts Medal

♦ Dr. Clarice D. Reid—Public Health Service Superior Service Award

♦ Cicely Tyson, Oprah Winfrey, and Suzanne de Passe—NAACP Image Award

◆ Marian Anderson, Dr. George Washington Carver, Jackie Robinson, Ernest E. Just, Dr. Louis T. Wright, Gordon Parks, James Weldon Johnson, Daisy Bates, Charles Young, Carl Murphy, Dr. Mary Bethune, Charles W. Chestnutt, Rosa Parks, and Dr. Martin Luther King, Jr.—Spingarn Medal

◆ Aretha Franklin's twenty-one gold records

Budget: Under $25

Sources:

Videos, such as *The Marva Collins Story, The Real Malcolm X,* and *Bob Marley and the Wailers;* Infotrac, Newsbank, and other online databases and microfilm reference sources; *Who's Who* and *Current Biography.*

African American Profiles, Visible Ink Press, 1997.

Baily, Cate, "Langston Hughes: How He Became America's Poet," *Scholastic Scope,* September 22, 1997, 14-17.

Bogle, Donald, *Dorothy Dandridge: A Biography,* Amistad, 1997.

Brady, James, "Oprah Winfrey," *Parade Magazine,* October 26, 1997, 12.

Corbin, Raymond M., *1,999 Facts About Blacks,* Madison Books, 1997.

Discovering Multicultural America (database), Gale Research, 1997.

Furtaw, Julia C, ed., *Black Americans Information Directory,* 3rd edition, Gale, 1993.

Hine, Darlene Clark, Elsa Barkley Brown, and Rosalyn Terborg-Penn, eds., *Black Women in America: An Historical Encyclopedia,* Carlson, 1993.

Hornsby, Alton, *Chronology of African-American History,* 2nd edition Gale, 1997.

Plowden, Martha, *Famous Firsts of Black Women,* Pelican, 1993.

"The Poetry of Rita Dove," *Scholastic Scope,* September 1997, 21-23.

Severson, Molly, ed., *Performing Artists.,* U•X•L/Gale, 1995.

Smith, Henrietta M., ed., *The Coretta Scott King Awards Book: From Vision to Reality,* American Library Association, 1994.

Smith, Jessie Carney, *Notable Black American Women,* Gale, 1992.

Terry, Ted, *American Black History,* Myles, 1991.

Alternative Applications: Have participants propose black leaders for awards, particularly for people who may have been passed over, such as heroes from the Persian Gulf War, spokespersons for AIDS research and prevention, peacekeepers, religious leaders, philanthropists, community role models, or noteworthy volunteers.

Black History Stamps

Age/Grade Level or Audience: All ages.

Description: Arrange a display of postal stamps from the United States, Africa, and the Caribbean.

Procedure: Select stamps that feature famous blacks, such as Marian Anderson, Nelson Mandela, Booker T. Washington, Toussaint-L'Ouverture, Charles Drew, Sarah Walker, Steven Biko, General Colin Powell, Winnie Mandela, Mahalia Jackson, and Martin Luther King, Jr. Place stamps on cards that detail the event or achievement that is featured on the stamp. Display where visitors can use a magnifying glass to examine stamps. Have art students enlarge drawings on stamps featuring famous black people. Place the enlargements on a bulletin board or feature them in a weekly newspaper column or website.

Budget: $25-$50

Sources:
African American Profiles, Visible Ink Press, 1997.
Branch, Muriel Miller, and Dorothy Marie Rice, *Pennies to Dollars: The Story of Maggie Lena Walker*, Linnet Books, 1997.
Harris, Henry E., *How to Collect Stamps*, Harris & Co., 1996.
Hinceman, Glenn, ed. *The Junior All American Stamp Album*, Novus Debut, 1993.
Malehorn, Merlin K, and Tim Davenport, *United States Sales Tax Tokens and Stamps: A History and Catalog*, Jade House Publications, 1993.
Severson, Molly, ed., *Performing Artists.*, U•X•L/Gale, 1995.

Alternative Applications: Have students propose a series of commemorative stamps. Organize groups to sketch individual plates featuring famous people and events, for instance Matthew Henson's arrival at the North Pole, Hattie McDaniel's Oscar for her role in *Gone with the Wind*, Garrett Morgan's invention of the gas mask, Lorraine Hale's work with needy infants and toddlers, the formation of the Buffalo Soldiers, Marcia Gillespie's editorials for *Ms.* magazine, Thurgood Marshall's service to the United States Supreme Court, or Mae Jemison's space flight.

Frederick Douglass

Age/Grade Level or Audience: High school or college history, literature, or journalism classes.

Description: Summarize Frederick Douglass's philosophy.

Procedure: Use quotations from Frederick Douglass's speeches and writings to illustrate his importance to the cause of black liberation. Present the following passages from *The North Star* in handout sheets, on a chalkboard, or by overhead projector as springboards to discussion. Pay particular attention to the italicized diction

- ♦ We solemnly dedicate the *North Star* to the cause of our long *oppressed* and *plundered* fellow countrymen.
- ♦ While it shall boldly advocate emancipation for our enslaved brethren, it will omit no opportunity to gain for the *nominally* free, complete *enfranchisement.*
- ♦ While advocating your rights, the *North Star* will strive to throw light on your *duties;* while it will not fail to make known your virtues, it will not *shun* to discover your faults. To be faithful to our foes it must be *faithful to ourselves,* in all things.
- ♦ Remember that *we are one,* that our cause is one, and that we must help each other if we would succeed.
- ♦ We have drunk to the dregs the *bitter cup of slavery;* we have worn the heavy *yoke;* we have sighed beneath our bonds, and writhed beneath the bloody lash—*cruel mementoes* of our oneness are *indelibly marked* in our flesh.
- ♦ When you suffer, we *suffer;* what you endure, we *endure.*

Also, present for debate Frederick Douglass's insistence that the Fourth of July is meaningless to slaves by discussing his core argument made in 1852, thirteen years before the end of the Civil War:

> What to the American slave is your Fourth of July? I answer, a day that reveals to him more than all other days of the year the gross injustice and cruelty to which he is the constant victim. To him your celebration is a sham; your boasted liberty an unholy license; your national greatness, swelling vanity; your sounds of rejoicing are empty and heartless; your denunciation of tyrants, brass-fronted impudence; your shouts of liberty and equality, hollow mockery; your prayers and hymns, your sermons and thanksgivings, with all your religious parade and solemnity, are to him mere bombast, fraud, deception, impiety, and hypocrisy—a thin veil to cover up crimes which would disgrace a nation of savages. There is not a nation of the earth guilty of practices more shocking and bloody than are the people of these United States at this very hour.

> Go where you may, search where you will, roam through all the monarchies and despotisms of the Old World, travel through South America, search out every abuse and when you have found the last, lay your facts by the side of the everyday practices of this nation, and you will say with me that, for revolting barbarity and shameless hypocrisy, America reigns without a rival.

Budget: Under $25

Sources:

Asante, Molefi K., and Mark T. Mattson, *Historical and Cultural Atlas of African Americans,* Macmillan, 1992.

Discovering Multicultural America (database), Gale Research, 1997.

Douglass, Frederick, *Autobiographies,* Library of America, 1994.

————, "I Hear the Mournful Wail of Millions," *A Treasury of the World's Great Speeches*, Houston Peterson, ed., Simon & Schuster, 1965.

————, *Narrative of the Life of Frederick Douglass, an American Slave, Written by Himself,* New American Library, 1968.

————, "Speech to the American Anti-Slavery Society" and "What to the Slave Is the Fourth of July?," *The American Reader Words That Moved a Nation*, HarperCollins, 1990.

"Frederick Douglass," http//www.webcom.com/~bright/source/fdougla.htm

"Frederick Douglass and John Brown," http//jefferson.village.virginia.ed/jbrown/douglass.html.

Rice, Alan, "Portrait of Frederick Douglass," http//www.keele.ac.uk/depts/as/Portraits/rice.douglass.html.

Thomas, Velma Maia, *Lest We Forget: The Passage from Africa to Slavery and Emancipation*, Crown, 1997.

Alternative Applications: Consider the years of service that Frederick put into abolitionism and rights for all people. Compose a theme justifying a national memorial to his work by commenting on this statement:

> We shall be the advocates of learning, from the very want of it, and shall most readily yield the deference due to men of education among us; but shall always bear in mind to accord most merit to those who have labored hardest, and overcome most, in the praiseworthy pursuit of knowledge, remembering "that the whole need not a physician, but they that are sick," and that "the strong ought to bear the infirmities of the weak". . . Shall this gift be blest to our good, or shall it result in our injury? It is for you to say. With your aid, cooperation and assistance, our enterprise will be entirely successful. We pledge ourselves that no effort on our part shall be wanting.

Freedom Fighters

Age/Grade Level or Audience: Elementary and middle school history classes; historical societies; civic presentations.

Description: Generate capsule biographies of great African American leaders.

Procedure: Have pairs of students pose as interviewers and civil rights leaders, such as these:

Ralph Abernathy	Daisy Bates	Black Panthers
H. Rap Brown	Stokely Carmichael	Paul Cuffee
Angela Davis	Martin Delany	Medgar Evers

James Farmer	Louis Farrakhan	James Foreman
Marcus Garvey	Fannie Lou Hamer	Josiah Henson
Anita Hill	Charlayne Hunter-Gault	Jesse Jackson
Coretta Scott King	Martin Luther King, Jr.	Thurgood Marshall
James Meredith	Carol Moseley-Braun	Constance Baker Motley
Elijah Muhammad	Rosa Parks	Adam Clayton Powell
Mary C. Terrell	C. Delores Tucker	Nat Turner
Faye Wattleton	Ida Wells-Barnett	Roy Wilkins
Malcolm X	Andrew Young	Whitney Young

Compose question and answer sessions between pairs of participants. Concentrate on the theme of progress and liberation for black people.

Budget: Under $25

Sources:
Films such as *Eyes on the Prize* (1986), *An Amazing Grace* (1974), *Malcolm X* (1992), *Mississippi Burning* (1988), and *Do the Right Thing* (1989).
Brown, Jeanne, *Medgar Evers*, Holloway, 1994.
Discovering Multicultural America (database), Gale Research, 1997.
Lazo, Caroline, *Martin Luther King, Jr.*, Macmillan Children's Group, 1994.
Medearis, Angela S., *Dare to Dream: Coretta Scott King and the Civil Rights Movement*, Dutton Child Books, 1994.
Plowden, Martha, *Famous Firsts of Black Women*, Pelican, 1993.
Rowan, Carl T., *Dream Makers, Dream Breakers: The World of Justice Thurgood Marshall*, Little, 1994.

Alternative Applications: Originate a newspaper, creative writing magazine, website, or daily public address feature from information about African American freedom fighters. Over individual strength and power, emphasize education, beliefs, courage, determination, religious faith, cooperation, and nonviolent collective action, as demonstrated by Malcolm X, Faye Wattleton, Adam Clayton Powell, Ida Wells-Barnett, Rosa Parks, and Martin Luther King.

Hats Off to the Abolitionists

Age/Grade Level or Audience: Elementary and middle school history classes; libraries or museums; religious schools.

Description: Create a wall display or bulletin board honoring famous abolitionists.

Procedure: On an oversized wall map, compile the names, home states, and work of noted abolitionists. Record information on hat-shaped cutouts. Include these examples:

- Reverend Richard Allen, founder of Philadelphia's Free African Society
- John Brown, who was hanged for leading a raid on the government arsenal at Harper's Ferry
- Samuel Cornish, organizer of Philadelphia's first black Presbyterian Church
- Alexander Crummell, Philadelphia abolitionist writer
- Dr. Martin Delany, Philadelphia writer for *Freedom's Journal* who tried to help blacks resettle in Africa
- Frederick Douglass, runaway from Maryland who fueled New England's abolitionist movement
- Reverend Hosea Eaton, Boston abolitionist pamphleteer
- Elihu Embree, publisher of *The Manumission Intelligencer* and *The Emancipator*, the first U. S. periodicals devoted to abolitionism
- James Forten, Philadelphia sailor who employed blacks in his sail-making business
- Henry Highland Garnet, Washington, D. C., minister and speaker
- William Lloyd Garrison, Bennington, Vermont abolitionist publisher and organizer
- Angelina Grimké, who in 1837 published *Letters to Catherine Beecher in reply to an Essay on Slavery and Abolitionism Addressed to S. A. Grimké*
- Frances Ellen Watkins Harper, Philadelphia activist for abolition and women's rights
- Reverend Absalom Jones, a founder of the Free African Society
- Haitian revolutionary Toussaint L'Ouverture
- James W. C. Pennington, Maryland blacksmith and brick mason who became an orator and writer for the abolitionist movement
- Robert Purvis, South Carolina landowner who founded anti-slavery societies
- Charles Lenox Redmond, official spokesman for the Massachusetts Antislavery Society
- David Ruggles, New York City writer for abolitionist papers
- John Russworm, Philadelphia founder of *Freedom's Journal*, the first black newspaper
- Dr. James McCune Smith, Philadelphia physician and abolitionist columnist
- Thaddeus Stevens, Lancaster, Pennsylvania, civil rights activist
- Harriet Beecher Stowe, Cincinnati, Ohio, anti-slavery writer and author of *Uncle Tom's Cabin*
- Sojourner Truth, Hurley, New York, orator and organizer
- Harriet Tubman, Auburn, New York, conductor for the Underground Railroad
- Richard Worrell, Germantown, Pennsylvania, Mennonite activist
- Theodore S. Wright, Rhode Island minister and conductor for the Underground Railroad

Budget: $25-$50

Sources:

Cantor, George Cantor, *Historic Landmarks of Black America*, Gale, 1991.

Coil, Suzanne M., *Slavery and Abolitionists*, TFC Books, 1995.

"Conflict of Abolition and Slavery," http//www.loc.gov/exhibits/african/confli.html.

Discovering Multicultural America (database), Gale Research, 1997.

Fitch, Suzanne Pullon, and Roseann M. Mandziuk, *Sojourner Truth As Orator: Wit, Story, and Song*, Greenwood, 1997.

Hornsby, Alton, *Chronology of African-American History*, 2nd edition Gale, 1997.

"The Influence of Prominent Abolitionists," http//www.loc.gov/exhibits/african/influ.html.

Metcalf, Doris Hunter, *African Americans: Their Impact on U. S. History*, Good Apple, 1992.

"Northeast Abolitionists," http//www.unl.edu/tcweb/altc/ staffpages/page3.html.

Rogers, James T., *The Antislavery Movement*, Facts on File, 1994.

Scott, Otto, *The Secret Six: John Brown and the Abolitionists*, Uncommon Books, 1993.

"Third Person, First Person Slave Voices," http//scriptorium, lib.duke.edu/slavery/

Thomas, Velma Maia, *Lest We Forget: The Passage from Africa to Slavery and Emancipation*, Crown, 1997.

Yellin, Jean F., and John C. Van Horne, *The Abolitionist Sisterhood: Women's Political Culture in Antebellum America*, Cornell University Press, 1994.

Alternative Applications:

Create a timeline of the abolition movement as it reached other parts of the world. Include these dates along with leaders, events, and personal testimonials that hastened an end to slavery:

- ◆ 1771—England
- ◆ 1779—France
- ◆ 1803—Haiti and Jamaica
- ◆ 1807—British colonies
- ◆ 1827—British Guiana
- ◆ 1829—Mexico
- ◆ 1831—Bolivia
- ◆ 1842—Uruguay
- ◆ 1842—West Indies
- ◆ 1851—Russia
- ◆ 1852—Colombia
- ◆ 1854—Venezuela
- ◆ 1856—Portugal
- ◆ 1860—Peru
- ◆ 1862—Paraguay
- ◆ 1865—United States
- ◆ 1872—Spain
- ◆ 1873—Puerto Rico

- 1888—Brazil
- 1898—Cuba
- 1923—Afghanistan
- 1924—Iraq
- 1924—Iran
- 1926—Nepal and Kalat
- 1929—Joran and Persia
- 1937—Bahrain
- 1942—Ethiopia

Malcolm X—Prophet and Martyr

Age/Grade Level or Audience: Middle school and high school history and English classes

Description: Summarize the life experiences of Malcolm X.

Procedure: Have students work in a group to research details about the life of Malcolm X. Assign each group a segment of his life, including childhood, young manhood, prison experience, conversion, ministry, travels, and martyrdom. Have students select a method of expressing their part of the group's chronological study of Malcolm X's life and historical significance. Suggest overhead projector, pantomime, skit, newspaper feature, ballad, formal outline, broadside, or video. Stress these facts about Malcolm X:

May 19, 1925	Malcolm Little was born to Reverend Earl Little and Louise Little in Omaha, Nebraska.
1931	After the family moved to Lansing, Michigan, Rev. Little was murdered.
1934	Malcolm turned to theft because his mother couldn't feed her eight children.
1937	He lived with the Gohannas, a foster family.
1939	He was confined to the Michigan State Detention Home.
1940	He visited his sister Ella in Roxbury, Massachusetts.
1941	Malcolm's junior high school teacher ridiculed the boy's choice of law for a career. Malcolm moved in with Ella, then worked as a busboy at the Parker House in Boston.
1941	He eluded the draft board by pretending to be crazy.
1942	He served as a steward aboard the "Silver Meteor" to Miami.
February 1946	He began an 8-10 year term in Charlestown State Prison for burglary.
1947	He studied with his cellmate, Bimbi.

1948	Ella got Malcolm transferred to the penal colony in Norfolk, Massachusetts.
1949	He joined the Nation of Islam
August 1952	After being paroled, he headed for Detroit and changed his name to Malcolm X.
summer 1953	He was named an assistant minister of the Nation of Islam.
March 1954	He served in Philadelphia and Harlem, New York.
1957	He started a temple in Los Angeles.
January 1958	He married Betty X.
1959	He led a protest outside a New York police station.
1960	He traveled to Egypt, Arabia, Sudan, Nigeria, and Ghana.
1961	He became a national minister.
1962	The Nation of Islam deliberately ignored his accomplishments.
1963	Alex Haley began writing Malcolm's life story.
November 22, 1963	He commented publicly on the assassination of John F. Kennedy.
January 1964	Malcolm took his family to visit Cassius Clay in Miami.
spring 1964	Malcolm journeyed to Cairo, Jedda, and Mecca and visits Beirut, Cairo, Alexandria, and Lagos. On return to New York, he established his own Islamic sect. He traveled to Mecca, Medina, and Africa. As a result of his travels he began to formulate a less judgmental attitude toward whites.
February 13, 1965	His residence was firebombed.
February 21, 1965	Three black gunmen shot him at the Audubon Ballroom in Harlem.

Budget: Under $25

Sources:

African American Voices, U•X•L/Gale, 1997.

Asante, Molefi K., *Malcolm X As Cultural Hero And Other Afrocentric Essays*, Africa World, 1993.

Carson, Clayborne, *Malcolm X The FBI File*, Carroll and Graf, 1991.

Crenshaw, Gwendolyn J., *Malcolm X: Developing Self-Esteem, Self-Love, and Self-Dignity*, Aesop Enterprises, 1991.

DISCovering Authors (CD-ROM), Gale, 1993.

Doctor, Bernard A., *Malcolm X for Beginners*, Writers and Readers, 1992.

Epps, Archie, *Malcolm X: Speeches at Harvard*, Marlowe & Co., 1994.

Friedly, *Malcolm X: The Assassination*, Ballantine, 1995.

Gallen, David, *Malcolm X As They Knew Him*, Carroll and Graf, 1992.

Kly, Y. N., *The Black Book: The True Political Philosophy of Malcolm X.* Clarity Press, 1986.

Leader, Edward R., *Understanding Malcolm: X His Controversial Philosophical Changes*, Vantage, 1992.

Malcolm X: By Any Means Necessary (CD-ROM), Scholastic, 1997.

Sagan, Miriam, *Malcolm X*, Lucent Books, 1996.

Smith, Sande, *Malcolm X*, Book Sales Inc., 1993.

Strickland, William, *Malcolm X: Make It Plain*, Viking Penguin, 1995.

Wolfenstein, Eugene V., *The Victims of Democracy: Malcolm X and the Black Revolution with a New Preface*, Colorado University Press, 1990.

Alternative Applications: Assign one group to outline the life and accomplishments of Malcolm X. Have a second group parallel his life with national and world events, including the beginning of the civil rights movement, Martin Luther King's leadership, and the rise of the Black Muslims in America and the world.

Martin Luther King, Jr.

Originators: Richard Kruglak and Robert DiAndreth, Linton Middle School, Pittsburgh, Pennsylvania.

Age/Grade Level or Audience: High school and college history and English classes; civic clubs; Scout troops.

Description: Present the life and writings of Martin Luther King, Jr.

Procedure: Using a computer disk or handouts, introduce a brief biography of Dr. King. Include these points:

- ♦ King, whose father was a Baptist minister and his mother a teacher, was born in 1929 in Atlanta, Georgia.
- ♦ The son and grandson of minister/activists, King absorbed the difficulty of the black struggle for freedom.
- ♦ A bright student at Booker T. Washington High School, he enrolled in sociology at Morehouse College at fifteen.
- ♦ He was ordained into the ministry in 1947.
- ♦ In 1948, King enrolled at Crozer Theological Seminary.
- ♦ He served as president of his class and won an award for leadership.
- ♦ While attending Boston University on a fellowship, King married voice major Coretta Scott.
- ♦ In 1954, he became pastor of Montgomery's Dexter Avenue Baptist Church.
- ♦ King was influenced by the writings of Gandhi and Henry David Thoreau to adopt a philosophy of nonviolent civil disobedience.
- ♦ He helped organize the Montgomery bus boycott in December 1955.
- ♦ King delivered his "Give Us the Ballot" speech before the Lincoln Memorial in Washington, D. C., on May 17, 1957.

◆ In 1959, King joined his father at Atlanta's Ebenezer Baptist Church and began a series of national and international travels and speaking engagements.

◆ He launched a desegregation movement in Albany, Georgia, in December 1961.

◆ Two years later, he delivered his most famous sermon, the "I Have a Dream" speech.

◆ In 1964, he won the Nobel Peace Prize.

◆ After denouncing the Vietnam war, he led the Poor People's March on Washington in March 1968.

◆ On April 4, James Earl Ray assassinated King at the Lorraine Motel in Memphis, Tennessee.

Complete the study of King's impact on civil rights and black unity by studying his "Letter from a Birmingham Jail." Consider this passage:

The question is not whether we will be extremists but what kind of extremist will we be. Will we be extremists for hate or will we be extremists for love? Will we be extremists for the cause of justice? In that dramatic scene on Calvary's hill, three men were crucified for the same crime—the crime of extremism. Two were extremists for immorality, and thus fell below their environment. The other, Jesus Christ, was an extremist for love, truth, and goodness, and thereby rose above his environment. So, after all, maybe the South, the nation and the world are in dire need of creative extremists.

Budget: $25-$50

Sources:
Discovering Multicultural America (database), Gale Research, 1997.

Fairclough, Adam, *Martin Luther King, Jr.,* University of Georgia Press, 1994.

King, Coretta, *The Words of Martin Luther King, Jr.,* Newmarket, 1992.

Lazo, Caroline, *Martin Luther King, Jr.,* Macmillan Children's Group, 1994.

Patterson, Little, *Martin Luther King, Jr., and the Freedom Movement,* Facts on File, 1993.

Alternative Applications: Have students analyze in a theme or oral report Dr. King's rhetorical style in the conclusion to his "Letter from the Birmingham Jail," which ends with an historical overview:

Before the Pilgrims landed at Plymouth, we were here. Before the pen of Jefferson etched across the pages of history the majestic words of the Declaration of Independence, we were here. For more than two centuries, our foreparents labored in this country without wages; they made cotton "king," and they built the homes of their masters in the midst of brutal injustice and shameful humiliation—and yet out of bottomless vitality, they continued to thrive and develop. If the inexpressible cruelties of slavery could not stop us, the opposition we now face will surely fail. We will win our freedom because the sacred heritage of our nation and the eternal will of God are embodied in our echoing demands.

 Native African Biographies

Age/Grade Level or Audience: Elementary and middle school students.

Description: Read aloud the biography of a native African.

Procedure: As you begin a life story, point out on a map the location of the protagonist's tribe or nation. Then develop incidents that shaped the life of the character. For instance, here are details about the life of Nana, an Itsekiri native of Benin:

- ◆ Nana was born in 1852 in Jakpa, Benin, and lived in Ebrohimi.
- ◆ He learned to speak English as well as the native languages of Ijo and Urhobo.
- ◆ He helped paddle his father's war canoe and served as his bodyguard.
- ◆ In 1876, after Nana's father was falsely accused of mistreating prisoners, Nana appeared in his father's behalf before the British consul.
- ◆ After Nana's father died in 1883, Nana became head of the household, which included ninety-two children, and grew to be a wealthy man.
- ◆ As an important chief, from 1851 to 1883, Nana served as governor of the Benin River and negotiated with emissaries of Queen Victoria.
- ◆ Disagreements with the British led to a war on August 3, 1894.
- ◆ Before the British cannon destroyed Ebrohimi, Nana escaped by a secret canal and fled to Lagos.
- ◆ The British captured and tried Nana in 1894; his punishment was exile to the Gold Coast and confiscation of most of his wealth.
- ◆ In 1906, Nana's son Johnson attended school in Accra.
- ◆ From 1898 to 1905, Nana petitioned the British consulate for pardon.
- ◆ In 1906, Nana was allowed to return home, where his people honored him.
- ◆ In his last years, he built a palace, which featured an open courtyard for ceremonies and dancing.
- ◆ In 1907, Nana promised to help spread the Christian faith.
- ◆ From 1914 to 1916, Nana was too ill to work. He died July 3, 1916.

Budget: Under $25

Sources:
"African Historical Biographies" series, Heinemann Educational Books (48 Charles Street, London WlX 8AH).

Curtin, P. D., *African History*, 2nd edition, Addison-Wesley, 1995.

Jackson, John G., *Introduction to African Civilizations*, Citadel Press, 1994.

McEvedy, Colin, *The Penguin Atlas of African History*, Penguin, 1996.

Steedman, Scott, *Pockets Ancient Egypt*, Dorling Kindersley, 1995.

Alternative Applications: Create a flow chart of world events that occurred during the subject's life. For example, while Nana was alive, the death of Queen Victoria in 1901 and the accession of her son Edward influenced African nations under England's control. Put a star beside items that would have affected English-African relations, particularly the invention of the steam engine, growth of the East India Company, exploration of river sources, expansion of Protestant and Catholic missions, and the beginning of World War I.

Role-Playing History

Age/Grade Level or Audience: Elementary and middle school drama and history classes; historical societies; civic club presentations.

Description: Organize mock replays of the events with which famous African Americans are connected.

Procedure: Have students pose as great black pioneers, such as these:

Ralph Abernathy	Marian Anderson	Ron Brown
Wilt Chamberlain	Ossie Davis	David Dinkins
Frederick Douglass	Marian Wright Edelman	Medgar Evers
Merlie Evers	Ernest J. Gaines	Mal Goode
Alex Haley	Sara Lou Harris	Josiah Henson
Anita Hill	Charlayne Hunter-Gault	Iman
Jesse Jackson	Mae Jemison	Elizabeth Keckley
Martin Luther King, Jr.	Patti LaBelle	Spike Lee
Miriam Makeba	Thurgood Marshall	Mark Mathabane
Donald McHenry	James Meredith	Anne Moody
Melba Moore	Jessye Norman	Rosa Parks
Donald Payne	Adam Clayton Powell	Colin Powell
Lloyd Richards	Sojourner Truth	Harriet Tubman
Faye Wattleton	Dionne Warwick	Maxine Waters
Nancy Wilson	Lawrence Winters	Tiger Woods
Andrew Young		

Capture greatness at particular moments in history, such as these:

- ◆ Marian Wright Edelman's creation of Child Watch
- ◆ Jean Baptiste Point du Sable's establishment of the city of Chicago
- ◆ Elizabeth Keckley's creation of Mary Todd Lincoln's inaugural gown
- ◆ Jessye Norman's first operatic role
- ◆ Lawrence Winters's debut in *Rigoletto* as first black performer in a leading operatic role
- ◆ Susie King Taylor's efforts as a volunteer army nurse during the Civil War
- ◆ Martin Luther King's march through Selma, Alabama
- ◆ Dorothea Towles's modeling career with top Paris designers
- ◆ Nella Larsen's receipt of a Guggenheim fellowship
- ◆ Edward Perkins's ambassadorship to South Africa
- ◆ Constance B. Motley's appointment as a federal judge
- ◆ Arsenio Hall's debut as a late-night television talk show host
- ◆ Rosa Parks's refusal to sit at the back of the bus
- ◆ Harriet Tubman's assistance of passengers on the Underground Railroad
- ◆ James Meredith's enrollment at the University of Mississippi
- ◆ Anne Moody's participation at the Greensboro lunch counter sit-ins
- ◆ Marian Anderson's performance with the Metropolitan Opera
- ◆ Medgar Evers's defiance of Ku Klux Klan intimidation
- ◆ Amy Kleinhans's receipt of the Miss South Africa title
- ◆ Mother Clara Hale's treatment of AIDS and crack babies
- ◆ Naylor Fitzhugh's receipt of an MBA from Harvard
- ◆ Willa Brown Chappell's pilot's license and training fliers for service in World War II
- ◆ John Murphy's founding of the Baltimore *Afro-American*
- ◆ A. Philip Randolph's organization of the Brotherhood of Sleeping Car Porters
- ◆ Mary Eliza Mahoney's entry into registered nursing
- ◆ W. C. Handy's publication of "The St. Louis Blues"
- ◆ Anita Hill's contributions to women's rights
- ◆ Josiah Henson's escape to Ontario and establishment of a trade school
- ◆ Charlayne Hunter's enrollment at the University of Georgia School of Journalism
- ◆ Ron Brown's appointment to President Bill Clinton's cabinet
- ◆ Florence B. Price's receipt of the Wanamaker Award for composing her *Symphony in E Minor*
- ◆ Mark Mathabane's entrance into all-white professional tennis.

Videotape these mini-dramas and present them for an assembly, open house, or museum display.

Budget: Under $25

Sources:

Videos, such as *An Amazing Grace* (1974), *Roots* (1977), *The Josephine Baker Story* (1990), and *Malcolm X* (1992).

Carvell, T., "Spike Lee: Madison Avenue's Gotta Have Him," *Fortune*, April 14, 1997, 84-86.

Dreifus, C., "Andrew Young On Life, Sin, and the Murder of Friends," *Modern Maturity*, March-April 1997, 52-59.

Gaines, Ernest J., *Timetables of History*, Random House, 1996.

Gurtman, Bill, *Tiger Woods: A Biography*, Pocket Books, 1997.

Harley, Sharon, *Timetables of African-American History: A Chronology of the Most Important People and Events in African-American History*, Simon & Schuster, 1996.

Hunter-Gault, Charlayne, *In My Place,* Farrar, Straus & Giroux, 1992.

Italia, Bob, *Anita Hill*, Abdo and Daughters, 1993.

Jackson, John G., *Introduction to African Civilizations*, Citadel Press, 1994.

Mathabane, Mark, *Kaffir Boy*, Penguin, 1986.

Nickson, Chris, *Denzel Washington*, St. Martin's Paperbacks, 1996.

Plowden, Martha, *Famous Firsts of Black Women*, Pelican, 1993. Severson, Molly, ed., *Performing Artists*, U•X•L/Gale, 1995.

Trager, James, *The People's Chronology*, revised edition, Henry Holt, 1996.

Alternative Applications: Create a database or website listing great figures from African American history. Fill in the following data on each entry name and photo or drawing; date; parents and birthplace; education and work experience; contributions and achievements; repercussions or outcomes of activism; recognition, awards, and honors; and sources.

Rosa Parks

Originators: Michael McSweeney, teacher, Auburn, Washington; Ellen Auten, teacher, Sandwich, Illinois.

Age/Grade Level or Audience: Middle school or high school history, literature, or black studies classes.

Description: Conduct an in-depth study of Rosa Parks.

Procedure: Organize a variety of methods to study the example set by Rosa Lee McCauley Parks, the woman who on December 1, 1955, refused to move to the back of a Montgomery city bus. For example:

♦ Read aloud "I Am Only One Person," an anonymous poem from *Ms.*, August 1974.

♦ Discuss experiences, education, and personal beliefs that prepare a person for making a public gesture for morality and justice

♦ Lead a discussion of the psychological impact of one person's rejection of racism.

◆ Have students speak extemporaneously on the statement Mrs. Parks made about racism:

Why can't we be treated like ordinary human beings? It's not me so much as the others—the ones the police hit over the head for no reason, the ones who won't have a lawyer to represent them in court. It's just the whole unbearable Jim Crow living week after week, year after year. If it will do any good, I'll just stay here in jail.

◆ Have students work as a team to design an appropriate monument to the quiet heroism of Rosa Parks. Select a small group to create an inscription honoring her achievement and an appropriate spot for the monument, such as the place where Rosa boarded the bus, her birthplace, or a state museum, government center, or library.

◆ Have a volunteer write to Mrs. Parks to express the group's reaction to her heroism. Address letters c/o Rep. John Conyers, 669 Federal Building, Detroit, MI 48226.

Budget: Under $25

Sources:

Hine, Darlene Clark, Elsa Barkley Brown, and Rosalyn Terborg-Penn, eds., *Black Women in America An Historical Encyclopedia,* Carlson, 1993.

Jackson, Garnet N., *Rosa Parks Hero of Our Time*, Modern Curriculum, 1992.

Metcalf, Doris Hunter, *African Americans: Their Impact on U. S. History*, Good Apple, 1992.

Rosa Parks, Did You Know Publications, 1992.

Smith, Jessie Carney, *Notable Black American Women,* Gale, 1992.

"Rosa Parks," http//www.grandtimes.com/rosa.html.

Alternative Applications: Play "Sister Rosa," a song on the Neville Brothers' album *Yellow Moon*. Discuss with students the influence of Martin Luther King's philosophy on Mrs. Parks. Have students make individual statements about the value of one person's example. Compose a chalkboard list of positive forces in Rosa Parks's life that prepared her for a challenge, such as religious and moral upbringing, stable home, and good attitudes toward unity and fairness.

 Sally Hemings

Age/Grade Level or Audience: High school or college American history classes.

Description: Study the influence of Sally Hemings on the life of Thomas Jefferson.

Procedure: Assign a report of the life of Sally Hemings, slave and common law wife of Thomas Jefferson. Include these data:

- ◆ born in Virginia in 1773 to Elizabeth Hemings, a mulatto slave, and John Wayles, a white man
- ◆ was the half sister of Thomas Jefferson's wife, Martha Wayles Jefferson, who died in 1782
- ◆ granddaughter of a white ship captain and an African slave
- ◆ lived and worked at Monticello, Jefferson's Virginia estate
- ◆ accompanied Jefferson to Paris in 1788 and is reputed to have been fluent in French
- ◆ is believed to have been the mother of Harriet (1795), Beverley (1798), Harriet (1801, named for the older daughter, who died in 1797), Eston (1805), and Madison (1805), all fathered by Jefferson, her owner
- ◆ was sensationalized as Jefferson's mistress by Thomson Callender on September 1, 1802, and during the political campaign of 1804
- ◆ passed to the ownership of Ellen Randolph Coolidge, Jefferson's grand-daughter
- ◆ sons Eston and Madison were freed in 1826 by Jefferson's will
- ◆ died a slave in 1835
- ◆ was memorialized by her sixth child, Madison Hemings, a carpenter
- ◆ was the subject of scurrilous racist attacks on Jefferson's ownership of slaves
- ◆ described in the fictionalized *roman à clef* of William Wells Brown, *Clotel, or The President's Daughter* (1853)

Note the circumstances under which Hemings entered Jefferson's life. Discuss the ambivalence of Jefferson and other nation planners toward slave ownership and their desire to write into the United States Constitution a clause forbidding further slave trade. Explain their reasons for leaving slavery out of laws protecting individual rights.

Budget: Under $25

Sources:
Burns, Ken, *Thomas Jefferson,* PBS video series, 1997.
Discovering Multicultural America (database), Gale Research, 1997.
Ellis, Joseph J., *American Sphinx: The Character of Thomas Jefferson,* 1997.
Hine, Darlene Clark, Elsa Barkley Brown, and Rosalyn Terborg-Penn, eds., *Black Women in America: An Historical Encyclopedia,* Carlson, 1993.
"Sally Hemings," http//www.monticello.org/Matters/people/Sally— Hemings.html.
"Thomas Jefferson and Sally Hemings An American Controversy," http//www.hnet. uci.edu/mclark/virginia.htm.
Smith, Jessie Carney, *Notable Black American Women,* Gale, 1992.

Alternative Applications: Compose a "What if" discussion based on these scenarios:

- ◆ Thomas Jefferson acknowledges his relationship with a common law slave wife.
- ◆ Thomas Jefferson publicly admits fathering children born to Sally Hemings.
- ◆ Sally Hemings persuades Thomas Jefferson to abolish slavery during the founding of the nation
- ◆ Thomas Jefferson refuses to support a national constitution that omits rights for non-white citizens
- ◆ Thomas Jefferson's slave children confront him publicly for denying their existence and for keeping them and their mother enslaved.

Shaka, the Zulu King

Age/Grade Level or Audience: Kindergarten and elementary classes; religious schools.

Description: Tell the story of Shaka, the Zulu king.

Procedure: Have volunteers use hand gestures, mimicry, and pantomime to tell the story of Shaka. Emphasize these facts:

- ◆ Shaka was born in 1787 and learned by age six to tend goats, sheep, and cows.
- ◆ One day a dog killed one of Shaka's sheep.
- ◆ Because Shaka's mother defended the child, Shaka's father drove her out of their village.
- ◆ Shaka and his mother lived with her parents.
- ◆ Other children made fun of Shaka.
- ◆ When a famine struck, Shaka and his mother moved on.
- ◆ While they lived with another clan, Shaka learned to be a warrior.
- ◆ He designed better weapons for his people to use against enemies and wild animals.
- ◆ After Shaka's father died, Shaka returned to take charge of the Zulus.
- ◆ An evil spy stabbed Shaka.
- ◆ A doctor visiting from England saved Shaka from death.
- ◆ After Shaka's mother died, he grieved for her.
- ◆ Shaka's enemies finally succeeded in killing him.
- ◆ Shaka's people honored him after his death because he was a great leader.

Budget: Under $25

Sources:

Ritter, E. A., *Shaka Zulu: The Rise of the Zulu Empire*, Stackpole, 1990.

"Shaka Stomps the World," http//marin.k12.ca.us/~parkweb/ShakaJesse.html.
"Shaka Zulu," http//main.emap.com/media/PFINDER/PFP52570.htm.
"This Week in Black History," *Jet*, November 2, 1992, 29.

Alternative Applications: Ask listeners to answer questions about Shaka and other leaders:

- ◆ Where did Shaka live?
- ◆ Why did Shaka grow to be a great man?
- ◆ What other great leaders have suffered before rising to power?
- ◆ How did Shaka's mother help him?
- ◆ How did Shaka help his tribe?
- ◆ Why would enemies want to kill someone who made their nation strong?
- ◆ How might the Zulus have honored their dead king?
- ◆ What could modern leaders learn from Shaka?
- ◆ What qualities and attitudes might a modern hero gain from Shaka?

Provide information on a more current leader to compare with Shaka such as freedom fighters Winnie Mandela and Nelson Mandela or Haile Selassie, the Ethiopian Emperor who was enthroned in 1930 and who created the nation's first written constitution, which outlawed slavery.

Star of the Week

Age/Grade Level or Audience: Middle school and high school language, history, mass media, or African American studies classes.

Description: During Black History Month present one famous actor or actress per week.

Procedure: Have a volunteer post photos, biographies, movie reviews, stills, or photocopied scenes from movies starring famous black actors and actresses. Note the contribution of the performer to the entertainment world. List honors, such as the Oscar, Golden Globe Award, and Emmy. Stress a diverse selection of performers Lawrence Fishburne, Halle Berry, Hattie McDaniel, Ethel Waters, Morgan Freeman, Lou Gossett, LaVar Burton, Paul Winfield, Sidney Poitier, Dorothy Dandridge, Yvonne de Carlo, Whoopi Goldberg, Bill Cosby, Billy Dee Williams, Butterfly McQueen, Stepin Fetchit, Cicely Tyson, Kevin Hooks, Danny Glover, Diahann Carroll, the Wayan brothers, Ice Cube, Diana Ross, Esther Rolle, and Denzel Washington.

Budget: Under $25

Sources:

Magazines such as *Jet, Time, Newsweek, Biography, Essence, U. S. News and World Report, Emerge,* and *Ebony.*

Craddock, James, *Video Hound's Golden Movie Retriever*, Visible Ink Press, 1998.

The Encyclopedia of Film, Random House, 1997.

Halliwell's Film Guide, Harper & Row, 1997.

Phelps, Shirelle, ed., *Who's Who Among Black Americans*, 10th edition, Gale, 1997.

Severson, Molly, ed., *Performing Artists.*, U•X•L/Gale, 1995.

Zaslow, Jeffrey, "Morgan Freeman," *USA weekend*, October 3-5, 1997, 26.

Alternative Applications: Hold a marathon movie month at the public library featuring a variety of these and other classic drama and comedy movies and videos:

◆ *Field of Dreams*
◆ *Beverly Hills Cop*
◆ *The Big Easy*
◆ *Diggstown*
◆ *White Nights*
◆ *Ghost*
◆ *Native Son*
◆ *Malcolm X*
◆ *To Sir With Love*
◆ *Cotton Comes to Harlem*
◆ *Birth of a Nation*
◆ *Jumpin' Jack Flash*
◆ *Juice*
◆ *The Little General*
◆ *Blacula*
◆ *Changing Places*
◆ *Autobiography of Miss Jane Pittman*
◆ *Coming to America*
◆ *Trading Places*
◆ *Mahogany*
◆ *Daughters of the Dust*
◆ *The Preacher's Wife*
◆ *Mississippi Burning*
◆ *Eve's Bayou*
◆ *The Associate*

◆ *Ragtime*
◆ *To Kill a Mockingbird*
◆ *Jungle Fever*
◆ *Member of the Wedding*
◆ *Mo' Money*
◆ *Glory*
◆ *The Fisher King*
◆ *Guess Who's Coming to Dinner*
◆ *The Color Purple*
◆ *Shaft*
◆ *In the Heat of the Night*
◆ *Sounder*
◆ *Boyz 'n the Hood*
◆ *Beverly Hills Cop*
◆ *A Patch of Blue*
◆ *Song of the South*
◆ *Places in the Heart*
◆ *Clara's Heart*
◆ *An Officer and a Gentleman*
◆ *Sarafina*
◆ *Pinky*
◆ *The Pelican Brief*
◆ *The Ghosts of Mississippi*
◆ *Waiting to Exhale*

Offer a different movie or video each evening. Hold an election to select the area's favorite living black cinema performer. Encourage fans to write to their favorites to express their opinions and thanks for good performances.

What's My Line?

Originator: Thea Sinclair, high school science teacher and writer, Hickory, NC.

Age/Grade Level or Audience: Middle school or high school science class.

Description: Play a version of the TV game show, *What's My Line?*

Procedure: Have one student pose as a notable African American scientist, engineer, doctor, astronaut, or inventor, such as Benjamin Banneker, Sarah Walker, Guion Bluford, Elijah McCoy, Ben Carson, James Walker, Ulysses Grant Dailey, Joycelyn Elders, Daniel Hale Williams, Garrett A. Morgan, Donald Cotton, Ernest Coleman, Mae Jemison, or Charles Drew, and have a panel guess the nature of the person's work.

Budget: Under $25

Sources:
Discovering Multicultural America (database), Gale Research, 1997.
Elders, Joycelyn, *Joycelyn Elders, M. D.: From Sharecropper's Daughter to Surgeon General of the United States of America*, William Morrow & Co., 1996.
Haber, Louis, *Black Pioneers of Science and Invention*, Harcourt Brace Jovanovich, 1991.
Hine, Darlene Clark, Elsa Barkley Brown, and Rosalyn Terborg-Penn, eds., *Black Women in America: An Historical Encyclopedia,* Carlson, 1993.
Plowden, Martha, *Famous Firsts of Black Women*, Pelican, 1993.
Severson, Molly, ed., *Performing Artists.*, U•X•L/Gale, 1995.
Smith, Jessie Carney, *Notable Black American Women,* Gale, 1992.
Terry, Ted, *American Black History Reference Manual*, Mylkes Publishing, 1991.
Weatherford, Doris, *American Women's History*, Prentice Hall, 1994.

Alternative Applications: Extend the game to include other important figures, such as these:

- ◆ television stars Esther Rolle and Bill Cosby
- ◆ editors Marcia Gillespie and Stephanie Stokes Oliver
- ◆ columnist William Raspberry
- ◆ educator Marva Collins
- ◆ cartoonists Walt Carr and Barbara Brandon
- ◆ politician Barbara Jordan
- ◆ authors Lorraine Hansberry and Richard Wright
- ◆ poets Mari Evans, Countee Cullen, Gwendolyn Brooks, and Langston Hughes
- ◆ dancers Bill Robinson, Katherine Dunham, Gregory Hines, Judith Jamison, and Josephine Baker

♦ actors Cicely Tyson, Lou Gossett, Jr., Danny Glover, and Hattie McDaniel
♦ athletes Tony Dorsett, Dominique Dawes, Sugar Ray Lenard, Wilma Rudolph, and William "Refrigerator" Perry
♦ astronauts Guion Bluford and Mae Jemison
♦ television host Bryant Gumbel
♦ newscasters Bernard Shaw and Ed Bradley

William Lloyd Garrison

Age/Grade Level or Audience: Middle school or high school history or language classes; religious schools.

Description: Study William Lloyd Garrison's reasons for fighting slavery.

Procedure: Present segments of William Lloyd Garrison's polemical newspaper *The Liberator*, which he published weekly in Boston from 1831 to 1865. Have volunteers explain why he made certain bold assertions such as these:

♦ I have a system to destroy, and I have no time to waste.
♦ I determined, at every hazard, to live up the standard of emancipation in the eyes of the nation, within sight of Bunker Hill and in the birthplace of liberty.
♦ That standard is now unfurled; and long may it float, unhurt by the spoliations of time or the missiles of a desperate force—yea, till every chain be broken, and every bondman set free!
♦ Let Southern oppressors tremble—let their secret abettors tremble—let their Northern apologists tremble—let all the enemies of the persecuted blacks tremble.
♦ I am aware that many object to the severity of my language; but is there not cause for severity?
♦ I will be as harsh as truth and as uncompromising as justice.
♦ On this subject I do not wish to think, or speak, or write with moderation. No! No!
♦ Tell a man whose house is on fire, to give a moderate alarm, tell him to moderately rescue his wife from the hands of the ravisher, tell the mother to gradually extricate her babe from the fire into which it has fallen—but urge me not to use moderation in a cause like the present.
♦ I am in earnest—I will not equivocate—I will not excuse—I will not retreat a single inch—AND I WILL BE HEARD.

Budget: Under $25

Sources:

"Conflict of Abolition and Slavery," http//www.loc.gov/exhibits/ african/confli.html.

Discovering Multicultural America (database), Gale Research, 1997.

Merrill, Walter N., *Against Wind and Tide: A Biography of William Lloyd Garrison,* Books Demand, 1996.

"William Lloyd Garrison," http//www.cc.columbia.edu/acis/bartleby/bartlett/409 .html.

Alternative Applications: Discuss why modern writers adopt a tone and approach similar to William Lloyd Garrison's when discussing current atrocities against black people, particularly famine in Ethiopia and Somalia, post-Apartheid trials in South Africa, political disruption in Haiti, revolution in Zaire, and unemployment, workplace discrimination, drug use, suppression, AIDS, and poverty among African Americans. Have students gather examples of letters to the editor, editorials, poetry, essays, novels, plays, and songs that parallel William Lloyd Garrison's forceful style of writing. Some likely comparisons are these:

- ♦ Richard Wright, *Black Boy* and "Between the World and Me"
- ♦ Maya Angelou, *I Know Why the Caged Bird Sings*
- ♦ Martin Luther King, "Letter from a Birmingham Jail"
- ♦ speeches by Nelson Mandela, Barbara Jordan, Louis Farrakhan, Shirley Chisholm, and Jesse Jackson
- ♦ Toni Morrison, *The Bluest Eye* and *Beloved*
- ♦ Gary Paulsen, *Nightjohn*
- ♦ Anne Moody, *Coming of Age in Mississippi*
- ♦ Ernest J. Gaines, *A Lesson Before Dying*
- ♦ Sonia Sanchez, *Does Your House Have Lions?*
- ♦ James Baldwin, *The Fire Next Time*
- ♦ Alice Childress, *A Hero Ain't Nothing But a Sandwich*

Wilma Rudolph

Age/Grade Level or Audience: All ages.

Description: Celebrate the success of Wilma Rudolph, Olympic gold medalist who overcame prejudice and polio to become a unprecedented track success.

Procedure: Invite a local black athlete or coach to introduce or comment on the values demonstrated by Rudolph as well as the personal strengths and family and community support that buoyed her to victory. Contrast her career with those of other athletes, such as Dick Gregory, Magic Johnson, Arthur Ashe, Jackie Joyner-Kersee, Michael Jordan, Muhammad Ali, Kareem Abdul Jabbar, and Carol Lewis. Close with one of these sports videos:

- *Clay vs. Liston*
- *Harlem Globetrotters: Six Decades of Magic*
- *The History of Great Black Baseball Players*
- *Jackie Robinson*
- *Jesse Owens Returns to Berlin*
- *Magic Johnson: Put Magic in Your Game*
- *Michael Jordan's Playground*
- *Michael Jordan: Come Fly with Me*
- *Muhammad Ali*
- *Muhammad Ali vs. Zora*
- *Ringside with Mike Tyson*
- *Sugar Ray Leonard*
- *Sugar Ray Robinson: Pound for Pound*

Budget: $25-$50

Sources:

Video rental services.

Ali, Muhammad, *Healing A Journal of Tolerance and Understanding*, HarperCollins, 1997.

Krull, Kathleen, and David Diaz, *Wilma Unlimited: How Wilma Rudolph Became the World's Fastest Woman*, Harcourt Brace, 1996.

"Muhammad Ali In the Biggest Fight of His Life," *Scholastic Scope*, October 20, 1997, 5.

Alternative Applications: Organize a writing contest with three categories—children, teens, and adult. Use the perseverance of Wilma Rudolph and Muhammad Ali as a writing theme. Emphasize Rudolph's difficulties overcoming polio and Ali's speech and coordination problems with Parkinson's disease. Have entrants apply their fight with disease to problems such as school drop-out, gang warfare, AIDS, random violence, poverty, and homelessness.

Words to Live By

Originator: Leatrice Pearson, retired teacher.

Age/Grade Level or Audience: All ages.

Description: Highlight the advice of famous black American women.

Procedure: Utilize quotations from notable black women as chalkboard slogans, banners, program focuses, bulletin and newsletter features, lapel buttons, and topics for discussion, debate, and writing. Select from the following memorable lines:

- I don't like the idea of the black race being diluted out of existence. I like the idea of all of us being here. (poet Gwendolyn Brooks)
- The black woman has deep wells of spiritual strength. She doesn't know how she's going to feed her family in the morning, but she prays and in the morning, out of thin air, she makes breakfast. (novelist Margaret Walker)
- In knowing how to overcome little things, a centimeter at a time, gradually when bigger things come, you're prepared. (dancer Katherine Dunham)
- I will die for my right to be human—just human. (actress Cicely Tyson)
- The only way I was going to make a difference for myself or any other black person is to say the hurdles were there and do what I had to do. (Olympic runner Wyomia Tyus)
- We don't have nothin', so we ain't losing nothin' and our life don't mean nothin' if we continue this way with no freedom. (former mayor of Mayersville, Mississippi, Unita Blackwell)
- It is the linkage of humanity which has to solve the problem. (former U.S. Senator Barbara Jordan)
- What you were born to do, you don't stop to think, should I? could I? would I? I only think will I? And, I shall. (choral director Eva Jessye)
- White people have suffered as much as we have. They just don't know it … (activist Anna Arnold Hedgeman)
- Most women that have to fight for survival get a special strength sooner or later. (sculptor and lithographer Elizabeth Catlett)
- I don't hate white people. I hate the idea that someone, black or white, condescends or looks down on me, on anyone. (activist Autherine Lucy)
- I weep a lot. I thank God I laugh a lot, too. The main thing in one's own private world is to try to laugh as much as you cry. (writer Maya Angelou)
- I am grateful and blessed because those women whose names made the history books, and a lot who did not, are all bridges that I've crossed over to get to this side. (entertainer Oprah Winfrey)
- … the struggle is to share the planet, rather than to divide it. (novelist Alice Walker)
- The cause of freedom is not the cause of a race or a sect, a party or a class—it is the cause of human kind, the very birthright of humanity. (teacher and activist Anna Julia Cooper)

Budget: Under $25

Sources:

Maggio, Rosalie, *The New Beacon Book of Quotations by Women*, Beacon Press, 1996.

Mullane, Deirdre, *Words to Make My Dream Children Live: A Book of African American Quotations,* Anchor Books, 1995.

Riley, Dorothy Winbush, *My Soul Looks Back, 'Less I Forget': A Collection of Quotations by People of Color*, Harper Perennial, 1993.

Alternative Applications: Select a famous quotation to illustrate with a political cartoon, woodcut, pen and ink drawing, watercolor, collage, sculpture, or other art form. Choose from these:

- ◆ ... I have no choice but to keep on. (activist Rosa Parks)
- ◆ It's a bitter experience when the assumption is that it's for all of us, and then you find out it's for some of us. (Spelman College president Johnnetta Betsch Cole)
- ◆ What I do concerns me, not what people think. (educator Marva Nettles Collins)
- ◆ Our proclamations and resolutions are great. We have yet to live them out. (Bishop Leontine Kelly)
- ◆ ... we balance on each others' shoulders and even if you stand on my head it's okay, if it will hold you up. (psychiatric nurse Rachel Robinson)
- ◆ You can focus on the obstacles, or you can go on and decide what you do about it. (president of Bennett College, Dr. Gloria Scott)
- ◆ God is good, that's what I'll say. (singer Sarah Vaughan)
- ◆ Racism just blinds us to the real problems that face us all. (actress Ruby Dee)
- ◆ The challenge is still there. (athlete Wilma Rudolph)
- ◆ This country couldn't call us Africans because if it had, we would have understood some things about ourselves. (poet Sonia Sanchez)
- ◆ The racism will continue. The coping will improve. (former mayor of Hartford, Connecticut, Carrie Saxon Perry)
- ◆ I have great belief in the fact that whenever there is chaos, it creates wonderful thinking. I consider chaos a gift. (activist Septima Clark)
- ◆ The time has come for a perception of compassion in this world. (actress Beah Richards)
- ◆ We're good people and we try. (activist Clara McBride Hale)
- ◆ [Happiness] comes from within. It was there all the time. (jazz singer Ernestine Anderson)

Business
and Advertising

African American Entrepreneurs

Age/Grade Level or Audience: High school or college math, business, or history classes.

Description: Organize a study of America's most successful African American entrepreneurs.

Procedure: Have students read and summarize books, Internet and other reference sources, newspapers, journals, and magazines for information about successful black businesses, for example:

♦ Madame C. J. Walker, Cornell McBride's M&M, Susan Taylor's Nequai, Comer J. Cottrell's Pro-Line, and Johnson Products, cosmetics and hair care

♦ Earl G. Graves, Black Enterprise Publications

♦ Sherry McGee, Apple Book Center Stores

♦ John H. Johnson, publishing and broadcasting

♦ Raymond V. Haysbert, Parks Sausage Company

♦ David Lloyd, Bay City Marine, shipbuilding and repair

♦ Fedco, Reginald L. Lewis, TLC Beatrice International, and STR, food processing and distribution

♦ Carl A. Brown, Mandex, telecommunications

♦ Al Watiker, highway and bridge construction

♦ Leamon M. McCoy, True Transport

♦ Edward Lewis, Essence Communications, magazine and television production

♦ midwife Biddy Mason's investment in Los Angeles properties

♦ Famous Amos cookies
♦ John Cornelius Asbury, burial society
♦ Thomy Lafon, H.C. Haynes, and John Jones, merchandising
♦ David Bing, Bing Steel
♦ Jacob Miles, Cultural Exchange
♦ Carol Green, Laracris Corporation
♦ Tony Haywood, A-1 Turbo Exchange
♦ John Williams, Biztravel.com
♦ Daphne Maxwell Reid and Tim Reid, New Millennium Studios
♦ Spike Lee, 40 Acres and a Mule Merchandising
♦ Herman J. Russell, construction and communications firm
♦ Ben Miles, president of Virginia Association of Broadcasters
♦ John Merrick and A. M. Moore's North Carolina Mutual Life Insurance
♦ Susan dePasse, president of Gordy/dePasse Productions
♦ Joshua Smith, Maxima, a computer service, and Gale Sayers's Crest Computer Supplies
♦ Naylor Fitzhugh, Small Business Center
♦ Paxton K. Baker, PKB Arts and Entermain Productions
♦ Oprah Winfrey, "AM Chicago" and "The Oprah Winfrey Show"
♦ Dr. Meredith Gourdine, Gourdine Industries, manufacturers of electro-gas dynamics equipment
♦ Larry A. Huggins, Ritway Construction
♦ Maggie Lena Walker, St. Luke Penny Savings Bank
♦ Bernard Beal, M. R. Beal Investments
♦ Richard R. Wright, Citizens and Southern Bank and Trust Company
♦ Berry Gordy, Motown Industries
♦ Ronald Brockett, Dover Graphics, advertising agency.

Conclude a consortium with general questions, such as these:

♦ How have black entrepreneurs helped stabilize and grow the American economy?
♦ What areas of business have produced the most success for black entrepreneurs?
♦ In what venues have black entrepreneurs been pioneers and innovators?
♦ What avenues of advertising have produced the greatest response to black business?
♦ How can schools promote similar entrepreneurial goals in future generations of black children?
♦ How can society assure equal success for black women?

Budget: Under $25

Sources:

Aitcheson, C., "Corporate America's Black Eye," *Black Enterprise*, April 1997, 109-110.
Brooks, T., "Entrepreneur on a Mission," *Michigan Chronicle*, December 11-17, 1996, 2-B.

"Businesses Unite to Celebrate National Black Bookstore Week," *Michigan Citizen*, June 15-21, 1997, B6.

Farley, Christopher John, "Cooking Up a Hit," *Time*, October 13, 1997, 86-88.

Gordy, Berry, *To Be Loved: The Music, the Magic, the Memories of Motown*, Time Warner, 1994.

"JPC Publisher Succeeds Against Odds," *Jet*, November 9, 1992, 6.

Kimbro, Dennis, and Napoleon Hill, *Think and Grow Rich A Black Choice*, Fawcett Crest, 1991.

Lovgren, Stefan, "Instead of Aid, Trade," *U. S. News and World Report*, October 13, 1997, 37-38.

Phelps, Shirelle, *Contemporary Black Biography*, Gale, 1997.

Phelps, Shirelle, *Who's Who Among African Americans*, 10th edition, Gale, 1997.

Randall, Eric D., "Black Financiers Gaining Good Education Adds Up," *USA Today*, September 22, 1992, 8B.

Shepherd, Paul, "Agenda Diverges from Women's Rights Tradition," *Charlotte Observer*, October 26, 1997, 10A.

Zagorin, Adam, "BET's Too Hot a Property," *Time*, October 20, 1997, 80.

Alternative Applications: Have groups of students examine current markets and suggest new areas in which black business people can be successful. Suggest these opportunities:

- ◆ import-export firms that encourage African or Caribbean trade
- ◆ publishers that appeal to the needs and tastes of Black Muslims, Million Man March/Million Woman March participants, black fraternities and sororities, and other black religious and ethical groups
- ◆ restaurants that feature spices, fruit, or other ingredients from black cuisines
- ◆ fashion designers and boutiques that offer Afrocentric clothing, hats, shoes, and jewelry in Kente cloth
- ◆ black-owned film companies that feature Afrocentric topics and black staff, musicians, and actors
- ◆ a professional consortium of black attorneys, doctors, dentists, surgeons, architects, and investors
- ◆ dance studios that teach African American and Caribbean dances.

African American Role Model of the Year

Age/Grade Level or Audience: All ages.

Description: Involve the black community in nominating and selecting a role model of the year.

Procedure: Invite businesses, industry, the Chamber of Commerce, and social or civic clubs to sponsor an annual African American Role Model of the Year Award. Follows these steps:

- ◆ Establish criteria, such as humanitarianism, dedication, high ideals, and patriotism.
- ◆ Publish the goals and aims of the award several months in advance.
- ◆ Offer prizes, scholarships, plaques, and certificates of excellence.
- ◆ Require nominations to be submitted in writing.
- ◆ Include individuals of all races and backgrounds in the evaluating committee. Complete the event with a press conference, community open house, reception, or banquet featuring a slide show or videotaped record of the recipient's activities.

Budget: $50-$75

Alternative Applications: Vary this idea to suit local needs, such as African American Volunteer of the Year or Outstanding Leader of Youth. Study the criteria of the Candace Award, Coretta Scott King Award, or Spingarn Medal, all of which honor distinguished black citizens. Ask local businesses and the media to support your award by displaying posters in store windows and on billboards, television, radio, newspapers, local newsmagazines, and websites.

African Money

Age/Grade Level or Audience: Middle school or high school business or economics class.

Description: Assemble an international money chart explaining the types of currency used in African countries.

Procedure: Have students work in pairs to create a money chart for Africa, listing country, names of greater and lesser forms of currency, and their international symbols. Obtain samples such as these currencies from banks to affix to the chart:

Country	Currency	Symbol
Algeria	dinar, centime	DA
Angola	new kwanza, lwei	Kw
Benin	franc, centime	Fr or F
Botswana	pula, thebe	P
Burundi	Burundi franc, centime	BFr

Cape Verde	escudo, centavo	Es
Comoros/Mayotte	Franc Comorien, centime	CFr
Djibouti	Djibouti franc, centime	DFr
Egypt	Egyptian pound, piastre	£E
Eritrea	Ethiopian birr, cent	EB
Ethiopia	birr, cent	E$ or EB
Gambia	dalasi, butut	D
Ghana	cedi, pesewa	¢
Guinea	Guinean franc, centime	GF
Guinea-Bissau	Guinea-Bissau peso, centavo	P
Kenya	shilling, cent	KSh
Lesotho	maloti, licente	M
Liberia	Liberian dollar, cent	L$
Libya	Libyan dinar, dirham	LD
Madagascar	Malagasy franc, centime	FMG
Malawi	kwacha, tambala	K
Mauritania	ouguiya, khoum	UM
Mauritius	rupee, cent	Re, *pl.* Rs
Morocco	dirham, fil	Dr
Mozambique	metical, centavo	Mt
Namibia	dollar, cent	N$
Pr'ncipe	dobra, centime	Db
Réunion	French franc, centime	FFr
Rwanda	Rwandan franc, centime	FR or RF
Sao Tomé	dobra, centime	Db
Seychelles	rupee, cents	Sr or Rs
Sierra Leone	leone, cent	Le
Somalia	Somali shilling, cent	Ssh
South Africa	rand, cent	R
Spanish North Africa	peseta, centimos	PTA
Sudan	Sudanese pound, piastre	S£
Swaziland	llilangeni *pl.* emalangeni, cent	E
Tanzania	Tanzanian shilling, cent	TSh
Tunisia	Tunisian dinar, millime	D
Uganda	Ugandan shilling, cent	USh
Zaïre	New zaïre, likuta, *pl.* makuta	NZ
Zambia	kwacha, ngwee	ZKw
Zimbabwe	dollar, cent	Z$

Include a separate chart of Francophone countries belonging to the Communauté Francière Africaine, which use an interchangeable CRA franc. Include Burkina Faso, Côte d'Ivoire, Mali, Niger, Senegal, and Togo, which use the *Banque Centrale des Etats de l'Afrique de l'Ouest* [Central Bank of the West African States] banknote and the monetary symbol CFA. Provide a parallel chart of Benin, Cameroun, Central African Republic, Chad, Congo, Equatorial Guinea, and Gabon, which recognize the banknote labeled *Banque des Etats de l'Afrique Centrale* [Bank of the Central African States] and the monetary symbol CFA.

Have students extend the chart to include other countries where the population is largely black, especially Haiti, Tobago, and Jamaica. Explain why travelers to these places will want to know the currency name, symbols, and exchange rate before they leave the United States.

Budget: Under $25

Sources:

Full service banks, government agencies, foreign embassies, Federal Reserve Bank, reference books on finance and currencies, travel guides, and websites on currency or world banking.

Africa A Lonely Planet Shoestring Guide, Lonely Planet, 1995.

"Currencies of the World, "http//pacific.commerces.ube.ca/tradecurrencies.html.

Edwards, Carolyn A., ed., *World Currency Yearbook*, 28th edition, Currency Data and Intelligence, Inc., 1996.

Gill, Dennis, *The Coinage of Ethiopia, Eritrea and Italian Somalia*, D. Gill, 1991.

Pick, Albert, *Standard Catalog of World Paper Money, Vol. 2 General Issues*, 7th edition, Krause Publications, 1996.

Webster's Tenth New Collegiate Dictionary, Merriam-Webster, Inc. 1993.

Alternative Applications: Have students trace the history of African money back to the earliest recorded forms, which suggests that shells, hides, goats, and cattle were the first trade premiums. Include the currencies of European invaders, particularly ancient Phoenicia, Syria, Greece, and Rome, Italy, Victorian England, Belgium, France, Portugal, and Germany. Compare sketches of African paper money and coins, denominations, metals, and weight. Decorate a historical African currency collection with drawings of notables and famous events connected with the history of the country. Stress prominent female figures.

The Atlantic Triangle

Age/Grade Level or Audience: Elementary and middle school history classes.

Description: Create a bulletin board outlining the trade arrangement known as the Atlantic Triangle.

Procedure: Post a map of the area bounded by Bristol, England, Africa's west coast, and the West Indies. Label each point of the triangle with its trade goods woolens and trinkets from Bristol, slaves from Africa, and sugar, rum, and tobacco from the West Indies. Estimate the distances on each segment of the triangle and the time it took clipper ships to cover each leg of the route. Discuss why the triangle was also known as the "Golden Triangle."

Budget: Under $25

Sources:

Asante, Molefi K., and Mark T. Mattson's *Historical and Cultural Atlas of African Americans*, Macmillan, 1991.

Bennett, Lerone, Jr., *Before the Mayflower: A History of Black America*, 6th edition, Penguin Books, 1993.

"Black Experience in America Slavery as Capitalism," http//www.iscrit.edu/~nrcgsh/bx/bx03a.html.

Parish, Peter, *Slavery*, Harper Collins, 1990.

"Slavery in America," http//ils.unc.edu/ingham/index.html.

Sullivan, George, *Slave Ship: The Story of the Henrietta Marie*, DuttonChild Books, 1994.

Alternative Applications: Have students prepare a time line of slavery, noting when it was protested and ultimately outlawed in different parts of the Atlantic Triangle. Include the importance of William Lloyd Garrison, Angelina Grimké, John Newton, Sarah Grimké, Mennonites and Quakers, Sojourner Truth, Frederick Douglass, Harriet Beecher Stowe, Abraham Lincoln, Toussaint L'Ouverture, and William Wilberforce.

Black Landmark Ad Campaign

Age/Grade Level or Audience: Middle school and high school writing, art, or journalism classes.

Description: Compose attractive magazine ads featuring African American historical or cultural tourist attractions.

Procedure: Select some places tourists or school groups might enjoy visiting in order to know more about black history. Highlight the area with a carefully planned ad campaign, including slogans, maps, drawings, descriptions, and other enticements. Consider these spots:

♦ Detroit's famed 24-foot-long sculpture, "The Fist," which symbolizes the black power movement and commemorates a native, Joe Louis, championship boxer. Also in Detroit is the Motown Museum at the Henry Ford Museum in Greenfield Village, a collection of memorabilia from some of the most successful black music stars, and the Hitsville Museum on West Grand Boulevard in Detroit; now a museum it was Motown's first office and recording studio.

♦ Buffalo Soldier Monument in Fort Leavenworth, Kansas.

♦ Scott Joplin's home in St. Louis, Missouri, which has been restored with accurate details from the early twentieth century.

♦ Mobile's Africa Town, where slaves brought illegally to the United States aboard the *Clothilde* in 1859 settled and maintained their African culture. Emphasize the statue of Cudjoe Lewis, the last surviving African passenger.

♦ Harriet Tubman Historical and Cultural Museum in Macon, Georgia, which contains photos and portraits of the famous conductor of the Underground Railroad.

♦ Lorraine Motel in Memphis, Tennessee, where Martin Luther King, Jr., was assassinated. Currently in use as a civil rights museum, the building houses displays about the Civil Rights Movement, including a bus commemorating the 1955 Mobile Transportation Strike.

♦ Walker Building in Indianapolis, Indiana, where Sarah Breedlove Walker manufactured the hair dressings and cosmetics that earned her over a million dollars.

♦ Historical section of Jamestown, Virginia, where the first black slaves were settled and where the first black child was born on New World territory.

♦ Phillis Wheatley Memorial at the H. T. Sampson Library in Jackson, Mississippi, which honors America's first black published author.

♦ Afro-American Museum of Chattanooga, Tennessee, where Bessie Smith and other black notables are honored.

♦ Robert Smalls Memorial at the Baptist Tabernacle Church in Beaufort, South Carolina, which captures the spirit of a slave who captained the *Planter*, a navy steamer, during the Civil War.

♦ Mann's Chinese Theatre, in Hollywood, California, where Sidney Poitier became the first black actor immortalized with his footprints in cement.

♦ Mary McLeod Bethune home in Daytona, Beach, Florida, where the famous educator and civil rights worker who created the National Council of Negro Women resided.

♦ Black Museum of Omaha, Nebraska, which honors Mary Fields, manager of a stagecoach station in Cascade, Montana.

♦ Pythias Hall, in Louisville, Kentucky, which dates to 1915 and houses the first African American fraternal group.

♦ New York's Apollo Theater, where many of the pioneers of black music entertained integrated audiences since the 1920s.

Budget: $25-$50

Sources:

Brochures, maps, and travel guides from area chambers of commerce and the Automobile Assocation of America (AAA).

Cantor, George, *Historic Black Landmarks A Traveler's Guide*, Gale, 1991.

Discovering Multicultural America (database), Gale Research, 1997.

Mabunda, L. Mpho, ed., *The African American Almanac*, 7th edition, Gale, 1997.

Sherr, Lynn, and Jurate Kazickas, *Susan B. Anthony Slept Here: A Guide to American Women's Landmarks*, Times Books, 1994.

Alternative Applications: Organize a field trip or walking tour to interesting black monuments and historic sites in your area. Have a group work together to create a schematic drawing or map of the tour. Supply information such as these facts:

- ◆ locations of cemeteries, battlegrounds, museums, churches, civic centers, libraries, schools, mills, businesses, or homes of famous people
- ◆ times that buildings are open and guided tours available
- ◆ admission fees
- ◆ locations of gift shops or book stores featuring African American lore
- ◆ suggestions for photographic opportunities, particularly sculpture, plaques, historic architectural styles, or reenactments of scenes from black history.

Write up the day's excursion in journal or letter form.

The Black Middle Class

Age/Grade Level or Audience: College economics classes; adult civic groups, such as the Business and Professional Women's League, Civitan, Optimist Club, or Rotary Club.

Description: Discuss the social burdens borne by the rising black middle class.

Procedure: Invite a business or economics expert to address an adult college, business, or civic group on the difficulties faced by the black bourgeoisie.

- ◆ emergence of a class within a class
- ◆ cultural gap between wealthy and poor blacks
- ◆ psychological problems, such as guilt and self-doubt
- ◆ response to Affirmative Action quotas
- ◆ hindrance to upward mobility due the "glass ceiling" and "pink collar" jobs
- ◆ accepting social and moral responsibility to the black race and the nation as a whole

Budget: $50-$75

Sources:

Du Bois, W. E. B., "The Talented Tenth." *Forbes*, September 14, 1992, 132-138.

Gates, Henry Louis, "Two Nations . . . Both Black," *Forbes*, September 14, 1992, 132-138.

Kimbro, Dennis, and Napoleon Hill, *Think and Grow Rich*, Fawcett Crest, 1991.

Kunjufu, Jawanza Kunjufu, *Black Economics: Building a Strong Economic Base*, Highsmith, 1992.

Lovgren, Stefan, "Instead of Aid, Trade," *U. S. News and World Report*, October 13, 1997, 37-38.

Mabunda, L. Mpho, ed., *The African American Almanac*, 7th edition, Gale, 1997.

"Minorities Treated Worse Than Whites When House Hunting in D. C. Area," *Jet*, May 5, 1997, 4-5.

Alternative Applications: Hold a round robin discussion exploring the problems of the black bourgeoisie. Present your findings in a local newspaper. Discuss ways to overcome prejudices among people of differing financial and educational standings, for example, monthly multicultural business luncheons and job fairs that include representative black entrepreneurs.

 ## Business Incubator

Age/Grade Level or Audience: Adult civic groups, city and county leaders, media.

Description: Organize a consortium to create methods of encouraging black enterprise.

Procedure: Invite participants to brainstorm methods of encouraging young people to establish their own businesses. Consider some of the following methods:

- ◆ Create an ongoing business referral service.
- ◆ Open money markets and small business loans to high-risk entrepreneurs.
- ◆ Staff 24-hour financial hotlines for advising first-time investors on market shifts and new regulations and tax laws.
- ◆ Offer reduced-rate advertising for minority and women-owned businesses.
- ◆ Organize think tanks for high school and college students interestedin business ventures.
- ◆ Revitalize dying city areas by offering young entrepreneursstorefront space at reduced rates in exchange for refurbishment.
- ◆ Meet with successful minority entrepreneurs from surrounding areasto share ideas and promote networking.

♦ Set up computer and Internet workshops to help young business leaders stay up to date on software, using e-mail, navigating and creating websites, and worldwide marketing and advertising via the Internet.

♦ Anticipate potential problems, such as unemployment, market shifts, insurance problems, street crime, non-English speaking clientale, and tight money.

Budget: $50-$75

Sources:

Federal Small Business Administration; volunteer agencies, civic groups, such as the Business and Professional Women's League, and philanthropical societies

"Black Business Initiative—Black to Business," http//bbi.ns.canewsletter/index.html.

"Black Business Network," http//www.ibsa.io.org/bblm.htm.

"Black Enterprise Online," http//www.blackenterprise.com.

"BlackSeek Black Business—Afro-Americans," http//www.blackseek.com.

Kunjufu, Jawanza Kunjufu, *Black Economics: Building a Strong EconomicBase,* Highsmith 1992.

Kimbro, Dennis, and Napoleon Hill, *Think and Grow Rich*, Fawcett Crest 1991.

Alternative Applications: Present ideas, campaigns, and suggestions in a regular newspaper column, business school newsletter, or website slanted toward minority beginners in the marketplace. Invite write-in questions. Establish a hotline staffed on a volunteer basis by financiers, political leaders, Chamber of Commerce, Business and Professional Women, American Association of University Women, and business and industrial managers.

The Economics of Slavery

Age/Grade Level or Audience: High school and college business, history, or economics classes; civic groups.

Description: Organize a panel to discuss how economics favored the institution of slavery in the Western Hemisphere.

Procedure: Present the following facts for discussion:

♦ Southern and Caribbean plantations depended on free slave work forces to plant, tend, and harvest labor-intensive crops such as cotton, sugar cane, spices, rice, indigo, corn, and tobacco.

♦ Plantation owners encouraged polygamy to increase the slave population, then bred and sold offspring like livestock to supplement agricultural income.

◆ Elite Southern American and Caribbean lifestyles, based on European notions of gentility and refinement, required substantial incomes, leisure time for travel and entertainment, elegant houses and grounds, libraries and art objects, gardeners and house staff, and cooks and table servers.

◆ Southerners and Caribbean plantation owners feared a wholesale freeing of slaves or a general uprising and retaliation against slave dealers, overseers, and owners.

◆ If Southern states had elected to end slavery, they would have faced the problem of housing, feeding, and educating blacks to become self-sufficient.

◆ Most of the churches and abolitionist societies that opposed slavery were in Pennsylvania, Ohio, and New England, far from the reality of the slave economy.

◆ Caribbean slave owners began emancipation proceedings decades before Southern planters.

Conclude with a discussion of the division of North and South and the ensuing Civil War. Debate the role of Caribbean privateers, who served successfully as blockade runners during the war.

Budget: Under $25

Sources:

"Black Experience in America Slavery as Capitalism," http//www.iscrit.edu/~nrcgsh/bx/bx03a.html.

A History of Slavery in America (video), Schlessinger Media.

Hornsby, Alton, *Chronology of African-American History*, 2nd edition Gale, 1997.

Metcalf, Doris Hunter, *African Americans: Their Impact on U. S. History*, Good Apple, 1992.

Parish, Peter, *Slavery*, Harper Collins, 1990.

"Slavery in America," http//ils.unc.edu/ingham/index.html.

Thomas, Velma Maia, *Lest We Forget: The Passage from Africa to Slaveryand Emancipation*, Crown, 1997.

Twining, Mary A., and Keith E. Baird, *African Presence in the Carolinas andGeorgia Sea Island Roots*, Africa World, 1990.

Alternative Applications: Extend the discussion of the economics of slavery to the collapse of the Southern economy during the Civil War and reasons why recovery has taken so long. Consider the following details in your examination of economic trends:

◆ General William Tecumseh Sherman's siege of Atlanta

◆ disruption of rail service and destruction of roads, trestles, and bridges

◆ loss of managers, technicians, and business leaders during the war

◆ dislocation of the labor force

◆ malaise among leaders who looked to a restoration of the past economy

- ◆ collapse of the Confederate monetary system
- ◆ the burden of wounded veterans, amputees, and victims of tuberculosis, malnutrition, and other diseases brought on by hunger, exposure, stress, and cold
- ◆ the inability of the federal government to decide on a workable plan of economic recovery
- ◆ confusion and dismay among free blacks who were deceived by promises of "forty acres and a mule"
- ◆ restrictive legislation such as *codes noirs*, or Black Codes, the Grandfather Clause, and Jim Crow laws
- ◆ the rise of sharecropping and tenant farming, which mimicked slavery in their control of black lives
- ◆ the rise of job opportunities during the world wars
- ◆ black migration to Northern industrial centers
- ◆ cultural support systems, particularly the extended family, schools, and churches

Getting the Public's Attention

Age/Grade Level or Audience: All ages.

Description: Organize a public awareness of Black History Month through advertisement.

Procedure: Suggest that local business and professional groups, civic clubs, visitors bureaus, and the Chamber of Commerce support black history awareness through a variety of banners, media announcements, shopping bags, yard markers, billboards, hats, paper napkins, cups, toys and giveaways, such as yo-yos, kites, key chains, luggage tags, posters, calendars, lapel pins, and bumper stickers. Have school art, history, and English classes provide drawings, maps, slogans, and quotations to serve as the basis of the campaign, which should continue throughout February. Offer a prize for the most creative display suggestion, drawing, or slogan. Display runners-up at a civic center, library, or museum.

Budget: $50-$75

Sources:
Survey the advertising market and adapt ideas from catalogs, displays, promotions, websites, and other sources to focus on black history.
"Africa Online," http//africaonline.com.
Dacey, Donna, "Crafts of Many Cultures Three Seasonal Art Projects with Global Appeal," *Instructor*, November-December 1991, 30-33.
Mabunda, L. Mpho, ed., *The African American Almanac*, 7th edition, Gale, 1997.

Alternative Applications: Organize a local contest to create a city seal, flag, banner, plaque, plaza, signboard, mural, slogan, or other symbol of community pride. Feature all racial groups involved in acts depicting good citizenship through racial harmony.

 Hi, Ho, Come to the Fair

Age/Grade Level or Audience: City planning board, Chamber of Commerce, and travel and tourism board.

Description: Establish an annual state or regional fair to honor black contributions to the area.

Procedure: Involve multiple groups in organizing a Black History Month state fair. On a computer design board, lay out an oval of events. Include food and craft booths, skills demonstrations, health and fitness booths, fashion shows, pet parade, and industrial and historical exhibits. Encourage black businesses, artisans, clubs, and fraternal organizations to sponsor special guests, including quick-sketch artists, storytellers, performers, animal trainers, cooks, and clothing designers.

Budget: $50-$75

Sources:
Consult planning manuals from the Chamber of Commerce or local library.

Alternative Applications: Create a "Festival of Black Contributions" brochure through a local newspaper, television station, civic group, college, or university. Feature articles on black contributors to the life and prosperity of the area, for example, jazz clubs, small businesses, educators, and homeowners.

Salute to Diversity

Age/Grade Level or Audience: Banks, factories, hospitals, airports, and other businesses.

Description: Hold a Diversity Day celebration.

Procedure: Invite workers to celebrate America's cultural heritage and to demonstrate respect and enthusiasm for Africa and the Caribbean by featuring flags, maps, regional foods, and music or by wearing native dress.

Budget: $25-$50

Sources:
Organize Diversity Day activities through Chamber of Commerce, human relations committees, churches, ministerials associations, libraries, and schools.

Alternative Applications: Extend Diversity Day activities to a celebration of all backgrounds.

Selling Stories

Age/Grade Level or Audience: Middle school and high school art classes; church school activities; scout troops and 4-H clubs.

Description: Create a market for African and African American stories.

Procedure: Present students a variety of black storytellers in print, audiocassette, CD, and video. Have students work in groups to determine an individualized ad campaign to boost the career of a beginning teller. Post examples of audiocassette and CD cover design, direct mail, website entries, magazine layout, and television ad campaign. Study the careers of these and other popular black storytellers for ideas:

Ron and Natalie Blaise	Brother Blue	Gladys Coggswell
Ken Corsbie	Ellaraino	Rex Ellis
Diane Ferlatte	Linda Goss	Grace Hallworth
Paul Keens-Douglas	Bobby Norfolk	Doug and Frankie Quimby
Shanta	Mary Carter Smith	Jackie Torrence

Budget: Under $25

Sources:
Miller, Corki, and Mary Ellen Snodgrass, *Storytellers: A Biographical Directory of 120 English-Speaking Storytellers Worldwide,* McFarland, 1998.
"National Storytelling Association," http//users.aol.com/storypagensa.htm.

Alternative Applications: Create a compendium, television docudrama, or film based on works by black storytellers that give an overview of Caribbean and African American history and lore. Include Anansi the Spider stories, reflections on slavery and the Underground Railroad, Emancipation and Reconstruction era hardships, and the Civil Rights Movement.

Cooking
and Nutrition

African Dessert-a-Thon

Originator: Gary Carey, teacher, writer, and editor, Lincoln, Nebraska.

Age/Grade Level or Audience: All ages.

Description: Organize a tasting booth of African desserts.

Procedure: For a street fair or other get-together in celebration of black history month, present a variety of African desserts for sampling and comparison. Use these recipes for food demonstrations at county fairs, appliance shows, and home economics projects. For example:

South African Rice with Raisins

Melt 2 tbs. butter in a skillet and brown 1 c. white rice. Add these ingredients:

> 2 c. boiling water
> 1 stick cinnamon
> ½ tsp. turmeric
> ⅛ tsp. saffron
> 1 tsp. salt
> ¾ c. sugar

Cover and simmer twenty minutes. Remove cinnamon stick. Add 1 c. raisins. Serve with cream.

Banana Sweeties

Slice bananas lengthwise. Coat inside with peanut butter and press halves together. Top with the following mixture:

> 2 tbs. molasses
> 1 c. sugar
> 1 tsp. cinnamon
> 1 c. whipped evaporated milk.

Tanzanian Fruit Whip

To 2 c. mashed banana add 3 whipped egg whites, ½ tsp. vanilla, and 1 tbs. sugar. Serve over mixed fruit slices, rice, or pudding.

South African Stewed Sweet Potatoes

Peel and slice 2 lbs. of sweet potatoes into ½-inch rounds. On the bottom of a 4-quart saucepan alternate slices and sprinkle with the following mixture:

> 1 tsp. salt
> 1 tbs. flour
> ¼ cs. brown sugar
> 1 tbs. butter

Slide 3 1-inch sticks of cinnamon under the potatoes. Pour in ½ c. water. Cook 45 minutes.

West African Banana Fritters

Whisk together the following ingredients

> 1 ½ c. flour
> 6 tbs. sugar
> 3 eggs

Puree 5 bananas and blend with the mixture.

Heat 3 inches deep of peanut or corn oil in a heavy dutch oven and drop in dollops of the banana mixture. When they are brown on all sides, drain on brown paper and sprinkle with confectioner's sugar.

Mozambique Papaya Pudding

Whirl the following ingredients in a blender:

> 1 ripe papaya, seeded and chopped
> ¼ c. lime or lemon juice
> ¼ c. water

Place in a small saucepan and add these ingredients

> 2 c. sugar
> 1 stick cinnamon
> 4 cloves

Cook, stirring constantly, until mix reaches 230°. Remove cinnamon and cloves and cool. Whisk 5 egg yolks until thick. Add the hot mixture in a thin stream and beat until smooth. Pour into dessert dishes and refrigerate.

Angolan Coconut Pudding

In a 5-quart saucepan, combine the following:

> 2 c. sugar
> 6 c. water
> 4 whole cloves

Boil until mixture reaches 230°. Discard cloves. Add 4 c. grated coconut. Cook 10 minutes, stirring constantly. Remove from heat. Whisk 12 egg yolks and blend into the hot mixture. Cook 10 minutes. Pour into dessert cups, sprinkle with ground cinnamon, and refrigerate until firm.

South African Figure Eight Cookies

Sift together the following:

> 1 ½ c. flour
> 1 tsp. baking powder
> 1 tsp. cinnamon
> ⅛ tsp. salt

In a separate bowl, cream 7 tbs. butter with ½ c. sugar. Beat in an egg; add the mixture to the dry ingredients. Knead dough into a ball. Roll out ¼-inch thick, cut into strips, and roll into cylinders. Shape into figure eights and place on cookie sheet. Spread with a mixture of lightly beaten egg white. Sprinkle with ½ c. slivered almonds and ¼ c. sugar. Chill for ½ hour; then bake 12 minutes at 400°.

South African Crullers

Prepare a syrup from the following ingredients:

> 4 c. sugar
> 2 c. water
> 3 sticks cinnamon
> 2 tbs. lemon or lime juice
> peel of 1 lemon
> ¼ tsp. cream of tartar mixed with 2 tsp. water
> ⅛ tsp. salt

Cook mixture until sugar melts. Cool immediately in container of ice.

Combine dry ingredients:

> 4 c. flour
> 4 tsp. baking powder
> ½ tsp. each cinnamon, nutmeg, and salt

Knead in 2 tbs. each butter and lard. Roll balls of dough into rectangles. Cut into three vertical strips and braid. Fry in 3 inches deep of hot peanut oil. Drain and dip into syrup.

Budget: $50-$75

Sources:
"African Recipes Home Page," http//www.africanrecipes.com.
Duckitt, Hildagonda, *Traditional South African Cookery*, Hippocrene Books, 1996.
Hafner, Dorinda, *A Taste of Africa*, Ten Speed Press, 1993.
"Recipes," http//www.africanews.org/cookbook/food.html.

Alternative Applications: Demonstrate African desserts and comment on common ingredients, particularly cream, rice, yogurt, fresh bananas, papayas, yams, coconut, peanuts, cinnamon, cloves, nutmeg, allspice, and coriander. Hold a workshop in which participants experiment with original recipes made from typical African ingredients. Maintain a database of original recipes. Publish the results of the workshop in a handout or booklet.

 African Lentils

Originator: Gary Carey, teacher, writer, and editor, Lincoln, Nebraska.

Age/Grade Level or Audience: All ages.

Description: Hold a neighborhood dinner or Africa Night PTA supper to celebrate Black History Month.

Procedure: Select volunteers to cook and serve an Egyptian or Zambian one-dish meal.

Kusherie

Heat two tbs. of peanut oil in a saucepan or covered skillet. Add 1 ¼ c. lentils. Brown for 5 minutes, stirring constantly. Blend in 3 c. boiling water or chicken stock, salt and pepper. Cook ten minutes at a slow boil. Add 1 ½ c. brown rice and 1 c. boiling water or chicken stock. Simmer 30 minutes.

While the main ingredients are cooking, heat these ingredients for the sauce:

    ¾ c. tomato paste
    3 c. tomato juice, puree, or sauce
    1 green, yellow, or red pepper, chopped

1 c. chopped celery leaves and heart
1 tbs. sugar
½ tbs. salt
1 tbs. cumin
¼ tbs. cayenne pepper or crushed chilis

Simmer sauce 30 minutes.

Heat three sliced onions and four minced garlic cloves in 2 tbs. oil. Serve rice and lentils with sauce and onion topping. Leftover rice and lentil mix can be eaten with plain yogurt or sour cream. Serves 6-8.

For other ways of cooking lentils, consider these variations.

Lentils Deluxe

Simmer for ½ hour the following:

1 c. lentils
2 ½ c. water
2 beef, chicken, or vegetable bouillon cubes
1 bay leaf
the tops of one bunch of celery
1 tbs. each salt and pepper

Cover with lentil curry topping:

Lentil Curry

Saute one chopped onion and one garlic clove in ¼ c. oil or margarine. Add 1 tbs. salt and 2 tbs. curry powder. Remove from heat, blend with chopped parsley and 2 tbs. lemon or lime juice.

Sweet and Sour Lentils

Cook lentils in 2 c. water. When lentils are cooked, add these ingredients:

¼ c. apple or pineapple juice
¼ c. cider vinegar
¼ c. brown sugar
1 crushed garlic clove
⅛ tbs. ground cloves
sautéed onion

Lentil Stew

To cooked lentils add the following:

½ lb. diced ham, browned ground or string beef, or sausage
¾ c. tomato paste
2 c. water
¼ tbs. oregano
1 tbs. salt
1 chopped onion

two stalks of celery, chopped
1 minced garlic clove

Bring ingredients to a boil, simmer until vegetables are tender. Serve over rice, couscous, or pita rounds.

Lentil Soup

Cook 1 c. lentils in 4 c. water seasoned with ½ tbs. cumin. Meanwhile sauté a chopped onion and garlic clove in 1 tbs. peanut of olive oil. Blend in 1 tbs. flour. Add mixture to cooked lentils and bring to a boil. Top off the soup with salt, pepper, and lemon or lime juice.

Lentil Salad

Season ½ lb. cooked lentils with the following ingredients:

3 tbs. wine vinegar
2 tbs. peanut or vegetable oil
1 tsp. salt
1 tsp. pepper
8 shallot cloves, peeled and halved
2 hot chilies stemmed, seeded, and cut into thin strips

Marinate salad for ½ hour, stirring gently. Serve with crackers or fresh vegetables.

If you prefer a green accompaniment, serve a Zambian side dish of chopped beet tops or leaves from beans, pumpkin vines, cauliflower, or broccoli. Boil greens with salt and chopped peanuts. Other alternatives include these:

Kenyan Cucumber or Onion Salad

Thinly slice 3 c. of cucumber or onion and dress with these ingredients:

2 tbs. dill weed
2 tbs. sour cream, yogurt, or mayonnaise
1 tbs. vinegar
2 tbs. olive, peanut, or corn oil
salt, pepper, chopped chilies, and paprika to taste

Serve chilled.

South African Beet and Onion Salad

Cut the leafy tops from 1 lb. of small fresh beets. Drop beets into boiling water and simmer ½ hour. Drain and skin beets. Slice into strips. Marinate ½ hour in the following dressing:

¼ c. wine vinegar
1 tsp. salt
½ tsp. sugar
¾ c. thinly sliced onion rings

Budget: $25-$50

Sources:

"African Recipes Home Page," http//www.africanrecipes.com.

Duckitt, Hildagonda, *Traditional South African Cookery*, Hippocrene Books, 1996.

Hafner, Dorinda, *A Taste of Africa*, Ten Speed Press, 1993.

"Recipes," http//www.africanews.org/cookbook/food.html.

Alternative Applications: Feature eggplant or other vegetables instead of lentils.

Eggplant Supreme

Peel and slice a large eggplant into 1/4-inch pieces. Heat in a large skillet with 1 tbs. peanut or corn oil or margarine, onion, and chopped or slivered green pepper. Sprinkle with chili powder and salt. As the eggplant slices cook, whip 5 eggs and stir in 2 large tomatoes, chopped. Pour over softened vegetables. When egg is cooked on one side, flip and brown the other side. Serve like crepes, frittatas, or pancakes.

Zambian One-Dish Pumpkin

In a large dutch oven combine these ingredients:

> lbs. chopped potato
> 1 lb. cooked pumpkin

or

> 2 lbs. chopped carrot or turnip
> 2 chopped onions
> 2 stalks of celery, chopped
> 3 tbs. fresh parsley, chopped
> 2 minced garlic cloves
> salt and pepper
> water or broth to moisten vegetables
> ¼ c. peanut or corn oil or margarine

When vegetables are tender, add 1 tbs. bouillon powder dissolved in ¼ c. water and ½ c. ground peanuts.

Egyptian Tabikh

Cook 6 c. of green beans or zucchini in 2 c. tomato juice. Add 2 tbs. tomato paste, sauteed onion, bits of ham or chicken. Cook 20 min. Serve over rice, orzo, or couscous.

West African Chicken and Peanut Stew

Cut a 6-lb. chicken into pieces and rub with 1 tbs. each salt and ground ginger. Brown in a lightly oiled dutch oven along with 1 c. chopped onions. Add the following ingredients:

> 5 puréed tomatoes
> ¼ c. tomato paste
> ½ c. dried ground shrimp

1 finely chopped garlic clove

¼ tsp. grated ginger

½ tsp. each white and hot red pepper or paprika

Simmer 5 minutes. Add these ingredients:

6 c. boiling water

¼ c. dried small fish

2 hot chilies

Coat chicken in the mixture and cook 15 minutes. Make a paste of 1 c. peanut butter and 1 c. water. Add along with 12 stemmed okra pods and cook 1 hour. Add 6 hard-boiled eggs and simmer 5 minutes. Serve stew along with a choice of garnishes, such as chopped onion, pineapple chunks, roasted peanuts, diced tomatoes, spiced okra, avocado chunks, plantain or papaya cubes, or fufu (mashed yams).

South African Cabbage Rolls

Boil 1 large head of cabbage for 10 minutes. Remove cabbage from liquid and peel off thick outside leaves. Spread leaves and cut out the tough ribs. Fill each leaf with a patty made from ⅓ c. of the following ingredients:

2 c. cooked ground lamb

½ c. bread crumbs

½ c. chopped onion

2 eggs

¼ tsp. nutmeg

1 tsp. coriander

2 tsp. salt

1 tsp. pepper

¼ c. peanut, corn, or vegetable oil

1 c. beef stock

1 tbs. flour

1 tbs. cold water

Wrap leaves around patties and tie with cotton cord. Place seam side down in a dutch oven. Cover with 2 c. beef or vegetable stock and simmer for 1 hour. Remove to platter. Whisk 2 tbs. flour with ½ c. water and add to stock. Cook sauce until thickened and pour over cabbage rolls.

Cooking for Kwanzaa

Originator: Roberta Brown, teacher, Fort Bragg, North Carolina.

Age/Grade Level or Audience: Kindergarten and elementary school students; church schools.

Description: Help students make simple foods to celebrate Kwanzaa.

Procedure: Begin with simple recipes. For instance:

Coconut Sudi

Blend the meat and milk of a fresh coconut with one tsp. each vanilla, nutmeg, and cinnamon.

Add an American touch. Explain to students how George Washington Carver helped change the South's economy by teaching people to rely on peanut butter to enrich their diet with protein. Then have students make their own peanut butter.

Peanut Butter

Shell enough roasted peanuts to fill 1 c. Put the nuts along with 1/2 tsp. salt and 3 tbs. corn or vegetable oil in a blender and process for 1 minute. Serve on small crackers.

Expand this lesson by introducing students to sweet potato recipes, including fufu dumplings and sweep potato soufflé.

Fufu Dumplings

Mash baked sweep potatoes and form paste into balls 2 inches in diameter. Drop into soup stock, stew, or broth.

Sweet Potato Soufflé

Blend a 1 lb. can of sweet potatoes with the juice of 1 lemon and 6 egg yolks. Whip 6 egg whites separately and blend in 1 c. sugar. Fold first mixture into sweetened whites. Bake in buttered casserole 30 minutes at 375°.

Budget: $25-$50

Sources:

Anderson, David A., *Kwanzaa An Everyday Resource and Instructional Guide*, Gumbs & Thoms, 1993.

Brady, April A., *Kwanzaa Karamu Cooking and Crafts for a Kwanzaa Feast*, Lerner Group, 1995.

Chocolate, Deborah, *My First Kwanzaa Book*, Scholastic, Inc., 1992.

Copage, Eric V., *Kwanzaa An African-American Celebration of Culture and Cooking*, Morrow, 1993.

Ford, Juwanda, *K Is for Kwanzaa*, Scholastic Books, 1997.

Karenga, Maulana, ed., *Kwanzaa, a Celebration of Family, Country, and Culture*, University of Sandore Press, 1996.

Medearis, *Kwanzaa Celebration Festive Recipes & Homemade Gifts from an African-American Kitchen*, New American Library, 1997.

Minnick, Kathleen, *Kwanzaa How to Celebrate It in Your Home*, Praxis Madison, 1994.

Alternative Applications: Encourage students to publish favorite Kwanzaa recipes by these methods:

♦ Using hole punchers and shoelaces or cord, fasten large pieces of tagboard into a Kwanzaa Big Book. Place in the school or local library.

♦ Reproduce ideas on Internet services, such as IRIS or Prodigy.

♦ Share original recipes by e-mail with a sister school or on a school website.

♦ Use desktop publishing software to create individual recipe handout sheets. Illustrate with drawings of Kwanzaa symbols. Distribute at a multi-cultural fair, PTA, library reading program, or open house.

♦ Videotape cooking sessions for other classes to view. File a copy in the school library.

♦ Keep a classroom database of recipes. Have students type in new recipes throughout the year.

♦ Submit Kwanzaa recipes for publication in children's magazines, such as *Cricket, Cobblestone,* or *Hopscotch.*

 **Food Clinic**

Age/Grade Level or Audience: All ages.

Description: Invite black cooks to staff a foods clinic.

Procedure: Invite black cooks to teach the fundamentals of cooking typical Caribbean, African, or African American menus. Provide the workshop free to assist indigent community members in improving their skills. Emphasize good health habits with these strategies:

♦ Trim meats and substitute vegetable oil for animal fats.

♦ Replace cream, whole milk, sour cream, and cream cheese with skim milk, yogurt, and reduced-calorie cheese.

♦ Emphasize spices over salt and sugar.

♦ Replace sugar with aspartame, fruit juice or pulp, honey, dried dates and raisins, or molasses.

♦ Encourage the addition of roughage, such as shredded green vegetables, unpeeled potatoes, corn, coconut, raisins, and nuts.

♦ Introduce uses for less familiar ingredients, such as couscous, lentils, curry, sun-dried tomatoes, yellow rice, saffron, coconut milk, banana liqueur, papaya, mango, currants, and fenugreek.

♦ Offer handouts featuring nutritional tips and recipes designed to meet a variety of needs, including small children, the elderly, and people with dental, metabolic, and other health problems.

Budget: $50-$75

Sources:

Consult local college and university home economics departments, home demonstration clubs, or county extension agents for suggested personnel to staff foods clinics.

Alternative Applications: Distribute information from the foods clinic by various media:

♦ Videotape foods demonstrations for later use.

♦ Coordinate handouts or a booklet featuring good health concepts and recipes from the foods workshop.

♦ Offer a collection of recipes to the foods section of a newspaper, newsletter, journal, or website.

♦ Share food ideas with other communities through Internet bulletin boards or services, such as IRIS or Prodigy.

Plan regular updates with new recipes and health advice.

Jamaican Specialties

Age/Grade Level or Audience: All ages.

Description: Invite friends to a Jamaican food tasting.

Procedure: Prepare a group of Jamaican foods, including baked sweet potatoes, red beans, rice, and cole slaw spiced with a touch of horse radish. Serve as accompaniments to Jamaican specialty dishes from the following authentic recipes:

Salmagundi

Soak 2 lb. pickled shad and ½ lb. each pickled herring and mackerel for 4 hours. Drain and cover with fresh water. Bring to a boil, then let stand 5 minutes. Drain and skin fish. Shred into small pieces. Arrange on a serving platter and top with a mixture of ⅓ c. oil, 1 ½ c. chopped onion, and 1 tsp. each red, white, and black pepper. Heat a sauce of 1 c. vinegar and 1 tbs. pimento seeds and drizzle over fish. Cover and leave unrefrigerated overnight. Serve with toast rounds, crackers, or wafers.

Pumpkin Soup

Heat 1 ½ lb. beef cubes or pickled pigtails in 2 quarts water. When meat is tender, add 2 lb. pumpkin cubes, 1 garlic clove, 2 whole scallions, and 1 chopped green, yellow, or red pepper. Boil until vegetables dissolve. Season with sprigs of thyme and parsley.

Marinated Chicken

Blend the following ingredients in a food processor:

1 ½ c. chopped onion or scallions

2 tsp. tyme
1 tsp. salt
2 tsp. sugar
1 tsp. allspice
½ tsp. each nutmeg and cinnamon
1 tsp. each black pepper and hot pepper or pepper sauce
1 tbs. vegetable or peanut oil
1 tbs. vinegar

Place 7 lb. chicken strips or pieces in a plastic bag. Pour in marinade. Refrigerate 4 hours. Grill, basting with leftover marinade.

Pork Roast

Marinate a 4-lb. pork roast with a tropical seasoning of the these ingredients:

1 chopped garlic clove
1 tbs. hot pepper sauce
½ tsp. each thyme and allspice

Bake at 3750 1 ½ hrs., basting frequently with leftover juice. Cool, then slice roast into ½-inch rounds and allow to soak up drippings.

Hushpuppies

Mix the following dry ingredients:

1 c. each plain flour and yellow corn meal
2 tsp. sugar
½ tsp. each salt and vanilla
¼ tsp. each nutmeg and baking soda

Stir in ½ c. milk to make a thick batter. Drop by teaspoonfuls into deep fat. When batter browns, drain on brown paper.

Plaintain Strips

Peel and slice 2 lb. plantain into 1-inch cylinders. Fry in vegetable or peanut oil until brown. Drain on brown paper.

Fruit Compote

Cut mangos, grapes, oranges, papayas, pineapple, and bananas into bite-sized pieces. Sprinkle with the juice of 1 lime and 1 c. freshly grated coconut. Serve chilled.

Fruit Punch

Blend 1 papaya, 1 mango, and 2 c. each orange and pineapple juice. Mix in 1 c. each sugar and guava juice, 12 ozs. club soda, and the juice of 2 limes. Serve over crushed ice with banana bread or fresh coconut cake.

Decorate tables with Jamaican flags, palm leaves, and fresh coconuts and bananas. Play reggae or calypso music. Finish the meal with hot Jamaican coffee topped with whipped cream and a sprinkle of nutmeg.

Budget: $50-$75

Sources:
Hafner, Dorinda, *A Taste of Africa*, Ten Speed Press, 1993.
"Jamaican Style Cooking," http//cyberramp.net/~kb2iqs/cooking.htm.
"Jamaican Tourist Food," http//www.jamaicans.com/food.htm.
Willinsky, Helen, *Jerk Barbecue from Jamaica*, Crossing Press, 1990.

Alternative Applications: Share the work by making a progressive dinner, with fruit punch and fruit kabob appetizers at one house, chicken at the next, and continuing down the menu at different residences. Conclude with an evening of reggae music and dancing.

A Slave's Diet

Age/Grade Level or Audience: Elementary science, health, and home economics classes.

Description: Lead a study of a slave's diet.

Procedure: Present to students a typical diet of plantation slaves in the rural South. Discuss with the class the benefits of a diet rich in honey, molasses, berries, yams, corn, potatoes, cabbage, wild greens, cornbread, herb teas, herbal dietary supplements, rice, fish, shellfish, game, pork, chicken, peanuts, milk, cheese, nuts, persimmons, muscadines, melons, and apples.

Budget: Under $25

Sources:
Ehlert, Lois, *Eating the Alphabet Fruits and Vegetables from A to Z*, HarBrace, 1996.
Nutrition, Chelsea House, 1996.

Alternative Applications: Have students lay out a vegetable and fruit garden for a slave compound. Include easy types of vegetables and herbs to grow parsley, mint, basil, dill, potatoes, corn, okra, tomatoes, cucumbers, squash, peppers, lettuce, turnips, peas, radishes, strawberries, blueberries, muscadines, melons. Have the group create a mural of the garden that includes trellises made from limbs and found objects.

LIFE | **Soul Food**

Age/Grade Level or Audience: High school home economics classes; gourmet and home demonstration clubs; civic displays or street fairs.

Description: Organize a cook-off or buffet of soul food for sale and/or sampling.

Procedure: Examine the importance of food as a unifying and bonding agent in black family and community life. Comment on Sunday dinners, holiday meals, church reunions, and gifts of foods to shut-ins, bereaved families, catastrophe victims, and the elderly and homeless. Stress the importance of barbecues, fish fries, cookouts, and picnics, particularly when these gatherings are linked to a single patriarch.

Using local cooks, create a colorful spread of traditional African American dishes for people to buy or sample, such as spoonbread, pork rinds, chitlins, turnip and mustard greens, corn fritters, field peas and ham hocks, hoppin' john, cracklins', pinto beans with chowchow, corn pudding, baked sweet potatoes, pralines, and pecan pie. To create a homey atmosphere, blend a variety of crockery, china, tinware, and wooden platters on a checkered cloth and decorate with a simple vase of wildflowers. Consider the following recipes:

Smithfield Ham

Soak a whole ham overnight in cold water, changing the water every few hours. Boil in fresh water along with these ingredients:

1 tbs. peppercorns
3 bay leaves
1 tbs. hot sauce
1 cinnamon stick
1 tbs. lemon rind
1 c. cider or apple juice
1 c. chopped celery or 1 tbs. celery seed

Cool and skin the ham. Mix the following:

½ c. ham drippings
3 egg yolks
2 tbs. brown sugar
1 tbs. hot sauce
1 tsp. dry mustard
1 c. of crushed cracker or bread crumbs

Coat the ham and bake at 450° until the crust browns. Serve thinly sliced in fresh split biscuits or Parker House rolls. Accompany with a variety of mustards.

Ham Hocks and Collard Greens

Cut stalks from leaves of 9 lb. of collard greens. Soak leaves in salted cold water. Rinse, then slice or chop leaves into 1-inch pieces and soak for another hour. Place six ham hocks and greens in 3 quarts of water. Add red pepper to taste, cover, and cook for 2 ½ hours, stirring occasionally. Serves 10.

Field Peas and Ham Hocks

Soak 2 c. of dried field peas in water overnight. Bring to a boil, then drain and return to 2 quarts of fresh water. Add 2 ham hocks or a meaty ham bone. Simmer 3-4 hours. Reduce pot liquor to a thick gravy. Garnish with home-canned dill pickles or hot peppers. Serve over rice or slices of day-old corn bread as a one-dish meal.

Corn Pudding

Shave kernels from 10 ears of corn. Make a paste of 3 tbs. of melted butter and 2 tbs. of plain flour. Stir in kernels plus these ingredients:

> 1 pt. cream or half-and-half
>
> 3 beaten egg yolks
>
> 1 tsp. salt
>
> ½ tsp. vanilla
>
> 3 tbs. sugar (optional)

Whip 3 egg whites into stiff peaks and fold into mixture. Bake in greased casserole at 350° for 45 minutes. Serve immediately.

Chow-Chow

Chop the following ingredients:

> 2 pts. each sweet red and green peppers
>
> 2 qts. cabbage
>
> 2 pts. onions
>
> 4 hot peppers

Sprinkle vegetables with 10 tbs. canning (non-iodized) salt. Marinate for 8 hours, then drain, pour into a kettle, and mix well with these flavorings:

> 8 tbs. mustard seed
>
> 4 tbs. celery seed
>
> 2 tbs. dill weed
>
> 1 c. sugar
>
> 2 qts. vinegar

Cook 15 minutes. Pack into sterilized jars and process for ten minutes. Cool and store. Serve with bland foods, such as pinto beans, field peas, hominy, or creamed corn.

Cornbread

Mix the following ingredients:

2 c. white or yellow cornmeal

2 eggs

1 tbs. sugar (optional)

2 tsp. baking powder

2 tbs. vegetable or peanut oil or bacon drippings

2 ½ c. Buttermilk

For added texture, add 1 c. of corn kernels or creamed corn. Bake in greased casserole for 25 minutes at 450°.

Ribs

Cook 3 or 4 lbs. of spareribs in a shallow pan at 325° for an hour. Baste every quarter hour with a mixture of four tbs. vinegar in 2 c. water. Cover with barbecue sauce and roast an additional half hour.

Candied Yams

Boil 6 yams in 6 c. water. Drain, cool, and peel. Cut yams into quarters or 1-inch slices. Coat with the following mixture:

3 c. sugar

4 tbs. melted butter

1 ½ tsp. cinnamon

½ tsp. each of nutmeg and cloves

1 c. pecan pieces (optional)

1 c. miniature marshmallows (optional)

Bake in a medium oven 1 ½ hours. Serves 4-6. An alternate method of candying yams is to replace sugar and marshmallows with a can of crushed pineapple or pineapple tidbits.

Sweet Potato Pie

Mix the following ingredients:

⅔ c. sugar

1 tsp. of cinnamon

½ tsp. each ginger and cloves

2 eggs

1 ½ c. milk

½ c. molasses or maple syrup

1 ½ c. cooked or canned pumpkin

1 tsp. lemon juice.

1 tsp. grated lemon rind

Pour into unbaked pie shell. Bake 10 minutes at 450°. Lower temperature to 350° and bake 40 minutes more. Serve with whipped cream.

Budget: $50-$75

Sources:

Ferguson, Sheila, *Soul Food Cuisine from the Deep South*, Grove-Atlantic, 1993.

Hafner, Dorinda, *A Taste of Africa*, Ten Speed Press, 1993.

O'Neill, Molly, "Southern Thanksgiving," *New York Times Magazine*, November 22, 1992, 75-76.

"Soul Food," http//www.ajlc.waterloo.on.ca/food/Soul_Food.html.

"What's Cooking," *USA Today*, September 23, 1992, 6D.

Alternative Applications: Organize a progressive dinner, with each participant preparing a part of the soul food meal. Conclude with pie and espresso coffee blended with a few drops of vanilla, curaçao, brandy, or klahua. Supply each participant with recipes or publish a booklet featuring recipes of the entire meal. Offer as a table favor for a club or civic convention, distribute through the state visitors bureau or city chamber of commerce, or sell at street fairs and book stores.

What's For Dinner?

Age/Grade Level or Audience: Kindergarten; church school.

Description: Present a tray of foods harvested and sold in predominantly black countries.

Procedure: Arrange a display of food samples that emphasize what foods are grown and harvested by black farmers around the world. Consider these choices:

- ◆ banana circles (Brazil)
- ◆ small cups of Blue Mountain coffee (Jamaica)
- ◆ sweet potato chips (Africa)
- ◆ coconut flakes (Caribbean)
- ◆ rice pudding (Louisiana)

Budget: $25-$50

Sources:

"For Wee Folks," *Highlights for Children*, November 1997, 35.

Alternative Applications: Have students list foods grown by black farmers. Appoint a small group to select menus made up exclusively of these foods. Letter the menus on poster paper.

Dance

African Dance Styles

Age/Grade Level or Audience: Middle school dance or physical education classes; dance schools or troupes; gymnastics classes.

Description: Have students evolve dances from the basic steps of African culture.

Procedure: Explain to students how African dance steps influenced the conga, samba, rhumba, and mambo. Invite an expert to demonstrate standard African rhythmic movements and steps, such as the Cameroon makossa, Haitian soca, Congolese drum dance, Nigerian afrobeat and juju, Senaglese mbalax, South African mbaqanga and mbube, Zaireian soukous, Zimbabwean chimurenga and jit-jive, and native steps from the Seychelles, including the sega, moutia, tinge, and komtale. Stress these basic movements:

- ◆ leaping
- ◆ dancing on stilts
- ◆ imitation of insects, birds, fish, reptiles, or other animals
- ◆ kneeling and sweeping arms and head sideways and back and forth
- ◆ standing shoulder to shoulder in a circle dance and sliding counterclockwise
- ◆ syncopation of the Juba or Jumba
- ◆ Muslim ring-shout, which dancers perform while holding lighted candles or pine knots
- ◆ dignified and formalized movements of chalk-line walks or cakewalk
- ◆ marching or imitating the python in single file formation
- ◆ solo and duo dances
- ◆ free-form expression to percussion rhythms
- ◆ block formation accompanied by humming, clapping, body slapping, and kazoos

    ◆ ritual prayer dance

    ◆ mystical interpretive dance

Accompany new combinations with authentic African music.

Budget: $25-$50

Sources:

Videos about Africa such as *Zulu, The Power of One,* and *Mister Johnson.* "C. K. Ladzekpo African Music and Dance," http//cnmat.cnmat.berkeley.edu/~ladzekpo/ test.html.

"Flashback (Xhosa Dancers)," *National Geographic,* July 1996, 132.

Fraser, Diane L., *Playdancing Discovering and Developing Creativity in Children,* Dance Horizons, 1990.

Gilbert, Anne G., *Creative Dance for All Ages,* AAHPERD, 1992.

Haskins, James *Black Dance in America; A History Through Its People,* Harper Trophy, 1990.

Long, Richard A., *The Black Tradition in American Dance,* Prion, 1995.

Medearis, Angela Shelf, and Michael R. Medearis, *Dance (African American Arts),* 21st Century Books, 1997.

Mitchell, Jack, *Alvin Ailey American Dance Theater: Jack Mitchell Photographs,* Andrews & McNeel, 1993.

Thorpe, Edward, *Black Dance,* Overlook Books, 1996.

Welsh-Asante, Kariamu, ed., *African Dance: An Artistic, Historical, and Philosophical Inquiry,* African World Press, 1997.

Alternative Applications: Contrast African dance movements with Native American ritual dances, such as those by the Hopi, Zuñi, Cherokee, Navajo, Sioux, Kwakiutl, and Ojibwa. Draw conclusions about what types of rhythms, steps, gestures, and movements seem to be universal, especially circles, lines, stamping and hopping, and mimicking human and animal behaviors. Categorize and illustrate examples of dances that relate to mourning, elation, victory, patriotism, romance and courtship, nature, childhood, and coming of age.

 Black Dance Troupes

Originator: Louis Nunnery, ballet instructor, Hickory, North Carolina.

Age/Grade Level or Audience: Cultural arts groups; dance classes.

Description: Present the background and accomplishments of these African American dancers:

♦ Alvin Ailey, Dance Company
♦ Pearl Primus, Earth Dance Company
♦ Katherine Dunham Troupe
♦ Judith Jamison's Jamison Project
♦ Bode Lawal's Sakoba Dance Theatre
♦ Arthur Mitchell, Dance Theatre of Harlem

Procedure: Illustrate the talent, discipline, and expression of a black dance troupe, for example:

♦ The Alvin Ailey Dance Company, which was organized in 1958, by showing video tapes of the group's performances, such as *District Storyville, Hidden Rites, Blues Suites, North Star, Forgotten Time Cry, Revelations,* or *Strange Fruit* or *Creole Giselle*, performed by the Dance Theatre of Harlem.
♦ Bode Lawal's Sakoba Dance Theatre, a British company that combines traditional African dance to Congolese drum with contemporary movement derived from tai ch'i, flamenco, and butoh in *Mystical Songs, New Moves in African Dance,* and *Afilu Soro.*
♦ The Katherine Dunham Troupe, which presented an original ballet, *L'Ag'Ya*, demonstrating Martinique's martial arts.

Budget: Under $25

Sources:

Video rental services.

"African american Dance Ensemble," http//www.agate.net/~ile/aade.html.

"Alvin Ailey," http//www.duke.edu/~sm/ailey.html.

"Arthur Mitchell," http//kennedy-center.org/explore/honors/html.

"Creole Giselle Dance Theater of Harlem," http//www.schoolroom.com/videos/V12277.htm.

Day, Jeffrey, "Spoleto '98 Features Paul Taylor Premiere," *Charlotte Observer*, November 2, 1997, 3F.

Haskins, James *Black Dance in America: A History Through Its People*, Harper Trophy, 1990.

"Josephine Baker," http//www.classicalmus.com/artistst/baker.html.

"Katherine Dunham," http//www.st-louis.mo.us/st-louis/walkofame/inductees/dunham.

"Katherine Dunham," http//www.duke.edu/~sm/dunham.html.

Long, Richard A., *The Black Tradition in American Dance*, Prion, 1995.

Mitchell, Jack, *Alvin Ailey American Dance Theater: Jack Mitchell Photographs*, Andrew & McNeel, 1993.

"Nubian Message," http//www.2.ncsu.edu/ncsu/stud_pubs/ nubian_message/History

"Paris Music Hall Collection," http//www.libs.uga.edu/darchive/hargrett/paris/baker.html.

Severson, Molly, ed., *Performing Artists.*, U•X•L/Gale, 1995.

Skoog, D., "Peru Negro Coastal Music and Dance in Peru," *American Visions*, June/July 1997, 24-27.

Alternative Applications: Lead a panel in contrasting the exuberance, energy, and choreography of Alvin Ailey, Katherine Dunham, Josephine Baker, Bode Lawal, and Judith Jamison with the more controlled, formalized movements of traditional troupes, such as the Folklorica of Spain, Bolshoi, Saddler's Wells, Kirov, Joffrey, Dance Theatre of Canada, or San Francisco Ballet. Discuss with dance students the difference in training and choreography between more expressive dance groups and the rigorously synchronized *corps de ballet* of classical dance. Include comment on partnering, soloing, character portrayal, individualized interpretation, and full company choreography.

 Caribana

Age/Grade Level or Audience: All ages.

Description: Organize a Trinidadian carnival.

Procedure: Invite participants to create refreshments, fantasy costumes, headdresses, and floats to celebrate the ten-day native West Indian carnival. Choose from the following events:

children's marching unit	costume competition
crafts	dance competition
marching bands	masked ball
parade	procession
tableau floats	talent display
West Indian food fest	

Budget: $50-$75

Sources:
"Caribana 30th Anniversary Official Web Site," http//www.caribana.com.

Cowley, John, *Carnival, Canboulay and Calypso Caribbean Traditions in the Making*, Cambridge University Press, 1996.

Doyle-Marshall, William, "Caribana Rocks Toronto with Music and Masquerade," *Emerge*, August 1992, 54.

"The Frenzy of Carnival," http//www.nando.net/prof/caribe/carnival.html.

Kinser, Samuel, *Carnival, American Style Mardi Gras at New Orleans and Mobile*, University of Chicago Press, 1990.

Skoog, D., "Peru Negro Coastal Music and Dance in Peru," *American Visions*, June/July 1997, 24-27.

Slater, Les, "25th Anniversary of West Indian-American Day Carnival," *Class*, July/August 1992, 57-58.

Alternative Applications: Invite a dance teacher to instruct small groups in the native dances of Caribana, which are often featured in United States festivals, such as Charleston, South Carolina's Spoleto and Mojo and the Mardi Gras celebrations of New Orleans and Mobile. Have students sketch and color costumes topped by fantastic headdresses featuring fruit, feathers, woven straw, beads, lace, ribbons, and sequins. Emphasize island colors—citrus yellow, orange, and lime, sunset red, sea blue, and palm green. Have a group work together on a cardboard or chalkboard backdrop depicting tropical trees, birds, flowers, and vines, sand, surf, and native homes.

Dance Workshop

Age/Grade Level or Audience: All ages.

Description: Locate black dancers to staff a dance workshop.

Procedure: Invite black dancers to instruct students in the fundamentals of ballroom, tap, ballet, acrobatic, jazz, rock and roll, limbo, reggae, and other forms of dance, for example:

- ◆ early syncopated forms of celebration, such as buck, pigeon wing, jig, cakewalk, ring dance, buzzard lope, and juba
- ◆ the New Orleans coonjine, chica, babouille, cata, voudou, and congo
- ◆ T. D. Rice's loose-limbed blackface caricatures of Jim Crow
- ◆ the emergence of more serious dancers, particularly William Henry Lane, Billy Kersands, and Ernest Hogan
- ◆ exotic dance postures by Josephine Baker, Judith Jamison, Pearl Primus, Bode Lawal, and Katherine Dunham
- ◆ tap routines by Bill "Bojangles" Robinson and Gregory Hines

Have participants imitate shuffling, jigging, cakewalking, and strutting. Introduce more complex dance steps, such as the Charleston, black bottom, shimmy, ballin' the jack, mooche, lindy hop, jitterbug, shag, funky chicken, camel walk, moon walk, hip-hop, breakdancing, and truckin'. Provide the workshop free to assist indigent community members in improving their skills and to provide exercise for children, handicapped, and the elderly.

Budget: $50-$75

Sources:
Consult local college and university dance departments and private studios for suggested personnel to staff dance workshops.

Alternative Applications: Videotape dance demonstrations. Place videos in local libraries, schools, and recreation centers for later use.

Everybody Limbo!

Age/Grade Level or Audience: Kindergarten and elementary children.

Description: Teach a class to limbo.

Procedure: Organize a line dance and teach participants how to limbo. Have them follow the leader as the limbo pole moves lower with each pass under it. Invite the other students to clap, shuffle, and sing calypso tunes, such as "Mary Ann," "Yellow Bird," or "The Banana Boat Song," as they wait their turn.

Budget: $25-$50

Sources:
Calypso albums by the Beach Boys and Harry Belafonte.

Alternative Applications: Have groups of students make up verses to limbo songs. Suggest birds, flowers, fish, boats, straw markets, vegetable stands, surf, strolling vendors, and Caribbean scenery as illustrations. Use the following prompts for starters:

Limber Limbo
Sing a limber tune,
Follow in a line . . .

Bright Stars
Caribbean sky, bright with many stars,
Shine on me . . .

String of Shells
I caught the clam in my net;
I opened it up to see . . .

Calypso Lou
Gotta friend, name-a Lou,
Calypso is his beat . . .

Interpretive Dance

Originator: Louis Nunnery, ballet teacher, Hickory, North Carolina.

Age/Grade Level or Audience: All ages.

Description: Present a religious interpretive dance.

Procedure: As part of a black history festival, multicultural arts presentation, worship service, or demonstration, organize a group of dancers to interpret Pablo Casals's "Nigra Sum," a choral work expressing the concerns of a female slave at the court of Solomon. Use costumes evocative of slave days.

Budget: $25-$50

Sources:
Casals, Pablo, "Nigra Sum," Tetra Music Corp, 1966.
Fraser, Diane L., *Playdancing Discovering and Developing Creativity in Children,* Dance Horizons, 1990.
Gilbert, Anne G., *Creative Dance for All Ages,* AAHPERD, 1992.
Long, Richard A., *The Black Tradition in American Dance,* Prion, 1995.
"Nigra Sum," sung by the San Francisco Gay Men's Chorus on *How Fair This Place* (CD), Golden Gate Performing Arts, Inc., 1991.

Alternative Applications: Apply this suggestion to other music, such as "Listen to the Lambs," "Nobody Knows the Trouble I See," "Poor Wayfarin' Stranger," "On That Great Gettin' Up Morning," "Good News," "Didn't It Rain," "Mary Had a Baby," "Joshua Fit the Battle of Jericho," "Standin' in the Need of Prayer," "I'm Just a Wanderer," "Sometimes I Feel Like a Motherless Child," "O Freedom," or other spirituals, anthems, and hymns.

Jivin' to the Oldies

Age/Grade Level or Audience: All ages.

Description: Hold a neighborhood sock hop.

Procedure: Revive the oldies and introduce young participants to dance to the great names of early rock by holding a sock hop. Use tapes, disc recordings, or CDs. Invite a local deejay to announce the songs and give background about periods, instrumentalists, dances, and singers. For example, stress these:

◆ Chubby Checkers's creation of the twist craze
◆ beach music and the shag
◆ Motown's early hits by Diana Ross and the Supremes, Smokey Robinson and the Miracles, Jackson Five, and Martha and the Vandellas
◆ the jitterbug and slam dances of World War II
◆ Michael Jackson and the moon walk
◆ reggae, limbo, and Caribbean rhythms
◆ breakdancing
◆ disco

Offer prizes for the best line dancers, funky chicken, Charleston, disco, moon walk, reggae, or stroll. Select a few volunteers to teach children the steps and hand motions of significant dances from the era.

Budget: $50-$75

Sources:
Films such as *The Glenn Miller Story* (1954), *The Cotton Club* (1984), *For the Boys* (1991), and *Malcolm X* (1992).
Long, Richard A., *The Black Tradition in American Dance*, Prion, 1995.
Severson, Molly, ed., *Performing Artists.*, U•X•L/Gale, 1995.

Alternative Applications: Have art students draw panels or a mural to typify the fashion, gestures, and background of dance crazes, such as the cloche hat, flapper chemise, fringe, bugle beads, and rolled hose of the 1920s, zoot suits and long watch chains of the late 1930s, slit skirts and off-shoulder blouses of Latin music and the tango craze, and elegant tuxedos and long gowns and corsages of the big band era, which led into the music of USO dances during World War II. Use the art as a backdrop for a neighborhood or club dance.

 Josephine Baker

Age/Grade Level or Audience: Civic groups; music and dance clubs.

Description: Present an overview of the career of dancer Josephine Baker.

Procedure: Assign a committee to report on Josephine Baker's contributions to entertainment and to the emancipation of black women. Stress these facts:

♦ born in Saint Louis on June 3, 1906
♦ began domestic work at age eight
♦ ran away from home in her early teens to escape an unsuitable marriage to Willie Wells
♦ danced with the Dixie Fliers
♦ performed in *Chocolate Dandies* in 1924 and the next year at the Plantation Club
♦ appeared in the *Revue Nègre* and the Folies Bergère in Paris
♦ opened the Chez Joséphine in Paris in 1926
♦ published an autobiography, *Les Mémoires de Joséphine Baker* the next year
♦ began a world tour in 1928
♦ returned to her Paris home and danced in *La Joie de Paris*
♦ danced in Offenbach's *La Créole* in 1934, the same year she appeared in the movie *Zouzou*
♦ accepted work with the Ziegfeld Follies two years later
♦ served as a spy for the French Resistance and traveled through Europe and North Africa during World War II
♦ suffered life-threatening illness following a hysterectomy in 1942
♦ was named NAACP's woman of the year for her demand for integrated audiences in the 1950s
♦ filled her French country house with twelve adopted children of a variety of ethnic backgrounds
♦ after two heart attacks, made a comeback in Monte Carlo at the age of sixty-eight
♦ died of cerebral hemorrhage April 14, 1975
♦ was honored by the French at a state funeral and buried in Monaco

Budget: Under $25

Sources:
The films *The Josephine Baker Story* (1990) and *Chasing a Rainbow The Life of Josephine Baker.*
Baker, Jean-Claude, and Chris Chase, *Josephine The Hungry Heart*, Random House, 1993.
"Josephine Baker," http//www.classicalmus.com/artistst/baker.html.
Long, Richard A., *The Black Tradition in American Dance*, Prion, 1995.
Papich, Steven, *Remembering Josephine Baker*, Bobbs, Merrill, 1976.
"Paris Music Hall Collection," http//www.libs.uga.edu/darchive/hargrett/paris/baker. html.
Rose, Phyllis, *Jazz Cleopatra Josephine Baker in Her Time,* Vintage Books, 1991.
Smith, Jessie Carney, *Notable Black American Women*, Gale, 1992.

Alternative Applications: Have a panel present a variety of lives of female performers, including Pearl Bailey, Katherine Dunham, Yvonne de Carlo, Sarah Vaughan, Ella Fitzgerald, Mahalia Jackson, Natalie Cole, Judith Jamison, Gladys Knight, Diana Ross, Bessie Smith, Ethel Waters, Tina Turner, Pearl Primus, Marian Anderson, Kathleen Battle, Jessye Norman, Janet Jackson, or Aretha Franklin. Contrast the struggles of each with those of Josephine Baker, who found receptive audiences in Europe when Americans ignored or exploited her.

Sign Troupe

Age/Grade Level or Audience: All ages.

Description: Organize a sign troupe to perform for a mixed audience of hearing and hearing impaired.

Procedure: Invite a sign troupe to perform memorable dance, tableau, mime, and signed history lessons for the deaf. Consider the following events as suitable material for representation:

- the voyage of the *Clothilde, Amistad,* or *Henriette Marie*
- Martin Luther King, *I Have A Dream* speech
- Frederick Douglass and Angelina Grimké's work as abolitionists
- James Weldon Johnson, *The Creation*
- Harriet Tubman's journeys on the Underground Railroad
- Sojourner Truth's speech "Ain't I a Woman"
- Maya Angelou, *Now Sheba Sings the Song*
- Robert Shaw's all-black regiment during the Civil War
- Alex Haley's search for his African roots
- Barbara Jordan's speech "Who Then Will Speak for the Common Good?"
- Mae Jemison's role as the first black female astronaut
- the arrival of Buffalo Soldiers to the American frontier

Budget: $50-$75

Sources:
Consult local school administrators and state bureaus of the handicapped or Deaf-REACH, 3722 12th St. NE, Washington, D.C., 20017 (202-832-6681) or National Theatre of the Deaf, P. O. Box 659, Chester, Connecticut 06412 (203-526-4971) (FAX 203-526-9732) (TDD 203-526-4974).

"Cultural Calendar for the Deaf Community," http//handson.org.

"Deaf D. C. Web," http//dww.deafworldweb.org.

"Deaf-REACH," http//deaf.reach.org.

Alternative Applications: Present a choreographed or mime overview of black history narrated for the hearing and interpreted for the deaf. Mix media by using slides, film clips, readers, storytellers, dancers, actors, and instrumentalists. Emphasize black experiences in the United States, Caribbean, Africa, South America, and Europe, particularly during the two world wars, the Korean War, Vietnam War, and Persian Gulf War. Conclude with a glimpse of the future of race relations in the United States and the world.

Tapping to Stardom

Originator: Charles L. Blockson, editor, Temple University, Philadelphia.

Age/Grade Level or Audience: Music schools; dance societies; civic groups; community festivals.

Description: Present an overview of America's great tap dancers.

Procedure: Assign a committee to report on these and other famous African American tap dancers:

Cholly Atkins	Clayton Bates
John W. Bubbles	Bunny Buggs
Charles "Honi" Coles	Leon Collins
Stepin Fetchit	Four Step Brothers
Chuck Green	Gregory Hines
Ernest Hogan	Billy Kersands
Florence Mills	Harold and Fayard Nicholas
Bill "Bo Jangles" Robinson	Sandman Sims
Lynn Whitfield	

Present a video showcase of black tap dancers by showing clips of films, such as *Stand Up and Cheer, Tap, The Josephine Baker Story, Malcolm X, The Cotton Club, Breakdance, Showboat,* and *White Nights.*

Budget: $25-$50

Sources:
Films such as *No Maps on My Taps* (1979), *Tapdancin'* (1982), *In a Jazz Way A Portrait of Mura Dehn* (1986), *Call of the Jitterbug* (1988), *Songs Unwritten A Tap Dancer Remembered,* and *Black Dance America.*

Haskins, James, *Black Dance in America; A History Through Its People,* Harper Trophy, 1990.

Kislan, Richard, *American Show Dance From Minstrels to MTV*, Chicago Review, 1994.

Long, Richard A., *The Black Tradition in American Dance*, Prion, 1995.

Seeger, Mike, *Talking Feet Solo Southern Dance; Buck, Flatfoot, and Tap*, North Atlantic, 1992.

Severson, Molly, ed., *Performing Artists.*, U•X•L/Gale, 1995.

Stearns, Marshall, and Jean Stearns, *Jazz Dance The Story of American Vernacular Dance*, Da Capo, 1994.

"Tap Dance Home Page," http//www.hahnemann.edu/tap.

"Tap Dance Page Subutilities," http//www.mcphu.edu/~corrp/tap/taputils/ghindex.html.

"Tap Dance Links," http//www.sapphireswan.com/dance/links/tap.htm.

Alternative Applications: Invite an expert to demonstrate variations of African American dance steps, particularly the buck, pigeon wing, jig, cake-walk, juba, black bottom, shimmy, moochie, suzi-q, camel walk, moon walk, truckin', breakdancing, lindy hop, jitterbug, shag, ballin' the jack, Charleston, big apple, hip-hop, and funky chicken. Have participants describe the emotions, naturalistic attitudes, mimicry, and posturing illustrated by each step.

 A Tribute to Judith Jamison

Originator: Louis Nunnery, ballet instructor, Hickory, North Carolina.

Age/Grade Level or Audience: Civic or school groups; dance classes.

Description: Present an overview of the career of Judith Jamison, African american prima ballerina.

Procedure: Comment on significant roles in Judith Jamison's career, particularly her work with Alvin Ailey. Note these facts:

- ♦ born May 10, 1944, in Philadelphia
- ♦ began dancing at age six
- ♦ attended Fisk University on an athletic scholarship and studied psychology
- ♦ dropped out in her sophomore year to enroll at the Philadelphia Dance Academy
- ♦ debuted in the ballet *Giselle*
- ♦ was mentored by Agnes de Mille at age twenty
- ♦ joined Alvin Ailey in November 1965 in *Congo Tango Palace*
- ♦ toured Europe and danced in Senegal the following year
- ♦ suffered an ankle injury in 1967 while dancing with the Harkness Ballet

♦ achieved stardom in Europe with the Hamburg Ballet, England's Royal Ballet, and the ballet company of the Vienna State Opera

♦ received an award from *Dance* magazine, presented by Katherine Dunham in 1972

♦ served on the board of the National Endowment for the Arts

♦ danced exclusively with Alvin Ailey's troupe until 1980

♦ partnered with Mikhail Baryshnikov in *Pas de Duke*

♦ danced on Broadway in Duke Ellington's *Sophisticated Ladies* in 1980

♦ presented *Divining*, an original choreography, in 1984

♦ organized her own company, the Jamison Project, in 1988

♦ replaced Alvin Ailey as head of his company after his death in 1989

Budget: Under $25

Sources:

Dunning, Jenniver, "Strong As Nails (and Soft of Heart)," *New York Times*, December 4, 1994, H34.

Haskins, James, *Black Dance in America: A History Through Its People,* Harper Trophy, 1990.

Hine, Darlene Clark, Elsa Barkley Brown, and Rosalyn Terborg-Penn, eds., *Black Women in America An Historical Encyclopedia,* Carlson, 1993.

"Judith Jamison," *Biography Today*, January 1996, 66-76.

"Judith Jamison Alvin Ailey's Inspiring Leader," *Amsterdam News*, December 28, 1996, 21-22.

Kelley, Janine, "The Dancing Spirits of Judith Jamison," *Black Elegance*, February/March 1994, 34-37.

Kisselgoff, Anna, "In an Ailey Premiere, Moving and Mugging Take on a Cartoonlike Esprit," *New York Times*, December 16, 1994, C3.

———, "Longtime Winner and a Premiere in an Ailey Gala," *New York Times*, December 9, 1995, 13.

Long, Richard A., *The Black Tradition in American Dance*, Prion, 1995.

Sancton, Thomas, "Back to Their Roots," *Time Australia,* July 14, 1997, 82-83.

Smith, Jessie Carney, *Notable Black American Women*, Gale, 1992.

Tobias, Tobi, "Standing Tall," *New York,* December 1990, 106.

Alternative Applications: Invite a local ballet teacher or dance historian to speak on the techniques that have set Judith Jamison apart from other black dance stars, particularly Pearl Primus, Geoffrey Holder, Carmen DeLavallade, Alvin Ailey, James Truitt, Lynn Whitfield, Gregory Hines, Miriam Makeba, Albert Evans, Rhonda Burke Spero, Katherine Dunham, and Janet Collins. Emphasize African rhythms, symbolic body language, and feminist themes, especially in Jamison's signature work, *Cry.*

Genealogy

Alex Haley's Genealogy

Originator: Leatrice Pearson, teacher, Lenoir, North Carolina.

Age/Grade Level or Audience: High school or college literature classes; literary societies.

Description: Organize a recreation of Alex Haley's family tree.

Procedure: Have volunteers read segments of Alex Haley's three family novels—*Roots The Saga of an American Family* (1976), *Roots The Next Generation* (1979), and *Queen* (1993). Plot Haley's family tree, noting particularly relatives who contribute to family pride, such as Chicken George, Kizzy, Easter, and Kunta Kinte.

Budget: $25-$50

Sources:
"African American Genealogy," http//ourworld.compuserve. com/homepages/Cliff_m.
Benberry, Cuesta, *Always There The African american Presence in American Quilts*, Kent Quilting, 1992.
"Black Family Heritage," http//www.afrinet.net/~hallh/afrotalk/afroaug95/1894.hml.
"Black Pioneers," http//www.localnet.com/~adonis2/pioall.htm.
"CLP Pennsylvania Department Resources in African American Genealogy," http//www.clpgh.org/CLP/Pennsylvania/oak_penna.32.html.
Haley, Alex, *The Autobiography of Malcolm X.*, Ballantine, 1964.
———, *Queen The Story of an American Family,* William Morrow and Co., 1993.
———, *Roots The Saga of an American Family*, Doubleday, 1976.
Santiago, Chiori, "A Story Underfoot," *American Style*, Fall 1997, 49.

Alternative Applications: Create a wall hanging, banner, cushion, rug, or quilt from the information gained from the genealogy. Display the finished product in a traveling show to school groups who are also reading Alex Haley's books or viewing videos of his works. Have participants conclude the activity with a discussion of Marcus Garvey's statement, "A people without a sense of their history is like a tree without roots."

The Family Tree

Originator: Leatrice Pearson, teacher, Lenoir, North Carolina.

Age/Grade Level or Audience: Middle School history or language classes.

Description: Have students collect information about family surnames, traditional first and middle names, traditions, lore, participation in historical events, reunions, recipes, military and birth records, deeds, family trees, slave lists and bills of sale, wills, tax records, letters, diaries and plantation daybooks, Bibles, ledgers, photographs, and albums; then organize the information into a scrapbook.

Procedure: Have collectors create a uniform questionnaire featuring a set of questions to jog the memories of family members, for example:

- Describe the schooling, courtship, and marriage of your parents and grandparents. Supply dates and places for graduations and weddings.
- List names and nicknames that recur in your family, such as Big Arthur and Little Art, Mama Lucille and Big-Mama Lucille. Comment on alternate spellings or shortened versions.
- Name major events in which your family has taken part, such as wars, political movements, and community development.
- Describe family reunions. List locations, branches of the family included in the gathering, numbers of attendees, and favorite foods. Supply traditional recipes, particularly for holiday foods.
- Summarize information from family albums, written histories, newspaper clippings, home movies and videos, uniforms and war medals, diplomas, awards, trophies, and other memorabilia.
- Detail geographical location of major branches of your family and shifts to new locations. Explain situations and events which caused a major migration, such as the Depression, new factories, or periods of prosperity.
- Sketch a family burial plot, noting locations of graves, birth and death dates, and characteristics of markers, headstones, and epitaphs.

♦ Characterize your family's celebration of graduations, birthdays, holidays, and other joyous occasions. Add information about how they note a death, catastrophe, or loss, such as a car accident or tornado or flood damage.

♦ List anecdotes and humorous stories which grow and change with passing time. Stress details that have been added or altered. Be sensitive to information which might embarrass or shock a family member.

♦ List questions about your background that you would like to have answered, even if there is not current source of information for you to consult. For example, inquire about a person who left home and never reunited with family members.

♦ Consult genealogical centers, especially the Family History Library in Salt Lake City, Utah, the world's largest collection of family information.

♦ Consult local sources, for example family papers, church records, county tax lists, jury pools, voter registration, fraternal memberships, graduation records, and inscriptions on tombstones.

♦ Note any informal adoptions, by which a family reared an abandoned or orphaned child or merged with a segment of the family which had been dispossessed by fire or loss of supportive family members.

♦ Describe colorful, eccentric characters from your family's past, for instance whistlers, taxidermists, hubcap collectors, and whittlers.

For advanced groups, this material could be included in an annotated family tree, complete with quotations and photographs.

Budget: $25-$50

Sources:
The video *Family Across the Sea* (1990).

"African American Genealogy," http//ourworld.compuserve. com/homepages/Cliff_m.

Benberry, Cuesta, *Always There The African american Presence in American Quilts*, Kent Quilting, 1992.

"Black Family Heritage," http//www.afrinet.net/~hallh/
afrotalk/afroaug95/1894.hml.

"Black Pioneers," http//www.localnet.com/~adonis2/pioall.htm.

Carlberg, Nancy E., *Getting a Quick Start Up Your Family Tree*, Carlberg Press, 1993.

"CLP Pennsylvania Department Resources in African American Genealogy," http//www.clpgh.org/CLP/Pennsylvania/oak_penna.32.html.

Croom, Emily, *The Genealogist's Companion and Sourcebook*, Betterway Books, 1994.

Florman, Kurt, *Take Your Place in History A Personal Chronology*, Heritage Books, 1993.

Giles, D., "Getting Together with Family," *Black Enterprise*, February 1997, 213-214.

Hill, C., "Keeping the Roots Alive," *Essence*, February 1997, 114.

Ki-Zerbo, Joseph, "Oral Tradition as a Historical Source," *UNESCO Courier*, April 1990, 43-46.

Ramazani, Mwanvuwa A., *African Names Claiming Your True Heritage*, Montecom Publishing, 1995.

Alternative Applications: Have students compose vignettes of family activities, including holidays, birthdays, anniversaries, church homecoming, school and cultural events, reunions, weddings, and births. Share these written vignettes with other classes via e-mail or on databases, websites, or Internet services, such as IRIS or Prodigy. For more information, consult Sandra Oehring's "Teaching with Technology," *Instructor*, November/December, 1992, 60.

Photo History

Originator: Leatrice Pearson, teacher, Lenoir, North Carolina.

Age/Grade Level or Audience: All ages.

Description: Organize a community album from donated photographs.

Procedure: Locate a single sponsor, such as a historical society, newspaper, library, or college, to create a community album celebrating blacks and their contributions to the area. Arrange the album in chronological order. Feature these items:

- ◆ initiation into school groups and fraternal organizations
- ◆ graduations
- ◆ gatherings at depots, bus stations, and airports
- ◆ new homes and farms
- ◆ beginning businesses
- ◆ opening professional offices
- ◆ anniversary parties
- ◆ family reunions
- ◆ church socials and homecomings
- ◆ street fairs
- ◆ political speeches and campaigns
- ◆ recreation and sports, such as swimming meets or wrestling tournaments.

Augment still photos with videos of family reunions, graduations, weddings, parades, block parties, and other memorable occasions. Keep a written record of names, dates, and places for later reference.

Budget: $50-$75

Sources:
Collect photographs from local black families, churches, schools, museums, businesses, newspapers, and county archives. Consult brochures from the United States Consumer Information Center "Using Records in the National Archives for

Genealogical Research," "Where to Write for Vital Records," and "Your Right to Federal Records."

Hill, C., "Keeping the Roots Alive," *Essence*, February 1997, 114.

Myers, Walter Dean, *One More River to Cross An African American Photograph Album*, Harcourt Brace, 1995.

Alternative Applications: Blend a photo gallery with a display of vintage clothing, books, school desks, radios, victrolas, medicine bottles, hair curlers, tools, crafts, farm machinery, automobiles, and other memorabilia. Have volunteers collect memoirs or interviews on audio or video tape from elderly community residents. For a model, follow "Aunt Airie" from Eliot Wigginton's *Foxfire*.

Quilted History

Age/Grade Level or Audience: All ages.

Description: Make a family quilt.

Procedure: Organize workers to create a family quilt or wall hanging. Select important events to fill separate blocks, such as the opening of a family business, an advanced degree or appointment, or the building of a local church, recreation center, or other involvement in local affairs. Embroider or paint information clearly on the block. Connect blocks into quilt form. Finish edge with edging in symbolic colors. Display at the family homeplace, a local museum or library, or in the lobby of a family business or city hall.

Budget: $50-$75

Sources:

Benberry, Cuesta, *Always There: The African-American Presence in American Quilts*, Kent Quilting, 1992.

"Black Family Heritage," http//www.afrinet.net/~hallh/afrotalk/afroaug95/1894.hml.

Doane, Gilbert H., and James B. Bell, *Searching for Your Ancestors: The How and Why of Genealogy*, University of Minnesota Press, 1992.

Florman, Kurt, *Take Your Place in History A Personal Chronology*, Heritage Books, 1993.

Giles, D., "Getting Together with Family," *Black Enterprise*, February 1997, 213-214.

Hill, C., "Keeping the Roots Alive," *Essence*, February 1997, 114.

Santiago, Chiori, "A Story Underfoot," *American Style*, Fall 1997, 49.

Alternative Applications: Create individual segments of needlework to honor family traditions, beliefs, background, or accomplishments, such as a visit to an African country symbolized by a national flag. Display finished products by a variety of methods:

♦ frame works to hang in a prominent place
♦ line a tray with needlework
♦ upholster as bolsters, chair backs, and seats
♦ form into pillows, mantlepieces, floor coverings, scatter rugs, or footstools
♦ enter in county fair or craft exhibits
♦ photograph and share prints of the design.

Sundiata and Family

Age/Grade Level or Audience: High school literature class.

Description: Draw the family tree of Sundiata, the Mandingan epic hero.

Procedure: During a reading of *Sundiata*, the epic of Mali, keep character notes in the form of a family tree that depicts multiple marriages. In addition to the warrior Sundiata, chart the position of these characters:

Dankaran Touman	Maghan Kon Fatta	Manding Bory
Namandjé	Nana Triban	Sassouma Bérété
Sogolon Djamarou	Sogolon Kedjou	Sogolon Kolonkan

Budget: Under $25

Sources:
Johnson, John William, *Oral Epics from Africa: Vibrant Voices from a Vast Continent*, Indiana University Press, 1997.
Lazzari, Marie, ed., *Epics for Students: Presenting Analysis, Context, and Criticism on Commonly Studied Epics*, Gale, 1997.
Naine, *Sundiata: An Epic of Old Mali*, Longman, 1965.
Wisniewski, David, *Sundiata: Lion King of Mali*, Houghton Mifflin, 1992.

Alternative Applications: Keep a scrapbook of character trees on numerous literary classics that contain large black families, particularly:

Chinua Achebe, *Things Fall Apart*
Maya Angelou, *I Know Why the Caged Bird Sings*
Maryse Condé, *The Children of Segu*

The Epic of Askia Mohammed

Ernest Gaines, *The Autobiography of Miss Jane Pittman*

Alex Haley, *Roots*

Lorraine Hansberry, *A Raisin in the Sun*

Zora Neale Hurston, *Their Eyes Were Watching God*

Margaret Walker, *Jubilee*

Richard Wright, *Black Boy*

Geography

An African Holiday

Age/Grade Level or Audience: Middle school or high school business classes.

Description: Have students create a four-week itinerary for a tour of Africa.

Procedure: Assign students to groups to work out the following details of an extended African vacation:

- ♦ itinerary
- ♦ alternate forms of land transportation
- ♦ campgrounds
- ♦ clothing advisory
- ♦ currencies and traveler's checks
- ♦ hotels, inns, and bed and breakfasts
- ♦ overseas airline schedule
- ♦ overseas telephone, FAX, and mail service
- ♦ travel and luggage restrictions
- ♦ vaccinations
- ♦ visas and passports
- ♦ water and food advisories

Budget: Under $25

Sources:

Travel agents, African embassies, video travel guides from Rand McNally or local dealers.

Adams, W. M., *The Physical Geography of Africa*, Oxford University Press, 1996.

Africa: A Lonely Planet Shoestring Guide, Lonely Planet, 1995.

"Africa Online," http//www.africaonline.com.

Binns, Tony, *The People and Environment in Africa*, John Wiley and Sons, 1995.

Bryjak, G. J., "Is It Possible to Rescue Sub-Saharan Africa?," *USA Today* (periodical), July 1997, 34-36.

Chadwick, Douglas H., "A Place for Parks in the New South Africa," *National Geographic*, July 1996, 2-41.

Cobb, Charles E., Jr., "Eritrea Wins the Peace," *National Geographic*, June 1996, 82-105.

Collins Nations of the World Atlas, HarperCollins, 1996.

Fodor's Kenya, Tanzania, Seychelles, Fodor's Travel Guides, 1997.

Halliburton, Warren J., and Kathilyn Solomon Probosz, *African Landscapes*, Crestwood House, 1993.

McEvedy, Colin, *The Penguin Atlas of African History*, Penguin, 1996.

Pope, Joyce, *The Children's Atlas of Natural Wonders*, Millbrook Press, 1995.

Salopek, Paul F., "Gorillas and Humans An Uneasy Truce," *National Geographic*, October 1995, 72-83.

Schaller, George B., "Gentle Gorillas, Turbulent Times," *National Geographic*, October 1995, 58-68.

"Serengeti," http//www.cyberatl.net/~young/.

"Tanzania, "http//www.africa.com/~venture/wildfron/wildtanz.htm.

"Uganda," http//imul.com/uganda/

Worldmark Encyclopedia of Cultures and Daily Life, Gale, 1997.

"Zimbabwe," http//www.mother.com/~zimweb/History.html.

Alternative Applications: Create a travel guide to Africa, denoting the peculiarities and problems of each country, such as travel and hunting restrictions, common foods, currencies, and local diseases, such as malaria, cholera, schistosomiasis, Ebola, and AIDS.

 African Peoples

Originator: Leatrice Pearson, teacher, Lenoir, North Carolina.

Age/Grade Level or Audience: Elementary or middle school history classes.

Description: Have student draw a large map of Africa and locate the most prominent tribes.

Procedure: Provide students with the names of African tribes, particularly these:

Afrikaners	Akan	Amhara	Angola
Ashanti	Azanda	Banum	Baule
Berbers	Bini	Bushmen	Chagga
Congo	Dogon	Edo	Ekoi
Ewe	Fali	Fanti	Fon
Fulbe	Ga	Grebo	Hausa
Hottentot	Ibo	Ikoma	Isoko
Jabo	Jie	Kikuyu	Kom
!Kung	Lozi	Mandinka	Mangbetu
Masai	Mbunder	Moor	Namib
Ndaka	Nuer	Nyanga	Osei
Ouadai	Pondo	Pygmies	Quimbande
Rendille	Serere	Shangaan	Shilluk
Soninke	Sotho	Tsonga	Tuaregs
Tutu	Twa	Uge	Vai
Wagenia	Watutsis	Wolof	Xhosa
Yedseram	Yombe	Yoruba	Zande
Zulu			

Have students put placards in the areas inhabited by these African peoples.

Budget: $25-$50

Sources:

Adams, W. M., *The Physical Geography of Africa*, Oxford University Press, 1996.

Africa: A Lonely Planet Shoestring Guide, Lonely Planet, 1995.

"Africa Online," http//www.africaonline.com.

"African Travel Gateway," http//africantravel.com/home.html.

"Africa TourNet," http//wn.apc.org/mediatech/tourism/TN090072.HTM.

Ajmera, Maya, and Anna Rhesa Versola, *Children from Australia to Zimbabwe*, Charlesbridge, 1997.

Binns, Tony, *The People and Environment in Africa*, John Wiley and Sons, 1995.

Bolz, D. M., "Picturing the Face of the African Diaspora," *Smithsonian*, February 1997, 26.

Demko, George J., *Why in the World Adventures in Geography*, Anchor Books, 1992.

"Flashback (Xhosa Dancers)," *National Geographic*, July 1996, 132.

Collins Nations of the World Atlas, HarperCollins, 1996.

Hammond New Century World Atlas, Hammond, 1996.

Jeunesse, Gallimard, *Atlas of Countries*, Cartwheel Books, 1996.

Labi, Esther, *Pockets World Atlas*, Dorling Kindersley, 1995.

Mason, Paul, ed., *Atlas of Threatened Cultures*, Raintree/Steck-Vaughn, 1997.

McEvedy, Colin, *The Penguin Atlas of African History*, Penguin, 1996.

Müller, Claudia, *The Costume Timeline: 5000 Years of Fashion History*, Thames and Hudson, 1993.

Oliver, Roland, *The African Experience*, IconEditions, 1992.

Theroux, Paul, "Down the Zambezi," *National Geographic*, October 1997, 2-31.

"Webcrawler Guide Travel Africa Travel Guides," http//webcrawler.com/select/trav. africa.html.

Worldmark Encyclopedia of Cultures and Daily Life, Gale, 1997.

"Zaire," http//www.spectortravel.com/Pages/about.html.

Alternative Applications: Have each student focus on a tribe and fill in the following data by creating a booklet or database on each group:

- ◆ styles of government, flag, and relations with the United States
- ◆ food and cooking styles
- ◆ music, musical instruments, dancing, and ceremonies
- ◆ storytelling, lore, and educational opportunities
- ◆ weapons, tools, and common utensils
- ◆ languages and alphabets
- ◆ religions, coming-of-age ceremonies, and seasonal rituals
- ◆ economy and currency
- ◆ hairstyles, jewelry, headdresses, tattooing, scarification
- ◆ housing, gardens, and domesticated animals

Assemble the booklets for a library, school, civic, or museum display or share databases via Internet bulletin boards, websites, and services, such as IRIS or Prodigy.

African Riches

Age/Grade Level or Audience: Elementary school or church school, scouts, or 4-H clubs.

Description: Assign groups to study reference books about Africa, name its most important products, and place symbols of these products on a map.

Procedure: Assemble reference books, films, filmstrips, and videos about Africa. Have students organize data disks African products, such as the following:

- ◆ **timber, fruit, and vegetables** palm oil, sisal, pyrethrum, yams, rice, vanilla, peanuts, millet, cocoa, barley, wheat, corn, sugar cane, cotton, tea, dates, bananas, figs, coffee, tobacco, grapes, olives, papyrus, sisal, hardwood
- ◆ **minerals** bauxite, phosphates, chemicals, mica, copper, petroleum, lead, platinum, tin, zinc, tungsten, cobalt, vanadium, lead, sulphur, uranium, graphite, chromium, silver, titanium, asbestos, diamonds
- ◆ **refined or manufactured materials and goods** rubber, cork, paper, building materials, jewelry, dyes, hydroelectric power, flavorings, packaged foods

♦ **woven goods** clothing, linen and cotton textiles, rugs, baskets, wall hangings

♦ **livestock and animal byproducts** sheep, cattle, camels, goats; ivory, hides, wool, dairy products, fish, seafood

Create symbols to represent each. Assign a few volunteers to place the symbols on disks labeled by main topics, *e. g.*, woven goods or livestock. Pin to the spot on a map where they are most common, such as diamonds from South Africa, goats in Kenya, and hydroelectric power in Egypt.

Budget: $25-$50

Sources:

Adams, W. M., *The Physical Geography of Africa*, Oxford University Press, 1996.

"African Geography" (software), KnowMaster.

"African Travel Gateway," http//africantravel.com/home.html.

"Africa TourNet," http//wn.apc.org/mediatech/tourism/TN090072.HTM.

Binns, Tony, *The People and Environment in Africa*, John Wiley and Sons, 1995.

"Botswana," *National Geographic*, December 1990.

Demko, George J., *Why in the World Adventures in Geography*, Anchor Books, 1992.

Halliburton, Warren J., and Kathilyn Solomon Probosz, *African Landscapes*, Crestwood House, 1993.

Collins Nations of the World Atlas, HarperCollins, 1996.

Hammond New Century World Atlas, Hammond, 1996.

Jeunesse, Gallimard, *Atlas of Countries*, Cartwheel Books, 1996.

Labi, Esther, *Pockets World Atlas*, Dorling Kindersley, 1995.

Lindquist, Tarry, "Create and Use 'Data Disks,'" *Instructor,* November/December 1997, 72.

Mason, Paul, ed., *Atlas of Threatened Cultures*, Raintree/Steck-Vaughn, 1997.

"Math of Africa" (poster), Dale Seymour

McEvedy, Colin, *The Penguin Atlas of African History*, Penguin, 1996.

Oliver, Roland, *The African Experience*, IconEditions, 1992.

Pope, Joyce, *The Children's Atlas of Natural Wonders*, Millbrook Press, 1995.

"Webcrawler Guide Travel Africa Travel Guides," http//webcrawler.com/select/trav. africa.html.

"Zaire," http//www.spectortravel.com/Pages/about.html.

Alternative Applications: Have students contrast exports common to the United States and other nations with those of Africa. For example, note these exports:

♦ British Isles, France and Italy—wine, cheese, tea, paper products, books, movies, records and tapes, perfume

♦ Germany and eastern Europe—electronics, laboratory equipment, and leather goods

♦ Sweden, Denmark, Finland, and Norway—fish, cheese, hides, movies, books

♦ Japan, Singapore, Hong Kong, and Korea—seafood, automobiles, and electronic equipment
♦ India—teak, jewelry, spices, madras, and cotton clothing
♦ Caribbean islands and Central and South America—carvings and other wood products, oil, coffee, beef, spices, bauxite, fruit, music
♦ Australia and New Zealand—wool, beef, fruit

Encourage students to realize that nations share in world trade by supplying what the other nations lack.

An African Travel Guide

Age/Grade Level or Audience: Elementary or middle school language or history classes.

Description: Have students create an organized travel guide to Africa.

Procedure: Suggest that students begin at a particular spot, such as Agra or Cairo, then move in a clockwise fashion around the continent, providing distances between points and suggesting methods of travel, such as camel, horse, train, car, plane, or boat. Focus on important tourist attractions such as these:

♦ Mt. Kilimanjaro, Kenya, Table Mountain, Aberdare, Ahaggar, Muchinga, Virunga, Cameroon, Tibesti, Drakesberg, Atlas, Futa Jallon, Ruwenzori Meru, and the Ethiopian Highlands
♦ Qattara Depression, Ngorongoro Crater, Zambezi Basin
♦ Watumu Beach
♦ Cape Verde, Cape Agulhas, Cape of Good Hope, Cape Blanc
♦ Ras Hafun, Ras Beni Sako
♦ Victoria Falls, Kebrabassa Falls, Stanley Falls, Stanley Pool
♦ Serengeti Plains
♦ Ituri Rain Forest
♦ Nile Delta, Gulf of Guinea, Strait of Gibraltar, Suez Canal
♦ Red Sea, Indian Ocean, Mediterranean Sea, Atlantic Ocean
♦ cities of Freetown, Abidjan, Durban, Mombasa, Casablanca, Khartoum, Cairo, Accra, Cape Town, Conakry, Addis Ababa, Lagos, Johannesburg, Kampala, Kinshasa, Port Elizabeth, Marrakesh, Pretoria, Brazzaville, Timbuktu, Alexandria, Tripoli, Tunis, Djibouti, Alwa, Nairobi, Dar-es-Salaam, Monrovia, and Dakar
♦ Marsabit Nature Reserve, Sabi Sabi, Rungwa, Ugalla River, Maswa, Losai, S. Turkana, and Kora Game Reserve, and Kruger, Amboseli, Serengeti, Masai Mara, Tsavo, and Kafue National Parks

- ◆ Cabora Bassa, Aswan, Asokombo Main, Ayame, Jos, Kainji, Kariba, and Inga dams
- ◆ the islands of Zanzibar, Madagascar, Mauritius, Seychelles, Saint Helena, Réunion, Comoros, Saint Helena, Ascension, São Tomé, Principe, Annobón, Bioko, Canaries, Madeiras, and Pemba
- ◆ gold mines of Ghana
- ◆ Snake Park, Koobi Fora, and Nairobi museums
- ◆ lakes Leopold, Assal, Victoria, Chad, Kivu, Tana, Tanganyika, Malawi, Mweru, Kariba, Kioga, Rudolf, Manyara, Baringo, Turkana, Natron, Bangweulu, Albert, and Edward
- ◆ Kalahari, Sahara, Libyan and Nubian deserts
- ◆ Great Rift Valley and Olduvai Gorge
- ◆ pyramids of Cheops and Khafre in Giza

Budget: Under $25

Sources:

Adams, W. M., *The Physical Geography of Africa*, Oxford University Press, 1996.

Africa: A Lonely Planet Shoestring Guide, Lonely Planet, 1995.

"Africa Online," http//www.africaonline.com.

Binns, Tony, *The People and Environment in Africa*, John Wiley and Sons, 1995.

Chadwick, Douglas H., "A Place for Parks in the New South Africa," *National Geographic*, July 1996, 2-41.

Cobb, Charles E., Jr., "Eritrea Wins the Peace," *National Geographic*, June 1996, 82-105.

Collins Nations of the World Atlas, HarperCollins, 1996.

Fodor's Kenya, Tanzania, Seychelles, Fodor's Travel Guides, 1997.

Halliburton, Warren J., and Kathilyn Solomon Probosz, *African Landscapes,* Crestwood House, 1993.

Hammond Students Atlas of the World, Hammond, 1995.

Jeunesse, Gallimard, *Atlas of Countries*, Cartwheel Books, 1996.

Pope, Joyce, *The Children's Atlas of Natural Wonders*, Millbrook Press, 1995.

Salopek, Paul F., "Gorillas and Humans An Uneasy Truce," *National Geographic*, October 1995, 72-83.

Schaller, George B., "Gentle Gorillas, Turbulent Times," *National Geographic*, October 1995, 58-68.

"Serengeti," http//www.cyberatl.net/~young/.

"Tanzania, "http//www.africa.com/~venture/wildfron/wildtanz.htm.

"Uganda," http//imul.com/uganda/.

"Zimbabwe," http//www.mother.com/~zimweb/History.html.

Alternative Applications: Have travel planners survey catalogs of safari clothing and footwear, tents, equipment, cameras, and other gear so that they can make useful suggestions about pre-travel purchases. Give advice about currency, inoculations, drinking water, swimming, and protection from heat, insects, disease, and poisonous snakes.

Africa's Great Rivers

Originator: Paula Montgomery, editor, Baltimore, Maryland.

Age/Grade Level or Audience: Elementary geography classes.

Description: On a large map, name and explore Africa's rivers.

Procedure: Post large topographical maps of Africa and have students name these rivers:

Aruwimi	Atbara	Benue	Congo
Gambia	Juba	Kasai	Kwando
Limpopo	Lualaba	Lwango	Niger
Nile	Ogooué	Orange	Senegal
Shire	Ubangi	Vaal	Volta
Zambezi			

Have participants trace by hand the main channels and branches. Lead a discussion of how each river influences the lifestyle of local tribes. Include commentary on the types of plants and animals that thrive on African river banks, particularly the hippopotamus, crocodile, flamingoes, fish, and water hyacinths and lilies.

Budget: Under $25

Sources:

Computer software such as Data Disc International's *World Data* or MECC's *World Geography.*

Adams, W. M., *The Physical Geography of Africa*, Oxford University Press, 1996.

Africa: A Lonely Planet Shoestring Guide, Lonely Planet, 1995.

Africa Inspirer (CD-ROM), Tom Snyder Productions.

"Africa Online," http//www.africaonline.com.

Bentsen, Cheryl *Maasai Days*, Anchor Books, 1991.

Binns, Tony, *The People and Environment in Africa*, John Wiley and Sons, 1995.

Bryjak, G. J., "Is It Possible to Rescue Sub-Saharan Africa?," *USA Today* (periodical), July 1997, 34-36.

Coleman, A. D., "Celebrating Survival," *Art News*, February 1997, 102-105.

Collins Nations of the World Atlas, HarperCollins, 1996.

Demko, George J., *Why in the World Adventures in Geography*, Anchor Books, 1992.

Fodor's Kenya, Tanzania, Seychelles, Fodor's Travel Guides, 1997.

Halliburton, Warren J., and Kathilyn Solomon Probosz, *African Landscapes,* Crestwood House, 1993.

Hammond New Century World Atlas, Hammond, 1996.

Jeunesse, Gallimard, *Atlas of Countries*, Cartwheel Books, 1996.

Labi, Esther, *Pockets World Atlas*, Dorling Kindersley, 1995.

"Lonely Planet," http//www.lonelyplanet.com.

"Mali," *National Geographic*, October 1990.

McEvedy, Colin, *The Penguin Atlas of African History*, Penguin, 1996.

"Serengeti," http//www.cyberatl.net/~young/.

"Tanzania, "http//www.africa.com/~venture/wildfron/wildtanz.htm.

"Uganda," http//imul.com/uganda/.

"Wild Egypt The Nile Adventure," http//www.interoz.com/egypt/wildegypt/
nile.html.

"Zaire," *National Geographic*, November 1991.

"Zimbabwe," http//www.mother.com/~zimweb/History.html.

Alternative Applications: Supply smaller maps to groups of two or three children and have them letter the names of the Congo, Niger, Nile, and other important waterways. Complete the assignment by writing in names of major cities that depend on rivers for drinking water, trade, recreation, irrigation, transportation, and water power.

Bean Bag Toss

Age/Grade Level or Audience: Kindergarten or elementary school geography classes.

Description: Organize games of bean bag toss on an oversized map of Africa.

Procedure: Outline a color-coded map of Africa approximately eight feet long on an asphalt or concrete playground. Color code the countries with chalk or paint. To protect the map from rain damage, spray with a fixative, such as polyurethane or water seal. This game could also be drawn on a tarp or piece of canvas and rolled up for storage, then played in a gymnasium, hallway, community center, church activities room, or neighborhood street festival.

Vary rules with each use. Have students toss bean bags onto the map or play variations of hopscotch. For example:

♦ Score points only for bags that land on a particular country or island, such as Benin, Comoros, Principe, Sao Tomé, or Mali. The smaller the country or island, the greater the number of points.

♦ Have students name the country they are aiming for before tossing bean bags. If they are successful, they win points.

◆ Have students continue tossing so long as they hit the countries they name beforehand. When the bean bag lands on another country, the turn passes to another player.

◆ Have students hop on one foot onto a series of countries without touching borders. In order to win points, they must call out the name of the country they land on.

◆ Have students name the capital of the nation they land on. Refer to this list:

Algeria—Algiers	Angola—Luanda
Benin—Porto-Novo	Botswana—Gaborone
Burkina Faso—Ouagadougou	Burundi—Bujumbura
Cameroon—Yaoundé	Cape Verde—Praia
Central African Republic—Bangul	Chad—N'Djamena
Comoros—Moroni	Congo—Brazzaville
Djibouti—Djibouti	Egypt—Cairo
Equatorial Guinea—Malabo	Eritrea—Asmara
Ethiopia—Addis Ababa	Gabon—Libreville
Gambia—Banjul	Ghana—Accra
Guinea—Conakry	Guinea-Bissau—Bissau
Ivory Coast—Abidjan	Kenya—Nairobi
Lesotho—Maseru	Liberia—Monrovia
Libya—Tripoli	Madagascar—Antananarivo
Malawi—Lilongwe	Mali—Bamako
Mauritania—Nouakchott	Mauritius—Port Louis
Morocco—Rabat	Mozambique—Maputo
Namibia—Windhoek	Niger—Niamey
Nigeria—Lagos	Réunion-Saint-Denis
Rwanda—Kigali	São Tomé and Principe—São Tomé
Senegal—Dakar	Seychelles—Victoria
Sierra Leone—Freetown	Somalia—Mogadishu
South Africa—Pretoria	Spanish North Africa—Ceuta, Melilla
Sudan—Khartoum	Swaziland—Mbabane
Tanzania—Dar es Salaam	Togo—Lomé
Tunisia—Tunis	Uganda—Kampala
Zaire—Kinshasa	Zambia—Lusaka
Zimbabwe—Harare	

Budget: $50-$75

Sources:

Computer software such as Data Disc International's *World Data* or MECC's *World Geography*.

Adams, W. M., *The Physical Geography of Africa*, Oxford University Press, 1996.

Africa: A Lonely Planet Shoestring Guide, Lonely Planet, 1995.

Africa Inspirer (CD-ROM), Tom Snyder Productions.

"Africa Online," http//www.africaonline.com.

Binns, Tony, *The People and Environment in Africa*, John Wiley and Sons, 1995.

Chadwick, Douglas H., "A Place for Parks in the New South Africa," *National Geographic*, July 1996, 2-41.

Collins Nations of the World Atlas, HarperCollins, 1996.

Demko, George J., *Why in the World Adventures in Geography*, Anchor Books, 1992.

Halliburton, Warren J., and Kathilyn Solomon Probosz, *African Landscapes*, Crestwood House, 1993.

Hammond New Century World Atlas, Hammond, 1996.

Jeunesse, Gallimard, *Atlas of Countries*, Cartwheel Books, 1996.

Labi, Esther, *Pockets World Atlas*, Dorling Kindersley, 1995.

Alternative Applications: Extend the use of the oversized African map with a whole world map covering an entire asphalt or concrete playground. Organize a PTA committee or other volunteers to lay out continents and color code countries. Lead students in comparative studies of Africa with other nations. For example:

- Use small steps to measure the Nile, Niger, Limpopo, or Congo river. Compare the length with that of the Amazon, Yalu, or Missouri river.
- Blindfold players and have them hop to a stopping point on a continent, country, or island populated primarily by black people, such as Jamaica, Haiti, Zaire, Barbados, or Guiana.
- Estimate, then walk the distance from Africa west to Brazil and east to India. Contrast the difference in numbers of steps.
- Name the countries directly north of Africa and the languages spoken in each, such as French in France, Greek in Greece, Italian in Italy and Sicily, Turkish in Turkey, and Spanish in Spain.
- Play follow-the-leader by pretending to fly over the whole world. Name countries in each continent where you intend to land.

Black Educational Institutions

Age/Grade Level or Audience: High school juniors and seniors; vocational classes; guidance offices.

Description: Create a map locating the nation's black colleges and universities.

Procedure: Establish a bulletin board where students, parents, guidance counselors, and teachers can locate black educational institutions or schools which maintain strong black studies departments. Mark with a push pin the location of each. For example:

♦ Alabama A & M University, Normal, Alabama
♦ Alabama State University, Montgomery, Alabama
♦ Albany State College, Albany Georgia
♦ Alcorn Sate University, Lorman, Mississippi
♦ Atlanta Metropolitan College, Atlanta Georgia
♦ Bethune-Cookman College, Daytona Beach, Florida
♦ Bowie state University, Bowie, Maryland
♦ Central State University, Wilberforce, Ohio
♦ Chicago State University, Chicago, Illinois
♦ Clark Atlanta University, Atlanta, Georgia
♦ Delaware State College, Dover, Delaware
♦ Dillard University, New Orleans, Louisiana
♦ Fisk University, Nashville, Tennessee
♦ Grambling State University, Grambling, Louisiana
♦ Hampton University, Hampton, Virginia
♦ Howard University, Washington, D.C.
♦ Johnson C. Smith University, Charlotte, North Carolina
♦ Langston University, Langston, Oklahoma
♦ Lincoln University, Jefferson City, Missouri
♦ Medgar Evers College of City University of New York, Brooklyn, New York
♦ Morehouse College, Atlanta, Georgia
♦ Morgan State University, Baltimore, Maryland
♦ Norfolk State University, Norfolk, Virginia
♦ North Carolina A & T, Greensboro, North Carolina
♦ Prairie View A & M University, Prairie View, Texas
♦ Roxbury Community College, Roxbury Crossing, Massachusetts
♦ Savannah State College, Savannah, Georgia
♦ Shaw University, Raleigh, North Carolina
♦ South Carolina State College, Orangeburg, South Carolina
♦ Southern University, Baton Rouge, Louisiana
♦ Tennessee State University, Nashville, Tennessee
♦ Texas Southern University, Houston, Texas
♦ Tuskegee Institute, Tuskegee, Alabama
♦ University of Arkansas, Pine Bluff, Arkansas
♦ University of the District of Columbia, Washington, D.C.
♦ Virginia State University, Petersburg, Virginia
♦ Wayne State University, Detroit, Michigan
♦ West Virginia State College, Institute, West Virginia
♦ Winston-Salem State University, Winston-Salem, North Carolina
♦ Xavier University of Louisiana, New Orleans, Louisiana

Attach a string from the pin to an index card listing essential information, such as size, range of majors, specialty courses, for example women's studies or urban planning, extracurricular activities, scholarship and work-study programs, tuition, required tests, and addresses of student aid officers and admissions directors.

Budget: Under $25

Sources:
Barron's Compact Guide to Colleges, Barrons Educational Series, 1996.
Black Student's Guide to Colleges, Madison Books, 1997.
Custard, Edward T., *The Best 311 Colleges-1998*, Princeton Review, 1997.
Mattson, Mark T., *Macmillan Color Atlas of the States*, Macmillan Library Reference/Simon & Schuster Macmillan, 1996.
Peterson's Guide to Four-Year Colleges-1998, Peterson's Guides, 1997.

Alternative Applications: To encourage interest in higher education, invite graduates of black educational institutions to address students and display slides, posters, and charts of pertinent data. Provide a table of handouts, brochures, college catalogs, and student aid forms.

The Black Flavor of New Orleans

Age/Grade Level or Audience: All ages.

Description: Hold a New Orleans festival.

Procedure: As a community celebration of Black History Month, create the atmosphere of New Orleans in language, architecture, fashion, song, food, instrumental music, dance, pageantry, and drama.

- ◆ Provide a list of words and terms that express New Orleans history, attitudes, and culture, particularly Big Easy, gris-gris, Vieux Carré, lagniappe, plantation society, gingerbread architecture, Cajun, Creole, *code noir*, and zydeco.
- ◆ Label festival booths with familiar names:

Bourbon Street	Cafe du Monde	Canal Street
Jackson Square	The Levee	Preservation Hall
The Quarter	Satchmo's Place	St. Charles Avenue
Storyville		

- ◆ Serve local foods such as poor boys, muffalettas, red beans and rice, crawfish etouffée, gumbo, beignets, pralines, and coffee with chicory.
- ◆ Play music that originated in New Orleans, particularly Dixieland Jazz, Cajun and Creole folk music, and zydeco. Invite volunteers to demonstrate dance steps that complement the music.
- ◆ Assign groups to draw murals and design fabrics that capture the style of the Mississippi Delta, bayou country, and Cajun and Creole folk culture.

♦ Stress how successfully African people have blended with Native Americans and French, Spanish, Portuguese, Irish, Acadian, and English settlers.

Budget: $50-$75

Sources:

The films *The Big Easy* (1987), *American Patchwork Jazz Parades* (1990), *American Patchwork The Land Where the Blues Began* (1990), or *Feet Don't Fail Me Now;* American Automobile Association (AAA) guidebooks to New Orleans, Louisiana.

Bultman, Bethany E., *New Orleans*, 2nd edition, Fodor's Travel Guides, 1996.

City Profiles USA 1996 A Travelers' Guide to Major US Cities., Omnigraphics, 1996.

Delehanty, Randolph, *New Orleans The ULtimate Guide*, Chronicle Books, 1997.

"HM USA Travel Guide—Louisiana," http//www.dedas.com/hm_usa/states/la.html.

New Orleans, Berlitz, 1994.

Raburn, Robert, *New Orleans*, Lonely Planet, 1997.

"Virtual Voyages New Orleans, Louisiana," http//www.virtualvoyages.com/usa/la/n_o/n_o.htm.

Alternative Applications: Launch a study of black influence on Harlem, Memphis, St. Louis, Atlanta, Detroit, Charleston, Chicago, Mobile, Louisville, Philadelphia, Boston, Indianapolis, the Mississippi Delta, or Washington, D. C. Highlight African American contributions to each area, such as Memphis's Beale Street, Mobile's Africatown, Charleston's Slave Market and Catfish Row, Detroit's Motown Records, Atlanta's Underground, or Harlem's Cotton Club.

Caribbean Idyll

Age/Grade Level or Audience: Elementary and middle school art and history classes; travel clubs.

Description: Create a Caribbean oasis.

Procedure: Create a display or bulletin board featuring the Caribbean's most famous historical spots, products, and tourist attractions. Have volunteers draw an oversized map of Caribbean islands, particularly tourist favorites such as these:

Anguilla	Antigua	Aruba
Bahamas	Barbados	Bonaire
British Virgin Islands	Curaçao	Dominica
Dominican Republic	Grand Caymans	Granada
Guadaloupe	Haiti	Jamaica
Martinique	Montserrat	Nevis

Puerto Rico	Saba	Santo Domingo
St. Bart	St. Eustatius	St. Kitts
St. Lucia	St. Martin	St. Thomas
St. Vincent	Tobago	Trinidad

Apply these activities to class study:

♦ Use colored markers and string to add posters and placards explaining the historical features, such as petroglyphs, ruins of Indian villages, sugar and indigo plantations, slave markets, fishing ports, and the birthplace of Toussaint L'Ouverture.

♦ Use a system of symbols to indicate leading products, particularly rum, perfume, oil, bauxite, fruit, fish, and vanilla.

♦ Indicate landmarks and tourist attractions, especially lighthouses, underwater parks, caves, peaks, rain forests, lagoons, ghost sightings, and the homes of famous freedom fighters.

♦ Read aloud from the writings of famous Caribbean authors, particularly James Berry, Jamaica Kincaid, V. S. Naipaul, and Derek Walcott, winner of the 1992 Nobel Prize for literature

♦ Play recorded stories performed by tellers Paul Keens-Douglas, Ken Corsbie, and Grace Hallworth.

Budget: Under $25

Sources:

Collins Nations of the World Atlas, HarperCollins, 1996.
Hammond New Century World Atlas, Hammond, 1996.
Jeunesse, Gallimard, *Atlas of Countries*, Cartwheel Books, 1996.
Labi, Esther, *Pockets World Atlas*, Dorling Kindersley, 1995.

Consult these tourist boards:

♦ Anguilla Department of Tourism
1208 Washington Drive
Centerport, NY 11721
phone 516-425-0900
fax 516-425-0903

♦ Antigua and Barbuda Department of Tourism
610 Fifth Avenue, Suite 311
New York, NY 10020
phone 212-541-4117
fax 212-757-1607
http//www.interknowledge.com/
antigua-barbuda

♦ Aruba Tourism Authority
1000 Harbor Boulevard
Weehawken, NJ
phone 800-TO-ARUBA, 201-330-0800
fax 201-830-8757
http//www. interknowledge.com/aruba

♦ Bahamas Tourist Office
150 East 52nd Street, 28th floor north
New York, NY 10022
phone 800-422-4262, 212-758-2777
fax 212-753-6531
http//www.interknowledge.com/
bahamas

◆ Bonaire Tourist Information Office
201 1/2 East 29th Street
New York, NY 10016
phone 800-8826-6247
http//www.interknowledge.com/
bonaire

◆ Barbados Tourism Authority
800 Second Avenue
New York, NY 10017
phone 212-986-6516, 800-221-9831
fax 212-573-9850

◆ Belize Tourist Board
421 Seventh Avenue, Suite 701
New York, NY
phone 212-563-6011, 800-624-0686
fax 212-563-6033
http//www.belize.com

◆ Bonaire Tourist Board
10 Rockefeller Plaza, Suite 900
New York, NY 10020
phone 212-956-5911/12, 800-826-6247
fax 212-956-5913

◆ British Virgin Islands
360 Lexington Avenue, Suite 416
New York, NY 10017
phone 212-696-0400, 800-835-8530
fax 212-949-8254

◆ Caribbean Tourism Organization
80 Broadway, 32nd Floor
New York, NY 10004
phone 212-635-9530
fax 212-635-9511
http//www.caribtourism.com

◆ Cayman Islands Department of
Tourism
420 Lexington Avenue, #2733
New York, NY 10170
phone 212-682-5582
fax 212-986-5123
http//www.caymans.com

◆ Curaçao Tourist Board
475 Park Avenue South, Suite 2000
New York, NY 10016

phone 212-683-7660, 800-270-3350
fax 212-683-9337
http//www.interknowledge.com/
curacao

◆ Dominica Consulate
820 Second Avenue, 9th Floor
New York, NY 10017
phone 212-599-8478
fax 212-808-4975

◆ Dominican Republic Tourist Office
1501 Broadway, Suite 410
New York, NY 10036
phone 212-575-4966
fax 212-575-5118

◆ Grenada Tourist Board
820 Second Avenue, Suite 900D
New York, NY 10017
phone 212-687-9554, 800-927-9554
fax 212-573-9731

◆ Guadeloupe/St. Barts
French Government Tourist Office
444 Madison Avenue, 16th Floor
New York, NY 10022
phone 212-838-7800 ext. 206,
800-391-4909
fax 212-838-7855

◆ Guyana Consulate
866 United Nations Plaza, 3rd Floor
New York, NY 10017
phone 212-527-3215
fax 212-935-7548

◆ Consulate of Haiti
271 Madison Avenue, 17th Floor
New York, NY 10016
phone 212-697-9767
fax 212-681-6991

◆ Jamaica Tourist Board
801 Second Avenue, 20th Floor
New York, NY 10017
phone 212-856-9727, 800-233-4582
fax 212-856-9655
http//www.jamaictravel.com

◆ Martinique Promotion Bureau
c/o French Government Tourist
Office
444 Madison Avenue, 16th Floor
New York, NY 10022
phone 212-838-7800 ext. 228
fax 212-838-7855
http//www.nyo.com/martinique

◆ Montserrat Tourist Information
Medhurst & Associates
1208 Washington Drive
Centerport, NY 11721
phone 516-351-4922, 800-646-2002
fax 516-425-0903
http//www.mrat.com/

◆ Puerto Rico Tourism Company
575 Fifth Avenue, 23rd Floor
New York, NY 10017
phone 212-599-6262, 800-223-6530
fax 212-818-1866

◆ Saba and Sint Eustatius
P. O. Box 6322
Boca Raton, FL 33427
phone 407-304-8580, 800-722-2394
fax 407-394-8588
http//www.turq.com/saba

◆ Saint Kitts and Nevis Tourist Board
414 East 75th Street, 5th Floor
New York, NY 100021
phone 212-535-1234, 800-582-6208
fax 212-734-6511
http//www.interknowledge.com/
stkitts-nevis

◆ St. Lucia Tourist Board
830 Second Avenue, 9th Floor
New York, NY 10017
phone 212-867-2950, 800-456-3984
fax 212-867-2795
http//www.interknowledge.com/
st-lucia

◆ Sint Maarten (St. Martin)
675 Third Avenue, 23rd Floor

New York, NY 10017
phone 212-953-2084, 800-786-2278
fax 212-953-2145
http//www.st.maarten.com

◆ St. Martin Tourist Office
c/o Marketing Challenges
10 East 21st Street, #600
New York, NY 10010
phone 212-529-8484
fax 212-460-8287
http//www.interknowledge.com/
st-martin

◆ St. Vincent and the Grenadines
801 Second Avenue, 21st Floor
New York, NY 10017
phone 212-687-1981, 800-729-1726
fax 212-949-5946

◆ Suriname Tourist Information
c/o Suriname Airways
8775 Blue Lagoon Drive, Suite 320
Miami, FL 33126
phone 305-262-9922, 800-327-6864
fax 305-261-0884

◆ Trinidad and Tobago Tourist
Information
7000 Boulevard East
Gottenberg, NJ 07093
phone 201-869-0060, 800-748-4224
fax 201-869-7628
http//www.tidco.co.it

◆ Turks and Caicos Islands
331 Madison Avenue
New York, NY
phone 800-241-0824
http//www.digimark.net/dundas/
turksog/

◆ U.S. Virgin Islands
1270 Avenue of the Americas #2108
New York, NY 10020
phone 212-332-2222
fax 212-332-2228
http//www.usvi.net

Alternative Applications: Feature a Caribbean island each week during black history month. Explain through posters and time lines how Africans came to populate the area and dominate its growth and culture, particularly in Jamaica, Haiti, Santo Domingo, and Antigua. Mention French, Dutch, Portuguese, English, and other colonizers. Indicate each area's struggle for civil rights.

The Drifting Continents

Age/Grade Level or Audience: Middle school and high school geography and earth science classes.

Description: Study the shifting continents of the globe.

Procedure: Have students make contrasting maps of the world before and after continental drift. Point out the following facts:

◆ During the Mesozoic era before continental drift, Africa was the center of a cluster of lands.
◆ This African cluster was known as Pangaea, which is Greek for "all lands."
◆ The first to separate during the Cretaceous era was South America, followed by Asia.
◆ The drifting continents formed North and South America, Europe, Asia, Australia, and Antarctica.
◆ Fossil plants and animals are evidence of the time this separation was completed.
◆ Fluctuations in the earth's crust have produced the Great Rift Valley, Lake Tanganyika, the Luangwa Valley of Zambia, and the Ethiopian Highlands.
◆ Louis, Mary, and Richard Leakey located the earliest human remains in the Olduvai Gorge, Kenya.

Budget: Under $25

Sources:
"Continental Drive," http//deimos.ucsd.edu/projects/cty/platetectonics/drift.html.
Kingdon, Jonathan, *Island Africa: The Evolution of Africa's Rare Animals and Plants*, Princeton University Press, 1992.
Pope, Joyce, *The Children's Atlas of Natural Wonders*, Millbrook Press, 1995.
Sereno, Paul C., "Africa's Dinosaur Castaways," *National Geographic*, June 1996, 106-119.

Alternative Applications: Have students cite geological and climatic reasons for the creation of the Sahara Desert, Zambezi Basin, Kalahari Desert, Namib Desert, Olifants Gorge, Batoka Gorge, Mount Kilimanjaro, and Okavango Swamps. Give evidence that the surface of Africa is continually shifting and changing, for instance in the newly arid areas of Somalia and Ethiopia, where famine endangers farmers and herders. Discuss how the Canaries, Seychelles, Cape Verde, Mauritius, Réunion, Principe, Sao Tomé, Comoros, Mayotte, and Madagascar formed offshore.

Learning on the Go

Age/Grade Level or Audience: Elementary and middle school writing and music classes.

Description: Create an Afro-centric travel tape for toddlers and young children.

Procedure: Brainstorm a series of songs, jingles, poems, rounds, fables, stories, counting rhymes, and audience participation ghost tales to entertain toddlers and young children on a long journey. Use material from the Caribbean and Africa or create models that focus on black experience, for example, riddles and handclapping songs such as "Who Can Climb the Coconut Palm?," "Naming the Elephant's Babies," "Cutting Sugar Cane," or "Sailing to Jamaica."

Budget: $25-$50

Sources:
Alexander, Lloyd, *The Fortune-Tellers*, Dutton Children's Books, 1992.
Arnold, Helen, *Kenya*, Raintree Steck-Vaughn, 1996.
Barchers, Suzanne I., *Storybook Stew*, Fulcrum, 1996.
Cabral, Len, *Anansi's Narrow Waist* (easy reader in English and Spanish), Addison-Wesley 1994.
Coggswell, Gladys, *Well Shut My Mouth* (audiocassette), Coggswell Communications 1995.
Goss, Linda, "Anansi and the Wisdom Tree," *The World & I*, February 1995, 272-273.
Labi, Esther, *Pockets World Atlas*, Dorling Kindersley, 1995.
Wolkstein, Diane, *The Magic Orange Tree and Other Haitian Folktales*, Schocken 1997.

Alternative Applications: Assemble travel games and tapes from numerous sources. Rewrite the stories and games with an Afro-centric focus. For example, instead of farm animals, use African and Caribbean animals.

Learning the Colors of Africa

Age/Grade Level or Audience: Pre-school and kindergarten children.

Description: Teach colors that represent Africa.

Procedure: Stress the colors of Africa by having children color and display objects that typify them:

- black—black-skinned African children, hippopotamus, coal, black pepper
- red—hibiscus, mango slices, smiles, melons
- yellow—sunlight, wheat, canaries, yams, desert sands, hemp
- green—grasslands, palm branches, grasshoppers, coffee plants

Budget: $25-$50

Sources:

Arnold, Helen, *Kenya*, Raintree Steck-Vaughn, 1996.

Labi, Esther, *Pockets World Atlas*, Dorling Kindersley, 1995.

Porter, A. P., *Kwanzaa*, Carolrhoda Books, 1991.

Stock, Catherine, *Armien's Fishing Trip*, Morrow Junior Books, 1990.

Alternative Applications: Present big books, posters, color prints, national flags, and fabrics. Have children point out objects or shapes by color. Discuss how the colors of Africa—black, red, yellow, and green—differ from the traditional American red, white, and blue. Explain why Africans stress colors from nature.

 **Liberia**

Age/Grade Level or Audience: Elementary or middle school history class.

Description: Lead a study of Liberia.

Procedure: Using lecture, film, filmstrips, posters, videos, and other materials, explain to students how freed American slaves founded the nation of Liberia. Discuss the following data:

- significance of the country's name
- arrival of Americo-Liberians in 1821
- emptying of slave ships
- Liberia's independence in 1847
- opening of the Firestone rubber plantation in 1927
- presidency of William Tubman, who fought discrimination again tribal members

◆ establishment of republican government in 1945

◆ extension of voting rights in 1947

◆ model of independence as the sole black republic in Africa until 1957

◆ becoming a charter member of the United Nations

◆ model African state serving the United Nations Security Council in 1960

◆ founding member of the Organization of African Unity in 1963

◆ the violent end of William Tolbert's corrupt government in 1980

◆ warring factions sign a peace accord in 1995

◆ peace fails as rival factions clash in 1996

Budget: $25-$50

Sources:

Adams, W. M., *The Physical Geography of Africa*, Oxford University Press, 1996.

Africa: A Lonely Planet Shoestring Guide, Lonely Planet, 1995.

"Africa Online," http//www.africaonline.com.

Binns, Tony, *The People and Environment in Africa*, John Wiley and Sons, 1995.

Chicoine, Stephen, *Liberian Family*, Lerner Group, 1997.

Dendel, Esther Warner, *You Cannot Unsneeze a Sneeze and Other Tales from Liberia*, University Press of Colorado, 1995.

Jeunesse, Gallimard, *Atlas of Countries*, Cartwheel Books, 1996.

"Liberia," http//dept.physics.upenn.edu/courses/gladdney/dex/ AboutLiberia.html.

"Liberia," http//www.odci.gov./cio/publications/nsdo/factbook/li.htm.

"Liberia," http//www.uis.edu/~dnimpson/liberia.

"Liberia News and Resources," http//www.africanews.org/liblinks.html.

McEvedy, Colin, *The Penguin Atlas of African History*, Penguin, 1996.

Alternative Applications: Have students celebrate Liberia's uniqueness by doing the following:

◆ dressing in Liberian costume

◆ listening to Liberian music and examining traditional musical instruments

◆ reading stories or poems by Liberian authors

◆ identifying plants and animals common to Liberia

◆ drawing a map illustrating the diversity of the brewing, chemical, farming, mining, timber, rubber, and palm industries

◆ trying some native recipes featuring rice, cassava, bananas, sweet potatoes, and cocoa

Life along the Nile

Age/Grade Level or Audience: Elementary or middle school language or history classes.

Description: Present the extensive history of the Nile.

Procedure: Assist students in preparing a database history, scroll, or time line of the Nile River, from its earliest inhabitants, the builders of the Pyramids and Sphinx, through colonial explorations to the removal of Abu Simbel to accommodate the building of the Aswan Dam, and more recent developments. Have groups of students contribute segments to the overall study of the Nile, then bind the finished reports into a single scrapbook about the river's rich history.

Budget: $25-$50

Sources:
Ancient Egypt and the Secrets of the Sun, Golden Obelisk, 1995.
Celesia, Denee, ed., *Ancient Egypt Photo Fun Activities*, Edupress, 1994.
Fischer, Henry G., *Ancient Egyptian Calligraphy: A Beginner's Guide to Writing Hieroglyphs*, Abrams, 1994.

Alternative Applications: Discuss how Western fiction and nonficiton writers celebrate the Nile in their works, including William Shakespeare in *Antony and Cleopatra* and the explorer Richard Francis Burton in *Goa, and the Blue Mountains* and *First Footsteps in East Africa*.

 ## Living in a Kenyan Village

Age/Grade Level or Audience: Kindergarten or elementary school craft classes or librarian lessons.

Description: Organize the building of a miniature Kenyan Village.

Procedure: Have students examine books about life in Kenya. Provide clay, wooden dowels or clothespins, twigs, straw, cardboard, and found objects to create a miniature Kenyan village. Stress the following details:

- ♦ fields of tea, coffee, sugar cane, hemp, wheat, sweet potatoes, and rice
- ♦ pastures grazed by cattle, sheep, oxen, and goats
- ♦ palm trees
- ♦ black leopard, elephant, bongo, and rhino at the Aberdare National Park
- ♦ hyrax and flamingo at Nakuru National Park
- ♦ giraffe, baboon, wart hog, spotted hyena, gray jackal, gazelle, impala, topi, hartebeest, and wildebeest at Masai Mara Game Preserve
- ♦ travel by dhow

- ♦ a camel derby
- ♦ safaris on foot, in a jeep, by camel, and by hot-air balloon travel to Ambosel, Tsavo, Samburu, Buffalo Springs, and Masai Mara
- ♦ coral reefs and sandy beaches
- ♦ flamingos, hot springs, crocodiles, hippos, and geysers at Lake Bogoria and Lake Baringo
- ♦ Kikuku, Luhia, Kikamba, and Luo people
- ♦ rail lines reaching from the heart of the country to the port of Mombasa
- ♦ carvings, fruit, and vegetables at Masai open-air market
- ♦ restaurants serving curry, thali, and tandoori.

Budget: $25-$50

Sources:

Arnold, Helen, *Kenya*, Raintree Steck-Vaughn, 1996.

Bailey, Donna, and Anna Sproule, *Kenya*, Raintree Steck-Vaughn, 1990.

Bertrand, Anne A., and Anne Spoery, *Kenya from the Air*, Vendome, 1994.

Burch, Joann J., *Kenya Africa's Tamed Wilderness*, Silver Burdett, 1996.

Dacey, Donna "Crafts of Many Cultures Three Seasonal Art Projects with Global Appeal," *Instructor*, November-December 1991, 30-33.

Halliburton, Warren J., and Kathilyn Solomon Probosz, *African Landscapes,* Crestwood House, 1993.

"An Introduction to Kenya," http//www.interknowledge.com/kenya/.

Jacobson, Karen, *Kenya*, Children's Press, 1991.

Jeunesse, Gallimard, *Atlas of Countries*, Cartwheel Books, 1996.

Kenya, American Geographical, 1995.

Kenya, Humanities, 1997.

"Kenya," http//www.rcbowen.com/kenya/.

Kenya in Pictures, Lerner Group, 1991.

Ng'Weno, Fleur, *Kenya*, Trafalgar, 1992.

"Travel Kenya," http//city.net/countries/kenya.

Worldmark Encyclopedia of Cultures and Daily Life, Gale, 1997.

Alternative Applications: Have students build two or three villages to illustrate life in contrasting parts of Africa, such as these:

- ♦ Ethiopia, Botwana, and Nigeria
- ♦ Ivory Coast, Lesotho, and Algeria
- ♦ Morocco, Uganda, and South Africa
- ♦ Niger, Muritania, and Swaziland
- ♦ Angola, Rwanda, and Mozambique
- ♦ Egypt, Benin, and Madagascar
- ♦ Togo, Senegal, and Sudan.

The Moors

Age/Grade Level or Audience: Middle school and high school geography or history classes.

Description: Organize a study group to describe the Moorish people, lands where they settled, and their influence on civilization.

Procedure: Have students present oral reports on Moorish civilization and its influence. For example:

♦ the origin of the term "Moor"

♦ Moorish migration to Iberia

♦ eleventh-century expulsion of Moors from Europe

♦ Moorish architecture around the Mediterranean

♦ Moorish mosques

♦ Moors and the Spanish Inquisition

♦ Moorish pottery, textiles, and metalwork

♦ Shakespeare's use of Othello, a Moorish general from Venice, as protagonist of a major English drama

♦ conversion of North African Berbers and blacks to Islam.

Budget: $25-$50

Sources:

Africa: A Lonely Planet Shoestring Guide, Lonely Planet, 1995.

"Africa Online," http//www.africaonline.com.

"Architecture and Design," http//physserv/physics.wisc.edu/~shalizi/notebooks/ arch.des.

McEvedy, Colin, *The Penguin Atlas of African History*, Penguin, 1996.

"Moors," *National Geographic*, July 1988.

Oliver, Roland, *African Experience*, Icon Editions, 1992.

Alternative Applications: Have participants sketch a series of posters illustrating Moorish styling in jewelry, metalwork, pottery, mosaic flooring, wall hangings, and architecture. Have a group write a round-robin short story or poem about the arrival of Moors in Spain and their experiences among people of a vastly different culture.

Puzzle Me Africa

Age/Grade Level or Audience: Elementary or middle school geography classes; religious schools; scouts.

Description: Put together an African map puzzle.

Procedure: Draw a map of Africa on tagboard, canvas, or wrapping paper. After individual countries are colored with markers, chalk, crayon, or paint, laminate the finished map, then cut apart along border lines. Have students work in teams to reassemble the map. The team that finishes in the shortest time wins.

Budget: Under $25

Sources:
Africa: A Lonely Planet Shoestring Guide, Lonely Planet, 1995.
"Africa Online," http//www.africaonline.com.
Binns, Tony, *The People and Environment in Africa*, John Wiley and Sons, 1995.
Collins Nations of the World Atlas, HarperCollins, 1996.
Hammond Students Atlas of the World, Hammond, 1995.
Jeunesse, Gallimard, *Atlas of Countries*, Cartwheel Books, 1996.
McEvedy, Colin, *The Penguin Atlas of African History*, Penguin, 1996.
Pope, Joyce, *The Children's Atlas of Natural Wonders*, Millbrook Press, 1995.

Alternative Applications: Have an individual hold up a single puzzle piece and report to the class on the wildlife, natural resources, products, people, culture, languages, religions, or landmarks of that country. As speakers finish, have them place their puzzle parts in correct order among the other map pieces. The finished map could serve as the focal point of a Black History Month open house, PTA program, civic display, foyer mural, or library or museum bulletin board.

Safari

Age/Grade Level or Audience: Kindergarten and elementary language classes; scout troops, or 4-H clubs.

Description: Organize a game of "I Spy" with an African touch.

Procedure: Select a leader to choose a letter of the alphabet from A to Z. Have the leader begin a game of "I Spy" at random, for example, "I spy something that begins with an M." Name as the new leader the first player to name an African place, fruit, craft, ritual object, people, language, or animal, such as Mozambique, mango, mats, mask, Moroccans, Masai, or monkey.

Budget: Under $25

Sources:

Adlerman, Dan, *Africa Calling*, Coyote Press, 1996.

"Africa Online," http//www.africaonline.com.

Alexander, Lloyd, *The Fortune-Teller*, Dutton, 1992.

Arnold, Caroline, *African Animals*, Morrow Junior Books, 1997.

Binns, Tony, *The People and Environment in Africa*, John Wiley and Sons, 1995.

Chadwick, Douglas H., "A Place for Parks in the New South Africa," *National Geographic*, July 1996, 2-41.

Cobb, Charles E., Jr., "Eritrea Wins the Peace," *National Geographic*, June 1996, 82-105.

Fodor's Kenya, Tanzania, Seychelles, Fodor's Travel Guides, 1997.

Halliburton, Warren J., and Kathilyn Solomon Probosz, *African Landscapes*, Crestwood House, 1993.

"Serengeti," http//www.cyberatl.net/~young/.

"Tanzania, "http//www.africa.com/~venture/wildfron/wildtanz.htm.

Theroux, Paul, "Down the Zambezi," *National Geographic*, October 1997, 2-31.

"Uganda," http//imul.com/uganda/.

"Zimbabwe," http//www.mother.com/~zimweb/History.html.

Alternative Applications: Play these word games:

♦ Assign students only one letter to find on their safari, such as C. Reward the person who names the most words in correct alphabetical order, such as these Cairo, Cameroon, Cape Verde, caracal, Chad, chevrotain, chimpanzee, civet, cobra, colobus, Comoros, Congo, cony, cork, cormorant, corn, Côte d'Ivoire, cotton, crane, and crocodile.

♦ Assign teams to name words about Africa and beginning with a particular letter. Give points for placing correctly spelled words under these headings foods, animals, plants, insects, places, landmarks, bodies of water, countries, languages, musical instruments, religions, and famous people.

♦ Work with a small group to play "Hang Man." Provide the first letter and ask for more letters until the word is completed or the hanged man drawn, for example, C H E E T A H.

 Sailing from Africa

Age/Grade Level or Audience: Elementary school geography and history classes.

Description: Imagine the route from Africa.

Procedure: Have students describe their mental pictures of the route from Africa to the Caribbean and on to Southern slave markets for sale and transfer to a plantation. Conclude by having students describe their fears of loving their freedom and their hopes of joining other slaves to live in a peaceful New World community or return to their homeland.

Budget: Under $25

Sources:

"Conflict of Abolition and Slavery," http//www.loc.gov/exhibits/african/confli.html.

"A History of Slavery in America" (video), *Schlessinger Media.*

Hornsby, Alton, *Chronology of African-American History*, 2nd edition Gale, 1997.

Metcalf, Doris Hunter, *African Americans: Their Impact on U. S. History*, Good Apple, 1992.

Thomas, Velma Maia, *Lest We Forget: The Passage from Africa to Slavery and Emancipation*, Crown, 1997.

"Slavery," http//www.afu.org/~afu43300/slave.html.

Alternative Applications: Have volunteers find on a map the sites of an oral history of slavery, from Africa to the American South and on to freedom. Conclude by having students sketch freehand the route new slaves took on their way from Africa into bondage.

Serving the Cities

Age/Grade Level or Audience: College and university city planning courses.

Description: Design a mobile assistance fleet to the black ghetto of a major American city.

Procedure: Using street maps of an American ghetto or a rural community with a predominantly black population, lay out a block-by-block program of assistance for the poor. Propose mobile assistance for varied needs. Design mobile units such as these assisted living for the handicapped bookmobile:

eldercare	homelessness assessment
home safety and fire prevention education	immunization and well baby care
jobs and career advice	legal aid

methadone and alcohol treatment
summer and vacation play centers
TB testing and mammography
voter registration

nutritional support
tax preparation and financial
  planning services

Note appropriate places for mobile units to stop and set up tutorials, examinations, counseling, distribution of leaflets, and activities centers. Place completed plans on display or mount on a website.

Budget: Under $25

Sources:
Consult city maps and online cartography.
Black Population in the United States, Gordon Press, 1995.
The Black Population in the U. S.: A Statistical Profile, Diane Publications, 1994.
City Planning, Watson-Guptil, 1996.
"Empowering Communities," http//www.usc.edu/Library/QF/diversity/communi-ties.html.
"Ghetto Education," http//www.sirius.com/~adisa/ghetto.html.
Hommann, Mary E., *City Planning in America Between Promise and Despair*, Greenwood, 1993.
"Start Your Own Tolerance Program," http//home.fia.net/~kjmoros/start.html.
"University of Michigan Program on Poverty and Social Welfare Policy," http//www. umich.edu/~socwk/poverty/index.html.
Wilson, William J., ed., *Ghetto Underclass Social Science Perspectives*, Sage, 1993.

Alternative Applications: Compose a hypothetical city council or county commission presentation on the needs of a minority community. Cite sources of statistics that prove black communities are under-served. Suggest better representation and methods of alleviating pockets of poverty.

 | **Simon Says**

Age/Grade Level or Audience: Kindergarten or elementary classes; religious schools; day-care centers.

Description: Play an African version of "Simon Says."

Procedure: Have students act out a game of "Simon Says" from an African point of view. For example, give these commands:

- Build like the termite.
- Flap like the emu.

- Climb like the gorilla.
- Giggle like the monkey.

- Growl like the lion.
- Run like the cheetah.
- Snort like the rhinoceros.
- Swim like the crocodile.
- Trumpet like the elephant.
- Wiggle like the cobra.

- Howl like the hyena.
- Scurry like the ant.
- Stretch like the giraffe.
- Trot like the hyena.
- Wallow like the hippopotamus.

Budget: Under $25

Sources:

Alexander, Lloyd, *The Fortune-Teller*, Dutton, 1992.

Arnold, Caroline, *African Animals*, Morrow Junior Books, 1997.

Kaaza, Keiko. *A Mother for Choco*, Putnam, 1992.

Kingdon, Jonathan, *Island Africa The Evolution of Africa's Rare Animals and Plants*, Princeton University Press, 1992.

Alternative Applications: Have students make up African games suited to life in particular climates and surroundings, such as these:

- steamy jungles of Zaire
- Kenyan plains and grasslands
- riverbanks of the Nile or Niger
- fortune-telling tents in the Cameroons
- sandy beaches of the Seychelles
- camel derbies in a Sudan desert
- Nigeria's thatched villages
- Sahara Desert oases.

Suggest guessing games and listening and speaking activities for keeping cool, watching animals, playing in sand or surf, picking bananas and mangoes, sipping coconut milk, making mud houses, digging for diamonds, hunting for dinosaur bones, playing drums and flutes, stringing beads and shells, braiding hair, taking photos, or drawing animal pictures.

What York Saw

Age/Grade Level or Audience: Middle school or high school history or writing class.

Description: Describe the Lewis and Clark expedition from the point of view of York.

Procedure: Rewrite the travels of Lewis and Clark through the eyes of York, the first black man to venture across the North American continent to the Pacific Ocean. Comment on the lives of Native Americans and their understanding of slavery. Include York's friendship with Sacajawea and his description of life for most American blacks in the eighteenth century.

Budget: Under $25

Sources:

Ambrose, Stephen E., *Undaunted Courage: Meriwether Lewis, Thomas Jefferson, and the Opening of the American West*, Simon & Schuster, 1996.

Bakeless, John E., *Lewis and Clark Partners in Discovery*, Dover, 1996.

Moulton, Gary, *Lewis and Clark and the Route to the Pacific*, Chelsea House, 1991.

Alternative Applications: Extend the writing assignment to other travels and expeditions, for example, the Buffalo Soldiers's experiences in the Indian Wars, landing of the *Clothilde*, mutiny on the *Amistad*, Guion Bluford's journey into space, creation of the Charleston slave market, sailing slavery's Golden Triangle, and spread of Toussaint L'Ouverture's spirited abolitionism throughout the Caribbean.

 World Races

Age/Grade Level or Audience: Elementary or middle school history or geography classes.

Description: Create a map illustrating the locations of major concentrations of black people.

Procedure: Have students research information about the locations of black people on the globe. Divide the class into six groups, one for each continent. Have students draw the continents and islands and indicate with a bar graph the distribution of black people among other races.

Budget: Under $25

Sources:

Adams, W. M., *The Physical Geography of Africa*, Oxford University Press, 1996.

Africa: A Lonely Planet Shoestring Guide, Lonely Planet, 1995.

"Africa Online," http//www.africaonline.com.

Binns, Tony, *The People and Environment in Africa*, John Wiley and Sons, 1995.

Demko, George J., *Why in the World Adventures in Geography*, Anchor Books, 1991.

Halliburton, Warren J., and Kathilyn Solomon Probosz, *African Landscapes,* Crestwood House, 1993.

Jeunesse, Gallimard, *Atlas of Countries,* Cartwheel Books, 1996.

Mason, Paul, ed., *Atlas of Threatened Cultures,* Raintree/Steck-Vaughn, 1997.

Statistical Abstract of the U.S. Department of Census, U. S. Department of Commerce, Bureau of the Census, 1992.

Alternative Applications: Have students apply this assignment to a study of races by state throughout the United States and the rest of North America. Note in particular the most cosmopolitan world cities, particularly New York, Atlanta, San Francisco, Seattle, Los Angeles, San Diego, Toronto, Mexico City, Montreal, and Miami. Have students draw conclusions about how diversity in large cities affects the following cultural aspects:

- community attitudes
- education
- government
- news gathering and publication
- transportation and housing

- currency and finance
- fashion, hairstyles, music, and dining
- literature and lore
- religion and holidays

History

African and World Events

Age/Grade Level or Audience: All ages.

Description: Create a wall chart pairing African events with happenings in other parts of the globe.

Procedure: Create a time line of significant events. Tie them to other areas of human development. Stress these important happenings:

- ♦ **5000-4000 B.C.** While Mesopotamian cities were thriving, the Egyptians devised a twelve-month, 360-day calendar.
- ♦ **4000-3000 B.C.** As Cretan mariners dominated Mediterranean trade routes, Middle Easterners were migrating to Africa across the Sinai Peninsula.
- ♦ **3000-2500 B.C.** While the Chinese were creating the bamboo flute, Egyptians were producing one of the first literary manuscripts.
- ♦ **2000 B.C.** As Ethiopia flourished, Indian civilization was beginning in the Indus Valley.
- ♦ **2000-1000 B.C.** Hammurabi was ruling Babylon and farmers were tilling Central American fields during the Egyptian invasion of Nubia.
- ♦ **1200 B.C.** Jews were exiting Egypt about the time of the Trojan War and the beginning of Peruvian culture.
- ♦ **1000-950 B.C.** While Egyptians were growing poppies for medicinal uses, King Solomon was ruling Judah.
- ♦ **814 B.C.** Greek city-states were flourishing while the Phoenicians were founding Carthage in North Africa, half a century before Rome was founded on the Tiber River.
- ♦ **690 B.C.** The Library at Nineveh collected Sumerian and Semitic texts while Taharka ruled Ethiopia.

◆ **500 B.C.** Hanno, a Carthaginian explorer, sailed the coast of Africa while Greece enjoyed its Golden Age.

◆ **250 B.C.** About the time that the Alexandrian lighthouse at Pharos came into use, Iron Age tribes were invading England.

◆ **100 B.C.** Shortly after the building of the Great Wall of China, North Africa came under Roman domination.

◆ **700 A.D.** Arabs simultaneously converted North Africa and Spain to Islam.

◆ **1250** Shortly after the Magna Carta came into use, the nation of Ghana was established on the African west coast.

◆ **1488** Bartholomeu Dias sailed around the Cape of Good Hope while the Aztec and Incan empires were reaching their height.

◆ **1607** While aboriginal peoples populated arid regions of Australia, the slave trade began in the United States and Caribbean Islands.

◆ **1800** In the years before and after the completion of the Suez Canal, colonizers from Britain, Belgium, France, Germany, and Italy staked out claims in Africa.

◆ **1950s** A decade after the end of World War II and the creation of a free Jewish state in Israel, twenty-seven African republics won their independence from colonialism.

◆ **1990s** At the same time that the United States launched an exploration of Mars, South Africa continued its struggle against racist oppression.

Budget: Under $25

Sources:

Bennett, Lerone, Jr., *Before the Mayflower: A History of Black America*, 6th edition, Penguin Books, 1993.

"Black History," http//www.slip.net/~rigged/history.html.

"Black History Month Let's Get Started," http//www.netnoir.comspotlight/bhm/jbhm. html.

Gates, Henry Louis, ed., *Chronology of African American History from 1445-1980*, Amistad Press, 1993.

Grun, Bernard, *The Timetables of History A Horizontal Linkage of People and Events*, Simon & Schuster, 1991.

Jackson, John G., *Introduction to African Civilizations*, Citadel Press, 1994.

Mabunda, L. Mpho. ed., *The African American Almanac*, 7th edition, Gale, 1997.

McEvedy, Colin, *The Penguin Atlas of African History*, Penguin, 1996.

Myers, Walter Dean, *Now Is Your Time! The African-American Struggle for Freedom*, Harper Trophy, 1991.

"The Roots of African Civilization" (video), Anti-Defamation League.

Steedman, Scott, *Pockets Ancient Egypt*, Dorling Kindersley, 1995.

Saari, Peggy, and Daniel B. Baker, *Explorers and Discoverers: From Alexander the Great to Sally Ride*, U•X•L/Gale, 1995.

Trager, James, *The People's Chronology*, revised edition, Henry Holt, 1996.

Alternative Applications: For a more detailed version of "African and World Events," divide a display into six segments, each representing the five continents plus the islands of the Pacific Rim. Synchronize histories of each continent, giving detailed information about time, place, participants, and events and emphasizing each area's struggles against oppression, exploitation, and tyranny, for example:

♦ building of the Anasazi culture in North America
♦ French and Russian revolutions in Europe
♦ Spanish conquest of Mexico and the American Southwest
♦ Celtic architects' creation of Stonehenge as a predictor of solar events
♦ Captain Cook's arrival in Australia
♦ Polynesian settlement of Hawaii
♦ Japan's air attacks on Nanking, China, during World War II

All Aboard!

Age/Grade Level or Audience: All ages.

Description: Organize a black history cavalcade.

Procedure: Offer the public a special city bus tour or motorcade to local black history centers, landmarks, and points of interest, particularly black colleges, historic churches and cemeteries, recreation and crafts centers, and family homes. Connect local history with the greater picture by pointing out how area figures participated in abolitionism, the Underground Railroad, agricultural and economic development, sit-ins, or civil rights marches. For example, consider the following points of interest in Louisville, Kentucky:

♦ fall Corn Island Storytelling Festival
♦ riverfront "Gateway to Freedom"
♦ Portland Museum's collection of photos and artifacts
♦ Hillerich and Bradsby's "Louisville Slugger," the bat used by Hank Aaron
♦ J. B. Speed Art Museum African art collection
♦ Quinn Chapel, named for Bishop Paul Quinn
♦ Muhammad Ali's home on Grand Avenue
♦ Kenbucky Derby Museum's displays featuring Isaac B. Murphy, three-time winner of the Kentucky Derby
♦ Louisville Free Public Library, the first established for black patrons
♦ Mammoth Life and Accident Insurance Company, established by black owners in 1915
♦ Russell Historic Neighborhood, featuring homes built by black contractor Samuel Plato
♦ Frank Stanley's *Louisville Defender*, the state's first black newspaper.

Budget: $50-$75

Sources:
Enlist the mayor and city council or county commission in offering this tour to citizens, student groups, and visitors. Consult county genealogical and historical societies, historical maps and websites, tax and records offices, newspapers, local colleges and universities, museums, libraries, church groups, and private collectors for information.

Alternative Applications: Using desktop publishing software print a walking tour, including map and markers or plaques indicating historic events and monuments, architectural landmarks, and noteworthy districts. Leave free copies at convention centers, the Chamber of Commerce, public libraries and museums, school administration offices, media centers, shopping malls, hotel complexes, and visitors bureaus.

The Antislavery Movement in England and the United States

Age/Grade Level or Audience: High school or college history class.

Description: Compose a double time line paralleling the United States Abolitionist Movement with England's Anti-Slavery Movement.

Procedure: Have students work in pairs to locate data for a double timeline.

- ◆ On the English side, emphasize the writings of Anna Laetitia Aikin Barbauld, William Pitt's speech before the House of Commons, and John Newton's confessional hymn "Amazing Grace," all of which influenced William Wilberforce to spearhead an anti-slavery movement.
- ◆ On the United States side, stress similar work by Quakers, Mennonites, Frederick Douglass, Harriet Beecher Stowe, Sojourner Truth, Reverend Richard Allen, John Brown, Harriet Ann Jacobs, Martin Delany, Elihu Embree, Sarah Grimké, William Ellery Channing, Harriet Tubman, William Lloyd Garrison, Frances Ellen Watkins Harper, John Russworm, Mary Anne Shadd Cary, Angelina Grimké, and Thaddeus Stevens.

Budget: $25-$50

Sources:
"African American History," http//www.msstate.edu/Archives/History/USA/Afro-Amer/afro.html.
American Eras, Gale, 1997.
"Anna Laetitia Aikin Barbauld," http//www.cs.cmu.edu/afs/cs.cmu.edu/user/mmbt/www/women/barbault/bal-biography.html.

Bennett, Lerone, Jr., *Before the Mayflower: A History of Black America*, 6th edition, Penguin Books, 1993.

Cantor, George Cantor, *Historic Landmarks of Black America*, Gale, 1991.

Channing, William Ellery, *The Abolitionist*, reprint of 1836 edition, Reprint Service 1990.

Coil, Suzanne M., *Slavery and Abolitionists*, TFC Books, 1995.

"Conflict of Abolition and Slavery," http//www.loc.gov/exhibits/ african/confli.html.

Evitts, William J., *Captive Bodies, Free Spirits: The Story of Southern Slavery*, Messner, 1985.

Fritz, Jean, *Harriet Beecher Stowe and the Beecher Preachers*, Putnam Publishing Group, 1994.

Gates, Henry Louis, ed., *Chronology of African-American History from 1445-1980*, Amistad Press, 1993.

"The History of the British Abolition Movement," http//miavxl.muohio.edu/~aronowml/ History.HTM.

Hornsby, Alton, *Chronology of African-American History*, 2nd edition Gale, 1997.

"The Influence of Prominent Abolitionists," http//www.loc.gov/exhibits/african/ influ.html.

Metcalf, Doris Hunter, *African Americans: Their Impact on U. S. History*, Good Apple, 1992.

Myers, Walter Dean, *Now Is Your Time!: The African-American Struggle for Freedom*, Harper Trophy, 1991.

"Northeast Abolitionists," http//www.unl.edu/tcweb/altc/ staffpages/page3.html.

Painter, Nell I., *Sojourner Truth: A Life, A Symbol*, W. W. Norton & Co., 1996.

Rogers, James T., *The Antislavery Movement*, Facts on File, 1994.

Scott, Otto, *The Secret Six: John Brown and the Abolitionists*, Uncommon Books, 1993.

Thomas, Velma Maia, *Lest We Forget: The Passage from Africa to Slavery and Emancipation*, Crown, 1997.

Wilberforce, William, "The Number of Deaths Speaks for Itself," *A Treasury of the World's Great Speeches*, Houston Peterson, edition, Simon & Schuster, 1965.

"William Wilberforce," http//www.scry.com/ayer/AFRO.AM/ 4602542.htm.

Yellin, Jean F., and John C. Van Horne, *The Abolitionist Sisterhood: Women's Political Culture in Antebellum America*, Cornell University Press, 1994.

Alternative Applications: Report facts about slavery's growth and abolishment in the Caribbean islands. Note the influence of places such as Jamaica, Haiti, the Dominican Republic, Aruba, St. Martin, Tortola, Cuba, Bermuda, Antigua, Martinique, and Nassau. Comment on the effects of home rule as colonial governments collapsed, were voted out, or abandoned each island.

Apartheid and the World

Age/Grade Level or Audience: High school and college history or economics classes.

Description: Have students study Apartheid and its effect on world trade and international relations.

Procedure: Provide a selection of resource material about Apartheid, including novels, biographies, newspaper and newsmagazine studies, and reference books. Have students complete the following activities:

- ◆ Outline the beginnings of colonialism in Africa, particularly in the rich diamond fields of South Africa.
- ◆ Compose an extended definition of Apartheid, its origins, and its ramifications in local and global relations.
- ◆ Contribute information and inferences about the nature of severe systems of racial segregation.
- ◆ Stress the irony of the South African flag, which features small insets of the Dutch, British, and Orange Free State flags in the center.
- ◆ Explain the role of Winnie Mandela, Nelson Mandela, and Steven Biko as national heroes.
- ◆ Account for Mark Mathabane's self-liberation from hunger and oppression in Alexandra, a squalid slum of Johannesburg.
- ◆ Discuss the future of colonialism in Africa and the Caribbean.
- ◆ Outline the post-Apartheid hearings and the revelations of former oppressors.
- ◆ Describe Nelson Mandela's post-prison role in state government.

Budget: Under $25

Sources:

"The History of Apartheid in South Africa," http//xenon.stanford.edu/~cale/cs201/ apartheid.hist.html.

"Instruments of Apartheid," http//www.unp.ac.za/UNPDepartments/politics/price4 .htm.

Mandela, Nelson, *The Long Walk to Freedom The Autobiography of Nelson Mandela*, Little, Brown, 1994.

Mathabane, Mark, *Kaffir Boy*, Macmillan Plume Books, 1986.

"Nelson Mandela's Address to the Rally in Cape Town on His Release from Prison," http//www.anc.org.za/ancdocs/speeches/release.html.

Pheko, Motsoko, *Apartheid: The Story of a Dispossessed People*, Pheko & Assocs., 1994.

Seavers, Corbin, *Apartheid: The Untold Story*, United Brothers and Sisters, 1997.

Alternative Applications: Have students present a school assembly program on Apartheid. Include posters, overhead transparencies, handouts, maps, taped sound bites, and mock interviews with significant figures, particularly the president of the United Nations, human rights leaders, Pope John Paul II, Nelson Mandela, Winnie Mandela, Steven Biko, Ian Smith, F. W. de Klerk, Mark Mathabane, and former secretaries of state and presidents of the United States. Stress forensic studies that prove that freedom fighters were beaten, abused, and murdered while in custody.

| **Atlanta-Bound** |

Age/Grade Level or Audience: All ages.

Description: Organize a trip to Atlanta's Freedom Walk.

Procedure: Organize a bus trip to Atlanta. Focus on the life and accomplishments of Martin Luther King, Jr., by beginning the group's tour at the King Center for Nonviolent Social Change. Include on your itinerary the Joel Chandler Harris Museum, office of the Atlanta *Constitution,* and Underground Atlanta. Narrate the role of Atlanta in important segments of African American history, such as the Civil Rights Movement, Sherman's siege, Reconstruction, the slave trade, and the New South economy.

Budget: $75-$100

Sources:
Atlanta Chamber of Commerce or Automobile Association of America (AAA) brochures, maps, websites, and travel guides.
Atlanta, Rand-McNally, 1996.
Atlanta, Time-Life Books, 1997.
"Atlanta History Center," http//www.athist.org.
Cantor, George, *Historic Landmarks of Black America*, Gale, 1991.
"Destination: Atlanta!," http//thomson.com/gale/atl.html.
Garrison, Webb, *Atlanta and the War*, Rutledge Hill Press, 1996.
King, Coretta Scott, *My Life with Martin Luther King, Jr.*, Henry Holt & Co., 1992.
"Margaret Mitchell's House,"http//www.gwtw.org/gwtw-attr.htm.
"Museums," http//www.grainn.com/atlanta/museum.html.

Alternative Applications: Present an historical overview of Atlanta through brochures, photos, maps, diagrams, film clips of *Gone with the Wind*, and media articles. Create a bulletin board featuring a street map of Atlanta and memorabilia from each area, such as programs from the diorama, a schematic drawing of Underground Atlanta, press photos of civil rights demonstrations, election information about the city's first black mayor, and literature from museums.

| **Black Heritage Trivia** |

Originator: Leatrice Pearson, teacher, Lenoir, North Carolina.

Age/Grade Level or Audience: Teenagers and adults.

Description: Organize a group into teams to play Black Heritage Trivia. Broadcast the event on local television or radio stations during Black History Month or distribute game cards at shopping centers, libraries, schools, and civic centers for a city-wide competition.

Procedure: Provide a list from which players may select answers to the following questions:

History

- Who was the first black born in the English colonies? (William Tucker)
- Who founded the Children's Defense Fund? (Marian Wright Edelman)
- What first is linked to Guion Bluford's career? (first black in space)
- Who was the first black woman in space? (Mae Jemison)
- What was the first Negro newspaper? (Freedom's Journal)
- What female agent helped form the Underground Railroad? (Harriet Tubman)
- In what city was the NAACP created? (New York)
- Who founded the National Council of Negro Women? (Mary McLeod Bethune)
- What was Malcolm X's real surname? (Little)
- In what year was the Civil Rights Act passed? (1964)
- Who was the U.S. President that year? (Lyndon B. Johnson)
- By what name is Isabella Baumfree known? (Sojourner Truth)
- Who was the first black general of the U.S. Army? (Benjamin Davis)
- Who was the first black female senator of the United States? (Carole Moseley Braun)
- What is the title of Martin Luther King's most famous speech? ("I Have a Dream")
- What does SCLC stand for? (Southern Christian Leadership Conference)
- Which constitutional amendment abolished slavery? (thirteenth)
- Who was the first black to be pictured on a postage stamp? (Booker T. Washington)
- Who was the first black millionaire? (Madame C. J. Walker)
- To what state were the first slaves brought? (Virginia)
- What school did Booker T. Washington establish? (Tuskegee Institute)
- For what is Jane Matilda Bolin famous? (first black female judge)
- What black man was the first to die at the Boston Massacre? (Crispus Attucks)
- For what is Iman famous? (fashion modeling)
- What black won the Nobel Peace Prize in 1964? (Martin Luther King)
- In what city did Elizabeth Eckford attempt to integrate an all-white high school? (Little Rock, Arkansas)

◆ Who was the first black to win a Nobel Peace Prize? (Ralphe Bunche)

◆ Who escaped from slavery and made nineteen return trips to the South to liberate slaves? (Harriet Tubman)

◆ In what city did Jesse Owens win four gold Olympic medals? (Berlin)

◆ Who led a bloody slave revolt in Virginia in 1831? (Nat Turner)

◆ What was Harriet Tubman's code name? (Moses)

◆ Whose fashion label was "Williwear"? (designer Willi Smith)

◆ Who spearheaded the "Back to Africa" movement? (Marcus Garvey)

◆ To what group was Edith Sampson the first black delegate from the United States? (United Nations)

◆ What famous regiment did Robert Gould Shaw command during the Civil War? (the only black regiment)

◆ In what field was Maggie Lena Walker a first? (female bank president)

◆ In what Southern city did black students stage sit-ins at a Woolworth's lunch counter? (Greensboro, NC)

◆ In what career was Bessie Coleman first? (female pilot)

◆ From what university did a group of famous World War II airmen come? (Tuskegee)

◆ What crime did journalist Ida B. Wells-Barnett fight? (lynching)

Music

◆ What is the title of the song that begins, "Lift every voice and sing"? (Negro National Anthem)

◆ Which film honored Scott Joplin's contribution to music? (*The Sting)*

◆ What singer dubbed her voice onto recordings made by her father? (Natalie Cole)

◆ What dance did Chubby Checker popularize? (the Twist)

◆ Who is called the "Queen of Soul"? (Aretha Franklin)

◆ What is Steveland Morris's stage name? (Stevie Wonder)

◆ Who was the first black star of the Metropolitan Opera? (Marian Anderson)

◆ What prominent organization humiliated Marian Anderson? (Daughters of the American Revolution)

◆ What prominent D.A.R. member resigned because of the humiliation of Marian Anderson? (Eleanor Roosevelt)

◆ Who tap danced with Mikhail Baryshnikov in the film *White Nights?* (Gregory Hines)

◆ Who is best known for scat? (Ella Fitzgerald)

◆ Who shocked filmgoers by holding hands with Shirley Temple while tap-dancing? (Bill "Bojangles" Robinson)

◆ What expatriate American dancer served with the French Resistance? (Josephine Baker)

◆ Who paid tribute to Duke Ellington with the song "Sir Duke"? (Stevie Wonder)

◆ What group sang "Soldier Boy" and "Mama Said" among fifteen top singles? (the Shirelles)

◆ What singer married Elvis Presley's only child? (Michael Jackson)
◆ Who sang "His Eye Is on the Sparrow" in a stage version of Carson McCullers's play *Member of the Wedding?* (Pearl Bailey)
◆ What instrument did Wynton Marsalis play? (trumpet)
◆ What female vocalist led the Supremes? (Diana Ross)
◆ Who pioneered bebop? (Charlie Parker)

Literature

◆ Who wrote *To Be Young, Gifted, and Black?* (Lorraine Hansberry)
◆ What work depicts the maternal side of Alex Haley's genealogy? *(Queen)*
◆ Who was the first black to receive a Pulitzer Prize? (Gwendolyn Brooks)
◆ For what book did Toni Morrison win a Pulitzer Prize? *(Beloved)*
◆ What novel won Ralph Ellison a National Book Award in 1952? *(Invisible Man)*
◆ What play did Zora Neale Hurston write with Langston Hughes? *(Mule Bone)*
◆ What play title is taken from Langston Hughes's "A Dream Deferred"? *(A Raisin in the Sun)*
◆ What playwright produced *A Hero Ain't Nothin' But a Sandwich?* (Alice Childress)
◆ Who was "the Brown Bomber" mentioned in *I Know Why the Caged Bird Sings?* (Joe Louis)
◆ What black Georgia state legislator is also a poet? (Julian Bond)
◆ What black writer shocked readers by publishing a novel about (female circumcision? (Alice Walker)
◆ What literary movement started in Harlem in the 1930s? (Harlem Renaissance)
◆ Where is Ann Petry's book *Tituba* set? (Salem, Massachusetts)
◆ What writer described himself as the "manchild in the promised land"? (Claude Brown)
◆ What neglected writer did novelist Alice Walker teach Americans to appreciate? (Zora Neale Hurston)
◆ What American novelist and author of *The Fire Next Time* felt more at home in Paris? (James Baldwin)
◆ What poet did President Bill Clinton invite to recite at his first inaugural? (Maya Angelou)
◆ For what art are Paul Keens-Douglas, Mary Carter Smith, Jackie Torrance, and Doug and Frankie Quimby best known? (storytelling)

Television and Movies

◆ Who portrayed Gale Sayers in *Brian's Song?* (Billy Dee Williams)
◆ What black singer starred in *Stormy Weather* and *Cabin in the Sky?* (Lena Horne)
◆ Who portrayed Mother Younger in the film *A Raisin in the Sun?* (Ruby Dee)
◆ What actor was the first black All-American football player? (Paul Robeson)

◆ What football star played a role in the film *The Dirty Dozen?* (Jim Brown)

◆ What black journalist stars on "60 Minutes"? (Ed Bradley)

◆ Who was the first black woman to win an Oscar? (Hattie McDaniel)

◆ For what film did she win the award? *(Gone with the Wind)*

◆ In what film did Sammy Davis, Jr., play Sportin' Life? *(Porgy and Bess)*

◆ Who starred as Idella in *Driving Miss Daisy?* (Esther Rolle)

◆ What black actor starred in *The Defiant Ones, To Sir with Love, Guess Who's Coming to Dinner,* and *In the Heat of the Night?* (Sidney Poitier)

◆ To what actor is singer Pauletta Pearson married? (Denzel Washington)

◆ Who won an Oscar for his supporting role in *An Officer and a Gentleman?* (Lou Gossett, Jr.)

◆ Who played the mother in *Sounder* and the centenarian protagonist of *The Autobiography of Miss Jane Pittman?* (Cicely Tyson)

◆ What black television star appeared on a televised special about AIDS and revealed the death of his son from the disease? (Robert Guillaume)

◆ What award-winning role did Maya Angelou play in *Roots?* (Kunta Kinte's grandmother)

◆ Who played the train conductor in *Silver Streak?* (Scatman Carruthers)

◆ What comedian created a character called Geraldine? (Flip Wilson)

◆ Who was the first black female to have her own TV show? (Diahann Carroll)

◆ Who were the first black male and female television talk show hosts? (Arsenio Hall and Oprah Winfrey)

◆ What black actor received starring roles in *Glory, Much Ado About Nothing,* and *Malcolm X?* (Denzel Washington)

◆ What black star played the Broadway stage role of Dolly Levi? (Pearl Bailey)

Sports

◆ In what sport was Cheryl White the first black female participant? (horse racing)

◆ What black comedian started out as a track star? (Dick Gregory)

◆ What female track star competed in the Olympics simultaneously with her brother? (Carol Lewis)

◆ Who was the first black coach of a major league team? (Bill Russell)

◆ Who was the first black tennis player to compete at Wimbledon? (Althea Gibson)

◆ Who broke Babe Ruth's batting record? (Hank Aaron)

◆ In what sport was Victoria Young Smith the first woman to hold a black belt? (judo)

◆ What black male tennis star was the first to win at Wimbledon? (Arthur Ashe)

◆ What Olympic star won a gold medal in the 1992 heptathlon? (Jackie Joyner-Kersee)

◆ Which major league baseball team was the first to hire a black athlete? (Brooklyn Dodgers)

◆ For what sport did Sheila Bonilla win a 1994 Most Valuable Player? (baseball)

◆ Who was the first black major league baseball player? (Jackie Robinson)

◆ In what sport does Dominque Dawes compete? (gymnastics)

◆ Who was the first black golfer admitted to the PGA? (Charlie Sifford)

◆ What disease did runner Wilma Rudolph overcome? (polio)

◆ What NBA star is nicknamed "Air"? (Michael Jordan)

◆ Who was the first black woman to earn an Olympic medal? (Audrey Patterson)

◆ What NFL star is nicknamed "Sweetness?" (Walter Payton)

◆ In what event did Alice Coachman win an Olympic medal? (high jump)

◆ What athlete was nicknamed "The World's Fastest Human?" (Bob Hayes)

◆ What black coach wrote *Track and Field for Girls and Women?* (Nell Jackson)

◆ What athlete was originally named Cassius Clay? (Muhammad Ali)

◆ What black tennis star announced that he contracted AIDS from a blood transfusion? (Arthur Ashe)

◆ Who was the first black heavyweight champion? (Jack Johnson)

◆ What black athlete did Adolf Hitler snub? (Jesse Owens)

◆ What black athlete is nicknamed "Mr. October?" (Reggie Jackson)

◆ What team did Magic Johnson twice retire from? (Lakers)

Politics and National Events

◆ What disease did the U.S. government study through injections to black human guinea pigs? (syphilis)

◆ Who was the first black U.S. senator? (Hiram Revels of Mississippi)

◆ Who was the first black woman elected to Congress? (Shirley Chisholm)

◆ In what year did black voters first cast their ballots in a presidential election? (1868)

◆ Who was the first black cabinet member? (Dr. Robert C. Weaver, HUD, under Franklin Roosevelt in 1941)

◆ What Texas legislator is best known for the speech "Who Then Will Speak for the Common Good?" (Barbara Jordan)

◆ Who was the first black justice of the Supreme Court? (Thurgood Marshall)

◆ What suffragist demanded "Ain't I a Woman?" (Sojourner Truth)

◆ What state did Senator Edward Brooke represent? (Massachusetts)

◆ What cabinet member shocked Americans by opinions on masturbation? (Dr. Joycelyn Elders)

◆ What U.S. President retired to build low-interest houses for poor blacks? (Jimmy Carter)

◆ Who was the first black female to serve as Secretary of Energy? (Hazel R. O'Leary)

◆ What controversial New York congressman published the *People's Voice?* (Adam Clayton Powell)

◆ What controversial group did NAACP leader Daisy Bates advise? (Little Rock Nine)

◆ What was the name of the black regiment formed to fight Indians? (Buffalo Soldiers)

◆ Who first invited the National Council for Negro Women to the White House? (Eleanor Roosevelt)

◆ What does the acronym PUSH stand for? (People United to Save Humanity)

◆ Who organized PUSH? (Jesse Jackson)

◆ What black woman advised President Franklin D. Roosevelt? (Mary McLeod Bethune)

◆ What do the letters NAACP stand for? (National Association for the Advancement of Colored People)

◆ What state did Congresswoman Barbara Jordan represent? (Texas)

◆ What do the letters SNCC stand for? (Student Nonviolent Coordinating Committee)

◆ Who founded SNCC? (Andrew Young)

◆ What United Nations post did Andrew Young hold? (United States Ambassador to the United Nations)

◆ What black activist described the Greensboro, North Carolina, student sit-ins in *Coming of Age in Mississippi?* (Anne Moody)

◆ What black Atlanta mayor has served two terms? (Maynard Jackson)

◆ In what state did black militants protest the jailing of the Wilmington Nine? (North Carolina)

Budget: $25-$50

Sources:

"African American History," http//www.msstate.edu/Archives/History/USA/Afro-Amer/afro.html.

African American History in the Press, 1851-1899, Gale, 1996.

American Eras, Gale, 1997.

"Black History," http//www.slip.net/~rigged/history.html.

"Black History Month: Let's Get Started," http//www.netnoir.com/spotlight/bhm/jbhm. html.

"Black Women Firsts," *Ebony,* April 1997, 78.

Bunzel, J. H., and A. S. Grossman, "Black Studies Revisited," *The Public Interest,* Spring 1997, 71-80.

Chappell, K., "How Black Inventors Changed America," *Ebony,* February 1997, 40.

Corbin, Raymond M., *1,999 Facts about Blacks: A Sourcebook of African-American Achievement,* 2nd edition, Madison Books, 1997.

Dean, Robbie, *The African American/Black Diaspora Word Search Puzzlebook,* Robbie Dean Press, 1997.

"The Faces of Science: African Americans in the Sciences," http//www. lib.lsu.edu/lib/chem/display/faces.html.

Fowler, Arlen L., *The Black Infantry in the West, 1869-1891*, University of Oklahoma Press, 1997.

Hine, Darlene Clark, Elsa Barkley Brown, and Rosalyn Terborg-Penn, *Black Women in America: An Historical Encyclopedia,* Carlson Publishing, 1993.

Leckie, William H., *The Buffalo Soldiers*, University of Oklahoma Press, 1997.

Nelson, Rebecca, and Marie J. MacNee, eds., *The Olympic Factbook: A Spectator's Guide to the Summer Games*, Visible Ink Press, 1996.

Saari, Peggy, and Daniel B. Baker, *Explorers and Discoverers: From Alexander the Great to Sally Ride*, U•X•L/Gale, 1995.

"This Person in Black History: Thurgood Marshall," http//www.ai.mit.edu/~isbell/ Hfh/black/events_and_people/001.thurgood_marshall.

Trager, James, *The People's Chronology*, revised edition, Henry Holt & Co., 1996.

"What Is Your Black History IQ?," *Ebony*, February 1997, 86-88.

Alternative Applications: As an exercise in the use of reference sources, provide students a variety of resource materials about black history, such as *Infotrac, Newsbank, Africa Watch, Ebony, Jet, Emerge, Black Business, Africa Online, Current Biography, Bartlett's Familiar Quotations, Statistical Abstract of the 1990 Census, Reader's Guide to Periodical Literature, Who's Who Among African Americans,* and *The Times Atlas*. Have groups create their own sets of trivia questions under these subject headings:

- ◆ activism and women's rights
- ◆ astronomy, medicine, inventions
- ◆ entertainment and sports
- ◆ international news and events
- ◆ politics, law, and government
- ◆ space exploration
- ◆ art, dance, architecture, sculpture
- ◆ education and the family
- ◆ geography, natural phenomena
- ◆ literature and journalism
- ◆ religion, ethics, and philosophy
- ◆ United States-African relations

Black History Bingo

Originator: Michele Spence, teacher, editor, and writer, Lincoln, Nebraska.

Age/Grade Level or Audience: Teenagers and Adults.

Description: Organize a game of bingo to determine how well students understand a study of black history.

Procedure: Have students prepare a blank gameboard similar to a bingo card containing a central free space and marked with a random arrangement of any twenty-four numbers from one to seventy-five in the remaining blanks. For example:

7	25	68	11	9
42	10	36	59	23
21	51	FREE	74	67
32	5	59	70	45
19	39	22	53	67

Prepare seventy-five questions, each on a separate slip of paper, then draw a slip and read aloud the number and question. Players locate the number on their cards and write the answer in the space. The first person to get a straight line of correct answers, either across, down, or diagonally, wins the game.

Budget: Under $25

Sources:

African American History in the Press, 1851-1899, Gale, 1996.

Asante, Molefi K., *Historical and Cultural Atlas of African Americans*, Macmillan, 1991.

Bennett, Lerone, Jr., *Before the Mayflower: A History of Black America*, 6th edition, Penguin Books, 1993.

"Black History," http//www.slip.net/~rigged/history.html.

"Black History Month Let's Get Started," http//www.netnoir.com/spotlight/bhm/jbhm.html.

"Black Women Firsts," *Ebony,* April 1997, 78.

Bunzel, J. H., and A. S. Grossman, "Black Studies Revisited," *The Public Interest,* Spring 1997, 71-80.

Corbin, Raymond M., *1,999 Facts about Blacks: A Sourcebook of African american Achievement,* 2nd edition, Madison Books, 1997.

Dean, Robbie, *Black Children's Parents Imparting Discipline/Heritage,* Robbie Dean Press, 1997.

Gates, Henry Louis, ed., *Chronology of African-American History from 1445-1980,* Amistad Press, 1993.

Hine, Darlene Clark, Elsa Barkley Brown, and Rosalyn Terborg-Penn, *Black Women in America An Historical Encyclopedia,* Carlson Publishing, 1993.

Jackson, John G., *Introduction to African Civilizations*, Citadel Press, 1994.

Nelson, Rebecca, and Marie J. MacNee, eds., *The Olympic Factbook: A Spectator's Guide to the Summer Games*, Visible Ink Press, 1996.

Steedman, Scott, *Pockets: Ancient Egypt*, Dorling Kindersley, 1995.

Saari, Peggy, and Daniel B. Baker, *Explorers and Discoverers: From Alexander the Great to Sally Ride*, U•X•L/Gale, 1995.

"This Person in Black History: Thurgood Marshall," http//www.ai.mit.edu/~isbell/ Hfh/black/events_and_people/001.thurgood_marshall.

Trager, James, *The People's Chronology*, revised edition, Henry Holt, 1996.

"What Is Your Black History IQ?," *Ebony*, February 1997, 86-88.

Alternative Applications: Make this game more interesting by playing T, I, L, U, X, cross, postage stamp, picture frame, ring of eight, and cover the card.

- ♦ T credits only the answers that fill the top horizontal row and the center vertical row.
- ♦ I requires that the top and bottom horizontal rows and the center vertical row be filled.
- ♦ L credits answers down the left vertical row and across the bottom.
- ♦ U is the same as L plus the right vertical row.
- ♦ X, a variation of T, requires players to complete the diagonal rows that pass through the free space.
- ♦ Cross recognizes the filling of horizontal and vertical rows that pass through the free space.
- ♦ Postage stamp requires winners to fill any block of four.
- ♦ Picture frame requires the player to fill the outer rim.
- ♦ Ring of eight recognizes answers on the inner square of eight blocks surrounding the free square.
- ♦ Covering the card requires that the player fill the board with correct answers.

 Black History Calendar

Age/Grade Level or Audience: Middle school class; 4-H or scout groups; or youth clubs.

Description: Have participants create a wall mural featuring an oversized calendar.

Procedure: Assign a specific area to research, such as politics, government, world events, awards, sports, entertainment, science and technology, medicine, religion, dance, or architecture. Using biographical dictionaries, clipping files, biographies, or other source material, have participants contribute significant entries to the calendar and fill blocks with important dates from black history, such as these:

♦ the Emancipation Proclamation
♦ Frederick Douglass's first abolitionist speech
♦ the first Million Woman March
♦ Jackie Robinson's entrance into major league baseball
♦ Greensboro, N.C., lunch counter sit-ins
♦ Thurgood Marshall's nomination to the U.S. Supreme Court
♦ the first patent obtained by a black inventor
♦ the first African American to run for United States President
♦ the first African American to earn an Academy Award
♦ the first African American to serve as an astronaut

Follow this model:

JANUARY

1 1862 Emancipation Proclamation	2	3	4 1965 Great Society Announced	5	6	7
8	9	10	11	12	13	14
15 1986 Martin Luther King holiday established	16	17 1917 United States purchases Virgin Islands	18	19	20	21
22	23 1981 Samuel Pierce becomes Sec. of HUD	24	25 1966 Constance B. Motley named federal judge	26	27	28
29	30	31				

Budget: $25-$50

Sources:

Students may refer to February issues of school and library journals, particularly *Instructor* and *Learning*, as well as *Jet*, *Emerge*, *Essence*, *Biography*, *Life*, *Smithsonian*, and *Ebony*.

African American History in the Press, 1851-1899, Gale, 1996.

"Black Women Firsts," *Ebony*, April 1997, 78.

Bunzel, J. H., and A. S. Grossman, "Black Studies Revisited," *The Public Interest*, Spring 1997, 71-80.

Corbin, Raymond M., *1,999 Facts about Blacks: A Sourcebook of African-American Achievement*, 2nd edition, Madison Books, 1997.

Deburg, William L, *Black Camelot: African American Culture Heroes in Their Times, 1960-1980*, University of Chicago Press, 1997.

Dean, Robbie, *Black Children's Parents Imparting Discipline/Heritage*, Robbie Dean Press, 1997.

Forge, Alice, and Karen E. Quinones Miller, "The Philadelphia Story," *People*, November 10, 1997, 123-124.

Hine, Darlene Clark, Elsa Barkley Brown, and Rosalyn Terborg-Penn, *Black Women in America: An Historical Encyclopedia*, Carlson Publishing, 1993.

Nelson, Rebecca, and Marie J. MacNee, eds., *The Olympic Factbook: A Spectator's Guide to the Summer Games*, Visible Ink Press, 1996.

Hornsby, Alton, *Chronology of African-American History*, 2nd edition Gale, 1997.

Terry, Ted, *American Black History: Reference Manual*, Myles Publishing, 1991.

Alternative Applications: Begin this project for Black History Month, then continue it as an ongoing compendium of facts. Illustrate with original drawings, political cartoons, and maps. Extend the effectiveness of the exercise with these activities:

- ◆ Carry over the group's work to the next February so that a subsequent celebration of Black History Month adds details to the original calendar.
- ◆ Place months on individual oversized sheets and bind into resource big books or preserve on a database.
- ◆ Place copies in libraries, churches, display cases, public meetings halls, museums, malls, and civic centers.

Black History in Miniature

Originators: Lela Coley and Gail Freeman, middle school teachers, Deerfield Beach, Florida

Age/Grade Level or Audience: All ages.

Description: Create a miniature black history museum.

Procedure: Organize volunteers to collect and display crafts and objects related to black history. Consider these items:

- ◆ jointed dolls, tops, marbles, hoops, puzzles, limberjacks, kites, jack rocks

- ◆ tobacco can, corncob pipe, drawstring bag of loose tobacco, rolling papers
- ◆ washboard and tub, bluing, cast-iron washpot, and bars of lye soap
- ◆ quilts, quilting frame, cotton batting, colored twill thread, needles and bodkins, and quilt rack
- ◆ curling irons and straightening combs
- ◆ kerosene lamp, wicks, coal oil can, lighter sticks
- ◆ bonnets, high-button shoes, gaiters, spats, suspenders, bowler hats
- ◆ military uniforms, patches, medals, parachutes, rifles
- ◆ spider, churn, coffee mill, grater, colander, potato masher, eggbeater, waffle iron, and other kitchen utensils
- ◆ early crystal set or radio
- ◆ Victrola and cylinders, jukebox, or 78 recordings of black artists
- ◆ lace tablecloths and napkins
- ◆ old baby bottles
- ◆ paper fans with Bible pictures and inscriptions

Provide posters or audiotaped guides to explain how each display relates to black history.

Budget: $50-$75

Sources:

Encourage participants to check attics, used clothing stores, yard sales, and Salvation Army and Goodwill stores. For missing items, substitute drawings, clay models, murals, or posters.

American Eras, Gale, 1997.

Cantor, George, *Historic Landmarks of Black America*, Gale, 1991.

Corbin, Raymond M., *1,999 Facts About Blacks*, Madison Books, 1997.

Myers, Walter Dean, *One More River to Cross: An African American Photograph Album*, Harcourt Brace, 1995.

Parks, Gordon, *Half Past Autumn: A Retrospective*, Bulfinch Press, 1997.

Alternative Applications: For a mini-museum in a hurry, have students create cardboard or clay copies of items or draw three-dimensional settings of kitchens, porches, sitting rooms, classrooms, church choir lofts, factories, sawmills, blacksmith forges, tanneries, woodworking shops, sugar mills, barns, granaries, military camps, bowing rings, baseball diamonds, playgrounds, and other locations connected with black history.

Black History Time Capsule

Age/Grade Level or Audience: All ages.

Description: Create a display of items to enter a black history time capsule.

Procedure: Collect items which epitomize the emancipation of the black race. Include the items:

- ◆ a chain and drawing of a slave ship
- ◆ early Mennonite and Quaker documents demanding abolition of slavery
- ◆ words and music to Negro spirituals
- ◆ newspaper editorials and speeches by Sojourner Truth, Frederick Douglass, Sarah Grimké, Angelina Grimké, and Elihu Embree
- ◆ Abraham Lincoln's Emancipation Proclamation
- ◆ amendments to the Constitution giving black citizens the right to vote
- ◆ James Weldon Johnson and Rosemond Johnson's "Negro National Anthem,"
- ◆ Alex Haley's *Roots* or *Queen*
- ◆ Margaret Walker's *Jubilee*
- ◆ covers of popular magazines featuring entertainers such as Cicely Tyson, Lou Gossett, Sammy Davis, Jr., Natalie Cole, Morgan Freeman, and Bill Cosby
- ◆ judgements and aphorisms of Thurgood Marshall
- ◆ CDs of Scott Joplin's music
- ◆ photos of Mae Jamison's space flight

Budget: $50-$75

Sources:

Drawings, political cartoons, photos, and clippings from the popular press; museum brochures.

American Eras, Gale, 1997.

Channing, William Ellery, *The Abolitionist*, reprint of 1836 edition, Reprint Service 1990.

Discovering Multicultural America (database), Gale Research, 1997.

Haley, Alex, *Roots: The Saga of an American Family*, Doubleday, 1976.

———, *Alex Haley's Queen*, Avon, 1994.

Ravitch, Diane, *The American Reader: Words That Moved a Nation*, HarperCollins, 1990.

Silverman, Jerry, *Songs of Protest and Civil Rights*, Chelsea House, 1992.

Alternative Applications: Hold an assembly in which you explain why each item to be placed in the time capsule deserves recognition by future generations. Open the last portion of the meeting for suggestions from the audience.

 | **A Black History Timeline** |

Age/Grade Level or Audience: High school social studies class.

Description: Have students prepare an exhaustive timeline of African American history.

Procedure: Organize students into groups to cover African American history from the beginning of European colonization of the United States until current times. Present findings through mixed media, including handmade filmstrips, transparencies, database, frieze or scroll, photographs, drawings, interviews, and taped speeches and songs. Begin with the following framework and enhance it with vivid details, such as locations, cause and effect, and interesting circumstances:

Thirteenth Century

◆ Skeletal evidence from a cemetery in the Virgin Islands suggests that Africans were present in the New World by 1250.

Fourteenth Century

◆ A Malinese oral history describes the Atlantic voyage of a Mandingo king in 1312.

Fifteenth Century

◆ In 1492, a black Spaniard, Pedro Alonzo Niño, accompanied Columbus on his voyage to the New World
◆ Columbus's son Ferdinand reported seeing blacks in Honduras.

Sixteenth Century

◆ In 1501, black explorers and seamen arrived in the New World.
◆ In 1502, Portugal transported black slaves to the New World.
◆ On September 25, 1513, a black, Nufo de Olano, accompanied Balboa's expedition to the Pacific Ocean.
◆ In 1526, black slaves fled a South Carolina settlement and took up residence with Indians.
◆ In 1538, Estevanico, a black explorer, entered Arizona and New Mexico.
◆ In 1562, British slaver John Hawkins sold blacks to Spanish planters.

Seventeenth Century

◆ In 1619, the first slaves—Antony, Pedro, and Isabella—were brought to Jamestown, Virginia, aboard a Dutch vessel.
◆ In 1624, William Tucker was the first black child born in the American colonies.
◆ In 1630, Massachusetts enacted laws to protect slaves from cruel masters.
◆ In 1639, slaver William Pierce exchanged Indian slaves for African in the West Indies.
◆ By 1640, the slave population of Barbados reached 6,000.
◆ In 1651, black planter Anthony Johnson attempted to establish a black village in North Hampton, Virginia.
◆ In 1672, a bounty was set on maroons, fugitive slaves.

♦ On February 18, 1688, Mennonite Quakers led the first abolitionist protest.

♦ In 1693, Quaker George Keith published the first abolitionist pamphlet.

Eighteenth Century

♦ By 1700, the colonial slave population was 5,000 in New England and 23,000 in the southern colonies.

♦ In 1712, a slave rebellion in New York City resulted in public execution of blacks by hanging or burning alive.

♦ In 1763, Gershom Prince and other blacks defended colonists during the French and Indian War.

♦ In 1770, Philadelphia Quakers opened a school for blacks.

♦ On March 5, 1770, Crispus Attucks was killed in the Boston Massacre.

♦ In 1774, Lemuel Haynes served with minutemen at the Battle of Lexington.

♦ In 1775, Peter Salem and Salem Poor fought with a company of black soldiers at the Battle of Bunker Hill.

♦ On February 2, 1776, George Washington answered a letter from black poet Phillis Wheatley.

♦ In 1777, Prince Hall petitioned the Massachusetts legislature to end slavery.

♦ In 1779, Pompey Lamb served the army as a spy.

♦ In 1780, Torrington, Connecticut, Rev. Lemuel Haynes became the first black minister of a white congregation.

♦ In 1791, Benjamin Banneker published an almanac.

♦ In 1793, Eli Whitney made slavery more profitable by inventing the cotton gin. Also, Bishop Richard Allen established the Mother Bethel African Methodist Episcopal Church in Philadelphia and Canada passed an anti-slavery law.

♦ In 1794, Andrew Bryan built the first black Baptist church.

♦ In 1796, Toussaint L'Ouverture commanded the French at Santo Domingo.

♦ In 1797, a slave named Doctor practiced medicine in Charleston, South Carolina.

Nineteenth Century

♦ In 1800, Philadelphia's free blacks influenced Congress to end slavery.

♦ On August 30, 1800, Gabriel Prosser led an assault on the arsenal in Richmond, Virginia.

♦ In 1803, American colonies doubled in size after the Louisiana Purchase.

♦ In 1807, laws ended the slave trade in the U.S. and Great Britain.

♦ In 1811, Paul Cuffe and his thirty-eight black passengers sailed the *Traveller* from Massachusetts to Sierra Leone.

♦ In 1815, Napoleon banned the slave trade in France and French possessions.

♦ In 1819, the slave trade thrived through an underground market system.

♦ By 1820, Congress enacted the Missouri Comprise to balance free and slave states.

♦ By 1820, abolitionists aired their protests in letters, speeches, and pamphlets.

♦ In 1821, the African Methodist Episcopal Zion Church was established.

♦ In July 1822, Denmark Vesey, a free black carpenter, was executed for launching a slave revolt in Charleston, South Carolina.

♦ In 1826 Edward Jones and John Russwurm became the first black college graduates.

♦ In 1827, the first black newspaper, *Freedom's Journal*, went to press.

♦ In 1831, New Englanders formed the Anti-Slavery Society and William Lloyd Garrison founded *The Liberator*, an abolitionist newspaper, in Boston.

♦ On August 21, 1831, Nat Turner led a slave revolt which terrorized Virginia.

♦ By 1840, thousands of slaves had escaped servitude and fled to Canada.

♦ In 1841, slaves who were forced aboard the *Amistad* gained their freedom by U.S. Supreme Court decree.

♦ In 1843, Henry Highland Garnett led a slave revolt.

♦ In 1844, the Dominican Republic was established.

♦ In 1847, Frederick Douglass launched the *North Star*, an abolitionist newspaper. Also, Green Flake, a black pioneer, was one of the first Mormons to settle Salt Lake City

♦ In 1850, pressure from the Fugitive Slave Act led William Still to organize the Underground Railroad.

♦ In 1851, delegates of the Women's Rights Convention welcomed Sojourner Truth as guest speaker.

♦ In 1852, Harriet Beecher Stowe's *Uncle Tom's Cabin* promoted anti-slavery sentiments.

♦ In 1854, Lincoln University, the first black college, opened its doors to students in Chester County, Pennsylvania.

♦ In 1857, the U.S. Supreme Court declared Dred Scott the property of his owner.

♦ On December 2, 1859, John Brown, a white abolitionist, was martyred after leading an abortive slave revolt at Harper's Ferry, Virginia.

♦ In 1861, Mary Peake began teaching former slaves under Emancipation Oak in Hampton, Virginia

♦ On April 12, 1861, civil war broke out at Fort Sumter, South Carolina.

♦ On January 1, 1863, Lincoln ended slavery by issuing the Emancipation Proclamation.

♦ On February 1, 1865, Dr. John S. Rock, a Massachusetts lawyer and physician, became the first black to plead a case before the U.S. Supreme Court.

♦ In 1870, the Fifteenth Amendment to the U.S. Constitution guaranteed the right to vote to males of all races.

♦ On February 25, 1870, Hiram Revels became the first black elected to the U.S. Senate.

♦ In 1873, Henry O. Flipper became the first black to graduate from West Point.

♦ On March 23, 1873, slavery was abolished in Puerto Rico.

♦ In 1878, Dr. Caroline Virginia Anderson became the first black woman to achieve a medical degree.

♦ In 1879, Dr. Mary Eliza Mahoney became the first black graduate nurse in the United States.

♦ In 1881, Booker T. Washington founded Tuskegee Institute.

♦ In 1883, Frederick Douglass made heavy demands on white society in a speech delivered in Washington, D.C.

♦ In 1886, Lucy Craft Laney opened Haines Normal Institute in Macon, Georgia.

♦ In 1888, the Capitol Savings Bank, the first U.S. bank operated by blacks, opened in Washington, D.C.

♦ In 1893, Dr. Daniel Hale Williams performed the first open heart surgery.

♦ In 1896, the National Association of Colored Women was founded.

♦ In 1898, North Carolina Mutual Life, the first black insurance company, opened.

Twentieth Century

♦ In 1903, Maggie Lena Walker became the first woman to establish a financial institution, the Saint Luke Penny Savings Bank.

♦ On April 6, 1909, Matthew Henson reached the North Pole.

♦ In 1910, the National Association for the Advancement of Colored People was begun to organize black political efforts.

♦ In 1917, the first black officers training camp was established at Fort Des Moines.

♦ On January 17, 1917, the United States purchased the Virgin Islands.

♦ The Harlem Renaissance reached its height from 1922 to 1929.

♦ In 1926, Dr. Carter G. Woodson inaugurated Negro History Week.

♦ In 1938, Pennsylvania's Crystal Bird Fauset was the first black woman elected to a U.S. state legislature.

♦ In 1939, Eleanor Roosevelt withdrew from the Daughters of the American Revolution because it refused Marian Anderson's bid to sing in Washington, D.C.

♦ In 1940, Booker T. Washington became the first black person pictured on a U.S. postage stamp, and Hattie McDaniel became the first black person to win an Academy Award.

♦ On December 7, 1941, in Pearl Harbor, Hawaii, messman Dorie Miller took over an anti-aircraft gun to ward off strikes on the *Arizona* by Japanese planes.

♦ In 1942, three black regiments helped construct the 1,400-mile Alcan Highway to protect Alaska from Japanese attack.

♦ In 1943, the first platoon of black paratroopers formed at Fort Benning, Georgia.

♦ In 1944, the United Negro College Fund was established.

♦ In 1948, Harry Truman ended segregation in the armed services.

◆ In 1950, poet Gwendolyn Brooks won a Pulitzer Prize.

◆ In 1950, Dr. Ralph Bunche, U.N. peacekeeper and mediator, won a Nobel Peace Prize.

◆ On May 17, 1954, segregated schools were outlawed.

◆ On December 2, 1955, Rosa Parks refused to give up her seat on a bus in Montgomery, Alabama, and Dr. Martin Luther King, Jr., an Atlanta minister, organized the Montgomery Bus Boycott.

◆ In 1957, Congress passed the Civil Rights Act.

◆ On February 15, 1957, the Southern Christian Leadership Conference was organized.

◆ In 1959, Lorraine Hansberry's *A Raisin in the Sun* opened on Broadway.

◆ On February 2, 1960, students from North Carolina A & T led sit-ins at a Woolworth's lunch counter in Greensboro, NC, to draw attention to segregation of public facilities.

◆ On August 28, 1963, Dr. Martin Luther King, Jr., led a march on Washington, D.C., and delivered his "I Have a Dream" speech.

◆ In 1964, the Nobel committee conferred its peace prize on Dr. Martin Luther King. Also, Bill Cosby became the first black actor to star in a dramatic series, "I Spy."

◆ In 1965, Elizabeth Duncan Koontz became the first black to head the National Education Association.

◆ On February 21, 1965, Muslim leader Malcolm X was assassinated.

◆ In 1967, Thurgood Marshall became the first black Supreme Court justice, and Robert Lawrence, the first black astronaut, was killed in a training exercise.

◆ On April 4, 1968, Dr. Martin Luther King, Jr., was assassinated.

◆ On October 18, 1968, Olympic track stars John Carlos and Tommy Smith were suspended for giving the black power salute at an awards ceremony in Mexico City.

◆ In 1972, Barbara Jordan of Texas became the first black woman to preside over a state legislature.

◆ On April 11, 1974, Jackie Robinson became the first black professional baseball player.

◆ In 1974, Hank Aaron set a homerun record.

◆ In 1983, Lt. Col. Guion S. Bluford, Jr., became the United States' first black astronaut.

◆ In 1986, January 15 was officially established as a legal holiday honoring Martin Luther King, Jr.

◆ In October 1991, construction workers unearthed an eighteenth-century black burial site in lower Manhattan containing 20,000 skeletons.

◆ In September 1992, astronaut Mae Jemison gave up her Los Angeles medical practice to become the first black woman in space.

◆ In January 1993, poet Maya Angelou delivered an original poem, "On the Pulse of the Morning," at the inauguration ceremony for 42nd President William Jefferson Clinton.

◆ In 1997, Tiger Woods became the first black golf superstar.

Budget: $25-$50

Sources:

African American History in the Press, 1851-1899, Gale, 1996.

American Eras, Gale, 1997.

Beck, Richard, *African-American History,* Royal Fireworks, 1994.

Brailsford, Karen, "Sacred Ground Dry Bones Speak," *Emerge,* October 1992, 73.

Corbin, Raymond M., *1,999 Facts about Blacks: A Sourcebook of African-American Achievement,* 2nd edition, Madison Books, 1997.

Cramer, Clayton E., *Black Demographic Data, 1790-1860 A Sourcebook,* Greenwood Press, 1997.

Dennis, Denise, *Black History for Beginners,* Highsmith, 1992.

Hine, Darlene Clark, Elsa Barkley Brown, and Rosalyn Terborg-Penn, *Black Women in America: An Historical Encyclopedia,* Carlson Publishing, 1993.

Mabunda, L. Mpho, ed., *The African American Almanac,* 7th edition, Gale, 1994.

Myers, Walter Dean, *Now Is Your Time!: The African-American Struggle for Freedom,* Harper Trophy, 1991.

Nelson, Rebecca, and Marie J. MacNee, eds., *The Olympic Factbook: A Spectator's Guide to the Summer Games,* Visible Ink Press, 1996.

Saari, Peggy, and Daniel B. Baker, *Explorers and Discoverers: From Alexander the Great to Sally Ride,* U•X•L/Gale, 1995.

Savage, Beth, et al., eds., *African-American Historic Places,* Wiley, 1994.

Thomas, Velma Maia, *Lest We Forget: The Passage from Africa to Slavery and Emancipation,* Crown, 1997.

Alternative Applications: Divide students into small groups to complete a similar time line of African or Caribbean history. Record information on a database. Throughout the school year, add data and retrieve information as students have need for it.

Black Holidays

Age/Grade Level or Audience: Middle school and high school history classes.

Description: Present an overview of major black holidays.

Procedure: Make a bulletin board, brochure, database, website, or display of holiday information. Beside each, give the date, purpose, and customs. Include these occasions:

◆ **Martin Luther King's Birthday** (celebrated on the third Monday in January). This holiday honors Nobel Peace Prize winner Martin Luther King, Jr., minister and freedom fighter who organized nonviolent boycotts and marches, the most memorable being the Montgomery Bus Boycott and the Selma Freedom Riders. The occasion is a federal holiday celebrated with speeches, community gatherings, and reflection on the advancement of civil rights.

◆ **Black History Month** (February). This celebration, begun in 1926 by Carter G. Woodson, the father of black history, promotes the Negro's place in history. Observances feature plays, special business and recreational programs, civic assemblies, church meetings, speeches, pageants, parades, and coverage in the media. The month can be divided into segments the first week honoring African heritage; the second week honoring people who died in slavery, lynchings, and riots; the third week honoring distinguished individuals; and the last week commemorating rites of passage as young people pledge to accept cultural, family, and religious values.

◆ **Malcolm X Day** (May 19). Since his assassination on February 21, 1965, Malcolm X has been honored for furthering the Black Muslim movement and for symbolizing hope to the lowest levels of society. Celebrants offer assistance to the homeless, prisoners, the poor, elderly, and unemployed.

◆ **African Liberation Day** (May 25). Selected by the Organization of African Unity in 1963, the day commemorates the liberation of African nations. Festivities feature parades, processions, conferences, and rallies to honor freedom fighters. Symbolized by the red, black, and green flag designed by Marcus Garvey, the holiday supports unity among black people everywhere.

◆ **Juneteenth** (June 19th). African American Emancipation Day, June 19, 1865, brought the message to Texas blacks that slavery had ended as of January 1. The occasion, first celebrated officially in 1972, honors the Thirteenth Amendment to the Constitution and recalls the exuberance of slaves as they danced, sang, and feasted in celebration of their new freedom. Starting with food and storytelling on the evening before, Juneteenth celebrations often feature parades, music, speeches, games, fairs, feasts, exhibits, pageants, and the drinking of strawberry soda, a traditional holiday drink.

◆ **Marcus Garvey's Birthday** (August 17). A reminder to followers of black history of the "Back to Africa" movement. Celebrants issue newsletters and articles about Pan-Africanism, a political, social, and economic movement that unites black people worldwide.

◆ **Umoja Karamu** (fourth Sunday in November). The unity feast, first celebrated in 1971, acknowledges the importance of the black family. Groups gather for feasts of blackeye peas, rice, tomatoes, greens, and sweet potatoes or corn. Decorations emphasize the five food colors black, white, red, green, and yellow. Candles and incense stress a spiritual atmosphere, enhanced by prayer and readings.

◆ **Kwanzaa** (December 26-January 1). Begun by Maulana Karenga in 1966, this harvest celebration reminds black people of their strengths through unity, sharing, responsibility, faith, talents, determination, and generosity.

Budget: $25-$50

Sources:

Chase, H., "Juneteenth in Texas," *American Visions*, June/July 1997, 44-49.

"Juneteenth," http//scuish.scu.edu/SCU/Programs/Diversity/june.html.

Medearis, Angela, *Holidays and Celebrations*, Henry Holt, 1997.

Oni, Sauda, *What Kwanzaa Means to Me*, DARE Books, 1996.

Robartson, Linda, *The Complete Kwanzaa Celebration Book*, Creative Acrylic, 1993.

Ross, Kathy, *Crafts for Kwanzaa*, Millbrook Press, 1994.

St. James, Synthia, *The Gifts of Kwanzaa*, A Whitman, 1994.

Winchester, Faith, *African American Holidays,* Capstone Press, 1996.

Alternative Applications: Insert these holidays into a study of the full spectrum of America's religious, patriotic, and secular festivals, including Easter, Hanukkah, Christmas, Rosh Hashanah, Halloween, Flag Day, Arbor Day, St. Patrick's Day, Yom Kippur, Ramadan, and New Year's Day. Arrange a group of symbols or drawings of celebrations, such as a shamrock, Star of David, pumpkin, menorah, Koran, bells, ram's horn, American flag, Kwanzaa table runner, and map of the world denoting the largest populations of black people.

Black Indians

Originator: Roberta Brown, teacher, Fort Bragg, North Carolina.

Age/Grade Level or Audience: Middle school and high school social studies classes; civic presentations; multicultural festivals.

Description: Make a group presentation concerning runaway slaves and the Indian tribes that gave them a home.

Procedure: Collect data about persons of mixed Native American and African American blood, for instance:

- ◆ rodeo star Bill Pickett, a black Cherokee
- ◆ pioneering black Kiowa Diana Fletcher, and Biddy Johnson Arnold, a black Apache
- ◆ singer Roland Hayes
- ◆ black Sioux Isaiah Dorman, army scout at the Battle of Little Big Horn
- ◆ black Seminole Chief John Horse, who defeated American troops at the Battle of Cheechebee in 1837 and helped negotiate the tribe's removal to Fort Dixon and Fort Duncan

- fifty black Seminole army scouts, including John Ward, Isaac Payne, and Pompey Factor
- Crispus Attucks, a black Natick, who, on March 5, 1770, became the first person to die during the Boston Massacre, a prelude to the American Revolution
- black Chippewa sculptor Edmonia Lewis, who is best known for "Forever Free."

Budget: Under $25

Sources:

"African and Native American Mix," http//www.bioc09.uthscsa.edu/natnet/archive/nl/9510/0370.html.

Banbury, Horace A., "Music Pouring Out of His Body," *Class*, July/August 1992, 59.

Black Cowboys Legends of the West, Chelsea House 1996.

"Black History," http//www.slip.net/~rigged/history.html.

"Black History Month Let's Get Started," http//www.netnoir.com/spotlight/bhm/jbhm.html.

"Black Seminole Indians," http//web.fie.com/~tonya/blkind.htm.

Cunningham, Teresa, and Montez De Carlo, *Black Indians: A Pictorial Essay of a Secret Heritage*, National Experience, 1996.

Fowler, Arlen L., *Black Infantry in the West, 1869-1891*, University of Oklahoma Press, 1996.

Katz, William Loren, *Black Indians*, Simon & Schuster, 1997.

———, *The Black West*, 3rd edition, Open Hand Publishers, 1987.

Knill, Harry, *Black Cowboy*, Bellerophon Books, 1993.

Noah, Belinda, *Black Seminoles: The Little-Known Story of the First Seminoles*, Belinda Noah Products, 1995.

Porter, Kenneth, W., ed., *Black Seminole: History of a freedom-Seeking People*, revised edition, University Press of Florida, 1996.

Preston, D., "Fossils and the Folsom Cowboy," *Natural History*, February 1997, 16-18.

Walton-Raji, Angela, *Black Indian Genealogy Research*, Heritage Books, 1993.

Alternative Applications: Comment on the fate of black Indians after the government forced tribes west to Oklahoma reservations, particularly those who married and bore children of mixed ancestry. Consult the Bureau of Indian Affairs or census figures to learn the size of the mixed African-Native American population.

Black Leaders of America

Age/Grade Level or Audience: Middle school and high school social studies classes; League of Women Voters; civic presentations.

Description: Present small biographies of famous African American politicians, activists, and leaders.

Procedure: Organize a scrapbook or website that pays tribute to black leaders. Include these:

Ralph Abernethy	Maria Baldwin	Mary McLeod Bethune
Julian Bond	Tom Bradley	Ron Brown
Blanche Kelso Bruce	Ralph Bunche	Mary Ann Shadd Cary
Shirley Chisholm	Septima P. Clark	Paul Cuffee
David Dinkins	Joycelyn Elders	Louis Farrakhan
Fannie Lou Hamer	Frances Ellen Harper	Benjamin Hooks
Jesse Jackson	Barbara Jordan	Martin Luther King, Jr.
William Lucy	Anne Moody	Carol Moseley-Braun
Rosa Parks	Adam Clayton Powell	Rupert Richardson
William Monroe Trotter	Fay Wattleton	Ida Wells-Barnett
Roy Wilkins	Andrew Young	Coleman Young

Budget: $25-$50

Sources:

African American History in the Press, 1851-1899, Gale, 1996.

American Eras, Gale, 1997.

"Black History," http//www.slip.net/~rigged/history.html.

"Black History Month Let's Get Started," http//www.netnoir.com/spotlight/bhm/jbhm. html.

Corbin, Raymond M., *1,999 Facts about Blacks: A Sourcebook of African-American Achievement*, 2nd edition, Madison Books, 1997.

Dennis, Denise, *Black History for Beginners*, Highsmith, 1992.

Discovering Multicultural America (database), Gale Research, 1997.

Elliot, Jeffrey M., *Encyclopedia of African-American Politics*, ABC-Clio, 1997.

Hine, Darlene Clark, Elsa Barkley Brown, and Rosalyn Terborg-Penn, *Black Women in America: An Historical Encyclopedia,* Carlson Publishing, 1993.

Mabunda, L. Mpho, ed., *The African American Almanac*, 7th edition, Gale, 1997.

Nelson, Rebecca, and Marie J. MacNee, eds., *The Olympic Factbook: A Spectator's Guide to the Summer Games*, Visible Ink Press, 1996.

Saari, Peggy, and Daniel B. Baker, *Explorers and Discoverers: From Alexander the Great to Sally Ride*, U•X•L/Gale, 1995.

Sarpong-Kumankumah, Jojo, "In Defense of Ethnic Studies," *Essence*, August 1992, 134.

Shapiro, William E., ed., *The Kingfisher Young People's Encyclopedia of the United States.*, Larousse Kingfisher Chambers, 1994.

Straub, Deborah Gillan, ed., *African American Voices*, U•X•L/Gale, 1996.

Taylor, Kimbelry H., *Black Civil Rights Champions*, Oliver Press, 1995.

"This Person in Black History Thurgood Marshall," http//www.ai.mit.edu/~isbell/ Hfh/black/events_and_people/001.thurgood_marshall.

Alternative Applications: Compose a theme contrasting the political difficulties of leaders from different centuries, particularly these:

- ♦ Senator Carole Moseley Braun and Sojourner Truth
- ♦ Frederick Douglass and Ron Brown
- ♦ Barbara Jordan and Ida Wells-Barnett
- ♦ Joycelyn Elders and Booker T. Washington
- ♦ Faye Wattleton and Roy Wilkins
- ♦ Shirley Chisholm and Susan B. Anthony

Black Military Parade

Originators: Leatrice Pearson, teacher, Lenoir, North Carolina; Roberta Brown, teacher, Fort Bragg, North Carolina; R. M. Browning, Jr., U. S. Coast Guard Headquarters; History and Museums Division, U. S. Marine Corps.

Age/Grade Level or Audience: Middle school and high school history classes.

Description: Organize an honor roll of black military leaders.

Procedure: Have students comb sources for names of black military leaders who have distinguished themselves both in peacetime and in war. Post the names on a bulletin board or prepare a scroll of names along with the branch of service each represents. For example:

♦ **Buffalo Soldiers**

Nurse Luticia P. Butler	George W. Williams	Emanuel Stance George Jordan
Thomas Jones	Jones Morgan	Fitz Lee
William Cathy, a woman disguised as a man		

♦ **Cavalry**

Charles Young	Horace Bivens	George Berry
Henry O. Flipper		

♦ **Army**

Colin Powell	Milton L. Olive, III	Nancy Leftenant
Robert Smalls	Michael Howard	Henry Johnson
Needham Roberts	William H. Carney	Harriet M. West
Clinton Greaves	Roscoe Robinson	Charles Rogers

William O. Flipper	Margaret E. Bailey	Louise Martin
Clifford Alexander	John Alexander	Hazel W. Johnson
Benjamin O. Davis, Sr.		

◆ **Air Force**

Otis B. Young	Guion S. Bluford	Daniel James, Jr.
Edward J. Dwight	George S. Robert	Joseph D. Alsberry
Benjamin O. Davis, Jr.		

◆ **Navy**

Samuel L. Gravely	Janie Mines	Wesley Brown
Joachim Pease	Bernard Robinson	Leonard Ray
Harmon Janie Mines	John Lee	Jesse Brown
Gerald Thomas	Brenda Robinson	Hazel P. McCree
John S. Lawson		

◆ **Marines**

John Martin	Frank E. Petersen	John Earl Rudder
Isaac Walker	Alfred Masters	George O. Thompson
Kenneth J. Tibbs	Frederick C. Branch	Herbert L. Brewer
Annie E. Graham	Ann E. Lamb	Gloria Smith
Kenneth H. Berthoud	Agrippa W. Smith	Edgar R. Huff
Rodney M. Davis	Ralph H. Johnson	

◆ **Coast Guard**

Daphie Reese	Linda Rodriquez	Bobby C. Wilks
Alex Haley	Pamela Autry	Thomasina Sconiers
Michael Healy	Joseph Jenkins	

◆ **National Guard**

Thomas J. Hargis

◆ **Merchant Marines**

Hugh Mulzac	John Godfrey	Adrian Richardson
Clifton Fostic		

Budget: Under $25

Sources:

"Afro-America: The Tuskeegee Airmen," http//www.afroam.org/ history/tusk/ tuskmain.html.

Christian, Garna L., *Black Soldiers in Jim Crow Texas, 1899-1917*, Texas A & M University Press, 1995.

"Colin Powell, Like Ike," http//www.jbs.org/vo11no06.htm.

Davis, Burke, *Black Heroes of the American Revolution*, Harcourt Brace Jovanovich, 1991.

Dennis, Denise, *Black History for Beginners*, Highsmith, 1992.

"Fort Davis History," http//nymedia.tddc.net/hot/bigbend/ftdavis/.

"Freedom Black Military Experience," http//www.inform.umd.edu/ARHU/depts/ History/Freedom/bmepg.htm.

"General Colin Powell," http//www2.lucidcafe.com/lucidcafe/library/96apr/powe ll.html.

"General Colin Powell Dedicates a Monument to the Buffalo Soldier—Unsung Black Heroes," *Jet*, September 7, 1992, 34-38.

Lanning, Michael Lee, *African-American Soldiers: From Crispus Attucks to Colin Powell*, Birch Lane, 1997.

"Limited Edition Photographic Series," http//www.coax.net/people/ lwf/bsphotos.htm.

Powell, Colin, *My American Journey*, Random House 1995.

Terry, Ted, *American Black History: A Reference Manual*, Myles Publishing, 1991.

Alternative Applications: Have students create a special medal honoring African American military members. Consider African American participants in all American conflicts Revolutionary War, Indian Wars, Mexican-American War, Civil War, World War I, World War II, Korean War, Vietnam War, and the Persian Gulf War, as well as active duty in Beirut, Granada, Panama, Haiti, and Bosnia. If participants have members of the community they wish to add to the list, note branch of service and distinguished conduct.

The Civil War

Age/Grade Level or Audience: All ages.

Description: Present a community study of the Civil War.

Procedure: Open a two-week session with the eleven-hour video series *The Civil War*, by Ken Burns. Intersperse small group discussion periods to determine whether African Americans receive proper credit for their role in preserving the American Union and ending slavery.

Budget: $25-$50

Sources:
The nine-part Public Broadcasting Service series *The Civil War* (1990).

"African american Civil War Websites," http//ccharity.com/indexes/ aacivilwar.htm.

American Eras, Gale, 1997.

"Civil War Chronology," http//www.coax.ent/people/lwf/cwchron.htm.

Davis, William C., *Civil War: A Historical Account of America's War of Secession*, Smithmark, 1996.

McFeeley, William *Civil War: As Seen*, Viking Penguin, 1997.

Murphy, Jim, *The Boy's War: Confederate and Union Soldiers Talk about the Civil War*, Clarion Books, 1990.

Robertson, James J., Jr., *Civil War*, Random House, 1996.

Ward, Geoffrey C., Ric Burns, and Ken Burns, *The Civil War: An Illustrated History*, Knopf, 1990.

Alternative Applications: Invite a panel of local social studies teachers, journalists, historians, and civil rights activists to comment on Ken Burns's intent in structuring his famous documentary. As a theme song for your session, have a pianist play "The Ashokan Farewell," which was written for the video series. Include other musical works from the 1860s, particularly Negro spirituals and period pieces such as "Eating Goober Peas," "Tenting on the Old Campground," "Aura Lee," "Maryland, My Maryland," and "The Bonnie Blue Flag."

Colonialism

Age/Grade Level or Audience: High school or college history, economics, or African American studies classes.

Description: Have students conduct an in-depth assessment of the rise of colonialism in Africa and its effect on culture, religion, and world trade.

Procedure: Have students work collaboratively on a study of colonialism and its impact on Africa. For example, consider these topics:

- ◆ changes in South African government under foreign governments
- ◆ decimation of the elephant and rhino populations by ivory hunters
- ◆ exportation of endangered species to zoos and private dealers
- ◆ griot of storyteller as tribal unifier in colonial Africa
- ◆ loss of human rights as a direct outgrowth of the diamond trade
- ◆ native deaths from hunger, mistreatment, and exposure to European diseases
- ◆ slaughter of animals for hides, teeth, claws, and skulls
- ◆ spread of colonialism in the Caribbean
- ◆ suppression of animism by missionaries and white governments
- ◆ women's roles in colonial African society

Conclude with a comparison to European decimation of Native American populations.

Budget: Under $25

Sources:

Achebe, Chinua, *Things Fall Apart*, Fawcett Crest, 1959.

Echewa, T. Obinkaram, *I Saw the Sky Catch Fire*, Plume, 1993.

Kirk-Greene, Anthony, "Decolonisation in British Africa," *History Today*, January 1992, 44-50.

McEvedy, Colin, *The Penguin Atlas of African History*, Penguin, 1996.

Mostert, Noël, *Frontiers: The Epic of South Africa's Creation and the Tragedy of the Xhosa People*, Knopf, 1992.

Oliver, Roland, *The African Experience*, IconEditions, 1992.

"Pan-Africanism: Yesteray and Today," http//www.columbia.edu/cu/iraas/pan-afri. html.

Saari, Peggy, and Daniel B. Baker, *Explorers and Discoverers: From Alexander the Great to Sally Ride*, U•X•L/Gale, 1995.

Alternative Applications: Organize a debate between history classes or area schools. Possible topics of the debate include:

- ♦ Greed as a motivating force in racism
- ♦ The trading company's role in introducing African nations to industrial development
- ♦ The influence of the missionary in keeping African nations subservient to European colonial overlords
- ♦ The gold-salt trade across the Sahara
- ♦ The role of Quakers and Mennonites in changing opinions about slavery
- ♦ Sources of cultural disintegration in Chinua Achebe's *Things Fall Apart*

The Constitution and Black America

Originator: Michael McSweeney, teacher, Auburn, Washington.

Age/Grade Level or Audience: Middle school or high school history or civics classes.

Description: Organize a study unit on the amendments to the U.S. Constitution that have most benefitted black Americans.

Procedure: Name the amendments which have promoted individual freedoms, such as the right to be free, to own property, and to vote. Explain the circumstances that caused these amendments to be added to the Constitution:

- ♦ Thirteenth Amendment (1865) freed the slaves
- ♦ Fourteenth Amendment (1868), passed three years after the Civil War to protect newly freed slaves, extended citizenship and due process to former

slaves and denied the rights of former Confederate sympathizers to run for congressional office. It also forbade states from differentiating among classes of people.

♦ Fifteenth Amendment (1870) allowed male citizens the vote
♦ Nineteenth Amendment (1920), gave women the right to vote
♦ Twenty-fourth Amendment (1964) ended poll taxes

Budget: Under $25

Sources:

"Civil War Chronology," http//www.coax.net/people/lwf/cwchron.htm.

Cramer, Clayton E., *Black Demographic Data, 1790-1860: A Sourcebook*, Greenwood Press, 1997.

"Decisions of the United States Supreme Court," http//supct.law.cornell.edu/supct/.

"Documents in the NAACP Story," http//www.wh.org/naacp/visit.htm.

"The History of the Supreme Court," http//www.oup.usa.org/ gcdocs/gc_019509 3879.html.

Freeman, Marilyn, *The Constitution*, Children's Press, 1995.

Hornsby, Alton, *Chronology of African american History*, 2nd edition Gale, 1997.

Alternative Applications: Have individual groups capture the spirit of a particular amendment in a collage or poster. Collect a series to honor these amendments and hang them in a prominent place, such as a city hall foyer, school hallway, mall, library showcase, or billboard.

Courts and Racial Justice

Contributor: Michael McSweeney, teacher, Auburn, Washington.

Age/Grade Level or Audience: High school and college civics and history classes.

Description: Create a bulletin board display or handout featuring significant court and legislative decisions.

Procedure: Post background data about the most important court cases and legislative decisions that affect black people. Include the following:

♦ **Plessy v. Ferguson** (1896), requiring equal schools for blacks
♦ **Smith v. Alwright** (1944), rejecting the exclusion of blacks from the Democratic party primary elections

◆ **Brown v. Board of Education** (1954), halting racial segregation in public schools

◆ **Hawkins v. Board of Control** (1956), forcing Florida to admit a qualified Negro to a state university graduate program

◆ **Edwards v. South Carolina** (1963), rejecting the state's interference with rights of assembly and freedom of speech by arresting demonstrators for disturbing the peace

◆ **Gideon v. Wainwright** (1963), providing free legal counsel to indigent defendants in criminal cases

◆ **Westberry v. Sanders** (1964), halting gerrymandering, the denial of representation by capricious variances in congressional districting

◆ **Civil Rights Act** (1964), declaring an end to discrimination in employment, school integration, voting, and federally funded projects

◆ **Voting Rights Act** (1965), ending literacy tests as a means of keeping blacks from registering, allowing the President to sent supervisers to register voters, and halting the requirement of poll taxes

◆ **Title VII** (1965), ending discrimination in private business

◆ **Miranda v. State of Arizona** (1966), requiring police to advise suspects of constitutional rights

◆ **Harper v. Virginia Board of Elections** (1966), halting poll taxes in state elections

◆ **Loving v. Virginia** (1967), overruling anti-miscegenation laws

◆ **Swann v. Charlotte-Mecklenburg Board of Education** (1971), upholding busing as a method ending segregation

Budget: Under $25

Sources:

"Affirmative Action," http//www.aclu.org/congress/affirmative.html.

"Affirmative Action Html," http//district.wachusett-rhs.wred.k12.ma.us/Echo/Feb96/affir.

"Decisions of the United States Supreme Court," http//supct.law.cornell.edu/supct/.

"Documents in the NAACP Story," http//www.wh.org/naacp/visit.htm.

"The History of the Supreme Court," http//www.oup.usa.org/gcdocs/gc_0195093879.html.

Mabunda, L. Mpho, ed., *The African American Almanac*, 7th edition, Gale, 1997.

Roberts, Dorothy, *Killing the Black Body Race, Reproduction, and the Meaning of Liberty*, Pantheon, 1997.

Sadler, A. E., ed., *Affirmative Action*, Greenwood, 1996.

Alternative Applications: Set up a bulletin board or website during a voter drive. Post and hand out printed copies of time lines detailing the rise in black rights. Post voter rights, residency and poll maps, dates, and mock ballots at a public library or other registration site. Encourage participation through local media announcements, yard signs, church bulletins, door-to-door campaigns, websites, and billboards.

⊡ ☐ Displaying Black History

Age/Grade Level or Audience: Elementary or middle school social studies class; public library group activity.

Description: Organize interactive museum displays of moments in black history.

Procedure: Have small groups select a moment in black history to recreate in miniature. Suggest the *Amistad* mutiny, creation of the Underground Railroad, arrival of the *Clothilde*, or Dred Scott court case. Using dolls, clay shapes, or mannequins, reproduce the dramatic moment. Work with a second group to provide recorded music and a taped voiceover to explain the location, time, participants, and outcome of the events, for example, Joseph Cinqué's return to Africa or Harriet Tubman's numerous trips into the antebellum South to free slaves. Group finished interactive displays in chronological order so viewers can discuss the scenes and play the recordings.

Budget: $25-$50

Sources:

"African American History," http//www.msstate.edu/Archives/History/USA/Afro-Amer/afro.html.

Aikman, D., "Slavery in Our Time: America Slowly Rediscovers Slavery—in Africa," *American Spectator*, February 1997, 52-53.

Bennett, Lerone, Jr., *Before the Mayflower: A History of Black America*, 6th edition, Penguin Books, 1993.

Cantor, George Cantor, *Historic Landmarks of Black America*, Gale, 1991.

Gates, Henry Louis, ed., *Chronology of African-American History from 1445-1980*, Amistad Press, 1993.

"A History of Slavery in America," *Schlessinger Media.*

Hornsby, Alton, *Chronology of African-American History*, 2nd edition Gale, 1997.

Metcalf, Doris Hunter, *African Americans Their Impact on U.S. History*, Good Apple, 1992.

Thomas, Velma Maia, *Lest We Forget The Passage from Africa to Slavery and Emancipation*, Crown, 1997.

Alternative Applications: Design a series of video or movie awards for historical presentation. Honor actors, costumes, scenes, music, photograph, fictional characters, historical figures, accuracy, background detail, special effects, and realism. Keep a cumulative class scrapbook of awards.

Dressing Up and Stepping Out

Age/Grade Level or Audience: Adults

Description: Hold a Black History Month costume ball.

Procedure: Join with an arts league, civic center, or historical society in hosting a Black History Month costume ball. Announce categories of prizes, for example, most authentic costume, best couple, best dancers, and most original headdress. Provide music from a black dance band or deejay. Post photographs in a civic center or publish in the society section of the newspaper or television news program.

Budget: $75-$100

Sources:
Bennett, Lerone, Jr., *Before the Mayflower: A History of Black America*, 6th edition, Penguin Books, 1993.
"Black History," http//www.slip.net/~rigged/history.html.
"Black History Month Let's Get Started," http//www.netnoir.com/spotlight/bhm/jbhm. html.
Dennis, Denise, *Black History for Beginners*, Highsmith, 1992.
Grun, Bernard, *The Timetables of History: A Horizontal Linkage of People and Events*, Simon & Schuster, 1991.
Hornsby, Alton, *Chronology of African-American History*, 2nd edition Gale, 1997.
Jackson, John G., *Introduction to African Civilizations*, Citadel Press, 1994.
Mabunda, L. Mpho, ed., *The African American Almanac*, 7th edition, Gale, 1997.
O'Halloran, Kate, *Hands-on Culture of Ancient Egypt*, Walch, 1997.
————, *Hands-on Culture of West Africa*, Walch, 1997.
Saari, Peggy, and Daniel B. Baker, *Explorers and Discoverers: From Alexander the Great to Sally Ride*, U•X•L/Gale, 1995.
Steedman, Scott, *Pockets Ancient Egypt*, Dorling Kindersley, 1995.

Alternative Applications: Hold a costume design contest. Have participants sketch outfits for famous black heroes and achievers. Display winning designs at an art museum, mall, or bank lobby.

Each One Teach One

Age/Grade Level or Audience: Adult teachers, librarians, museum curators, or community and religious leaders.

Description: Organize a tutorial to educate leaders in black history.

Procedure: Create a consortium of black history experts to present a workshop for teachers, civic leaders, ministers, social workers, doctors, writers, editors, and others who need to know more about the subject in order to perform their jobs adequately.

Budget: $50-$75

Sources:

Bennett, Lerone, Jr., *Before the Mayflower: A History of Black America*, 6th edition, Penguin Books, 1993.

"Black History," http//www.slip.net/~rigged/history.html.

"Black History Month Let's Get Started," http//www.netnoir.com/spotlight/bhm/jbhm. html.

Brailsford, Karen, "Sacred Ground: Dry Bones Speak," *Emerge*, October 1992, 73.

Dennis, Denise, *Black History for Beginners*, Highsmith, 1992.

Grun, Bernard, *The Timetables of History: A Horizontal Linkage of People and Events*, Simon & Schuster, 1991.

Hornsby, Alton, *Chronology of African-American History*, 2nd edition Gale, 1997.

Jackson, John G., *Introduction to African Civilizations*, Citadel Press, 1994.

Mabunda, L. Mpho, ed., *The African American Almanac*, 7th edition, Gale, 1997.

Saari, Peggy, and Daniel B. Baker, *Explorers and Discoverers: From Alexander the Great to Sally Ride*, U•X•L/Gale, 1995.

Steedman, Scott, *Pockets Ancient Egypt*, Dorling Kindersley, 1995.

Alternative Applications: Have a consortium produce a pamphlet, website, or syllabus to assist immigrants and other newcomers to the area in appreciating local, state, and national black history. Videotape consortium members' speeches or lessons and place them in local schools, public libraries, and databases for students, teachers, and others to use as an impetus to future black history celebrations.

 The Emancipation Proclamation

Age/Grade Level or Audience: Middle school or high school history or language students.

Description: Study the Emancipation Proclamation.

Procedure: Provide an array of works on early nineteenth-century America, the presidency of Abraham Lincoln, fugitive slave laws, the Abolitionist Movement, the Missouri Compromise, and the beginnings of the Civil War. Encourage students to form their own opinions as to why Lincoln chose to free the slaves. Compose a hand-out sheet or website featuring the following facts:

♦ At first, Lincoln did not sympathize with slaves, but pressure from aboli-tionists and Republicans eventually changed his position on white supremacy.

♦ Congress began weakening slavery by freeing slaves from the Confederate military, those in the District of Columbia and federal territories, and those belonging to traitors.

♦ By July 1862, Lincoln revealed to his cabinet his plans to emancipate slaves.

♦ He announced his plans to end slavery on September 22, 1862.

♦ Lincoln used the proclamation as a means of justifying a war to end slav-ery.

♦ Following the Union Army's success as Antietam, the Emancipation Proclamation was issued January 1, 1863.

♦ Its central message was simple:

And by virtue of the power and for the purpose aforesaid, I do order and declare that all persons held as slaves within said designated States and parts of states are, and henceforward shall be, free; and that the executive government of the United States, including the military and naval authorities thereof, will recognize and maintain the freedom of said persons.

♦ slaves living in Confederate states, *i.e.* Alabama, Arkansas, Florida, Georgia, Mississippi, North Carolina, South Carolina, Texas, and parts of Louisiana and Virginia, were freed.

♦ The 800,000 slaves in border states or areas captured by Union troops were not covered.

♦ To offset further violence, the proclamation urged newly freed slaves to "abstain from all violence, unless in necessary self-defense."

♦ The proclamation opened the U.S. Army and Navy to 180,000 black volun-teers, who helped turn the tide of the war.

♦ Southern rebels ignored Lincoln's proclamation.

♦ As Union forces liberated territories, more slaves gained their freedom, adding to the growing problem of refugees fleeing the war zone.

♦ The complete abolition of slavery did not occur until December 18, 1865, when Congress passed the Thirteenth Amendment to the Constitution.

Budget: Under $25

Sources:
Charnwood, Lord, *Abraham Lincoln A Biography*, Madison Books, 1996.
"The Emancipation Proclamation," http//rain.org/~Karpeles/EmancipationPr.html.

"The Emancipation Proclamation," http//www.accusd.edu/~sakkinen/ abe10.html.

"The Emancipation Proclamation," http//www.winternet.com/~orion/text/emanproc. txt.

"The Emancipation Proclamation," National Archives and Records, 1993.

Hummel, Jeffrey R., *Emancipating Slaves, Enslaving Free Men A History of the American Civil War*, Open Court, 1996.

Rhodes, Elisha Hunt, *All for the Union: The Civil War Diary and Letters of Elisha Hunt Rhodes*, Vintage Books, 1992.

Wellman, Sam, *Abraham Lincoln*, Barbour & Co., 1994.

Young, Robert, *The Emancipation Proclamation: Why Lincoln Really Freed the Slaves*, Silver Burdett, 1994.

Alternative Applications: Explain why the creation of a Freedman's Bureau was necessary to enforce the liberation of slaves and ease their emergence into free society. List hindrances to their progress, for example, illiteracy, poverty, poor health, separation of families, violent opposition, homelessness, and unemployment.

Events and Outcomes

Age/Grade Level or Audience: Middle school or high school history classes.

Description: Chart the cause and effects of events influencing black history.

Procedure: Explain to students how to draw cause-and-effect maps, flow charts, cycle diagrams, and sequence chains. Have students select a graphic style to express the importance of these events to black history:

Amistad trial	black military units
Brown vs. Board of Education	desegregated public transportation
Dred Scott Decision	Emancipation Proclamation
establishment of Howard University	Freedman's Bureau
"I Have a Dream" speech	integration of Supreme Court
Jim Crow laws	manumission of Frederick Douglass
martyrdom of Medgar Evers	Missouri Compromise
publication of *Uncle Tom's Cabin*	raid on Harper's Ferry
voyage of the *Clothilde*	women receive the right to vote

Have students conclude the exercise with an annotated bibliography of reference works, hypertexts, and websites used in their research.

Budget: Under $25

Sources:

"African American History," http//www.msstate.edu/Archives/History/USA/Afro-Amer/afro.html.

African American History in the Press, 1851-1899, Gale, 1996.

Asante, Molefi K., *Historical and Cultural Atlas of African Americans*, Macmillan, 1991.

"Black History," http//www.slip.net/~rigged/history.html.

"Black History Month Let's Get Started," http//www.netnoir.com/spotlight/bhm/jbhm.html.

Corbin, Raymond M., *1,999 Facts about Blacks: A Sourcebook of African american Achievement*, 2nd edition, Madison Books, 1997.

"The Faces of Science African Americans in the Sciences," http//www.lib.lsu.edu/lib/chem/display/faces.html.

Hine, Darlene Clark, Elsa Barkley Brown, and Rosalyn Terborg-Penn, *Black Women in America: An Historical Encyclopedia,* Carlson Publishing, 1993.

Mabunda, L. Mpho, ed., *The African American Almanac*, 7th edition, Gale, 1997.

Saari, Peggy, and Daniel B. Baker, *Explorers and Discoverers: From Alexander the Great to Sally Ride*, U•X•L/Gale, 1995.

Trager, James, *The People's Chronology*, revised edition, Henry Holt & Co., 1996.

"What Is Your Black History IQ?," *Ebony*, February 1997, 86-88.

Alternative Applications: Have students create a flow chart or series of cause-and-effect maps for a period of time, for example, the settlement of New England or the end of the Civil War. Highlight events that influence black history.

Explorers of Africa

Age/Grade Level or Audience: Middle school and high school history, geography, and social studies classes; civic presentations; multicultural festivals; museum displays.

Description: Create an illustrated time line of noted Europeans who explored the "dark continent."

Procedure: Collect names and nationalities of famous African explorers, noting where they went, how long they stayed, and what they accomplished. Some major figures include the following:

◆ **Belgium** Maurice Adolphe Linant de Bellefonds (1827), Boer settlers

◆ **England and Scotland** Mungo Park (1795-1797, 1805-1806), Hugh Clapperton (1822-1827), Richard L. Lander (1825-1827, 830), Alexander Gordon Laing (1825-1826), Richard Pococke (1737-1740), James Bruce (1769-1772), Richard Francis Burton (1857-1859), John Henning Speke (1857-1863), David Livingstone (1841-1856, 1865-1873), John Kirk (1841-1855), James A. Grant (1860-1863), Dr. Samuel Baker (1863-1865), Henry Morton Stanley (1871, 1874-1877), Joseph Thomson (1883-1884)

◆ **France** Napoleon Bonaparte (1798-1801), René Callié (1827-1828), Gaspard T. Mollien (1796-1872), Louis Léon César Faidherbe (1850s), Louis Binger (1887-1889), Parfait Louis Monteil (1890-1892), Paul Du Chaillu (1840s-1860s)

◆ **Germany** Dr. Ludwig Krapf (late 1840s), Rev. John Rebmann (late 1840s), Dr. Heinrich Barth (1850-1855), Adolf Overweg (1852), Friedrich Gerhard Rohlfs (1831-1896), Gustav Nachtigal (1834-1885), Carl Peters, Count Samuel Teleki von Szek

◆ **Italy** Pierre Savorgnan de Brazza (1975-1978)

◆ **Portugal** Henry the Navigator (1441-1460), Nuno Tristao (1442), Alvise da Cadamosto (1456), Pedro de Cintra (1462), Diego Cao (1482-1484), Bartholomew Dias (1487-1488), Vasco da Gama (1497-1498) Finao Gomes (1469-1471), Fernao da Po

Budget: Under $25

Sources:

"David Livingstone's Birthplace and Museum of African Exploration,"http//www.kid-snet.co.uk/scotland/davidliv.shtml.

"Geographical Timeline," http//www.utexas.edu/depts/grc/ustudent/ frontiers/ fall95/blackford/blackford.html.

McEvedy, Colin, *The Penguin Atlas of African History*, Penguin, 1996.

"Mungo Park," http//www.microsoft.com/corpinfo/press/1996/sept96/MUNGOPR.htm.

Saari, Peggy, and Daniel B. Baker, *Explorers and Discoverers: From Alexander the Great to Sally Ride*, U•X•L/Gale, 1995.

Steedman, Scott, *Pockets Ancient Egypt*, Dorling Kindersley, 1995.

"Voice of Africa," http//www.scry.com/ayer/AFRO-AM/4401185.htm.

Alternative Applications: Pinpoint on a large map of Africa these explorations:

◆ David Livingstone crosses the Kalahari Desert

◆ James Bruce searches for the source of the Nile

◆ Mungo Park searches for the Niger

◆ Nuno Tristao explores the Gambia River

◆ Richard Burton journeys down the White Nile

Filming Ancient Africa

Age/Grade Level or Audience: Elementary or middle school history, art, or humanities classes.

Description: Begin preliminary work on a film about ancient Africa.

Procedure: Divide participants into three major groups one to design sets, another to create costumes, and a third to select props for a movie or video about one of the following topics:

- ◆ discovery of King Tut's tomb
- ◆ building of the Aswan Dam
- ◆ court visits of the Queen of Sheba
- ◆ discovery of the Hope Diamond
- ◆ first Africans to settle in Guyana
- ◆ first Africans to trade with European slavers
- ◆ first Europeans to visit Kilwa
- ◆ horse traders of Kanem-Bornu
- ◆ Life in the court of the Oba of Benin
- ◆ Queen Nzingha's life as a warrior-ruler
- ◆ Shaka's kingdom
- ◆ Sundiata's diplomatic triumphs
- ◆ Worship and ritual at the temple at Great Zimbabwe

Bring together the three groups and map out story boards to guide the director of the movie your group plans to make. Suggest appropriate titles, then propose how the movie will be advertised to draw a large audience.

Budget: $25-$50

Sources:
Curtin, P. D., *African History*, 2nd edition, Addison-Wesley, 1995.
Jackson, John G., *Introduction to African Civilizations*, Citadel Press, 1994.
McEvedy, Colin, *The Penguin Atlas of African History*, Penguin, 1996.
Steedman, Scott, *Pockets: Ancient Egypt*, Dorling Kindersley, 1995.

Alternative Applications: Assign students a period of African history to visualize. Have them outline on paper a film, documentary television drama, miniseries, website, or video detailing why that period was crucial to black history. Invite students to suggest names of actors to play important roles.

George Washington's Will

Age/Grade Level or Audience: Middle school or high school language or history classes.

Description: Organize a study of George Washington's will.

Procedure: Read aloud or present by overhead projector George Washington's will, which manumitted his slaves. Invite volunteers to restate in simpler terms the following crucial lines:

- ◆ Upon the decease of my wife, it is my will and desire that all the slaves which I hold in my own right, shall receive their freedom.
- ◆ And whereas among those who will receive freedom according to this devise, there may be some, who from old age or bodily infirmities, and others who on account of their infancy, that will be unable to support themselves; it is my will and desire that all who come under the first and second description shall be comfortably clothed and fed by my heirs while they live ...
- ◆ The Negroes thus bound are (by their masters or mistresses) to be taught to read and write; and to be brought up to some useful occupation, agreeably to the laws of the commonwealth of Virginia, providing for the support of orphans and other poor children.
- ◆ And I do hereby expressly forbid the sale, or transportation out of said commonwealth of any slave I may die possessed of, under any pretense whatsoever.
- ◆ And to my mulatto man William (calling himself William Lee) I give immediate freedom; or if he should prefer it (on account of the accidents which have befallen him, and which have rendered him incapable of walking or of any active employment to remain in the situation he now is), it shall be optional in him to do so. In either case however, I allow him an annuity of thirty dollars during his natural life, which shall be independent of the victuals and clothes he has been accustomed to receive, if he chooses the last alternative; but in full, with his freedom, if he prefers the first;—and this I give him as testimony of my sense of his attachment to me, and for his faithful services during the Revolutionary War.

Budget: Under $25

Sources:

Alden, John R., *George Washington: A Biography*, Louisiana State University Press, 1996.

Cramer, Clayton E., *Black Demographic Data, 1790-1860 A Sourcebook*, Greenwood Press, 1997.

"George Washington," http//history.hanover.edu/18th/washingt.htm.

"George Washington Links," http//www.vms.utexas.edu/~jdedman/xing/lnks.htm.

Mabunda, L. Mpho, ed., *The African American Almanac*, 7th edition, Gale, 1997.

Walvin, James, *Slavery and the Slave Trade: A Short Illustrated History*, University Press of Mississippi, 1983.

Alternative Applications: Have students discuss the meaning and purpose of manumission and to consider the consequences for a black slave who has never known freedom. Make a separate study of each of the following cases:

- ◆ handicapped or aged slaves
- ◆ illiterate slaves
- ◆ slaves born of white parentage
- ◆ slaves guilty of crimes against their owners, such as rape, stealing, assault, poisoning, or arson.
- ◆ slaves who do not speak English
- ◆ slaves who prefer to remain in their master's care
- ◆ slaves who wish to return to Africa
- ◆ women with small children

Harlem: Black America's Home Town

Originator: Janet M. Donaldson, Upper Midwest Women's History Center for Teachers, St. Louis Park, Minnesota.

Age/Grade Level or Audience: High school or college black history classes; arts societies.

Description: Compose an historical overview of Harlem.

Procedure: Using photographs, filmstrips, books, diaries and memoirs, art prints, sculpture, brochures, or movies, account for the importance of Harlem to the cultural survival of black America. Include famous people and places and a timeline of events. Stress important contributors, such as these:

- ◆ writers Countee Cullen, Zora Neale Hurston, Claude McKay, James Weldon Johnson, Jean Toomer, Jessie Faucet, Claude Brown, Rudolph Fisher, Nella Larsen, Langston Hughes
- ◆ musicians Duke Ellington, Eubie Blake, Noble Sissle, Roland Hayes, F. E. Miller, Aubrey Lyle, Billie Holiday, Jelly Roll Morton
- ◆ editors Carter Woodson and W. E. B. Du Bois
- ◆ composers W. C. Handy, J. Rosamond Johnson, Harry J. Burleigh
- ◆ actors Charles Gilpin, Florence Mills, and Paul Robeson
- ◆ dancers Josephine Baker and Katherine Dunham

- ◆ NAACP activist and policewoman Ethel Ray Nance
- ◆ entrepreneur Madame C. J. Walker and her style-conscious daughter A'Lelia Walker
- ◆ minister and leader Malcolm X

Create a scrapbook of quotations, aphorisms, poems, memoirs, vignettes, and dialogues created by residents of Harlem, such as the poems of Langston Hughes, plays and stories of Zora Neale Hurston, Josephine Baker's memoirs, speeches of Malcolm X, or essays by W. E. B. DuBois.

Budget: Under $25

Sources:

Bradbury, Malcolm, gen. ed., *The Atlas of Literature,* De Agostini, 1996.

Cantor, George, *Historic Landmarks of Black America,* Gale, 1991.

Delany, Sarah L., and A. Elizabeth Delany, *Having Our Say,* Dell, 1993.

Haley, Alex, *The Autobiography of Malcolm X,* Ballantine Books, 1992.

Harlem Renaissance, Chelsea House, 1996.

"The Harlem Renaissance," http//www.usc.edu/Library/Ref/Ethnic/harlem.html.

Haskins, James, *Harlem Renaissance,* Millbrook Press, 1996.

McCanlies, Tim, *Harlem,* Holloway, 1994.

Morrison, Toni, *Jazz,* Knopf, 1992.

Myers, Walter Dean, *Harlem,* Scholastic, Inc., 1997.

"Uptown Harlem Online," http//www.cldc.howard.edu/~he/fall95s/ page17.html.

Alternative Applications: Organize a group to create a walking tour, website, or tourist guide to Harlem. Include the following landmarks:

- ◆ Abyssinian Baptist Church at 132 West 138th Street, once the pulpit of Adam Clayton Powell, Jr.
- ◆ Apollo Theater on West 125th Street, home to black dancers, singers, and instrumentalists from the 1920s to current times
- ◆ Cotton Club, Lenox Avenue and 143rd Street, where Duke Ellington and Count Basie performed for uptown white audiences.
- ◆ Black Fashion Museum at 155 W. 126th Street, which features garments covering the entire history of black residence in the New World
- ◆ Schomburg Center for Research in Black Culture at Lenox Avenue and 135th Street, which displays published materials which influenced the Harlem Renaissance
- ◆ St. Nicholas Historical District, an area extending from 137th to 139th streets and from Frederick Douglass Boulevard to Adam Clayton Powell Boulevard, which was once home to Noble Sissle, Claude McKay, James Weldon Johnson, Florence Mills, Eubie Blake, Will Marion Cook, and W. C. Handy, father of the blues
- ◆ Studio Museum of Harlem at 144 W. 125th Street, a folk art center which was once an artists' center containing a lecture hall, concert stage, and studio.

Hear Ye! Hear Ye!

Age/Grade Level or Audience: Elementary or middle school social studies or history classes.

Description: Appoint a town crier to relate weekly additions to black history.

Procedure: Collect items for a black history bulletin board or database. Assign a student to present items of interest each week and to follow up on developing stories, for example, black participation in Olympic games, civil rights protests, scientific experiments, or space flights.

Budget: Under $25

Sources:
Online magazines, news sources, and major links, such as "Africa Online"; newspapers, *Time, Newsweek, U. S. News and World Report, Jet, Ebony, Essence, Emerge,* or *Biography*.

Alternative Applications: Have groups design broadside sheets of news briefs and features from a particular period, for example, Lorraine Hale and Clara Hale's work with infants during the rise of AIDS or Colin Powell's consideration as a presidential candidate. Include original ballads of black achievers as well as maps, photos, and drawings scanned in from history books and current sources.

 The Ku Klux Klan

Age/Grade Level or Audience: High school or college social studies, psychology, and sociology classes; history societies; professional and religious groups.

Description: Organize a multimedia study of hate groups, featuring the formation and development of the Ku Klux Klan.

Procedure: Collect information on Ku Klux Klan-sponsored propaganda and violence from a variety of sources, including books, websites, newspaper and magazine articles, histories, movies, videos, brochures, leaflets, and interviews. Present findings in a series of illustrated lectures. Illustrate the following facts:

◆ Six Confederate veterans founded the Klan in late spring of 1866 in Pulaski, Tennessee.

◆ The name "Ku Klux" is a corruption of the Greek word "cyclos" for circle.

◆ A major facet of Klan membership was secrecy, which was assured by the donning of white robes with pointed caps pierced by two eyeholes.

◆ The purpose was to harass, humiliate, and otherwise degrade newly freed blacks.

◆ The idea caught on with low-class whites, who felt economically threatened by hordes of emancipated blacks and who sought empowerment through membership in a secret society.

◆ Other "Old South" supporters, including landowners, judges, doctors, lawyers, and politicians, joined the Klan cause by night while wearing the mask of respectability by day.

◆ To legitimize their hate of blacks, Catholics, Jews, Italians, and other outsiders in the South, Klansmen made a show of religiosity, family devotion, and patriotism.

◆ Methods of annoying blacks worsened to nightriding, cross burning, arson, horsewhipping, rape, emasculation, shooting, tarring and feathering, and lynching.

◆ Targets were usually people who owned land or possessed status, such as a successful forge or woodcarving shop or a bid for public office.

◆ The conservative press condoned Klan violence on the pretext of protecting Southern women.

◆ Some victims of Klan violence were condemned for a minor slight, such as bumping against a white woman on the street or demanding a receipt in payment of a debt to a white lender.

◆ The Ku Klux Klan Acts of 1870 and 1871 quelled the movement's growth.

◆ From 1882 to 1968, lynchings were common occurrences in Southern states and not unknown as far north as New England. The totals in order of frequency include forty-three states:

Mississippi	581
Maryland	29
Georgia	531
South Dakota	27
Texas	493
Ohio	26
Louisiana	391
Washington	26
Alabama	347
Oregon	21
Arkansas	284
Idaho	20
Florida	282
Iowa	19
Kentucky	205

North Dakota	16
South Carolina	160
Minnesota	9
Missouri	122
Michigan	8
Oklahoma	122
Pennsylvania	8
North Carolina	101
Utah	8
Virginia	100
Nevada	6
Montana	84
Wisconsin	6
Colorado	68
New Jersey	2
Nebraska	57
New York	2
Kansas	54
Delaware	1
West Virginia	48
Maine	1
Indiana	47
Vermont	1
California	43
New Mexico	36
Wyoming	35
Arizona	31
Maryland	29
TOTAL	**4709**

[States not credited with lynching include Hawaii, New Hampshire, Alaska, Massachusetts, Iowa, Connecticut, and Illinois.]

♦ D. W. Griffith's *Birth of a Nation* spawned a resurgence of Klan activity in 1915.

♦ Outraged whites, spurred by the anti-lynching movement led by Ida Wells-Barnett and Jessie Daniel Ames, fought Klan violence.

♦ The Civil Rights Movement of the late 1950s and 1960s inspired Klan bombings, often of black churches.

♦ On January 23, 1957, Klansmen forced Montgomery truck driver Willie Edwards, Jr., to jump from a bridge spanning the Alabama River. No one was found guilty of the crime.

♦ On April 25, 1959, eight masked white males dragged Mack Charles Parker from a cell in the Poplarville, Mississippi, jail three days before he was to be tried for raping a white woman. Members of the mob included a Baptist minister, health department worker, and jailer. Juries refused to find the men guilty.

◆ On May 2, 1964, Meadville, Mississippi, Klansmen kidnapped Charles Moore and Henry Dee, beat and mutilated them, and threw their bodies into the Mississippi River. Charges against two suspects were dismissed.

◆ On June 12, 1963, Byron De La Beckwith was charged with murdering civil rights activist Medgar Evers at his Jackson, Mississippi, home. On February 5, 1994, Beckwith was convicted of murder and sentenced to life in prison.

◆ Four young black girls were killed in the bombing of Birmingham's 16th Street Baptist Church on September 15, 1963. Klansman Robert Chambliss was imprisoned until 1977.

◆ On June 10, 1966, Klansmen shot and killed 67-year-old caretaker Ben Chester White in Natchez, Mississippi. Even with a confession from one Klan member, the jury failed to reach a verdict.

◆ In the 1990s, former Klan official David Duke failed to downplay his earlier role in hate groups in his bid for the governorship of Louisiana.

Publish findings in a series of newspaper articles or professional journals, such as a state legal or journalism society or a civil liberties newsletter.

Budget: $25-$50

Sources:

Films or videos of *Places in the Heart* (1984) *The Ghosts of Mississippi* (1997), *Mississippi Burning* (1988), or *Birth of a Nation* (1915).

"Extremist Groups The Ku Klux Klan," http//www.acsp.uic.edu/gangs/kkk/aka. shtml.

Frederickson, Karl, *The Ku Klux Klan of the 1920s*, M. E. Sharpe, 1997.

"The Ku Klux Klan," http//www.unix-ag.umi-pl.de/~moritz/ alatm/artikel/kukluxkl.art.

Alternative Applications: Contrast the rise and fall of Klan activity with similar hate groups in the United States, Russia, Germany, Ireland, Pakistan, India, Afghanistan, and South Africa. Note extremist behavior and religious overtones in an attempt to conceal the seriousness of racist crimes. Discuss the importance of such peacekeeping groups as the United Nations, Amnesty International, Klan Watch, and the American Civil Liberties Union.

Library Scavenger Hunt

Originator: Kay Paisley-Callender, teacher and writer, Columbus, Ohio.

Age/Grade Level or Audience: Elementary or middle school.

Description: Pose a series of questions about black leaders, civil rights history, entertainers, or sports figures.

Procedure: In order to strengthen library resource skills, have the librarian assemble a group of books, magazines, journals, filmstrips, disc recordings, CDs, software, databases, website URLs, and other materials on black history. Have participants locate answers and list sources from which each came. Some significant questions include these subjects:

- ◆ the name of the first abolitionist newspaper
- ◆ the setting of Martin Luther King's "I Have a Dream" speech
- ◆ the singer who popularized "Old Man River" in the musical *Showboat*
- ◆ product that made Madame C. J. Walker America's first black millionaire
- ◆ first state to abolish slavery
- ◆ first free African nation
- ◆ date that Rosa Parks refused to move to the back of the bus
- ◆ first black female to seek the U.S. presidency
- ◆ Constitutional amendment allowing black males to vote
- ◆ state that refused to make Martin Luther King, Jr.'s birthday a legal holiday
- ◆ U.S. Supreme Court justice who spearheaded civil rights
- ◆ first black author to win a Pulitzer Prize
- ◆ black attorney who accused a U.S. Supreme Court nominee of sexual harassment
- ◆ first black female astronaut

The first student to list answers and sources will win a prize and/or recognition as a black history expert.

Budget: $25-$50

Sources:
African American History in the Press, 1851-1899, Gale, 1996.

Asante, Molefi K., *Historical and Cultural Atlas of African Americans*, Macmillan, 1991.

"Black History," http//www.slip.net/~rigged/history.html.

"Black History Month Let's Get Started," http//www.netnoir.com/spotlight/bhm/jbhm.html.

Corbin, Raymond M., *1,999 Facts about Blacks A Sourcebook of African-American Achievement*, 2nd edition, Madison Books, 1997.

Hine, Darlene Clark, Elsa Barkley Brown, and Rosalyn Terborg-Penn, *Black Women in America: An Historical Encyclopedia*, Carlson Publishing, 1993.

Mabunda, L. Mpho, ed., *The African American Almanac*, 7th edition, Gale, 1997.

Nelson, Rebecca, and Marie J. MacNee, eds., *The Olympic Factbook: A Spectator's Guide to the Summer Games*, Visible Ink Press, 1996.

Saari, Peggy, and Daniel B. Baker, *Explorers and Discoverers: From Alexander the Great to Sally Ride*, U•X•L/Gale, 1995.

Shapiro, William E., ed., *The Kingfisher Young People's Encyclopedia of the United States.*, Larousse Kingfisher Chambers, 1994.

"This Person in Black History Thurgood Marshall," http//www.ai.mit.edu/~isbell/ Hfh/black/events_and_people/001.thurgood_marshall.

Alternative Applications: Present black history data through a "Question of the Day" contest, which may be accompanied by a list of hints, photo, drawing, map, documents, or video- or audiotaped clue, such as a segment of a speech or scene from the docudrama *Eyes on the Prize*. Awards should be something small, but meaningful, for example, a bookmark or listing on a bulletin board.

Matthew Henson

Age/Grade Level or Audience: Elementary or middle school history and science classes.

Description: Present the history of North Pole exploration, highlighting the contribution of Matthew Henson.

Procedure: Explain to students how Matthew Henson became the first explorer to reach the North Pole. Emphasize these points:

- ◆ Henson, born in Charles County, Maryland, in 1866, lived in New York.
- ◆ At age twelve he went to sea.
- ◆ Hired as an explorer of Nicaragua in 1887, Henson assisted Robert E. Peary.
- ◆ Henson became the first to reach the North Pole on April 6, 1909.
- ◆ He took readings and placed the U.S. flag at the correct spot before Peary arrived.
- ◆ In 1912, Henson wrote *A Negro Explorer at the North Pole*.
- ◆ He was admitted to the Explorer's Club in 1937.
- ◆ President Truman honored his achievements in 1950 at a Pentagon ceremony.
- ◆ Four years later, President Eisenhower honored Henson at the White House.
- ◆ Pushed aside as unimportant, he died poor in 1955.
- ◆ A plaque erected in 1961 in Annapolis, Maryland, honors Henson's contribution.

Have students draw a map illustrating the entire Peary-Henson voyage.

Budget: Under $25

Sources:

Asante, Molefi K., and Mark T. Mattson, *Historical and Cultural Atlas of African Americans*, Macmillan, 1991.

Bigelow, Barbara Carlisle, ed., *Contemporary Black Biography*, Vol. 2, Gale, 1992.

"A Black Man Reaches the North Pole," http//marin.k12.ca.us/~parkweb/ MatthewKevin.html.

Dolan, Sean, *Matthew Henson*, Chelsea House, 1992.

"A Final Resting Place for Matthew Henson," *Ebony*, July 1988, 108-112.

"Matthew Henson," http//www.schoolroom.com/videos/v6775.htm.

"Matthew Henson, Polar Explorer," http//www.matthewhenson.com.

Straub, Deborah G., *Contemporary Heroes and Heroines, Book II*, Gale, 1992.

Williams, Jean, *Matthew Henson, Polar Adventurer*, Watts, 1994.

Alternative Applications: Have students draw illustrations of how they imagine Henson's journey to the North Pole. To stir their thinking, read aloud from a biography of Matthew Henson or display films, filmstrips, websites, or *National Geographic* pictures of the North Pole.

Report Writing

Originator: Leatrice Pearson, teacher, Lenoir, North Carolina.

Age/Grade Level or Audience: High school or college literature, history, or African American studies class.

Description: Have students assemble detailed reports on important aspects of African American history, such as crucial periods of political influence.

Procedure: Have students utilize media resources and complete a library or research paper or an outline for an oral report on one of the following topics:

- ◆ African Diaspora
- ◆ "Black Is Beautiful" Movement
- ◆ Black Muslims in the United States
- ◆ Black Soldiers During the Civil War
- ◆ Black Women and the Women's Movement
- ◆ Buffalo Soldiers and the Settlement of the West
- ◆ Carter G. Woodson and Negro History Week
- ◆ Civil Rights Act of 1875
- ◆ Civil Rights Acts of 1957 and 1960
- ◆ Creation of the Civil Rights Act of 1866

- ◆ Creation of the Freedman's Bureau
- ◆ Creation of the NAACP
- ◆ Dred Scott Case
- ◆ First Reconstruction Act of 1867
- ◆ Harlem Renaissance
- ◆ Jim Crow Laws
- ◆ Ku Klux Klan From Bedford Forest to David Duke
- ◆ Marcus Garvey and the "Back to Africa" Movement
- ◆ Matthew Henson, North Pole Explorer
- ◆ Million Man March and Million Woman March
- ◆ Nature and Purpose of the Black Codes
- ◆ Speeches of Frederick Douglass

Assemble individual reports on significant black history topics into an in-house journal, newsletter, assembly program, or database. Retain student writing as resource material. Share reports by e-mail or on websites.

Budget: Under $25

Sources:

African American History in the Press, 1851-1899, Gale, 1996.

Asante, Molefi K., *Historical and Cultural Atlas of African Americans*, Macmillan, 1991.

"Black History," http//www.slip.net/~rigged/history.html.

"Black History Month Let's Get Started," http//www.netnoir.com/spotlight/bhm/jbhm. html.

Cramer, Clayton E., *Black Demographic Data, 1790-1860: A Sourcebook*, Greenwood Press, 1997.

Forge, Alice, and Karen E. Quinones Miller, "The Philadelphia Story," *People*, November 10, 1997, 123-124.

Gillespie, Marcia Ann, "Men on My Mind," *Ms.*, November/December 1997, 1.

Hine, Darlene Clark, Elsa Barkley Brown, and Rosalyn Terborg-Penn, *Black Women in America: An Historical Encyclopedia*, Carlson Publishing, 1993.

Mabunda, L. Mpho, ed., *The African American Almanac*, 7th edition, Gale, 1997.

Miller, Randall, M., and John David Smith, *Dictionary of Afro-American Slavery*, Greenwood, 1997.

McKissack, Patricia, and Frederick L. McKissack, *Rebels Against Slavery: American Slave Revolts*, Scholastic, 1996.

"Slavery." http//www.afu.org/~afu43300/slave.html.

Alternative Applications: Organize an annual contest for the best researched scholarly paper on black history. Invite schools throughout the state to participate. Nominate a multiracial panel to read and evaluate submissions. Offer a stipend, prize, ribbon, medallion, or trophy at a black history assembly or civic function. Name the contest after a prestigious black community member, for example an educator, inventor, civil rights leader, or entrepreneur.

Slavery and the Caribbean

Age/Grade Level or Audience: Middle school and high school geography and history classes; civic and travel groups.

Description: Create a timeline of the history of slavery in the Caribbean.

Procedure: Have students search a variety of sources for information about the Caribbean slaves' experiences. Include these data:

◆ By 1635, French planters on Guadeloupe were staffing their sugar plantations with African workers.

◆ By 1640, Nevis's plantation owners were growing rich off the work of black slaves.

◆ By 1650, France had already established on Martinique a thriving sugar trade, replacing Carib laborers with African slaves.

◆ By 1667, African slaves staffed sugar plantations in Antigua.

◆ In 1680, English planters began importing slaves to provide labor for Virgin Gorda's sugarcane and cotton fields.

◆ As early as 1700, Guadeloupe, utilizing slave work gangs, established itself as a major sugar producer, particularly the Zévalos plantation near St. François.

◆ In 1726, British sovereignty on Grenada brought the need of more slaves to work the spice mills.

◆ In 1733, slaves chose to drown in the seas around Minna Neger Ghut, St. John, rather than live in bondage.

◆ In 1750, Antiguan slave laborers completed a building which now houses the Museum of Antigua and Barbuda. Also, sugar barons of Montserrat, St. Lucia, and St. Kitts were importing West African slaves to work the fields.

◆ In 1787, Will Blake used slave labor to build Wallblake, his plantation mansion, on Anguilla.

◆ During the 1790s, Charlotte Amalie, Virgin Islands, was a thriving slave market.

◆ In 1794, Victor Hugues routed the British from Guadeloupe, liberated the slaves, and sent their masters to the guillotine.

◆ By 1800, slaves marooned on Bonaire's Rode Pan occupied wretched thatched huts and harvested salt for their European masters. Jamaican maroons evolved their famous jerked meat as they hid in remote areas and smoked wild pigs for food.

◆ In 1804, a slave revolt in the Dominican Republic resulted in the creation of Haiti, the first black republic, on the western portion of the island.

◆ In 1807, the slave trade was abolished in Jamaica.

◆ By 1815, Napoleon had reestablished slavery in Guadeloupe.

♦ In 1816, British colonial overseers forced Anguilla into a confederation with St. Kitts and Nevis.

♦ In 1824, runaway slaves from the Freeman Sisters' underground railroad sailed aboard the *Turtle Dove* and foundered in Samaná, Dominican Republic, where they made a permanent black settlement.

♦ In 1833, after the demise of slavery in Virgin Gorda, whites abandoned the island to black slaves, who farmed and fished.

♦ In 1834, slavery was abolished on Montserrat.

♦ In 1838, Jamaican slaves were freed.

♦ In 1848, Alsatian Victor Schoelcher helped abolish slavery in Guadeloupe, as did the governor of St. Thomas.

♦ After the American Civil War ended in 1865, planters tried to resurrect the genteel antebellum lifestyle by importing slaves on the Turks and Caicos islands.

Budget: Under $25

Sources:

Beckles, Hilary, and Verene Shepherd, eds., *Caribbean Slave Society and Economy: A Student Reader*, New Press New York, 1994.

Fodor's Caribbean: A Complete Guide to 27 Island Destinations, Fodor's Travel Guides, 1997.

Miller, Randall, M., and John David Smith, *Dictionary of Afro-Americna Slavery*, Greenwood, 1997.

"Slavery," http//www.afu.org/~afu43300/slave.html.

Sullivan, George, *Slave Ship: The Story of the Henriette Marie*, Dutton Children's Books, 1994.

Thomas, Velma Maia, *Lest We Forget: The Passage from Africa to Slavery and Emancipation*, Crown, 1997.

Alternative Applications: Organize a discussion group to consider why freedom came to some Caribbean slaves decades before the Emancipation Proclamation released American slaves. Consider the following possibilities:

♦ Black populations outnumbered white populations.

♦ Black leaders were able to overwhelm small islands.

♦ European overseers governed ineffectively.

♦ Island militias were inadequate.

♦ The urge for freedom in one island quickly spread to others as sailors carried news from port to port.

Slavery Diorama

Age/Grade Level or Audience: High school or college history, sociology, and psychology classes.

Description: Create a diorama or multimedia display describing the African slave trade.

Procedure: Have students depict realistic views of the slave trade, for instance:

- ◆ slave capture in nets and placement in baracoons
- ◆ shackling in coffles for overland transportation to ports
- ◆ horizontal arrangement of slaves in the holds of slave ships
- ◆ shackling of neck, wrists, and ankles and confinement in stacked layers
- ◆ deck dancing to prevent death from inactivity
- ◆ drowning of troublemakers
- ◆ extermination of aged, deformed, or diseased slaves
- ◆ display at large auction centers, such as the Charleston slave market, where blacks were oiled, coated with tar, and branded before being offered for sale
- ◆ bidding, loading on transport wagons, and removal to plantations
- ◆ training in trades, such as blacksmithing, carpentry, cooking and house service, child care, laundry, sugar milling, grain binding, tobacco planting, cotton picking, logging, construction, road building, tanning, and livestock management and slaughter
- ◆ punishment by whipping, amputation, branding, castration, and hamstringing
- ◆ breeding slaves like prize livestock by selecting strong males to mate with young, vigorous females
- ◆ separation of families as children and elderly slaves were sold to enhance profitability.

Budget: $25-$50

Sources:

Fritz, Jean, *Harriet Beecher Stowe and the Beecher Preachers*, Putnam Publishing Group, 1994.

Gaines, Ernest, *The Autobiography of Miss Jane Pittman*, Bantam Books, 1971.

Haley, Alex, *Roots The Saga of an American Family*, Doubleday, 1976.

———, *Alex Haley's Queen*, Avon, 1994.

"The History of the British Abolition Movement," http//miavxl. muohio.edu/~ aronowml/History.HTM.

Hornsby, Alton, *Chronology of African-American History*, 2nd edition Gale, 1997.

Miller, Randall,, M., and John David Smith, *Dictionary of Afro-Americna Slavery*, Greenwood, 1997.

Morrison, Toni, *Beloved*, Knopf, 1987.

Thomas, Velma Maia, *Lest We Forget: The Passage from Africa to Slavery and Emancipation*, Crown, 1997.

Walker, Margaret, *Jubilee*, Bantam Books, 1984.

Alternative Applications: Have students study the psychological effects of dehumanization. Carry this study into the Reconstruction Era when newly emancipated blacks tried to cope with these challenges:

- responsibilities of caring for themselves and their families
- countering racist attacks
- learning to manage money
- learning trades and getting jobs
- locating housing
- managing health needs
- migrating from plantations and hostile communities
- obtaining an education
- reuniting scattered families

Draw conclusions about how Darwin's concept of survival of the fittest applies to the ex-slaves who were most successful at reshaping their lives to conform to white expectations.

  What If

Age/Grade Level or Audience: Elementary or middle school history classes.

Description: Organize a thinking game to expand student awareness of racism.

Procedure: Have students name specific changes in United States and world history that would have differed if major events had been altered. For example, what if:

- African explorers had discovered America
- Mennonite and Quaker activists had succeeded in ending slaving in the late seventeenth or early eighteenth century
- the first colonial slaves seized control of New England
- Creek, Choctaw, Seminole, and Cherokee joined with slaves to overpower European settlers in the Carolinas, Georgia, and Florida
- Frederick Douglass had become President of the United States or a cabinet member under Abraham Lincoln
- Nelson Mandela had been martyred
- trade embargoes had ended Apartheid
- black athletes had been barred from Olympic participation in 1992
- Clarence Thomas's nomination to the U.S. Supreme Court had been defeated
- Barbara Jordan had been elected Bill Clinton's vice president

◆ Jesse Jackson had led a United Nations team in eradicating famine in Somalia or Haiti

◆ Colin Powell had run for president against Bill Clinton

Budget: Under $25

Sources:

Indexes such as *Infotrac* and *Newsbank;* periodicals such as *Jet, Ebony, Emerge, Life, Time, Newsweek, U. S. News and World Report, Forbes,* and *Black Business;* Internet Sources, particularly "Africa Online."

Asante, Molefi K., and Mark T. Mattson, *Historical and Cultural Atlas of African Americans*, Macmillan, 1991.

Bache, Ellyn, *The Activist's Daughter*, Spinsters Ink, 1997.

Chiasson, Lloyd, ed., *The Press on Trial: Crimes and Trials as Media Events*, Greenwood, 1997.

Hill, Anita, *Speaking Truth to Power*, Dougleday, 1997.

Hornsby, Alton, *Chronology of African-American History*, 2nd edition Gale, 1997.

Alternative Applications: Assign students to compose a news item, tableau, interview, website, short story, play, poem, hymn, song, movie, or dance expressing a rewritten historical event from the black point of view. For instance:

◆ Anita Hill's testimony before the Senate committee

◆ composition of "Dixie"

◆ Denzel Washington's role in the film *Malcolm X*

◆ establishment of a holiday honoring Christopher Columbus

◆ Gettysburg Address

◆ Jefferson Memorial

◆ John Newton's composition of "Amazing Grace"

◆ Lincoln-Douglas debates

◆ O. J. Simpson trial

◆ unveiling of the Vietnam Memorial

◆ Virginia Reel

◆ William Styron's publication of *The Confessions of Nat Turner*

Journalism

Africa in the News

Age/Grade Level or Audience: Elementary and middle school language, writing, and journalism classes.

Description: Create an "Africa in the News" bulletin board.

Procedure: Have students comb the popular press for items about Africa. Group stories on similar topics, such as these:

- ♦ successful African sports figures, particularly tennis pro Mark Mathabane
- ♦ fighting the spread of AIDS, malaria, and Ebola
- ♦ hunger relief efforts in Somalia, Ethiopia, and Sahel
- ♦ Nelson Mandela's speeches and public appearances
- ♦ literature by Wole Soyinka, Chinua Achebe, Bessie Head, and other African artists
- ♦ musical performances and recordings by Angelique Kidjo, Aster Aweke, Cesaria Evora, Sijeba, Tarika, and Miriam Makeba
- ♦ Kwanzaa and other African celebrations, rituals, and holidays
- ♦ African cooking and recipes
- ♦ design, furniture, fashion, and hair styles
- ♦ new markets for African products, for instance, kinte cloth and wood carvings
- ♦ visits to Africa by world leaders and entertainers
- ♦ attempts to rescue endangered African species, such as the elephant and mountain gorilla

Have students compare articles from different sources.

Budget: Under $25

Sources:

Consult *Time, Newsweek, Ebony, Biography, Jet, Emerge, Wall Street Journal, U. S. News and World Report, Traveler, USA Today,* and other newspapers, magazines, and internet sources.

"Africa Online," http//www.africaonline.com.

"The African Diaspora," http//www.pitt.edu/~cedst10/.

"African Documents," http//www.halcyon.com/FWDP/africa.html.

"African Writers," http//www.africaonline.com/AfricaOnlinegriotstalk/writers/series. html.

"Blackseek," http//www.blackweek.com/index.html.

"Diaspora Art," http//www.diaspora.com/art.html.

Alternative Applications: Have students submit letters to the editor, political cartoons and comic strips, columns, obituaries, mock interviews, feature articles, fashion sketches, recipes, children's page quizzes and games, sports and concert schedules, calendars of events, and editorials in response to news from Africa or the Caribbean.

African Americans in the Media

Age/Grade Level or Audience: High school or community college journalism, language, sociology, economics, or history classes.

Description: Launch a study and discussion of the emerging role of African Americans in the popular press.

Procedure: Assign pairs of scholarly journals, magazines, and newspapers—one from the 1950s-1980s and a current issue. Useful choices of publications include these:

AMA Journal	*American Scholar*	*Atlanta Constitution*
Boston Globe	*Chicago Tribune*	*Christian Science Monitor*
English Journal	*Forbes*	*Lancet*
Life	*National Geographic*	*New York Times*
Newsweek	*People*	*Popular Science*
Reader's Digest	*Saturday Evening Post*	*Smithsonian*
Sports Illustrated	*Time*	*U. S. News and World Report*
Wall Street Journal	*Washington Post*	

Have students prepare a set of questions to guide their thinking:

◆ What percent of the total advertising space features black models?

◆ How many leading articles or news stories depict black Americans in a positive light?

◆ What subtle commentary does each publication make about race relations in the United States?

◆ Which articles refer specifically to black leaders and heroes, both male and female?

◆ How are black youths and women portrayed?

◆ What contributions by black artists, scientists, scholars, and entrepreneurs receive cover or lead stories?

◆ How thoroughly do graphs and statistics cover black opinions and data?

Budget: Under $25

Sources:

Chiasson, Lloyd, ed., *The Press on Trial Crimes and Trials as Media Events*, Greenwood, 1997.

Doob, Christopher B., *Racism: An American Cauldron*, 2nd edition, Addison-Wesley, 1995.

Gabriel, *Racism, Culture, Markets*, Routledge, 1994.

Gray, Herman, *Watching Race TV and the Struggle for the Sign of Blackness*, University of Minnesota Press, 1997.

Guillaumin, Colette, *Racism, Sexism, Power and Ideology*, Routledge, 1995.

Hester, Joseph P., *Encyclopedia of Values and Ethics*, ABC-Clio, 1996.

Senna, Carl, *The Black Press and the Struggle for Civil Rights*, Franklin Watts, 1993.

Solomos, John, and Les Back, *Racism in Society*, St. Martin, 1996.

Weinberg, Meyer, comp., *Racism in Contemporary America*, Greenwood, 1996.

Alternative Applications: Conduct an exhaustive investigation of a single day, week, or month from any period. Examine a broad spectrum of news and features about blacks in newspapers, magazines, scholarly journals, government publications, films, radio and television programs, billboards, mass mailings, and internet news and events from that period.

African Heroes

Age/Grade Level or Audience: Middle school and high school journalism, creative writing, communications, or language classes.

Description: Study great African leaders of the past and present.

Procedure: Provide a selection of resource material about African history. Have each students select a particular hero or heroine to describe for a school newspaper feature. Some good choices are Sundiata, Patrice Lamumba, Hathshepsut, Mansa Musa, Desmond Tutu, Nelson Mandela, Shaka, Oliver Tambo, Stephen Biko, Sunni Ali Ber, Askia Muhammad, Winnie Mandela, Affonso I, Idris Alaoma, and Makeda, the Queen of Sheba.

Budget: $25-$50

Sources:

"Africa Online," http//www.africaonline.com.

Curtin, P. D., *African History*, 2nd edition, Addison-Wesley, 1995.

"Dinizulu at the Time of His Trial," http//www.pinetreeweb.com/bpdinizulu3.htm.

Jackson, John G., *Introduction to African Civilizations*, Citadel Press,1994.

Kunjufu, Jawanza, *Lessons from History: A Celebration in Blackness,* African American Images, 1987.

Multicultural America (database), Gale Research, 1997.

"Nzinga Warrior Queen," http//www.netins.net80/showcase/alurir/nzinga.html.

Saari, Peggy, and Daniel B. Baker, *Explorers and Discoverers: From Alexander the Great to Sally Ride*, U•X•L/Gale, 1995.

"Shaka's Children: A History of the Zulu People," http//www.amazon.com/exec/ obidos.

Steedman, Scott, *Pockets: Ancient Egypt*, Dorling Kindersley, 1995.

"The Story of Sheba," http//www.cs.com/sheba/html/sheba/story.htm.

"Uthongathi," http//www.shaka.iafrica.com/~uthong/.

"Voice of Africa," http//www.scry.com/ayer/AFRO-AM/4401185.htm.

"World History Archives; History of Southern Africa in General," http//www.hartford-hwp.com/archives/37/index-1.html.

Alternative Applications: Have students prepare mock interviews with their heroes and heroines. Suggest the following questions:

- ♦ Were your parents leaders?
- ♦ How did you prepare to lead your people?
- ♦ What are the qualifications for your office?
- ♦ What was your hardest challenge?
- ♦ What have you learned from facing difficult tasks?
- ♦ What are your rewards?
- ♦ What has fame cost you?
- ♦ Has your family suffered as a result of your political role?
- ♦ What would bring you and your people the greatest happiness?

Videotape the students in costume as they ask questions and learn more about African history.

Backing Police Efforts

Age/Grade Level or Audience: Civic groups, human relations committees.

Description: Lead a campaign backing law enforcement efforts.

Procedure: Organize a meeting between local media leaders and city and county officials to consider poor neighborhoods and crime deterrent programs such as these:

♦ increased hiring of minority men and women

♦ intense training for inner-city crime prevention

♦ pairing black and white officers for community foot patrol

♦ opening police annexes in troubled communities where drug dealers or gangs threaten citizens

♦ stepping up surveillance to protect the elderly, handicapped, single women, and children

♦ aiding immigrants in a hostile or confusing environment

♦ increasing Neighborhood Watch programs

♦ establishing an ombudsman to mediate controversial issues, particularly complaints of police brutality

Budget: $25-$50

Sources:
Consult library sources and state and federal law enforcement agencies for suggestions and models.

Chiasson, Lloyd, ed., *The Press on Trial Crimes and Trials as Media Events*, Greenwood, 1997.

Cox, Steven M., and Jack D. Fitzgerald, *Police in Community Relations: Critical Issues*, Brown & Benchmark, 1991.

Hester, Joseph P., *Encyclopedia of Values and Ethics*, ABC-Clio, 1996.

———, *Law Enforcement Ethics*, ABC-Clio, 1997.

Kronenwetter, Michael, *Encyclopedia of Twentieth-Century American Social Issues*, ABC-Clio, 1997.

Police and Policing, Chelsea House, 1996.

Alternative Applications: Offer a reward or citation for Minority Police Officer of the Year or for individual heroic deeds performed by city officials, including fire fighters, social service workers, parks and recreation employees, and rescue departments.

Be an Angel

Age/Grade Level or Audience: Civic and church groups, volunteers, philanthropic societies, individuals.

Description: Create an angels program to support black history.

Procedure: Launch a media drive to support black history. Solicit donors, volunteers, and supporters to underwrite school, library, and museum programs by collecting and raising funds for additional books, magazine subscriptions, maps, globes, posters, videos, slides, databases, computers, software, CD-ROMs, field trips, and guest speakers.

Budget: $50-$75

Sources:
Emulate the volunteer and donor programs of arts councils, Friends of the Library, museum docents, and Angels of the Theater.

Alternative Applications: Help local educational groups and teachers' unions launch a drive to raise funds and collect donated materials, for instance sculpture, art prints, maps, books, magazines, computers and software, CD-ROMs, and photographs, for schools or libraries that lack adequate materials on black history.

Black Cartoonists

Age/Grade Level or Audience: High school or college journalism classes; local newspaper editors or columnists.

Description: Lead a discussion comparing the work of white and black cartoonists.

Procedure: Have participants compare cartoons by Charles Schulz, Kevin Siers, Doug Marlette, or Hanna-Barbera with the work of these black cartoonists:

- ◆ Elmer Simms Campbell's cartoons for *Esquire*
- ◆ Ray Billingsley's "Curtis"
- ◆ Robin Harris and Bruce Smith's animated "Bebe's Kids"
- ◆ Barbara Brandon's "Where I'm Coming From"
- ◆ Walt Carr and Gerald Dye's humor in *Ebony*
- ◆ Ron Bryant's political cartoons in *Emerge*

Comment on social values, satire, caricature, dialect, slang, and styles of humor from the black and white perspective.

Budget: Under $25

Sources:
"Bruce Smith Drawing on a Vision," *Essence*, September 1992, 54.
"Cartoonist Directory," http//pages.prodigy.com/inkwave/.
"Daryl Cagle's Professional Cartoonist Index," http//www.cagle.com.
Marschall, Richard, ed., *America's Great Cartoon Strip Artists, From the Yellow Kid to Peanuts*, Stewart Tabori and Chang, 1997.
"Old Time Comics," http//www.netexas.net/white/Comics.html.
"Philadelphia Online Choose Your Own Comics," http//interactive.phillynews.com/comics/.
"UExpress Marketplace," http//www.uexpress.com/catalog/.

Alternative Applications: Have a panel study the frequency with which black characters appear in single-cell cartoons, political cartoons, and cartoon strips, particularly "Peanuts," "Kathy," "Beetle Bailey," "The Wizard of Id," "Sally Forth," "Doonesbury," "For Better or Worse," "Garfield," "Shoe," "Big Jake," "Dagwood and Blondie," and "Kudzu." Comment on the need for positive images in black humor, especially in large metropolitan newspapers and magazines.

Black History Month Newspaper

Age/Grade Level or Audience: Middle school, high school, or community college journalism, communications, or language classes.

Description: Devote the February issue(s) of a regular school newsletter, newspaper, or magazine to black history.

Procedure: Have student reporters write features, news, and editorials on issues relating to black history, for instance:

- ◆ interviews with local civil rights leaders and activists
- ◆ features about little known American blacks, such as Sally Hemings, Crispus Attucks, Harriet Jacobs, Daniel Hale Williams, Edmonia Lewis, Gordon Parks, Edward W. Brooke, Sarah and Elizabeth Delany, Jean Baptiste Pointe du Sable, Dominique Dawes, Toussaint L'Ouverture, Althea Gibson, Denmark Vesey, Faye Wattleton, Reverend Richard Allen, Ida Wells-Barnett, Jan Matzeliger, Marcia Gillespie, Joseph Cinque, or Shirley Chisholm
- ◆ editorials concerning affirmative action programs or the need for greater diversity in the study of world history and American history

♦ cartoons and comic strips on black themes

♦ critiques of black films and literature

♦ quizzes, puzzles, or a question for the day about black inventors, entertainers, film makers, Olympic champions, politicians, educators, activists,
or sports figures.

Offer a prize to the first entrant who submits correct answers.

Budget: $25-$50

Sources:

African American History in the Press, 1851-1899, Gale, 1996.

"Black History," http//www.slip.net/~rigged/history.html.

"Black History Month Let's Get Started," http//www.netnoir.comspotlight/bhm/jbhm.
html.

Corbin, Raymond M., *1,999 Facts about Blacks: A Sourcebook of African-American
Achievement,* 2nd edition, Madison Books, 1997.

Dennis, Denise, *Black History for Beginners,* Highsmith, 1992.

Elliot, Jeffrey M., *Encyclopedia of African-American Politics,* ABC-Clio, 1997.

Hine, Darlene Clark, Elsa Barkley Brown, and Rosalyn Terborg-Penn, *Black Women
in America: An Historical Encyclopedia,* Carlson Publishing, 1993.

Mabunda, L. Mpho, ed., *The African American Almanac,* 7th edition, Gale, 1997.

Nelson, Rebecca, and Marie J. MacNee, eds., *The Olympic Factbook: A Spectator's
Guide to the Summer Games,* Visible Ink Press, 1996.

Saari, Peggy, and Daniel B. Baker, *Explorers and Discoverers: From Alexander the
Great to Sally Ride,* U•X•L/Gale, 1995.

Shapiro, William E., ed., *The Kingfisher Young People's Encyclopedia of the United
States.,* Larousse Kingfisher Chambers, 1994.

"This Person in Black History: Thurgood Marshall," http//www.ai.mitedu/~isbell/
Hfh/black/events_and_people/001.thurgood_marshall.

Alternative Applications: For schools that have no newspaper, the
February Black History Month Newsletter might be a useful beginning to encourage
journalism with a multicultural tone and outreach. A single broadside filled with
information about African American history should include positive information, for
instance a description of Kwanzaa activities, fads and fashions, and community projects such as Habitat for Humanity, Meals on Wheels, Mother's Day out programs, literacy campaigns, foster grandparents, Big Brother Big Sister, and voter registration.

 Black Media

Age/Grade Level or Audience: High school or college journalism
classes.

Description: Assign research on major African American publications.

Procedure: Have students select a key African American publication, such as these newspapers:

Amsterdam News	*Atlanta Daily World*
Baltimore Afro-American	*Berkeley Post Group*
Black Panther	*Black Progress Shopper News*
Buckeye Review	*Capitol Spotlight*
Charlotte Post	*Chicago Citizen*
Chicago Defender	*Chicago South Suburban News*
Forward Times	*Iowa Bystander*
Jamaica's Voice	*Los Angeles Sentinel*
Louisville Defender	*Manhattan Tribune*
Memphis Citizen	*Metro-Sentinel*
Michigan Chronicle	*Muhammad Speaks*
New Pittsburgh Courier	*New York Courier*
Norfolk Journal and Guide	*Seattle Afro-American Journal*
Philadelphia Tribune	*Southern Mediator Journal*
St. Louis Mirror	*Tampa Sentinel-Bulletin*
Tri-State Defender	

and these journals and magazines:

American Visions	*Black Academy Review*
Black Careers	*Black Enterprise*
Black Scholar	*Black Theatre*
Black World	*CLA Journal*
Crisis	*Ebony*
Ebony Jr.	*Emerge*
Essence	*Freedomways*
Harambee	*Homefront*
Jet	*Journal of Negro Education*
Journal of Negro History	*Journal of African Civilizations*
National Medical Association	*Journal Negro History Bulletin*
Negro Traveler and Conventioneer	*New Lady*
Phylon	*Sepia*
Star of Zion	

Trace the publication's beginning, philosophy, format, intended audience, and readership. If publication has ceased, note dates and reasons for its demise. Report findings in the form of a library paper, speech, or term paper, complete with outline, thesis statement, annotated text, and exhaustive bibliography.

Budget: Under $25

Sources:

African-American Book of Lists, Putna, 1997.

African-American Resource Guide, Barricade, 1994.

African-American Yellow Pages, Henry Holt & Co., 1996.

Encyclopedia of Associations, Gale, 1997.

Guy, Pat, "Magazines Seek Minorities," *USA Today*, October 22, 1992, 4B.

Katz, Bill, and Linda Sternberg Katz, *Magazines for Libraries*, Bowker, 1993.

Senna, Carl, *The Black Press and the Struggle for Civil Rights*, Franklin Watts, 1993.

Smith, Jessie Carney, ed., *Notable Black American Women*, Gale, 1992.

Alternative Applications: Compose a database of the addresses and producers of black broadcast media, such as Black Entertainment TV, Essence TV, Tony Brown's Journal, and Ebony/Jet Showcase, and publishing houses, notably Empak Enterprises, Third World Press, Afro-American Distributors, Africa World/Red Sea Press, Black Classic Press, Just Us Books, African American Images, Kitchen Table Women of Color Press, and New Day Press/KARAMU. Use the information to generate an oral report, which could be delivered along with tapes and critiques of the medium and capsule biographies of key figures.

 Covering Future News

Age/Grade Level or Audience: Middle school composition or journalism classes.

Description: Write a series of features on future black achievements.

Procedure: Assign individuals to cover black history for a special edition dated fifty years in the future. Include these projected accomplishments:

◆ the unveiling of a ship, plane, or satellite named for a black hero
◆ multiple gold medals won by black Olympic athletes
◆ Oscars, Grammys, Emmys, and Golden Globes given to black entertainers
◆ the first black president of the United States

Budget: Under $25

Sources:

Predict areas of national achievement in which black participants will make breakthroughs.

Alternative Applications: Have students role-play on-the-scene coverage of the first black person to win the United States presidency, invent a new fuel, cure a disease, or establish a multi-national corporation.

Editorials from the Black Perspective

Originators: Leatrice Pearson, teacher, Lenoir, North Carolina.

Age/Grade Level or Audience: High school or college journalism and communications classes; local newspaper editors or columnists.

Description: Provide prompts that will encourage strong editorial writing.

Procedure: Obtain responses to the following opinions:

♦ There are no bonds so strong as those which are formed by suffering together. (Harriet Jacobs)

♦ If one managed to change the curriculum in all the schools so that negroes learned more about themselves and their real contributions to this culture, you would be liberating not only negroes, you'd be liberating white people who know nothing about their history. (James Baldwin)

♦ It is scarcely possible to enumerate the many ways in which an ambitious colored young woman is prevented from being all that she might be in the higher directions of life in this country. (Fannie Barrier Williams)

♦ Slavery was the black gold that produced America's first wealth and power. Slavery was the breeding ground for the most contagious and contaminating monster of all time—racism. (from *Malcolm X The Man and His Times*)

♦ Every Black woman in America lives her life somewhere along a wide curve of ancient and unexpressed anger. (Audre Lorde)

♦ Hunger has no principles; it simply makes men, at worst, wretched, and at best, dangerous. (James Baldwin)

♦ When you kill the ancestor, you kill yourself. (Toni Morrison)

♦ A riot is the language of the unheard. (Martin Luther King, Jr.)

♦ Seeking no favors because of our color or patronage because of our needs, we knock at the bar of justice and ask for an equal chance. (Mary Church Terrell)

♦ A school system without parents at its foundation is just like a bucket with a hole in it. (Jesse Jackson)

♦ What the people want is very simple—they want an America as good as its promise. (Barbara Jordan)

Budget: Under $25

Sources:

Chiasson, Lloyd, ed., *The Press on Trial Crimes and Trials as Media Events*, Greenwood, 1997.

Delamotte, Eugenia, Natania Meeker, and Jean O'Barr, eds. *Women Imagine Change: A Global Anthology of Women's Resistance, 600 B. C. E. to Present*, Routledge, 1997.

Diggs, Anita Doren, ed., *Talking Drums: An African-American Quote Collection*, St. Martin's, 1995.

Maggio, Rosalie, *The New Beacon Book of Quotations by Women*, Beacon Press, 1996.

Mullane, Deirdre, *Words to Make My Dream Children Live: A Book of African American Quotations*, Anchor Books, 1995.

Riley, Dorothy Winbush, *My Soul Looks Back, 'Less I Forget': A Collection of Quotations by People of Color*, Harper Perennial, 1993.

Alternative Applications: Have students create political cartoons or comic strips to illustrate the following bits of wisdom:

- ◆ He who starts behind in the great race of life must forever remain behind or run faster than the man in front. (Dr. Benjamin E. Mays, former president of Morehouse College, Atlanta, Georgia)
- ◆ We've got to decide if it's going to be this generation or never. (Daisy Bates)
- ◆ Education is our passport to the future, for tomorrow belongs to the people who prepare for it today. (Malcolm X)
- ◆ There is no menial work, only menial spirits. (Mary McLeod Bethune)
- ◆ Anger is like the blade of a sword. Very difficult to hold without harming oneself. (Charles Johnson)
- ◆ Our children are what they are taught just as we are what we eat. (Marva Collins)
- ◆ The unprecedented recognition of black male talent in America . . . is perhaps the greatest story never told by the white media. (Leroy Keith)
- ◆ The culture I come from is just as rich as any Western European culture. (Kathleen Battle)
- ◆ We cannot get too comfortable in our houses. The hawk of intolerance still hovers in the air, and restless bigots still talk bigotry in their secret rooms. (Gordon Parks)
- ◆ To acknowledge our ancestors means we are aware that we did not make ourselves, that the line stretches all the way back, perhaps to God, or to gods. (Alice Walker)

The Editorials of Joel Chandler Harris and Henry W. Grady

Age/Grade Level or Audience: High school or college journalism classes; literary societies or book clubs.

Description: Organize a round table reading and discussion of Joel Chandler Harris's editorials.

Procedure: Read individual editorials from Joel Chandler Harris's writings for the *Atlanta Constitution*. Explain why he seeks to ameliorate black/white relations during Reconstruction. Discuss how each editorial might prove healing to Georgians during the bitter era following General William T. Sherman's march to the sea and General Robert E. Lee's surrender to General Ulysses S. Grant at Appomattox Courthouse. Also, invite analysis of Harris's short story "Free Joe and the Rest of the World," which contains this observation:

> The problems of one generation are the paradoxes of a succeeding one, particularly if war, or some such incident, intervenes to clarify the atmosphere and strengthen the understanding.

> Comment on complementary writings by Henry W. Grady, fellow writer for the *Atlanta Constitution*. Discuss segments of "The New South," Grady's speech to the New England Society, December 21, 1886, which contains this paragraph:

> But what of the Negro? Have we solved the problem he pre-sents or progressed in honor and equity toward solution? Let the record speak to the point. No section shows a more prosperous laboring population than the Negroes of the South, none in fuller sympathy with the employing and land-owning class. He shares our school fund, has the fullest protection of our laws and the friendship of our people.

Budget: Under $25

Sources:

Bickley, R. Bruce, Jr., *Joel Chandler Harris*, University of Georgia Press, 1987.

Davis, Harold E., *Henry Grady's New South Atlanta, a Brave and Beautiful City*, University of Alabama Press, 1990.

"Joel Chandler Harris," http//xroads.virginia.edu/~UG97/remus/jch.html.

Meredith, James, "A Challenge to Change," *Newsweek*, October 6, 1997, 18.

O'Shea, Brian, "Joel Chandler Harris Home Page,"http//www.ajc.com/staff/oshea/preswalk.htm.

Raspberry, William, "Why do Black Americans Feel Connected to Africa?," *Springfield Journal Register*, October 27, 1997, 7.

Alternative Applications: Contrast Joel Chandler Harris and Henry W. Grady's humanistic editorial commentaries with those of cartoonist Walt Carr, William Raspberry, columnist for the Washington *Post*, or Barbara Reynolds, columnist for *USA Today*. Note similarities in their style and attitudes toward racial harmony.

 Extra! Extra!

Age/Grade Level or Audience: High school and college history, writing, and journalism classes.

Description: Relate major American headlines to black Americans.

Procedure: Organize a round table or symposium to discuss how important events affected the lives of African Americans. Consider these examples:

- ◆ Battleship Maine Destroyed (February 16, 1898)–black soldiers join whites in fighting a common enemy during the Spanish-American War.
- ◆ German U-Boat Sunk During Attack on U.S. Transports (July 4, 1917)–emphasis on war in Europe drew attention away from the demand for civil rights.
- ◆ Negro Lynched in Mississippi (May 21, 1927)–increased pressure on law enforcement to provide equal protection to all citizens.
- ◆ Nazis Surrender (May 8, 1945)–returning black soldiers demand more freedom and opportunity.
- ◆ Russia Puts Man in Space (April 12, 1961)–the United States puts less emphasis on social programs.
- ◆ Martin Luther King Shot to Death (April 5, 1968)–black citizens lose a spokesman, but gain a hero and rallying points.
- ◆ "That's One Small Step for Man"–Armstrong (July 21, 1969)–civil rights leaders complain that the growing space program robs poor Americans of funds for education, health, and welfare.

Budget: Under $25

Sources:

African American History in the Press, 1851-1899, Gale, 1996.

Asante, Molefi K., *Historical and Cultural Atlas of African Americans*, Macmillan, 1991.

"Black History," http//www.slip.net/~rigged/history.html.

"Black History Month Let's Get Started," http//www.netnoir.com/spotlight/bhm/jbhm.html.

Corbin, Raymond M., *1,999 Facts about Blacks: A Sourcebook of African-American Achievement*, 2nd edition, Madison Books, 1997.

Grun, Bernard, *The Timetables of History: A Horizontal Linkage of People and Events*, Simon & Schuster, 1991.

Hine, Darlene Clark, Elsa Barkley Brown, and Rosalyn Terborg-Penn, *Black Women in America: An Historical Encyclopedia,* Carlson Publishing, 1993.

Hornsby, Alton, *Chronology of African-American History*, 2nd edition Gale, 1997.

Mabunda, L. Mpho, ed., *The African American Almanac*, 7th edition, Gale, 1997.

Straub, Deborah Gillan, ed., *African American Voices*, U•X•L/Gale, 1996.

Alternative Applications: Have students project future issues that will affect black Americans and other citizens, such as the following:

- ◆ pharmaceutical discoveries relating to the treatment of AIDS and other sexually transmitted diseases, drug addiction, alcoholism, cancer, sickle cell anemia, cystic fibrosis, tuberculosis, diabetes, high blood pressure, and heart disease

◆ legislation affecting the availability of handguns

◆ Justice Department investigations of police brutality and interference in suspects' civil rights

◆ international strategies to end female genital mutilation

◆ laws to end domestic violence and child abuse and neglect

◆ Olympic records, award-winning films, and black-centered entertainment channels

◆ widespread Internet availability in public schools and libraries

◆ an increase in the birth rate of all non-white citizens

◆ an increase in racially mixed marriages

◆ an increase in the immigration of non-whites to the United States

◆ greater representation of blacks in law-making bodies and among mayors, sheriffs, the FBI, highway patrols, and local civic bureaus

Faces of Racial Progress

Age/Grade Level or Audience: Elementary or middle school journalism or media project.

Description: Post a display of pioneers in race relations.

Procedure: Post a series of photos and brief captions honoring leaders in race relations. Note the contributions of Jesse Jackson, Joycelyn Elders, Lyndon Baines Johnson, Clara Hale, Bill Cosby, Ida Wells-Barnett, Colin Powell, Barbara Jordan, Jackie Robinson, Diahann Carroll, Spike Lee, Whoopi Goldberg, and Louis Armstrong. Arrange the display on a folding screen or room divider, photo album, poster, or bulletin board or scan onto a website.

Budget: Under $25

Sources:
Online news sources and newsmagazines, particularly *Jet, Emerge, Essence, Ebony, Time, Newsweek, U. S. News and World Report, Sport Illustrated, People,* and *Biography.*

Alternative Applications: Arrange a series of pictures that form a photo essay on a life or event, for example:

◆ Colin Powell's contribution to the Persian Gulf War

◆ Zora Neale Hurston and the Harlem Renaissance

♦ Tiger Woods and American sports

♦ Clara Hale and Lorraine Hale's method of aiding critically ill or neglected children

♦ Carl Lewis and Carol Lewis at the Olympic Games

♦ Lena Horne or Gregory Hines on Broadway or in film

♦ Maya Angelou touring Ghana

♦ Ralph Ellison and black literature

♦ Mary Carter Smith or Rex Ellis and black storytelling

♦ Guion Bluford or Mae Jemison and the space program

Choose a theme. Provide sidebars to contain information and statistics, for example, the number of awards Carol Lewis has won, Ralph Ellison's posthumous publications, and the titles of Mary Carter Smith's stories.

A Future in the Media

Age/Grade Level or Audience: High school and college cinema, journalism, art, and management students; camera clubs.

Description: Circulate information encouraging young journalists, cinematographers, and directors.

Procedure: Spread information about opportunities in the media. Include the following scholarship and fellowships:

♦ W. Eugene Smith Memorial Fund Grand in Humanistic Photography
e/o International Center of Photography
1130 Fifth Avenue
New York, New York, 10128

♦ Ed Bradley Scholarship
1000 Connecticut Avenue NW, Suite 615
Washington, D. C. 20036
phone 202-467-5212

♦ James Lawrence Fly Scholarship
1771 N. Street NW
Washington, D. C. 20036
phone 202-429-5354

♦ Shane Media Scholarship
1771 N Street NW
Washington, D. C. 20035
phone 202-429-5354

♦ WTOL-TV Broadcast and Communications Scholarship
University of Toledo
Financial Aid Office
Toledo, Ohio 43606
phone 419-537-2056

Budget: Under $25

Sources:

"A-Infos Radio Project," http//www.tao.ca/ainfo/radio/0235.html.

Bucher, Douglas, intro., *Scholarships 1997-1998*, Simon & Schuster 1996.

Ekeler, William J., ed., *The Black Student's Guide to High School Success*, Greenwood Press, 1997.

"National Scholarships in Broadcasting," http//www.usn.edu/~bea/descrip.html.

"Scholarships and Grants—AIME," http//ideanet.doe.state.in.us/aime/scholgra.

"Scholarships, Grants and Loans," http//www.birchwood.com/.

Schwartz, John, ed., *College Scholarships and Financial Aid*, 6th edition, Macmillan, 1995.

"Virtual Library Journalism," http//www.cais.com/makulow/vlj.html.

Alternative Applications: Invite media specialists to address journalism and media classes. Promote small group discussion with experts on how minority students should prepare for a career in film, television news, sportscasting, weather, fashion commentary, cartooning, advertising, editing, website creation, and electronic news.

Guest Columnist

Age/Grade Level or Audience: All ages.

Description: Establish a guest column written by a local black leader.

Procedure: Invite a leader of the black community to write a guest column for the local newspaper or city website or deliver it on radio or television. Suggest a number of topics:

♦ the purpose of celebrating black history and black holidays
♦ building consensus among citizen groups
♦ methods of promoting racial harmony
♦ the role of cultural diversity in community life
♦ the future of minorities in the community

> ◆ support for black political candidates and issues
> ◆ minority youth achievement
> ◆ black history as a year-round project
> ◆ strengths of the black family
> ◆ black contributions to the area

Distribute the material on brochures at street fairs, through the Chamber of Commerce, via e-mail, on websites, or as inserts to the daily newspaper. Include a calendar of events for Black History Month.

Budget: Under $25

Sources:

Local newspapers, newsletters, media news programs, in-house business publications, or websites.

Black Community, 3rd edition, Addison-Wesley, 1991.

Black Community Crusade and Covenant for Protecting Children, Children's Defense, 1995.

Dandy, Evelyn B., *Black Communications: Breaking Down the Barriers,* African American Images, 1992.

Kretzmann, John P, and John L. McKnight, *Building Communities from the Inside Out: A Path Toward Finding and Mobilizing a Community's Assets,* ACTA Publications, 1993.

Ravitch, Diane, *The American Reader: Words That Moved a Nation,* HarperCollins, 1990.

Sandoz, Ellis, *Political Sermons of the American Founding Era,* Liberty Press, 1991.

Alternative Applications: Have local media reprint speeches by strong black leaders, particularly Medgar Evers, Marcia Gillespie, Martin Luther King, Jr., Sojourner Truth, Frederick Douglass, Faye Wattleton, Jesse Jackson, Ida Wells-Barnett, Thurgood Marshall, Maya Angelou, Carole Moseley Braun, Louis Farrakhan, Fannie Lou Hamer, Ralph Abernathy, Myrlie Evers, Colin Powell, or Barbara Jordan. Print these speeches or excerpts from them in a Black History Month feature. Expand this program to appear in church bulletins, civic newsletters, or PTA publications.

 Honoring the Past

Age/Grade Level or Audience: All ages.

Description: Establish a "Five, Ten, and Twenty-Five Years Ago in the Black Community" section in the newspaper.

Procedure: During Black History Month, feature events and photographs of individuals, businesses, church, school, and social activities, and other evidence of community contributions in a special column that looks to the past. Update information with stories about famous people and how their lives have been affected by the events, for example, war heroes or scholarship winners who have returned to serve in public office or to establish local professional practices or businesses.

Budget: $25-$50

Sources:

Newspaper and Internet archives; library, museum, and private collections; diaries, clipping files, and photo albums; census reports.

"African American History," http//www.msstate.edu/Archives/History/USA/Afro-Amer/ afro.html.

African American History in the Press, 1851-1899, Gale, 1996.

"Black History," http//www.slip.net/~rigged/history.html.

"Black History Month Let's Get Started," http//www.netnoir.com/spotlight/bhm/jbhm. html.

Corbin, Raymond M., *1,999 Facts about Blacks A Sourcebook of African-American Achievement*, 2nd edition, Madison Books, 1997.

"The Faces of Science: African Americans in the Sciences," http//www.lib.lsu.edu/lib/ chem/display/faces.html.

Gates, Henry Louis, ed., *Chronology of African-American History from 1445-1980*, Amistad Press, 1993.

Hine, Darlene Clark, Elsa Barkley Brown, and Rosalyn Terborg-Penn, *Black Women in America: An Historical Encyclopedia,* Carlson Publishing, 1993.

Hornsby, Alton, *Chronology of African-American History*, 2nd edition Gale, 1997.

Mabunda, L. Mpho, ed., *The African American Almanac*, 7th edition, Gale, 1997.

Nelson, Rebecca, and Marie J. MacNee, eds., *The Olympic Factbook: A Spectator's Guide to the Summer Games*, Visible Ink Press, 1996.

Saari, Peggy, and Daniel B. Baker, *Explorers and Discoverers: From Alexander the Great to Sally Ride*, U•X•L/Gale, 1995.

Trager, James, *The People's Chronology*, revised edition, Henry Holt & Co., 1996.

Alternative Applications: Compose a demographic study of local citizens. Include a study of population by race, personal income, home ownership, literacy, leadership roles, black-owned businesses and newspapers, churches and synagogues, public and private schools, segregated country clubs and social organizations, street gangs, and crime. Have newspapers, radio, and television editors and website managers prepare feature articles stressing the growth and achievement of the black community, including the following data:

◆ number of churches and church attendance
◆ increase in educational attainment through literacy programs
◆ number and diversity of the local work force

♦ professional awards and attainments

♦ architectural refinements in black neighborhoods

♦ recreational facilities and opportunities for youth

♦ anti-crime, domestic violence, wellness, and drug awareness programs

♦ support for families, including outreach to single mothers

♦ philanthropic and volunteer organizations, particularly soup kitchens, halfway houses, and shelters for the homeless, runaway children, AIDS victims, or battered women

Publish your findings during Black History Month by newspaper, television, or radio. Invite reader write-in or call-in.

Lead Story Roundup

Age/Grade Level or Audience: Middle school or high school English, history, communications, or journalism classes.

Description: Have students create headlines about civil rights.

Procedure: Provide students with information about famous black Americans. Then assign individuals or groups to compose twenty-five headlines about famous events in African American history along with the date that each occurred. Follow these models:

♦ Diego el Negro sails with Columbus aboard the *Capitana* (July, 1502).

♦ Maryland passes the first anti-miscegenation law (September 20, 1664).

♦ The Declaration of Independence is approved after the deletion of an anti-slavery clause (July 4, 1776).

♦ William Lloyd Garrison begins publishing *The Liberator* (January 1, 1831).

♦ Harried Tubman escapes slavery in Maryland (July 1849).

♦ James Stone becomes the first black to fight for the Union Army (August 23, 1861).

♦ Richard T. Greener becomes the first black to graduate from Harvard (November 1873).

♦ Harry T. Burleigh wins the Spingarn Medal for creative music (November 1917).

♦ Dr. Percy Julian joins Glidden staff (1936).

♦ Dr. Ruth Love is named superintendent of Chicago schools (March 1981).

♦ Dusable Museum of African-American History opens in Chicago (1972).

♦ Andy Razaf enters the Songwriters Hall of Fame (May 1972).

♦ Fannie Lou Hamer registers to vote (December, 1962).

♦ Thousands march in Selma (1955).

♦ Muhammad Ali takes the heavyweight boxing championship from George Formen in Kinshasa, Zaire (October 26, 1974).

◆ Loretta Glickman elected mayor of Pasadena (May 6, 1982).

◆ Max Robinson, American network television's first black anchor, dies of AIDS (December 20, 1988).

◆ Nelson Mandela tours the United States (June 20-30, 1990).

◆ Whoopi Goldberg stars in *Sister Act* and *Sarafina!* (1992).

◆ Daryl Jones is nominated as secretary of the Air Force (1997).

Budget: Under $25

Sources:

"African American History," http//www.msstate.edu/Archives/History/USA/Afro-Amer/afro.html.

African American History in the Press, 1851-1899, Gale, 1996.

"Black History," http//www.slip.net/~rigged/history.html.

"Black History Month: Let's Get Started," http//www.netnoir.com/spotlight/bhm/jbhm.html.

Corbin, Raymond M., *1,999 Facts about Blacks: A Sourcebook of African-American Achievement,* 2nd edition, Madison Books, 1997.

"The Faces of Science: African Americans in the Sciences," http//www.lib.lsu.edu/lib/chem/display/faces.html.

Hine, Darlene Clark, Elsa Barkley Brown, and Rosalyn Terborg-Penn, *Black Women in America: An Historical Encyclopedia,* Carlson Publishing, 1993.

Hornsby, Alton, *Chronology of African-American History,* 2nd edition Gale, 1997.

Nelson, Rebecca, and Marie J. MacNee, eds., *The Olympic Factbook: A Spectator's Guide to the Summer Games,* Visible Ink Press, 1996.

Saari, Peggy, and Daniel B. Baker, *Explorers and Discoverers: From Alexander the Great to Sally Ride,* U•X•L/Gale, 1995.

Thomas, Evan, and Gregory L. Vistica, "A Question of Respect," *Newsweek,* October 27, 1997, 32-33.

Trager, James, *The People's Chronology,* revised edition, Henry Holt, 1996.

Alternative Applications: Organize an overview of African American history through a series of banner headlines for front page leads. For instance:

♦ First Slaves Auctioned in the Western Hemisphere
♦ Plantation System Thrives on Cheap Slave Labor
♦ Virginia Slave Revolts Signal Unrest
♦ Underground Railroad Leads Captives to Freedom in Canada
♦ President Lincoln Signs Emancipation Proclamation
♦ Hard Times for Newly Freed Blacks
♦ Rise of Klan Activity Rids the Midwest of Many Black Immigrants
♦ West Offers Opportunities for Former Slaves
♦ Rising American Black Middle Class Nets Higher Standard of Living
♦ Shirley Chisholm Runs for United States Presidency
♦ Jesse Jackson Organizes Rainbow Coalition

◆ Colin Powell Rejects Presidential Bids from Either Party

 Race and Controversy

Age/Grade Level or Audience: College civics and journalism classes; letters to the editor; public debate.

Description: Study public reaction to controversial or pornographic references in works by black artists and entertainers during the late twentieth century.

Procedure: Determine the limits on freedom of speech, which is guaranteed in the First Amendment of the Bill of Rights. Examine the outcry over expressions by evangelists, artists, photographers, homosexuals, feminists, rock and rap performers, comedians, radio talk shows, Internet users, or film stars, particularly Arsenio Hall's television show, comedy routines by Eddie Murphy and Richard Pryor, Malcolm X's speeches, Louis Farrakhan's recruitment of followers, Sister Souljah's public interviews, Eldridge Cleaver's prison memoir *Soul on Ice,* poetry by Nikki Giovanni and Sonia Sanchez, RuPaul's stage and talk show appearances, Joycelyn Elders's public comments about masturbation, and Ice-T's "Cop Killer." Compare your definitions of freedom with those of the Religious Right, Citizens for the American Way, Citizens for Decency, Dan Quayle's public statements about gay rights, and media crusades led by Tipper Gore and Anita Bryant. Debate the use of these curbs on individual freedom:

♦ movie and television ratings
♦ television and Internet filters
♦ wrappers on sexually explicit magazines and newspapers
♦ censorship of public and school libraries
♦ warning labels on records, tapes, and CDs that are sold to minors
♦ crusades against liberal textbooks

Budget: $25-$50

Sources:
"The American Civil Liberties Union," http//www.aclu.org.
"The Blue Ribbon Campaign for Online Free Speech," http//www.eff.org/blueribbon.html.
Chiasson, Lloyd, ed., *The Press on Trial Crimes and Trials as Media Events,* Greenwood, 1997.
"Freedom of Expression Links," http//insight.mcmaster.ca/org/exc/pages/chronicle/censor.html.
Hester, Joseph P., *Encyclopedia of Values and Ethics,* ABC-Clio, 1996.
———, *Law Enforcement Ethics,* ABC-Clio, 1997.
"Internet Censorship and Freedom of Expression," http//www.surfwatch.com/surfwatch/censorship.html.

Kronenwetter, Michael, *Encyclopedia of Twentieth-Century American Social Issues*, ABC-Clio, 1997.

Rooney, Terrie, *Contemporary Newsmakers*, Gale Research.

Sherrow, Victoria, *Censorship in Schools*, Enslow Publications, 1996.

Stay, Byron, ed., *Censorship*, Greenhaven, 1996.

"VTW Free Speech Page," http//www.vtw.org/speech.

Alternative Applications: Organize a local panel to suggest ways in which parents can protect children from controversy without violating the rights of others to express dissent. Consider these options:

♦ television and Internet filters

♦ limiting Internet use to public or high traffic areas

♦ late-night scheduling of violent television programs

♦ rating and labeling systems for television, movies, and recorded music

♦ pre-approval of T-shirts with explicit messages

♦ school and public dress codes

Understanding the News

Age/Grade Level or Audience: Elementary school current events class.

Description: Explain how to analyze news from the black perspective.

Procedure: Summarize daily news as it applies to black history. Include these categories military deployment, nomination of a diplomat or Supreme Court justice, sports championships, proposed candidates for national offices, FBI crime reports, legislative changes in welfare and affirmative action, fads and fashions, and controversial television programs and film.

Budget: Under $25

Sources:

Internet news; newspapers and news magazines, including *Time, Newsweek, U. S. News and World Report, USA Today, Jet, Ebony, Essence, Emerge,* and *Biography*.

Chiasson, Lloyd, ed., *The Press on Trial Crimes and Trials as Media Events*, Greenwood, 1997.

Alternative Applications: Have students brainstorm a list of the best ways for citizens to read news about blacks. Include national weeklies, black sports and news channels, Internet sources, separate pages in the *Wall Street Journal* or *USA Today*, separate listings of bestsellers and music by blacks, and reviews of movies that reflect black life and history.

Volunteers Without Borders

Age/Grade Level or Audience: All ages.

Description: Compose a newspaper feature or guest column on *Medicins sans Frontiers* or *Aviation sans Frontiers.*

Procedure: Research in online, newspaper, or magazine articles the history and purpose of Doctors Without Borders or Pilots Without Borders, both Belgian-based medical relief and evacuation agencies. Compose a journalistic feature or guest column on this European volunteer medical group's work in Africa.

Budget: Under $25

Sources:
"Crisis in Central Africa," http//www.interaction.org/zrcrisis.html.
"Global Hunger and Food Security after the World Food Summit," http//oneworld.
  org/odi/briefing/1_97.html.
"Human Rights," http//www.igc.org80/igc/issues/hr/index.html.
"Robert E. Ford's Bookmarks," http//www.geog.utah.edu/~hdgcsg/fordmark.html.
"World Food Programme," http//wfp.org/vamhome.html.

Alternative Applications: Compose editorials to encourage local support for relief efforts by publishing names, addresses, and photos of agencies that assist the poor, sick, illiterate, neglected, endangered, or oppressed. Include these:

American Civil Liberties Union	Amnesty International
Big Brothers of America	Big Sisters of America
Christian Children's Fund	Habitat for Humanity
Junior Police	Meals on Wheels
Quilt Project	Reading Is Fundamental
Salvation Army	Save the Children
UNICEF	United Negro College Fund

Who's Writing News

Age/Grade Level or Audience: Elementary and middle school writing classes.

Description: Create an in-house newsletter.

Procedure: During Black History Month, have students create a school newsletter featuring news of the day. Include in each issue a thumbnail sketch of a noted black journalist, editor, cartoonist, cinema director, or sportscaster, especially Walt Carr, Ida Wells-Barnett, Ed Bradley, Spike Lee, Alice Dunnigan, Bernard Shaw, Cheryl Miller, Mal Goode, Bryant Gumbel, Barbara Brandon, Stephanie Stokes Oliver, Ahmad Rashad, William Raspberry, Barbara Reynolds, or Venice Tipton Spraggs.

Budget: $50-$75

Sources:
Chiasson, Lloyd, ed., *The Press on Trial Crimes and Trials as Media Events*, Greenwood, 1997.
Phelps, Shirelle, ed., Who's Who among Black Americans, 108th edition, Gale, 1997.
Phelps, Shirelle, ed., *Contemporary Black Biography*, Gale, various volumes.
Smith, Jessie Carney, ed., *Notable Black American Women*, Gale, 1992.

Alternative Applications: Collect thumbnail sketches of black journalists, editors, cartoonists, movie directors, or sportscasters in a scrapbook or database. Next to each, cite an original essay, editorial, article, or familiar quotation.

You Are There

Age/Grade Level or Audience: High school journalism, drama, or American history classes.

Description: Organize an on-the-spot interview with participants at major events of African American history.

Procedure: Assign students to work in pairs or small groups to role-play and interview famous black Americans at the scene of some major occurrence. For example:

- ◆ Rosa Parks's famous bus ride
- ◆ the promotion of Colin Powell to general
- ◆ the publication of Lewis Latimer's textbook on electric lighting systems
- ◆ a performance by Odetta
- ◆ Daisy Bates's encouragement of nine students to integrate Central High in Little Rock, Arkansas
- ◆ Quincy Jones's honors at the 24th Annual Grammy Awards in Los Angeles
- ◆ Hank Aaron's achievement of the nickname "Home Run King"
- ◆ Diahann Carroll's TV series "Julia"

◆ Guion Bluford's medical experiments in outer space
◆ Fanny Jackson Coppin's leadership of the Black Women's Rights Movement
◆ Spike Lee's film *Malcolm X*
◆ Carol Moseley Braun's election to the U.S. Senate.

Play the tape over local radio stations in celebration of Black History Month.

Budget: $25-$50

Sources:

"African American History," http//www.msstate.edu/ArchivesHistory/USA/Afro-Amer/afro.html.

African American History in the Press, 1851-1899, Gale, 1996.

"Black History," http//www.slip.net/~rigged/history.html.

"Black History Month: Let's Get Started," http//www.netnoir.comspotlight/bhm/jbhm.html.

Corbin, Raymond M., *1,999 Facts about Blacks: A Sourcebook of African-American Achievement*, 2nd edition, Madison Books, 1997.

"The Faces of Science: African Americans in the Sciences," http//www.lib.lsu.edu/lib/chem/display/faces.html.

Gates, Henry Louis, ed., *Chronology of African-American History from 1445-1980*, Amistad Press, 1993.

Hine, Darlene Clark, Elsa Barkley Brown, and Rosalyn Terborg-Penn, *Black Women in America: An Historical Encyclopedia,* Carlson Publishing, 1993.

Hornsby, Alton, *Chronology of African-American History*, 2nd edition Gale,1997.

Nelson, Rebecca, and Marie J. MacNee, eds., *The Olympic Factbook: A Spectator's Guide to the Summer Games*, Visible Ink Press, 1996.

Saari, Peggy, and Daniel B. Baker, *Explorers and Discoverers: From Alexander the Great to Sally Ride*, U•X•L/Gale, 1995.

Trager, James, *The People's Chronology*, revised edition, Henry Holt, 1996.

Alternative Applications: Form a panel of students impersonating famous black Americans to discuss one of these crucial topics:

◆ improvement of life in the inner city
◆ low-income housing
◆ daycare for single parents
◆ formation of black-owned businesses
◆ films by and about blacks
◆ abortion rights for poor women
◆ community literacy
◆ voter registration programs
◆ equal rights in the military
◆ drugs, alcohol, gang violence, AIDS, and other killers of the young
◆ issues facing your own community
◆ black history as an ongoing focus of school curricula

Language

Afrocentrism

Age/Grade Level or Audience: All ages.

Description: Invite a guest speaker or panel to present a program on Afrocentrism.

Procedure: Have participants explain the meaning and purpose of Afrocentrism and its effect on black people. Include information about these topics:

- ◆ Black Muslims
- ◆ Afrocentric schools and curricula
- ◆ reclaiming the black culture from Eurocentrism
- ◆ reducing family stress and street violence
- ◆ identifying and conquering self-destructive behavior, particularly drug dependence, alcoholism, and smoking
- ◆ strengthening the black family
- ◆ creating a stronger self-image in young people
- ◆ Afrocentrism as a cohesion mechanism
- ◆ Afrocentrism as a means of combatting ghetto mentality
- ◆ cultivating safer, more enjoyable cities.

Conclude with handouts, press releases, and brochures to be distributed through black history classes, museums, libraries, Scout troops, police youth clubs, churches, and the Chamber of Commerce.

Budget: $50-$75

Sources:
Adler, Jerry, "African Dreams," *Newsweek*, September 23, 1991, 43-45.

"Altculture: Afrocentrism," http://www.pathfinder.com/altculture/aentries/a/afrocentrism.html.

The Ancient Kingdoms of Africa, Whole World Language Catalog.

Bray, Rosemary, "Reclaiming Our Culture," *Essence,* December 1990, 84-87.

"Building Bridges to Afrocentrism," http://www.sas.upenn.edu/African_Studies/Articles_Gen/afrocen.

"Fallacies of Afrocentrism," http://www.chss.montclair.edu/ english/furr/afrocent.html.

Lefkowitz, Mary, *Not Out of Africa: How Afrocentrism Became an Excuse to Teach Myth,* Basic Books, 1996.

Powers, Jamilla, and Tyson Gibbs, *Afro-Centric Guide to Reflections, Affirmations, Meditations, and Prayers,* Jamilla Powers, 1994.

Sanders, Cheryl J., ed., *Living the Intersection: Womanism and Afrocentrism in Theology,* Fortress Press, 1995.

Alternative Applications: List other ethnic groups who have been slighted by Eurocentric American history. For example, include Native Americans, Hispanics, and Asian Americans, particularly the victims of Japanese internment camps, which imprisoned blameless American citizens during much of World War II.

Apartheid

Age/Grade Level or Audience: High school or college sociology or world civilization classes; religious groups; civic organizations.

Description: Define and explain Apartheid.

Procedure: Provide participants with background information on apartheid, South Africa's formal segregation of races, including its origins, purpose, and social and political ramifications Provide handouts of the following timeline:

- ◆ As early as 1652, white settlers of South Africa supported a system of apartness from black natives.
- ◆ "Apartheid" became the Afrikaner National Party slogan in the 1940s.
- ◆ In 1948, separation of races intensified as Nationalists gained power.
- ◆ In 1956, Miriam Makeba sang in the anti-Apartheid documentary *Come Back Africa.*
- ◆ In 1961, because of United Nations condemnation, South Africa withdrew from the English Commonwealth.
- ◆ During the 1970s, public condemnation of Apartheid-style racism brought boycotts and trade embargos from many nations.

♦ In 1990 Miriam Makeba and Nelson Mandela were allowed to return to South Africa.

♦ On February 11, 1990, Nelson Mandela gained his freedom after 27 years of imprisonment.

♦ In February 1991, President De Klerk announced an end to racial segregation.

♦ In June 1991, the Race Registration law was repealed.

♦ In 1992, Nelson Mandela toured the United States to raise funds to fight Apartheid.

♦ In 1993, all factions began planning a new constitution.

♦ In 1994, Nelson Mandela was elected president of South Africa.

Read aloud from books and magazine articles describing rigid laws affecting land ownership, inheritance, schools, public transportation, government representation, medical care, and marriage. Lead a discussion of the moral implications of a political and social system that allowed a white minority to tyrannize a black majority.

Budget: Under $25

Sources:

Films *Cry Freedom* (1987), *The Power of One (1991),* and *Sarafina! (1992*).

Dobroey, Steven, *South Africa: To the Sources of Apartheid,* University Press of America, 1989.

"The History of Apartheid in South Africa," http://xenon.stanford.edu/~cale/cs201/apartheid.hiss.html.

"Instruments of Apartheid," http://www.unp.ac.za/UNPDepartments/politics/price4.htm.

Mandela, Nelson, *The Long Walk to Freedom: The Autobiography of Nelson Mandela,* Little, Brown, 1994.

Mathabane, Mark, *Kaffir Boy,* Macmillan Plume Books, 1986.

Mostert, Noel, *Frontiers: The Epic South Africa's Creation and the Tragedy of the Xhosa People,* Knopf, 1992.

"Nelson Mandela's Address to the Rally in Cape Town on His Release from Prison," http://www.anc.org.za/ancdocs/speeches/release.html.

Ndibe, Okey, "South Africa's Circle of Violence," *Emerge,* December 1992, 15-16.

Pheko, Motsoko, *Apartheid: The Story of a Dispossessed People,* Pheko & Assocs., 1994.

Seavers, Corbin, *Apartheid: The Untold Story,* United Brothers and Sisters, 1997.

Woods, Donald, *Apartheid: A Graphic Guide,* Henry Holt & Co, 1988.

———, *Biko,* Henry Holt & Co, 1991.

Alternative Applications: Turn this study into a public forum by inviting public officials and business leaders to debate the issues that questioned trade with South Africa. Include the following topics:

♦ Were liberal nations morally obligated to boycott trade with South Africa?

♦ Did the cessation of trade do more harm than good to the black cause?

♦ Were white South African leaders moving toward an end to racism?

♦ How could bloodshed have been stopped during the transition years?

♦ What should the United States have done to alleviate racism in Soweto, Alexandra, and other slums of Johannesburg, South Africa?

♦ What could outside agencies have done to promote better living conditions for black citizens of South Africa?

♦ Why was Steven Biko martyred?

♦ How did his martyrdom aid freedom fighters?

♦ What does Mark Mathabane's example prove about ambition and determination?

Black English

Age/Grade Level or Audience: High school and college language classes

Description: Study the emergence of Ebonics, a separate branch of English spoken by black people.

Procedure: Lead students in a group study of black linguistic patterns, such as the use of the verb "to be," idioms such as "sweet mouth," "bloods," "bro'," "home-boy," "po' white trash," "soul food," and "juke and jive," and characteristic pronunciations, particularly "ahnt" for "aunt" and "ax" for "ask."

♦ Outline the evolution of ebonics, a lingual subset hybridized from archaic white speech, pidgin English, and creole language.

♦ Select examples of black English from writings by authors Margaret Walker, Langston Hughes, Alice Walker, Zora Neale Hurston, Mark Twain, Gwendolyn Brooks, Harriet Beecher Stowe, William Armstrong, Toni Morrison, Alfred Uhry, Sonya Sanchez, Alice Childress, Walter Dean Myers, Harriet Jacobs, Edgar Allan Poe, Maya Angelou, and Ernest Gaines. For instance, list on a chalkboard the black English usage in Frederick Douglass's poem "Jubilee-Beaters":

We raise de wheat
Dey gib us de corn;
We bake de bread
Dey gib us de cruss;
We sif de meal
Dey gib us de huss;
We peel de meat
Dey gib us de skin,

And dat's de way
Dey takes us in.
We skim de pot
Dey gib us de liquor
And say dat's good enough for nigger.
Walk over! Walk over!
Tom butter and de fat;
Poor nigger you can't get over dat;
Walk over!

Budget: Under $25

Sources:

Anderson, Monica F., *Black English Vernacular: From "Ain't" to "Yo Mama"–The Words Politically Correct Americans Should Know*, Rainbow Books, 1994.

Cross, Theodore, "Suppose There Was No Affirmative Action at the Most Prestigious Colleges and Graduate Schools," *Journal of Blacks in High Education,* Spring 1994, 44-51.

Crystal, David, *The Cambridge Encyclopedia of the English Langauge,* Cambridge University Press, 1995.

Draper, James P., *Black Literature Criticism,* Gale, 1992.

Duneier, Mitchell, "Earning Another Chance," *Chicago Tribune,* December 29, 1994, 1.

"Ebonica," http://linguist.emich.edu/topics/ebonics/Isa-ebonics. html.

"Ebonics Lectric Library Table of Contents," http://www.NovusOrdo.com/.

"Ebonics: Rush to Judgment?," *Education Digest,* April 1997, 24-28.

Garwood, Alfred, ed., *Black Americans: A Statistical Sourcebook,* Numbers & Concepts, 1992.

"History of Black English," http://www.princeton.edu/~bclewis /blacktalk.html.

"History of Ebonics," http://www2.shore.net/~shai/origins.html.

Lee, Felicia R., "Lingering Conflict in the Schools: Black Dialect vs. Standard Speech," *New York Times,* January 5, 1994, A1.

Massey, D. S., and N. A. Denton, *American Apartheid,* Harvard University Press, 1993.

Perry, Theresa, and Lisa Delpit, eds, "The Real Ebonics Debate Power, Language, and the Education of African-American Children," *Rethinking Schools,* Fall 1997.

Alternative Applications: Study spirituals and the works of dialect writers, particularly these:

- ◆ Margaret Walker, *Jubilee*
- ◆ Paul Keens-Douglas, "Tanti Merle at de Oval"
- ◆ Alice Walker, *The Color Purple*
- ◆ Ernest Gaines, *A Lesson Before Dying*
- ◆ Mary Carter Smith, "Cindy Ellie"
- ◆ Zora Neale Hurston, *Mule Bone*
- ◆ the poetry of Mari Evans, Langston Hughes, Sonya Sanchez, and Nikki Giovanni

◆ Edgar Allan Poe, "The Gold Bug"
◆ Alice Childress, *A Hero Ain't Nothin' But a Sandwich*
◆ Joel Chandler Harris, Uncle Remus tales
◆ Susan Straight, I *Been in Sorrow's Kitchen and Licked out All the Pots*
◆ Virginia Hamilton, *Drylongso*
◆ Theodore Taylor, *The Cay.*

List variances in dialect by comparing phrases and words to standard English. Note the dropping of letters and endings and the alteration of inflections and auxiliary verbs. Characterize the cadence and energy of black dialect.

Black History Glossary

Age/Grade Level or Audience: Middle school or high school history or language class.

Description: Generate an alphabetized glossary of terms crucial to African American history.

Procedure: Assign individual students to maintain an open database of terms along with definitions and origins. Include these terms:

A.N.C.	affirmative action
afrocentrism	apartheid
"Back to Africa" Movement	Black Is Beautiful
Black Power	block busting
Brown vs. Board of Education	Buppy
chickenbone special	church burning
civil disobedience	civil rights
code noir	copperhead
dark continent	*de facto* segregation
diaspora	Dred Scott decision
ebonics	equal opportunity employer
Fifteenth Amendment	Freedmen's Bureau
garbage workers' strike	grandfather clause
Great Society	Harlem Renaissance
hate crimes	high tech lynching
indentured servant	Islam
Jim Crow laws	Ku Klux Klan
maroons	miscegenation
Motown	mulatto
multiculturalism	NAACP
negrito	Negro National Anthem

nightriders

non-violence

O. J. Simpson trial

octoroon

Oreo

Pan-Africanism pass

patroller

Poor People's March

PUSH

quotas

Rainbow Coalition

Reconstruction

Rodney King

separate but equal

slave trade triangle

SNCC

Symbionese Liberation Army

tokenism

Uncle Tom

WASP

Watts riot

white flight

white flight academy

white man's burden

Willie Horton ads

work fair

Where possible, have students supply a date or an era to which these terms apply and place each term and a definition on a poster. Arrange posters chronologically in a display to indicate their importance in history and politics, particularly election campaigns, civil rights victories, wars, and periods of racial unrest. For example, place nightriders during Reconstruction, Great Society during Lyndon Johnson's presidency, Rodney King during George Bush's presidency, high tech lynching during Anita Hill's testimony against Clarence Thomas, and the O.J. Simpson trial and church burnings during the Clinton administration.

Budget: Under $25

Sources:

African American History in the Press, 1851-1899, Gale, 1996. "Black History," http://www.slip.net/~rigged/history.html.

"Black History Month: Let's Get Started," http://www.netnoir.com/spotlight/bhm/jbhm. html.

Corbin, Raymond M., 1,999 *Facts about Blacks: A Sourcebook of African American Achievement,* 2nd edition, Madison Books, 1997.

Hine, Darlene Clark, Elsa Barkley Brown, and Rosalyn Terborg-Penn, *Black Women in America: An Historical Encyclopedia,* Carlson Publishing, 1993.

Hornsby, Alton, *Chronology of African-American History,* 2nd edition Gale, 1997.

Mabunda, L. Mpho, ed., *The African American Almanac,* Gale, 1997.

Straub, Deborah Gillan, ed., *African American Voices,* U•X•L/Gale, 1996.

"Woman Who Changed Laws That Prevented Mixed Marriage Tells What It Was Like Then," *Jet,* November 9, 1992, 12-15.

Zivkovich, Pride V., "Building Vocabulary with a *3-D* Word Wall," Fralick, *Teaching K-8,* October 1997, 58-59.

Alternative Applications: Place a "Term of the Day" on the chalkboard. Explain and discuss each, such as "separate but equal," "white flight academy," and "*de facto* segregation." Review terms from previous days and show their relationship to each other and to the current state of race relations. At the end of the study, collect terms in a database or publish a handbook of terms from black history. Exchange the handbook with sister schools in other areas of the country and hold an interschool spelling bee.

Black Language Roundup

Age/Grade Level or Audience: Middle school and high school language, history, or black studies classes.

Description: Have students name and locate geographically the languages spoken by members of the black race.

Procedure: Students will utilize media resources to identify the languages spoken by most of the world's black peoples, including these:

Acholi	Afrikaan	Akan	Arabic
Bambara	Bantu	Bari	Cajun
Dinka	Dyula	Ewe	French
Fulani	Gambai	Gbaya	Gullah
Hausa	Hindi	Ijo	Kanuri
Khoisan	Kiswahili	Kongo	Krio
Kwa	Lendu	Lingala	Lugbara
Luo	Madi	Malinka	Mande
Mangbetu	Masai	Mende	Mossi
Lango	Nandi	Nubian	Portuguese
Rwanda	Sango	Shona	Swahili
Tswana	Twi	Voltaic	Wolof
Xhosa	Yoruba	Zulu	

Budget: Under $25

Sources:

African Language Collection: Indiana Universities, Bloomington, Indiana Africa, 1994.

" African Language Sites," http://polyglot.Iss.wisc.edu/lss/lang/african.html.

Crystal, David, *The Cambridge Encyclopedia of the English Langauge,* Cambridge University Press, 1995.

"Hausa," http://ah.soas.uk/LanguageGuide/Hausa.html.

"Kamusi Project: Swahili Dictionary," http://www.yale.edu/swahili.

McCrum, Robert, *The Story of English,* Penguin Books, 1993.

Alternative Applications: Assign students to prepare a word list of English terms which came from African languages. Provide numerous dictionaries, language histories, and etymologies for participants to compare histories. Have them choose a word to illustrate on a poster. For example:

- ◆ **aardvark**, the Afrikaan term from "earth pig" dating to 1833, names a large digging animal.
- ◆ **aardwolf**, the Afrikaan term from "earth wolf" and dating to 1833, names a striped mammal of the hyena family.
- ◆ **apartheid**, an Afrikaan term from the Dutch "apart-hood" dating to 1947, naming a policy of racial segregation or separation.
- ◆ **banana**, an African term dating to 1597, names a soft tropical fruit.
- ◆ **banjo**, from the Kimbandu word mbanza end dating to 1739, is a four- or five-string musical instrument.
- ◆ **baobab**, an African name dating from 1640, names a broad tropical tree.
- ◆ **basenji**, from the Bantu word dating from 1933, names a small brown barkless dog.
- ◆ **benne**, from the Mandingo *bene* and dating *to* 1769, is a synonym for sesame.
- ◆ **bongo**, from the Bobangi *mbangani* to 1861, names a small central African antelope.
- ◆ **boogie**, a 1902 black American slang term denoting a good time or spirited dance.
- ◆ **bwana**, a Swahili term from the Arabic "our father" dating to 1878, the equivalent of sir, master, or boss.
- ◆ **chimpanzee**, from the Kongo wore *chimpenzi* to 1738, names a small tree ape.
- ◆ **cocktail**, from the Krio term *kakte* to 1806, which derives from a scorpion with a stinger on its tail and refers to an alcoholic drink.
- ◆ **dashiki**, from the Yoruba *danshiki* dating to 1968, names a loose tunic.
- ◆ **dik-dik**, an East African name dating to 1883, refers to a small antelope.
- ◆ **duiker**, from the Afrikaan *duik* meaning "dive" and dating to 1777, names a family of antelopes.
- ◆ **ebony**, from the Egyptian *hbnj* dating to the fourteenth century, denotes a tropical hard wood.
- ◆ **eland**, the Afrikaan work dating to 1600, names a spiral-horned elk.
- ◆ **gerenuk**, from the Somali *garanung* dating to 1895, denotes an east African antelope.
- ◆ **gnu**, from the Bushman *nqu* and dating to 1777, names a large African antelope with curved horns.
- ◆ **goober**, from the Kongo *nguba* and dating to 1833, is a synonym for peanut.
- ◆ **guinea**, African place name dating to 1664, which was transferred to the coins made from native gold and also refers to plants and animals, such as guinea hens and guinea corn.

◆ **gumbo**, a Bantu word derived from *ochinggombo* and dating to 1845. A synonym for okra, it also refers to soup thickened with okra or to a mixed Creole dialect.

◆ **harmattan**, a Twi term from the seventeenth century naming a dusty Atlantic wind.

◆ **hoodoo**, from the Hausa *hu'du'ba* and dating to 1875, a jinx or evil spell.

◆ **Hottentot**, an Afrikaan word dating to 1677, refers to Bush people and Bantu natives in south Africa.

◆ **impala**, a nineteenth-century Zulu name for a large brown antelope.

◆ **indri**, a Malagasy term meaning "look!," which the black and white femur of Madagascar.

◆ **juju**, from the Hausa *djudju* and dating to 1894, is a synonym for amulet, fetish, or charm.

◆ **juke**, derived from the Bambara term *dzagu* end dating to 1939, originally meant "wicked" and was applied to roadhouses and jukeboxes. Currently, it is used as a verb meaning to dance or frolic.

◆ **kopje**, from the Afrikaan *koppie* and dating to 1848, is a hillock.

◆ **kraal**, an Afrikaan term from the Portuguese, naming an enclosed or fenced stockyard or animal pen; also, a village or compound.

◆ **kudu**, the Afrikaan *koedoe* and dating from 1777, names a large spiral-horned antelope.

◆ **mamba**, the Zulu *im-amba* dating from 1862, names a venomous snake of the cobra family.

◆ **marimba**, the Bantu from the Kimbundu for native xylophone, a term that entered English in 1704.

◆ **mojo**, a black teenage expression of the 1960s, refers to a seasoning, potion, or concoction that has power over the emotions.

◆ **mumbo-jumbo**, an African deity mentioned in 1738, currently refers to complex rituals or language.

◆ **nyala**, the Zulu *inxala* dating to 1894, names a southeasern African antelope.

◆ **obeah**, derived from Twi *abia*, a vine used to make a charm, and dating from 1760, is a general term for voodoo or sorcery.

◆ **okapi**, the Mbuti term from *o'api* dating from 1900, names a shortnecked member of the giraffe family that is marked by a striped rump and reddish skin.

◆ **okra**, an African word dating to 1679 which names a tall vegetable plant and its edible pods.

◆ **Rastafarian**, derived from the Ethiopian name of Haile Selassie and dating to 1955, refers to a Jamaican religious cult.

◆ **safari**, an Arabic term for trip, currently referring to the equipment and caravan of a hunting party or non-military expeditionary force.

◆ **springbok**, the Afrikaan term dating from l775, names a graceful gazelle.

◆ **steenbok**, the Afrikaan term dating from 1775, names a small antelope.

◆ **tote**, dating to 1677, is a synonym for carry. It is also the noun referring to a burden, load, or satchel.

◆ **trek**, the Afrikaan term from the Dutch for pull or haul, now meaning a complex journey, expedition, or organized migration.

◆ **tsetse**, from the Tswana word dating to 1849, names a south African fly.

◆ **veldt**, the Afrikaan term for field dating from 1852, is a synonym for grassland or savanna.

◆ **voodoo**, from the Ewe *vodu* and dating to 1850, names an African form of ancestor worship.

◆ **wildebeest**, from the Afrikaan dating from 1838, is a synonym for gnu.

◆ **yum yum**, an African lip sound dating to 1883, expresses delight or anticipation.

◆ **zombie**, from the Kongo *nzembi* dating to 1871, refers to a corpse reanimated by a supernatural power.

Extend the list to include Caribbean terms, such as reggae, buckra, grisgris, and dreadlocks. Assist students in making an oversized crossword puzzle to decorate a wall for a banquet, assembly, or celebration.

Black Language Trees

Age/Grade Level or Audience: High school or college linguistics classes.

Description: Coordinate a world chart of languages spoken by predominantly black populations.

Procedure: Have individuals provide a skeleton history of a black language or dialect, for example, Afrikaans or Bantu. Appoint a scribe to graph entries on a world web of languages. Print out the finished graph to use as a wall chart.

Budget: Under $25

Sources:

African Language Collection: Indiana Universities, Bloomington, Indiana Africa, 1994.

"African Language Sites," http://polyglot.lss.wisc.edu/lss/lang/african.html.

Bennett, T., and Y. Moya-Gutierrez, "Speaking Across the Divide," *New Yorker,* January 27, 1997, 35-42.

Crystal, David, *The Cambridge Encyclopedia of the English Langauge,* Cambridge University Press, 1995.

Duneier, Mitchell, "Earning Another Chance," *Chicago Tribune,* December 29, 1994, 1.

"Ebonica," http://linguist.emich.edu/topics/ebonics/lsa-ebonics. html.

"Ebonies Lectric Library Table of Contents," http://www.NovusOrdo.comI:,

"Ebonies: Rush to Judgment?," *Education Digest,* April 1997, 24-28.

Gibbs, W. W., "A Matter of Language," *Scientific American,* April 1997, 24-28.

"Hausa," http://ah.soas.uk/LanguageGuide/Hausa.html.

"History of Black English," http://www.princeton.edu/~bclewis /blacktalk.html.

"History of Ebonics," http://www2.shore.net/~shai/origins.html.

"Kamusi Project: Swahili Dictionary," http://www.yale.edu/swahili.

Mills, D. J., "Bashing Black English," *Commonweal,* February 28, 1997, 10-11.

Alternative Applications: Generate a traveler's glossary of travel terms, phrases, and names of things from an African or Caribbean language. Consider Haitian Creole, Swahili, or Bambara.

Expatriates

Age/Grade Level or Audience: High school or college English or history classes.

Description: Assign an extended definition of expatriate by examining the lives of several black expatriates.

Procedure: Have students define the expatriate's purpose by using as examples actor/singer Paul Robeson, dancer Josephine Baker, and novelist James Baldwin. Explain the social, political, and economic reasons for each defection:

- ◆ Paul Robeson's investigation by the House Un-American Activities Commission
- ◆ James Baldwin's ease with French artists
- ◆ Josephine Baker's open reception by the people of Paris, whom she aided as a spy during World War II.

Discuss what social and professional advantages these people gained by leaving their homeland and living elsewhere.

Budget: Under $25

Sources:

"African American History," http://www.msstate.edu/Archives/History/USA/Afro-Amer/ afro.html.

"Black History, "http://www.slip. net /~rigged/history. html.

"Black History Month: Let's Get Started," http://www.netnoir.com/spotlight/bhm/ jbhm.~\html.

Corbin, Raymond M., *1,999 Facts about Blacks: A Sourcebook of African American Achievement*, 2nd edition, Madison Books, 1997.

Dean, Philip H., *Paul Robeson*, Dramatists Play, 1996.

Duberman, Martin, *Paul Robeson*, New Press New York, 1996.

Hine, Darlene Clark, Elsa Barkley Brown, and Rosalyn Terborg-Penn, *Black Women in America: An Historical Encyclopedia*, Carlson Publishing, 1993.

"Josephine Baker," http://www.classicalmus.com/artistst/baker.html.

Papich, Steven, *Remembering Josephine Baker*, Bobbs, Merrill, 1976.

"Paris Music Hall Collection," http://www.libs.uga.edu/darchive/hargrett/paris/baker. html.

Rose, Phyllis, *Jazz Cleopatra: Josephine Baker in Her Time*, Vintage Books, 1991.

Smith, Jessie Carney, *Notable Black American Women*, Gale, 1992.

Takach, James, *James Baldwin*, Lucent Books, 1996.

Alternative Applications: Lead a discussion of World War II and the liberating influence on black Americans through contact with Europeans, particularly the French, who welcomed non-white people, including their own Algerian citizens. Describe how the return of veterans to the United States altered attitudes toward inclusion and multiculturalism.

Gullah

Age/Grade Level or Audience: High school or college language or literature classes; literary societies; reading theaters.

Description: Study literary works that depict Gullah.

Procedure: Discuss the following data about black language:

- ◆ the isolation felt by slaves from differing lingual groups
- ◆ the advantage to slave owners in keeping workers ignorant of each other's language
- ◆ the advantage to slaves of creating a mutually understood language
- ◆ the creation of pidgin or creole languages as a means of communication among people of varying lingual backgrounds
- ◆ stylistic and linguistic mechanisms of Gullah that set it apart from the other prominent Southern dialects, notably Tidewater, Southern Mountain, Uncle Remus, Geechee, Cajun, and Creole and from Caribbean languages, particularly Krio and Afrish
- ◆ minority groups' need to be bilingual when dealing with business, government, or the media.

Conclude with a study group reading aloud from Frankie and Doug Quimby's "The Ibo Landing Story," Carlie Towne's "It's a Cultural Affair: My Journey to My Gullah People," Theodore Taylor's young adult novels The Cay and *Timothy of the* Cay, Susan Straight's novel *I Been in Sorrow's Kitchen and Licked out All the Pots,* Edgar Allan Poe's short story "The Gold Bug," Pat Conroy's *The Water Is Wide,* or Virginia Hamilton's children's book *Drylongso.*

Budget: $25-$50

Sources:

Films *Conrack* (1974) and *Daughters of the Dust (1992).*

"Georgia Sea Island Singers Deliver Message of Dignity," *Jacksonville Times-Union,* March 3, 1996.

Gewertz, Daniel, "Black History Alive in Singers Act," *Boston Herald,* April 12, 1991, S22.

"The Gullah Connection," http://www.afrinet.net/~halih/ afrotalk/afrooct95/1090. html.

"Gullah People and Culture," http://www.tezcat.com/~ronald/gullah.html.

Hamilton, Virginia, *Drylongso,* Harcourt Brace Jovanovich, 1992.

Hanson, Trudy Lewis, "United in Story and Song: The Power of Music in Storytelling," *Storytelling Magazine,* May 1997, 14-15.

Jones, Charles C., Jr., and Roger D. Abrahams, *Gullah Folktales from the Georgia Coast,* University of Georgia Press, 1997.

Morgan, Bruce, "In Georgia: Through the Gospel Grapevine," *Time,* September 12, 1988, 12-13.

Ogunleye, Tolagbe, "Afro-American Folklore," *Journal of Black Studies,* March 1997, 435-456

Quimby, Doug, and Frankie Quimby, "The Ibo Landing Story" in *Talk That Talk,* Simon & Schuster, 1989.

Straight, Susan, *I Been in Sorrow's Kitchen and Licked Out All the Pots,* Hyperion, 1992.

Taylor, Theodore, *The Cay,* Cornerstone Books, 1990.

——, *Timothy of the Cay,* Avon, 1993.

Alternative Applications: Present black filmmaker Julie Dash's film *Daughters of the Dust,* which describes the migration of a Gullah family northward from their home in Sea Islands, Georgia. Organize a panel to describe feminist themes, for example:

 ◆ Gullah women's concepts of morality and social order
 ◆ the courage of women in leading their families during hard times
 ◆ the role of matriarch or elder female leader
 ◆ women and rites of passage
 ◆ the mother's role in stabilizing a fragmented family.

Hieroglyphics

Age/Grade Level or Audience: Elementary and middle school language classes.

Description: Have students study the origin and meaning of hieroglyphics.

Procedure: Point out the existence of a highly developed black civilization which evolved pictographs five thousand years ago as the written alphabet of a pharaonic language. Have students create a website on the hieroglyphic form of writing. Incorporate the writing of common words and names in Egyptian pictographs. Decorate greeting cards, posters, and jewelry with hieroglyphs.

Budget: $25-$50

Sources:
Betro, Mario C., *Hieroglyphics: The Writing of Ancient Egypt*, Abbeville Press, 1996.
"Egyptian Hieroglyphs," http://galaxy.cau.edu/tsmith/eghier.html.
Manuelian, Peter Der, *Hieroglyphs from A to Z*, Scholastic, Inc., 1996.
"See Your Name in Hieroglyphic Language," http://www.idsc.gov.eg/tourism/tortm.htm.
Spence, Lewis, *Ancient Egyptian Myths and Legends*, Dover Publications.
Steedman, Scott, *Pockets: Ancient Egypt*, Dorling Kindersley, 1995.
Weatherill, Steve, and Sue Weatherill, *Hieroglyph It! Set*, Barron, 1995.

Alternative Applications: Have students duplicate an Egyptian frieze written in pictographic form or create a new frieze delineating a great moment in Egyptian history, such as these:

- ♦ the internment of a pharoah or princess
- ♦ a harvest or coming-of-age ritual
- ♦ arrival of a visiting dignitary from the south
- ♦ capture and display of jungle animals
- ♦ the Queen of Sheba's visit to Solomon's court
- ♦ creation of a bust, temple, or obelisk to honor Cleopatra, Hatshepsut, Tutankhamen, or Ramses II.

Jump Rope Rhymes

Age/Grade Level or Audience: Elementary school students.

Description: Have students evolve their own jump rhymes by imitating the rhyming ditties of black children.

Procedure: Present a two-line prompt to establish style and rhythm. Have children work in small groups to supply more couplets. For instance:

◆ I was born in a frying pan
  Just to see how old I am . . .
◆ Little Sally Walker
  Sitting in the saucer . . .
◆ Hey girl
  Whatcha got? . . .
◆ My momma and your momma
  Live across the street . . .
◆ Miss Sue, Miss Sue
  Miss Sue from Alabama
◆ I have a boyfriend
  Nabisco . . .
◆ Oh, sailor went to sea sea sea
  To see what he could see see see
◆ I wish I had a nickel
  I wish I had a dime
◆ Apples on a stick
  Make me sick
◆ Miss Mary Mack Mack Mack
  All dressed in black black black
◆ Way down yonder,
  On the East Coast Line . . .
◆ Mister Brown, Mister Brown,
  I come to court your daughter . . .
◆ Teddy bear, teddy bear, What's your name?

Then have students use their rhymes to keep time with activities involving hopscotch, jumping rope, hand clapping partner games, hula trooping, bean bag toss, line and circle dancing, rhythm bands, circle games, ball passing, and follow-the-leader.

Budget: Under $25

Sources:

Brunvand, Jan Harold, ed., *American Folklore: An Encyclopedia*, Garland, 1996.
"Jump Rope Resource Center," http://www.aei.ca/~jumprope/center.html.
"Jump Rope Rhymes," http://www.corpcomm.net/~gnieboer/jump_little_puppy. htm.
Jump Rope Rhymes, Western Publications, 1995.
Lankford, Mary D., *Hopscotch Around the World,* Morrow Junior Books, 1992.

Loredo, Elizabeth, *Jump Rope Book and Jump Rope*, Workman Publications, 1996.
Vecchione, Glen, *Jump Rope Book,* Sterling, 1996.

Alternative Applications: Use Africa American folk rhymes as the basis of choral reading during which children act out, clap, pantomime, and sway to the words they recite. For example:

Hambone

>Hambone, Hambone, where you been?
>Around the world and I'm goin' agin.
>Hambone, Hambone, what'd you do? I caught the train and the ferry too.
>Hambone, Hambone, where'd you go?
>Sailed right up to Lucy's door.
>I asked sweet Lucy would she be mine,
>She said she's willin' if Papa don't mind.

Kwanzaa Flash Cards

Originator: Dr. Laurie Rozakis, teacher, editor, and writer, Farmingdale, New York.

Age/Grade Level or Audience: Elementary school language classes; religious schools.

Description: Create a set of flash cards to illustrate the seven lessons or *ngazo saba* of Kwanzaa, a holiday created in 1966 by African American leader Maulana Karenga.

Procedure: Begin with a large card with the word "Kwanzaa" surrounded by pumpkins, beans, gourds, cabbages, onions, corn, bananas, coconuts, pineapples, and other harvested vegetables and fruits. Explain that Kwanzaa means "first fruits of the harvest" and that it takes place annually from December 26 until January 1. Have students compare the December festival with the American concept of Thanksgiving. Then introduce the seven lessons of Kwanzaa, one per card.

> ◆ **brotherhood**–Have students pantomime a scene featuring brothers and sisters playing a ring game or jumping rope in harmony.
> ◆ **self-determination**–Ask a volunteer what it means to be determined. Explain why determination must begin with the individual and radiate out to the community.
> ◆ **cooperation**–Have two students lock hands on the other's wrists to form a chair. Ask a third student to sit on the improvised seat.

- **sharing**–Make an oral list of places in the United States where people share with those who are poor, homeless, sick, or in danger, such as the Red Cross, Goodwill, UNICEF, Salvation Army, and church charities.
- **creativity**–Ask students how they would spend a rainy Saturday if they could have any supplies they needed, such as paper, cardboard, crayons, markers, string, and glue.
- **purpose**–Have a volunteer explain why it is important to set personal goals and achieve them. Ask every student to name at least three goals for the school year.
- **faith**–Have students explain why they trust their country, neighbors, families, and churches to make the best possible world.

Budget: Under $25

Sources:

"The Complete Kwanzaa Celebration Basket," http://lainet3.1ainet. com/~joejones/ kwanzaa/htm.

"Kwanzaa," http://www.dca.net/~areid/kwanzaa.htm.

"Kwanzaa Bazaar," http://shops.net/shops/Kwanzaa/item-5.html.

"Kwanzaa Links," http://new.melanet.com/kwanzaa/links.html.

Oni, Sauda, *What Kwanzaa Means to Me*, DARE Books, 1996.

Porter, A. P., *Kwanzaa*, Carolrhoda Books, 1991.

Robartson, Linda, *The Complete Kwanzaa Celebration Book*, Creative Acrylic, 1993.

Ross, Kathy, *Crafts for Kwanzaa*, Millbrook Press, 1994.

St. James, Synthia, *The Gifts of Kwanzaa*, A Whitman, 1994.

Alternative Applications: For older groups, place the African terms for the seven lessons on the backs of each card. They should read as follows:

- unity–umoja [u . mow' jah]
- self-determination–kujichagulia [koo' . jee . she. goo' Iyah]
- cooperation–ujima [u. gee' mah]
- sharing–ujamma [u . jahm' mah]
- creativity–koumba [koo. oom' bah]
- purpose–nia [nee' ah]
- faith–imani [ee. mah'nee]

Have the students read the words with you as you identify the meaning of each and explain its importance to the holiday and to the idea of community. Note that celebrants exchange gifts, give thanks, share a feast, and look forward to another year. Discuss how this idea relates to the first Thanksgiving, when Native Americans shared their food with Pilgrims. Then have students explain why the world as a whole needs to develop a sense of brotherhood, self-determination, cooperation, sharing, creativity, purpose, and faith.

Language Pairs

Age/Grade Level or Audience: Middle school or high school foreign language classes or clubs.

Description: Make a chart of Swahili words and their equivalent in a target language.

Procedure: Have French, Spanish, German, Italian, or Latin classes create a chart pairing Swahili with the language they are studying. For example:

French
- ◆ habari/bon jour–hello
- ◆ buba/chemise–blouse
- ◆ chakulan/nouriture–food
- ◆ loppa/joupe–skirt
- ◆ kofi/chapeau–hat
- ◆ Hujambo/comment ça va–How are you?

German
- ◆ karibu/willkommen–welcome
- ◆ tafadali/bitte–please
- ◆ toto/kind–child
- ◆ tutaonana/auf wiedersehen–good-bye
- ◆ peya/birne–pear

Italian
- ◆ jambo/buon giorno–hello
- ◆ kanzu/vestito–robe
- ◆ wototo/ragazzi–children
- ◆ tufa/mela–apple
- ◆ asante/grazie–thanks
- ◆ kwaheri/arrivaderci–goodbye
- ◆ tafadhali/per favore–please

Latin
- ◆ simba/leo–lion
- ◆ rafiki/amicus–friend
- ◆ boga/melopepo–pumpkin
- ◆ dashiki/tunica–tunic
- ◆ matunda/frumentum–fruit
- ◆ zazibu/uvae–grapes

Spanish
- ◆ fundi/maestro or maestra–teacher
- ◆ gele/adorno–turban
- ◆ karamu/fiesta–feast
- ◆ nanasi/anana–pineapple

- ◆ rafiki/amigo–friend
- ◆ sana/muy–a lot

Teach counting and the days of the week in multiple langauges:

English: one, two, three, four, five, six, seven, eight, nine, ten
Swahili: moja, mbili, tatu, nne, tang, site, saba, nane, tisa, kumi
Italian: uno, due, tre, quattro, cinque, setto, otto, nove, dieci
English: Sunday, Monday, Tuesday, Wednesday, Thursday, Friday, Saturday
Swahili: jumapili, jumatatu, jumane, jumatano, alhamisi, ijumaa, jumamosi
French: dimanche, lundi, mardi, mercredi, jeudi, vendredi, samedi

Translate the seven Swahili concepts of Kwanzaa into a target language. For example, in Latin:

- ◆ unity–umoja/concordia
- ◆ self-determination/constantia
- ◆ cooperation–ujima/consociatio
- ◆ sharing–ujamma/partiens
- ◆ creativity–kuumba/cogitatio
- ◆ purpose–nia/consilium
- ◆ faith–imani/fides

Budget: Under $25

Sources:

Awde, Nicholas, *Swahili-English, English-Swahili Practical Dictionary,* Hippocrene Books, 1996.
"Kamusi Project: Swahili Dictionary," http://www.yale.edu/swahili.
Perrott, D. Y., *Swahili Dicitonary,* NTC Publishing Group, 1995.
Swahili Cassette Pack, Berlitz, 1995.
Swahili Phrase Book, Berlitz, 1995.

Alternative Applications: Listen to the French-African poems read by Paul Mankin, which is available on cassette from Smithsonian/Folkways. Compare to the rhythms, images, and diction of poems by Baudelaire, Hugo, Verlaine, Rimbaud, and other French poets.

 New Names for Old

Age/Grade Level or Audience: Middle school and high school history classes.

Description: Collect early names for African countries.

Procedure: Make a list of current countries of Africa. Beside each, give former names. Include these out-of-date names:

Abyssinia	Ashanti	Basutoland
Bechuanaland	Cape Colony	Congo Free State
Dahomey	Darfur	Eritrea
French Somalia	German East Africa	Gold Coast
Kamerun	Madagascar	Merina
Northern Rhodesia	Nyasaland	Orange Free State
Portuguese Guinea	Southern Rhodesia	Southwest Africa
Spanish Sahara	Tanganyika	Togoland
Transvaal	Ubangui-Shari	United Arab Republic

Budget: Under $25

Sources:

Adams, W. M., *The Physical Geography of Africa,* Oxford University Press, 1996.

Africa: A Lonely Planet Shoestring Guide, Lonely Planet, 1995.

"Africa Online," http://www.africaonline.com.

Ayo, Yvonne, *Ancient Africa,* Random House, 1995.

Binns, Tony, *The People and Environment in Africa,* John Wiley and Sons, 1995.

Jeunesse, Gallimard, *Atlas of Countries,* Cartwheel Books, 1996.

Alternative Applications: Create a series of color-coded maps of colonies that were once ruled by Belgium, France, Germany, Great Britain, Italy, Portugal, Spain, and Turkey. Show them in chronological order by decades to demonstrate the gradual withdrawal of colonial governments as African nations obtained freedom.

Sharing Words from Different Worlds

Originator: Dr. Laurie Rozakis, teacher, editor, and writer, Farmingdale, New York.

Age/Grade Level or Audience: Elementary or middle school language class; church school.

Description: Have students learn Swahili terms.

Procedure: Make illustrated handouts demonstrating the meaning of the following Swahili words:

◆ **asante** [ah.sahn' tay]–thank you

◆ **bendera** [ben. de' rah]–the red, black, and green-striped flag of Africa

◆ **bibi** [bee' bee]–Mrs.

◆ **boga** [bo' gah]–pumpkin

◆ **buba** [boo' buh]–an African blouse

◆ **bwana** [bwah' nuh]–mister

◆ **chakula** [sha. koo' lah]–food

◆ **chungwa** [chuhng' wah]–orange

◆ **daktari** [dahk. tah' ree]–doctor

◆ **duma** [doo' mah]–cheetah

◆ **duka** [doo' kuh]–shop

◆ **fundi** [fuhn' dee]–teacher or mentor

◆ **habari** [hah. bah' ree]–How are you?

◆ **jambo** [jahm' bo]–hello

◆ **kima** [kee' mah]–monkey

◆ **kofi** [ko' fee]–an African hat

◆ **kondoo** [kohn' doo]–sheep

◆ **kwaheri** [kwa. heh' ree]–goodbye

◆ **loppa** [lahp' pah]–an African skirt

◆ **matunda** [mah. toon' dah]–fruit

◆ **mbune** [muh. boo' nay]–ostrich

◆ **mia** [mee' ah]–one hundred

◆ **myoko** [myoh' koh]–snake

◆ **nanasi** [nah. nah' see]–pineapple

◆ **nazi** [nah' zee]–coconut

◆ **ndizi** [nuh. dee' zee]–banana

◆ **nyati** [nyah' tee]–buffalo

◆ **nzuri** [nuh. zoo' ree]–I am well

◆ **peya** [pay' yah]–pear

◆ **punda milia** [poon' dah mee' lee. ah]–zebra

◆ **rafiki** [rah. fee' kee']–friend

◆ **sana** [sah' nah]–a lot

◆ **simba** [sihm' buh]–lion

◆ **tafadali** [tah. fah. dah' lee]–please

◆ **toto** [toh' toh]–child

◆ **tufa** [too' fah]–apple

◆ **tutaonana** [too. tow. nah' nah]–good-bye

◆ **wototo** [wo. to' to]–children

◆ **zazibu** [zah. zee' boo]–grapes

Budget: Under $25

Sources:

Awde, Nicholas, *Swahili-English, English Swahili Practical Dictionary*, Hippocrene Books, 1996.

"Kamusi Project: Swahili Dictionary," http //www yale edu/swahili.

Perrott, D. Y., *Swahili Dicitonary,* NTC Publishing Group, 1995.

Swahili Cassette Pack, Berlitz, 1995.

Swahili Phrase Book, Berlitz, 1995.

Alternative Applications: Assign a group of students to draw a mural illustrating an African harvest feast where participants wear traditional dress. Have them label examples from the word list above plus these terms:

- ◆ **dashiki** [dah. shee' kee]–an African man's open-necked tunic
- ◆ **gele** [gay' lay]–an African's woman's head cloth or turban
- ◆ **kanzu** [kan' zoo]–an African man's robe
- ◆ **karamu** [kah. rah' moo]–a thanksgiving or harvest feast, held on the last day of Kwanzaa week
- ◆ **kikomba cha umoja** [kee. kohm' bah chain u. moh' jah]–the shared juice cup
- ◆ **kinara** [kee. nah' rah]–a candleholder
- ◆ **mazao** [mah. zow']–fresh vegetables and fruit
- ◆ **mishumaa saba** [mee. shoo' mah sah' bah]–seven holiday candles, with three red on the left, a black in the middle, and three green on the right
- ◆ **mkeka** [muh. key' kah]–table mat
- ◆ **muhindi** [moo. heen' dee]–corn
- ◆ **zawadi** [zah wah' dee]–presents to exchange with friends

Translating Lyrics

Age/Grade Level or Audience: Middle school or high school foreign language classes.

Description: Have students listen to Cajun songs and isolate phrases they can translate into French.

Procedure: Present works by a black zydeco group, such as Queen Ida and the Bon Temps Zydeco Band, Chubby Carrier and the Bayou Swamp Band, Clifton Chenier and His Red-Hot Louisiana Band, Rockin' Dopsie and the Zydeco Twisters, and Buckwheat Zydeco. Have French students contrast Cajun lyrics with standard French. On the chalkboard, make a list of differences, such as the elision of *mes amis* into *zamis or* the Cajun pronunciation of *cher* [chahr] and *Louisiane* [loo . zahn'].

Budget: $25-$50

Sources:

Records, cassettes, and compact discs from local libraries; French dictionaries.

Casals, Pablo, "Nigra Sum," Tetra Music Corp., 1966.

"Nigra Sum" sung by the San Francisco Gay Men's Chorus on *How Fair This Place* (CD), Golden Gate Performing Arts, Inc., 1991.

Reneaux, J. J., *LifeLine* (CD), Reneaux Productions, 1998.

Woodard, Josef, "Tales-and Tunes-From the Swamp," *Los Angeles Times,* February 6, 1997, 3.

Alternative Applications: Present Latin grammar and derivation lessons based on phrases from the Latin canticle "Nigra Sum" (I am a black woman). Include these activities:

◆ name the tense and pronoun of each verb in these phrases-

ideo dilexit	et introduxit me	nigra sum
surge et veni	hiems transiit	imber abiit
flores apparuerunt	perfect he	present, I
[perfect, he	perfect, it	perfect, it
present command, you		
perfect, they]		

◆ Give an English derivative from the underlined words in each phrase:

<u>filiae</u> Jerusalem	sed <u>formosa</u>	in <u>cubiculum</u>
in <u>terra</u> nostra	<u>tempus</u> putationis	<u>surge</u> et veni

◆ Underline singular forms in this list: <u>sum</u>, filiae <u>amica</u>, <u>dixit</u>, apparuerunt, <u>hiems</u>, <u>nigra</u>, ideo, sed, <u>mea</u>, jam, <u>imber</u>, <u>nostra</u>

Understanding Lincoln

Age/Grade Level or Audience: Middle school or high school language and history classes.

Description: Study the language and syntax of the Emancipation Proclamation.

Procedure: Read aloud from the Emancipation Proclamation or listen to a recorded version. Select a few phrases and terms to explain, especially these:

abstain	aforesaid	by virtue of
countervailing testimony	deemed	enjoin
executive government	garrison forts	henceforward
hereby	in accordance with	suppressing
thenceforward	thereof	thereto
warranted	wherein	

Have students restate Lincoln's basic idea in their own words.

Budget: Under $25

Sources:
Charnwood, Lord, *Abraham Lincoln: A Biography*, Madison Books, 1996.
EmancipationPr.html.
"The Emancipation Proclamation," http://rain.org/~Karpeles/.
"The Emancipation Proclamation," http://www.accusd.edu/~sakkinen/ abe10.html.
"The Emancipation Proclamation," http://www.winternet. com/~orion/text/ emanproc.txt.
"The Emancipation Proclamation," National Archives and Records, 1993.
Hummel, Jeffrey R., *Emancipating Slaves, Enslaving Free Men: A History of the American Civil War,* Open Court, 1996.
Rhodes, Elisha Hunt, *All for the Union: The Civil War Diary and Letters of Elisha Hunt Rhodes,* Vintage Books, 1992.
Wellman, Sam, *Abraham Lincoln,* Barbour & Co., 1994.
Young, Robert, *The Emancipation Proclamation: Why Lincoln Really Freed the Slaves,* Silver Burdett, 1994.

Alternative Applications: Select a few students to draw up a similar document and post it on a bulletin board, chalkboard, or website.

Literature

African Authors

Age/Grade Level or Audience: Middle school and high school literature classes; literary societies, library programs.

Description: Provide a wide selection of noted African literature for perusal, small group discussion, and writing and art projects.

Procedure: Guide readers in the selection of materials from the following possibilities:

- Peter Abraham, *Wild Conquest, Mine Boyu, The Path of Thunder, Tell Freedom,* and *Return to Goli*
- Chinua Achebe, "The Voter," "Dead Man's Path," *Things Fall Apart, Girls at War, No Longer at Ease, Arrow of God,* "Civil Peace," and *Man of the People*
- Mongo Beti, *Le Pauvre Christ de Bomba, Mission Terminée,* and *LeRoi Miraculé*
- J .P. Clark, *Song of a Goat, The Masquerade,* and *The Raft*
- H. I. E. Dhlomo, *Valley of the Thousand Hills*
- Muga Gicaru, *Land of Sunshine*
- Bessie Head, "Woman from America"
- A. C. Jordan, *The Wrath of the Ancestors*
- Joseph Kariuki, *Mau Mau Detainee*
- Barbara Kimenye, *Kalasanda, Kalasanda Revisited,* and "The Winner"
- Alex la Guma, *A Walk in the Night* and *And a Threefold Cord*
- Camara Laye, *The Dark Child, The Radiance of the King,* and *a Dream of Africa*
- Naguib Mahfouz, *New Cairo, Midaq alley,* and his Cairo Trilogy—*Between the Two Palaces, The Palace of desire,* and *The Sugar Bowl*

♦ Mark Mathabane, *Kaffir Boy, Kaffir Boy in America,* and *Love in Black and White*

♦ Thomas Mofolo, *Pitseng, Chaka,* and *Traveler to the East*

♦ Ezekiel Mphahlele, *Down Second Avenue, The African Image, Man Must Live, The Living and Dead,* and *Shaka Zulu*

♦ James Ngugi, *Weep Not Child* and *The River Between*

♦ Abioseh Nicol, *The Truly Married Woman and Other Stories*

♦ Grace Ogot, "The Rain Came"

♦ Ben Okri, *The Famished Road, Flowers and Shadows, The Landscapes Within, Stars of the New Curfew,* and *Songs of Enchantment*

♦ Sembene Ousmane, *Le Docker Noir, O Pays, Mon Beau Peuple!, Les Bouts de Bois de Dieu,* and *L'Harmattan*

♦ Ferdinand Oyono, *Le Vieux Nègre et la M´daille, Une Vie de Boy,* and *Chemins d'Europe*

♦ Okot p'B'Tek, *Are Your Teeth White*

♦ Sol T. Plaatje and Mwalimu Joseph Nyerere, translations of Shakespeare's plays

♦ Tayeb Salih, *The Wedding of Zein and Other Stories* and *Season of Migration to the North*

♦ Wole Soyinka, *The Interpreters, The Road, A Dance of the Forests, Kongi's Harvest, The Strong Breed, The Lion and the Jewel, The Trials of Brother Jero* and *The Swamp Dwellers*

♦ Amos Tutuola's *The Palm Wine Drunkard* and *My Life in the Bush of Ghosts.*

♦ B. W. Vilakazi, *In the Gold Mines, Zulu Horizons,* and *Zulu Songs*

♦ the poems of Jacob Stanley Davies, Adelaide Casley-Hayford, Mabel Dove Danquah, Léopold Sédar Senghor, Léon Damas, David Diop, Édouard Maunick, Elolongué Epanya-Yondo, Oswalk Mbuyiseni Mtshali, Tchicaya U'Tamsi, Malick Fall, and A. B. C. Merriman Labor

♦ anthologies, particularly *Contos d'Africa, Novos Contos d'Africa,* and *Poesia Negra de Expressäo Portuguesa*

Budget: $25-$50

Sources:

"African Writers," http//www.africaonlline.com/AfricaOnlinegriotstalk/writers/series.html.

Day, Frances Ann, *Multicultural Voices in Contemporary Literature,* Heinemann, 1994.

Draper, James P., *Black Literature Criticism,* Gale, 1992.

Gale, Steven H., *West African Folktales,* National Textbook, 1995.

Jackson, *Black Writers and the Hispanic Canon,* Twayne, 1997.

Malinowski, Sharon, ed., *Black Writers,* 2nd edition, Gale, 1994.

Osa, Osayimwense, *African Children's and Youth Literature,* Twayne, 1995.

Ousby, Ian, *Cambridge Paperback Guide to Literature in English,* Cambridge University Press, 1996.

Rosenberg, Donna, *Folklore, Myths, and Legends: A World Perspective*, National Textbook Company, 1997.

———, *World Literature*, National Textbook Company, 1992.

Sturrock, John, ed., *The Oxford Guide to Contemporary World Literature*, Oxford University Press, 1996.

Alternative Applications: Hold a reading circle in which volunteers cite passages by black African authors and compare or contrast similar segments by white writers. For example, consider the following paired readings:

- ◆ the Dahomey "Song for the Dead" and Christina Rossetti's "Song" or "Remember"
- ◆ Adelaide Casely-Hayford's "Mista Courifer" and George Orwell's "Shooting an Elephant"
- ◆ Bernard Dadié's "Dry Your Tears, Africa" and Carl Sandburg's "Chicago"
- ◆ David Diop's "Africa" and Walt Whitman's "I Hear America Singing" or Emma Lazarus's "The New Colossus"
- ◆ Chinua Achebe's "Marriage Is a Private Affair" and Rudyard Kipling's "Without Benefit of Clergy" or Zora Neale Hurston's *Their Eyes Were Watching God*
- ◆ Mark Mathabane's *Kaffir Boy* and Dori Sander's *Clover*

Have participants locate lines illustrating rhetorical devices, such as personification, metaphor, extended metaphor, image, simile, sense impression, parallel construction, onomatopoeia, euphony, cacophony, paradox, alliteration, rhyme, caesura, apostrophe, rhetorical question, and symbolism.

The African Epic Hero

Age/Grade Level or Audience: High school or college literature classes.

Description: Propose a modern recreation of an African national hero.

Procedure: Rewrite in modern form the Mandingan epic *Sundiata*, a heroic verse cycle that existed orally in Mali from the late thirteenth century until griot Djeli Mamoudou Kouyaté helped a folklorist produce a formal composition in the 1950s. Other oral epics of Africa include the Soninkan *The Dausi*, the Songhay *Epic of Askia Mohammed*, and the Bambaran *Monzon and the King of Kore.*

Budget: Under $25

Sources:

Hale, Thomas A., *The Epic of Askia Mohammed*, Indiana University Press, 1996.

Johnson, John William, *Oral Epics from Africa: Vibrant Voices from a Vast Continent,* Indiana University Press, 1997.

Lazzari, Marie, ed., *Epics for Students: Presenting Analysis, Context, and Criticism on Commonly Studied Epics,* Gale, 1997.

Naine, *Sundiata: An Epic of Old Mali,* Longman, 1965.

Wisniewski, David, *Sundiata: Lion King of Mali,* Houghton Mifflin, 1992.

Alternative Applications: Working with a group, make a comparative chart of standard world epics. Select examples from this chronological list of folk and literary epics:

Sumerian *Gilgamesh* (1200 B.C.)

Finnish *Kalevala* (1100 B.C.)

Greek *Iliad* and *Odyssey* (ca. 850 B.C.)

Hebrew *Exodus* (ca. 600 B.C.)

Indian *Ramayana* (300 B.C.) and *Mahabharata* (200 B.C.)

Naevius's *Annales* (ca. 265 B.C.)

Appollonius's *Argonautica* (235 B.C.)

Virgil's *Aeneid* (19 B.C.)

Lucan's *Pharsalia* (65 A.D.)

Ossian's *Fingal* (ca. 300)

Balinese *Bhima Swarga* (400)

Anglo-Saxon *Widsith* (ca. 450)

Anglo-Saxon *Beowulf* (600)

Russian *Lay of the Host of Igor* (ca. 870)

Persian *Shahnamah* (1000)

French *Chanson de Roland [The Song of Roland]* (1080)

Irish epic tale "The Destruction of Dá Derga's Hostel" (ca. 1100)

Spanish *El Cid* (1150)

Slavic *Edda* (1150-1250)

Japanese *The Tale of Heike* (ca. 1225)

Hungarian romantic epic, *Berta of Hungary* (ca. 1270)

Mali *Sundiata* (ca. 1275)

Dante's *Divina Commedia [The Divine Comedy]* (1314-1317)

John Barbour's *Bruce* (1375)

Ariosto's *Orlando Furioso* (1516)

Luis Vaz de Camoëns's *Os Lusiadas [The Luciad]* (1572)

Torquato Tasso's *Jerusalem Delivered* (1575)

Edmund Spenser's *Faerie Queene* (1590-1596)

John Milton's *Paradise Lost* (1667)

Zulu *Shaka* (late eighteenth century)

Joel Barlow's *The Vision of Columbus* (1787) and *The Columbiad* (1807)

Delaware pictographic *Walum Olum* (1820)

Adam Kidd's *The Huron Chief* (1830)

Henry Wadsworth Longfellow's *The Song of Hiawatha* (1855)

Alfred Tennyson's *Idylls of the King* (1859-1885)

Frances Ellen Watkins Harper's *Moses A Story of the Nile* (1869)
Stephen Vincent Benet's *John Brown's Body* (1928)
John Dos Passos's *USA* (1936)
Derek Walcott's *Omeros* (1990)

Emphasize a description of the hero, location, national crisis, military service, catalog of weapons, journeys, verse style, history, language, supernatural elements, family involvement, tests of character, and speeches.

Assessing Historical Literature

Age/Grade Level or Audience: High school or college literature classes; literary societies.

Description: Organize a great books symposium or discussion of works by black and white authors that depict black history.

Procedure: Beginning with a reading list of fiction and nonfiction works by black and white authors, contrast the accuracy of historical fiction accounts of black history. Include these works:

♦ Zora Neale Hurston, *Mule Bone*
♦ Suzanne Jurmain, *Freedom's Sons: The True Story of the Amistad Mutiny*
♦ Gustavus Vassa, *The Interesting Narrative of the Life of Olaudah Equino, or Gustavus Vassa, the African, by Himself*
♦ Julius Lester, *To Be a Slave*
♦ Dubose Heyward, *Porgy*
♦ Harriet Jacobs, *Incidents in the Life of a Slave Girl, Written by Herself*
♦ Gary Paulsen, *Nightjohn*
♦ Alice Childress, *A Hero Ain't Nothin' But a Sandwich*
♦ Toni Morrison, *Beloved* and *Jazz*
♦ George Washington Cable, *The Grandissimes*
♦ Fredericks Douglass, *Narration of the Life of Frederick Douglass*
♦ Robert Penn Warren, *Band of Angels*
♦ William Wells Brown, *Clotelle: A Tale of Southern States*
♦ William Blinn, *Brian's Song*
♦ Susan Straight, *I Been in Sorrow's Kitchen and Licked Out All the Pots*

Budget: Under $25

Sources:
A variety of fiction and nonfiction by black and white authors describing black history.

African Americans Who Made a Difference: 15 Plays for the Classroom, Scholastic Books, 1996.

Bontemps, Arna, ed., *American Negro Poetry*, Hill & Want, 1974.

Gates, Henry Louis, gen. ed., *The Norton Anthology of African American Literature*, W. W. Norton & Co., 1997.

Halliburton, Warren J., *Historic Speeches of African Americans*, Franklin Watts, 1993.

Segal, Aaron, Carole Berotte Joseph, and Marie-José N'Zengou-Tayo, *Caribbean Literature: An Anthology*, National Textbook, 1998.

Worley, Demetrice A., and Jesse Perry, Jr., eds. *African-American Literature: An Anthology*, 2nd edition, National Textbook, 1998.

Alternative Applications: As a follow-up exercise to an in-depth study of black society as described by black and white writers, keep an open website for write-in comments on the authenticity and validity of literature that depicts black history.

 ### "Between the World and Me"

Originator: Leatrice Pearson, teacher, Lenoir, North Carolina.

Age/Grade Level or Audience: Middle school or high school literature classes; literary societies.

Description: Discuss the imagery of Richard Wright's "Between the World and Me."

Procedure: Explain what rhetorical devices Wright uses to communicate the speaker's horror at discovering the scene of a recent lynching. Have readers answer the following questions:

- ◆ How does the speaker give life to inanimate objects?
- ◆ Where and when did the lynching take place?
- ◆ How was the victim tormented?
- ◆ How and why does the speaker identify with the victim?
- ◆ What irony attaches to his "baptism"?
- ◆ How does the event affect the speaker's attitude?
- ◆ Why does the ground grip his feet?
- ◆ Why does the burned trunk appear to point upward?
- ◆ What does the sun symbolize?

Explain how Richard Wright's use of sense impressions—sound, taste, smell, sight, and touch—enables the reader to identify with both the speaker and the victim.

Contrast the mood and tone of "Between the World and Me" with Richard Wright's "I Have Seen Black Hands" "The FB Eye Blues," and "Red Clay Blues" or Dudley Randall's "Ballad of Birmingham," which eulogizes four black children who were murdered in Birmingham, Alabama, in 1963.

Budget: Under $25

Sources:

Chapman, Abraham, ed., *Black Voices: An Anthology of Afro-American Literature*, St. Martin's Press, 1970.

Fabre, Michel, *Richard Wright Books and Writers*, University Pressof Mississippi, 1990.

"Richard Wright—Black Boy," http//www.itvs.org/programs/RW/more_info.html.

"Richard Wright—Black Boy," http//www.pbs.org/rwbb/teachgd.html.

"Richard Wright 1908-1970," http//educeth.ethz.ch/english/Reading List/EducETH-Wright, Ricahrd, html.

"Richard Wright—Black Boy," (video) Mississippi Educational TV/BBC, 1994.

Snodgrass, Mary Ellen, *The Encyclopedia of Southern Literature*, ABC-Clio, 1998.

Trotman, James C., *Richard Wright: Myths and Realities*, Garland, 1989.

Walker, Margaret, *Richard Wright: Daemonic Genius,* Warner, 1988.

Alternative Applications: Compose a round robin short story based on the dramatic situation in Richard Wright's poem "Between the World and Me." Provide character names, location, and motivation for violence. Add details about police investigation and burial services for the unnamed victim of lynching.

Black Book Fair

Age/Grade Level or Audience: All ages.

Description: Help Friends of the Library organize a black book fair.

Procedure: Obtain sponsorship for a black book fair. Offer shoppers calendars, bookmarks, videos, storytelling tapes, software, games, comics, posters, art prints, magazines, journals, newspapers, photographs, greeting cards, and other memorabilia as well as fiction and nonfiction by and about blacks. Help black families select works to introduce children to their heritage, such as atlases of Africa, explanations of Kwanzaa, biographies of great black entertainers, scholars, and sports figures, taped stories by black storytellers, and collections of stories, myths, and poems by Caribbean, African, and African American authors. Make the black book fair an annual event during Library Week, American Education Week, or Martin Luther King Day.

Budget: $50-$75

Sources:

Request assistance from professional booksellers, particularly B. Dalton, Scholastic, Media Play, Barnes and Noble, and Waldenbooks.

"African Writers," http//www.africaonlline.com/AfricaOnlinegriotstalk/writers/series. html.

Day, Frances Ann, *Multicultural Voices in Contemporary Literature*, Heinemann, 1994.

Diefendorf, Elizabeth, ed., *The New York Public Library's Books of the Century*, Oxford University Press, 1996.

Draper, James P., *Black Literature Criticism*, Gale, 1992.

Gillespie, John T., and Corinne J. Naden, *Characters in Young Adult Literature*, Gale, 1997.

Jackson, *Black Writers and the Hispanic Canon*, Twayne, 1997.

Osa, Osayimwense, *African Children's and Youth Literature*, Twayne, 1995.

Alternative Applications: Further the reading of literature by black authors by publishing helpful websites in a newspaper or newsletter. Request that local department stores, discount markets, and booksellers provide a shelf or corner devoted to black literature. Encourage others to patronize vendors who feature black authors, newspapers and periodicals, children's books, and bestsellers.

 Black History Book Collection

Age/Grade Level or Audience: All ages.

Description: Organize a special room dedicated to books by and about black history.

Procedure: Invite local book clubs, civic groups, Friends of the Library, and donors to add books to a special collection of works on black history. Include reference books, atlases, poster collections, recordings, photographs, sculpture, software, videos, and other material. Raise money for costly volumes by selling donated books, magazines, prints, or other items.

Budget: $50-$75

Sources:

"African Writers," http//www.africaonlline.com/AfricaOnlinegriotstalk/writers/series. html.

Diefendorf, Elizabeth, ed., *The New York Public Library's Books of the Century*, Oxford University Press, 1996.

Draper, James P., *Black Literature Criticism*, Gale, 1992.

Gillespie, John T., and Corinne J. Naden, *Characters in Young Adult Literature*, Gale, 1997.

Osa, Osayimwense, *African Children's and Youth Literature*, Twayne, 1995.

Alternative Applications: Post notices on the library bulletin board or in local newspapers encouraging people to donate a book, periodical, or software as a memorial to a community member or to honor a birthday, graduation, Mother's Day, Father's Day, Boss's Day, or Kwanzaa and other holidays. Offer a prioritized list of materials that the library needs. Supply an appropriate bookplate to mark memorial books.

Black on White

Age/Grade Level or Audience: High school or college literature or black studies classes; literary societies or book clubs; library workshops.

Description: Organize a study of literature that depicts how blacks get along with people of other races.

Procedure: Select short stories or books that detail a black/white relationship, such as these:

- ◆ Bette Greene, *Summer of My German Soldier*
- ◆ Mark Twain, *Pudd'nhead Wilson* or *Huckleberry Finn*
- ◆ Margaret Mitchell, *Gone with the Wind*
- ◆ William Styron, *The Confessions of Nat Turner*
- ◆ Jean Rhys, *Wide Sargasso Sea*
- ◆ William Blinn, *Brian's Song*
- ◆ E. R. Braithwaite, *To Sir with Love*
- ◆ Elizabeth Kata, *A Patch of Blue*
- ◆ J. H. Griffith, *Black Like Me*
- ◆ Eddy L. Harris, *Native Stranger*
- ◆ Thomas Tryon, *Lady*
- ◆ Toni Morrison, *Beloved*
- ◆ Alan Paton's *Cry the Beloved Country*
- ◆ William Faulkner, "That Evening Sun Go Down," *Intruder in the Dust, The Unvanquished,* or *The Sound and the Fury*
- ◆ William E. Barrett, *Lilies of the Field*
- ◆ Chinua Achebe, *Things Fall Apart*

- ◆ Jess Mowry, *Way Past Cool*
- ◆ Theodore Taylor, *The Cay*
- ◆ Carson McCullers, *The Member of the Wedding*
- ◆ Harper Lee, *To Kill a Mockingbird*
- ◆ Gary Paulsen, *Nightjohn* and *Sarny*
- ◆ Kaye Gibbons, *Ellen Foster*
- ◆ Alfred Uhry, *Driving Miss Daisy*
- ◆ Theodore Taylor, *The Cay*
- ◆ Terry McMillan, *Mama*
- ◆ Maya Angelou, *Even the Stars Look Lonesome*

Complete the study with a roundtable discussion of the coping mechanisms that facilitate peaceful coexistence.

Budget: $25-$50

Sources:

Consult the Multicultural Catalog or Perma-Search (CD-ROM) from Perma-Bound, Vandalia Road, Jacksonville, Illinois 62650, 800-637-6581, fax 800-551-1169, e-mail perma-bound@worldnet.att.net, websitehttp//www.perma-bound.com.

Draper, James P., *Black Literature Criticism*, Gale, 1992.

Gillespie, John T., and Corinne J. Naden, *Characters in Young Adult Literature*, Gale, 1997.

Segal, Aaron, Carole Berotte Joseph, and Marie-José N'Zengou-Tayo, *Caribbean Literature: An Anthology*, National Textbook, 1998.

Worley, Demetrice A., and Jesse Perry, Jr., eds. *African-American Literature: An Anthology*, 2nd edition, National Textbook, 1998.

Alternative Applications: Have readers select these and other significant passages of dialogue to read aloud, pantomime, or dramatize:

- ◆ Dilsey's interaction with the Compson children in *The Sound and the Fury*
- ◆ Homer Smith's arguments with the nuns in *Lilies of the Field*
- ◆ Jem Finch's attempts to understand the plight of a black man accused of raping a white woman in *To Kill a Mockingbird*
- ◆ Philip's attitude toward black people before and after the hurricane in *The Cay*
- ◆ Berenice's rejection of the orange dress in *A Member of the Wedding*
- ◆ Brian Piccolo's first meeting with his roommate, Gale Sayers, in *Brian's Song*
- ◆ Celie's experiences in the dry goods store in *The Color Purple*
- ◆ the unnamed boy's visit to his father's jail cell in *Sounder*
- ◆ Hoke's application for work in *Driving Miss Daisy*.

Black Study Group

Age/Grade Level or Audience: Adult literary society.

Description: Organize serious readers into a black study group.

Procedure: Consult the Internet or *Encyclopedia of Associations* for organizations that might be interested in supporting a black study group. Consider studying current black voices, such as these:

- ◆ cinematographer Spike Lee
- ◆ composer Quincy Jones
- ◆ columnists Marcia Gillespie and William Raspberry
- ◆ autobiographers Maya Angelou and Della Reese
- ◆ novelists Gordon Parks, Chinua Achebe and Terry McMillan
- ◆ playwright Alice Childress
- ◆ memoirist Jamaica Kincaid and V. S. Naipaul
- ◆ poets Sonia Sanchez, Nikki Giovanni, Anna Ruth Henriques, or Derek Walcott
- ◆ young adult authors Walter Dean Myers, Mildred Taylor, Dori Sanders, and Christopher Paul Curtis.

Advertise the creation of a black study group on college or university bulletin boards, in the media, on websites, and through newsletters of Mensa, League of Women Voters, and American Association of University Women. Hold an organizational meeting to decide what types of studies will be included, such as current fiction, feminism, civil rights, political issues, community improvement, film, or a variety of programs. Create a spin-off black studies group for high school or grade school students. Have volunteers from the parent group involve young members in readings, skits, discussions, and debates.

Budget: $50-$75

Sources:

Abrahams, Roger, D., *African Folktales*, Pantheon, 1983.

Brown, Stewart, ed., *Caribbean Poetry Now*, Edward Arnold, 1992.

"African Writers," http//www.africaonlline.com/AfricaOnlinegriotstalk/writers/series. html.

Diefendorf, Elizabeth, ed., *The New York Public Library's Books of the Century*, Oxford University Press, 1996.

Draper, James P., *Black Literature Criticism*, Gale, 1992.

Rosenberg, Donna, *Folklore, Myths, and Legends: A World Perspective*, National Textbook Company, 1997.

———, *World Literature*, National Textbook Company, 1992.

Schuman, Michael, "We've Come a Long Way . . .," *Forbes*, February 14, 1992, 196-214.

Segal, Aaron, Carole Berotte Joseph, and Marie-José N'Zengou-Tayo, *Caribbean Literature: An Anthology*, National Textbook, 1998.

Senanu, K. E., and T. Vincent, eds., *A Selection of African Poetry*, Longman, 1990.

Worley, Demetrice A., and Jesse Perry, Jr., eds. *African-American Literature: An Anthology*, 2nd edition, National Textbook, 1998.

Alternative Applications: Design a library, college, or university bulletin board featuring a map of the following countries and their black authors. Place a star by those writing in French. For example:

AFRICA

Benin

Olympe Bhely-Quénum

Cameroon

Mongo Beti*, Elolongué Epanya-Yondo*, Ferdinand Oyono*

Cape Verde Islands

Nuno Miranda

Congo

Tchicaya U Tam'si*

Egypt

Naguib Mahfouz

French Guiana

Léon-Gontran Damas

Gambia

Lenrie Peters

Ghana

Ama Ata Aidoo, Ayi Kwei Armah, George Awooner-Williams, Adelaide Casely-Hayford, Mabel Dove Danquah, Ngugi Wa Thiong'o, Michael Ofori-Mankata

Guinea

Camara Laye*, Léon Damas*

Ivory Coast

Bernard Binlin Dadié

Kenya

Muga Gicaru, Josiah Kariuki, M. O. Macoye, James Ngugi, Grace Ogot

Lesotho

Thomas Mofolo

Mauritius

Édouard Maunick, Gutto Shadrack

Nigeria

Chinua Achebe, Timothy Aluko, Elechi Amadi, John Pepper Clark, Cyprian Ekwensi, Onuora Nzekwu, Gabriel Okara, Christopher Okigbo, Ben Okri, Wole Soyinka, Amos Tutuola

Nyasaland

James D. Rubadiri

Rhodesia

Dennis Brutus

São Tomé

Francisco Jose Tenreiro

Senegal

Birago Diop*, David Diop*, Malick Fall*, Cheikh Hamidou Kane, Sembène Ousmane*, Léopold Sédar Senghor*

Sierra Leone

Jacob Stanley Davies, A. B. C. Merriman Labor, Abioseh Nicol

South Africa

Peter Abrahams, H. I. E. Dhlomo, Bessie Head, A. C. Jordan, Mazisi Kunene, Alex La Guma, Mark Mathabane, Ezekiel Mphahlele, S. E. K. Mqhayi, Oswald Mbuyiseni Mtshali, Sol T. Plaatje, B. W. Vilakazi

Sudan

Tayeb Salih

Uganda

Barbara Kimenye, Okot p'Bitek

Zaire

Vumbi Yoka Mudimbe

Zimbabwe

Charles Mungoshi

CARIBBEAN

Antigua

Jamaica Kincaid

Barbados

Edward Brathwaite, George Lamming

Dominica

Cesteros

Haiti

Jacques-Stéphen Alexis, Pierre Marcelin, Jacques Roumain, Philippe Thoby-Marcelin

Jamaica

Peter Abrahams, Claude McKay, Anna Ruth Henriques

Martinique

Aimé Césaire*, René Maran

St. Lucia

Derek Wolcott

Tobago

Grace Hallworth

Trinidad

Okot p'Bitek, Paul Keens-Douglas, V. S. Naipaul

SOUTH AMERICA

Guyana

Ken Corsbie, Wilson Harris, E. R. Braithwaite, Edgar Mittelholzer

NORTH AMERICA

United States

Maya Angelou	William Armstrong	William Attaway
James Baldwin	Toni Cade Bambara	Amiri Baraka
Arna Bontemps	Gwendolyn Brooks	Sterling A. Brown
Ed Bullins	Jeanette Caines	Charles W. Chesnutt
Alice Childress	Countee Cullen	Rita Dove
Paul Laurence Dunbar	Ralph Ellison	Mari Evans
Ernest J. Gaines	Nikki Giovanni	Virginia Hamilton
Lorraine Hansberry	Robert Hayden	Chester Himes
Langston Hughes	Zora Neale Hurston	James Weldon Johnson
William Melvin Kelley	John Oliver Killens	Audre Lorde
Terry McMillan	Toni Morrison	Walter Dean Myers
Ishmael Reed	Wallace Thurman	Melvin B. Tolson
Jean Toomer	Alice Walker	Margaret Walker
John A. Williams	Richard Wright	

Create a display of articles, poems, short stories, plays, speeches, children's literature, novels, autobiography, and nonfiction in print and on tape for visitors to browse and sample.

Books for Africa

Age/Grade Level or Audience: All ages.

Description: Launch a "Books for Africa" project.

Procedure: Assist emerging African nations in learning about black history and their place of black peoples in the moden world by collecting books to donate to a national or international book project such as these:

Books for Africa
5233 Silver Maple Circle
Minneapolis, MInnesota 55343
phone 612-939-9889
e-mail bfa@mtn.org

Books for All
Brunhildenstrasse 34, D-80639
München, Germany
phone 011-49-89-172383
fax 011-49-89-2607896

Brother's Brother Foundation
1501 Reedsdale Street, Suite 3005
Pittsburgh, Pennsylvania 15233
phone 412-321-3160
fax 412-321-3325
e-mail BBF@charitiesusa.com
http//www.brothersbrother.com/educate.htm

CODE
321 Chapel Street

Ottawa, Ontario
Canada K1N 7Z2
phone 613-232-3569
fax 613-232-7435
e-mail codehq@codecan.com
http//www.web.net/~code/

Darien Book Aid Plan, Inc.
1926 Post Road
Darien, Connecticut 06820
phone 203-655-2777
fax 203-656-3939

International Book Bank
813 Central Avenue, Suite F
Linthicum, Maryland 21090
phone 410-636-6895
fax 410-636-6898
e-mail ibbusa@worldnet.att.net

International Book Project, Inc.
1440 Delaware Avenue
Lexington, Kentucky 40505
e-mail ibp@iglou.com

Project HOPE International Textbook
Distribution Program
Scott Crawford
Route 255
Millwood, Virginia 22646
phone 800-544-4673
e-mail scrawford@projhope.org

Sabre Foundation, Inc.
Scientific Assistance Project
872 Massachusetts Avenue, Suite 2-1
Cambridge, Massachusetts 02139
phone 617-868=3510
fax 617-868-7916
e-mail colin@sabre.org
http//www.sabre.org/SAP/book.journal.html.

World Bank Volunteer Book Project
1818 H Street, N. W., Room NB1-105
Washington, D. C. 20433
phone 202-473-8960
fax 202-522-0301

Budget: $75-$100

Sources:
Watkins, Christine, "Changing the World Through Books," *American Libraries*, October 1997, 52-54.

Alternative Applications: Work with a charity to collect used and donated reference books to send to a developing African or Caribbean nation.

Books for Summer

Age/Grade Level or Audience: All ages.

Description: Organize a summer reading program.

Procedure: Create a special collection of library books about black history or by black authors. Offer prizes at different levels for number of books read, for example, coloring books, posters, magazine subscriptions, or paperbacks to readers who reach a target number of books in a three-month period. Include books on tape for handicapped or illiterate readers. Provide titles in foreign languages to serve local populations who don't read English.

Budget: $50-$75

Sources:

Recruit volunteers, particularly the Friends of the Library, to donate books or help raise funds to add to the library's collection of works suited to the summer reading program. Consult the Multicultural Catalog or Perma-Search (CD-ROM) from Perma-Bound, Vandalia Road, Jacksonville, Illinois 62650, 800-637-6581, fax 800-551- 1169, e-mail permabound@worldnet.att.net, website http//www.perma-bound.com.

Coles, Y. R., "Recent and Relevant Children's Books," *American Visions*, December 1996-January 1997, 28-31.

Dickey, Shelly, ed., *What Do Children Read Next?,* volume 2, Gale, 1997.

Dickey, Shelly, ed., *What Do Young Adults Read Next?,* volume 2, Gale, 1997.

Diefendorf, Elizabeth, ed., *The New York Public Library's Books of the Century*, Oxford University Press, 1996.

Fralick, Katharine G., ed., "Character and Citizenship: An Annotated Bibliography of Children's and Young Adults' Literature," *Teaching K-8,* October 1997, 50-52.

Gillespie, John T., and Corinne J. Naden, *Characters in Young Adult Literature*, Gale, 1997.

Osa, Osayimwense, *African Children's and Youth Literature*, Twayne, 1995.

"The Poetry of Rita Dove," *Scholastic Scope*, September 1997, 21-23.

Alternative Applications: Organize volunteers to start a clipping file for the local library, museum, school library, or historical society. Have a regular staff of volunteers comb newspapers, magazines, travel guides, journals, internet, and other print sources for materials to comprise a clipping file on black history. Laminate articles, especially maps and charts, to facilitate their use before groups and to lessen wear on fragile newsprint. Ask local readers to donate or photocopy articles that will bolster local collections of books and other print material, particularly those in color, such as maps and articles from *National Geographic, Discovery,* and *Biography.*

 | **Comparing Wisdom**

Age/Grade Level or Audience: Middle school or high school language classes; civic groups, book clubs, or literary societies.

Description: Compare common American aphorisms with the wise sayings of Africans.

Procedure: Present the group with a list of African aphorisms. For example:

♦ The head of a man is a secret storage place. (Chagga)

♦ The heart of a man is like an intricately woven net. (Tswana)

♦ The fool says, 'This world is a virgin girl'; the wise man knows the world is old. (Hausa)

♦ The heart of the wise man lies quiet like limpid water. (Cameroon)

♦ There is no medicine to cure hatred. (Ashanti)

♦ The humble pay for the mistakes of their betters. (Baguirmi)

♦ It is best to bind up the finger before it is cut. (Lesotho)

♦ He who hunts two rats, catches none. (Buganda)

♦ What is said over the dead lion's body, could not be said to him alive. (Zaire)

♦ The frog wanted to be as big as the elephant, and burst. (Ethiopia)

♦ Move your neck according to the music. (Galla)

♦ If there were no elephant in the jungle, the buffalo would be a great animal. (Ghana)

♦ One camel does not make fun of the other camel's hump. (Guinea)

♦ Save your fowl before it stops flapping. (Ivory Coast)

♦ Thunder is not yet rain. (Kenya)

♦ A little rain each day will fill the rivers to overflowing. (Liberia)

♦ The end of an ox is beef, and the end of a lie is grief. (Madagascar)

♦ A cutting word is worse than a bowstring; a cut may heal, but the cut of the tongue does not. (Mauritania)

♦ There is no medicine against old age. (Niger)

♦ Some birds avoid the water, ducks seek it. (Nigeria)

♦ One little arrow does not kill a serpent. (Malawi)

♦ The monkey does not see his own hind parts; he sees his neighbors'. (Zimbabwe)

♦ In a court of fowls, the cockroach never wins his case. (Rwanda)

♦ If a centipede loses a leg, it does not prevent him from walking. (Senegal)

♦ Only a monkey understands a monkey. (Sierra Leone)

♦ In the ocean, one does not need to sow water. (Somalia)

♦ Let rats shoot arrows at each other. (Sudan)

♦ A sheep cannot bleat in two different places at the same time. (Tanzania)

♦ A roaring lion kills no game. (Uganda)

♦ A horse has four legs, yet it often falls. (Zululand)

Have volunteers restate the idea with American images.

Budget: Under $25

Sources:

Delamotte, Eugenia, Natania Meeker, and Jean O'Barr, eds. *Women Imagine Change A Global Anthology of Women's Resistance, 600 B. C. E. to Present*, Routledge, 1997.

Diggs, Anita Doren, ed., *Talking Drums: An African-American Quote Collection*, St. Martin's, 1995.

Maggio, Rosalie, *The New Beacon Book of Quotations by Women*, Beacon Press, 1996.

Mullane, Deirdre, *Words to Make My Dream Children Live: A Book of African American Quotations,* Anchor Books, 1995.

Riley, Dorothy Winbush, *My Soul Looks Back, "Less I Forget": A Collection of Quotations by People of Color*, Harper Perennial, 1993.

Alternative Applications: Have participants work in pairs to create a comparative list of African and American sayings, such as one of Poor Richard's sayings, a verse from the book of Proverbs, or one of Aesop's moral tags. Select the most striking pairs to write in calligraphy on poster paper or on wall hangings or book markers. Transfer some to cloth and create needlework to be framed, hung as banners, or made into pillows and floor coverings. For example:

- ◆ Seeing is different from being told. (Kenya)
  Seeing is believing.
- ◆ Before healing others, heal thyself. (Nigeria)
  Physician, heal thyself.
- ◆ Evil knows where evil sleeps. (Nigeria)
  Evil begets evil.
- ◆ A little shrub may grow into a tree. (Sudan)
  The mighty oak was once an acorn.
- ◆ Hunger is felt by a slave and hunger is felt by a king. (Ashanti)
  All men put on their pants one leg at a time.
- ◆ Little by little grow the bananas. (Zaire)
  The best way to eat an elephant is one bite at a time.

"D. P."

Age/Grade Level or Audience: Middle school or high school literature or humanities classes.

Description: Lead a discussion of Kurt Vonnegut's short story, "D. P."

Procedure: Read Kurt Vonnegut's story aloud. Lead a discussion of the author's purpose in choosing the orphaned "blue-eyed colored boy" as his focus.

Budget: Under $25

Sources:

"Biracial Children," http//www.korealink.com/public/general/messages/2468.htm.

"The Interracial Family and Social Alliance," http//www.flash.net/~mata9/ifsa.htm.

"Multiethnic Presence," http//ils.unc.edu/inls110/projects/brisj/ multieth.html.

Simmons, John S., and Malcolm E. Stern, *The Short Story and You: An Introduction to Understanding and Appreciation,* National Textbook Co., 1986.

Vonnegut, Kurt, *Welcome to the Monkey House,* Franklin Library, 1981.

Alternative Applications: Organize discussion groups to ponder the fate of multiracial children, particularly the offspring of black G. I.s in Korea, Vietnam, Panama, Granada, the Persian Gulf, and Bosnia.

- ◆ List suggestions for how the United States can prevent racial discrimination against multiracial children.
- ◆ Report on the Pearl Buck Foundation, which was established to ease the burden of the children born to Asian mothers and American G. I. fathers.
- ◆ Locate source material explaining the hard life of unwanted biracial children in Asia, especially Vietnamese orphans known as "the dust."
- ◆ Discuss the Census Bureau's use of single racial categories.

Derek Walcott

Age/Grade Level or Audience: College literature class; literary society, book club.

Description: Hold a public reading of the works of Derek Walcott, 1992 Nobel Prize winner for literature.

Procedure: Hold a Derek Walcott reading at a school, library, museum, or public assembly. Select some of his verse, such as segments of *Omeros,* his 325-page Caribbean epic, or short works, such as *The Light of the World, The Lighthouse,* "Sea Grapes," "A Far Cry from Africa," or "Sunday Lemons." Concentrate on thought-provoking, evocative lines, for instance:

> Where shall I turn, divided to the vein?
> I who have cursed
> the drunken officer of British rule, how choose
> Between this Africa and the English tongue I love?
> Betray them both, or give back what they give?

Have participants note syncopated cadences, slang, Creole patois, sense impressions, paradox, and rich island images. Conclude the reading with a comparison of Walcott's view of Caribbean life with that of other literary views, such as Jamaica

Kincaid's *Annie John* or *My Brother*, Paul Keens-Douglas's "Tanti Merle at de Oval," Lynn Joseph's *Coconut Kind of Day,* Theodore Taylor's *The Cay*, Jean Rhys's *Wide Sargasso Sea*, or Ernest Hemingway's *The Old Man and the Sea* or *Islands in the Stream.*

Budget: Under $25

Sources:

Brown, Stewart, ed., *Caribbean Poetry Now*, Edward Arnold, 1992.

"Derek Walcott," http//hsl.hst.msu.edu/~cal/celeb/walcott.html.

"Derek Walcott," http//www.smau.it/nobel/biograph/bwalc.htm.

"Derek Walcott, Famed Poet, Playwright, awarded 1992 Nobel Prize in Literature," *Jet*, October 26, 1992, 14.

Goring, Rosemary, ed., *Larousse Dictionary of Writers*, Larousse Kingfisher Chambers, 1994.

Gray, Paul, "Bard of the Island Life," *Time*, October 19, 1992, 65.

Hamner, Robert D., *Derek Walcott,* revised edition, Scribners Reference, 1993.

Lazzari, Marie, ed., *Epics for Students: Presenting Analysis, Context and Criticism on Commonly Studied Epics*, Gale, 1997.

Ousby, Ian, *Cambridge Paperback Guide to Literature in English*, Cambridge University Press, 1996.

Sturrock, John, ed., *The Oxford Guide to Contemporary World Literature*, Oxford University Press, 1996.

Terada, Rei, *Derek Walcott's Poetry: American Mimicry*, Nebraska University Press, 1992.

Walcott, Derek, *The Arkansas Testament,* Farrar, Straus, 1978.

———, *Collected Poems, 1945-1984,* Farrar, Straus, 1986.

———, *Dream on Monkey Mountain and Other Plays*, Farrar, Straus, 1970.

———, *The Fortunate Traveller,* Farrar, Straus, 1981.

———, *The Joker of Seville and O Babylon!: Two Plays,* Farrar, Straus, 1980.

———, Midsummer, Farrar, Straus, 1984.

———, *Odyssey, a Stage Version,* Farrar, Straus, 1993.

———, *Omeros*, Farrar, Straus, 1992.

———, Remembrance and Pantomime Two Plays, Farrar, Straus, 1980.

———, *The Star-Apple Kingdom,* Farrar, Straus, 1979.

———, *Three Plays,* Farrar, Straus, 1986.

———, *Viva Detroit*, Farrar, Straus, 1992.

Alternative Applications: As an introduction to an influential poet and playwright, post a bulletin board display of facts about the life and career of Derek Walcott. Include these data:

- ♦ Derek Walcott was born of Dutch, English, and African ancestry in 1930 in Castries, St. Lucia.
- ♦ Educated at St. Mary's College and the University of the West Indies, Kingston, Jamaica, he published his first book of verse at the age of eighteen.

- ◆ He followed with nine more volumes in his lengthy career as poet, playwright, and teacher and stresses the blend of African and European influences on Caribbean thought and culture.
- ◆ In 1959, he founded the Trinidad Theatre Workshop.
- ◆ Spending equal amounts of time in Boston, Massachusetts, and Port of Spain, Trinidad, he teaches literature and creative writing at Boston University.
- ◆ His first significant prize was the MacArthur Foundation grant in 1981.
- ◆ In October 1992, Walcott won the Nobel Prize for literature, totaling $1.2 million.

Feminist Writers

Originator: Leatrice Pearson, teacher, Lenoir, North Carolina.

Age/Grade Level or Audience: High school and college literature students; literary societies.

Description: Present a program of female African American poets.

Procedure: Read aloud from Nikki Giovanni, Mari Evans, Gwendolyn Brooks, Naomi Long Madgett, Clarissa Scott Delany, Helene Johnson, Margaret Walker, Julia Fields, Audre Lorde, Toni Morrison, Rita Dove, Brandi Barnes, Helen Armstead Johnson, Lucille Clifton, and Maya Angelou. Focus on particular lines and chapters, for example, Mona Lake Jones's "Room Full of Sisters," which proclaims "A sisterhood of modern sojourners today/Still out in front, blazing the way" and on "Black Culture," which drolly comments "'Black folks don't have any culture' I heard somebody say/and I just put my hand on my hip, rolled my eyes and looked the other way."

Budget: $25-$50

Sources:

Carroll, Rebecca, *I Know What the Red Clay Looks Like: The Voice and Vision of Black Women Writers*, Carol Southern Press, 1995.

Diefendorf, Elizabeth, ed., *The New York Public Library's Books of the Century*, Oxford University Press, 1996.

Hine, Darlene Clark, Elsa Barkley Brown, and Rosalyn Terborg-Penn, *Black Women in America: An Historical Encyclopedia,* Carlson Publishing, 1993.

Segal, Aaron, Carole Berotte Joseph, adn Marie-José N'Zengou-Tayo, *Caribbean Literature: An Anthology*, National Textbook, 1998.

Smith, Jessie Carney, *Notable Black American Women*, Gale, 1992.

Worley, Demetrice A., and Jesse Perry, Jr., eds. *African-American Literature: An Anthology*, 2nd edition, National Textbook, 1998.

Alternative Applications: Lead a discussion of the black woman's unique point of view as demonstrated by her poetry. Determine how hardship has made her strong and humor has preserved her balance, as described in Mari Evans's poem "I Am a Black Woman." Compare these assertions to Sojourner Truth's "Aint' I a Woman" speech, Helen Reddy's popular song, "I Am Woman," Gloria Steinem's introduction to *Revolution from Within,* or Maya Angelou's lyric poem *Now Sheba Sings the Song.*

Freedom's Journal

Age/Grade Level or Audience: High school or college literature or writing classes.

Description: Discuss *Freedom's Journal.*

Procedure: Read aloud from the first edition of Samuel Cornish and John B. Russworm's *Freedom's Journal,* the first black newspaper in the United States. Have students discuss the significance of the following paragraphs:

> We wish to plead our own cause. Too long have others spoken for us. Too long has the public been deceived by misrepresentations, in things which concern us deeply, though in the estimation of some mere trifles; for though there are many in society who exercise towards us benevolent feelings; still (with sorrow we confess it) there are others who make it their business to enlarge upon the least trifle, which tends to the discredit of any person of colour and pronounce anathemas and denounce our whole body for the misconduct of this guilty one. We are aware that there are many instances of vice among us, but we avow that it is because no one has taught its subjects to be virtuous; many instances of poverty, because no sufficient efforts accommodated to minds contracted by slavery, and deprived of early education have been made, to teach them how to husband their hard earnings, and to secure to themselves comfort.
>
> Education being an object of the highest importance to the welfare of society, we shall endeavour to present just and adequate views of it, and to urge upon our brethren the necessity and expediency of training their children, while young, to habits of industry, and thus forming them for becoming useful members of society. It is surely time

that we should awake from this lethargy of years, and make a concentrated effort for the education of our youth. We form a spoke in
the human wheel, and it is necessary that we should understand our
dependence on the different parts, and theirs on us, in order to perform our part with propriety.

If ignorance, poverty and degradation have hitherto been our unhappy
lot; has the eternal decree gone forth, that our race alone are to remain
in this state, while knowledge and civilization are shedding their
enlivening rays over the rest of the human family? The recent travels of
Denham and Clapperton in the interior of Africa, and the interesting
narrative which they have published; the establishment of the republic
of Haiti after years of sanguinary warfare; its subsequent progress in all
the arts of civilization; and the advancement of the liberal ideas in South
America, where despotism has given place to free governments, and
where many of our brethren now fill important civil and military stations, prove the contrary.

Budget: Under $25

Sources:
"African-American Periodicals and Periodical Reference Materials," http//www.unc.
   edu/~bsemonch/blackpress.html.
"Black Periodical Literature Project," http//web-dubois.fas.harvard.edu/DuBois/
   Research/BPLP/BPLP.H.
Mabunda, L. Mpho, ed., *The African American Almanac*, 7th edition, Gale, 1997.

Alternative Applications: Have students contribute paragraphs,
essays, editorials, or letters to the editor of the first issue of the newspaper in which
they support Russworm's fight to abolish slavery and cite other reasons why slavery
should be abolished. Suggest these types of submissions:

   ◆ expository writing about the time span of the slave trade
   ◆ personal essay about experiences with slaves and slave owners
   ◆ journal entry on observations at a slave market
   ◆ letter to the editor agreeing with Cornish and Russworm
   ◆ biographical essay written about a slave overseer or auctioneer
   ◆ travelogue describing the slave trade on Africa's west coast
   ◆ a feature on African American readers in the mid-nineteenth century

Judging Fact and Fiction

Age/Grade Level or Audience: Book clubs, literary symposiums,
and library study groups.

Description: Hold a symposium comparing black history in history and fiction.

Procedure: Provide a sampling of literature by historians, biographers, autobiographers, playwrights, and fiction writers. Lead a discussion of these issues:

- ◆ Which gives a more accurate picture of black history, nonfiction or fiction?
- ◆ What is truer to actual events?
- ◆ Which is timelier for recreational readers?
- ◆ What advantages does the fictional biographer have over the historian?

Budget: Under $25

Sources:
Offer a list of suggested works from classic literature by and about black history. Mount the list on a library website or post on a bulletin board.

Carroll, Rebecca, *I Know What the Red Clay Looks Like: The Voice and Vision of Black Women Writers*, Carol Southern Press, 1995.

————, *Swing Low: Black Men Writing*, Carol Southern Press, 1995.

Jackson, *Black Writers and the Hispanic Canon*, Twayne, 1997.

Osa, Osayimwense, *African Children's and Youth Literature*, Twayne, 1995.

Alternative Applications: Have a reading circle brainstorm a believable character and background for one of these literary genres: detective or spy story, fantasy adventure, sci-fi thriller, historical romance, young adult novel, children's storybook, epic poem, musical comedy, or episodic romance.

The Latest by Black Authors

Age/Grade Level or Audience: All ages.

Description: Advertise current works by black authors.

Procedure: Create a bulletin board or scan a website of book jackets from works by Caribbean, African, or African American authors. Organize the display by age and interest level. Stress a variety of books from reference and nonfiction to poetry, drama, novels, and short stories, for example:

- ◆ poems by Nobel winner Derek Wolcott, Audre Lorde, Sonia Sanchez, and Rita Dove
- ◆ Henry Louis Gates, Jr., and Cornel West, *The Future of the Race*
- ◆ Patricia McKissack, *Jesse Jackson*

- ◆ Anna Kosof, *The Civil Rights Movement and Its Legacy*
- ◆ Mildred D. Taylor, *Roll of Thunder, Hear My Cry*
- ◆ John Agard, *The Calypso Alphabet*
- ◆ Joyce Powzyk, *Tracking Wild Chimpanzees*
- ◆ Donna Bailey and Anna Sproule, *We Live in Nigeria*
- ◆ Judith Hoffman Corwin, *African Crafts*
- ◆ Martin Gibrill, *African Food and Drink*
- ◆ Toni Morrison, *Jazz*
- ◆ Ralph Ellison, *Flying Home and Other Stories*
- ◆ Dori Sanders, *Dori Sanders' Country Cooking*
- ◆ Christopher Paul Curtis, *The Watsons Go to Birmingham—1963*

Budget: Under $25

Sources:

Collect book jackets from the technical services division of a city, county, or school library. For more information about books, consultthe Multicultural Catalog or Perma-Search (CD-ROM) from Perma-Bound, Vandalia Road, Jacksonville, Illinois 62650, 800-637-6581, fax 800-551-1169, e-mail permabound@worldnet.att.net,website http//www.perma-bound.com.

Baily, Cate, "Langston Hughes: How He Became America's Poet," *Scholastic Scope*, September 22, 1997, 14-17.

DiConsiglio, John, "Taking It Easy with Walter Mosley," *Literary Cavalcade*, November/ December 1997, 4-5.

Ellis, Roger, *Multicultural Theatre: Scenes and Monologues from New Hispanic, Asian, and African-American Plays*, Meriwether Publications, 1996.

Kruse, Ginny M., and Kathleen T. Horning, eds., *Multicultural Literature for Children and Young Adults: A Selected Listing of Books 1980-1990 by and about People of Color*, Diane Publications, 1993.

Naipaul, V. S., "The Raffle," *Literary Cavalcade*, November/December, 1997, 16-19,

Naylor, Gloria, *Children of the Night: The Best Short Stories by Black Writers, 1967 to the Present*, Little, Brown & Co., 1996.

Miller-Lachmann, Lyn, *Our Family, Our Friends, Our World: An Annotated Guide to Significant Multicultural Books for Children and Teenagers,*Bowker, 1992.

"The Poetry of Rita Dove," *Scholastic Scope*, September 1997, 21-23.

Polette, Nancy, *Multicultural Readers Theatre*, Book Lures, 1994.

Alternative Applications: Encourage more readers to sample black authors. Use these methods:

- ◆ Perform a skit or scene from a play over a public address system, such as V. S. Naipaul's "The Raffle" or a scene from one of Walter Mosley's mysteries, for example, *Devil in a Blue Dress* or *Always Outnumbered, Always Outgunned.*
- ◆ Distribute book lists by mail, on a library or school website, or at the checkout desk of the library.

- ◆ Share the information with the book editor of a local newspaper.
- ◆ Have the Friends of the Library include new book information in their newsletters.
- ◆ Include suggested titles that the library would like to purchase and that donors or support groups may supply as gifts or memorials.
- ◆ Hold a pre-holiday Afrocentric book fair.
- ◆ Make Afrocentric bookmarks to distribute free. List a book title on each.

Lyndon Johnson and the Black Panthers

Age/Grade Level or Audience: High school and college history and literature classes; civic clubs.

Description: Compare the philosophy of Lyndon Johnson's voting rights address of 1965 with the Black Panther Manifesto of 1966.

Procedure: Note the differences in phrasing and intent in these two works. Consider Johnson's comments and goals:

- ◆ There is no Negro problem. There is no Southern problem. There is no Northern problem. There is only an American problem.
- ◆ There is no issue of states rights, or national rights. There is only the struggle for human rights.
- ◆ We must preserve the right of free speech and the right of free assembly.
- ◆ We will guard against violence, knowing it strikes from our hands the very weapons which we seek—progress, obedience to law, and belief in American values.
- ◆ So we want to open the gates to opportunity. But we're also going to give all our people, black and white, the help that they need to walk through those gates.
- ◆ I want to be the President who helped to feed the hungry and to prepare them to be taxpayers instead of tax eaters.

Contrast these thoughts with the Black Panther Party's demands

- ◆ We want freedom. We want power to determine the destiny of our Black Community.
- ◆ We want full employment for our people.
- ◆ We want an end to the robbery by the capitalist of our Black Community.
- ◆ We want decent housing, fit for shelter of human beings.
- ◆ We want education for our people that exposes the true nature of this decadent American society. We want history that teaches us our true history and our role in the present-day society.
- ◆ We want an end to police brutality and murder of black people.

◆ We want land, bread, housing, education, clothing, justice and peace.

Budget: Under $25

Sources:

Jones, Charles, *Black Panther Party Reconsidered Reflections and Scholarship*, Black Classic, 1996.

Mabunda, L. Mpho, ed., *The African American Almanac*, 7th edition, Gale, 1997.

Schulman, Bruce J., *Lyndon B. Johnson and American Liberalism: A Brief Biography with Documents*, St. Martin, 1994.

Seale Bobby, *Seize the Time: The Story of the Black Panther Party and Huey P. Newton*, Random House, 1970.

Alternative Applications: Debate the more extreme of the Black Panther demands:

◆ We want all black men to be exempt from military service.

◆ We want freedom for all black men held in federal, state, county and city prisons and jails.

◆ We want all black people when brought to trial to be tried in court by a jury of their peer group or people from their black communities, as defined by the Constitution of the United States.

◆ ... when a long train of abuses and usurpations, pursuing invariably the same object, evinces a design to reduce [black people] under absolute despotism, it is their right, it is their duty, to throw off such government, and to provide new guards for their future security.

Melville and Slavery

Age/Grade Level or Audience: High school or college literature classes; literary societies; book clubs.

Description: Analyze the themes of Herman Melville's novella Benito Cereno.

Procedure: Launch a thorough study of the theme of Benito Cereno, Herman Melville's novel concerning the debilitating effect of the slave trade on European adventurers Consider several controlling motifs:

◆ the imprisoning microcosm of the ship
◆ miscommunication between Captain Delano and Don Benito
◆ desperation of transported slaves
◆ evil begetting evil
◆ the duplicity and greed that undergird the foundations of America

> ◆ eventual disaster awaiting both whites and blacks involved in the slave trade

Budget: $25-$50

Sources:

"Accounting for the Caprices of Madness," http://www.anderson.ucla.edu/research/conferences/scos/abstract.

Adamson, Joseph, Melville, Shame, and the Evil Eye: Psychoanalytic Reading, State University of New York Press, 1997.

Gale, Robert *L., Herman Melville Encyclopedia,* Greenwood, 1995.

Melville, Herman, *Benito Cereno,* Imprint Society, 1972.

"Melville Online," http://www.melville.org/download.htm.

Parker, Hershel, *Herman Melville: A Biography, Vol.* 7: 7879-7857, Johns Hopkins, 1996.

Alternative Applications: Contrast Melville's horrific tale with other authors' views of slavery and its aftermath. Consider these titles:

- ◆ Ernest Gaines, The Autobiography of Miss Jane Pittman
- ◆ William Faulkner, *Absalom, Absalom*
- ◆ Paula Fox, *Slave Dancer*
- ◆ Gustavus Vassa, *The Interesting Narrative of the Life of Olaudah Equiano, or Gustavus Vassa*
- ◆ Harriet Jacobs, *Incidents in the Life of a Slave Girl*
- ◆ Harriet Beecher Stowe, *Uncle Tom's Cabin*
- ◆ Arthur Miller, *The Crucible*
- ◆ Toni Morrison, *Beloved*
- ◆ Margaret Walker, *Jubilee*
- ◆ Gary Paulsen, *Nightjohn*
- ◆ William Styron, *The Confessions of Nat Turner*
- ◆ Ann Petry, *Tituba of Salem Village*
- ◆ Alex Halex, *Roots* and *Queen*

Incorporate into your study the words of W. E. B. Du Bois on race:

> The problem of the twentieth century is the problem of color. This double-consciousness, this sense of always looking at one's self through the eyes of others, of measuring one's soul by the tape of a world that looks on in amused contempt and pity. One ever feels his twoness-an American, a Negro; two souls, two thoughts, two unreconciled strivings, two warring ideals in one dark body, whose dogged strength alone keeps it from being torn asunder.

Decide whether Du Bois's description of "twoness" is still relevant to American life.

Militant Verse

Originator: Leatrice Pearson, teacher, Lenoir, North Carolina.

Age/Grade Level or Audience: High school or college literature classes; literary societies.

Description: Assess the tone and accuracy of Raymond R. Patterson's poetry.

Procedure: Invite volunteers to read aloud stanzas of Raymond Patterson's "A Traditional Ballad," "Birmingham 1963," "For the Bombed Negro Children," and "Riot Times U.S.A.," which concludes:

> Yes, I trust the things one hears-
> Times will get better
> Than they presently are-
> About as far as I can throw
> Three hundred years,
> And up to now
> That hasn't been far.

Encourage each reader to make a personal response or evaluation of each verse, particularly as it applies to recurrent urban unrest, as seen in the Los Angeles riots in spring 1992.

Budget: Under $25

Sources:
Hester, Joseph P., Encyclopedia of Values and Ethics, ABC-Clio, 1996.
———,*Law Enforcement Ethics,* ABC-Clio, 1997.
Kronenwetter, Michael, *Encyclopedia of Twentieth-Century American Social Issues,* ABC-Clio, 1997.
Patterson, Raymond R., 26 *Ways of Looking at a Black Man and Other Poems,* Award Books, 1969.
Segal, Aaron, Carole Berotte Joseph, and Marie-Jose N'Zengou-Tayo, *Caribbean Literature: An Anthology,* National Textbook, 1998.
Worley, Demetrice A., and Jesse Perry, Jr., eds. *African-American Literature: An Anthology,* 2nd ed., National Textbook, 1998.

Alternative Applications: Invite creative writers to append their own stanzas concerning restlessness, racism, hatred, and vengeance. Collect responses on a single handout and share with the group. Have students compare their style with Patterson's command of rhythm, tone, point of view, image, and diction.

| **Models from Black Literature** |

Age/Grade Level or Audience: High school or college literature class; book club or literary society.

Description: Illustrate literary terms with models by black authors.

Procedure: Have participants make a study chart or series of posters illustrating rhetorical devices. Draw illustrations from poems, essays, short stories, plays, novels, or speeches by black writers. For example:

◆ **metaphor**

Hope is a crushed stalk
Between clenched fingers.
(Paul) Murray, "Dark Testament")

◆ **simile**

I'm certain that if she could
Tutor these potential protégés, as
Quick as Aladdin rubbin his lamp, she would.
(Margaret Danner, "Dance of the Abakweta")

◆ **aphorism**

Much growth is stunted by too careful prodding,
Too eager tenderness.
The things we love we have to learn to leave alone.
(Naomi Long. Madgett, "Woman with Flower")

◆ **slang**

she slid past
so fly and outtasight
that whistles
didn't phase her
(Marvin Wyche, "And She Was Bad")

◆ **onomatopoeia**

I want to tell you what hills are like in October when colors gush down mountainsides and little streams are freighted with a caravan of leaves.
(Margaret Walker, "October Journey")

◆ **hyperbole**

Lately, I've become accustomed to the way
The ground opens up and envelops me
Each time I go out to walk the dog.
(LeRoi Jones, "Preface to a Twenty Volume Suicide Note")

◆ **parallel structure**

I am an invisible man. No, I am not a spook like those who haunted Edgar Allan Poe; nor am I one of your Hollywood-movie ectoplasms. I am a man

of substance, of flesh and bone, fiber and liquids-and I might even be said
to possess a mind.
(Ralph Ellison, Invisible Man)

◆ **dialect**

You sang:
Walk togedder, chiller,
Dontcha git weary . . .
(Stirling A. Brown, "Strong Men")

◆ **periodic sentence**

Consciousness of my environment began with the sound of talk.
(J. Saunders Redding, *No Day of Triumph*)

◆ **allusion**

I
am the result of
President Lincoln
World War I
and Paris
the
Red Ball Express
white drinking fountains
sitdowns and
sit-ins ...
(Mari Evans, "Status Symbol")

◆ **repetition as humor**

It seemed that everything to eat in our house was stamped Not To Be Sold.
All Welfare food bore this stamp to keep the recipients from selling it. It's a
wonder we didn't come to think of Not To Be Sold as a brand name.
(Alex Haley, *The Autobiography of Malcolm X*)

◆ **dialogue**

"Jim, I cannot let my baby go." Her mother's words, although quiet, were
carefully pronounced.

"Maybe," her father answered, "it's not in our hands. Reverend Davis and I
were talking day before yesterday how God test the Israelites, maybe he's
just trying us."

"God expects you to take care of your own," his wife interrupted.
(Diane Oliver, "Neighbors")

◆ **rhyme**

However,
even the F. F. V. pate
is aware that laws defining a Negro
blackjack each other within and without a state.
(Melvin B. Tolson, "PSI")

◆ **alliteration**

The lariat Iynch-wish I deplored.

The loveliest lynchee was our Lord.

(Gwendolyn Brooks, "The Chicago Defender Sends a Man to Little Rock")

♦ **apostrophe**

O that I were free! 0, that I were on one of your gallant decks, and under your protecting wing! Alas! betwixt me and you, the turbid waters roll. Go on, go on. O that I could also go! Could I but swim! If I could fly. 0, why was I born a man, of whom to make a brute!

(Frederick Douglass, *Narrative of the Life of Frederick Douglass*)

♦ **balanced sentence**

Cholly Breedlove is dead; our innocence too. The seeds shriveled and died; her baby too.

(Toni Morrison, *The Bluest Eye*)

♦ **call and response**

caller: Gather 'round, my people

response: *Well, well.* caller: Gonna tell you a story.

response: *Well, well.*

caller: Listen now, my children.

response: *Well, well.* all: *Well, well, well, well.*

(storytelling warm-up by Linda Goss)

♦ **paradox**

We're an African people

hard softness burning black

the earth's magic color our veins.

(Haki Madhubuti, "African Poem")

Have students work in small groups to collect more illustrations of rhetorical devices and styles of versification, such as cacophony, masculine and feminine rhyme, blank verse, metonymy, caesura, enjambment, antithesis, and internal rhyme.

Budget: Under $25

Sources:

Ashabranner, Brent K., ed., The Lion's Whiskers and Other Ethiopian Tales, Linnet Books, 1997.

Day, Frances Ann, *Multicultural Voices in Contemporary Literature,* Heinemann, 1994.

Delamotte, Eugenia, Natania Meeker, and Jean O'Barr, eds. *Women Imagine Change: A Global Anthology of Women's Resistance, 600 B. C. E. to Present,* Routledge, 1997.

Diggs, Anita Doren, ed., *Talking Drums: An African-American Quote Collection,* St. Martin's, 1995.

Hile, Kevin, ed., *Novels for Students,* Gale, 1997.

Kim, Elaine H., Lilia V. Villaneuva, eds., *Making More Waves: New Writing by Asian American Women,* Beacon Press, 1997.

Maggio, Rosalie, *The New Beacon Book of Quotations by Women,* Beacon Press, 1996.

Mullane, Deirdre, *Words to Make My Dream Children Live: A Book of African American Quotations,* Anchor Books, 1995.

Myers, Walter Dean, *The Story of the Three Kingdoms* (fable), Harper Trophy, 1995.

Naylor, Gloria, *Children of the Night: The Best Short Stories by Black Writers, 1967 to the Present,* Little, Brown & Co., 1996.

Riley, Dorothy Winbush, *My Soul Looks Back, Less I Forget: A Collection of Quotations by People of Color,* Harper Perennial, 1993.

Segal, Aaron, Carole Berotte Joseph, and Marie-Jose N'Zengou-Tayo, *Caribbean Literature: An Anthology,* National Textbook, 1998.

Trudeau, Lawrence, ed., *Literature and Its Times,* Gale, 1997.

Worley, Demetrice A., and Jesse Perry, Jr., eds. *African-American Literature: An Anthology,* 2nd ed., National Textbook, 1998.

Alternative Applications: Have students survey a variety of literary works by black authors in numerous genres. Organize a group to propose the table of contents for an anthology of works by black authors. Promote the list as a genre study or reading guide for a literature or English education class, city website, or local library.

New Settings for Old

Age/Grade Level or Audience: Middle school or high school reading or literature classes.

Description: Reset a European classic in an African or Caribbean locale.

Procedure: Have students report on Euro-centric literary classics, for example, *Jane Eyre, Cyrano de Bergerac, Withering Heights, Frankenstein, Beowulf, Les Misérables, Great Expectations, All Quiet on the Western Front, The Mayor of Casterbridge, Romeo and Juliet,* or *A Tale of Two Cities.* Conclude the assignment with a theme that resets the action in a predominantly black setting, for example, Morocco, South Africa, Tobago, or the Virgin Islands. To begin, imagine the laboratory and city streets of *Dr. Jekyll and Mr. Hyde* reset in the Mombasa, Lagos, Cairo, Casablanca, Kingston, Jamaica, or Bridgetown, Barbados. Highlight differences in transportation, language, sights, costume, foods, currency, and lifestyles.

Budget: Under $25

Sources:
A variety of European literary classics.
Gillespie, John and Corinne J. Naden, *Characters in Young Adult Literature,* Gale, 1997.

Page, Clarence, *Showing My Color: Impolite Essays on Race and Identity,* HarperCollins, 1996.

Salzman, Jack, and Pamela Wilkinson, gen eds., *Major Characters in American Fiction,* Henry Holt & Co., 1994.

Alternative Applications: Compose an Afrocentric title, setting, and character list for a popular classic, such as *Gone with the Wind, The Thorn Birds, Like Water for Chocolate, House of the Spirits, Alice in Wonderland,* or *Crime and Punishment.* Rename characters with common given names and surnames of a predominantly black nation.

Reading the Black Female Writer

Age/Grade Level or Audience: College women's studies groups; adult civic clubs, such as Business and Professional Women's League, American Association of University Women, National Organization of Women, and League of Women Voters.

Description: Organize a reading circle to discuss black feminism as revealed through current fiction.

Procedure: Have different members volunteer to read short works by contemporary black female authors, particularly Margaret Walker's "Lineage," Nikki Giovanni's "Mothers," June Jordan's "For My Mother," and Alice Walker "Women," "Uncles," and "For My Sister Molly Who in the Fifties" Provide each reader a list of themes and issues to examine, for example:

- ◆ achievement
- ◆ alienation
- ◆ commitment
- ◆ community solidarity
- ◆ education issues
- ◆ emotional strengths
- ◆ employment issues
- ◆ empowerment
- ◆ family violence
- ◆ health issues
- ◆ male/female parental roles
- ◆ reproductive issues
- ◆ social equality
- ◆ spirituality
- ◆ workplace harassment

Budget: $25-$50

Sources:

Provide a wide selection from these choices:

Angelou, Maya, *And Still I Rise*, Random House, 1978.

———, *A Brave and Startling Truth*, Random House, 1995.

———, *Now Sheba Sings the Song*, Dial Books, 1987.

———, *I Know Why the Caged Bird Sings*, Random House, 1970.

Campbell, Bebe Moore, *Your Blues Ain't Like Mine*, Putna, 1992. Carey, Lorene, *Black Ice*, Vintage Books, 1992 Fitch, Suzanne Pullon, and Roseann M Mandziuk, *Sojourner Truth As*

Orator: Wit, Story, and Song, Greenwood, 1997.

Giovanni, Nikki, *My House*, Morrow, 1972.

Golden, Marita, *And Do Remember Me*, Doubleday, 1992.

Guy-Sheftall, Beverly, ed., *Words of Fire: An Anthology of African-American Feminist Thought*, New Press, 1995.

Hunter-Gault, Charlayne, *In My Place*, Vintage Books, 1995.

Jordan, June, *Things That I Do in the Dark: Selected Poetry*, Random House, 1977.

Lewis, Mary, *Herstory: Black Female Rites of Passage*, African American Images, 1988.

McMillan, Terry, *Waiting to Exhale*, G. K. Hall, 1993.

Morrison, Toni, *Beloved*, Knbopf, 1987.

———, *Jazz*, Knopf, 1992.

———, Song of Solomon, Knopf, 1977.

———, Sula, Knopf, 1973.

Naylor, Gloria, *Mama Day*, Vintage Books, 1994.

———, The Women of Brewster Place, Viking, 1982.

Pemberton, Gayle, *The Hottest Water in Chicago: On Family, Race, Time, and American Culture*, Faber & Faber, 1992.

Petry, Ann, *Tituba of Salem Village*, Crowell, 1964.

Stetson, Erlene, *Black Sister: Poetry by Black American Women, 1746-1980*, Indiana University Press, 1981.

Walker, Alice, *The Color Purple*, Harcourt Brace Jovanovich, 1982.

———, *Possessing the Secret of Joy*, Harcourt Brace Jovanovich,

———, Revolutionary Petunias and Other Poems, Harcourt Brace Jovanovich, 1973.

Walker, Margaret, *Jubilee*, Houghton, 1965, reprinted, Bantam, 1981.

Alternative Applications: Study pairs of feminist poets, essayists, novelists, dramatists, journalists, orators, storytellers, and short story writers, one black and one non-black. Some likely pairs include:

Maya Angelou/Margaret Atwood

Terri McMillan/Anne Tyler

Gayle Ross/Mary Carter Smith

Margaret Sanger/lda Wells-Barnett

Kate Chopin/Bebe Moore Campbell

Gloria Steinem/Marcia Gillespie
Edith Wharton/Margaret Walker
Cynthia Rylant/Dori Sanders
Susan B. Anthony/Sojourner Truth
Bette Greene/Mildred Taylor
Olive Ann Burns/Sarah Delany and Elizabeth Delany
Sara Teasdale/Mari Evans
Heather Forest/Jackie Torrence
Molly Yard/Barbara Jordan
Carolyn Kiser/Nikki Giovanni
Amy Lowell/Rita Dove
Susan Straight/Ann Petry
Hilda Doolittle/Audre Lorde

Determine the relative significance of racism and sex discrimination to each writer's work.

Read, Read, Read

Originator: Dr. Sandra E. Gibbs, Director of Special Programs, National Council of Teachers of English.

Age/Grade Level or Audience: All ages.

Description: Launch a community African American read-in.

Procedure: Encourage community members to familiarize themselves with African American authors. Use a variety of methods, including these:

- ◆ Help public libraries prepare for the event by holding bake sales, silent auctions, progressive dinners, yard sales, and book swaps to raise money for additional books and magazines by black authors and publishers.
- ◆ For large gatherings, provide an interpreter to sign for the deaf.
- ◆ In bilingual settings, provide a translator.
- ◆ Organize reading circles for families and clubs.
- ◆ Print selections and excerpts in newspapers.
- ◆ Have local radio announcers read selections on the air, for instance, works included in David Lewis's Portable Harlem Renaissance Reader.
- ◆ Mount a website and add entries by black authors each day, for example, science fiction writer Octavia Butler.
- ◆ Get a sorority or fraternal organization to sponsor free paperbacks for under-privileged people.

◆ Select a team of young readers to visit retirement homes, hospitals, and veterans' homes to read aloud.

◆ Provide large print volumes or books on tape for visually impaired and illiterate people.

◆ Create a separate shelf of books in translation for non-English speaking readers.

◆ Offer small rewards to children who read twenty-five books during Black History Month.

◆ Pair readings with movies, for instance, read aloud from Maya Angelou's *I Know Why the Caged Bird Sings,* Terry McMillan's *Waiting to Exhale,* William R. Braithwaite's *To Sir, With Love,* William Armstrong's *Sounder,* Ernest Gaines's *The Autobiography of Miss Jane Pittman* or *A Gathering of Old Men,* Alex Haley's *Queen, Roots,* or *The Autobiography of Malcolm X,* or Alice Walker's *The Color Purple;* then show the video.

◆ Introduce a book club to the novels and shorter works of Chester Himes, including *If He Hollers Let Him Go, The Heat's On, A Rage in Harlem, Cotton Comes to Harlem, Black on Black, Run Man Run,* and *Pinktoes* or to the detective novels of Walter Mosley, such as *Butterflyor Devil in a Blue Dress.*

◆ Organize a book swap among romance readers. Keep on hand works by Rochelle Alers, Beverly Jenkins, Francis Ray, Eboni Snoe, Sandra Kitt, Shelby Lewis, Terris Grimes, Layle Giusto, Gwynne Forster, Anita Bunkley, Angela Benson, Lynn Emery, Percival Everett, Bette Ford, Felicia Mason, and Margie Walker.

◆ Tape readings and create a reference collection for use by schools, book clubs, and church groups.

Budget: $75-$100

Sources:

For information about the National African American Read-In Chain, contact Dr. Jerrie C. Scott, African American Read-In Chain, University of Memphis, Memphis, Tennessee 38152 (901-678-5146),

e-mail jcscott@cc.memphis.edu or Dr. Sandra E. Gibbs, Director of Special Programs, National Council of Teachers of English, 1111 Kenyon Road, Urbana, Illinois 61801 (217-328-3870, ext. 230), e-mail sgibbs@ncte.org.

Perma-Bound multicultural catalog, Vandalia Road, Jacksonville, Illinois 62650 (800-637-6581).

Diefendorf, Elizabeth, ed., The New York Public Library's Books of the Century, Oxford University Press, 1996.

Fralick, Katharine G., ed., "Character and Citizenship: An Annotated Bibliography of Children's and Young Adults' Literature," *Teaching* K-8, October 1997, 50-52.

Gale, Steven *H., West African Folktales,* National Textbook, 1995.

Segal, Aaron, Carole Berotte Joseph, and Marie-Jose N'Zengou-Tayo, *Caribbean Literature: An Anthology,* National Textbook, 1998.

Spirited Mlnds: African American Books for Our Sons and Our Brothers, W. W. Norton, 1997.

Worley, Demetrice A., and Jesse Perry, Jr., eds. *African-American Literature: An Anthology,* 2nd edition., National Textbook, 1998.

Alternative Applications: Launch the "Year of the Black Author." Divide the calendar into segments, allotting different time spans for novels, young adult literature, short stories, tales, plays, essays, poems, Iyrics, speeches, sermons, editorials, biography, autobiography, and aphorism. For example, begin with these titles:

- ◆ Lorene Cary, *Black Ice*
- ◆ Walter Dean Myers's western *The Righteous Revenge of Artemis Bonner*
- ◆ Jackie Torrence's autobiography *The Importance of Pot Liquor*
- ◆ tales such as Mary Carter Smith's "Cindy Ellie" or Paul Keens-Douglas's "Tanti Merle at de Oval"
- ◆ Toni Cade Bambara's short story "Blues Ain't No Mockingbird"
- ◆ plays such as Useni Perkins's *Black Fairy,* Ntozake Shange's *For Colored Girls Who've Considered Suicide,* or August Wilson's *Piano Lesson.*
- ◆ Langston Hughes's juvenile classic *Tales of Simple*
- ◆ Margaret Walker's novel *Jubilee*
- ◆ the spiritual "Oh, Freedom"
- ◆ Gwendolyn Brooks's poem "We Real Cool"
- ◆ Derek Walcott's epic poem *Omeros*
- ◆ Alain Locke's essay "The New Negro"
- ◆ the prologue to Ralph Ellison's psychological novel *Invisible Man*
- ◆ Darwin Turner's critical essay, "The Negro Dramatist's Image of the Universe, 1920-1960"
- ◆ Toni Morrison's literary treatise *Playing in the Dark: Whiteness and the Literary Imagination*
- ◆ Martin Luther King's sermon, "I Have a Dream"
- ◆ Lerone's Bennett, Jr's *Before the Mayflower: A History of Black America*
- ◆ Lorraine Hansberry's play *A Raisin in the Sun*
- ◆ Dori Sander's young adult classic *Clover*

Steinbeck on American Racism

Age/Grade Level or Audience: Middle school or high school history or literature classes; civic groups; literary societies or book clubs.

Description: Give readings from John Steinbeck's *Travels with Charley* and *America and Americans.*

Procedure: Read aloud from John Steinbeck's observations of forced integration in New Orleans, found in Book Four of *Travels with Charley*. Follow up with his essay on slavery in *America and Americans*. Make the following interpretive comments:

◆ While traveling America during the volatile 1960s, Steinbeck chose to watch the forced integration of public schools.

◆ He described the blatant racism of white women directed at small black children "a kind of frightening witches' Sabbath. These were crazy actors playing to a crazy audience."

◆ He compared his own childhood experiences in Salinas, California, but had too little contact with black people to place himself in the position of Southerners.

◆ He commented, "I knew I was not wanted in the South When people are engaged in something they are not proud of, they do not welcome witnesses In fact, they come to believe the witness causes the trouble."

◆ In *America and Americans,* he accounted for the strength of black people by explaining how humble diet, hard work, and struggle accomplished what Charles Darwin described as strengthening of the race by "survival of the fittest."

Budget: Under $25

Sources:
Steinbeck, John, America and Americans, Viking Press, 1966.
———, *Travels with Charley: In Search of America,* Viking Press, 1962, reprinted, Penguin Books, 1986

Alternative Applications: Ask students to role-play their own part in the first forced integrations of public schools. Display photographs of the era showing state police, governors George Wallace, Lester Maddox, and Orville Faubus, and students James Meredith and Autherine Lucy, all of whom played prominent parts in the mixing of races in schools.

Math

An African American Profile

Age/Grade Level or Audience: High school or community college math, computer, or economics classes.

Description: Present an audio-visual overview of the black American's standard of living in contrast with whites, Asian-Americans, Hispanics, and Native Americans.

Procedure: Have students create overhead transparencies, computer disks and databases, websites, or original filmstrips of charts, graphs, and maps featuring data about the lifestyle of the United States' black population. Individual graphics should cover these topics:

- ◆ population numbers and distribution among states
- ◆ family size
- ◆ property and business ownership
- ◆ entrepreneurial success
- ◆ birth, death, marital, and health statistics
- ◆ participation in the military
- ◆ literacy and educational attainment
- ◆ crime and prison population
- ◆ welfare statistics
- ◆ representation in the Senate and House of Representatives
- ◆ numbers of black police chiefs, mayors, governors, judges, and other municipal and state authorities projected for future elections and other pertinent governmental facts.

Budget: $25-$50

Sources:

Africa Online and software programs such as *Get S.M.A.R.T., Census-USA,* and *Statmaster Desktop Demographics.*

"African-American Census Schedules Online," http//www.mindspring.com/~smoters/ AACensus.htm.

"Blacks Grow to 12.8 Percent of Population," *Jet,* July 14, 1997, 4.

Chambers, Veronica, "Minority Women: The New Boss," *USA Weekend,* Oct. 31-Nov. 2, 1997.

"Department of Commerce Bureau of the Census on the African-American Population," http//fr.counterpoint.com8000/fr/1996/0610/00042.htm.

Kish, Leslie, *Survey Sampling,* John Wiley & Sons, 1995.

Sourcebook America 1998 (CD-ROM), Gale, 1997.

Alternative Applications: Present an oral report contrasting the lifestyles of all races. Draw correlations between these topics:

- ◆ education and attainment
- ◆ urban residence and crime
- ◆ major illnesses and availability of health care
- ◆ infant morality and prenatal care
- ◆ dietary deficiency and household income.

Use facts and figures as a basis for developing computer graphics in line, vertical bar, and horizontal bar graphs and pie charts. For example, consider this horizontal bar graph:

Life Expectancy in the First Three Quarters of the 20th Century

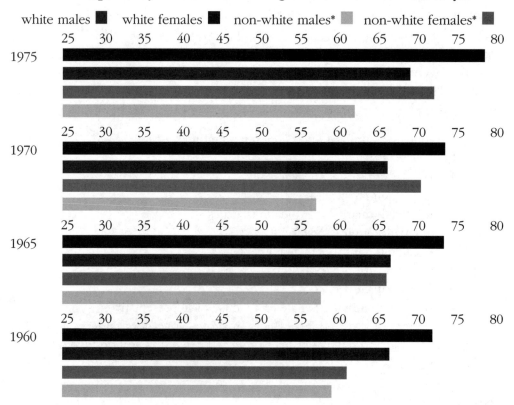

white males ■   white females ■   non-white males* ▨   non-white females* ▨

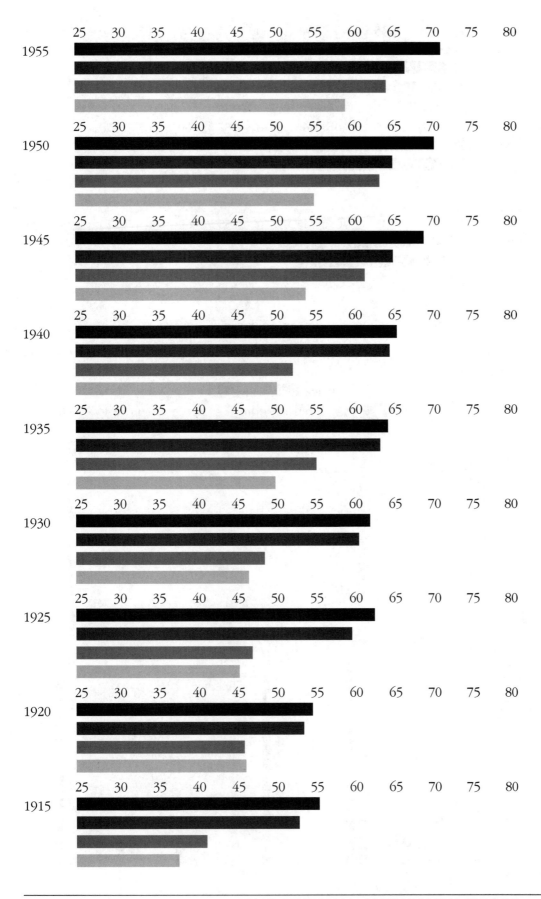

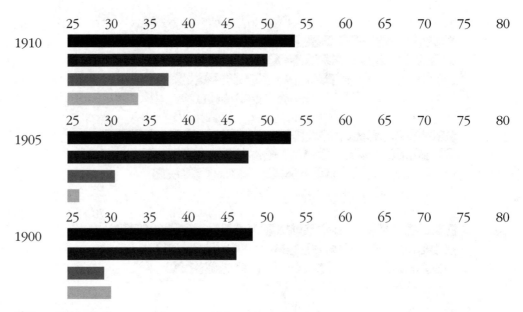

*[Note 90% of all non-whites are African Americans.]

A vertical bar graph of soldiers refused by the military during World War II shows these data:

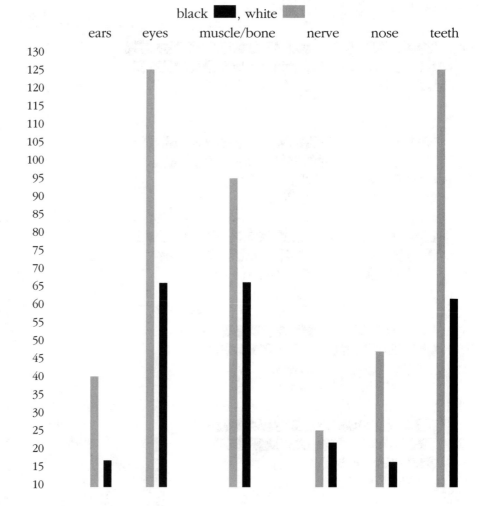

A statistical table of population growth projected for Anchorage, Alaska, shows these racial breakdowns:

	Total (thousands)	White	Black	Hispanic	Other
1970	128.03	116.34	5.48	3.49	6.21
1980	176.54	153.47	9.47	4.83	13.60
1990	226.47	186.98	14.55	9.26	24.95
1995	236.33	192.94	17.04	11.45	26.35
2000	257.33	207.80	20.63	16.15	28.90
2005	281.47	225.31	25.12	19.96	31.04
2010	308.59	245.39	30.57	23.75	32.64
2015	338.65	268.23	36.98	23.80	33.44

An African American Theme Park

Age/Grade Level or Audience: High School geometry, computer, business, or drafting classes.

Description: Lay out an African American theme park.

Procedure: Utilize computer equipment or drafting boards to plot a schematic drawing of a large theme park based on the culture, history, lifestyle, and interests of African Americans. Emulate the layout and appeal of Disneyland, Disney World, Six Flags over Georgia, Busch Gardens, and other theme parks. Use geometric shapes to balance roads, parking ares, and exhibits. Design attendant uniforms in native styles, for example, a Ghanian dress and matching turban. Include the following attractions:

- ◆ maze marked with models and posters of events in African American history, such as Joe Louis's championship bouts or Althea Gibson's achievements
- ◆ halls of history displaying the four-way stop signal, hot comb, and other items invented by African Americans
- ◆ murals and art displays from Detroit, New York, Birmingham, Atlanta, Miami, and other cities rich in African American art
- ◆ soul food courts and tasting booths featuring foods and recipes from Africa and the Caribbean
- ◆ trading centers featuring African commodities and African American books, tapes, jewelry, pottery, carvings, decorations, tableware, and clothing.

Budget: Under $25

Sources:
Refer to visual stimuli, such as "Black Odyssey: Migration to the Cities" (filmstrip) by Center for the Humanities, or "The History of Africa" (software) by KnowMaster.

Alternative Applications: Have students divide into groups and make mock attractions of an African American theme park out of cardboard, clay, balsa wood, styrofoam, or other light, malleable material. Conclude by assembling the attractions on a sandtable or library display case. Invite students to plan websites, posters, TV and radio spots, billboards, T-shirts, coffee mugs, tote bags, magazine layouts, and other forms of advertisement for the park. Use actuarial tables to project the numbers of visitors, parking spaces needed, and the park's peak hours and days. Make a calendar that encourages visits on off-peak times by offering reduced fares and package deals to families, senior citizens, handicapped visitors, and other target groups.

An African Museum

Age/Grade Level or Audience: High school or college art, history, drafting, computer, physics, or architecture class.

Description: Design a museum to house a black art collection.

Procedure: Have students select a focus for a museum collection, such as early African art, African culture, African American lifestyles and art, African influences on Caribbean watercolor, architecture, and nature photography, or other topics. Then have the group design a building to display the collection so that people of all ages and backgrounds can gain from the experience of visiting and viewing the displays. Include the following data:

- ◆ accessible entries for the handicapped
- ◆ accoustical enhancements
- ◆ art workshops
- ◆ height and angle of ceilings
- ◆ interactive showings for children
- ◆ lengths of hallways
- ◆ lighting sources and types
- ◆ revolving display cases for delicate objects, particularly woven goods, carvings, and delicate masks
- ◆ security systems
- ◆ special groupings, such as African basketry of the pre-colonial period

Create a brochure that will guide visitors to the displays. Arrange materials in logical order, for example chronologically or by type of displays, such as African clothing, cooking vessels, jewelry, weapons, musical instruments, and games.

Budget: $25-$50

Sources:

Abusabib, Mohamed A., *African Art: An Aesthetic Inquiry*, Coronet Books, 1995.

Arnold, Marion, *Women and Art in South Africa*, St. Martin's Press, 1997.

Clarke, Duncan, *African Art*, Random House Value Books, 1995.

"Diaspora Art," http//www.diaspora.com/art.html.

"The History of Kente Cloth," http//webusers.anet-chi.com/~midwesthistory.html.

"Musical Instruments of Africa," http//www.eyeneer.comworld/af/instruments.

Poyner, Robin, *African Art at the Hara Museum: Spirit Eyes, Humanj Hands*, University Press of Florida, 1995.

Roberts, Allen F., *Animals in African Art: From the Familiar to the Marvelous*, International Books Import Services, 1997.

"Shelia Collectibles," http//www.erinet.com/granio/key03.html.

"University of Texas at Austin Center for African and African-American Studies," http//www.utexas.edu/depts/cadds/.

Vogel, Susan, *Africa Explores: Twentieth Century African Art*, International Books Import Services, 1997.

"WoYaal—Afrique Arts," http//www.woyaal.com/TreeFR/arts/.

Alternative Applications: Create a memorable, functional monument to African American contributions. Design a geometric shape that will appeal to the eye and establish a cohesive impression, for example, an obelisk, geodesic dome, or pyramid. Select building materials, landscaping, sculpture, bas-relief, signage, and inscriptions. Choose a significant location, such as a city on the banks of the Mississippi River, opposite the Caribbean Sea, or near the Charleston Slave Market Museum.

City Comparisons

Age/Grade Level or Audience: Elementary or Middle school math or computer classes.

Description: Have students chart and compare the black urban population centers of the United States.

Procedure: Have students collect census figures on the growth of urban centers, particularly New York, Chicago, Los Angeles, Seattle, Detroit, Philadelphia, Washington, D. C., Baltimore, Houston, Atlanta, Dallas, Newark, St. Louis, San Francisco, New Orleans, Memphis, Cleveland, Miami, Birmingham, Norfolk, Pittsburgh, and Portland. Assign charts illustrating shifts in racial concentrations in these areas, including the growth of Hispanic, Native American, and Asian populations. Have students highlight figures on areas that have the least diversity of racial population, especially the upper midwest.

Budget: Under $25

Sources:

Africa Online and software programs such as *Get S.M.A.R.T., Census-USA,* and *Statmaster Desktop Demographics.*

"African-American Census Schedules Online," http//www.mindspring. com/~smothers/AACensus.htm.

"Blacks Grow to 12.8 Percent of Population," *Jet*, July 14, 1997, 4.

"Department of Commerce Bureau of the Census on the African-American Population," http//fr.counterpoint.com8000/fr/1996/0610/00042.htm.

Kish, Leslie, *Survey Sampling*, John Wiley & Sons, 1995.

Sourcebook America 1998 (CD-ROM), Gale, 1997.

Alternative Applications: Organize a roundtable to discuss the "what-ifs" of demographics. Consider these possibilities:

- ◆ affirmative action for colleges and universities
- ◆ enforcement of equal opportunity laws
- ◆ equal distribution of races among all states
- ◆ increase in non-white home ownership
- ◆ integrated housing patterns
- ◆ job opportunities and small business starts for nonwhites
- ◆ more mixed race people

 ## Counting in Swahili

Age/Grade Level or Audience: Kindergarten through primary grades

Description: Teach students to count from one to ten in Swahili.

Procedure: Present a brief description of Swahili, how old a language it is, where it is spoken, and who speaks it. Then repeat the first ten numbers in Swahili until students have them memorized.

1. **moja** [mow' jah]
2. **mbili** [uhm . bee' lee]
3. **tatu** [tah' too]
4. **nne** [uhn' nay]
5. **tano** [tah' no]
6. **sita** [see' tah]
7. **saba** [sah' buh]
8. **nane** [nah' nay]
9. **tisa** [tee' suh]
10. **kumi** [koo' mee]

Refer to these numbers in future counting exercises or for bean bag toss, hopscotch, jumping rope, car travel games, and other counting activities.

Budget: Under $25

Sources:

"African Language Sites," http//polyglot.lss.wisc.edu/lss/lang/african.html.

Feelings, Muriel L, *Jambo Means Hello: Swahili Alphabet Book*, Dial Books for Young Readers, 1992.

Haskins, Jim, *Count Your Way Through Africa*, Carolrhoda Books, 1989.

Alternative Applications: Use each number alongside its pronunciation and a uniquely African representation of the meaning:

one Mount Kilimanjaro or Niger River
two wildebeest or gnus
three ostriches or emus
four yams or bowls of fufu
five grass huts or village compounds
six Ashanti drums or finger pianos
seven diamonds or pyramids
eight Masai women or Mali children
nine hyenas or hippos
ten baobab trees or palms

Graphing Racial Data

Age/Grade Level or Audience: Middle school or high school college mathematics, economics, or computer classes.

Description: Have students create a series of hand-drawn or computer-generated graphs that depict African or Caribbean lifestyles.

Procedure: Have students locate and discuss demographic studies of African and African American peoples, particularly these topics:

- ♦ commerce and standard of living
- ♦ disease, death, and birth rates
- ♦ education and literacy
- ♦ location and patterns of migration from black nations to the United States
- ♦ marriage and divorce
- ♦ religions
- ♦ urbanization and industrialization

Refer to *USA Today, Time, Black Business, Forbes, Newsweek,* and *U. S. News and World Report* for ideas on graphing. Have students utilize these facts as they practice drawing, illustrating, and coloring horizontal and vertical bar, pie, or line graphs, either by hand or on the computer. Suggest captions for each graph. Arrange the finished graphs on a website or in a school, museum, civic, library display, or newspaper feature.

Budget: $25-$50

Sources:

Africa Online; software programs such as *Get S.M.A.R.T., Census-USA,* and *Statmaster Desktop Demographics;* the video "Immigration to the U. S." (Schlessinger Media).

"African-American Census Schedules Online," http//www.mindspring.com/~smothers/AACensus.htm.

"Analysis of Immigration and Naturalization Service Data," http//www. | usatoday.com.

Chambers, Veronica, "Minority Women The New Boss," *USA Weekend,* Oct. 31-Nov. 2, 1997.

"Department of Commerce Bureau of the Census on the African-American Population," http//fr.counterpoint.com8000/fr/1996/0610/00042.htm.

Kish, Leslie, *Survey Sampling,* John Wiley & Sons, 1995.

Sourcebook America 1998 (CD-ROM), Gale, 1997.

"The USA's New Immigrants," *USA Today,* October 13, 1997.

Alternative Applications: Have students present a select body of data using all four methods of computer graphing. For example, present the following facts and assign groups of students to think of ways to demonstrate their implications about white and black people in the United States:

Date	%Black	Black	White
1620	1.0	20	2,180
1630	2.0	60	4,586
1640	2.2	597	26,037
1650	3.2	1,600	47,768
1660	3.9	2,920	72,138
1670	4.0	4,535	107,400

1680	4.6	6,971	144,536
1690	8.0	16,729	193,643
1700	11.1	27,000	223,000
1710	13.5	44,000	286,000
1720	14.8	68,000	397,000
1730	14.5	91,000	538,000
1740	17.7	160,000	745,000
1750	20.2	236,000	934,000
1760	20.4	325,000	1,267,000
1770	21.4	459,000	1,688,000
1780	20.7	575,000	2,204,000
1790	19.3	757,000	3,172,000
1800	18.9	1,002,000	4,306,000
1810	19.0	1,378,000	5,862,000
1820	18.4	1,772,000	7,867,000
1830	18.1	2,329,000	10,537,000
1840	16.8	2,874,000	14,196,000
1850	15.7	3,639,000	19,553,000
1860	14.1	4,442,000	26,923,000
1870	13.5	5,392,000	33,589,000
1880	13.1	6,581,000	43,403,000
1890	12.3	7,389,000	55,101,000
1900	11.6	7,760,000	66,809,000
1910	10.7	9,827,000	81,364,000
1920	9.9	10,463,000	94,120,000
1930	9.7	11,891,000	108,864,000
1940	9.7	12,865,000	118,214,000
1950	9.9	15,042,000	134,982,000
1960	10.5	18,871,000	158,831,000
1970	11.1	22,530,000	177,748,000
1980	11.7	26,495,000	227,061,000
1990	12.1	29,986,000	249,924,000

Have groups work together to answer the following questions utilizing conclusions drawn from a study of the data:

♦ Why do population shifts occur, such as migrations, epidemics, or resettlements?

♦ What missing information skews this study of racial population, such as ways of categorizing mixed blood people?

♦ How could war, disease, natural catastrophes, and laws affect a rise or fall in population percentage?

♦ What change in figures might a demographer predict for the coming century?

♦ How might methods of studying census affect future data?

Also, have students create color-coded graphs of information by race, for example, these sets of figures about racial migration in 1995:

Washington, D.C.

El Salvador	434
Ethiopia	294
Vietnam	217
Nigeria	166
China	117
Dominican Republic	98
Jamaica	97
Philippines	83
United Kingdom	66
Guatemala	52
Total	3,042

U. S. Immigrants by Country of Origin (1995)

Mexico	86,960
Philippines	50,962
Vietnam	41,752
Dominican Republic	38,392
China	35,459
India	34,715
Cuba	17,932
Ukraine	17,432
Jamaica	16,335
Korea	16,034
Russia	14,560
Haiti	13,892
Poland	13,804
Canada	12,913
United Kingdom	12,311
El Salvador	11,563
Colombia	10,780
Pakistan	9,743
Taiwan	9,374
Iran	9,178

Measuring Monuments

Age/Grade Level or Audience: Elementary or middle school math classes.

Description: Appoint a committee to arrange a bulletin board display, mural, or website entry on converting U.S. measurements to the Metric System.

Procedure: Introduce a class to metric measure. Use as models a series of inventions by black scientists and engineering marvels and monuments to black history. Include the Pyramid of Cheops, Sphinx, African petroglyphs, or archeological sites in Africa, the Caribbean, and the United States, for example, the measurements of the Joe Louis fist statue in Detroit or the size of the docking area of the *Clothilde*, the last slave ship to arrive on United States shores.

Budget: Under $25

Sources:
Aaseng, Nathan, *Black Inventors*, Facts on File, 1997.
Caselli, Giovanni, *Wonders of the World*, Dorling Kindersley, 1992.
Cox, Reg, et al., *The Seven Wonders of the Ancient World*, Silver Burdett Press, 1996.
Gibbs, C. R., *Black Inventors: From Africa to America Two Million Years of Invention and Innovation*, Three Dimensional Publications, 1995.
Hudson, Wade, and Thomas Hudson, *Five Notable Inventors*, Cartwheel Books, 1995.
"Inventors," http//www.slip.net/~rigged/history.html#invent.
Kahn, Jetty, *African-American Inventors: Lonnie Johnson, Frederick McKinley Jones, Marjorie Stewart Joyes, Elijah McCoy, Garrett Augustus Morgan*, Capstone Press, 1996.
McKissack, Patricia, and Fredrick McKissack, *African-American Inventors*, Millbrook Press, 1994.
Towle, Wendy, *The Real McCoy: The Life of an African-American Inventor*, Scholastic Publications, 1995.

Alternative Applications: Apply the study of distance to expeditions or journeys from black history. Include Mae Jemison or Guion Bluford's space flight, circumference of the Atlantic Triangle, total mileage of Martin Luther King's marches, and the approximate distance covered by Harriet Tubman on the Underground Railroad.

The Migrant Scene

Age/Grade Level or Audience: High school or college sociology or history classes.

Description: Write a history of the evolution of migrant labor as a significant aspect of southern agriculture.

Procedure: Organize a paper to cover the following aspects of the history of migrant labor. Through computer graphics, generate facts and figures to depict the migrant situation state by state, which clearly indicates that black people do *not* comprise a major portion of seasonal agricultural workers. Include data on race, age, earnings, work and travel schedules, health, education, on-the-job injuries, and longevity. Mention these facts:

- Because of the demands of the job, 70% of migrant workers are young, averaging 31 years.
- Only 4% are under the age of eighteen.
- The average age of African American migrants is 40.
- Only 29% of seasonal farm workers are women.
- 64% of migrants are married.
- 29% have never been married.
- Only 38% are United States-born, the rest coming from Asia, the Caribbean, and Latin America.
- Only 2% of American migrants are black.
- Of U.S. citizens who follow the harvests for a living, 60% are white, 34% Hispanic, 5% black, and the remaining 1% Asian and Native American.

Budget: Under $25

Sources:

Africa Online and software programs such as *Get S.M.A.R.T., PCensus-USA,* and *Statmaster Desktop Demographics.*

"African-American Census Schedules Online," http//www.mindspring. com/~smothers/AACensus.htm.

Altman, Linda J., *Migrant Farm Workers: The Temporary People*, Watts, 1994.

"Analysis of Immigration and Naturalization Service Data," http//wwwusatoday.com.

Cramer, Clayton E., *Black Demographic Data, 1790-1860 A Sourcebook*, Greenwood Press, 1997.

Hahamovitch, Cindy, *Fruits of Their Labor: Atlantic Coast Farmworkers and the Making of Migrant Poverty*, University of North Carolina Press, 1997.

Mitchell, Don, *The Lie of the Land: Migrant Workers and the California Landscape*, University of Minnesota Press, 1996.

Sourcebook America 1998 (CD-ROM), Gale, 1997.

Alternative Applications: In the text of an analytic paper, indicate the following conclusions:

- how migrant labor replaced slave labor during the Reconstruction Era
- where migrant labor has become most profitable in the South
- a racial breakdown of the migrant labor force by decades, including illegal workers from Haiti and other parts of the Caribbean
- lifestyles of migrant families

◆ debilitating problems faced by migrants, notably interruption of education, alcoholism and illegal drug use, infant mortality, malnutrition, health problems, substandard housing and sanitation, domestic violence, and work-related accidents

◆ congressional, state, and private efforts to improve life for migrants

◆ effectiveness of these and other private philanthropic groups in assisting migrants in breaking the poverty cycle: Habitat for Humanity, National Farm Worker Ministry, National Migrant Workers Council, National Association of State Directors of Migrant Education, Migrant Dropout Reconnection Program, Interstate Migrant Eduction Council, Farmworker Justice Fund, East Coast Migrant Health Project, Association of Farmworker Opportunity Programs, and Amnesty International.

Schematic Drawings

Age/Grade Level or Audience: Middle school or high school geometry or computer drafting classes.

Description: Create a gallery of schematic drawings of inventions by African Americans.

Procedure: Study important inventions by black scientists and engineers, such as these:

◆ Virgie Ammons, Fireplace damper tool
◆ Benjamin Banneker, wooden clock
◆ Andrew J. Beard, automatic railcar coupler
◆ Henry Blair, corn and cotton planters
◆ Sarah Boone, folding ironing board
◆ Otis Boykin, stimulator for an artificial heart
◆ Henrietta Bradbury, torpedo discharger
◆ Marie Van Brittan Brown, home security system
◆ David N. Crosthwait, vacuum heating system
◆ Sarah E. Goode, folding bed
◆ Meredith C. Gourdine, electradyne paint spray gun
◆ Elijah J. McCoy, automatic lubricating cup
◆ Garrett Augustus Morgan, four-way traffic signal and gas mask
◆ Norbert Rillieux, sugar refiner
◆ Lewis Temple, improved whaling harpoon
◆ Sarah Walker, hot comb
◆ Ozzie S. Williams, radar search beaconor
◆ Granville T. Woods, railroad telegraph

Produce multiple views of the mechanisms. Label moving parts.

Budget: $25-$50

Sources:

Aaseng, Nathan, *Black Inventors*, Facts on File, 1997.

Gibbs, C. R., *Black Inventors: From Africa to America Two Million Years of Invention and Innovation*, Three Dimensional Publications, 1995.

Haber, Louis, *Black Pioneers of Science and Invention*, Harcourt Brace Jovanovich, 1970, reprinted, 1992.

Hayden, Robert C., *African-American Inventors*, 21st Century Books, 1992.

Hudson, Wade, and Thomas Hudson, *Five Notable Inventors*, Cartwheel Books, 1995.

"Inventors," http//www.slip.net/~rigged/history.html#invent.

James, Portia P. James's *The Real McCoy: African-American Invention and Innovation, 1619-1930*, Smithsonian Institution Press, 1989.

Kahn, Jetty, *African-American Inventors: Lonnie Johnson, Frederick McKinley Jones, Marjorie Stewart Joyes, Elijah McCoy, Garrett Augustus Morgan*, Capstone Press, 1996.

McKissack, Patricia, and Fredrick McKissack, *African-American Inventors*, Millbrook Press, 1994.

Towle, Wendy, *The Real McCoy: The Life of an African-American Inventor*, Scholastic Publications, 1995.

Alternative Applications: Pair drawings illustrating earlier models that these inventions improved on. For example, illustrate these:

- the more primitive sugar-making systems used on Caribbean and Southern plantations as opposed to Norbert Rillieux's modernized version, which reduced the tedium of labor intensive work and spared the workers from falls, burns, drowning, and scalding
- contrast Benjamin Banneker's wooden clock with time systems of earlier civilizations, such as water clocks, slotted candles, and sundials
- sketch early methods of hair straightening with Madame Sarah Walker's hot comb.

Music

African Musical Instruments

Age/Grade Level or Audience: Elementary and middle school, religious schools, scouts, and 4-H groups.

Description: Present pictures and information about African musical instruments.

Procedure: Using reference books, tapes, disc recordings, films, filmstrips, and videos, acquaint students with the sounds and uses of African musical instruments, such as the notched flute, kalimba, musical bow, gondje, kalungu, double gong, drumstick, xylophone, tambourine, apentemma drum, atumpan or talking drum, fontomfrom drum, donno drum, harp, lyre, zither, trumpet, bells, fiddle, mibra or thumb piano, and hand rattle. Point out that traditional audiences play their own bodies by slapping their hands and legs, stamping their feet, vibrating their tongues against the roofs of their mouths, and clicking their fingers and tongues. Divide African musical instruments into four categories:

♦ aerophones—instruments which make music from air vibration, such as the notched flute, animal horn or calabash trumpet, reed flute, oboe, clarinet, double-reed pipe, mouth bow, and whistle

♦ chordophones—instruments which coax musical tones from string vibrations, such as the lyre, zither, lute, one-string fiddle, earth-bow, hand piano, kalimba, molo, and harp

♦ idiophones—instruments which vibrate in every part, as with the thumb piano, calabash rattles, scrapers, xylophones, marimbas, beaded nets, lithophones, clappers, sistrum, or bells

♦ membranophones—instruments which require a tightly stretched membrane or skin to carry the vibration caused by a blow of the hand or a stick, as with the talking drum, tension drum, hourglass drum, slit drum, friction drum, water drum, or iron gong.

Note that a few instruments combine techniques, as with the tambourine, which mates a vibrating membrane with the sound of clashing metal disks.

Budget: $25-$50

Sources:

Authentic Ethnic Music, Whole World Language Catalog.

Ewens, Graema, *Africa O-Ye!,* Da Capo, 1992.

"Musical Instruments of Africa," http//www.africaonline.com.

"Musical Instruments of Africa," http//www.eyneer.com/World/Af/Instuments/ index.html.

Rubin, Janet E., and Margaret Merrion, *Creative Drama and Music Methods*, Linnet Books, 1996.

"Sing Children Sing Songs of the Congo," from Caedmon Records.

"zZounds African Musical Instruments," http//www.zzounds.com/WorldMusic Center/Africa/.

Alternative Applications: Present recorded African songs for special occasions, such as homecomings, weddings, harvest festivals, coming-of-age ceremonies, coronations, and funerals.

◆ Discuss the mood that each song invokes, such as playfulness, patriotism, pride, grief, gratitude, curiosity, hope, or joy.
◆ Have students write their reactions to each song. Discuss the roles of the cantor or leader and the griot, the tribal narrator who educates citizens by reciting the tribe's history.
◆ Differentiate between monotonal Arab style, polyphonic Negro style, and polyphonic Bushman-Pygmy style or yodeling.
◆ Include technical information, such as the importance of syncopation, rhythmic patterns, call-and-response, lined hymns, ring shouts, and descant.
◆ Have a volunteer group make a finger piano from strips of bamboo cut in varied lengths and laid across a half gourd, which serves as echo chamber.

African Music American Style

Age/Grade Level or Audience: Adult music societies.

Description: Lead a discussion of similarities between traditional African music and the styles of famous black North American singers.

Procedure: Play recordings of traditional African and Afro-Caribbean music, then play the works of these performers:

Marian Anderson	Louis Armstrong	Pearl Bailey
Ysaye Barnwell	Count Basie	Kathleen Battle
Harry Belafonte	Brook Benton	Cab Calloway
Ray Charles	Natalie Cole	John Coltrane
Miles Davis	Bo Diddley	Fats Domino
Ella Fitzgerald	Roberta Flack	Lionel Hampton
Roland Hayes	Jimi Hendrix	Billie Holiday
Lena Horne	Janet Jackson	Mahalia Jackson Louis
Jordan	Ronny Jordon	B. B. King
LL Cool J	Bob Marley	Jelly Roll Morton
Faith Nolan	Leontyne Price	Charlie Pride
Lou Rawls	Bernice Johnson Reagon	Toshi Reagon
Otis Redding	Lionel Ritchie	Chris Rock
Diana Ross	Smokey Robinson	Samana
Bessie Smith	Sunsplash	Sweet Honey in the Rock
Linda Tillery	Sarah Vaughan	Ethel Waters
Mary Wells	BeBe and CeCe Winans	Stevie Wonder

Lead a discussion of hints of African tradition in American soul, calypso, ragtime, reggae, plena, zydeco, opera, minstrelsy, urban blues, disco, musical theater, black country, jazz, hip-hop, be-bop, doowop, swing, hymns, scat, gospel, spirituals, protest songs, funk, and rhythm and blues.

Budget: $25-$50

Sources:

Recordings such as: the soundtrack from the PBS series *The Civil War;* "Great Gospel Performances, Vols. 1 & 2;" "Count Basie and His Orchestra Ain't Misbehavin';" "Nat King Cole The Trio Recordings;" "Happy Birthday Duke, Vols. 1-5;" "The Essential Jimi Hendrix;" "The Rhythm of Resistance Music of Black South Africa;" "Ladysmith Black Mambazo Journey of Dreams;" "Sing! The Songs of Joe Raposo;" and "Louis Armstrong The California Concerts."

Ayres, B. Drummond, "On Bayou, Non-Cajuns Fight for Recognition," *New York Times,* November 23, 1997, 10.

Caldwell, Hansonia, *African American Music—A Chronology 1619-1995*, Ikoro Communications, 1996.

Heilbut, Anthony, *Gospel Sound: Good News and Bad Times*, Limelight Editions, 1997.

Jones, Steve, "LL Cool J's Album," *USA Today*, November 10, 1997, 3D.

McCorkle, Susannah, "Back to Bessie," *American Heritage*, November 1997,54-75.

Merlis, Bob, and Davin Seay, *Heart and Soul: A Celebration of Black Music Style in America 1930-1975*, Stewart, Taboori and Chang, 1997.

Pruter, Robert, *Doowop: The Chicago Scene*, University of Illinois Press, 1996.

Southern, Eileen, *Music of Black America: A History*, W. W. Norton & Co., 1997.

Spencer, Jon Michael, *Protest and Priase: Sacred Music of Black Religion*, Fortress Press, 1997.

Vincent, Rickey, *Funk: The Music, the People, and the Rhythm of One*, St.Martin's Press, 1996.

Alternative Applications: Organize a panel to discuss recurrent themes in African, Caribbean, and African American music, such as love, relationships between men and women, community spirit, discrimination, hardship, yearning for freedom, trust in God, and work. Compare themes of Appalachian folk tunes, country and western, movie themes, and show tunes to those of traditional black music. For example:

Nobody Knows de Trouble I See
Nobody knows de trouble I see,
Nobody knows but Jesus;
Nobody knows de trouble I see,
Glory hallelujah.
Sometimes I'm up
Sometimes I'm down,
Oh, yes, Lord;
Sometimes I'm almost to de groun',
Oh, yes, Lord.
Altho' you see me goin' 'long so,
Oh, yes, Lord;
I have my troubles here below,
Oh, yes, Lord.

 African Rhythm Band

Age/Grade Level or Audience: Kindergarten and elementary music and crafts classes; religious schools; classes for the handicapped.

Description: Create and play African instruments.

Procedure: Help participants make their own African musical instruments. For example, try these:

♦ Make a banjo from a shoe box lid with a hole cut in it. Stretch thick and thin rubber bands lengthwise across the box. Pluck strings separately or strum them in a series.

◆ Make a xylophone from wooden tomato stakes cut into two one-foot lengths. Lay them parallel and about three inches apart. Place varying lengths of aluminum or plastic pipe or bamboo strips horizontally across the two stakes. Tap with a mallet made from wooden dowels with a rubber ball pushed onto the end.

◆ Make a thumb piano by gluing bamboo strips or popsicle sticks of varying lengths between two wooden blocks or a hollow gourd. Play by plucking with the fingers.

◆ Make pairs of finger cymbals by pushing thick rubber bands through holes cut in two bottle caps or metal lids.

◆ Make bongos from oatmeal boxes with the ends removed. Attach two rubber circles cut from heavy balloons by fitting them over each end and lacing with heavy twine. Play with the tips of your fingers.

◆ String noisemakers on rubber bands and tie around wrists and ankles.

Budget: $50-$75

Sources:

Burgess, Anna, *Do-It-Yourself Project Book*, Troll Associates, 1994.

Corwin, Judith H., *Kwanzaa Crafts*, Watts, 1995.

Dahlstrom, Lorraine M., *Doing the Days: A Year's Worth of Creative Journaling, Drawing, Listening, Reading, Thinking, Arts and Crafts Activities for Children*, Free Spirit Publications 1994.

Deshpande, Chris, and Iain Macleod-Brudenell, *Festival Crafts*, Gareth Stevens, 1996.

Drake, Jane, and Ann Love, *The Kids' Summer Handbook*, Ticknor and Fields Books, 1994.

Kallen, Stuart A., *Eco-Arts and Crafts*, Abdo & Daughters, 1993.

Lohf, Sabine, *Things I Can Make*, Chronicle Books, 1994.

Mason, Kate, *Make Your Own Cool Crafts*, Troll Associates, 1994.

McLean, Margaret, *Make Your Own Musical Instruments*, Lerner Group, 1988.

Zweifel, Frances, *The Make-Something Club: Fun with Crafts, Food, and Gifts*, Viking Child Books, 1994.

Alternative Applications: Give a concert of African or Caribbean songs. Have band members play melodies and keep time with homemade or purchased rhythm band instruments. Include simple rhythm instruments, such as rhythm sticks, cymbols, rain sticks, scrapers, gourds, tambourines, shakers, triangles, shakeres, and rattles.

Antiphonal Chant

Age/Grade Level or Audience: Elementary or middle school music classes; music societies.

Description: Acquaint participants with the African system of arranging songs into antiphonal chants.

Procedure: Hand out song sheets which depict the separation of lines into those sung by the cantor or leader and the reply of the assembly or chorus.   For example:

Go Down Moses

cantor:	When Israel was in Egypt's land,
chorus:	Let my people go.
cantor:	Oppress'd so hard they could not stand,
chorus:	Let my people go.
cantor:	Go down, Moses,
	Way down in Egypt lan'
	Tell ole Pharoah,
chorus:	Let my people go!

I Ain't Gwine Study War No More

cantor:	Gwine to lay down my burden,
chorus:	Down by the riverside,
	Down by the riverside,
	Down by the riverside.
cantor:	Gwine to lay down my burden,
chorus:	Down by the riverside.
	Ain't gonna study war no more.

Swing Low, Sweet Chariot

cantor:	I looked over Jordan and what did I see,
chorus:	Comin' fo' to carry me home.
cantor:	A band of angels comin' after me,
chorus:	Comin' fo' to carry me home.
cantor:	If you get there before I do,
chorus:	Comin' fo' to carry me home.
cantor:	Tell all my friends I'm comin' too,
chorus:	Comin' fo' to carry me home.

Brother Rabbit

cantor:	Brother rabbit, brother rabbit your ears mighty long,
chorus:	Yes, brother possum, I b'lieve they're put on wrong, however,
unison:	Ev'ry little soul must shine, shine,
	Ev'ry little soul must shine,
	Rise and shine, rise and shine, rise and shine.

Wade in the Water

cantor:	See that ban' all dress'd in white?
chorus:	It look lak the childr'n of the Israelite.

cantor: See that ban' all dress'd in red?

chorus: It look lak the ban' that Moses led.

unison: Wade in de water

Wade in de water,

Wade in de water.

God's a-gonna trouble de water.

I'm Gonna Sing

cantor: Oh, I'm a-gonna sing,

chorus: Gonna sing, gonna sing,

Gonna sing all along the way.

cantor: One day you'll hear the trumpet sound

chorus: Gonna sing all along the way.

cantor: The trumpet sound the world around

chorus: Gonna sing all along the way.

cantor: Oh, Jordan's stream is wide and cold,

chorus: Gonna sing all along the way.

cantor: It chills the body but not the soul,

chorus: Gonna sing all along the way.

Budget: Under $25

Sources:

Videos or audio cassettes of the films *Glory* (1990) and the nine-part PBS series, *The Civil War* (1990).

Heilbut, Anthony, *Gospel Sound: Good News and Bad Times*, Limelight Editions, 1997.

Merlis, Bob, and Davin Seay, *Heart and Soul: A Celebration of Black Music: Style in America 1930-1975*, Stewart, Taboori and Chang, 1997.

Silverman, Jerry, *Spirituals,* Chelsea House, 1995.

Southern, Eileen, *Music of Black America: A History*, W. W. Norton & Co., 1997.

Spencer, Jon Michael, *Protest and Priase: Sacred Music of Black Religion*, Fortress Press, 1997.

Spirituals We Play and Sing, Bks. 1 and 2, Lillenas, 1993.

Alternative Applications: Lead a discussion of the interplay between a cantor or spokesperson and an assembly. Play a recording or videotape of these examples:

♦ storytelling by Mary Carter Smith, Linda Goss, Rex Ellis, Gladys Coggswell, or Doug and Frankie Quimby

♦ Martin Luther King's "I Have a Dream Speech"

♦ speeches by Jesse Jackson and Barbara Jordan

Discuss how antiphony affects American assemblies where black people follow African patterns by replying to the cantor's statements.

Band Music

Originator: Bob Taylor, trumpeter, band director, retired teacher, Hickory, North Carolina.

Age/Grade Level or Audience: Community band or jazz ensemble.

Description: Offer a program of serious or classical band music expressing black themes and created by black composers.

Procedure: Present a program of works by black composers. Some possibilities include these:

- ♦ Count Basie, "One O'Clock Jump," "Swingin' the Blues," "Send for You Yesterday, and Here You Come Today," and "Boogie-Woogie"
- ♦ Harry T. Burleigh, "Six Plantation Melodies"
- ♦ Tad Dameron, "If You Could See Me Now," "Dial B for Beauty," "Our Delight," and "The Scene Is Clean"
- ♦ Duke Ellington, "Cotton Tail," "Black and Tan Fantasy," "Mood Indigo," "Satin Doll," "Black, Brown and Beige," "Liberian Suite," "A Drum Is a Woman," "My People," and "New Orleans Suite"
- ♦ W. C. Handy, "St. Louis Blues"
- ♦ Erskine Hawkins, "Tuxedo Junction"
- ♦ James P. Johnson, "Carolina Shout" or "Mule Walk"
- ♦ Quincy Jones, *The Pawnbroker, For Love of Ivy, The Wiz, Cactus Flower, In Cold Blood,* "Even When You Cry," "Grace," and "Ironsides"
- ♦ Meade Lux Lewis, "Honky Tonk Train Blues"
- ♦ Thelonius Monk, "Criss Cross," "Misterioso," and "Round Midnight"
- ♦ Jelly Roll Morton, "Black Bottom Stomp"
- ♦ Kid Ory, "Society Blues"
- ♦ Pinetop Smith, "Pinetop's Boogie-Woogie"
- ♦ Billy Strayhorn, "Take the A Train," "Chelsea Bridge," "Warm Valley," and "Jack the Bear"
- ♦ Thomas "Fats" Waller, "Ain't Misbehavin'"
- ♦ "When the Saints Go Marchin' In"
- ♦ Stevie Wonder, *Songs in the Key of Life,* "Love's in Need of Love Today," "Sir Duke," and "Isn't She Lovely"
- ♦ Trummy Young, "It Ain't What You Do, It's the Way That You Do It"

Budget: $50-$75

Sources:

Caldwell, Hansonia, *African American Music—A Chronology 1619-1995,* Ikoro Communications, 1996.

Heilbut, Anthony, *Gospel Sound: Good News and Bad Times*, Limelight Editions, 1997.

Merlis, Bob, and Davin Seay, *Heart and Soul: A Celebration of Black Music Style in America 1930-1975*, Stewart, Taboori and Chang, 1997.

Pruter, Robert, *Doowop : The Chicago Scene*, University of Illinois Press, 1996.

Southern, Eileen, *Music of Black America: A History*, W. W. Norton & Co., 1997.

Spencer, Jon Michael, *Protest and Praise: Sacred Music of Black Religion*, Fortress Press, 1997.

Vincent, Rickey, *Funk: The Music, the People, and the Rhythm of One*, St. Martin's Press, 1996.

Black Music Videos

Age/Grade Level or Audience: All ages.

Description: Present a music video at a Black History Month celebration.

Procedure: Hold a neighborhood, church, civic, or school celebration featuring a great black musician or musical movement. Show a music video, for example:

- ◆ *Aretha Franklin: Queen of Soul*
- ◆ *Aretha Franklin: Ridin' on the Freeway*
- ◆ *B. B. King and Friends: A Night of Red Hot Blues*
- ◆ *B. B. King: Live at Nicks*
- ◆ *B. B. King: Live in Africa*
- ◆ *Chaka Khan: Live*
- ◆ *Diana Ross: In Concert*
- ◆ *Diana Ross: Visions of Diana*
- ◆ *Fats Domino and Friends*
- ◆ *Harlem Harmonies*
- ◆ *Herbie Hancock: Jazz Africa*
- ◆ *Ike and Tina Turner Show*
- ◆ *The Incomparable Nat King Cole, Volumes I and II*
- ◆ *Johnny Mathis: Chances Are*
- ◆ *Konkombe: The Nigerian Pop Music Scene*
- ◆ *La Toya Jackson*
- ◆ *Louis Armstrong: Satchmo*
- ◆ *Mahalia Jackson*
- ◆ *Marvin Gaye: Greatest Hits Live*
- ◆ *Marvin Gaye: Motown Presents*
- ◆ *Natalie Cole: The Unforgettable Concert*
- ◆ *Otis Redding: Live in Monterey*
- ◆ *Pointer Sisters: Live in Africa*

    ◆ *Quincy Jones: A Celebration*
    ◆ *Reggae Superstars in Concert*
    ◆ *Spike Lee: A Cappella*
    ◆ *Thelonious Monk: Music in Monk's Time*
    ◆ *Whitney Houston: Welcome Home Troops*
    ◆ *Wynton Marsalis: Blues and Swing*
    ◆ *Ziggy Marley and the Melody Makers*

Budget: $50-$75

Sources:

"African American Composer Series," http//cwis.usc.edu/dept/news—Service/chronicle—html/1996.02.

"Best of Jazz 'Round Midnight" (CD), Verve, 1996.

Caldwell, Hansonia, *African American Music—A Chronology 1619-1995*, Ikoro Communications, 1996.

Coleman, M., "The New Edition," *Rolling Stone*, July 10-24, 1997, 36-38.

"Duke Ellington: Live at the Blue Note" (CD), Roulette, 1997.

Heilbut, Anthony, *Gospel Sound: Good News and Bad Times*, Limelight Editions, 1997.

"John Coltrane: The Heavyweight Champion—The complete Atlantic Recordings" (CD), Rhino, 1995.

Jones, Steve, "LL Cool J's Album," *USA Today*, November 10, 1997, 3D.

"Louis Armstrong Plays W. C. Handy" (CD), Columbia Jazz Legacy, 1997.

"Louis Armstrong: The Complete RCA Victor Recordings" (CD), RCA, 1997.

McCorkle, Susannah, "Back to Bessie," *American Heritage*, November 1997,54-75.

Merlis, Bob, and Davin Seay, *Heart and Soul: A Celebration of Black Music Style in America 1930-1975*, Stewart, Taboori and Chang, 1997.

"Miles Davis: Kind of Blue" (CD), Columbia Jazz Legacy, 1997.

"Ray Charles: Genius and Soul—The 50th Anniversary Collection" (CD), Rhino, 1997.

"Scores: Archives of African American Music and Culture," http//www.indiana.edu/~aaamc/undine.html.

"Still Going On: An Exhibit Celebrating the Life and Times of William Grant Still," http//scriptorium.lib.duke.edu/sg/start.html.

"Wade in the Water: African American Sacred" (CD), Smithsonian Folkways, 1996.

Alternative Applications: Have a volunteer outline on an overhead projector or website the contributions of black musicians to major musical movements, such as American soul, calypso, ragtime, reggae, minstrelsy, urban blues, disco, musical theater, black country, jazz, hip-hop, bebop, doowop, swing, opera, hymns, patriotic songs, scat, gospel, spirituals, protest songs, funk, Motown, and rhythm and blues. List top performers in each category, for example:

    ◆ ballads—Nat "King" Cole, Andy Bey
    ◆ bebop—Charlie "Bird" Parker
    ◆ country—Charlie Pride

- ♦ disco—Donna Summer
- ♦ gospel—Mahalia Jackson and Ethel Waters
- ♦ hymns and patriotic songs—Marian Anderson
- ♦ jazz—John Coltrane, Dinah Washington, Miles Davis, Errol L. Garner, Cannonball Adderley, Art Tatum
- ♦ movie music—Quincy Jones
- ♦ opera—Jessye Norman, Leontyne Price, and Kathleen Battle
- ♦ rap—Ice-T
- ♦ reggae—Bob Marley and the Wailers, Ziggy Marley
- ♦ rhythm and blues—Aretha Franklin, Ray Charles, Etta James, and Lou Rawls
- ♦ rock—Chuck Berry, James Brown, Little Richard, Chubby Checker
- ♦ scat—Ella Fitzgerald
- ♦ show tunes—Pearl Bailey and William Warfield
- ♦ spirituals—Harry T. Burleigh

Choral Music

Age/Grade Level or Audience: High school, college, or community chorus; church choir.

Description: Offer a program of serious or classical choral music by black composers or arrangers.

Procedure: Present a variety of choral works and solos that underscore the hardships and joys of black experience. A worthy modern composer to feature is Leslie Adams (1932-), creator of *Psalm 21, The Ode to Life, Hosanna to the Son of David, Madrigal, Creole Girl, The Heart of a Woman, I Want to Die Easy, Man's Presence, Prayer, The Righteous Man, Since You Went Away, Under the Greenwood Tree, Vocalise, We Shall Overcome, For You there Is No Song, Dunbar Songs, There Was an Old Man, Tall Tales*, and the opera *Blake*.

Other possibilities include these:

- ♦ Lee Adams and Charles Strouse, "No More," from the Broadway musical *Golden Boy*
- ♦ James A. Bland, "Carry Me Back to Old Virginny"
- ♦ Edward Boatner, *The Story of the Spirituals*
- ♦ Harry T. Burleigh, *Spirituals,* "Southland Sketches," "The Lovely Dark and Lonely One," "Little Mother of Mine," "Deep River," "The Prayer"
- ♦ Will Marion Cook, operetta *Clorinda*
- ♦ Robert de Cormier, "Wayfaring Stranger" and "Ain'-a That Good News"

- ◆ Anthony Davis, opera *The Life and Times of Malcolm X*
- ◆ Robert Nathaniel Dett, *The Chariot Jubilee*
- ◆ Thomas A. Dorsey, "Precious Lord, Take My Hand," "There'll Be Peace in the Valley," "If I Don't Get There," and "Say a Little prayer for Me"
- ◆ Harry Lawrence Freeman, *Voodoo* or *Martyr*
- ◆ Jester Hairston and Harry Robert Wilson, *Negro Spirituals and Folk Songs*
- ◆ Edwin Hawkins Singers, "Oh Happy Day"
- ◆ Tramaine Hawkins, "Spirit Fall Down on Me"
- ◆ Quincy Jones, *The Wiz, Give Me the Night, E.T.,* "We Are the World"
- ◆ Charles Harrison Mason, "I'm a Soldier in the Army of the Lord" and "My Soul Loves Jesus"
- ◆ Wallace Saunders, "Casey Jones"
- ◆ William Grant Still, "Troubled Island" and "Plain Chant for America"

Comment on the background of black composers and arrangers, particularly Harry T. Burleigh, Jester Hairston, and Edward Boatner.

Budget: $50-$75

Sources:

Caldwell, Hansonia, *African American Music—A Chronology 1619-1995*, Ikoro Communications, 1996.

Heilbut, Anthony, *Gospel Sound: Good News and Bad Times*, Limelight Editions, 1997.

Merlis, Bob, and Davin Seay, *Heart and Soul: A Celebration of Black Music Style in America 1930-1975*, Stewart, Taboori and Chang, 1997.

Southern, Eileen, *Music of Black America: A History*, W. W. Norton & Co., 1997.

Spencer, Jon Michael, *Protest and Priase: Sacred Music of Black Religion*, Fortress Press, 1997.

Vincent, Rickey, *Funk: The Music, the People, and the Rhythm of One*, St.Martin's Press, 1996.

Alternative Applications: Coordinate a program on the subject of justice and liberty. Feature the following choral works:

- ◆ Randall Thompson, *Testament of Freedom* or *The Last Words of David*
- ◆ Howard Hanson, *Song of Democracy*
- ◆ Pablo Casals, "Nigra Sum"
- ◆ William Grant Still, "Plain Chant for America"

Age/Grade Level or Audience: All ages.

Description: Hold a piano solo competition.

Procedure: Divide entrants into beginner, intermediate, and advanced categories. Have each performer play one personal choice and one selection from a required list, such as these:

- ◆ Harry Lawrence Freeman's opera "Martyr"
- ◆ William Grant Still's ballet *Sahdji*
- ◆ Harry Lawrence Freeman, *Voodoo*
- ◆ Scott Joplin, "Bethena," "The Entertainer," or "Maple Leaf Rag"
- ◆ Thomas Dorsey, "Precious Lord, Take My Hand"
- ◆ Nat King Cole, "Straighten Up and Fly Right"
- ◆ Francis Hall Johnson's folk opera *Run Little Children*
- ◆ Edwin Hawkins Singers, "Oh Happy Day."

Provide judges with a professional evaluation sheet rating students from one to ten on musicality, stage presence, rhythm, fingering, and phrasing.

Budget: $25-$50

Sources:
Brodt Music Company, P. O. Box 9345, Charlotte, N.C. 28299 (800-438-4129).

Alternative Applications: Include other types of keyboard performance categories, particularly duet, duo piano, vocal accompaniment, choral accompaniment, pipe or electric organ, electronic keyboard, moog, and piano and another instrument, such as violin, viola, or flute.

A Hero's Oratorio

Age/Grade Level or Audience: College music composition class.

Description: Create a musical oratorio to laud a black hero.

Procedure: Appoint a small group to write melodies and words honoring a black hero. Select a real person, for example, Nelson Mandela, Frederick Douglass, Ida Wells-Barnett, Kunte Kinte, Harriet Tubman, Mark Mathabane, Sojourner Truth, or Joseph Cinqué, or choose a noble character from literature, such as Bras-Coupé, the African prince in George Washington Cable's novel *The Grandissimes*, or Sethe, heroine of Toni Morrison's *Beloved*. Perform the work as part of a Black History Month musicale. Attach an overview of the hero's life and accomplishments to the program notes.

Budget: $25-$50

Sources:
Cable, George Washington, *The Grandissimes*, Viking Penguin 1988.
Haley, Alex, *Roots: The Saga of an American Family*, Doubleday, 1976.
———, *Alex Haley's Queen*, Avon, 1994.
King, Coretta Scott, *My Life with Martin Luther King, Jr.*, Henry Holt & Co., 1992.
Mandela, Nelson, *The Long Walk to Freedom: The Autobiography of Nelson Mandela*, Little, Brown, 1994.
Mathabane, Mark, *Kaffir Boy*, Macmillan Plume Books, 1986.
Morrison, Toni, *Beloved*, Knopf, 1987.

Alternative Applications: Work with a class to compose individual choral anthems that salute the heroism of famous blacks. Perform the works at a convocation or graduation concert.

A History of African American Music

Age/Grade Level or Audience: Middle school or high school college music classes; music societies; civic groups.

Description: Create an audio-visual music festival to celebrate the history of African American music.

Procedure: Assign participants a particular segment of music history to study and portray through an audio-visual presentation. Assemble the segments into a chronological whole, beginning with slave songs, hymns, work songs, and minstrel performances and working up through jazz, bebop, doo-wop, soul, rock, black show music, rhythm and blues, opera, reggae, zydeco, black country, West Indian soca, disco, hip-hop, and rap. Include these facts:

- ♦ In the 1870s, the Fisk Jubilee Singers of Nashville, Tennessee, popularized spirituals among white audiences.
- ♦ In 1871, John Esputa organized the Colored Opera company.
- ♦ In 1875, Massachusetts blacks formed the Boston Musical Union.
- ♦ In 1876, black musicians organized the Philharmonic society of New York.
- ♦ In 1893, Harry Lawrence Freeman's opera "Martyr" was performed in Denver. That same year, Frederick Douglass's grandson, violinist Joseph Douglass, toured the United States for the Victor Talking Machine Company.
- ♦ In 1897, Joplin produced the first ragtime hit, "Maple Leaf Rag."
- ♦ By 1903, the Samuel Coloridge-Taylor Musical Society of Washington, D.C., reached a membership of 200.

◆ In 1908, Shepard N. Edmons founded a black-owned music publishing house.

◆ In 1912, Robert Nathaniel Dett composed *Magnolia*, a five-piano suite.

◆ In 1921, Thomas Dorsey began writing gospels with "If I Don't Get There."

◆ In 1925, Florence B. Price became the first black woman to win the Wanamaker Award for musical composition.

◆ In 1928, Harry Lawrence Freeman's *Voodoo* was produced on Broadway.

◆ In 1932, Thomas Dorsey was proclaimed father of gospel after publishing "Precious Lord, Take My Hand."

◆ In 1943, Nat King Cole sold half a million copies of his first composition, "Straight Up and Fly Right," and, in 1948, he was the first black to star in his own radio series.

◆ In 1946, Pearl Bailey debuted on stage in *St. Louis Woman*.

◆ In 1947, Nat King Cole recorded "Christmas Song."

◆ In 1955, Leontyne Price sang in a televised production of *Tosca*.

◆ In 1960, Odetta performed at Carnegie Hall.

◆ In 1969, Edwin Hawkins Singers brought gospel to the pop charts with "Oh Happy Day."

◆ In 1968, Thomas J. Anderson composed his *Chamber Symphony*.

◆ In the fall of 1992, Kathleen Battle sang at the New York Philharmonic's 150th anniversary.

Budget: $50-$75

Sources:

Films such as *Lady Sings the Blues* (1972), *Mahogany* (1976), *Roots* (1977), *Glory* (1990), and *The Songs Are Free* (1991).

Caldwell, Hansonia, *African American Music—A Chronology 1619-1995*, Ikoro Communications, 1996.

Heilbut, Anthony, *Gospel Sound: Good News and Bad Times*, Limelight Editions, 1997.

McLane, Daisann, "Caribbean Soul: From Calypso to Reggae, Salsa to Soca," *Black Enterprise*, May 1991, 92-93.

Merlis, Bob, and Davin Seay, *Heart and Soul: A Celebration of Black Music Style in America 1930-1975*, Stewart, Taboori and Chang, 1997.

Pruter, Robert, *Doowop: The Chicago Scene*, University of Illinois Press, 1996.

Southern, Eileen, *Music of Black America: A History*, W. W. Norton & Co., 1997.

Spencer, Jon Michael, *Protest and Praise: Sacred Music of Black Religion*, Fortress Press, 1997.

Vincent, Rickey, *Funk: The Music, the People, and the Rhythm of One*, St.Martin's Press, 1996.

Alternative Applications: Invite local talent to illustrate each segment of the chronological study with songs or lip-syncing.

Joplin Expo

Age/Grade Level or Audience: All Ages

Description: Present a discussion and performance of the music of Scott Joplin.

Procedure: Present an overview of Scott Joplin's life, including these facts:

- The son of a former slave, Joplin was born November 24, 1868, in Texarkana, Texas.
- He moved to St. Louis in 1885 to play ragtime piano and tour on the vaudeville circuit.
- At George Smith College, he studied harmony and music theory.
- In 1897, while working at the Maple Leaf Club in Sedalia, Missouri, he composed his greatest hit, "Maple Leaf Rag," which sold over a million copies.
- From 1899 to 1909 he played marches, two-steps, ragtime, serenades, cake walks, and waltzes in saloons and bordellos.
- In 1903, he composed his first opera, *Guest of Honor.*
- In 1904 he wrote "The Cascades" for the 1904 World's Fair.
- Settled in St. Louis, in 1911 he wrote two operas, *The Entertainer* and *Treemonisha,* which he dedicated to his mother.
- Seriously mentally ill, he died penniless in a New York hospital in 1917 and was buried in an unmarked grave in St. Michael's Cemetery, Brooklyn.
- The Atlanta Symphony performed *Treemonisha* in 1972.
- In 1974, Joplin tunes were revived by Gunther Schuller.
- "The Entertainer" made the Top Forty and won Oscars for best title song and best sound track for the movie *The Sting.*

Play recordings of Joplin's ragtime originals, particularly "Bethena," "Maple Leaf Rag," "The Chrysanthemum," "The Cascades," "The Entertainer," "Swipesy," and "Solace." Compare them with other typically African American styles, such as reggae, plena, soca, rhythm and blues, calypso, spirituals, hip-hop, bebop, doowop, or soul tunes.

Budget: $25-$50

Sources:
Sound track from the film *The Sting* (1973).

Berlin, Edward A., *King of Ragtime—Scott Joplin and His Era*, Oxford University Press, 1996.

Caldwell, Hansonia, *African American Music—A Chronology 1619-1995*, Ikoro Communications, 1996.

Curtis, Susan, *Dancing to a Black Man's Tune: A Life of Scott Joplin*, University of Missouri Press, 1994.

Merlis, Bob, and Davin Seay, *Heart and Soul: A Celebration of Black Music Style in America 1930-1975*, Stewart, Taboori and Chang, 1997.

Otfinoski, Steven, *Scott Joplin: A Life in Ragtime*, Franklin Watts, 1995.

"Ragtime Related Links," http//www.ragtimers.org.

"Scott Joplin Archives," http//www.webcom.com/~jeff/Joplin—Archives/intro.html.

Steppin' on the Blues: The Visible Rhythms of African American Dance, University of Illinois Press, 1996.

"Treemonisha Home Page," http//www.midcoast.com/~bog/treemonisha.html.

Alternative Applications: Study the works of Scott Joplin alongside those of Thomas Milton Turpin or James Scott's "Ragtime Oriole." Expand the study to include background music in the videos *Ragtime* and *The Sting*.

Lullaby Pictures

Age/Grade Level or Audience: Elementary school integrated music and art classes.

Description: Pair recordings of lullabies with original art of the singers and subjects.

Procedure: Play recordings of lullabies from Africa or the Caribbean. Have listeners provide a series of illustrations to coordinate with the theme, subject, and atmosphere of each song. Group art and music for a PTA program.

Budget: Under $25

Sources:
Ernst, Karen, "What a Picture Can Be," *Teaching K-8,* October 1997, 26.
Lullabies Around the World: Featuring Designs from the Hallmark Collection, Hal Leonard Corp., 1995.
Lullabies from Around the World, When & Where, 1997.

Alternative Applications: Play recorded lullabies or read aloud the lullabies of Africa and the Caribbean. Include the lyrics of these songs:

> "Abiyoyo" (South Africa)
> "All Me Rock" (Jamaica)
> "Child of Mine, Hush" (Uganda)
> "Mama Gone A-mountin" (Tobago)

"O Rari, O Rari" (Morocco)

"Oh, My Little Dove" (Dominican Republic)

"Oh, Son, Son" (Tanzania)

"Sleep, Mosquitoes, Sleep" (Haiti)

"Ushururu My Child" (Ethiopia)

"Whose Child Is This Baby?" (Ghana)

Have participants act out the dramatic scenes in each, then capture in art with fingerpaint, water colors, colored markers, charcoal, crayons, or colored chalk. Post the finished art in a lullaby art collection.

 Motown

Age/Grade Level or Audience: Middle school or high school college music or music history classes.

Description: Prepare a history of Motown.

Procedure: Organize students into groups to take notes on the history of Motown, Berry Gordy's African American corporation which turned many singing groups and soloists into recording and performing stars. Assign individual groups to study Smokey Robinson and the Miracles, Diana Ross and the Supremes, Martha and the Vandellas, Temptations, Jackson Five, and Four Tops. Have the groups create wall charts of each group's most popular hits and the numbers sold. Use symbols to indicate gold and platinum records. Include important dates such as these:

- ◆ In 1957, former boxer Barry Gordy co-wrote "Reet Petite," his first modest hit.
- ◆ The next year Gordy wrote "Lonely Teardrops."
- ◆ At age thirty, he borrowed $800 in 1959 to start his Detroit recording business.
- ◆ In 1960, his first major success, "You Got What It Takes," was recorded by Marv Johnson.
- ◆ In 1961, he made his first gold record with the Miracles' "Shop Around."
- ◆ In 1962, Motown reached a major portion of the recording audience with "Two Lovers," "You Beat Me to the Punch," "Do You Love Me," and "You Really Got a Hold on Me."
- ◆ A record year, 1964, saw the production of "My Guy, " "Baby Love," "Where Did Our Love Go," "Chapel of Love," and "Hello Dolly."
- ◆ By 1966, three-quarters of Motown's output was successful, ranging from doo-wop to soul, Rhythm & Blues, gospel, rock and roll, and pop.
- ◆ In 1972, Motown moved to Los Angeles.
- ◆ Gordy sponsored the filming of *Lady Sings the Blues*, starring Diana Ross as Billie Holiday.

Budget: Under $25

Sources:

Davis, Sharon, *Motown, the History*, Guinness Superlatives, 1989.

Gordy, Berry, *To Be Loved: The Music, the Magic, the Memories of Motown*, Warner Books, 1994.

"Motown Home Page," http//motown.com/motown/.

"Motown Memories," *Rolling Stone*, August 23, 1990, 79-83.

"Rearview Mirror," http//detnews.com/history/motown/motown.htm.

Alternative Applications: Hold a Motown Day. Organize a variety of activities such as these:

♦ Have students demonstrate dances associated with the rise of Motown, such as the shag and the funky chicken.

♦ Suggest that groups dress up like famous groups, particularly Diana Ross and the Supremes, Temptations, Four Tops, Spinners, Gladys Knight and the Pips, Martha and the Vandellas, Four Seasons, Isley Brothers, Rare Earth, Junior Walker and the All Stars, Marvelettes, Pointer Sisters, Smokey Robinson and the Miracles, Commodores, or Jackson Five.

♦ Invite groups to sing or lip sync Motown favorites, such as "Under the Boardwalk" and "My Guy."

♦ Post charts of the numbers of records sold by Stevie Wonder, Diana Ross, Marvin Gaye, Smokey Robinson, Tammi Terrell, Billy Eckstine, Mary Wells, Lionel Ritchie, Chaka Khan, Rick James, and other Motown successes.

Music Workshop

Age/Grade Level or Audience: All ages.

Description: Locate black musicians to staff a music workshop.

Procedure: Invite black professionals to teach the fundamentals of guitar, piano, electronic keyboard, trumpet, banjo, drums, string bass, harmonica, or vocal music. Provide the workshop free to assist indigent community members in improving their skills. For the youngest participants, teach note reading, scales, and beginning harmonics. Conclude the music workshop with a group performance.

Budget: $50-$75

Sources:
Consult local school, college, and university music departments, night clubs, private music teachers, or bands for suggested personnel to staff music workshops.

A New Negro National Anthem

Age/Grade Level or Audience: High school music or creative writing classes.

Description: Compose an updated "Negro National Anthem."

Procedure: Working in groups, determine the events, attitudes, and accomplishments that should go into a new black anthem. Consider these changes and additions:

- ♦ "Afro-American," "African American" or "black" in place of "negro"
- ♦ tributes to civil rights leaders in several verses
- ♦ a new melody and more invigorating rhythm
- ♦ a title keyed to black pride

Budget: Under $25

Sources:
Heilbut, Anthony, *Gospel Sound: Good News and Bad Times*, Limelight Editions, 1997.

Merlis, Bob, and Davin Seay, *Heart and Soul: A Celebration of Black Music Style in America 1930-1975*, Stewart, Taboori and Chang, 1997.

Silverman, Jerry, *Spirituals,* Chelsea House, 1995.

Southern, Eileen, *Music of Black America: A History*, W. W. Norton & Co., 1997.

Spencer, Jon Michael, *Protest and Praise: Sacred Music of Black Religion*, Fortress Press, 1997.

Spirituals We Play and Sing, Bks. 1 and 2, Lillenas, 1993.

Alternative Applications: Compose jacket copy or a media blitz to accompany the release of a series of audiocassettes or CDs on the history of African American music. Include gospel, calypso, jazz, blues, reggae, hip hop, black country, pop, rock, rap, classical, and opera.

"N'Kosi sikelel' i Afrika"

Age/Grade Level or Audience: Kindergarten and elementary school music classes; church school.

Description: Teach children to sing "N'Kosi sikelel' i Afrika."

Procedure: Introduce "N'Kosi sikelel' i Afrika," the new official South African national anthem, which contains words of Xhosa, Zulu, and Swahili. Explain that the song, written by Enoch Sontonga in 1897, was a children's song in South African elementary classes. It was first performed publicly two years later and became a popular tune and ritual anthem in Johannesburg. Spread by the Ohlange Zulu Choir, it gained favor with the African National Congress, led by Nelson Mandela. Conclude the lesson by teaching the song by rote.

Budget: Under $25

Sources:
"N'Kosi sikelel' i Afrika" on *Postcards* (CD), Turtle Creek Chorale, Box 77225X, San Francisco, California 94107, phone 800-336-8866.

Alternative Applications: Use "N'Kosi sikelel' i Afrika" as the theme song for a rhythm band or choir.

Patois

Originator: Susan L. Henry, librarian and book dealer, Charlotte, North Carolina.

Age/Grade Level or Audience: Middle school college music classes; music societies, civic choruses.

Description: Sample African music that mixes languages other than English.

Procedure: Distribute song sheets containing the original words to songs in Louisiana Creole or Gullah patois. Discuss how the lyrics blend English with other tongues and dialects. For example, "Aurore Pradère," "Fais Do Do, Colas," "Kum Ba Yah," and "Sanguree."

Kum Ba Yah
Someone's singin', Lord, Kum ba yah.

Someone's singin', Lord, Kum ba yah.
Someone's shoutin', Lord, Kum ba yah.

Fais Do Do, Colas
Fais do do, Colas, mon 'tit frere.
Fais do do, chere cochon, mon 'tit frere.
T'auras du gateau Papa e aura,
Et moi j'un aurai,
Fais do do, mon chere.

Budget: $25-$50

Sources:

Recordings such as Sweet Honey in the Rock, *All for Freedom,* and Warren-Mattox Production, *Shake It to the One That You Love the Best.*

"The Gullah Connection," http//www.afrinet.net/~hallh/afrotalk/afrooct95/1090. html.

"Gullah People and Culture," http//www.tezcat.com/~ronald/gullah.html.

Alternative Applications: Organize a rhythm band to accompany *a capella* singing to these and other taped or recorded African songs:

"Alunde and the Story of Ono"	"Amen"
"Bob-a-Needle"	"Calypso Freedom"
"Gone to the Mailboat"	"Ise Oluwa"
"Juba"	"Kum Ba Yah"
"The Little Shekere"	"Loop de Loop"
"Ya, Ya, Ya"	"Yellow Bird"

Include cymbals, bongo drums, sticks, bells, tambourines, and triangles.

Porgy and Bess

Age/Grade Level or Audience: High school music classes; music clubs.

Description: Present a short version of the folk opera *Porgy and Bess.*

Procedure: Begin with a time line of the published versions of Porgy's story:

◆ In 1925, Dubose Heyward publishes his tragic dialect novella *Porgy.*
◆ Two years later, Heyward and his collaborator, playwright Dorothy Hartzell Kuhns Heyward, adapted *Porgy* into a brighter, more hopeful musical.

◆ In 1935, the Dubose Heyward collaborated with George and Ira Gershwin to produce *Porgy and Bess* as a vibrant three-act folk melodrama.

◆ In 1959, Samuel Goldwyn filmed *Porgy and Bess* for Columbia pictures. Otto Preminger directed the film version, which starred Pearl Bailey, Diahann Carroll, Sidney Poitier, Dorothy Dandridge, and Sammy Davis, Jr.

Discuss the historical foundations of the plot, the setting on Catfish Row and islands off the South Carolina coast, then summarize the action of the opera, interspersing recorded lyrics, particularly "Summertime," "I Got Plenty of Nothing," "I'm on My Way," "It Ain't Necessarily So," and "Bess, You Is My Woman." Note the following social, religious, and economic themes:

◆ community solidarity

◆ faith and determination.

◆ importance of family

◆ poverty and fatalism

◆ drug culture and gambling

◆ fate and superstition

◆ male and female roles

◆ religious societies

Budget: $25-$50

Sources:

Erb, Jane, "Porgy and Bess," http//www.classicalnet/~music/comp.1st/ works/gershwin/porgy&bess.html.

Gershwin: Porgy and Bess (3 CDs), EMI, 1988.

"Goat Cart Sam, aka Porgy," httpdarwin.clas.virginia.edu/~kh4d/porgy.html.

Heyward, Dubose, *Porgy,* George H. Doran Co., 1929.

———, *Porgy and Bess* (recording), Phillips, 1985.

Jones, Steve, "Top Players Jazz Up Broadway Classics," *USA Today*, October 14, 1997, 8D.

Snodgrass, Mary Ellen, *The Encyclopedia of Southern Literature*, ABC-Clio, 1998.

Alternative Applications: Perform the play in tableau shadow screen style, a technique requiring little stage preparation and rehearsal and minimal costs. As the narrator summarizes each segment of the action, have actors take their places on a stage or behind a screen. Pass out song sheets and invite the audience to sing along the familiar show tunes.

Presenting Black Musicians

Age/Grade Level or Audience: Middle school or high school music or humanities classes.

Description: Compose introductions to great works of music by black composers.

Procedure: Assign individual students to compose programs notes for a musical work by a black composer, for example :

> Dubose Heyward and George and Ira Gershwin, *Porgy and Bess*
> Harry T. Burleigh, *Spirituals*
> Will Marion Cook's operetta *Clorinda*
> Anthony Davis's opera *The Life and Times of Malcolm X*
> Jester Hairston and Harry Robert Wilson, *Negro Spirituals and Folk Songs,*
> Quincy Jones, *The Wiz*
> William Grant Still, "Troubled Island" and "Plain Chant for America"

Conclude the exercise with illustrations, photos, or a musical motif around the cover.

Budget: $25-$50

Sources:

Heilbut, Anthony, *Gospel Sound Good News and Bad Times*, Limelight Editions, 1997.

Merlis, Bob, and Davin Seay, *Heart and Soul: A Celebration of Black Music Style in America 1930-1975*, Stewart, Taboori and Chang, 1997.

Silverman, Jerry, *Spirituals,* Chelsea House, 1995.

Southern, Eileen, *Music of Black America: A History*, W. W. Norton & Co., 1997.

Spencer, Jon Michael, *Protest and Praise: Sacred Music of Black Religion*, Fortress Press, 1997.

Spirituals We Play and Sing, Bks. 1 and 2, Lillenas, 1993.

Alternative Applications: Create an online songbook of music by black composers, particularly Harry T. Burleigh, Scott Joplin, Will Marion Cook, Anthony Davis, Jester Hairston, Harry Robert Wilson, Quincy Jones, or William Grant Still. Intersperse notes and commentary on the era in which the work was composed, its reception, and revivals of the tunes and style, particularly the Burleigh's spirituals and Joplin's rags.

Rap Wrap-Up

Age/Grade Level or Audience: Civic, church, or school groups.

Description: Explore the purpose and style of rap music.

Procedure: Play some rap recordings or tapes, such as recordings by Snoop Doggy Dogg, Soul Sonic Force, Ice Cube, M. C. Hammer, Kurtis Blow, Fat Boys, Salt N Peppa, 2 Live Crew, Sons of the Ghetto, Tupac Shakur, LL Cool J., Takagi Kan's *Hip Hip Fork,* or Yolanda "Yo Yo" Whitaker's "Black Pearl." Invite local rap groups to perform. Encourage a discussion of pervasive themes, particularly outrage, poverty, and pride. Stress the importance of first-person observation, energy, feeling, and wit in the creation of rap lyrics. List rap slang, which has permeated the culture of France, Italy, Japan, Russia, and Brazil.

Budget: $25-$50

Sources:

Taped segments of local radio shows; record shops; films such as *Boyz 'n the Hood* (1991), *Grand Canyon* (1991), and *Yo! MTV Raps*.

Blair, M. Elizabeth, "Commercialization of the Rap Music Youth Subculture," *Journal of Popular Culture*, Winter 1993, 21-34.

Chambers, Veronica, "Rapping on Their Own," *Newsweek*, October 27, 1997, 72.

Collum, Danny Duncan, "Roots to Rap—A Mother Lode in the Ethnic Gap," *National Catholic Reporter*, February 28, 1992, 14.

Contemporary Musicians, Gale, 1997.

Cool J, L. L., *I Make My Own Rules*, St. Martin's Press, 1997.

Farley, Christopher John, "Reborn to Be Wild," *Time*, January 22, 1996.

Henry, Laurie, *The Fiction Dictionary*, Story, 1995.

Krohn, Franklin B., and Frances L. Suazo, "Contemporary Urban Music: Controversial Messages in Hip-Hop and Rap Lyrics," *Review of General Semantics*, Summer 1995, 139-155.

Popular Music, Gale, 1996.

"R&B, Hip Hop, Rap Music Page," http//www.cs.ucr.edu/~marcus/music.html.

"RRC Archives," http//www.kaiwan.com/rockrap/archive/index.html.

White, Armond, *Rebel for the Hell of It: The Life of Tupac Shakur*, Thunder's Mouth Press, 1997.

Alternative Applications: Organize a round robin rap session. Have one participant compose opening lines, then pass the poem to the next writer. Have a recorder reproduce a list of stanzas and distribute to readers, print in booklet form, or post on a bulletin board or website.

Rhythm of Resistance

Age/Grade Level or Audience: High school or college music or social studies classes; literary or music societies; library study groups.

Description: Hold an African music festival.

Procedure: Play recordings by African musicians, such as these:

Maria Alice	Aster Aweke	Balafon
M'Bella Bel	Ladysmith Black	Stella Chiwese
Fanta Damba	Sona Diabate	Nahawa Doumbia
Cesaria Evora	Umthombowase Golgota	Hassan Hakmoun
Irene and the Melodians	Angelique Kidjo	Amy Koita
Sanougue Kouyate	Tata Bambo Kouyate	Lijadu Sisters
Miriam Makeba	Perefere Malomba	Mambazo
Dumisani Maraire	Sipho Mchunu	Sophie Mgcinas
Babsy Mlangeni	Tshala Muana	Youssou N'Dour
Ebenezer Obey	Mahotella Queens	Mthembu Queens Tabu
Ley Rochereau	Oumou Sangare	Sibeba
Ali Sidibe	Douamba Sidibe	Foday Musa Suso
Tarika	Lilly Tchlumba	Zap Mama

Have students draw conclusions about how rhythm, repetition, and musical style communicate personal, social, and political opinions.

Budget: $25-$50

Sources:

The Videos "Rhythm of Resistance: Music of Black South Africa" and "Johnny Clegg and Savuka: Cruel, Crazy, Beautiful World"; consult Ladyslipper, 3205 Hillsborough Road, Durham, N. C. 27705 (800-634-6044), orders@ladyslipper.org, http//www.lady slipper.org.

"African Music and Dance," http//www.bmrc.berkeley.edu/people/ladzekpo.

"African Music Sources," http//www.matisse.net/~jplanet/ajmx//sources.htm.

"Africa Online," http//www.africaonline.com.

Barlow, Sean, et al., *Afropop: An Illustrated Guide to Contemporary African Music*, Book Sales, 1995.

Erlmann, Veit, *Nightsong: Performance, Power and Practice in South Africa*, University of Chicago Press, 1996.

"Sahel's Music Page," http//www.sahel.com/music.html.

Alternative Applications: Contrast African protest songs with Caribbean protest music. Consult works by these Reggae singers:

Lillian Allen	Amazulu	Ranking Ann
Cedelia Marely Booker	Foxy Brown	Deltones
Marcia Griffiths	I-Three	Linton Kwesi Johnson
Bob Marley	Rita Marley	Judy Mowatt
Sister Carol	Burning Spear	Peter Tosh

Bunny Wailer   Ziggy Marley

Screen the documentary *Time Will Tell*, which describes Marley's fervent fans, who extended from Jamaica outward to distant parts of the world and shows footage of his 1978 "One Love" Peace Concert, held in Kingston, Jamaica, and attended to Ethiopian emperor Haile Selassie. Have volunteers research Marley's role in the Rastafarian movement. Assign small groups to discuss protest themes in Marley's most famous songs, "I Shot the Sheriff," "Lively Up Yourself," "War," and "Them Belly Full."

 1776

Age/Grade Level or Audience: High school or college black studies or American history classes; adult music or civic groups.

Description: Discuss the premise of the musical comedy *1776*.

Procedure: Screen the video *1776*. Lead a group discussion of the movie's implications for later episodes in American history, particularly the abolitionist movement, Harriet Beecher Stowe's *Uncle Tom's Cabin*, Missouri Compromise, Dred Scott decision, raid on Harper's Ferry, Civil War, and Emancipation Proclamation. Have volunteers answer these questions:

- ◆ How might the nation have been different if Rutledge's proposal had failed?
- ◆ What does Rutledge's song "Molasses, Rum, and Slaves" imply about the purity of New England abolitionism?
- ◆ How does colonial economics impinge on the Declaration of Independence?
- ◆ What stand does slave-holder Jefferson take in the controversy?
- ◆ Why does John Adams capitulate to the Southern bloc?
- ◆ In what respect does the argument against King George's tyranny condemn the colonists's attitude toward slavery?

Budget: $25-$50

Sources:
The musical comedy *1776* (1972), and other tapes from video rental services.
Coil, Suzanne M., *Slavery and Abolitionists*, TFC Books, 1995.
"Conflict of Abolition and Slavery," http//www.loc.gov/exhibits/african/confli.html.
Hornsby, Alton, *Chronology of African-American History*, 2nd edition Gale, 1997.
"The Influence of Prominent Abolitionists," http//www.loc.gov/exhibits/african/influ.html.

Metcalf, Doris Hunter, *African Americans: Their Impact on U. S. History*, Good Apple, 1992.

"Northeast Abolitionists," http//www.unl.edu/tcweb/altc/staffpages/page3.html.

Rogers, James T., *The Antislavery Movement*, Facts on File, 1994.

Scott, Otto, *The Secret Six: John Brown and the Abolitionists*, Uncommon Books, 1993.

"Third Person, First Person Slave Voices," http//scriptorium, lib.duke.edu/slavery/.

Thomas, Velma Maia, *Lest We Forget: The Passage from Africa to Slavery and Emancipation*, Crown, 1997.

Yellin, Jean F., and John C. Van Horne, *The Abolitionist Sisterhood: Women's Political Culture in Antebellum America*, Cornell University Press, 1994.

Alternative Applications: Screen the film *1776*, starring Ken Howard and Blythe Danner as Thomas and Martha Jefferson. Evaluate the text from a modern perspective. Decide how modern legislators would vote on these ethical matters:

- ◆ the right of Southern states to import slaves
- ◆ the value of the slave trade to the economy
- ◆ the moral implications of slave ownership and breeding
- ◆ owners' responsibilities to educate, house, feed, and care for slaves
- ◆ national responsibilities to newly freed slaves.

Sing-along

Age/Grade Level or Audience: All ages

Description: Organize musicians and singers for a singalong to honor Black History Month. Citizens will assemble in a hall, auditorium, gymnasium, or church and join in the singing of a variety of familiar songs, spirituals, hymns, ring shouts, call-and-response, and patriotic anthems.

Procedure: Distribute song sheets featuring known and less familiar lyrics to songs by and about Negroes, such as these:

"Amazing Grace"	"The Battle Hymn of the Republic"
"Deep River"	"Elijah Rock"
"Follow the Drinking Gourd"	"Good News"
"Great Day"	"I'm So Glad"
"Joshua Fit the Battle of Jericho"	"The Negro National Anthem"
"Oh, Freedom"	"Soon I Will Be Done"
"Swing Low, Sweet Chariot"	"We Shall Overcome"

Relate the backgrounds of these works and note their significance to the Civil Rights Movement. For instance:

- ◆ "The Negro National Anthem" is also known as "Lift Ev'ry Voice and Sing."

♦ The theme of the song is faith, perseverance, and hope.

♦ It was written by James Weldon Johnson (1871-1938).

♦ The author's brother, Rosamond Johnson, set the lyrics to music.

♦ The first performance was at a Lincoln Day celebration on January 12, 1900, where 500 school children sang it in unison.

♦ By 1920, the anthem spread through the South and into other parts of the United States and the Caribbean.

♦ Maya Angelou honors the song in *I Know Why the Caged Bird Sings* (1970) with her memories of the uplifting lyrics sung at her eighth-grade graduation in Stamps, Arkansas.

Budget: $25-$50

Sources:

Heilbut, Anthony, *Gospel Sound: Good News and Bad Times,* Limelight Editions, 1997.

Merlis, Bob, and Davin Seay, *Heart and Soul: A Celebration of Black Music Style in America 1930-1975,* Stewart, Taboori and Chang, 1997.

Silverman, Jerry, *Spirituals,* Chelsea House, 1995.

Southern, Eileen, *Music of Black America: A History,* W. W. Norton & Co., 1997.

Spencer, Jon Michael, *Protest and Praise: Sacred Music of Black Religion,* Fortress Press, 1997.

Spirituals We Play and Sing, Bks. 1 and 2, Lillenas, 1993.

Alternative Applications: Show these or other video or movies:

Amistad	*The Associate*
The Autobiography of Miss Jane Pittman	Boyz 'n the Hood
Conrack	Daughters of the Dust
Driving Miss Daisy	Ghosts of Mississippi
Glory	I Know Why the Caged Bird Sings
The Learning Tree	Places in the Heart
The Preacher's Wife	Sounder

Follow with a songfest. To strengthen community participation, feature local soloists, instrumentalists, singing or dancing groups, storytellers, or folklorists. Conclude with a panel discussion of the importance of music to movies about African American life, both past and present.

 ## Slavery and Negro Spirituals

Age/Grade Level or Audience: Middle school or high school music classes; adult music societies; church or civic groups.

Description: Study the lyrics of Negro spirituals for clues to the hardships and longings inherent in slavery.

Procedure: Invite singing groups to present a medley of Negro spirituals in elegaic, philosophical, and exuberant moods, including "Sweet Little Jesus Boy," "Soon I Will Be Done with the Troubles of the World," "Get on Board, Little Children," "Steal Away," "Listen to the Lambs," and "De Gospel Train." Pass out song sheets including lyrics and commentary on how each song relates to these and other aspects of slavery:

◆ community solidarity
◆ despair
◆ expectation of liberation
◆ fear of the future
◆ boring, dirty, and dangerous labor
◆ hunger
◆ orphaned children
◆ poor health
◆ reliance on religious faith.
◆ separation of families

Budget: $25-$50

Sources:

Heilbut, Anthony, *Gospel Sound: Good News and Bad Times,* Limelight Editions, 1997.

Merlis, Bob, and Davin Seay, *Heart and Soul: A Celebration of Black Music Style in America 1930-1975,* Stewart, Taboori and Chang, 1997.

Silverman, Jerry, *Spirituals,* Chelsea House, 1995.

Southern, Eileen, *Music of Black America: A History,* W. W. Norton & Co., 1997.

Spencer, Jon Michael, *Protest and Praise: Sacred Music of Black Religion,* Fortress Press, 1997.

Spirituals We Play and Sing, Bks. 1 and 2, Lillenas, 1993.

Alternative Applications: Introduce the words to "Oh, Freedom" or "This Train."

Oh, Freedom!

Oh, freedom! Oh, freedom!
Oh freedom over me.
An' before I'd be a slave
I'd be buried in my grave,
An' go home to my Lord
An' be free, an' be free.

This Train

This train is boun' for glory, this train,

This train is boun' for glory, this train
This train is boun' for glory.
If you want to get to heb'n
Then you got to be holy.
This train is boun' for glory, this train.

Stress the work of Harry T. Burleigh in collecting and preserving the lyrics. Invite professional musicians to discuss the musical, religious, and thematic structure of the songs, particularly dialect, repetition, escapism, and affirmation of faith.

Songs of Protest

Age/Grade Level or Audience: All ages.

Description: Create a bulletin board display featuring lyrics from songs sung by protesters and civil rights marchers.

Procedure: Select a song to place at the center of a display or website of facts, maps, photographs, drawings, and memorabilia from the Civil Rights Movement. Some likely verses include the following:

If You Miss Me from the Front of the Bus
If you miss me from the front of the bus,
And you can't find me nowhere,
Come on up to the driver's seat,
I'll be drivin' up there.

We Are Soldiers in the Army
I'm glad I am a soldier,
I've got my hand on the gospel plow;
But one day I'll get old, I can't fight anymore,
I'll just stand here and fight on anyhow.

Carry It On
If you can't go on no longer,
Take the hand held by your brother;
Every victory gonna bring another,
Carry it on, carry it on.

My People Will Rise
Let's all unite
And make a stand
And share in the profit
Of our grand, rich land.

Budget: Under $25

Sources:

Heilbut, Anthony, *Gospel Sound: Good News and Bad Times*, Limelight Editions, 1997.

Merlis, Bob, and Davin Seay, *Heart and Soul: A Celebration of Black Music Style in America 1930-1975*, Stewart, Taboori and Chang, 1997.

Silverman, Jerry, *Spirituals*, Chelsea House, 1995.

Southern, Eileen, *Music of Black America: A History*, W. W. Norton & Co., 1997.

Spencer, Jon Michael, *Protest and Praise: Sacred Music of Black Religion*, Fortress Press, 1997.

Spirituals We Play and Sing, Bks. 1 and 2, Lillenas, 1993.

Alternative Applications: Have students write new verses to describe these and other aspects of the struggle for freedom:

- ◆ abolition of slavery in Haiti
- ◆ clean-up efforts and enterprise zones following urban riots in Los Angeles
- ◆ court cases such as Brown vs. the Board of Education
- ◆ end of segregation in the United States Military
- ◆ famous firsts, particularly Thurgood Marshall's appointment to the U.S. Supreme Court or Mae Jemison's space flight
- ◆ fight to end famine in Somalia, Haiti, and Ethiopia
- ◆ Ron Brown's role in the cabinet of President Bill Clinton
- ◆ support of the victims and survivors of Apartheid

We Shall Overcome

Age/Grade Level or Audience: All ages.

Description: Arrange a viewing of the Emmy Award-winning documentary musical, *We Shall Overcome*, narrated by Harry Belafonte.

Procedure: Have the audience respond individually to the film and its statement of powerful emotions and segments of history. Encourage participants to answer the following questions:

- ◆ Where did the song originate?
- ◆ Why did it become a rallying cry of tobacco workers of the 1930s and 1940s?
- ◆ Why was the song suitable for campus sit-ins and civil rights marches of the 1960s and 1970s?
- ◆ Why is the song often sung while people stand together and hold hands?
- ◆ What role did the following people play in its use: Pete Seeger, Martin Luther King, Jr., Guy Carwan, Joan Baez, the Freedom Singers?

◆ How does the song compare to other statements of purpose and beliefs, for example "Eyes on the Prize"?

◆ What do varying rhythms indicate about the song?

◆ Why has the song spread to oppressed peoples in India, South Africa, Lebanon, Moscow, and Korea?

◆ How does the song relate to anti-war and nuclear protest rallies?

Budget: $25-$50

Sources:

Documentary musical *We Shall Overcome* (1988).

Heilbut, Anthony, *Gospel Sound: Good News and Bad Times*, Limelight Editions, 1997.

Merlis, Bob, and Davin Seay, *Heart and Soul: A Celebration of Black Music Style in America 1930-1975*, Stewart, Taboori and Chang, 1997.

Silverman, Jerry, *Spirituals,* Chelsea House, 1995.

Southern, Eileen, *Music of Black America: A History*, W. W. Norton & Co., 1997.

Spencer, Jon Michael, *Protest and Praise: Sacred Music of Black Religion*, Fortress Press, 1997.

Spirituals We Play and Sing, Bks. 1 and 2, Lillenas, 1993.

Alternative Applications: Discuss why this song has been called unifying, stabilizing, reassuring, connecting, uplifting, and sustaining. Explain why the following variations are meaningful:

> We are not afraid.
> I will see the Lord.
> I will overcome.
> Blacks and whites together.
> We will win our rights.

Teach a group the most common set of lyrics to *We Shall Overcome*:

> We shall overcome,
> We shall overcome,
> We shall overcome someday.
> Oh, deep in my heart
> I do believe
> That we shall overcome some day.

Work Songs

Originators: Rick Glover, First Sergeant, U. S. Army, Retired, Hickory, North Carolina; Roberta Brown, teacher, Fort Bragg, North Carolina; Susan L. Henry, librarian and book dealer, Charlotte, North Carolina; Dennis Buff, video consultant, Hickory, North Carolina.

Age/Grade Level or Audience: Middle school or high school music classes or adult music societies.

Description: Lead a discussion of the emotional release found in work, marching, hunting, rowing, or convict songs.

Procedure: Present recordings and songsheets of the work songs "Water Boy," "Hammer Man," "Tol' My Cap'n," "Pick a Bale of Cotton," "You Can Dig My Grave with a Silver Spade," "We Raise the Wheat," and "Trouble Don't Last Always." Have a small group present their reactions to the emotionalism, injustice, despair, and protest inherent in the lyrics and describe the dramatic scenario which the song portrays.

Hammer Man
Take this hammer, carry it to the cap'n,
Tell him I'm gone, tell him I'm gone.
Cap'n called me lazy good fer nothin'
Aint's my name, ain't my name.
If he asks you, was I runnin'
Tell him I'm flyin', tell him I'm flyin'.

Tol' My Cap'n
Tol' my cap'n my han's wuz swole,
"Devil take yo' han's, boy,
Let the wheelers roll!"
Tol' my cap'n my feet wuz sore,
"Devil take yo' feet, boy,
Bother me no more."

Trouble Don't Last Always
Keep your eye on the sun
See how she run
Don't let me catch you with your work undone.
I'm a-troubled, I'm a-troubled,
Trouble don't last always.

Water Boy
Water boy, where you been hidin'?
If you don't come, gwine tell yo' Mammy.
There ain't no hammer
That's on this mount'in
That ring like mine, son,
That ring like mine.

We Raise the Wheat
We raise the wheat,

They give us corn;
We bake the loaf,
They give us crusts.
We skim the pot,
They give us the liquor.
Say "That's good enough
For the nigger."

You Can Dig My Grave with a Silver Spade
You can dig my grave with a silver spade
'Cause I ain't gonna be here no longer!
There's a little white robe in the heb'n for me
'Cause I ain't gonna be here no longer!
There's a golden harp in the heb'n for me.
You just touch one string and the whole heb'n rings
'Cause I ain't gonna be here no longer!

Budget: Under $25

Sources:
The songs "John Henry," "Dinah," "Shrimp Boat's a-Comin'," and "Banana Boat Song"; Gardner Read's "You Can Dig My Grave"; Jester Hairston's "Hold My Mule While I Dance, Josey," "Dis Ol' Hammer," and "Pay Me My Money Down"; Avery Robinson's "Water Boy"; Eugene Thamon Simpson's "Hold On"
Lester, Julius, *To Be a Slave*, 1969, reprinted, Scholastic, Inc., 1986.
Silverman, Jerry, *Spirituals,* Chelsea House, 1995.
Spencer, Jon Michael, *Protest and Praise: Sacred Music of Black Religion*, Fortress Press, 1997.
Spirituals We Play and Sing, Bks. 1 and 2, Lillenas, 1993.

Alternative Applications: Assign a committee to compose a work song based on a particular local job, such as truck driving, grave digging, heavy construction, tobacco planting and harvesting, cutting sugar cane, milling rice and cotton, fishing or shrimping, farm labor, selling produce and seafood door-to-door, livestock management, lumbering, mining, or marching. Stress the importance of cadence and repetition to fit natural work rhythms and repetitious hand and body motions, as with the stacking of lumber, hauling of fish nets, or the placement of items in crates. For example:

Tain't No Mo' Sellin' Today
Tain't no mo' sellin' today.
Tain't no mo' hirin' today.
Tain't no mo' pullin' off shirts today.
It's stomp down freedom today.
Stomp it down!
Stomp down freedom today.

Many Thousand Gone
[Marching song of the First Arkansas Unit]
No more iron chain for me
No mroe, no more,
No more iron chain for me,
Many thousand gone.

Airborne Running Cadence
[Sung to "Bo Diddley"]
Bo Diddley, Bo Diddley, have you heard
We're going to jump from a big iron bird.
Refrain Hey Bo Diddley, Hey hey Bo Diddley Bo.
C130 sitting on the strip
Airborne trooper going to take a little trip
Stand up, hook up shuffle to the door
Jump right out and count to four.
If my main don't open wide,
I've got another one by my side.
If that one don't open too,
Look out below I'm coming through.
If I die on the old drop zone,
Box me up and send me home.
Pin my wings upon my chest;
Tell my friends I done my best.

Marching Cadence
I used to wear some old blue jeans
Now I'm wearing army green
Hey, Mom, I want to go—
But they won't let me go—
Home.
I used to drive a Chevrolet;
Now I'm marching every day.
Hey, Mom, I want to go—
But they won't let me go—
Home.
I used to date a teenage queen;
Now I pack an M16.
Hey, Mom, I want to go—
But they won't let me go—
Home.

Drill Sergeant's Favorite, Fort Ord, California
[Sung to "Poison Ivy"]
Smoke is in the air;
Trainee begins to sigh.
Somebody's head is getting high.

Hippies on the corner
They're always shouting "pig."
Trainee on the scene wears a wig.
Foxy lady waitin'
She wants a real good time.
Trainee ain't even got a dime.
Refrain
California, California
Late at night while you're sleepin'
All the hippies come a-creepin'.
California, California.

Marching Song
[Marching song of the 1st Arkansas Unit, set to tune of "John Brown's Body"]
We have done with hoeing cotton;
We have done with hoeing corn.
We are color Yankee soldiers now
As sure as you are born.
When the Master hears us yelling,
They'll think it's Gabriel's horn,
As we go marching on.

Blood on the Risers, as sung by Airborne-school graduates
He was just a rookie trooper
And he surely shook with fright.
As he checked all his equipment
And made sure his pack was tight.
He had to sit and listen to those awful engines roar.
You ain't gonna jump no more.
"Is everyone happy?" cried the sergeant, looking up.
Our Hero, feebly answered "yes" and then they stood him up.
He leaped right out into the blast, his static line unhooked.
He ain't gonna jump no more.

Sweet Potatoes
Sweet potato, yellar yam,
Lord have mercy
Heah I am!
String beans, green corn, I got okra too.
Ev'rything is fresh for you.

Sandy Anna
Hey heave hi ho.
Work on the levee all day.
Seaman what's the matter? Heave ray hooray heave!
Seaman what's the matter? Heave Sandy Anna heave.

Street Medley
Chairs to men, old chairs to mend,

Rush or cane-bottomed.
New mackerel, new mackerel.
Old rags, any old bones,
Take money for your rags,
Any hard skins or rabbit skins.

Seller's Chant
Here's yo col' ice lemonade,
It's made in de shade,
It's stirred wid a spade.
Come buy my col' ice lemonade.
It's made in de shade
An' sol' in de sun.
Ef you hain't got no money,
You cain't git none.
One glass fer a nickel,
An' two fer a dime,
Ef you hain't got de chink,
You cain't git mine.
Come right dis way,
Fer it sho' will pay
To git candy fer de ladies
An' cakes fer de babies.

Religion and Ethics

Advice from Marion Edelman

Age/Grade Level or Audience: All ages.

Description: Promote good attitudes through displays and handouts.

Procedure: Create a bulletin board or series of posters illustrating advice from Marian Wright Edelman. Highlight these twenty-five concepts with illustrations, pictures cut from magazines, or paper flowers:

♦ Don't expect anything for free. Work for what you get.
♦ Choose your aims wisely and make a workable plan for achieving them.
♦ Take charge of what you do.
♦ Work for reasons other than pay or prestige.
♦ Allow room for failure and disappointments.
♦ Think of parenting as a serious responsibility.
♦ Accept your spouse as an equal and a friend.
♦ Create families to last.
♦ Be truthful, even when it is inconvenient or painful.
♦ View yourself as part of the entire human race.
♦ Give up pretense for the real you.
♦ Keep trying.
♦ Accept a crucial role in change.
♦ Keep learning.
♦ Show your children that hard work is necessary.
♦ Let yourself enjoy life.
♦ Select friends you can be proud of.
♦ Keep a positive attitude.
♦ Let go of painful memories.

◆ Assist those in need.

◆ Let your voice speak for the real you.

◆ Take charge of your outlook.

◆ Honor the family, state, nation, and race to which you belong.

◆ Don't be a quitter.

◆ Remember that you are not alone.

Budget: Under $25

Sources:

Burch, Joann J., *Marian Wright Edelman, Children's Champion*, Millbrook Press, 1994.

"Children of a Lesser Country," *New Yorker*, January 15, 1996, 26.

Edelman, Marian Wright, *Families in Peril: An Agenda for Social Change*, Harvard University Press, 1987.

———, *Guide My Feet: Prayers and Meditations on Loving and Working for Children*, Beacon Press, 1995.

———, "We Must Not Lose What We Knew Was Right Then," *Ebony*, November 1995.

Old, Wendie, *Marian Wright Edelman: Fighting for Children's Rights*, Enslow Publications, 1995.

Otfinoski, Steve, *Marian Wright Edelman: Defender of Children's Rights*, Blackbirch Press, 1992.

"She's Taking Her Stand," *Newsweek*, June 10, 1996, 32.

Siegel, Beatrice, *Marian Wright Edelman: The Making of a Crusader*, Simon& Schuster, 1995.

Straub, Deborah Gillan, ed., *African American Voices*, U•X•L/Gale, 1996.

Alternative Applications: Present Edelman's twenty-five precepts as topics for a writing, photography, speech, or poster contest. Distribute the statements on handouts or fliers around the community; advertise them in the newspaper. Publish the results in a booklet or on a web site devoted to Edelman's advice to live by. Hold a public reading at a PTA meeting, club gathering, or radio or television broadcast. Invite participants to suggest additions to the original list.

 African Meditation Methods

Age/Grade Level or Audience: All ages.

Description: Study the importance of meditation in African religions.

Procedure: Collect data on the method and use of meditation in African religion, particularly the "ankh" life-force in Egypt, "ntu" in South Africa, and "nkra" in Ghana. Contrast with meditative methods arising from other religions:

> Buddhist mandala
> Catholic rosary and retreats
> charismatic Christian laying on of hands and prayer circles
> Christian Science prayer for spontaneous healing
> Hasidic recitation
> Jewish Kabbalah
> Lao Tzu's water method
> Native American sweat lodge ceremony and vision quest
> Russian Orthodox contemplation of icons
> Taoist tai-chi
> transcendental meditation
> yoga postures and breath control
> Zen koan

Budget: Under $25

Sources:

Chidester, David, *Religions of South Africa*, Routledge, 1992.

Jamal, Isma'el, "African Meditation," *Upscale*, June/July 1992, 60-61

Kamalashila, *Meditation*, Windhorse Publications, 1996.

Lopez, Donald S., *Religions of China in Practice*, Princeton University Press, 1996.

"Mystic Massage," http//hypn.com/africanculture/mystic. meditations.html.

Nielson, Niels C., *Religions of the World*, 3rd edition, St. Martin Press, 1993.

Alternative Applications: Using an African method, lead a group in meditation. Stress breath control, posture, relaxation, visualization of a positive image, focus, and awareness of revitalization. Discuss the effects on heartbeat, body temperature, blood pressure, attitudes, fears, and thought processes. Discuss how folk practice has improved health and well being without recourse to medical intervention.

"Amazing Grace" and the Slave Trade

Age/Grade Level or Audience: Middle school or high school history or black studies classes; church gatherings.

Description: Present a chalk talk about the composition of the classic Christian hymn "Amazing Grace."

Procedure: Outline on a chalkboard, overhead projector, or handout the life of John Newton, religious convert who abandoned the slave trade. Include data such as these:

- ◆ John Newton was born July 24, 1725, in England.
- ◆ At age eleven, he followed the trade of his father, a sea captain.
- ◆ By fifteen, Newton have become so wicked and profane that he lost a job in Alicant, Spain.
- ◆ In 1742, he fell in love with Mary Catlett, a sweet-natured fourteen-year-old who influenced his behavior.
- ◆ The next year, Newton was impressed into the British navy aboard the *Harwich*.
- ◆ He deserted. After his capture, he was put in irons and whipped.
- ◆ In shame, he fled England and lived in Guinea.
- ◆ In Sierra Leone, he joined a white slaver and stood guard over 600 victims per ship, only 300 of whom survived the voyage.
- ◆ Aboard a vessel bound for Brazil, Newton read about Christianity.
- ◆ During a storm, he believed that he had been saved so that he could perform important Christian work.
- ◆ Newton married Mary Catlett in 1742; they adopted a daughter.
- ◆ To rid himself of the taint of the slave trade, he became a minister.
- ◆ In 1764, he wrote *An Authentic Narrative,* confessing his role in slavery and referring to himself as "the old African blasphemer."
- ◆ In 1779, he and William Cowper composed 281 hymns, including "Amazing Grace."
- ◆ He served English pulpits until his death in 1807.

Conclude the presentation with a discussion of the hymn and its emotional response to the slave trade, which Newton considered his greatest sin.

Budget: Under $25

Sources:

"Amazing Grace," http//www.bath.ac.uk/~chpjpv/grace.htm.

"Amazing Grace, the Story of John Newton," http//www.wilsonweb.com/archive/misc/newton.htm.

Haskins, John, *Amazing Grace: The Story Behind the Song,* Millbrook Press, 1992.

Hindmarsh, D, B., *John Newton and the English Evangelical Tradition: Between the Conversions of Wesley and Wilberforce,* Oxford University Press, 1996.

Sendberg, Anne, ed., *John Newton,* Barbour & Co., 1996.

Snodgrass, Mary Ellen, *Late Achievers: Famous People Who Succeeded Late in Life,* Libraries Unlimited, 1992.

Alternative Applications: Lead a discussion of Abraham Lincoln's famous assertion, "As I would not be a slave, so I would not be a master." Explain how these words describe the evil that corrupted John Newton's life. Comment on the return of his self-esteem and sense of purpose after he left the slave trade and confessed his crimes. Discuss how evangelism suited his need to confess and cleanse himself of complicity with the evils of the slave trade.

Black Evangelism

Age/Grade Level or Audience: High school or college religion or history classes; religious study groups; museums; historical societies.

Description: Generate a database or timeline detailing major periods of black evangelism.

Procedure: Assign particular decades to volunteers to research. Assemble data, including names, places, styles of evangelism, and impact in a database or on a wall frieze to hang in a church, library, museum, school, or public building during Black History Month. Note the following events:

- ◆ David George's description of black worship in 1773.
- ◆ The first black Baptist church, built in Augusta, Georgia, in 1773.
- ◆ Absalom Jones's rejection of segregation in the St. George's Methodist Episcopal Church of Philadelphia in 1787.
- ◆ Ordination of Absalom Jones as the first black Episcopal priest in 1804.
- ◆ Josiah Bishop's purchase of freedom and in 1810 his pastorate of the Abyssinian Baptist Church of New York.
- ◆ In 1807, John Gloucester's founding of the first African Presbyterian Church in Philadelphia.
- ◆ Richard Allen's establishment of the African Methodist Episcopal Church in 1816.
- ◆ In 1843, Henry Highland Garnet delivered "Address to the Slaves of the United States of America," a thundering denunciation of enslavement, at the National Convention of Colored Citizens, a meeting of free blacks in Buffalo, New York.
- ◆ Daniel Alexander Payne's election as bishop of the African Methodist Episcopal Church in 1852.
- ◆ The establishment of the Church of God in Christ in Lexington, Mississippi, in 1897
- ◆ In 1977, Pauli Murray becomes the first women ordained in the Episcopal faith.

Budget: Under $25

Sources:

Baer, Hans A., and Merrill Singer, *African-American Religion in the Twentieth Century: Varieties of Protest and Accommodation*, University of Tennessee Press, 1992.

Goodstein, Laurie, "Across a Great Divide: Bridging Racial Chasms in America's Churches," *International Herald Tribune*, September 30,1997, 4.

Hornsby, Alton, *Chronology of African-American History*, 2nd edition Gale, 1997.

Straub, Deborah Gillan, ed., *African American Voices*, U•X•L/Gale, 1996.

Traub, James, "Floyd Flake's Middle America," *New York Times Magazine*, October 19, 1997, 60-65.

Walker, Alice, "The Only Reason You Want to Go to Heaven Is That You Have Been Driven Out of Your Mind," *Humanist*, September/October 1997,29-33.

Alternative Applications: Invite a historian or specialist in liturgy to comment on periods of revival and evangelism in American history, such as the evangelism of these:

- ◆ Charles Emanuel "Sweet Daddy" Grace, founder of the United House of Prayer
- ◆ Jesse Jackson
- ◆ Martin Luther King, Jr.
- ◆ Charles Harrison Mason, one of the founders of the Church of God in Christ
- ◆ Adam Clayton Powell, Jr.

Black Moses

Age/Grade Level or Audience: Elementary or middle school writing class; Sunday School or Bible School class.

Description: Assign students to compose an explanation of Harriet Tubman's nickname, "Black Moses."

Procedure: Have students compare the accomplishments of Harriet Tubman and Moses, the epic leader of the Hebrew people. Suggest that they include the following items of interest:

- ◆ Harriet Tubman's escape from bondage
- ◆ Moses's role in leading the Israelites out of Egypt
- ◆ routes followed by Tubman on the Underground Railroad
- ◆ Moses's route out of Egypt
- ◆ laws that hampered Tubman's crusade for freedom
- ◆ Moses's racial problems after his adoption into the royal Egyptian court

♦ Tubman's place in history

♦ Moses's position as a Biblical patriarch

Budget: Under $25

Sources:

Bradford, Sarah, *Harriet Tubman: The Moses of Her People*, Carol Publishing Group, 1995.

Burns, Bree, *Harriet Tubman: And The Fight Against Slavery*, Chelsea House, 1993.

Carter, Polly, *Harriet Tubman and Black History Month*, Silver Burdett Press, 1996.

"Harriet Tubman,"http//www.geog.umd.edu/EdRes/TopicWomensStudies/Reading Room

"Harriet Tubman," http//www.n.c-bmc.com/gale/tubmanh.html.

"Harriet Tubman_African American Historical Figures," http//www.webcom.com/ ~bright/source/htubman.html.

Johnson, LaVerne C., *Harriet Tubman: Writer*, Empak Publications, 1992.

Kinard, Lee, *Harriet Tubman's Famous Christmas Eve Raid*, Winston-Derek, 1993.

Petry, Ann, *Harriet Tubman: Conductor on the Underground Railroad*, HarperCollins Children's Books, 1996.

Alternative Applications: Have students describe other leaders who parallel Harriet Tubman's bravery, such as these:

♦ Mary Baker Eddy, founder of the Christian Science Church

♦ Corrie ten Boom, savior of Jews fleeing Nazis

♦ Miep van Santen, concealer of Anne Frank's family

♦ Joseph Smith, leader of Mormon pioneers to Utah

♦ Black Elk, Lakota spiritual leader

Black Muslims

Age/Grade Level or Audience: High school or college sociology or religion classes; religious schools, civic groups.

Description: Describe the emergence of the Black Muslims.

Procedure: Note the impetus to a strong body of Black Muslim worshippers. Include these facts:

♦ In 1897, Robert Poole, later called Elijah Muhammad, began a study of the causes of black poverty.

♦ In the 1920s, the Nation of Islam, founded by Wallace Delaney Fard and headquartered in Detroit, insisted on the superiority of the black race.

◆ Fard, also known as F. Muhammad Ali, insisted that the earliest humans were black and that whites will one day face divine retribution for mistreatment and suppression of blacks

◆ Elijah Muhammad replaced Fard in 1934 and at a second temple in Chicago served as messenger of Allah.

◆ Fard disappeared.

◆ The Nation of Islam carried its message to prisoners, street people, and the hopeless.

◆ In 1942 Muhammad went to jail in Michigan when he failed to register for the draft.

◆ In 1946, he left prison and began recruiting followers, many from large urban centers and prisons.

◆ One of the most significant converts was Malcolm Little, a 21-year-old native of Omaha, Nebraska, who was imprisoned in Massachusetts in February 1946 for robbery and selling drugs.

◆ Little began studying Islam and corresponding with Muhammad.

◆ In 1952, Little, renamed Malcolm X to symbolize his loss of identity through slavery, obtained parole and ministered to blacks in New York and Philadelphia.

◆ C. Eric Lincoln published *The Black Muslims in America,* an overview of the Islamic sect, in 1961.

◆ Dr. Mohammed Abdul-Rauf allied Black Muslims with Muslims worldwide.

◆ Following the death of President John F. Kennedy in 1963, Malcolm X rejoiced. His remarks caused a permanent rift with Muhammad, who banned him from public speaking.

◆ By 1964, Malcolm X chose separatism and formed the Organization of Afro-American Unity, a more radical group.

◆ He journeyed to Mecca and renamed himself El-Hajj Malik El-Shabazz.

◆ Abandoning the fiery anti-white rhetoric of his earlier days, Malcolm X supported the Civil Rights Movement and change through non-violence. In his words, "Nobody can give you freedom. Nobody can give you equality ... if you're a man, you take it."

◆ On February 21, 1965, while delivering a speech at Harlem's Audubon Ballroom, Malcolm X was assassinated by three black gunmen—Norman Butler, Thomas Johnson, and Thomas Hagan—associated with the Nation of Islam. The three were found guilty and jailed.

◆ Malcolm X left six daughters and a wife, Betty Shabazz.

◆ By the 1970s, the Black Muslims, headquartered in Chicago, had built segregated schools, churches, businesses, and community networks among America's blacks.

◆ In 1975, Muhammad died. His son Warith Deen began his own version of Islam based on the tenets of Malcolm X.

◆ Louis Farrakhan perpetuated Muhammad's views.

◆ Gradually, the middle class began to accept the Islamic faith for its push for decency and lawful behavior.

◆ In 1988, Black Muslim teams helped suppress drug dealing in Washington, D.C.

◆ In 1992, Deen became the first Muslim to pray in the United States Senate.

◆ By 1992, Thomas Hagan remained in jail. His accomplices were paroled.

Budget: Under $25

Sources:
The films *The Story of Islam* (1989) and *Malcolm X* (1992).

Banks, William H., *Black Muslims*, Chelsea House, 1996.

"Farrakhan Addresses Philadelphia Rally on Racial Healing," *Jet*, May 5,1997, 16-17.

"Islam in America," http//www.colostate.edu/Orgs/MSA/docs.iia.html.

Lee, Marthe F., *Nation of Islam: An American Millenarian Movement*, Syracuse University Press, 1996.

Lincoln, E. Eric, *Black Muslims in America*, 3rd. revised edition, Africa World, 1993.

Sagan, Miriam, *Malcolm X*, Lucent Books, 1996.

"The Thinker, National of Islam," http//www-leland.stanford.edu/group/thinker/v2/v2n3/NO/Backg.

Alternative Applications: Lead a workshop on the differences between religious philosophy and political activism. Incorporate the following activities:

◆ Discuss the rise in jealousy, violence, and infighting that characterized the growth of the Black Muslims.

◆ Compare the Islamic beliefs concerning self-help and family values with traditional Christian, Jewish, and Mormon ideals.

◆ Account for the Black Muslim call for segregation of whites and black and a condemnation of whites as devils.

◆ Account for the controversy concerning the appeal of Louis Farrakhan.

◆ Contrast white and black reactions to Spike Lee's film *Malcolm X*.

Quakers and the Underground Railroad

Age/Grade Level or Audience: Adult discussion group.

Description: Study the reasons for the Quakers' assistance to runaway slaves.

Procedure: Research different denominations during slave times and their response to the slave trade, Missouri Compromise, Dred Scott decision, Fugitive Slave Law, abolitionism, and other issues crucial to the ending of the institution of slavery. Feature the work of Levi Coffin and other Quakers, who were the first to press for an end to slavery. Emphasize the role of Quakers in organizing and staffing the Underground Railroad. Mention specifically the activism of Mormons, Unitarians, Baptists, Mennonites, Methodists, Presbyterians, Lutherans, Episcopalians, Catholics, and Jews.

Budget: Under $25

Sources:

The novels or film versions of Jessamyn West's *Except for Me and Thee* (Harcourt 1969).

"Abolition," http/rs7.loc.gov/exhibits/african/abol.html.

Coil, Suzanne M., *Slavery and Abolitionists*, TFC Books, 1995.

Hornsby, Alton, *Chronology of African-American History*, 2nd edition Gale, 1997.

"The Influence of Prominent Abolitionists," http//www.loc.gov/exhibits/african/influ.html.

"The North Star Tracing the Underground Railroad," http//www.ugar.Org/.

Rogers, James T., *The Antislavery Movement*, Facts on File, 1994.

"The 1783 Quaker Petition to Congress Requesting the Abolition of Slavery," http//www.rootsweb.cm/~quakers/petition.htm.

"The Underground Railroad in Iowa," http//www.sos.state.ia.us/register/r7/r7undrr.thm.

Yellin, Jean F., and John C. Van Horne, *The Abolitionist Sisterhood: Women's Political Culture in Antebellum America*, Cornell University Press, 1994.

Alternative Applications: Compose a newsletter or newspaper article about the benevolent work of these Quaker abolitionists:

Anthony Benezet	Levi Coffin	George Fox
Garrett Henderich	George Keith	Abram Op de Graeff
Derick Op de Graeff	Francis Daniel Pastorius	William Penn
John Woolman	Richard Worrell	

Contrast the abolitionist movement with the assistance of Jews in escaping Nazi death camps, underground groups helping fleeing victims of oppression in Cuba and Guatemala, Haitian rescue operations, and aid to the victims of the war in Bosnia-Herzegovina.

The Religions of Africa

Age/Grade Level or Audience: High school or college history, religion, or sociology classes; church groups; literary societies.

Description: Have participants study the variety of religious customs and practices throughout Africa's history.

Procedure: Provide participants with guest lecturers, art prints, photographs, travelogues, videos, filmstrips, films, and reference books on these and other African religions:

Amenism	animism	Atenism
Baha'i	Catholicism	Copt
fetishism	Islam	Mormonism
Protestantism	Santeria	totemism
voodoo		

Organize discussion groups to consider these topics:

- ◆ Pharaoh Akhenaten's establishment of monotheism through the worship of Amon-Ra
- ◆ contrasts between Eastern Orthodox, Roman Catholicism, Russian Orthodox, Protestantism, and Coptic Christianity
- ◆ the Black Muslim emphasis on the family
- ◆ Baha'i activism against prejudice and racism
- ◆ differences in style of worship through symbols such the ankh, idols, shrines, particularly Spain's Shrine of the Black Madonna, which was adapted from the Moors, singing and clapping, ceremonies and feasts, processions, musical accompaniment, rites of passage, scarification, and circumcision
- ◆ effects of religion and ethics on cultural, social, and governmental structures
- ◆ Zulu methods of divination by "throwing the bones"
- ◆ Yoruba voodoo and witchcraft as outgrowths of nature lore
- ◆ Santeria and animal sacrifice

Note the influence of outside influences from Mormons, Seventh Day Adventists, Presbyterians, Lutherans, Catholics, Baptists, Moravian Brethren, and Methodists.

Budget: $50-25

Sources:

Aunapu, Greg, "Shedding Blood in Sacred Bowls," *Time*, October 19, 1992, 60.

Brown, Karen McCarthy, *Mama Lola: A Vodou Priestess in Brooklyn*, University of California Press, 1991.

Budge, E. A. Wallis, *Tutankhamen Amenism, Atenism and EgyptianMonotheism with Hieroglyphic Texts of Hymns to Amen and Aten*, B.Blom, 1971.

Chidester, David, *Religions of South Africa*, Routledge, 1992.

Jamal, Isma'el, "African Meditation," *Upscale*, June/July 1992, 60-61

Mbiti, John S., *African Religions and Philosophy*, 2nd edition, Heinemann, 1990.

"Mystic Massage," http;hypn.com/africanculture/mystic. meditations.html.
"Santería," http//www.nando.net/prof/caribe/santeria.html.
Spence, Lewis, *Ancient Egyptian Myths and Legends*, Dover Publications, 1990.
"Yoruba Religion and Myth," http//www.stg.brown.edu/projects/hypertext/
    landow/post/nigeria/yorubarel.html.

Alternative Applications: Have participants study and discuss the purpose of icons, headdresses, masks, priests' robes, ritual vessels, face paint, kente cloth, asipim chairs, umbrellas, and other artifacts connected with African worship. Present materials detailing music, dance, processions, divination, marriage and funeral rites, coming-of-age and healing ceremonies, naming rituals, and tableaux as African methods of worship.

Religious Themes in Negro Spirituals

Age/Grade Level or Audience: High school or college literature class, book club, church group, or literary society.

Description: Have participants listen to recordings of common Negro spirituals, then discuss prevalent Biblical scenes and themes.

Procedure: Present songsheets of classic Negro Spirituals, especially these:

"All God's Chillun"
"By an' By"
"Couldn't Hear Nobody Pray"
"De Blin' Man Stood in de Road and Cried"
"De Gospel Train"
"Deep River"
"Ev'ry Time I Feel De Spirit"
"Good News"
"I'm Jus' a Wanderer"
"Joshua Fit de Battle of Jericho"
"Little David, Play on Your Harp"
"Oh Dem Golden Slippers"
"Rock-a-My Soul"
"Roll, Jordan, Roll"
"Sometimes I Feel Like a Motherless Child"
"Stan' Still Jordan"
"Steal Away"
"Wade in de Water"
"Weepin' Mary"
"Were You There"

Invite volunteers to explain connections between names, places, and events in the songs with similar incidents in the Bible, for example, frequent mention of the Children of Israel, Pharaoh, Moses, Daniel, Gabriel, King David, Joshua, Mary, Joseph, Christ's birth and crucifixion, Paul and Silas, and the Jordan River.

Budget: $50-25

Sources:

Caldwell, Hansonia, *African American Music—A Chronology 1619-1995*, Ikoro Communications, 1996.

Heilbut, Anthony, *Gospel Sound: Good News and Bad Times*, Limelight Editions, 1997.

Merlis, Bob, and Davin Seay, *Heart and Soul: A Celebration of Black Music Style in America 1930-1975*, Stewart, Taboori and Chang, 1997.

Southern, Eileen, *Music of Black America: A History*, W. W. Norton & Co., 1997.

Spencer, Jon Michael, *Protest and Praise: Sacred Music of Black Religion*, Fortress Press, 1997.

Alternative Applications: Organize a Black History Month hymn sing. Invite multi-ethnic church groups to join in singing the most familiar songs. Select a hymn as feature of the week. Provide handouts to explain the background and significance of spirituals to slave morale. Indicate black code terms, such as River Jordan for underground railroad, Pharaoh for slave owners, Moses for leaders and abolitionists, and Hebrew children for slaves

Things Fall Apart

Age/Grade Level or Audience: High school or college literature class, book club, or literary society.

Description: Have participants read and discuss the religious implications of China Achebe's *Things Fall Apart*.

Procedure: After participants have read the book, organize round table discussions of the stabilizing influence of traditional religions. Concentrate on the theme of change and its destruction of the main characters' lives. Propose the following questions:

   ◆ What is the religious and ethical system before the arrival of missionaries?
   ◆ Why is childbirth significant to the tribe?
   ◆ Why are the souls of dead children suspect?
   ◆ How does life change during the main character's exile?
   ◆ Why is the main character estranged from his son?

♦ Why does the main character help murder his foster son?
♦ What forces lead to the main character's suicide?
♦ How does the new missionary destroy black pride and tradition?
♦ What is ironic about the reduction of the action to a footnote in history?

Budget: Under $25

Sources:

Achebe, Chinua, *Things Fall Apart*, Heinemann, 1958, reprinted, Fawcett, 1988.

"Chinua Achebe," http/ccat.upenn.edu/Complit/coml100/achebe.

"Chinua Achebe and Things Fall Apart," http//www.stg.brown.edu/projects/hypertext/landow/post/achebe.

Chinua Achebe Revisited, Scribner's Reference, 1997.

Moses, Knolly, "A Dialogue with Chinua Achebe," *Emerge*, December 1992,11-13.

Royal, Pat, "Review of *Things Fall Apart*," *School Library Journal*, December 1992, 146.

"Voyager The Art of Fiction Chinua Achebe," http//www.voyager.cocom/PR/witer94/chinua.html.

Winkler, Karen J., "An African Writer at a Crossroads," *Chronicle of Higher Education*, January 12, 1994, A9-12.

Alternative Applications: Have participants discuss why Achebe gave his book the name *Things Fall Apart*. Consider whether similar institutional changes are damaging African family life and worship, particularly industrialization, modernization, independence, communications, depletion of animal and plant species, and pollution.

Science

African and Caribbean Fruits and Spices

Age/Grade Level or Audience: Middle school or high school college biology or life science classes.

Description: Make an oral presentation about the cultivation, harvesting, and use of African and Caribbean spices, fruits, and vegetables.

Procedure: Have students select a particular plant to describe, such as these:

banana	cabbage	cardamom	cassava
cinnamon	coconut	coriander	corn
cumin	date	eggplant	egusi
ginger root	gourd	jujube	mango
millet	olive	onion	papaya
peanut	pepper	pineapple	plantain
pomegranate	pumpkin	rice	squash
spinach	tamarind	tomato	Turmeric

Supply information from a variety of sources, including textbook photos, Internet reports, and pronunciation of difficult names. Arrange samples of fragrant or tasty plants for students to smell and taste. Stress coconut, onion, cumin, turmeric, coriander, various types of pepper, banana oil, dates, ginger, and coriander. Then blindfold participants and have them identify substances by taste and smell.

Budget: Under $25

Sources:
"African Recipes Home Page," http//www.africanrecipes.com.

Duckitt, Hildagonda, *Traditional South African Cookery*, Hippocrene Books, 1996.

Fitzsimmons, Cecilia, *Fruit*, Silver burdett Press, 1996.

"Fruit Facts," http//www.crfg.org/pubs/frtfacts.html.

Hafner, Dorinda, *A Taste of Africa*, Ten Speed Press, 1993.

"Nishan Wijesinha," http//nova.uel.ac.uk/pers/1492m/

Raichlen, Steven, *Caribbeann Pantry Cookbook: Condiments and Seasonings from the Land of Spice and Sun*, Artisan, 1995.

Sookia, Devinia, *Caribbean Cooking*, Book Sales, Inc., 1994.

Alternative Applications: Make a chart of ways in which native plants are used in industry. For example, demonstrate these transformations:

- ◆ baobab trees—used in the manufacture of rope, rubber, fertilizer, soap, and cloth and provide packing materials and wood for canoes and musical instruments
- ◆ coconut palms—stripped of leaves and bark for rope and weaving material and parts are cooked as a vegetable
- ◆ flax—made into linen for bags, rope, cloth, and wallpaper
- ◆ gourds—carved into utensils, bowls, and musical instruments
- ◆ papyrus—formed into paper
- ◆ peanuts—made into oil, makeup, mulch, and fertilizer
- ◆ rice powder—added to cosmetics, puddings, paper, and baby foods

African Butterflies and Moths

Age/Grade Level or Audience: High school or college biology, entomology, life science, or art classes.

Description: Describe the habitats and life cycles of African butterflies.

Procedure: Isolate the most common butterflies of Africa by name and describe where and how they live. Emphasize adaptive coloration, which enables the delicate insects to elude predators. Include these species:

- ◆ black-bordered charaxes
- ◆ false acraea
- ◆ deilephila nerii or oleander hawk
- ◆ euchloron megaera
- ◆ bunaea alcinio
- ◆ papilio dardanus
- ◆ lycaenidae kallimoides or hairstreak
- ◆ danaidae linnaeus or tiger butterfly
- ◆ papilio demoleus or orange-dog swallow-tail

◆ morpho portis

◆ gonepteryx rhamni or brimstone butterfly

◆ pieris brassicae or white and yellow cabbage butterfly

◆ vanessa atalanta or red admiral butterfly

◆ cupido minimus or small blue butterfly

◆ lycaena phlaeas or small copper butterfly

◆ iphiclides podalirius or scarce swallowtail

◆ papilio antimachus or giant swallowtail

◆ satyridae elymnias or brown butterfly

◆ nudaurelia zambesina or giant silkworm moth

◆ argema mittrei or moon moth

◆ hemaris fuciformis or bee hawk moth

Sketch posters of the most colorful species. Use the sketches for a bulletin board display, to decorate tables, napkins, invitations, or thank-you notes, or to illustrate a display on African wildlife.

Budget: $25-$50

Sources:

"Butterfly Web Site Picture Gallery III," http//mgfx.com/butterfly/gallery/gallery3. htm.

D'Abrera, Bernard, *Butterflies of the Afrotropical Region*, Lansdown Editions, 1980.

Kingdon, Jonathan, *Island Africa: The Evolution of Africa's Rare Animals and Plants*, Princeton University Press, 1989.

Larsen, Torben B., *Butterflies of Kenya: And Their Natural History*, Oxford University Press, 1996.

Preston-Mafham, Rod, and Ken Preston-Mafham, *Butterflies of the World*, Facts on File, 1988.

"South America's Threatened Wildlife," http//www.infoweb.co.za/enviro/ewtbook/ page6.htm.

"Wildlife," http//www.southafrica.net/tourism/wildlife.html.

Alternative Applications: Conduct detailed research on these and other insects that are indigenous to the African ecosystem:

aedes aegypti mosquito	anopheles mosquito	botfly
caddis fly	cerbalus spider	cicada
desert locust	driver ant	dung beetle
honeybee	grasshopper	grub
Guinea threadworm	locust	mantid
silverfish	simulium fly	tenebrionid beetle
termite	tick	trapdoor spider
tsetse fly		

Note connections between insect infestations and disease, as with these:

♦ Aedes aegypti mosquito and yellow fever

♦ anopheles mosquito and malaria

♦ botfly and respiratory diseases of sheep, cattle, horses, and humans

♦ ticks and encephalitis

African Habitats

Age/Grade Level or Audience: High school or college biology or life science classes.

Description: Divide students into two teams to study variations in African habitats.

Procedure: Have students collect data on the requirements for survival in two widely contrasting areas of the African continent, including these:

bush	coastal	desert
jungle	mountain	nyika or wilderness
savanna	semi-arid scrub	swamp
tropical rain forest	woodland	

Subjects of research should include geology, weather, sources of water and fuel, plants, animals, predators, disease, and human adaptation.

Budget: Under $25

Sources:

Adams, W. M., *The Physical Geography of Africa*, Oxford University Press, 1996.

Africa A Lonely Planet Shoestring Guide, Lonely Planet, 1995.

"Africa Online," http//www.africaonline.com.

"African Travel Gateway," http//africantravel.com/home.html.

"Africa TourNet," http//wn.apc.org/mediatech/tourism/TN090072.HTM.

Binns, Tony, *The People and Environment in Africa*, John Wiley and Sons, 1995.

Bryjak, G. J., "Is It Possible to Rescue Sub-Saharan Africa?," *USA Today* (periodical), July 1997, 34-36.

Collins Nations of the World Atlas, HarperCollins, 1996.

Hammond New Century World Atlas, Hammond, 1996.

Jeunesse, Gallimard, *Atlas of Countries*, Cartwheel Books, 1996.

Labi, Esther, *Pockets World Atlas*, Dorling Kindersley, 1995.

Mason, Paul, ed., *Atlas of Threatened Cultures*, Raintree/Steck-Vaughn,1997.

Müller, Claudia, *The Costume Timeline: 5000 Years of Fashion History*, Thames and Hudson, 1993.

Murray, Jocelyn, *Cultural Atlas of Africa*, Facts on File, 1989.

Oliver, Roland, *The African Experience*, IconEditions, 1992.

Theroux, Paul, "Down the Zambezi," *National Geographic*, October 1997, 2-31.

"Webcrawler Guide Travel Africa Travel Guides," http//webcrawlercom/select/trav.
 africa.html.

"Zaire," http//www.spectortravel.com/Pages/about.html.

Alternative Applications: Have students augment their research by simulating a desert or jungle habitat in a terrarium or greenhouse. Collect these and other local flora and house plants common to Africa African:

daisy	African violet	bamboo
bird of paradise	calceria	crassula
dracaena	erica	eucalyptus
ficus	fishtail fern	gloriosa daisy
hibiscus	ixia	kalanchoe
lantana	lithops	nicodemia
oxalis	papyrus	pentas
philodendron	pink cissus	sea onion
star window plant	toad plant	zebrina

For large habitats, add indigenous toads, lizards, snakes, and birds or models made of clay.

African Healers

Age/Grade Level or Audience: High school or college biology or life science classes.

Description: Report on ethnobiology and African plants that are beneficial to medicine.

Procedure: In an oral presentation, give details about ginger, chinaberry, ouabain vine, snakeroot, calamus, and wormseed, which eighteen- and nineteenth-century African healers revered and transplanted to the American south and the Caribbean. Include details of these and other natural treatments:

- ◆ *African cherry*, which relieves prostate inflammation
- ◆ *baobab trees* of Zimbabwe and Zambia provide a curative for sores that promotes the immune system and fights viruses
- ◆ *castor oil* to combat warts, lesions, and bronchitis
- ◆ *copper salt* solution to ease eye infection

♦ *datura* for breast cancer

♦ *enantia* from Cameroon as an anti-malarial compound

♦ *fara*, a Senegalese cure for malaria, eye diseae, and stomachache

♦ *katirao* for snakebite

♦ *maytenus vine*, a treatment for cancer gathered from the Shimba Hills of Kenya

♦ *mold* on bread to encourage healing

♦ *mousingi* from the Central African Republic as a possible cure for AIDS

♦ *ox liver* roasted and applied to improve eyesight

♦ *palinkumfo* for intestinal parasites

♦ *pomegranate* and *wormseed* for intestinal parasites

♦ *poppy juice* to ease colic

♦ *rosy periwinkle* from Ghana and Madagascar to treat liver disorders and save children suffering from leukemia

♦ *sea onion juice* to strengthen a weak heart

♦ *squill* to treat ulcers and swelling in Egypt

♦ *tabernanthe iboga* shrub native to Ghana produces a substance that quells addiction and eases withdrawal symptoms

♦ *voacanga* and *strohanthus gratus* to stimulate the heart

♦ *water lily bulbs* to combat fever

♦ *willow bark* to treat infection and asthma

Budget: Under $25

Sources:

"Africa Express The Medical Man," httpww.channel14.co.7k/1QVKjkbi/backup/bss/ stuck/xpress/xpconn2/xpmedt2.html.

"Healing Plants of Africa," http//sdearthtimes.com/et0496/et0496s11.html.

Kingdon, Jonathan, *Island Africa: The Evolution of Africa's Rare Animals and Plants*, Princeton University Press, 1989.

"Nishan Wijesinha," http//nova.uel.ac.uk/pers/1492m/.

Pahlow, Manfred, *Healing Plants*, Barron, 1993.

Sindiga, Isaac, *Traditional Medicine in Africa*, Africa Books Collective, 1996.

"South Africa Country Report," http//web.icppgr.fao.org/Cr/CRSAF/2.htm.

Alternative Applications: Extend the study of folk cures with additional treatments derived from other parts of Africa, New Zealand, Japan, China, Australia, and Central, North, and South America. Create drawings and brief explanations of each treatment for a database or library, school, museum, hospital or clinic showcase, or civic display.

An African Window Garden

Age/Grade Level or Audience: Kindergarten or elementary school science classes, religious schools; 4-H clubs; Brownie or Cub Scouts; retirement homes; or classes for the handicapped.

Description: Establish a window garden of African plants.

Procedure: Provide participants with a variety of pottery dishes, peat pots, or glass containers in which to cuttings, slips, bulbs, or seeds of the following plants common to Africa:

acacia	acanthus	arum lily	bamboo
clivia	coffee	cowpea	deiffenbachia
eucalyptus	fern	flax	gourd
guava	heather	hemlock	hibiscus
hydrangea	lantana	laurel	liana
mallow	milkweed	millet	mint
moss	myrtle	nettle	okra
oleander	palm	papyrus	pepper
philodendron	pumpkin	rose	rubber tree
sedge	squash	yam	

Budget: $50-$75

Sources:

Berry, James, *The First Palm Trees*, Simon & Schuster, 1997.

Binns, Tony, *The People and Environment in Africa*, John Wiley and Sons, 1995.

Fitzsimmons, Cecilia, *Fruit*, Silver burdett Press, 1996.

"Fruit Facts," http//www.crfg.org/pubs/frtfacts.html.

Kingdom, Johnathan, *Island Africa: The Evolution of Africa's Rare Animals and Plants*, Princeton University Press, 1990.

Alternative Applications: Highlight an African display with massed sweet potato plants growing in water or deiffenbachia, fern, African violet, African daisy, hibiscus, philodendron, aloe, or coffee plant borrowed from local gardeners or grown from cuttings. Add paper cutouts of butterflies, snakes, lizards, toads, monkeys, and other animals.

All That Glitters

Age/Grade Level or Audience: High school or college natural science or geology classes.

Description: Present a unit on the African diamond trade.

Procedure: Use a variety of media to emphasize the importance of the diamond to the history and economics of Africa. For example:

♦ Present handouts explaining how diamonds, the world's hardest substances, are formed, mined, and shaped.

♦ Make a chalkboard list of industrial uses, such as crushing, grinding, sanding, polishing, drilling, and cutting.

♦ Name the trades which depend on diamonds, particularly auto and aircraft manufacturers, electronics, petroleum, mining, tool and dye, dentistry, and glass and optical laboratories.

♦ Explain how diamonds are graded and why they come in shades of yellow, pink, black, blue, gray, and champagne.

♦ Organize a small group to draw examples of famous African diamonds, notably the largest, the Cullinan (1905), from which the Star of Africa was cut and set in the British royal scepter, as well as the Eureka (1867), Excelsior (1893), Jonker, Jubilee, Star of Sierra Leone (1972), Star of South Africa (1869), Tiffany, and Victoria.

♦ Have several volunteers make geometric sketches of common crystalline configurations of shaped diamonds, notably the marquise, baguette, brilliant, round, pear, teardrop, and emerald cuts.

♦ Present and discuss technical terms connected with diamonds, especially facet, lapidary, schist, isometric, mineralogy, pipe, carat, Mohs scale, alluvial, diatreme spinel, adamantine, refraction, and octahedron.

♦ Assign reports on the following topics kimberlite, peridotite, olivine, garnet, pyroxene, ilmenite, serpentine, chlorite, calcite, and mica.

♦ Discuss how in 1880 James Ballantyne Hannay, a Scottish chemist, synthetized diamonds from lithium.

♦ Locate on a map the African cities and mines most closely connected with the diamond trade:

Bafi-Sewa	Bakwanga	Beyla	Birim River Brazzaville
Bultfontein	Bushimale	Cafunfo	Carnot
Chicapa	Chiumbe	De Beers	Dutoitspan
Elandsfontein	Hopetown	Jagersfontein	Kanshi
Kimberley	Kissidougou	Luachimo	Luembe
Marahoue River	Mwadui	Namaqualand	Nzako

Oranjemund	Ouadda	Premier	Shinyanga
Tortiya	Wesselton		

Budget: Under $25

Sources:

"Diamonds How and When They Were Created," http//www.tyleradam.com/40.html.

Frazier, Si and Ann, "South of the Equator," *Lapidary Journal*, August1990, 36-47.

"Geobase Abstract," http//webhost1.cerf.net/journals/epsl/jnlembase/abstrafcts/
  html/1029299_94k_04077.html.

"The Science of Diamonds," http//www.diamondcutters.com/sciencehtml.

"The World's Most Famous Diamonds," http//www.love-story.com/ fd14.htm.

Alternative Applications: Discuss social and economic issues that cluster about the diamond trade, particularly Apartheid, colonialism, and smuggling. Name people who have made their fortunes in diamonds, especially Barney and Harry Barnato, Cecil Rhodes, Ernest Oppenheimer, and Anton Dukelsbuhler. Explain how the diamond has been both boon and curse to Africans of Ghana, Guinea, Sierra Leone, Angola, Zaire, Liberia, Ivory Coast, the Central African Republic, Tanzania, and South Africa.

Animal Express

Age/Grade Level or Audience: Elementary or middle school science classes; ecology clubs; animal preservation societies.

Description: Study African animals.

Procedure: Open the session with a National Geographic Society videotape of *Gorillas in the Mist* (1988) or *Gorilla, African Wildlife, Africa Wilds of Madagascar,* or *Lions of the African Night; Animals of Africa Series, Secrets of an African Jungle, Jane Goodall's Chimpanzees,* and *The Lion's Kingdom* from the Library Video Company. Lead a discussion of the importance of preserving African animals in their natural habitats. Consider the following topics:

- ◆ embargoes and importation bans on hides, teeth, bones, genitals, glands, and horns of endangered species
- ◆ frozen sperm banks, frozen embryos, cloning, and artificial insemination to propagate endangered species
- ◆ media campaigns aimed at preserving wildlife and raising money for protective measures, such as anti-poaching patrols and border guards
- ◆ providing food for endangered species

◆ raising endangered species in game reserves or laboratories
◆ tagging migratory animals to determine habits
◆ treatment centers for injured or diseased animals
◆ vaccination programs

Budget: $25-$50

Sources:

Carty, Winthrop P., and Elizabeth Lee, *The Rhino Man and Other Uncommon Environmentalists,* Sevne Locks Press, 1992.

Chadwick, Douglas H., "A Place for Parks in the New South Africa," *National Geographic,* July 1996, 2-41.

Cobb, Charles E., Jr., "Eritrea Wins the Peace," *National Geographic,* June 1996, 82-105.

Endangered Wildlife of the World, 11 vols., Marshall Cavendish, 1993.

Ginsberg, J., "Family Ties," *National Geographic World,* August 1997, 21-23.

Halliburton, Warren J., and Kathilyn Solomon Probosz, *African Landscapes,* Crestwood House, 1993.

Kingdon, Jonathan, *Island Africa: The Evolution of Africa's Rare Animals and Plants,* Princeton University Press, 1992.

"Serengeti," http//www.cyberatl.net/~young/.

Sherry, Clifford J., *Endangered Species,* ABC-Clio, 1996.

"Tanzania, "http//www.africa.com/~venture/wildfron/wildtanz.htm.

Theroux, Paul, "Down the Zambezi," *National Geographic,* October 1997, 2-31.

"Uganda," http//imul.com/uganda/.

"Wild Africa Okavango, Chobe, Makgadikgadi" (CD-ROM), Library Video Company, 1995.

Williams, Wendy, "Of Elephants and Men," *Animals,* November/December 1997, 24-30.

"Zimbabwe," http//www.mother.com/~zimweb/History.html.

Alternative Applications: Conduct a study of the endangered species of Africa and the United States. Compare the ecological problems of both nations, such as these:

◆ acid rain
◆ deforestation and clear-cutting
◆ erosion
◆ forest fire
◆ highways, rail lines, and airports
◆ illegal ivory and antler trade
◆ industrialization
◆ poachers and hunters
◆ polluted air, streams, and rivers
◆ strip mining
◆ swamp draining

Baobab: The Tree of Life

Age/Grade Level or Audience: Elementary school children, scouts, 4-H, or religious schools.

Description: Describe to students the importance of the baobab tree to Africans.

Procedure: Read aloud a book about the baobab or monkey-bread tree. Point out the difference between biological facts and legends about the tree. Emphasize these facts:

- The baobab is one of the world's oldest plants.
- It can live as long as a thousand years.
- It can grow sixty feet high, forty feet wide, and ten feet thick.
- It is sometimes called the upside-down tree because, when the leaves fall, its stunted limbs, protruding from a grotesquely thickened trunk, look like roots pointing at the sky.
- The baobab is a succulent plant so soft that a bullet can pass through it.
- Its spongy inner tissue stores water to help it survive drought.
- The tree produces a gourd-like fruit hanging from long twigs.
- The baobab's ability to adapt to changes in the environment accounts for its long life.

Budget: $25-$50

Sources:
Attenborough, David, *Atlas of the Living World,* Houghton Mifflin, 1989.
Bash, Barbara, *Tree of Life: The World of the African Baobab*, Little, Brown, 1989.
Cochrane, Jennifer, *Trees of the Tropics*, Steck-Vaughn, 1990.
Hunter, Bobbi Dooley, *The Legend of the African Bao-Bab Tree*, Africa World Press, 1995.
"Nishan Wijesinha," http//nova.uel.ac.uk/pers/1492m/.
"What is a Baobab?," http//www.science.uwaterloo.ca~r3tang/baobab.html.

Alternative Applications: Explain why Africans revere the gnarled baobab and its role in the African ecosystem. Mention these facts:

- The baobab is a nesting place for birds, such as the yellow-collared love-bird, mosque swallow, orange-billed parrot, lilac-breasted roller, red-headed buffalo weaver, honey guide bird, pygmy falcon, superb starling, and yellow-billed hornbill.
- Insects make their homes in the bark, limbs, and leaves of the baobab.
- Bats pollinate the baobab's flowers.

♦ Natives pick the leaves and cook them like spinach.

♦ Elephants eat the smooth, glossy purplish-gray bark.

♦ Waxy flowers turn into firm-shelled fruit, which can be cracked and eaten.

♦ Parts of the tree are used for soap, weaving, drinks, fertilizer, packaging, drinking cups, musical instruments, rope, and candy.

♦ The spongy wood is light enough to make fishing floats, canoes, and housing material.

♦ As a medicine, the baobab is used to boost the immune system and to cure sores, malaria, dysentery, fever, earache, and kidney infection.

♦ The acid in the baobab nut is used to curdle milk or harden rubber.

♦ A burning solution of baobab pulp rids animals of insect pests.

Brainstorming

Age/Grade Level or Audience: High school or college science classes.

Description: Brainstorm the design and use of significant inventions.

Procedure: Assemble models or drawings of items and processes invented or improved by black engineers and scientists. Have students work in groups to examine the items and discover why they save labor. Discuss scientific principles that undergird the design of each. Include the following:

♦ James S. Adams, airplane propeller

♦ George E. Alcorn, semiconductors

♦ Benjamin Banneker, wooden clock

♦ James A. Bauer, coin changer

♦ Andrew J. Beard, automatic railcar coupler

♦ Dr. Keith Black, method of removing brain tumors

♦ Henry Blair, corn and cotton planters

♦ Otis Boykin, stimulator for an artificial heart

♦ Henrietta Bradbury, torpedo discharger

♦ Leander M. Coles, mortician's table

♦ Cap B. Collins, portable electric light

♦ David N. Crosthwait, vacuum heating system

♦ Joseph Hunter Dickinson, player piano

♦ Charles Richard Drew, blood bank

♦ James Forten, sail raising device

♦ Albert Y. Garner, flame retardant

♦ Dr. Meredith C. Gourdine, electradyne paint spray gun

♦ Edward Hawthorne, heart monitor

♦ Harry C. Hopkins, hearing aid

♦ Thomas L. Jennings, dry-cleaning process

♦ John Arthur Johnson, monkey wrench

♦ Frederick M. Jones, portable x-ray machine

♦ Percy Lavon Julian, glaucoma treatment

♦ J. L. Love, pencil sharpener

♦ Elijah J. McCoy, automatic locomotive lubricator

♦ Garrett Augustus Morgan, gas mask or four-way traffic signal

♦ W. B. Purvis, machine to make paper bags

♦ Norbert Rillieux, sugar refiner

♦ Adolphus Samms, space travel systems

♦ Dewey S. C. Sanderson, urinalysis meter

♦ J. H. Smith, lawn sprinkler

♦ P. D. Smith, mechanical potato digger

♦ Richard Spikes, automatic transmission

♦ Lewis Temple, improved whaling harpoon

♦ Sarah Walker, hair straightener

♦ Ozzie S. Williams, radar search beacon

♦ Granville T. Woods, railroad telegraph

♦ Louis Tompkins Wright, treatment for head and neck injuries.

Budget: $50-$75

Sources:

Aaseng, Nathan, *Black Inventors*, Facts on File, 1997.

Branch, Muriel Miller, and Dorothy Marie Rice, *Pennies to Dollars: The Story of Maggie Lena Walker*, Linnet Books, 1997.

Chappell, K., "How Black Inventors Changed America," *Ebony*, February1997, 40.

"The Faces of Science: African Americans in the Sciences," http//www. lib.lsu.edu/lib/chem/display/faces.html.

Gibbs, C. R., *Black Inventors; From Africa to america Two Million Years of Invention and Innovation*, Three Dimensional Publications, 1995.

Haber, Louis, *Black Pioneers of Science and Invention*, Harcourt Brace Jovanovich, 1970, repinted, 1992.

Hayden, Robert C., *African-American Inventors*, 21st Century Books, 1992.

Hine, Darlene Clark, Elsa Barkley Brown, and Rosalyn Terborg-Penn, *BlackWomen in America: An Historical Encyclopedia,* Carlson Publishing, 1993.

Hudson, Wade, and Thomas Hudson, *Five Notable Inventors*, Cartwheel Books, 1995.

"Inventors," http//www.slip.net/~rigged/history.html#invent.

Kahn, Jetty, *African-American Inventors: Lonnie Johnson, Frederick McKinley Jones, Marjorie Stewart Joyes, Elijah McCoy, Garrett Augustus Morgan*, Capstone Press, 1996.

Lemonick, Michael D., "The Tumor War," *Time*, Special Issue, Fall 1997, 46-53.

Massaquoi, H. J., "Blacks in Science and Technology," *Ebony*, February 1997, 172-173.

McKissack, Patricia, and Fredrick McKissack, *African-American Inventors*, Millbrook Press, 1994.

Saari, Peggy, and Daniel B. Baker, *Explorers and Discoverers*, UXL/Gale, 1995.

Towle, Wendy, *The Real McCoy: The Life of an African-AmericanInventor*, Scholastic Publications, 1995.

Alternative Applications: Have students compose a group report on how one of these inventions could be improved by applying these and other examples of current technology:

biotechnology	cloning	digital readout
enzymes	fiber optics	laser
microchips	remote control	solar panels
solid state construction	space age metals	voice synthesizer

 ## Deadly Organisms

Age/Grade Level or Audience: High school or college biology or life science classes.

Description: Organize a study of diseases caused by fungi, protozoa, spirochetes, bacteria, and viruses carried by such organisms as the snail, rat, tsetse fly, blood fluke, tick, louse, flea, sandfly, blackfly, and Aedes aegypti, Aedes africanus, and anopheles mosquito.

Procedure: Lead students in a study of the tropical organisms responsible for these ills:

bacterial meningitis	black water fever	cholera
dengue fever	diphtheria	Ebola virus
encephalitis	filariasis	hemorrhagic fever
hepatitis A	hepatitis B	hookworm
leishmaniasis	leprosy	malaria
nagana	onchocerciasis	plague
polio	Q-fever	rabies
schistosomiasis	syphilis	tetanus
trachoma	trypanosomiasis	typhus
yaws	yellow fever	

Show on maps the yellow fever belt of Africa and the malaria belt of Haiti, the Dominican Republic, Africa, and other parts of the world. Create a time line of the resurgence and eradication of major diseases through organism control. Feature these data:

♦ A crippled Egyptian mummy dating to 3700 B.C. may be the world's oldest evidence of polio.

♦ During the fifth century B.C., Hippocrates classified varieties of malaria.

♦ Smallpox ravaged north Africa in A.D. 647.

♦ European explorers brought malaria to the Western Hemisphere in the fifteenth century.

♦ In the 1630s, Spanish missionaries discovered that quinine, extracted from the cinchona tree, prevented malaria.

♦ The Dutch first infected South Africans with smallpox in 1713.

♦ In 1734, John Atkins described the neurological symptoms of sleeping sickness.

♦ From 1764 to 1778, yellow fever surfaced in Sierra Leone and Senegal.

♦ The importation of African slaves to Cuba in 1803 brought sleeping sickness to the Caribbean.

♦ In 1822, Fever J. Campbell reported that Rhodesians inoculated healthy people with smallpox to weaken the disease.

♦ In the 1820s, African slaves carried yellow fever to American port cities.

♦ Dengue from Africa first attacked the Caribbean and coastal U.S. in 1827.

♦ In 1852, Bilharz discovered the microbe which causes schistosomiasis.

♦ In 1872, Armauer G. Hansen discovered the bacteria that cause leprosy or Hansen's disease.

♦ In 1880, Charles Laveran discovered that protozoa infested the blood of Algerian malaria victims.

♦ In the 1880s, David Bruce studied the organisms which cause tetanus, sleeping sickness, and nagana.

♦ From 1881 to 1882, cholera swept through Egypt.

♦ In 1884, Loffler isolated the diphtheria microbe.

♦ In 1885, Pfeiffer isolated the bacteria which cause typhus and typhoid fever.

♦ Nigerians first suffered sleeping sickness in 1890.

♦ In the 1890s, Juan Finlay hypothesized that the Aedes aegypti mosquito spread yellow fever.

♦ In 1898, Ronald Ross of Great Britain connected the bite of female Anopheles mosquito with transmission of malaria. That same year, Italians Amico Bignami, Giuseppe Bastianelli, and Giovanni Battista Grassi made detailed studies of how the disease develops in the human body.

♦ Plague invaded South Africa in 1899.

♦ By 1900, Dr. Walter Reed proved Juan Finlay's ideas by isolating the virus that causes yellow fever.

♦ In 1905, William Gorgas initiated a program of insecticide spray and draining of standing pools of water to control mosquitoes.

♦ From 1912 to 1946, plague killed seventy percent of the residents of French West Africa.

♦ A London commission studied the eradication of sleeping sickness in 1925.

♦ From 1925 to 1936, hygienists attempted to eradicate hookworm among South African miners.

♦ The mortality rate for diphtheria in Egypt in 1932 was over 45 percent.

♦ In 1939, Paul Miller, a Swiss chemist, created DDT to control the mosquitoes that carry malaria.

♦ In 1940, a yellow fever epidemic afflicted the Nuba Mountains of the Sudan.

♦ During World War II, more effective malaria treatments replaced quinine.

♦ In 1947, cholera again swept Egypt.

♦ By 1948, sleeping sickness was virtually eradicated in the Congo.

♦ In 1954, yellow fever beset Trinidad.

♦ In 1955, the World Health Organization (WHO) attempted to conquer malaria by spraying DDT over areas infested with mosquitoes.

♦ In 1959, yellow fever returned to Trinidad. Also, rifampicin is discovered as a treatment for leprosy.

♦ In 1961, a severe yellow fever epidemic hit Ethiopia.

♦ In 1965, the Rockefeller Foundation signed an agreement with the government of St. Lucia to study the control of schistosomiasis by treating the sick and eradicating the disease-bearing snail.

♦ An outbreak of cholera in 1971 ravaged seventeen African countries.

♦ In 1980, researchers studied an anti-malaria vaccine.

♦ By 1984, WHO declared the St. Lucia method of schistosomiasis control a success.

♦ In the mid-1990s, Dr. Jill Seaman fought a deadly epidemic of kala-azar or visceral leishmaniasis in remote sections of the Sudan.

♦ Zaire reported an Ebola outbreak in 1995.

♦ Throughout 1996, the Ebola virus threatened Gabon.

Budget: Under $25

Sources:

"CDC Travel Information," http//www.cdc.gov/travel/Travel.html.

Close, William T., *Ebola*, Ivy Books, 1995.

Dowell, William, "Rescue in Sudan," *Time*, Special Issue, Fall 1997, 78- 82.

"Ebola Outbreaks," http://www.bocklabs.wics.edu/outbreak.html.

"Global Programme on AIDS," http//gpawww.who.ch/whademo/index.htm.

Hover, G. Henry, *Ebola Factor*, Pentland Press, 1996.

"Travel Health Information," http//www.intmed.mcw.edu/ITC/Healthhtml.

Alternative Applications: Make a similar study of Africa's most dangerous insects and reptiles, particularly the locust, scorpion, crocodile, cobra, viper, and black mamba. Determine the effects of their poisons on humans, impairment to systems, how victims are treated, and their chances of surviving attack. Note modern chemicals that ward off insects and protect swimmers from crocodiles.

Early Humans in Africa

Age/Grade Level or Audience: High school or college biology or life science classes.

Description: Lead a study of early human remains found in Africa, which date back over five million years.

Procedure: Discuss why knowledge of primitive social institutions, nutrition, disease, warfare, and survival methods are significant to the survival of homo sapiens on this planet. Include the following breakthroughs in cultural anthropology in your presentation:

- ◆ England's A. R. Radcliffe-Brown's study of social cohesion and ritual in African tribal society
- ◆ The 1925 discovery of the Taung Baby in South Africa
- ◆ Explorations of Louis and Mary Leakey on Rusinga Island, where remains of Proconsul led to a fuller understanding of human evolution from primates
- ◆ the Leakeys' study of the Kikuyu of Kenya from 1937 to 1939
- ◆ the Leakeys' extensive work in 1942 in the Olduvai Gorge of Tanzania, where hominid fossils and obsidian tools attested to the existence of the *Zinjanthropus boisei*, peoples living nearly two million years ago.
- ◆ The significance of *Australopithecus boisei*, a prehuman life form establishing Africa as the homeland of the world's oldest human life
- ◆ The discovery in the Olduvai Gorge between 1959 and 1965 of *Homo erectus*, who dates back a million years
- ◆ Evidence of toolmaking in *Homo habilis* in 1960
- ◆ In 1975, Mary Leakey's discovery of the Zinj skull of the "Nutcracker Man" in Laetoli, Tanzania
- ◆ Mary Leakey's discovery of bipedal hominid footprings in 1979 in Laetoli, Tanzania
- ◆ The establishment of the Coryndon Memorial Museum in Nairobi
- ◆ Studies of *Ramapithecus* and *Kenyapithecus Wickeri* near Fort Ternan and Rusinga near Lake Victoria
- ◆ the Leakeys' encouragement of Jane Goodall and Dian Fossey in studies of primates, particularly chimpanzees and gorillas
- ◆ The continuation of the Leakey family's interest in anthropology with the work of their son Richard, who concentrated on *Australopithecines* of East Africa and the Omo River region of Ethiopia and Lake Turkana, Kenya
- ◆ Yael Rak's discovery of one of the earliest skull fragments in Hadar, Ethiopia.

Budget: $25-$50

Sources:

The video *Nova: In Search of Human Origins*, Pacific Arts Publishing.

"African Web Links: An Annotated Resource List," http//www.sasupenn.edu/African_ Studies/Home_Page.www_Links.html.

Cove, John J., *What the Bones Say: Tasmanian Aborigines, Science and Domination*, Carleton University Press, 1995.

Friend, Tim, "New Skull Illuminates Early Man," *USA Today*, March 31,1994, D1-2.

Heiligman, Deborah, and Janet Hamlin, *Mary Leakey In Search of Human Beginnings*, W. H. Freeman & Co., 1995.

Johanson, Donald, *Lucy's Child: The Discovery of a Human Ancestor*, Avon, 1990.

Leakey, Louis, *White African: An Early Autobiography*, Doubleday, 1984. Leaky, Mary, *Africa's Vanishing Art: The Rock Paintings of Tanzania*, Doubleday, 1983.

Leakey, Richard, *The Making of Mankind*, Dutton, 1981.

"Louis Leakey Discovering the Secrets of Humankind's Past," http/ccwf.cc.utexas.edu/ ~tweiman/leakey.html.

"Mary Leakey," http//www.netsrg.com/~dbois/leakey.html.

Morell, Virginia, *Ancestral Passions The Leakey Family and the Quest for Humankind's Beginnings,* Simon & Schuster, 1995.

Morgan, Elaine, *The Scars of Evolution: What Our Bodies Tell Us about Human Origins*, Oxford University Press, 1990.

"Origins Reconsidered In Search of What Makes Us Human—Richard Leakey," http// california.com/~rpcman/or.htm.

"Richard Leakey," http//www.sunlink.net/~skip/leakey.html.

Alternative Applications: Select one of these writing projects:

♦ a history of the search for the !Kung and San peoples, who may have been Africa's original inhabitants.

♦ varying racial types of Africa, including the Forest Negroids, Nilotics, Pygmies, Bushman-Hottentots, Fulani, Somali, and Caucasoids

♦ illustrated definitions of *A. Africanus, East African homo, East African robustus, South African gracile,* and *South African robustus.*

♦ human "missing links," such as *Homo erectus, Homo habilis,* and *Homo sapiens,* and the significance of each.

Elephant Lore

Age/Grade Level or Audience: Elementary or middle school life science classes.

Description: Organize a group presentation of elephant lore.

Procedure: Compile scientific data as well as history, stories, films, cartoons, and poems about elephants, such as *Dumbo* or Rudyard Kipling's "The Elephant Child." Make a bulletin board display, database, booklet, research paper, or multimedia show from your findings. Include different types of elephants as well as their uses in agriculture, logging, zoos, and circus acts. Include the following facts:

- ♦ The elephant uses its trunk to gather food and as a sensory organ.
- ♦ The trunk is also called a proboscis.
- ♦ A trunk can siphon water.
- ♦ Because of their rounded legs and sturdy feet, elephants can move rapidly over rough terrain.
- ♦ Savanna elephants are larger than their cousins, the forest elephants.
- ♦ Diet consists of fresh greenery.
- ♦ All elephants fight off enemies with their tusks.
- ♦ Calves take nearly twenty-two months to gestate.
- ♦ Elephants, which are social animals, live in clans.
- ♦ Because they gradually wear out their molars, aged elephants starve to death.
- ♦ The clan gathers to help and comfort wounded or dying members.

Budget: $25-$50

Sources:

"African Wildlife News," http//www.awf.org/nf.ele.numbers.html.

Butterfield, Moira, *Big, Rough, and Wrinkly (What Am I)*, Raintree/Steck-Vaughn, 1997.

"Marine World Africa USA," http//www.freerun.com/napavalley/outdoor/marinewo/marinewo.html.

Penner, Lucille Recht, *Baby Elephant*, Grossett & Dunlop, 1997.

Pringle, Laurence P., *Elephant Woman: Exploring the World of Elephants*, Atheneum, 1997.

"Spook's Elephant Gallery," http//sailfish.exis.net/~spook/ele.html.

Alternative Applications: Have students compare the size, strength, and habits of elephants with other work mammals, such as burros, mules, horses, oxen, llamas, camels, goats, and dogs.

George Washington Carver, Inventor

Age/Grade Level or Audience: Middle school or high school college biology class; garden clubs; museums; agricultural societies; 4-H clubs.

Description: Present a study of George Washington Carver's contributions, discoveries, and inventions.

Procedure: Present an illustrated lecture on how George Washington Carver aided poor farmers by teaching them about nutrition and about turning a profit from the peanut. Mention that peanuts are rich sources of protein, vitamin B, polyunsaturated fat, no cholesterol, and significant amounts of magnesium, iron, calcium, phosphorus, and potassium. Illustrate your lecture with a large poster showing how peanuts form underground from low-growing bushes.

Name varieties of peanuts, particularly Virginia, Runner, Spanish, and Valencias. Note that peanut production is still associated with black farmers, particularly those of North and South Carolina, Georgia, Florida, Alabama, Texas, and Oklahoma as well as Malawi, Nigeria, Senegal, Sudan, and South Africa.

Budget: $25-$50

Sources:

"Carver, George Washington," http//msn.yahoo.com/Arts/HumanitiesHistory/U_S_History/People/Carver_George_Washington_1861_1943.

"George Washington Carver National Monument," http//www.coax.net/people/lwf/carver.htm.

"George Washington Carver National Monument Home Page," http//npsgov/gwca/

"George Washington Carver, the Saint Scientist," http//www.erols.comrpdiges/02049.htm.

Graham, Shirley, *George Washington Carver*, African World, 1995.

Gray, James M. Gray, ed., *George Washington Carver*, Silver Burdett Press, 1997.

Nicholson, Louis P., *George Washington Carver, Botanist and Ecologist*, Chelsea House, 1994.

Alternative Applications: Create a display tracing the arrival of the peanut in Africa, Europe, and Asia from its origination point in Brazil, South America. Note the following facts about peanuts:

◆ The word *goober* derives from the Kongo word *nguba*.
◆ The peanut formed a significant part of the soldier's diet during the Civil War, when meat and other protein sources were in short supply.
◆ Peanut growing was originally associated with poverty, particularly in the South.
◆ Peanuts rose in popularity as a snack food around 1875.
◆ By 1900, inventors had devised machines to plant, cultivate, harvest, and shell peanuts.
◆ As peanut production became cheaper and less labor intensive, the kernels were used for oil, peanut butter, candy, and salted snack food.
◆ Demand for peanut products grew during World War II.

◆ Peanuts can be made into other foods, for example milk, cheese, and ice cream.

◆ Nonfood uses for peanuts include face cream, shaving cream, ink, bleach, metal polish, washing powder, wallboard, shoe polish, medicine, cosmetics, linoleum, rubber, soap, and salve.

Include these and other facts about Carver's career:

◆ In 1869, Booker T. Washington hired George Washington Carver to teach at Tuskegee Institute in Tuskegee, Alabama.

◆ Carver began raising living standards for poor black farmers by teaching them to rotate crops by planting sweet potatoes, corn, cowpeas, soybeans, and peanuts along with cotton.

◆ Carver, a professor at Tuskegee Institute, developed over 300 uses for peanuts.

◆ In 1921, Carver urged the Congressional Ways and Means Committee to protect American peanut farmers from foreign competition.

◆ As unofficial champion of poor blacks, he influenced newspaper publishers, liberal congressmen, agricultural commissions, and other notables.

◆ Carver received honorary doctorates and numerous prestigious awards, including the Theodore Roosevelt medal, honors from the Edison Foundation and London's Royal Society of Arts, and the NAACP's Spingarn Medal.

◆ In 1936, Tuskegee honored his fortieth year on the faculty as the school's most productive teacher and researcher. Both the Prince of Wales and President Theodore Roosevelt visited Carver's lab.

◆ In 1940, to honor of his service to humanity, the Carver Foundation established the Carver Memorial Museum and preserved the Tuskegee laboratory.

◆ In 1973, Carver was elected to the Hall of Fame for Great Americans.

◆ Congress designated January 5 as George Washington Carver Day.

Health Tips

Age/Grade Level or Audience: All ages.

Description: Post health tips for handy reference.

Procedure: Keep a continuing series of news about black health problems on a central bulletin board at a school, post office, medical center, restaurant, retirement home, recreation department, library, or civic center. Include data such as these:

◆ Smoking during pregnancy causes low infant birth weight.

◆ Drinking alcohol during pregnancy can harm a newborn for life.

- ◆ AIDS spreads from shared needles and unprotected sex.
- ◆ A balanced diet of protein, vitamins, and calcium is essential for unborn babies.
- ◆ Drugs and violence are the most common killers of young blacks.
- ◆ Lead poisoning is a silent destroyer of poor children who chew on plaster and paint flakes.
- ◆ New treatments can ease the pain of sickle cell anemia.
- ◆ Children need a second vaccination against measles.
- ◆ To prevent death from stroke, adults should get regular blood pressure evaluations.
- ◆ To control weight, people should eat more steamed and broiled foods and less fatty, fried meats.
- ◆ Colon, rectal, and prostatic cancer kills more black men than white men because black men seek help too late.
- ◆ Women over forty need annual mammograms to detect breast cancer.
- ◆ Adults and children can lower stress and ease depression by exercising with a group.
- ◆ Certain groups—the elderly, people who have had pneumonia, heavy smokers, asthma and emphysema sufferers, teachers, and health care workers—should get a flu shot every fall.

Budget: $25-$50

Sources:

Gavin, James R., "Diabetes," *Ebony*, March 1997, 115-116.

Henry, Walter L., et al., *Black Health Library Guide to Diabetes*, Henry Holt & Co., 1993.

Johnson, Kirk, *Black Health Library Guide to Obesity*, Henry Holt & Co., 1993.

Jones, Paul, and Angela Mitchell, *Black Health Library Guide to Heart Disease*, Henry Holt & Co., 1993.

Kashef, Z., "What's Ailing Our Kids: Five Health Issues," *Essence*, May 1997, 184.

Rossellini, Lynn, "Joycelyn Elders Is Master of Her Domain," *U. S. News & World Report*, November 3, 1997, 65.

Singleton, Lafayette, and Kirk Johnson, *Black Health Library Guide to Stroke*, Henry Holt & Co., 1993.

Alternative Applications: Hold a health fair. Post national health statistics by race for accident, violence, stroke, heart attack, cancer, AIDS, emphysema, and diabetes. Distribute free brochures from these and other groups:

AIDS Coalition	Alzheimer's Foundation
American Arthritis Foundation	American Cancer Society
American Heart Association	March of Dimes
Meals on Wheels	National Institute of Mental Health
Planned Parenthood	Weight Watchers

Staff a booth with volunteers to provide free blood pressure checks, breast exams, prostate cancer test, stool sample kits, urinalysis, Mantoux tests, flu shots, pre-natal care, and vaccinations. To create a positive image of health care, offer coffee and pastries for adults and juice, cookies, balloons, pages to color, and other favors for children.

Herbs, Tonics, Teas, and Cures

Age/Grade Level or Audience: All ages.

Description: Demonstrate Southern black folk remedies.

Procedure: Collect examples of the following herbal preparations, which slaves and rural blacks relied upon when medical care was not available, for instance:

- ◆ Add **bergamot** to shampoo and hair pomade to promote healthy growth. Also, dice bergamot leaves in salads or boil into tea.
- ◆ Make a tea of **catnip** to ease pain and cure cough, flu, or bronchitis.
- ◆ Rely on **chamomile** tea to ease menstrual cramps and to sooth the nerves.
- ◆ Mix **chamomile** with **ground ivy** for a tea to cure heartburn.
- ◆ Blend **chamomile** with grease or lotion for a poultice to draw out inflammation.
- ◆ To cure gout, rheumatism, and joint pain, slice **dandelion** root and leaves in salads, boil as a bracing drink, or shred into stews and soups
- ◆ Simmer **dill** weed or seed and drink to settle a queasy stomach.
- ◆ Tie **fatback** over a splinter to make it rise to the surface.
- ◆ Drink **fennel** tea to rid the intestines of gas, promote a healthy sexual appetite, and cure hiccups.
- ◆ Drink **feverfew** tea to rid the intestines of worms, settle nerves, or regulate menstrual periods.
- ◆ Add **garlic** to stew, beans, and other foods to stop asthma attacks and to boost the immune system.
- ◆ Drink hot **ginger** tea for relief of painful menstrual cramps.
- ◆ Use ground **ginger root** as a nutritious additive to roast pork, turkey, or chicken.
- ◆ Stir honey into **horehound** tea to loosen a rattling chest cough or ease sore throat.
- ◆ Make a tea of **lemon mint** to add to bubble bath or shampoo.
- ◆ Give **mint** tea to invalids to relieve depression and weakness.
- ◆ Place **nightshade** leaves over a sore to promote healing.
- ◆ Promote healthy mucous membranes by adding **paprika** to foods.

♦ Serve **parsley** tea to rid the body of excess fluid.

♦ Ease a head cold or sinus infection by eating foods with lots of **pepper**.

♦ Soak or boil **persimmon** bark in water and sip as a cure for diarrhea.

♦ Bind **plantain** leaves on boils or abscesses.

♦ Blend **pine bark** with boiling water for a strong spring tonic.

♦ Keep **rosemary** in corn meal and flour as a deterrent to bugs.

♦ Rinse hair in **rosemary** and **borax** to promote shine.

♦ Place a compress of **rosemary** tea on the forehead to stop sinus headache or add to bath water to ease head and chest congestion.

♦ Keep dry **sage** on hand as an additive to tea. Sweeten with honey to relieve arthritis and chest colds.

♦ Drink **sassafras** tea to cure constipation.

♦ Sip **tansy** tea to kill intestinal parasites.

♦ Make a paste of wet **tobacco** to draw the sting out of chiggers, mosquito bites, or bee stings.

♦ Soak brown paper in **vinegar** and place over a bruise or stiff joint to ease soreness.

♦ Sip **vinegar** water sweetened with honey every morning to prevent arthritis.

Budget: $25-$50

Sources:

Evans, Mark, *Herbal Plants: Their History and Uses,* Smithmark, 1996.

Magic and Medicine of Plants, Reader's Digest Association, 1986.

Schiller, Carol, and David Schiller, *Aromatherapy Oils: A Complete Guide,* Sterling Publishing, 1996.

Alternative Applications: Compare black herbal lore with the folk remedies of Native Americans, who often relied on similar local plants for medication and nutrition.

 In the Rice Fields

Age/Grade Level or Audience: Middle school or high school college biology or life science classes.

Description: Make a display describing the labor-intensive nineteenth-century method of rice culture.

Procedure: Create a bulletin board delineating slaves performing each stage of rice culture. Feature how seed was rolled underfoot to mix it with clay and how workers sowed, hoed, flooded, and harvested the crop. Draw scenes of hulling, winnowing, and storage. Explain in side notes why rice was a profitable crop and nutritious dish. Give similar facts about tobacco, indigo, corn, jute, hemp, and cotton.

Budget: Under $25

Sources:

"Connections Enslavement," http//asu.alasu.edu/academicadvstudies/41.html.

Fretz, S. J., *Rice*, Wellspring, 1995.

Littlefield, Daniel C., *Rice and Slaves: Ethnicity and the Slave Trade in Colonial South Carolina*, University of Illinois Press, 1991.

———, *Rice and the Making of South Carolina: An Introductory Essay*, South Carolina Department of Archives and History, 1995.

Straight, Susan, *I Been in Sorrow's Kitchen and Licked out All the Pots,* Hyperion, 1992.

Hess, Karen, *The Carolina Rice Kitchen: The African Connection,* University of South Carolina Press, 1992.

Alternative Applications: Compile facts about rice plantations on a handout along with drawings of the plant during different stages of its growth. Give useful information about rice, such as:

♦ varieties, including Orgyza sativa, Orgyza globerrima, and Zizania aquatica
♦ high starch content, low protein, and vitamins
♦ use of rice to make oil, beer, flour, baby food, cereal, nonallergenic food, makeup, fuel, mulch, fertilizer, solvent, fodder, chicken feed, thatch, brooms, rope, mats, bedding, sandals, hats, paper, mats, bags, and plastics
♦ cultivation of rice in Tennessee, Florida, Missouri, Oklahoma, South Carolina, Louisiana, Mississippi, Arkansas, and California
♦ introduction of rice to South Carolina after Captain J. Turber's ship was blown off course in 1685
♦ how South Carolina led the nation in rice production.

Invent-O-Rama

Originator: Roberta Brown, teacher, Fort Bragg, North Carolina.

Age/Grade Level or Audience: Elementary or middle school history or science classes; scout troops; 4-H clubs.

Description: Have participants display the names of African American inventors alongside objects or drawings to illustrate their work.

Procedure: Arrange on a shelf or in a display case objects, drawings, or pictures cut from magazines representing the discoveries and designs of the following inventors, designers, and technologists:

- ♦ James S. Adams—airplane propeller
- ♦ George E. Alcorn—semiconductors
- ♦ Archie Alexander—Whitehurst Freeway, Washington, D. C.
- ♦ Virgie M. Ammons—fireplace damper tool
- ♦ Charles S. Bankhead—composition printing
- ♦ Benjamin Banneker—America's first clock
- ♦ James A. Bauer—coin changer
- ♦ Andrew J. Beard—automatic railcar coupler
- ♦ Charles R. Beckley—folding chair
- ♦ Alfred Benjamin—scouring pads
- ♦ Miriam E. Benjamin—signal chair
- ♦ J. W. Benton—oil derrick
- ♦ Henry Blair—corn and cotton planters
- ♦ Sarah Boone—folding ironing board
- ♦ Otis Boykin—stimulator for an artificial heart
- ♦ Henrietta Bradbury—torpedo discharger
- ♦ Phil Brooks—disposable syringe
- ♦ Marie Van Brittan Brown—home security system
- ♦ Robert F. Bundy—signal generator
- ♦ J. A. Burr—lawn mower
- ♦ George Washington Carver—crop rotation, recycling, paint, cosmetics and lotions, wood stain
- ♦ Albert J. Cassell—method of manufacturing silk
- ♦ W. Montague Cobb—color chart of the human heart
- ♦ Leander M. Coles—mortician's table
- ♦ Cap B. Collins—portable electric light
- ♦ David N. Crosthwait—vacuum heating system
- ♦ Joseph Hunter Dickinson—player piano
- ♦ Charles Richard Drew—blood bank
- ♦ James Forten—sail raising device
- ♦ Albert Y. Garner—flame retardant
- ♦ Sarah E. Goode—folding bed
- ♦ Dr. Meredith C. Gourdine—smoke control, electradyne paint spray gun
- ♦ W. S. Grant—curtain rod support
- ♦ Solomon Harper—thermostatic hair curlers
- ♦ M. C. Harvey—lantern
- ♦ Dr. Lincoln Hawkins—coatings for communication cable
- ♦ Edward Hawthorne—heart monitor; blood pressure control
- ♦ H.C. Haynes—improved razor strop
- ♦ Dr. William Hinton—test for syphilis
- ♦ Dorothy E. Hoover—aeronautical research

♦ Harry C. Hopkins—hearing aid

♦ Thomas L. Jennings—dry-cleaning process

♦ John Arthur Johnson—monkey wrench

♦ Frederick M. Jones—truck refrigeration, starter generator, portable x-ray machine

♦ Leonard Julian—sugar cane planter

♦ Percy Lavon Julian—glaucoma treatment, synthetic cortisone

♦ Ernest Everett Just—studies of cell division

♦ Dr. Samuel L. Kountz—improvement to kidney transplants

♦ Robert Benjamin Lewis—oakum picker

♦ J. L. Love—pencil sharpener

♦ Elijah J. McCoy—automatic locomotive lubricator

♦ James Winfield Mitchell—method of purifying chemicals

♦ Garrett Augustus Morgan—gas mask, four-way traffic signal

♦ Benjamin T. Montgomery—boat propellor

♦ George Olden-postage stamp

♦ W. B. Purvis—fountain pen, machine to make paper bags

♦ J. W. Reed—dough roller and kneader

♦ Norbert Rillieux—sugar refiner

♦ G. T. Sampson—folding clothes dryer

♦ Dewey S. C. Sanderson—urinalysis meter

♦ C. B. Scott—street sweeper

♦ J. H. Smith—lawn sprinkler

♦ P. D. Smith—mechanical potato digger

♦ Richard Spikes—automatic carwash, car directional signals, beer keg, automatic transmission

♦ J. A. Sweeting—cigarette roller

♦ Stewart and Johnson—metal bending machine

♦ Lewis Temple—improved whaling harpoon

♦ Charles H. Turner—method of studying the habits of insects

♦ Sarah Walker—hair straightener, face cream, hot comb

♦ Anthony Weston—improved threshing machine

♦ Daniel Hale Williams—first emergency open-heart surgery

♦ Ozzie S. Williams—radar search beacon

♦ J. R. Winter—fire escape ladder

♦ Granville T. Woods—railroad telegraph

♦ Louis Tompkins Wright—treatment for head and neck injuries

Budget: Under $25

Sources:

Branch, Muriel Miller, and Dorothy Marie Rice, *Pennies to Dollars: The Story of Maggie Lena Walker*, Linnet Books, 1997.

Chandler, Ann, *Black Women: A Salute to Black Inventors*, revised edition, Chandler White, 1992.

Chappell, K., "How Black Inventors Changed America," *Ebony*, February 1997, 40.

Day, Lance, and Ian McNeil, eds., *Biographical Dictionary of the History of Technology*, Routledge, 1996.

"The Faces of Science: African Americans in the Sciences," http//www.lib.lsu.edu/lib/chem/display/faces.html.

Gibbs, C. R., *Black Inventors: From Africa to America, Two Million Years of Invention and Innovation*, T. D. Publications, 1995.

Hine, Darlene Clark, Elsa Barkley Brown, and Rosalyn Terborg-Penn, *Black Women in America: An Historical Encyclopedia*, Carlson Publishing, 1993.

Mabunda, L. Mpho, ed., *The African American Almanac*, 7th edition, Gale, 1997.

Massaquoi, H. J., "Blacks in Science and Technology," *Ebony*, February1997, 172-173.

Saari, Peggy, and Daniel B. Baker, *Explorers and Discoverers*, UXL/Gale, 1995.

Alternative Applications: Use inventors' names as subjects for individual written or oral reports or scientific studies of how mechanical devices work. As subjects for science fairs or computer drafting projects, have students replicate the theory behind a particular device or treatment, such as these:

- ◆ Charles Drew's blood bank
- ◆ Otis Boykin's stimulator for an artificial heart
- ◆ Louis Wright's neck brace
- ◆ Garrett Augustus Morgan's gas mask
- ◆ Percy Julian's glaucoma treatment

Feature drawings and scientific explanations in a series of school, radio, television, or newspaper public address spots highlighting an inventor a day throughout Black History Month.

The Palm Tree

Age/Grade Level or Audience: Middle school or high school biology or life science classes.

Description: Create a bulletin board display of facts about the palm tree and its role in tropical societies.

Procedure: Post drawings of various types of palm trees, fronds, flowers, and fruit, especially the date and coconut palms. Include a map detailing where palm trees are most common, such as the African coast and Madagascar as well as the Caribbean. Emphasize facts about the trees:

- ◆ Palms vary from other trees because they have no branches, only a leafy crown of fan-shaped or elongated fronds.

◆ Dating back 220 million years, the palm is one of the earth's oldest trees.

◆ About 117 species are native to Africa.

◆ Palm trees are said to have a thousand uses. For centuries, people have woven palm huts, sunhats, mats, brooms, flooring, fans, umbrellas, clothing, and visors, bags and baskets, plaited rope and twine, and planted palms for shade, wind protection, and ornament.

◆ Palm wood is useful for making walls and buildings, garden tools, and utensils.

◆ Palm also provides coconuts for food and milk and sap for drinking and plant matter for fertilizer.

◆ The African palm also provides copra, which is made into oil for drugs and ointments, soap, candles, cosmetics, margarine and vegetable oil, vinegar, candies, tin-plating, rattan furniture, and lubricants.

◆ The leaf of the African toddy palm can be cooked as a vegetable.

Budget: Under $25

Sources:

Berry, James, *The First Palm Trees*, Simon & Schuster, 1997.

Binns, Tony, *The People and Environment in Africa*, John Wiley and Sons, 1995.

Cochrane, Jennifer, *Trees of the Tropics*, Steck-Vaughn, 1990.

Cote, Nancy, *Palm Trees*, Simon & Schuster Children's Books, 1993.

Demko, George J., *Why in the World: Adventures in Geography*, Anchor Books, 1992.

Halliburton, Warren J., and Kathilyn Solomon Probosz, *African Landscapes,* Crestwood House, 1993.

Hunter, Bobbi Dooley, *The Legend of the African Bao-Bab Tree*, Africa World Press, 1995.

Jones, David L., *Palms Throughout the World*, Smithsonian, 1995.

"Palm Trees," http//miavx1.muoh9o.edu/~dragonfly/itb/palm_tree.htmlx.

Alternative Applications: Make an illustrated report or website comparing the variety of uses for the palm with those of the oak, birch, pecan, walnut, sugar maple, rubber tree, pine, teak, and other trees. Comment on which plants are most disease resistent, most adaptable to varied habitats, widest spread, fastest growing, and easiest to harvest and replant.

Saving Africa's Past

Age/Grade Level or Audience: High school or college anthropology, archeology, or life sciences course.

Description: Outline an archeological dig to uncover and preserve African history.

Procedure: Using a variety of sources, map a spot of African history to preserve, such as a pygmy village. Organize these activities:

♦ List methods of preserving village walls and buildings, artifacts, jewelry, burial places, temples and worship centers, food and water sources, quarries, city centers, and roads and trails.
♦ Anticipate recovery methods and storage needs for bones and teeth, pottery, beadwork, excavations, language, oral epics, and genealogies.
♦ Anticipate methods of recording for future retrieval these data tribal events, wars, epidemics, earthquakes, droughts, comets and meteor showers, eclipses, and floods.
♦ Suggest methods of dating raw materials. Include carbon and arbon dating, eyewitness diaries, petroglyphs and cave drawings, diaries, land studies, and tribal griots.

Budget: Under $25

Sources:
Coulson, D., and A. Alexander, "Etched in Stone," *Time*, June 2, 1997, 66-69.
Leakey, Mary, *Olduvai Gorge, Vol. 5*, Cambridge University Press, 1995.
Nova: In Search of Human Origins (video), Pacific Arts Publishing.
"Pygmies Hunter Gatherers in the Jungle," http//www.ouottherenewscom/congo/glossary/pygmies.htm.
Rachlin, Harvey, *Lucy's Bones, Sacred Stones, and Einstein's Brain: The Remarkable Stories Behind the Great Objects*, Henry Holt, 1996.
"The Story of the Virungas," http//davem2.cotf.edu/ete/modulesmgorilla/mgtribal.html.
Thomas, *Archeology: Down to Earth*, HarBrace, 1997.
Tobias, Philip V., *Olduvai Gorge, Vol. 4*, Oxford University Press, 1991.

Alternative Applications: Focus on the Leakeys' discovery of Lucy, the hominid remains from the Olduvai Gorge. Characterize her life, dimensions, characteristics, and significance to anthropology. Contrast her human remains to those discovered in Australia, China, Europe, and the Americas. Propose an interactive CD-ROM that will introduce young researchers to Lucy and her contributions to the study of humankind

 Sickle Cell Anemia

Age/Grade Level or Audience: High school or college science or pre-med classes; museum or science center.

Description: Present facts about the occurrence and treatment of sickle cell anemia.

Procedure: Make available a series of posters and graphs delineating the virulence and effects of the disease and the percentage of black people who suffer from it. Include the following information:

- ♦ a map showing parts of North, Central, and South America, Africa, Asia, and Europe where the disease occurs
- ♦ a drawing of a normal cell and the crystallization of the twisted rod-like shapes of sickle cells, which impede absorption of oxygen and obstruct small blood vessels
- ♦ a list of causes of abnormal hemoglobin in red blood cells
- ♦ an explanation of how the disease, through chemical malfunction, affects victims, such as abdominal, skeletal, and muscle pain, kidney stress, tissue damage, anemia, shortness of breath, jaundice, fever, and bleeding
- ♦ a discussion of the genetic transference of the disease
- ♦ the relationship between sickle cells and malarial infection
- ♦ definitions of *HbA, HbS, heterozygous,* and *homozygous*
- ♦ a description of treatment, involving antibiotics, analgesics, rest, hot packs, and blood transfusion
- ♦ a chart contrasting the number of carriers (1 in 10) with the 65,000 U.S. victims (1 in 400)

Budget: Under $25

Sources:

Bloom, Miriam, *Understanding Sickle Cell Disease*, University Press of Mississippi, 1995.

"Sickle Cell Anemia," http//www.kumc.edu/gec/support/sickle_c.html.

"Sickle Cell Questions and Answers," http//www.medaccess.com/h_child/siclde/sa_03.htm.

Silverstein, Alvin, *Sickle Cell Anemia*, Enslow Publications, 1997.

Walker, Dava, *Puzzles*, Lollipop Power, Inc., 1996.

Alternative Applications: Describe the search for a cure for sickle cell anemia, such as Dr. Linus Pauling's study of blood cells. Note any breakthroughs in protecting families from transferring the tendency, particularly pre-conception screening and amniocentesis. Also, study other diseases that ravage black people in Africa and the Caribbean, including these:

AIDS	amebiasis	amoebic dysentery
bejel	bilharziasis	black water fever
brucellosis	cholera	dengue fever
diphtheria	Ebola	filariasis

Guinea threadworm	hemorrhagic fever	hepatitis A
hepatitis B	hookworm	kwashiorkor
Lassa fever	leishmaniasis	leprosy
malaria	marasmus	meningitis
onchocerciasis	plague	polio
Q fever	rabies	schistosomiasis
sleeping sickness	smallpox	syphilis
trachoma	tuberculosis	typhoid fever
typhus	yaws	yellow fever

Note that all of these diseases are spread or exacerbated by malnutrition, unsanitary conditions, intravenous drug use, risky sexual behavior, bacteria, virus, insects, and protozoa.

Two-Feet, Four-Feet, Wings, Fins, and Tail

Age/Grade Level or Audience: Kindergarten or elementary science classes.

Description: Have students draw a frieze that categorizes two-footed, four-footed, winged, crawling, and finned animals from Africa.

Procedure: Make available a collection of illustrated children's dictionaries, reference books, and posters, story books, filmstrips, and computer programs which classify animals. Have students select animals from Africa from each category to draw on a frieze.

Budget: $25-$50

Sources:
"African Wildlife News," http//www.awf.org/nf.ele.numbers.html.

Arnold, Caroline, *African Animals*, Morrow Junior Books, 1997.

Butterfield, Moira, *Big, Rough, and Wrinkly (What Am I)*, Raintree/Steck- Vaughn, 1997.

Hartmann, Wendy, *One Sun Rises: An African Wildlife Counting Book*, Dutton Child Books, 1994.

Hopcraft, Xan, "What I Learned from a Cheetah," *Scholastic Storyworks*, September 1997, 6-13.

"Marine World Africa USA," http//www.freerun.com/napavalley/outdoor/marinewo/marinewo.html.

McClung, Robert M., *Last of the Wild: Vanished and Vanishing Giants of the Animal World*, Linnet Books, 1997.

Penner, Lucille Recht, *Baby Elephant*, Grossett & Dunlop, 1997.

Pinter, Helmut. *African Grey Parrots ... as a Hobby*, T. F. H. Publications 1995.

Pringle, Laurence P., *Elephant Woman: Exploring the World of Elephants*, Atheneum, 1997.

"Spook's Elephant Gallery," http//sailfish.exis.net/~spook/ele.html.

Theroux, Paul, "Down the Zambezi," *National Geographic*, October 1997, 2-31.

Williams, Wendy, "Of Elephants and Men," *Animals*, November/December 1997, 24-30.

Alternative Applications: Have students create five separate over-sized booklets from poster paper, one each for two-footed, four-footed, winged, crawling, and finned animals. Assign separate groups to letter names of animals and add details of their habitats, such as lakes and rivers, sandy soil, mountain tops, burrows, cliffs, grassland, deserts, and vines.

Who Has Seen a Coelocanth?

Age/Grade Level or Audience: Elementary or middle school science classes.

Description: Study extinction with a unit on the coelocanth.

Procedure: Introduce students to the coelocanth, an archaic salt-water fish found only on the southeast coast of Africa off the islands of Cormoros and Madagascar. It dates back 350 million years and was thought extinct until a positive identification of a five-foot specimen in 1939. An Osteichthye and member of the sarcopterygians, this bony, tough-finned relative of the lungfish has surprised scientists by surviving from ancient times. Lead a discussion of pockets of surviving animals once thought extinct.

Budget: Under $25

Sources:

"Action Comores Home Page," http//bix.nott.ac.uk/ActionComores/achomepage 11f.html.

Benton, Michael J., *Vertebrate Paleontology*, Routledge, Chapman & Hall, 1990.

"Biogeography," http//sunflower.bio.indiana.edu/~bsinervo/S318Biogeography_and_Models.html.

"Lungfish and Coelocanths," http//www.anglia.co.uk/prehist/.

Alternative Applications: Profile the habitat of the coelocanth by studying the salt water off southeast Africa.

Zoo's Who

Age/Grade Level or Audience: Elementary or middle school science classes.

Description: Have students prepare posters picturing African animals and describing their habits.

Procedure: Have students draw one animal per poster and position it in a natural setting, such as on a plain, hill country, or mountain slope or in a lake, wetland, seashore, or river. Include these:

aardvark	aardwolf	alcelaphine	antelope
baboon	bongo	bat-eared fox	blackfly
black mamba	boomslang	buffalo	bushbaby
bushpig	bush warbler	caracal	cheetah
chevrotain	chimpanzee	civet	obra
colobus	cony	cormorant	crane
crocodile	dik-dik	duiker	dung beetle egret
eland	elephant	flamingo	ruit bat
gazelle	gekko	gemsbok	genet
gerenuk	giant frog	gnu	gorilla
guinea fowl	hartebeest	heron	hippo
hirola	hornbill	hyena	hyrax
jacana	jackal	kestrel kingfisher	klipspringer
kob	kongoni	korhaan	kudu
leopard	lion	mandrill	marabou stork
mongoose	mousebird nyala	okapi	oryx
ostrich	peacock	pelican	plover
porcupine	puff adder	python	reedbuck
rhino	scarab beetle	secretary bird	serval
shrew sitatunga	springbok	springhare	squirrel steenbok
vervet	tickbird	topi	tsetse fly
turaco	vulture	warthog	waterbuck
wildebeest	zebra	zebu	

Divide animal posters into identifiable groups and subgroups, i. e. scavenger, migratory, nocturnal, hoofed, insectivore, herbivore or browser, carnivore, omnivore, ruminant, feline, and primate. Have each student add a paragraph to the back of the poster telling about the animal's habits, diet, size, color, and natural enemies. For example, feature one of these unusual species:

♦ arboreal boomslang, a venomous tree snake that feeds on birds and chameleons

♦ southern carmine bee eater, a long-billed bird with deep rose body and
  blue head and underside, which breeds on banks overlooking rivers
♦ whistling rat, a burrowing rodent of the Kalahari
♦ rangei, a web-footed nocturnal desert lizard.

Budget: $25-$50

Sources:

"African Wildlife News," http//www.awf.org/nf.ele.numbers.html.

Arnold, Caroline, *African Animals*, Morrow Junior Books, 1997.

Butterfield, Moira, *Big, Rough, and Wrinkly (What Am I)*, Raintree/Steck-Vaughn,
  1997.

Diakité, Baba Wagué, *The Hunterman and the Crocodile*, Scholastic Books, 1997.

Hartmann, Wendy, *One Sun Rises: An African Wildlife Counting Book*, Dutton Child
  Books, 1994.

Kingdon, Jonathan, *Island Africa: The Evolution of Africa's Rare Animals and Plants*,
  Princeton University Press, 1992.

"Marine World Africa USA," http//www.freerun.com/napavalley/outdoor/
  marinewo/marinewo.html.

McClung, Robert M., *Last of the Wild: Vanished and Vanishing Giants of the Animal
  World*, Linnet Books, 1997.

Pinter, Helmut. *African Grey Parrots ... as a Hobby*, T. F. H. Publications 1995.

Pringle, Laurence P., *Elephant Woman: Exploring the World of Elephants*, Atheneum,
  1997.

"Spook's Elephant Gallery," http//sailfish.exis.net/~spook/ele.html.

Theroux, Paul, "Down the Zambezi," *National Geographic*, October 1997, 2-31.

Williams, Wendy, "Of Elephants and Men," *Animals*, November/December 1997, 24-
  30.

Alternative Applications: Organize a large frieze depicting the unique
animals of Africa set in their natural habitats. Include plants such as these:

acacia	acanthus	arum lily	bamboo
banana tree	baobab	bindweed	breadfruit
camellia	chickweed	cinnamon	clivia
clover	coffee	cowpea	deiffenbachia
ebony	epiphyte	eucalyptus	fern
flax	guava	guinea	grass
heather	hemlock	hibiscus	hydrangea
lantana	laurel	liana	lichen
mahogany	mallow	milkweed	millet
mint	moss	myrtle	nettle
Nile cabbage	okra	oleander	palm
papyrus	pepper	philodendron	pococa
quinine	rattan	rice	rose

| rubber tree | sedge | teak | vanilla |
| water | hyacinth | yam | ziziphus |

Have students present their part of the frieze orally to a parents' group or another class or videotape for later presentation.

Sewing and Fashion

 | **Banner Bolster**

Age/Grade Level or Audience: Middle school or high school sewing or crafts class; museum workshop; church school, scouts, civic club, or 4-H project.

Description: Create a series of uplifting banners to counter racism, community tensions, or elitism.

Procedure: Have groups of volunteers sew or paint an inspiring banner, such as a quotation from a variety of sources, for example the Bible, Mahandas Gandhi, Martin Luther King, Jr., Maya Angelou, Abraham Lincoln, Toni Morrison, Louis Armstrong, Marian Wright Edelman, Malcolm X, Joycelyn Elders, Jesse Jackson, Ida Wells-Barnett, Frederick Douglass, Barbara Jordan, Faye Wattleton, or Langston Hughes.

Budget: $25-$50

Sources:

Delamotte, Eugenia, Natania Meeker, and Jean O'Barr, eds. *Women Imagine Change: A Global Anthology of Women's Resistance, 600 B. C. E. to Present*, Routledge, 1997.

Diggs, Anita Doren, ed., *Talking Drums: An African-American Quote Collection*, St. Martin's, 1995.

Maggio, Rosalie, *The New Beacon Book of Quotations by Women*, Beacon Press, 1996.

Mullane, Deirdre, *Words to Make My Dream Children Live: A Book of African American Quotations*, Anchor Books, 1995.

Riley, Dorothy Winbush, *My Soul Looks Back, 'Less I Forget': A Collection of Quotations by People of Color*, Harper Perennial, 1993.

Alternative Applications: Organize a march, candlelight vigil, or informational picket in which groups carry inspirational banners to encourage community involvement, neighborliness, voting, parent involvement in education, literacy, concern for world hunger, or campaigns against drugs, alcohol, guns, AIDS, racism, or gang violence.

Corn Rows

Age/Grade Level or Audience: All ages.

Description: Organize a demonstration of how to cornrow hair.

Procedure: Create a booth at a street fair or neighborhood festival where volunteers cornrow hair for a small fee. Post a sign explaining these facts:

- ◆ Cornrowing dates to the reign of early Egyptian and Ethiopian queens, such as Sheba and Nefertiti.
- ◆ The rows symbolize order and symmetry.
- ◆ Hair plaiting is common among the Yoruba, Jamaicans, and Haitians.
- ◆ It often tops the heads of queens, priestesses, and dignitaries.
- ◆ The first cornrowing indicates a young girl's place among women.
- ◆ Marriage is symbolized by elaborate cornrowing, which winds to a small crown on the back of the head.
- ◆ Elaborate or ceremonial cornrowing often follows a conical shape rising to a crown.

Add other services, such as face painting for small children. Establish a goal and use the money from the cornrowing and face painting to pay for a school, museum, library, or recreation center project. Advertise the purpose of the booth in local media, newsletters, bulletin boards, and PTA meetings.

Budget: $25-$50

Sources:

Bonner, Lonnice B., *Good Hair: For Colored girls Who've Considered Weaves When the Chemicals Became Too Ruff*, Sapphire Publications, 1992.

———, *Plaited Glory: For Colored Girls Who've Considered Braids, Locks, and Twists*, Crown Publishing Group, 1996.

Brown, Carla, and Valerie Thomas-Osborne, *Accent African Traditional and Contemporary Hairstyles for the Black Woman*, Cult Express, 1991.

"Cornrow," http//www.m-w.com81/mw/art/cornrow.htm.

Rooks, Noliwe M., *Hair Raising: Beauty, Culture, and African American Women*, Rutgers University Press, 1996.

Alternative Applications: Using wigs, create a school, museum, or mall display of traditional African hair styles for men, women, and children, including braids and plaits, locs, interlocs, African twists, Nubian twists, cones, and corkscrews. Present an illustrated pamphlet with each style giving step-by-step instructions plus grooming tips.

A Handful of Puppets

Age/Grade Level or Audience: Kindergarten or elementary school classes; religious schools; Scout troups; or classes for the handicapped.

Description: Present a Black History Month puppet theater.

Procedure: Place hands flat on brown paper. Draw around palm, little finger, the three middle fingers, and thumb. Leave a two-inch margin. Trace the pattern on two pieces of felt and cut out. Sew front and back of puppets. Have students draw or stitch faces with crayons, liquid markers, embroidery, cross-stitch, buttons, and scraps of fabric, raffia, cord, or felt. Select favorite Afrocentric stories to tell with hand puppets.

Budget: $50-$75

Sources:
Duch, Mabel, *Easy-to-Make Puppets: Step-by-Step Instructions*, Plays, 1993.
"Folkmanis Puppets," http//www.idis.com/puppets/
"Handilinks to Puppets," http//www.ahandyguide.com/cat1/p/p100.htm.
Janes, Susan Niner, *Puppet Theater Funstation*, Price Stern Sloan, 1996.
Sierra, Judy, *Fantastic Theater: Puppets and Plays for Young Performers and Young Audiences*, H. W. Wilson, 1991.

Alternative Applications: Use puppets in tableaux or skits to teach young children health and safety tips about vaccinations, clean teeth, diet, study, friendship, after-school safety advice, using seat belts, and avoidance of drugs, alcohol, tobacco, guns, unwelcome touching, and violence.

Kite Flags

Age/Grade Level or Audience: Middle school or high school sewing classes, Brownie or Cub scouts, religious schools, handicapped students.

Description: Create kites featuring the colors and designs of African flags.

Procedure: Lead a study of reference books on African flags, then select individual styles to emulate in a simple rectangular kite with colored streamers for tails, such as the Liberian flag designed by Marcus Garvey and featuring red, black and green stripes to symbolize struggle, the black race, and the green of Africa. This project might also apply to the making of banners and windsocks, wall designs, jackets, T-shirts, tote bags, and other items displaying pride in Africa.

Budget: $25-$50

Sources:

"African Web Links: An Annotated Resource List," http//www.sasupenn.edu/African_ Studies/Home_Page.www_Links.html.

"Country-Specific Pages for Africa," http//www.sas.upenn.eduAfrican— Studies/Home—Page/Country.html.

Gibbons, Gail, *Catch the Wind: All about Kites*, Little, Brown, 1989.

Horn, Diane V., *African Printed Textile Designs*, Stemmer House, 1996.

Twenty Little Four-Patch Quilts, Dover, 1997.

Alternative Applications: Have flag makers sew copies of African flags from scraps of silk, polyester, or cotton or draw or paint flag designs on plain muslin or paper. Use the finished flags as the focal point of a Black History Month banquet, convocation, or multimedia presentation, such as a travelogue. Have a reader present the following facts on a chalkboard, handout, or overhead projector:

- ◆ Angola, which is red and black, features a machete, cog wheel, and star to symbolize farmers, industrial workers, and socialism.
- ◆ Benin's flag, which copies the flag of Ethiopia and was adopted in 1960, contains three rectangles in green, yellow, and red.
- ◆ After Botswana gained independence in 1966, the people of this desert land chose a blue flag halved by a black stripe edged in white to represent their need for water.
- ◆ In 1984, Burkina Faso designed a flag featuring a red top over a green bottom and a gold star at the center.
- ◆ Independent since 1962, Burundi adopted a complicated flag split into four sections by a white cross, its top and bottom portions are red and its side portions green. At the center of the cross is a white circle and three red stars edged in green symbolizing unity, peace, and progress.
- ◆ Cameroon's flag is divided vertically into thirds. The colors are green, red, and yellow. A yellow star, representing unity, adorns the center.
- ◆ The Cape Verde Islands sport a simple design decorated with an ornate insignia. To the right are horizontal rectangles of yellow and green. The left portion is a vertical stripe of red centered with a black star surrounded by corn husks, two ears of corn, and a seashell at the connecting point.

◆ The Central African Republic flag, adopted in 1960, is split by a vertical strip of red. To the left and right are four rectangles in blue, white, green, and yellow. On the first blue stripe to the left gleams a yellow star, symbol of unity.

◆ Chad, which once was governed by the French, adopted a simple flag in 1960. It is divided into three vertical rectangles colored blue, yellow, and red.

◆ The flag of the Comoro Islands, adopted in 1978, is a green background centered with a white crescent moon and four stars.

◆ The flag of Djibouti, designed in 1972, features a white triangle radiating from the left and bordering two strips, blue at the top and green at the bottom. Centering the triangle is a red star.

◆ Gambia's flag, composed of five horizontal stripes, features red at the top, blue in the middle, and green at the bottom. Separating these bright colors are two smaller white stripes.

◆ One of Africa's most artistic flags is that of Kenya: like Gambia's flag, it has five horizontal stripes, the top black, the center red, and the bottom green. Separating these three rectangles are two white stripes. At the center is a red, white, and black shield covering crossed spears.

◆ In 1966, Lesotho, also creative with its flag design, chose a diagonal design. The left rectangle, centered with a brown shield, crossed club and spear, and crocodile, is white, the center stripe blue, and the right rectangle green.

◆ Because Liberia was colonized by American slaves, its flag reflects the colors and shape of the U.S. flag. Eleven horizontal stripes alternate red with white. A blue square occupies the left corner and is topped by a white star.

◆ In contrast to these elaborate flags, the Libyan banner is solid green.

◆ Namibia's flag, like Lesotho's, is a diagonal design. A red stripe edged with white separates two triangles, the top blue and the bottom green. In the upper left corner shines a twelve-rayed gold sunburst.

◆ Nearly square in shape, Niger's flag, adopted in 1959, is comprised of three horizontal stripes ranging from orange at the top to white in the center and green at the bottom. In the center is an orange circle, symbolic of the sun.

◆ The flag of Rwanda, divided vertically into thirds, ranges from red to yellow to green. In the center stands a large black "R."

◆ One of the most graceful banners symbolizes the Seychelles and appeared in 1977. A wide red top and narrower green bottom are separated by a white curve.

◆ Reflecting the influence of the United Nations is Somalia's flag, adopted in 1960, a simple blue rectangle centered by a large white star.

◆ A complex design adorns Uganda's flag. Six horizontal stripes, colored black, yellow, red, black, yellow, red, set off a white circle containing a crane, the national bird, which is yellow, red, black, and gray.

◆ Zaire, possessor of one of the most romantic flag motifs, adopted a green background centered with a yellow circle, which holds a forearm clenching a flaming torch of freedom.

Finished flags might be used as decorations for a Black History Month processional or street fair. Place the speaker's comments along with colored model flags on hand-outs or favors for a banquet, reception, or conference.

 Native Fashions

Age/Grade Level or Audience: Civic, church, or school groups; 4-H clubs; sorority assemblies; department stores.

Description: Sponsor an African American fashion show.

Procedure: Select models to display fashions with a distinctive Caribbean, African, or African American flair. Invite a black fashion consultant to narrate. Use native African music and decor as background, such as Kente cloth, jungle animal prints, Kwanzaa symbols, transvaal daisies, palms, hibiscus, native birds and butter-flies, or displays of fruit and vegetables.

Budget: $75-$100

Sources:
"African Center," http//www.nubacom.com.
Rooks, Noliwe M., *Hair Raising: Beauty, Culture, and African American Women*, Rutgers University Press, 1996.
Samuels, Allison, "Black Beauty's New Face," *Newsweek*, November 24, 1997, 68.
"Ujamaa Fashions," http//shops.net/shop/Ujamaa—Fashions/

Alternative Applications: Sponsor a jewelry fair featuring native African accessories, particularly torques, armbands, bracelets, necklaces, barrettes, earrings, hair clusters, finger and toe rings, and anklets. Display on mannequins. Invite area crafters to sell their work. Suggest that part of the fair's profits be donated to a scholarship to help a black student study fashion history or design.

 Proud Stitches

Age/Grade Level or Audience: Home economics classes or adult sewing classes.

Description: Develop sewing techniques while cultivating black pride.

Procedure: Introduce basic sewing techniques by teaching beginning sewers to emulate the hallmarks of Afrocentric fashions. Display fashions along with pattern numbers that will produce similar designs. Feature the following African touches:

- ◆ animal prints
- ◆ appliqued X's to honor Malcolm X
- ◆ batiked fabrics
- ◆ bells, beading, and metal ornaments
- ◆ ethnic prints and colors, particularly black, red, gold, and purple
- ◆ jalabas and dashikis (tunics)
- ◆ kangas and kanzus (caftans)
- ◆ Kente trim
- ◆ kikois and kitenges (sarong skirts) and harem pants
- ◆ metallic braid
- ◆ regal headdresses and headbands with matching belts and sashes

Budget: $50-$75

Sources:

"African Center," http//www.nubacom.com.
Rooks, Noliwe M., *Hair Raising: Beauty, Culture, and African American Women,*
  Rutgers University Press, 1996.
"Ujamaa Fashions," http//shops.net/shop/Ujamaa—Fashions/.

Alternative Applications: Offer an award to the designer or sewing student who creates the best example of Afrocentric fashion for man, woman, or child. Display finished ensembles as sketches on a website or on a model, mannequin, or doll. Feature notable examples in a shop window, county fair, mall, library, school home-economics department, textile show, or museum display.

Sociology

African Culture in the Sea Islands

Age/Grade Level or Audience: High school and college history, sociology, and black studies classes; civic groups.

Description: Present an overview of African influence on black communities along the Atlantic coast.

Procedure: Using crafts, recordings of Gullah songs and stories, videos, and handouts, present information about African culture on the Atlantic islands off the coasts of Georgia and North and South Carolina. Include the following facts:

- ♦ perpetuation of an extended family rather than the European nuclear family
- ♦ living African style in compounds and enclaves rather than separate residences
- ♦ group work habits, such as laughter, conversation, and singing among groups weaving baskets, harvesting, cooking, or repairing fishing nets
- ♦ husbands taking more than one wife and maintaining more than one household
- ♦ matriarchs serving as teachers of culture, religion, and ethics to community children
- ♦ outside influences, particularly service in World War II and changes brought about by the Civil Rights Movement, such as the Headstart Program
- ♦ use of Gullah among old and young, with people of middle age adapting to standard English to facilitate relations with mainland business
- ♦ perpetuation of African names, for example Kojo, Fiba, Cunjie, Ayo, Yao, Twia, Minna, Jibba, Boogah, Bodick, Kiya, and Yacky

♦ erratic patterns of school attendance

♦ syncretism of Christian worship with African Santeria, Umbunda, and Voodoo

♦ beliefs in "haints" and "ghosses"

♦ decoration and annual cleaning of family graves

♦ reliance on herbal and folk remedies

♦ family disruption through migrant labor

♦ seasonal rhythms tied to rice and cotton culture, oyster and crab gathering, livestock and poultry raising, and vegetables such as potatoes, beans, tomatoes, cucumbers, cabbage, broccoli, squash, turnips, and melons.

Budget: $25-$50

Sources:

Films *Conrack* (1974) and *Daughters of the Dust* (1992).

Barnes, Marian E., "The Georgia Sea Island Singers Frankie and Doug Quimby," *Talk That Talk*, Simon & Schuster, 1989.

Brunvand, Jan Harold, ed., *American Folklore: An Encyclopedia*, Garland, 1996.

"Georgia Sea Island Singers Deliver Message of Dignity," Jacksonville *Times-Union*, March 3, 1996.

Gewertz, Daniel, "Black History Alive in Singers Act," *Boston Herald*, April 12, 1991, S22.

Grogan, David, "Frankie and Doug Quimby Sing Songs of Slavery to Keep Alive the Lore of Their Forebears," *People*, October 12, 1987.

"The Gullah Connection," http//www.afrinet.net/~hallh/ afrotalk/afrooct95/ 1090.html.

"Gullah People and Culture," http//www.tezcat.com/~ronald/gullah.html.

Hamilton, Virginia, *Drylongso*, Harcourt Brace Jovanovich, 1992.

Hanson, Trudy Lewis, "United in Story and Song: The Power of Music in Storytelling," *Storytelling Magazine*, May 1997, 14-15.

Jones, Charles C., Jr., and Roger D. Abrahams, *Gullah Folktales from the Georgia Coast*, University of Georgia Press, 1997.

Ogunleye, Tolagbe, "Afro-American Folklore," *Journal of Black Studies*, March 1997, 435-456.

Quimby, Doug, and Frankie Quimby, "The Ibo Landing Story" in *Talk That Talk*, Simon & Schuster 1989.

Straight, Susan, *I Been in Sorrow's Kitchen and Licked Out All the Pots*, Hyperion, 1992.

Alternative Applications: Present a map delineating the strongest African influence and highlighting the location and cultural significance of these places:

Butler	Darien	Dataw
Daufuskie	Edisto	Harris Neck
Hilton Head	James	Jekyll Island Ladies

Johns	Kiawah	Mt. Pleasant
Ossabaw	Ridgeway	Sapelo
Skidaway	St. Catherines	St. Helena
St. Simons	Thunderbolt	Tybee
Wadmalaw	Yamacraw	Younge's Island

Black Excellence

Age/Grade Level or Audience: All ages.

Description: Organize a workshop spotlighting black excellence.

Procedure: Screen the *Ebony/Jet Guide to Black Excellence,* an inspirational video featuring Oprah Winfrey, Joshua Smith, and John Johnson, with Avery Brooks narrating. Appoint a panel of local business and civic leaders, educators, and ministers to discuss how and why black people are achieving. Compose a task force to target areas in which adults can lead young people toward excellence. For example:

♦ Form a neighborhood watch to report crime and drug trade.

♦ Organize a support system of parents and neighbors to keep children in school.

♦ Organize a Friends of the Library to boost worthy reading materials about black success and to encourage participation at library activities.

♦ Petition city, county, state, and federal officials to support black business, scholarships, health clinics, and community development.

♦ Appoint a committee of local stringers to report area successes to newspapers, radio and TV stations, newsletters, magazines, and websites. Suggest that each story be accompanied by photographs or videos of such events as groundbreaking ceremonies, openings of new businesses, wellness clinics, and scholarship ceremonies.

Budget: $25-$50

Sources:

Dean, Robbie, *Black Children's Parents Imparting Discipline/Heritage*, Robbie Dean Press, 1997.

"Ebony/Jet Guide to Black Excellence Series," http//www.specialvideoscom/an/dbpage.pl/3721/yyx4654.116029.

"Jet Online," http//ebonymag.com/jethome.html.

"Johnson Publishing Company," http//ebonymag.com/jpcindex.html.

Alternative Applications: Invite a local camera club to create an overview of local examples of black excellence. Display pictures or films in shopping malls, business and college recruitment fairs, church assemblies, civic club meetings, or school festivals. Select a deejay, sports announcer, drama student, or speech teacher to narrate a tape to accompany the display.

The Black Experience

Originator: Leatrice Pearson, teacher, Lenoir, North Carolina.

Age/Grade Level or Audience: High school or college history, sociology, or anthropology classes; historical societies; museums.

Description: Organize a colloquium on the unique position of African Americans in United States history.

Procedure: Open a roundtable consideration of Malcolm X's statement, "Education is our passport to the future; for tomorrow belongs to the people who prepare for it today." Present the following ideas for discussion:

- Slavery prevented Africans from retaining a knowledge of their past.
- To squelch communication and the possibility of a revolt, slaveholders separated members of the same tribe or purchased members of different tribes.
- To quell revolts and halt religious practices, slaves were forbidden to own drums or firearms and stopped from assembling in large groups without a white person present.
- Slaves were not allowed to engage in enterprise, such as selling carvings and baskets or bartering vegetables for clothing or furniture.
- To maintain order, lawmakers forbade slaves to learn to read and write or from writing in their native languages.
- Families were often split up and sold to owners in different parts of the country.
- Black testimony was rejected in courts.
- Blacks were not allowed to ward off white attackers or to strike white people.
- Black Americans grew up with a hunger for their roots, which had been forcefully taken from them.
- Even free blacks who made new lives in the North and Canada did not feel welcome in white society.
- Runaway slaves who went south found acceptance among the Seminole, Creek, and Cherokee.

◆ Discrimination, bigotry, and hatred discourage black Americans from participating fully in citizenship, particularly at election time.

Conclude with an explanation of why black and white citizens should ponder these statements and learn more about racism in the United States.

Budget: Under $25

Sources:

Videos such as Alex Haley's *Roots* (1977), *Eyes on the Prize* (1986), *Mississippi Burning* (1988), *Malcolm X.* (1992), *The Civil War* (1990), and *The Ghosts of Mississippi* (1997).

"African American Genealogy," http//ourworld.compuserve. com/homepages/Cliff_m.

Benberry, Cuesta, *Always There: The African-American Presence in American Quilts*, Kent Quilting, 1992.

"Black Family Heritage," http//www.afrinet.net/~hallhafrotalk/afroaug95/1894.hml.

"Black Pioneers," http//www.localnet.com/~adonis2/pioall.htm.

Chase, H., "Festivals: Black Film, Then and Now," *American Visions*, June-July 1997, 38-39.

David, Jay, ed., *Growing Up Black: From Slave Days to the Present Twenty-five African-Americans Reveal the Trials and Triumphs of Their Childhoods*, Avon Books, 1992.

Haley, Alex, *The Autobiography of Malcolm X.*, Ballantine, 1964.

———, *Queen: The Story of an American Family*, William Morrow and Co., 1993.

———, *Roots: The Saga of an American Family*, Doubleday, 1976.

"Haley 'Malcolm X' Manuscript Is Auctioned for $100,000," *Jet*, October19, 1992, 14-15.

Kim, Elaine H., Lilia V. Villaneuva, eds., *Making More Waves: New Writing by Asian American Women*, Beacon Press, 1997.

Ki-Zerbo, Joseph, "Oral Tradition as a Historical Source," *UNESCO Courier*, April 1990, 43-46.

Morrison, Toni, *Beloved*, Knopf, 1987.

Roberts, Dorothy, *Killing the Black Body: Race, Reproduction, and the Meaning of Liberty*, Pantheon, 1997.

Sandoz, Ellis, *Political Sermons of the American Founding Era*, Liberty Press, 1991.

Santiago, Chiori, "A Story Underfoot," *American Style*, Fall 1997, 49.

Shipler, David K., *A Country of Strangers*, Knopf, 1997.

Wyatt, Gail Elizabeth, *Stolen Women: Reclaiming Our Sexuality, Taking Back Our Lives*, John Wiley & Sons, Inc., 1997.

Alternative Applications: Discuss why both black and white students need black history so that both races can appreciate contributions to history, culture, and citizenship. Select priorities that will enable black youth to develop a strong self-image and to achieve. For instance, introduce Paul Cuffee and Martin Delany's concept of Pan-Africanism through which black people everywhere share fellowship and unity. Discuss Frederick Douglass's reminder, "If there is no struggle, there is no progress."

Black Pride Day

Originator: Leatrice Pearson, teacher, Lenoir, North Carolina.

Age/Grade Level or Audience: All ages.

Description: Organize a procession to demonstrate black pride.

Procedure: Delegate tasks to organizers. Include these:

- ◆ Invite bands, majorettes, and pep clubs.
- ◆ Make posters and banners with uplifting quotations from memorable African Americans
- ◆ Invite civic, church, and school groups to make floats or dress as clowns, ride unicycles and go-carts, juggle, perform magic tricks, dance, or walk on stilts.

Begin the parade at a central location, such as City Hall or a railroad depot, and march to a significant location in the black community, for example a school, library, civic center, retirement home, housing project, monument, or museum. Hold the black pride procession in the morning so that activities can culminate at a food court, where vendors sell soul food, homemade pies and cakes, and lemonade.

Budget: $75-$100

Sources:

Call on the Chamber of Commerce and visitors bureau to support the procession, which will draw outsiders to your area.

Dean, Robbie, *Black Children's Parents Imparting Discipline/Heritage*, Robbie Dean Press, 1997.

Hine, Darlene Clark, Elsa Barkley Brown, and Rosalyn Terborg-Penn, eds., *Black Women in America: An Historical Encyclopedia*, Carlson, 1993.

Mabunda, L. Mpho, ed., *The African American Almanac*, 7th edition, Gale, 1997.

Smith, Jessie Carney, *Notable Black American Women,* Gale, 1992.

Weatherford, Doris, *American Women's History*, Prentice Hall, 1994.

Alternative Applications: Hold a miniature black pride parade in a shopping mall, school, civic center, auditorium, gymnasium, retirement home, or street. Invite civic clubs, school groups, scout troops, or churches to decorate a wagon, wheelbarrow, bicycles, or cart to depict some aspect of black pride, such as the achievements of early African civilizations, African American participation in the Olympics, or the role black women have played in gaining women's rights. Invite a local civil rights advocate or elected official to serve as grand marshall. Include marching units, such as junior police or hospital candy stripers, musicians, clowns, acrobats, and balloons. Have the parade pass a reviewing stand. Offer prizes for the most original, the best display of black pride, the youngest participant, and the most spirited performer.

Black Social Doctrine

Age/Grade Level or Audience: High school and college sociology classes; adult study groups.

Description: Discuss the implications of opinions expressed by black leaders.

Procedure: Read aloud the social philosophies of important black leaders on various topics. Lead a discussion of their applicability to all people. For example:

Feminism

♦ Black women are not here to compete or fight with you, brothers. If we have hangups about being male or female, we're not going to be able to use our talents to liberate all of our black people. (Shirley Chisholm)

♦ I want the same thing for blacks, Hispanics, and white that I want for myself and my child. And that is the ability to take charge of our lives and not be victimized by reproduction. (Faye Wattleton)

♦ Look at me! Look at my arm! I have plowed and planted, and gathered into barns, and no man could head me—and ain't I a woman? I could work as much and eat as much as a man (when I could get it), and bear de lash as well—and ain't I a woman? I have borne thirteen chillern and seen 'em mos' all sold off into slavery and when I cried out with a mother's grief, none but Jesus heard—and ain't I a woman? (Sojourner Truth)

Civil Rights

♦ The major threat to blacks in America has not been oppression, but rather the loss of hope and absence of meaning. (Cornel West)

♦ The challenge is to become part of the struggle, to make a positive difference. (David Satcher)

Racism

♦ This constant reminder by society that I am "different" because of the color of my skin, once I step outside my door, is not my problem—it's theirs. I have never made it my problem and never will. I will die for my right to be human—just human. (Cicely Tyson)

♦ To be black is to shine and aim high. (Leontyne Price)

Budget: Under $25

Sources:

Delamotte, Eugenia, Natania Meeker, and Jean O'Barr, eds. *Women Imagine Change: A Global Anthology of Women's Resistance, 600 B. C. E. to Present*, Routledge, 1997.

Diggs, Anita Doren, ed., *Talking Drums: An African-American Quote Collection*, St. Martin's, 1995.

Maggio, Rosalie, *The New Beacon Book of Quotations by Women*, Beacon Press, 1996.

Mullane, Deirdre, *Words to Make My Dream Children Live: A Book of African American Quotations,* Anchor Books, 1995.

Riley, Dorothy Winbush, *My Soul Looks Back, 'Less I Forget': A Collection of Quotations by People of Color*, Harper Perennial, 1993.

Alternative Applications: Contrast comments by black philosophers, lecturers, teachers, and writers with those of Socrates, Marcus Aurelius, Solomon, Confucius, Buddha, Susan B. Anthony, Black Elk, Chief Seattle, Chief Joseph, Gandhi, John Kennedy, Abraham Lincoln, Gloria Steinem, Henry David Thoreau, or Eleanor Roosevelt. During February, pair comments daily on the chalkboard or a bulletin board.

Black Towns

Age/Grade Level or Audience: High school and college sociology and history classes; civic and historical groups.

Description: Discuss the formation of all-black towns and communities.

Procedure: Present information about the creation of all-black towns and communities. Emphasize these facts:

- ◆ General Rufus Saxon's creation of a black peasant community on Georgia's Sea Islands following the Civil War
- ◆ John Eaton's establishment of a black community in Davis Bend, Mississippi
- ◆ South Carolina's creation of black communities through its Land Commission during the decade following the Civil War
- ◆ formation of Nicodemus, Kansas, a black town, in 1877
- ◆ Isaiah Montgomery's creation of Mound Bayou, Mississippi, in 1888
- ◆ Edward P. McCabe's establishment of Langston, Oklahoma, in 1890
- ◆ incorporation of Boley, Oklahoma, in 1904

Budget: Under $25

Sources:

Bethel, Elizabeth Rauh, *Promiseland: A Century of Life in a Negro Community*, Temple University Press, 1981.

Wilson, Charles Reagan, and William Ferris, *Encyclopedia of Southern Culture*, University of North Carolina Press, 1981.

Alternative Applications: Lead a debate of the practicality of an all-black town. Consider the following difficulties:

♦ commercial relationships with outside suppliers, labor unions, and financial institutions

♦ representation in county, state, and national government

♦ legal entanglements with anti-discrimination laws

♦ loss of contact with national values

♦ cultural and educational isolation

Contrast the formation of all-black towns with Indian reservations.

Black Women in the Third World

Originator: Janet M. Donaldson, Upper Midwest Women's History Center for Teachers, St. Louis Park, Minnesota.

Age/Grade Level or Audience: High school or college sociology or women's studies classes; adult study groups.

Description: Hold a workshop centered on the struggles of black women in the third world.

Procedure: Present handouts, activities, posters, discussion topics, slide programs, and videos detailing serious social inequalities for black women in the third world, particularly these:

♦ fatherless families

♦ female circumcision and genital mutilation

♦ lack of empowerment

♦ limited career expectations

♦ low self-esteem

♦ male preference

♦ manual labor

♦ patriarchal religions and fundamentalist beliefs

♦ physical strictures, such as the chador, veil, and curfews

◆ sexism
◆ subsistence farming

Budget: $50-$75

Sources:

Bender, David, *Third World: Opposing Viewpoints*, Greenhaven Press, 1995.

Fister, Barbara, *Third World Women's Literature: A Dictionary and Guide to Materials in English*, Greenwood, 1995.

Mason, Paul, ed., *Atlas of Threatened Cultures*, Raintree/Steck-Vaughn, 1997.

Mohonty, Chandra T., *Third World Women and the Politics of Feminism*, Indiana University Press, 1991.

Alternative Applications: Compare unhealthy and discriminatory practices in Africa to problems in the United States, notably these:

diminished academic performance	eating disorders
fundamentalist strictures	glass ceiling
high suicide rates	incest
low career expectations	low self-esteem
patriarchal family hierarchies	rape
sexual harassment	workplace exploitation

Make up a list of positive suggestions to benefit young black women. For example:

◆ budget workshops that feature details on how to establish credit
◆ centralized referral information on athletic and academic scholarships, grants, loans, and other inducements
◆ community, school, and church support of sex education
◆ GED programs to encourage older women to complete their education.
◆ halfway houses for substance abusers
◆ job placement and child care assistance for young mothers
◆ shelters for homeless or abused women
◆ support for women who are HIV positive
◆ tutorials for female students, particularly in science and math

Cities for All

Age/Grade Level or Audience: All ages.

Description: Hold a city-wide study of racial equality in the metropolitan center of the future.

Procedure: Have small groups look at present standards and racial equity in jobs, business recruitment, streets and highways, transportation centers, airports, medical facilities, schools, entertainment centers, malls, banking, recreation, parks, and recycling centers. Brainstorm proposals that will limit segregation or preferential treatment.

Budget: Under $25

Sources:

Aitcheson, C., "Corporate America's Black Eye," *Black Enterprise*, April 1997, 109-110.

The Black Population in the United States, Gordon Press, 1995.

The Black Population in the U.S.: A Statistical Profile, Diane Publications, 1994.

City Planning, Watson-Guptil, 1996.

Connerly, W., "All Americans Are Entitled to Equal Treatment," *Vital Speeches of the Day*, April 1, 1997, 370-372.

"Empowering Communities," http//www.usc.edu/Library/QF/diversity/communities. html.

Farley, Christopher John, "Kids and Race," *Time*, November 24, 1997, 88-91.

"Ghetto Education," http//www.sirius.com/~adisa/ghetto.html.

Hommann, Mary E., *City Planning in America: Between Promise and Despair*, Greenwood, 1993.

"Minorities Treated Worse Than Whites When House Hunting in D.C. Area," *Jet*, May 5, 1997, 4-5.

Randolph, L. B., "Colin Powell's Challenge to Black America," *Ebony*, June 1997, 20.

"Start Your Own Tolerance Program," http//home.fia.net/~kjmoros/start.html.

Tafoya, William L., "Perspectives on Community Policing," *Crime & Justice International*, July 1997, 7-14.

"University of Michigan Program on Poverty and Social Welfare Policy," http//www. umich.edu/~socwk/poverty/index.html.

Wilson, William J., ed., *Ghetto Underclass: Social Science Perspectives*, Sage, 1993.

Alternative Applications: Design an evaluative instrument for judging the inclusiveness of a metropolitan area. Set standards to apply to cities seeking grants and special permits. Enumerate racially blind requirements and assessments of civic strengths and prosperity.

Coping Through Story and Imagination

Age/Grade Level or Audience: College psychology or education class or human systems class.

Description: Analyze the coping mechanisms of black fable.

Procedure: Have students work independently with traditional black fables, particularly the works of Aesop, Joel Chandler Harris's Uncle Remus, West African and Caribbean stories of Anansi the Spider, and the heroics of High John the Conqueror. Conclude the research and study with a symposium on coping mechanisms, for example, outright trickery, humor, rationalizing, indirect confrontation, and reverse psychology.

Budget: Under $251

Sources:

The video "Rabbit Ears Koi and the Kola Nuts."

Abraham, Roger D., *African Folktales*, Pantheon Books, 1983.

Alexander, Lloyd, *The Fortune-Tellers*, Dutton Chidlren's Books, 1992.

Alston, Charlotte Blake, "Introducing African Storytelling" in *Tales as Tools: The Power of Story in the Classroom,* National Storytelling Press, 1994, 174-175.

Bankole, Adisa, "Afrika's Melanin Melody," *National Black Storytellers Newsletter*, Fall 1996, 3.

Cabral, Len, *Anansi's Narrow Waist* (easy reader in English and Spanish), Addison-Wesley, 1994.

Coggswell, Gladys, *Well Shut My Mouth* (audiocassette), Coggswell Communications, 1995.

Goss, Linda, "Anansi and the Wisdom Tree," *World & I*, February 1995, 272-273.

————, et al., *Jump Up and Say; Anthology of African-American Storytelling*, Simon & Schuster, 1995.

Hallworth, Grace, et al., *Our Favourite Stories From Around the World*, Longman, 1994.

Hamilton, Virginia, *The People Could Fly*, Knopf, 1985.

Harrington, Janice, *Janice N. Harrington, Storyteller* (audiocassette), Pogo Studio, 1996.

Norfolk, Bobby, "Anansi the Spider and His Six Sons" in *We Like Kids*, Good Year Books, 1995.

Spalding, Henry D., comp. and ed., *Encyclopedia of Black Folklore and Humor*, J. David Publishers, 1990.

Weiss, Jim, *Animal Tales* (audiocassette and CD), Greathall Production, 1990.

Wolkstein, Diane, *The Magic Orange Tree and Other Haitian Folktales*, Schocken, 1997.

Alternative Applications: Read aloud stories and poems of Anansi, Stag 'o Lee, John Henry, or High John the Conqueror. Lead a discussion of superhuman traits and their importance to lyrics, verse, stories, legend, and children's literature. Explain how readers adapt coping skills from the texts.

 ## Crisis Intervention

Age/Grade Level or Audience: Elementary and middle school social studies classes.

Description: Plan a day camp for racially tense communities.

Procedure: Assign a group to create an after-school or summer activity center for racially troubled areas. Include these activities:

art projects	board games	cooking
crafts	gymnastics	reading
role-playing	singing	storytelling
swimming	team sports	water games

Appoint a panel to discuss how each activity will improve self-esteem, discourage violence and gang activity, and head off future confrontations over racism.

Budget: Under $25

Sources:

Burrow, David, *Camp Counselor's Handbook of Over Ninety Games and Activities Just for Rainy days*, 2nd edition, McElroy Publications, 1992.

Hamilton, Robyn, ed, *Africa Activity Book: Arts, Crafts, Cooking and Historical Aids*, Edupress, 1996.

Kallen, Stuart A., *Eco-Arts and Crafts*, Abdo & Daughters, 1993.

Meier, Joel F., and Viola Mitchell, *Camp Counseling: Leadership and Programming for the Organized Camp*, 7th edition, Brown & Benchmark, 1992.

Alternative Applications: Propose a permanent day-care center, after-school study program, eldercare, or hobby center for a poor or troubled neighborhood.

Famine in Ethiopia and Somalia

Age/Grade Level or Audience: High school or college sociology classes; adult study groups; journalists.

Description: Compose a short history of famine in Somalia.

Procedure: Utilizing local sources, draw up a timeline of events that have devastated Ethiopia and Somalia and of the relief efforts launched by the United Nations, Red Cross, Disaster Relief, WHO, UNICEF, *Medecins sans Frontieres,* Church World Service, and other groups. Explain how malnutrition affects not only this generation, but the next as well. Include the slow, painful bodily depletion brought on by marasmus or starvation:

- ◆ Without nutrition, the body begins to devour its reserves of fat.
- ◆ Growth is stunted.
- ◆ Hunger encourages desperation and violent behavior and discourages learning.
- ◆ The heart loses strength.
- ◆ The immune system, weakened by loss of protein, fails.
- ◆ Diseases such as colds and flu become life-threatening.
- ◆ Communicable diseases such as measles and tuberculosis quickly spread among the malnourished.
- ◆ Skin loses its elasticity.
- ◆ Boils, lesions, and other eruptions increase discomfort.
- ◆ Flies and maggots corrupt the eyes, mouth, and open sores.
- ◆ Appetite is suppressed.
- ◆ Decreased brain activity causes loss of concentration.
- ◆ The eyes are unable to focus.
- ◆ The victim's hair falls out.
- ◆ Unclean water introduces gastrointestinal infection.
- ◆ Diarrhea robs the body of strength.
- ◆ Extreme diarrhea leads to rectal prolapse and further risks of infection.
- ◆ Dehydration may lead to unconsciousness or death.

Publish your findings in a local newspaper or church bulletin or deliver your data in an oral report to a civic or philanthropic organization. Encourage contributions to the American Red Cross, CARE, CARITAS, International Medical Corps, Mennonite Board of Missions, UNICEF, and World Concern.

Budget: Under $25

Sources:

"ACG Ethiopia Page," http//www.cs.indiana.edu/hyplan/dmulhollethiopia/ethiopia. html.

"ACG Somalia Page," http//www.cs.indiana.edu/hyplan/dmulhollSomalia/Somalia. html.

"Agriculture and Ethiopia's Development," http//etonline.netnation.comaddis-tri-bune/1997/03/20-03-97/editorial.html.

"Aid Donors Comment on Ethiopia's Reforms," http//www.worldbank.orghtml/extdr/ exte/afrl212.htm.

Electronic sources, including *Infotrac, Newsbank, Silver Platter, Africa Online,* and other Internet sources; the video *We Are the World.*

"Hunger and Poverty," http//www.plattsburgh.edu/legacyhunger_thesis.html.

"HungerWeb," http//www.brown.edu/Departments/World_HungerProgram/.

Mason, Paul, ed., *Atlas of Threatened Cultures*, Raintree/Steck-Vaughn, 1997.

"Somalia Somalia Somalia," http//www2.uic.edu/~aaffil/.

Alternative Applications: Use information about Somalia's famine to launch a club, church, or community project to help people trapped in a cycle of rebellion and political unrest, disease, starvation, migration, over-population, and death. Collect nonperishable food, dry milk, medicines, blankets, money, and volunteers to bring relief to the hopeless or support a child through Christian Children's Fund or social services in your area.

Human Relations Report Card

Age/Grade Level or Audience: All ages.

Description: Post a giant race relations report card.

Procedure: Utilize an electronic bulletin board, wall sign, banner, website, or other central location to post a community race relations report card. Select people of all races, ages, educational backgrounds, and income levels to participate on the evaluation committee. Have them consider the following points:

- ◆ number of community-sponsored events throughout the year
- ◆ museums, historic sites, and concerts featuring multicultural themes and offered free to the public
- ◆ sensitivity of press, television, and radio to racial issues, such as hiring practices, availability of public transportation, polling information, and health and economic resources
- ◆ percentage of non-whites appointed to standing committees, study commissions, and other honors
- ◆ non-white membership in civic clubs
- ◆ quality of educational facilities in all parts of town
- ◆ sports events featuring non-white players
- ◆ relationships between citizens and law enforcement officers and judges.

Budget: $50-$75

Sources:
Chamber of Commerce, League of Women Voters, or community relations committees.

Alternative Applications: Encourage the local newspaper editor to run the race relations report card in a February issue. Post an update within three to six months to show progress in weak areas, for example, minority hiring in city departments. Provide a wish list of items that would improve life for black citizens, such as stockpiles of emergency food and water, medicine, furniture, and clothing for disaster victims, telephone homework help, one-on-one tutorial services, organized activities and sports for young children, computer classes, AIDS and drug prevention, and mobile wellness clinics for infants, the handicapped, and the elderly.

Maasai Seasons

Age/Grade Level or Audience: High school or college literature, history, or sociology classes.

Description: Chart the seasons from the Maasai point of view.

Procedure: Have participants volunteer to submit information about various aspects of Maasai life as it reflects the seasons. Include the following details:

- ◆ acquiring firewood for July and August, the cold months
- ◆ anticipating May's short rains
- ◆ dressing meat for cooking
- ◆ drinking blood when milk is scarce
- ◆ feasting during initiation ceremonies
- ◆ going on retreat to garner strength for battle
- ◆ making useful items from horn, hides, and gourds
- ◆ moving herds to available water
- ◆ pasturing, branding, and tending cattle, goats, and sheep
- ◆ preparing to hunt game
- ◆ repairing fences and *kraals* or compounds
- ◆ repairing huts with dung after the November rainy season
- ◆ storing water for the May to October dry season
- ◆ watching for predators and rustlers

Budget: Under $25

Sources:

Anderson, David M., *Maasai People of Cattle*, Chronicle Books, 1995.
Bentsen, Cheryl, *Maasai Days*, Anchor Books, 1991.
Hetfield, Jamie, *Maasai of East Africa*, Rosen Group, 1996.
"KenyaWeb-People and Culture," httpwww.kenyaweb.com/peoplenilotes/maasai/maasai.html.
"Tom & Beth's Kenya Page-Maasai," http//www.blissites.comkenya/people/maasai.html.
Zeleza, Tiyambr, *Maasai*, Rosen Group, 1994.

Alternative Applications: Join with several partners to write a poem or song defining the periods of time that comprise the Maasai seasons. Alter tone and images to indicate hope and thanks to the gods for plenty of grass and rain. Chant your poem to the accompaniment of drum, flute, shekere, finger cymbals, scrapers, or thumb piano.

Mr. Johnson

Age/Grade Level or Audience: All ages.

Description: Study the film *Mr. Johnson.*

Procedure: Present the seriocomic film *Mr. Johnson.* Invite a panel to discuss themes in the movie, particularly colonial exploitation of West African people and the methods by which subject people adapt to colonialism.

Budget: Under $25

Sources:
The film *Mr. Johnson* (1991).
Gyekye, Kwame, *African Cultural Values: An Introduction,* Sankofa Publishing, 1996.
Kirk-Greene, Anthony, "Decolonisation in British Africa," *History Today* January 1992, 44-50.
Osterhammel, Jurgen, *Colonialism,* Wiener Publications Inc., 1996.

Alternative Applications: Have small groups consider various aspects of the filming of *Mr. Johnson,* which is set in Nigeria:

◆ bureaucracy	◆ clothing
◆ dance and entertainment	◆ food and hospitality
◆ Hausa hierarchy	◆ rites, ceremonies, and worship
◆ women's rights	◆ work styles and methods

Conclude the study with an explanation of Mr. Johnson's actions and the reasons he dies for his efforts. Compare with the videos *The Power of One, La Vie Est Belle, Heritage Africa, Daughters of the Dust, Sarafina!,* and *Come Back Africa.*

Out of Africa

Age/Grade Level or Audience: High school or college literature or mass media classes; book clubs.

Description: Discuss paternalistic attitudes toward African natives in Isak Dinesen's *Out of Africa.*

Procedure: Screen the video or film version of *Out of Africa,* and invite participants to sample some of Isak Dinesen's essays about life among the Kikuyu in her books *Out of Africa* and *Shadows on the Grass.* Lead a discussion of her attitude toward hiring, educating, healing, and defending the Kikuyu as English colonialism usurped increasing amounts of their land. Compare their status during the World War I era to current conditions.

Budget: $25-$50

Sources:
The film *Out of Africa* (1985).
Dinesen, Isak, *Out of Africa,* Putnam, 1937, reprinted, Crown, 1987.
———, *Shadows on the Grass,* Random House, 1961.
Thurman, Judith, *Isak Dinesen: The Life of a Storyteller,* St. Martin's Press, 1985.

Alternative Applications: Report on Karen Blixen's relationship with African neighbors. Contrast her coexistence and altruism with these visitors to Africa:

- ◆ animal activists Dian Fossey and Jane Goodall
- ◆ explorers Mungo Park, Henry Stanley, and David Livingstone
- ◆ medical missionary and minister Dr. Albert Schweitzer
- ◆ scientific investigators and paleontologists Louis, Mary, and Richard Leakey
- ◆ writers Joseph Conrad, Maya Angelou, and Ernest Hemingway

Peoples of Africa

Age/Grade Level or Audience: Middle school or high school sociology or history classes; adult study groups.

Description: Study the varied lifestyles of African peoples.

Procedure: Outline important aspects of African life. Include the following:

- ◆ adaptation to climate and topography
- ◆ extended families
- ◆ groups allied by marriage
- ◆ matrilineal and patrilineal descent
- ◆ population distribution
- ◆ sedentary vs. nomadic peoples

♦ stateless societies based on clan and kinship

♦ tribal societies

Keep a database of research information for future reference.

Budget: $25-$50

Sources:

Gyekye, Kwame, *African Cultural Values: An Introduction*, Sankofa Publishing, 1996.

Mason, Paul, ed., *Atlas of Threatened Cultures*, Raintree/Steck-Vaughn, 1997.

Owomoyela, Oyekan, *African Difference: Discourses on Africanity and the Relativity of Cultures*, P. Lang Publishers, 1996.

Alternative Applications: Have students draw comparisons between African lifestyles and other social groups, particularly the varied lifestyles of these groups:

♦ Australian aborigines

♦ Haitian refugees

♦ Kurds

♦ Montagnards and Hmong

♦ New Zealanders

♦ stateless Palestinians

♦ Gypsies and migrant workers

♦ Korea's divided people

♦ Lapps

♦ Native Americas

♦ Polynesians

The Rights of the Child

Age/Grade Level or Audience: High school and college sociology, history, and literature classes; civic and church groups.

Description: Organize a study of the United Nations Declaration of the Rights of the Child, adopted November 20, 1959.

Procedure: Lead a group discussion of the goal and effectiveness of the U.N. declaration which promises a better world to children. Comment on these tenets:

♦ Mankind owes the child the best it has to give.

♦ Children deserve equal treatment, regardless of race, sex, national origin, religion, and political background.

♦ Each should be protected and treated with dignity.

♦ Each deserves a name and nationality.

♦ Each has a right to care, nutrition, and medicine before and after birth.

♦ Handicapped children should receive special treatment and education.

   ◆ Each deserves loving, responsible parents.

   ◆ Each deserves free and compulsory education.

   ◆ Each deserves a chance to play and grow un the guidance of adults.

   ◆ Each should be protected from neglect, cruelty, and exploitation.

Compare these precepts with the ideas of Marian Wright Edelman.

Budget: Under $25

Sources:

Barn, Ravinder, *Black Children in the Public Care System*, Trafalgar, 1993.

"Black Family Heritage," http//www.afrinet.net/~hallhafrotalk/afroaug95/1894.hml.

"Black Pioneers," http//www.localnet.com/~adonis2/pioall.htm.

David, Jay, ed., *Growing Up Black: From Slave Days to the Present Twenty-five African-Americans Reveal the Trials and Triumphs of Their Childhoods*, Avon Books, 1992.

Newton, David E., *Gun Control: An Issue for the Nineties*, Enslow Publishers, 1992.

Alternative Applications: Discuss how these precepts have failed to protect the poor and abused of Somalia, South Africa, Haiti, Jamaica, the Dominican Republic, Antigua, and parts of the United States. Ask volunteers to join a panel to discuss key problems in child protection:

   ◆ early truancy and delinquency

   ◆ improper parenting and supervision

   ◆ incomplete immunization against serious disease

   ◆ irregular or absent preventative health care and medical treatment

   ◆ lack of quality reading materials and entertainment

   ◆ limited aspirations

   ◆ malnutrition

   ◆ poor self-image

   ◆ random shootings and other unpredictable forms of violence

  Stayin' Alive

Age/Grade Level or Audience: High school or college sociology or psychology classes; adult study groups.

Description: Lead a study of coping mechanisms that enabled slaves to endure bondage.

Procedure: Discuss in small groups the efficacy of these methods:

◆ breaking tools

◆ crippling horses and wagons

◆ deliberately losing, hiding, or dropping into a river important equipment and tools

◆ fouling wells and cisterns

◆ joking and lampooning

◆ leaving gates and fences open so animals could wander

◆ leaving the spigots of kegs open

◆ organizing sit-down strikes and other forms of mutiny

◆ poisoning or murdering overseers and masters

◆ pretending to be dimwitted, sick, hard of hearing, or obsequious and sub-servient

◆ punishing or killing black turncoats and spies

◆ sabotaging farm machinery and chimneys

◆ self-mutilation of toes, fingers, eyes, and teeth

◆ setting fires to barns, silos, warehouses, or ripening cane and cotton fields

◆ singing folk rhymes, ironic work songs, spirituals, and hymns

◆ telling symbolic stories, particularly the Uncle Remus fables

◆ untying boats from their moorings

◆ use of code names, such as Moses and the children of Israel for the underground railroad conductor and escapees or Canaan for Canada

◆ using a light-skinned slave as a cover for an escape

Budget: Under $25

Sources:

Best, Felton O., *Black Resistance: Movements in the United States and Africa, 1800-1993 Oppression and Retaliation*, E. Mellen, 1995.

Brunvand, Jan Harold, ed., *American Folklore: An Encyclopedia*, Garland, 1996.

Alternative Applications: Read aloud from slave narratives and rhymes that exemplify coping mechanisms. For instance, in his memoir, Peter Randolph describes an exchange with his master:

"Pompey, how do I look?"

"Oh, massa, mighty!"

"What do you mean by 'mighty,' Pompey?"

"Why, Massa you look noble."

"What do you mean by 'noble'?"

"Why, sar, you look just like one lion."

"Why, Pompey, where have you ever seen a lion?"

"I seen one down in yonder field the other day, massa."

"Pompey, you foolish fellow, that was a jackass."

"Was it, massa? Well you look just like him."

An ironic rhyme recited by William Wells Brown in *My Southern Home* depicts the slave blend of dialect, good humor, and satire:

> De big bee flies high,
> De little bee makes de honey,
> De black man raise de cotton,
> An' de white man gets de money.

A more pointed rhyme, recounted in William Wells Brown's *Clotel* describes the glee of slaves celebrating the master's death:

> Hang up the shovel and the hoe—
> Take down the fiddle and the bow.
> Old master has gone to the slaveholder's rest;
> He has gone where they all ought to go.

Conclude with a tribute to black history from the final chapter of Eldridge Cleaver's *Soul on Ice:*

> I watched the Slaver's lash of death slash through the
> opposing air and bite with teeth of fire into your delicate
> flesh, the black and tender flesh of African Motherhood,
> forcing the startled Life untimely from your torn and out-
> raged womb, the sacred womb that cradled primal man,
> the womb that incubated Ethiopia and populated Nubia and
> gave forth Pharaohs unto Egypt, the womb that painted the
> Congo black and mothered Zulu, the womb of Mero, the womb
> of the Nile, of the Niger, the womb of Songhay, of Mali, of
> Ghana, the womb that felt the might of Chaka before he saw
> the sun.

"Stop the Drugs" Campaign

Age/Grade Level or Audience: All ages.

Description: Organize a "Stop the Drugs" campaign.

Procedure: Sponsor a writing contest requiring students to state in 2,000 words or less the physical, moral, and psychological damage of alcohol and illegal drugs in a community. Emphasize the damage to the unborn, particularly fetal alcohol syndrome and crack babies. Make the connection between AIDS and shared needles. Offer prizes for winning contributions in three divisions—children, teens, and adults.

Budget: $50-$75

Sources:

Drug Crime, Chelsea House, 1996.

Washburne, Carolyn K., *Drug Abuse*, Lucent Books, 1996.

Wilson, Richard W., and Cheryl A. Kolander, *Drug Abuse Prevention: A School and Community Partnership*, Addison-Wesley, 1996.

Wittenberg, Erica, *Drug Proofing the Family: A Guide for Parents*, revised edition, Do It Now, 1995.

Alternative Applications: Assist science students in creating anti-drug, gun, alcohol, and tobacco projects for science fairs. Consider the following topics:

- ◆ alcoholism as substance abuse
- ◆ cocaine and respiration
- ◆ designer drugs and their effects on the nervous system
- ◆ emotional problems among the children of alcoholics
- ◆ guns and violence
- ◆ marijuana and its debilitation of users' offspring
- ◆ Methadone and recidivism
- ◆ methods of ending drug dependency
- ◆ poverty and street gangs
- ◆ smoking and cancer of the lip and tongue
- ◆ smoking and its effects on the unborn

Support each project with charts and graphs divided by race, age, sex, and location.

Studying the Bones

Age/Grade Level or Audience: College religion classes.

Description: Demonstrate the Zulu method of divination.

Procedure: Explain how Zulu diviners studied the animal ankle and knuckle bones, fruit pits, seeds, shells, bits of glass, horn, ivory, fangs, wooden carvings, claws, beaks, hooves, stones, and coins to make predictions about marriage, work, planting, dream interpretation, and spirits. Comment on the importance of these elements:

- ◆ selection of the correct pieces to make up a set of thirteen
- ◆ protecting the pieces
- ◆ designation of five special bones man, woman, warrior, chief, and cattle
- ◆ determination of purpose, whether to heal, interpret, advise, or curse
- ◆ phrasing a question for the bones to answer
- ◆ chanting or crooning to accompany a trance
- ◆ shaking the container

◆ blowing four breaths on the pieces
◆ pouring out the pieces onto a table or mat
◆ choosing pieces that are worth reading and pieces that refuse to cooperate
◆ assessment of location and spacing of bones
◆ counting the points, which carry these messages:

1. Freedom
2. Separation
3. good sign
4. Cooperation
5. Caution
6. strength and wisdom
7. trust God
8. prepare for a fight
9. creativity
10. wish fulfillment
11. communion with spirits
12. abundance
13. harmony

Budget: Under $25

Sources:

Brunvand, Jan Harold, ed., *American Folklore: An Encyclopedia*, Garland, 1996.
"Religions of the World: African Religions," http//jupiter.rowan.edu~banner/afrterm.html.
Ulufudu, *The Zulu Bone Oracle*, Wingbow Press, 1989.

Alternative Applications: Contrast the use of bone oracles with other types of divination, for example I Ching, Tarot, Ouija, nature lore, seances, palmistry, reading tea leaves, phrenology, astrology, dream interpretation, and ancient Roman systems of studying the flight of birds and the pattern of smoke in the sky.

Voting Patterns

Age/Grade Level or Audience: High school or college sociology, civics, black studies, or American history classes.

Description: Study the racial voting patterns in your area.

Procedure: Study factors affecting the racial voting patterns of your city, county, and state. Note periods when voter registration was heaviest and comment on these and other influential factors:

- ◆ emergence of bloc voting
- ◆ campaigns to enlist registration
- ◆ college drives to attract young voters
- ◆ distribution of materials on local issues
- ◆ mobile registration sites
- ◆ neighborhood advertising encouraging involvement

Budget: Under $25

Sources:

League of Women Voters, NAACP, courthouse records, almanacs and legislative records, local registrars, newspaper articles.

Alternative Applications: Generate a report on subjects including bloc voting, liberal vs. conservative candidates, one-issue voters, Christian Coalition, Rainbow Coalition, and hate crimes, church burning, and other forms of overt racism. Interview people who vote consistently and find out how their attitudes toward participation have varied over time. Present your findings in a series of school or local newspaper articles.

Welcoming Black Leaders

Age/Grade Level or Audience: Elementary and middle school writing and history classes.

Description: Welcome leaders from African and Caribbean nations to the United States.

Procedure: Take turns role-playing a formal welcome to a dignitary from a predominantly black nation, for example, Gabon, Haiti, Jamaica, or Guyana. Give an overview of the racial advancement of the past fifty years. Name particular accomplishments of the dignitary.

Budget: Under $25

Sources:

Almanacs and online sources that list countries and their leaders.

Africa: A Lonely Planet Shoestring Guide, Lonely Planet, 1995.

"African Language Sites," http//polyglot.lss.wisc.edu/lss/lang/africanhtml.

"Africa Online," http//www.africaonline.com.

Alternative Applications: Design banners to welcome foreign dignitaries from black nations. Include national flags, mottoes, and banners displaying words of welcome in the nation's language, for example, "Jambo" in Swahili.

 ## Who Does the Work?

Age/Grade Level or Audience: High school or college sociology, economics, or labor history classes.

Description: Research statistics on the types of jobs held by black Americans.

Procedure: Study the labor markets that are traditionally open to black workers. Research these economic periods:

- ◆ Depression
- ◆ Eisenhower Era
- ◆ Great Society
- ◆ post-World War II boom
- ◆ Reconstruction

Separate data by sex, age, state, and other factors, such as handicaps, skilled, semi-skilled, professional, unskilled, rural, suburban, and urban. Use this study to launch a local campaign to improve job opportunities for black workers. Present findings to key personnel managers, job fair coordinators, and school counselors.

Budget: Under $25

Sources:
Brown, Tony, *Black Labor-White Wealth: The Search for Economic Justice*, Duncan & Duncan, 1994.
Coleman, Jonathan, *A Long Way to Go*, Atlantic Monthly Press, 1997.
Smith, Jesse Carney and Robert L. Johns, *Statistical Record of Black Americans*, 3rd edition, Gale, 1995.
Simon, David, and Edward Burns, *The Corner*, Broadway Books, 1997.

Alternative Applications: Invite black entrepreneurs, lawyers, teachers, scholars, engineers, doctors, dentists, accountants, and other authority figures to compile advice to young people seeking to break out of stereotypical black jobs. Distribute the information through school and job counselors, ministers, libraries, and the Chamber of Commerce.

Speech, Debate, and Drama

Acting Out Black Poetry

Age/Grade Level or Audience: Middle school or high school literature class.

Description: Improvise scenes from a poem by a black author.

Procedure: Have students read a variety of works by black poets. Assign groups to select a pictorial poem to act out or pantomime. Choose from these titles:

- Nikki Giovanni, "The Funeral of Martin Luther King, Jr."
- Paul Laurence Dunbar, "My Sort o' Man"
- Lucille Clifton, "Good Times"
- Fenton Johnson, "A Negro Peddler's Song"
- Gwendolyn Brooks, "The Chicago Defender Sends a Man to Little Rock, Fall, 1957"-
- Melvin B. Tolson, "Dark Symphony"
- Richard Wright, "Between the World and Meff"
- Mari E. Evans, "When in Rome"
- Langston Hughes, "The Negro Speaks of Rivers"
- Margaret Walker, "For My People"

Budget: Under $25

Sources:
Gates, Henry Louis, gen. ed., *The Norton Anthology of African American Literature*, W. W. Norton & Co., 1997.

Halliburton, Warren J., *Historic Speeches of African Americans,* Franklin Watts, 1993.

Hudson, Wade, *Pass It On: African-American Poetry for Children,* Scholastic, Inc., 1993.

Killens, John Oliver, and Jerry W., Ward, Jr., eds., *Black Southern Voices: An Anthology of Fiction, Poetry, Drama, Nonfiction, and Critical Essays,* Meridian Books, 1992.

Linthwaite, Illone, ed., *Ain't I a Woman: A Book of Women's Poetry from Around the World,* Wings Books, 1993.

Rubin, Janet E., and Margaret Merrion, *Creative Drama and Music Methods,* Linnet Books, 1996.

Alternative Applications: Choose a scene or vignette to act out or pantomime. Select from the work of a black playwright or novelist, particularly Terry McMillan, William Armstrong, Zora Neale Hurston, Walter Dean Myers, Alice Childress, John Williams, or Lorraine Hansberry.

Action and Words

Originator: Theodore Shorack, teacher, Los Angeles, California.

Age/Grade Level or Audience: Kindergarten and elementary school students; PTA and parent night programs; religious schools; scout, 4-H, and other club programs.

Description: Teach young children to recite and act out the poem "Boats, Boats."

Procedure: Have students perform the following actions as they recite Theodore Shorack's "Boats, Boats." Note the gestures for the group and for its student leader.

> Boats, Boats
> Boats, boats off the coast,
> robbing Africans of what they love most.
> (rowing; leader shading eyes and gazing toward shore)
> Chains, chains, choking their throats
> packed in tight on the slavery boats.
> *(pulling at chains on throats; leader raising hands to the sky)*
> Dollars, dollars, the auctioneer hollers.
> White men taking Blacks by their collars.
> *(counting out money; leader stuffing bills into imaginery wallet)*
> Whip, whip, they long to break free,

doing what they can to escape and flee.

(lashing out with imaginary whips; leader cowering in pain and fear)

North, north follow that star,

safe in the darkness, traveling far.

(looking skyward; leader pointing to the North Star)

Danger, danger, during the day,

hound dogs and hunters along the way.

(holding hands up like dog ears and lolling their tongues; leader

guiding an imaginery dog by a leash)

Train, train, not on a rail,

Going house to house on the freedom trail.

(circular chugging motions; leader knocking on door)

Home, home, where can that be?

North in Canada, they can be free!

(hugging each other; leader waving to audience)

Invite students to create new verses which follow the same pattern of repetition, rhythm, mimicry, and rhyme.

Budget: Under $25

Sources:

Original verse.

Hudson, Wade, *Pass It On: African-American Poetry for Children*, Scholastic, Inc., 1993.

Linthwaite, Illona, ed., *Ain't I a Woman?: A Book of Women's Poetry from Around the World*, Wings Books, 1987.

Alternative Applications: Organize an elementary or middle school group to decide on gestures and dramatization for a choral reading of "Remember the Preacher-man."

Remember the Preacher-man

On a bus rode a woman named Rosa Parks.

'had to give up her seat because her skin was dark.

A white man saw Rosa in a seat he desired, but she wouldn't get up-she said, "my feet are tired!" The driver-man said, "you're going to jail, unless you give that seat to the man who's pale!".-~ So she went to jail-as if she'd done something bad.

Black folks in Montgomery were fighting mad.

A young preacher-man, Dr. Martin Luther King, said, "Rosa, my friend, you did the right thing!" He told all the Black folks who were ready to fight, "Let's get what we deserve, but let's do it right." Dr. King knew his history-indeed, he was a scholar.

He said, "Don't fight with guns; trust the Lord and use the dollar. " So dark-skinned people chose to walk instead of ride

and the buses lost the battle to a growing Black pride. There were many more battles and many remain today. Sharing his dream of justice, Dr. King led the way. But the power of hate couldn't resist temptation while this man of love was changing a nation. While he was taking his dream to Memphis town, a white man with a rifle gunned the peaceful man down. Now as we decide how to do the right thing, remember the preacher-man, Dr. Martin Luther King.

Africa's Liberation

Age/Grade Level or Audience: High school or college speech, drama, language classes; banquets, civic meetings, church assemblies; Toastmaster's Club.

Description: Present a speech on the evolving freedom among African countries.

Procedure: Deliver an address covering the liberation of African countries. Include the following details:

- ◆ On March 6, 1957, Ghana evolved from the former Gold Coast and three years later became a republic.
- ◆ Gambia dropped its colonial ties with England and became a free nation on February 18, 1965.
- ◆ On March 12, 1968, the island of Mauritius abandoned 158 years of British control and declared independence.
- ◆ Uganda evolved slowly, freeing itself of British control in 1962, but requiring five more years to become a republic.
- ◆ Also slow to achieve freedom, Zimbabwe struggled against British control from 1966 to 1972 and claimed independence on April 18, 1980.
- ◆ Breaking with Rhodesia, Zambia became a republic on October 24, 1964.
- ◆ After ending Belgian control in the Congo on June 30, 1960, the nation named Zaire suffered tribal squabbles until 1965.
- ◆ Zanzibar threw off British rule in 1961 and, as Tangan ylka, became independent.
- ◆ German Togoland became a free Republic on April 27, 1960.
- ◆ Free of its miserable history as a source of slaves, Nigeria embraced freedom on October 1, 1960.
- ◆ In 1958, Guinea voted to separate itself from French control.
- ◆ Gabon, also a French possession, became free on August 17, 1960.
- ◆ Another French territory, Chad achieved freedom in 1960.
- ◆ Upper Volta, which separated from French control in 1960, adopted the name Burkina Faso on August 4, 1984.

◆ Following four years of turmoil, Burundi stabilized as a republic in 1966.

◆ The former Bechuanaland, once controlled by the British, became the free nation of Botswana in 1966.

◆ The former Dahomey suffered repeated uprisings until 1975, when it achieved independence and was named Benin.

◆ On February 11, 1990, Nelson Mandela gained his freedom after 27 years imprisonment.

◆ In February 1991, President De Klerk announced an end to racial segregation in South Africa.

◆ In June 1991, the Race Registration law was repealed.

◆ In 1992, Nelson Mandela toured the United States to raise funds to fight Apartheid.

◆ In 1993, all factions began planning a new constitution.

◆ In 1994, Nelson Mandela was elected president of South Africa.

Read aloud from books and magazine articles describing rigid laws affecting land ownership, inheritance, schools, public transportation, government representation, medical care, and marriage. Lead a discussion of the moral implications of a political and social system that allowed a white minority to tyrannize a black majority.

Budget: Under $25

Sources:

Films *Cry Freedom* (1987), *The Power of One (1991),* and *Sarafina! (1992)*

Bayly, C A, *Atlas of the British Empire,* Hamlyn Publishing, 1989.

Curtin, P. D., *African History,* 2nd edition, Addison-Wesley, 1995.

"The Freedom Charter," http://www.anc.org.za/ancdocs/history/charter.html.

Grun, Bernard, *The Timetables of History: A Horizontal Linkage of People and Events,* Simon & Schuster, 1991.

"The History of Apartheid in South Africa," http://xenon.stanford.edu/~cale/cs201/ apartheid.hiss.html.

"Instruments of Apartheid," http://www.unp.actza/UNPDepartments/politics/price4. htm.

Jackson, John G., *Introduction to African Civilizations,* Citadel Press, 1994.

Mandela, Nelson, *The Long Walk to Freedom: The Autobiography of Nelson Mandela,* Little, Brown, 1994.

Mostert, Noel, *Frontiers: The Epic South Africa's Creation and the Tragedy of the Xhosa People,* Knopf, 1992.

Seavers, Corbin, *Apartheid: The Untold Story,* United Brothers and Sisters, 1997.

Alternative Applications: Select individuals to describe each nation's struggle in a short presentation. Arrange the program in the order of each country's liberation. Include details about colonial history, languages, peoples, customs, leaders, flags, natural resources, and current outlook. As each contributor concludes, pin the colored shape of the country to a blank map of Africa.

At Home in Africa

Age/Grade Level or Audience: Pre-school and kindergarten classes.

Description: Have students describe their lives as African animals.

Procedure: Display pictures, read stories, or show videos or filmstrips about African animals. Have students select an animal with which to identify. Have each participant answer the following questions:

- ◆ What color are you?
- ◆ What do you eat?
- ◆ Where do you live?
- ◆ What do you do all day?

Budget: $25-$50

Sources:

"African Wildlife News," http://www.awf.org/nf.ele.numbers.html.

Arnold, Caroline, *African Animals,* Morrow Junior Books, 1997.

Butterfield, Moira, *Big, Rough, and Wrinkly (What Am I),* Raintree/SteckVaughn, 1997.

Hartmann, Wendy, *One Sun Rises: An African Wildlife Counting Book,* Dutton Child Books, 1994.

Kingdon, Jonathan, *Island Africa: The Evolution of Africa's Rare Animals and Plants,* Princeton University Press, 1992.

"Marine World Africa USA," http://www.freerun.com/napavalley/outdoor/marinewo/marinewo.html.

Pinter, Helmut. *African Grey Parrots ... as a Hobby,* T. F. H. Publications, 1995.

Pringle, Laurence P., *Elephant Woman: Exploring the World of Elephants,* Atheneum, 1997.

"Spook's Elephant Gallery," http://sailfish.exis.net/~spook/ele.html.

Theroux, Paul, "Down the Zambezi," *National Geographic,* October 1997, 231.

Williams, Wendy, "Of Elephants and Men," *Animals,* November/December 1997, 24-30.

Alternative Applications: Have each student select an African animal to have as an imaginary pet. Distribute art supplies so that students can create the following drawings:

- ◆ a home for the pet
- ◆ a bath and pedicure
- ◆ a collar and leash
- ◆ competition at an African pet show
- ◆ feeding time
- ◆ brushing, combing, fluffing
- ◆ training

Attitudes and Issues

Age/Grade Level or Audience: All ages.

Description: Hold a public forum on community harmony and racial animosity.

Procedure: Open the session with a videotape of Bill Moyers's documentary *Beyond Hate*, featuring Jimmy Carter, Myrlie Evers, and John Kenneth Galbraith. Conclude with an open forum to air local opinions and address mutual problems, such as crime, ghettos, and city and county hiring practices. Carry the project to completion with a series of responses on a civic website, in local newspapers, and on radio and television talk shows.

Budget: $25-$50

Sources:
The videos *Beyond Hate, Hate on Trial,* and *Facing Hate.*

Alternative Applications: Conduct a week-long forum, including videotapes *Hate on Trial,* featuring white supremacists Tom and John Metzger, and *Facing Hate,* a discussion between Bill Moyers and Dr. Elie Wiesel, survivor of the Auschwitz and Buchenwald death camps and winner of the 1988 Nobel Peace Prize. Involve local students in a concluding discussion of why hate continues to resurface, impeding human progress and harmony.

Benjamin Franklin and Slavery

Age/Grade Level or Audience: High school or college speech, history, or writing classes.

Description: Discuss Benjamin Franklin's condemnation of slavery.

Procedure: Have students form small groups to discuss the following comments from an address on November 9, 1798, to the Pennsylvania Society for Promoting the Abolition of Slavery and the Relief of Free Negroes Unlawfully Held in Bondage, in which the group's president, Benjamin Franklin, castigated the Constitutional Convention for failing to include Thomas Jefferson's antislavery proposal. Emphasize these lines:

◆ Slavery is such an atrocious abasement of human nature, that its very extirpation, if not performed with solicitous care, may sometimes open a source of serious evils.

◆ The unhappy man, who has long been treated as a brute animal, too frequently sinks beneath the common standard of the human species. The galling chains that bind his body do also fetter his intellectual faculties, and impair the social affections of his heart.

◆ Accustomed to move like a mere machine, by the will of a master, reflection is suspended; he has not the power of choice; and reason and conscience have but little influence over his conduct because he is chiefly governed by the passion of fear.

◆ He is poor and friendless; perhaps worn out by extreme labor, age, and disease.

Budget: Under $25

Sources:

Jennings, Francis, *Benjamin Franklin, Politician: The Mask and the Man,* Norton, 1996.

Mabunda. L. Mpho, ed., *The African American Almanac,* 7th edition, Gale, 1997.

Middlekauff, Robert, *Benjamin Franklin and His Enemies,* University of California Press, 1996.

Alternative Applications: Have students make a brief oral explanation of the method by which abolitionists could alleviate the following difficulties inherent in manumission:

◆ how to teach slaves to utilize their freedom
◆ how to train former slaves for the labor market
◆ how to provide employment suitable to people of different ages, sexes, and talents
◆ how to provide education to black children
◆ how to protect newly freed blacks from racist violence

 Black Philosophies

Age/Grade Level or Audience: High school or college American history or speech class or debate society.

Description: Have students present opinion papers supporting or refuting the views of controversial black leaders.

Procedure: Have students study the speeches, essays, and philosophies of famous black leaders, particularly these:

Mary McLeod Bethune	Carol Moseley-Braun
Claude Brown	H. Rap Brown
Blanche Kelso Bruce	Ralph Bunche
Stokely Carmichael	Ben Carson
Shirley Chisholm	Eldridge Cleaver
Angela Davis	Frederick Douglass
Rita Dove	W. E. B. Du Bois
Marian Wright Edelman	Joycelyn Elders
Louis Farrakhan	Henry Highland Garnet
Marcus Garvey	Anita Hill
Jesse Jackson	Barbara Jordan
Martin Luther King, Jr.	Spike Lee
Thurgood Marshall	Adam Clayton Powell, Jr.
Colin Powell	Mary Church Terrell
Clarence Thomas	Sojourner Truth
Harriet Tubman	Booker T. Washington
Faye Wattleton	Ida Wells-Barnett
George H. White	Malcolm X
Whitney M. Young, Jr.	

Encourage each student to select an idea to support or refute by logic and example.

Budget: Under $25

Sources:

Asante, Molefi *K., Historical and Cultural Atlas of African Americans,* Macmillan, 1991.

"Black History," http://www.slip.net/~rigged/history.html.

"Black History Month: Let's Get Started," http://www.netnoir.com/spotlight/bhm/jbhm.html.

Corbin, Raymond M., *1,999 Facts about Blacks: A Sourcebook of African-American Achievement,* 2nd edition, Madison Books, 1997.

Dennis, Denise, *Black History for Beginners,* Highsmith, 1992.

Elliot, Jeffrey *M., Encyclopedia of African-American Politics,* ABC-Clio, 1997.

Fitch, Suzanne Pullon, and Roseann M. Mandziuk, *Sojourner Truth As Orator: Wit, Story, and Song,* Greenwood, 1997.

Harris, Robert L. Jr., *African American History in the Press, 1851-1899,* Gale, 1996.

Hine, Darlene Clark, Elsa Barkley Brown, and Rosalyn Terborg-Penn, *Black Women in America: An Historical Encyclopedia,* Carlson Publishing, 1993.

Mabunda, L. Mpho, ed., *The African American Almanac,* 7th edition, Gale, 1997.

McKinley, James C., Jr., "A Black Panther's Mellow Exile: Farming in Africa," *New York Times,* November 23, 1997, 3.

Saari, Peggy, and Daniel B. Baker, *Explorers and Discoverers: From Alexander the Great to Sally Ride,* U•X•L/Gale, 1995.

Shapiro, William E., ed., *The Kingfisher Young People's Encyclopedia of the United States.,* Larousse Kingfisher Chambers, 1994.

Straub, Deborah Gillan, ed., *African American Voices,* U•X•L/Gale, 1996.

Taylor, Kimberly H., *Black Civil Rights Champions,* Oliver Press, 1995.

"This Person in Black History: Thurgood Marshall," http://www.ai.mit.edu/~isbell/ Hfh/black/events_and_people/OO1.thurgood_marshall.

Alternative Applications: Pair students who choose opposite sides of a particular issue, such as the Back to Africa movement, black pride, nonviolence, gun control, neighborhood schools, Million Man March, Million Woman March, Black Power, leadership of Louis Farrakhan, or the rise of the Nation of Islam. Organize a formal debate that focuses on the black point of view. Videotape the results and discuss the strengths and weaknesses of each participant.

Black Sentiments

Originator: Leatrice Pearson, teacher, Lenoir, North Carolina.

Age/Grade Level or Audience: Middle school or high school college literature or drama classes; drama or literary societies.

Description: Have participants use quotations as springboards to oral interpretation, skits, or dialogues.

Procedure: Consider the following examples:

♦ "So de white man throw down de load and tell de nigger man tuh pick it up. He pick it up because he have to, but he don't tote it. He hand it to his womenfolks. De nigger woman is de mule uh de world so fur as she can see ..." (from Zora Neale Hurston's Their Eyes Were Watching God)

♦ "Power concedes nothing without demand. It never did and never will. People might not get all that they work for in this world, but they must certainly work for all they get." (Frederick Douglass)

♦ "So Baby's eight children had six fathers ... what she called nastiness of life was the shock she received upon learning that nobody stopped playing checkers just because the pieces included her children ..." (from Toni Morrison's *Beloved*)

♦ "Racism seems ageless, like the passion of those who war against it." (Gordon Parks)

- ◆ "A cynical young person is almost the saddest sight to see, because it means that he or she has gone from knowing nothing to believing nothing." (Maya Angelou)
- ◆ "Black people are the only segment in American society that is defined by its weakest elements. Every other segment is defined by its highest achievement." (Jewell Jackson McCabe)
- ◆ "Service is the rent that you pay for room on this earth." (Shirley Chisholm)
- ◆ "Never take a step backward or you never stop running." (W. E. B. Du Bois)
- ◆ "The better we feel about ourselves, the fewer times we have to knock somebody down in order to stand on top of their bodies and feel tall." (Odetta)

Budget: Under $25

Sources:

Edelman, Marian Wright, *Guide My Feet: Prayers and Meditations on Loving and Working for Children,* Beacon Press, 1995.

————, "We Must Not Lose What We Knew Was Right Then," *Ebony,* November 1995.

Maggio, Rosalie, *The New Beacon Book of Quotations by Women,* Beacon Press, 1996.

Mullane, Deirdre, *Words to Make My Dream Children Live: A Book of African American Quotations,* Anchor Books, 1995.

Pitts, Barbara, "Reading, Writing, and Freedom" (play), *Scholastic Storyworks,* September 1997, 26-30.

Riley, Dorothy Winbush, *My Soul Looks Back, 'Less I Forget: A Collection of Quotations by People of Color,* Harper Perennial, 1993.

Alternative Applications: Organize an extemporaneous speaking contest as a part of Black History Month. Use the citations above as a free selection of prompts for three-minute impromptu responses. Assign points to contestants based on these criteria:

- ◆ composure
- ◆ coverage of theme
- ◆ gestures
- ◆ posture
- ◆ stage presence
- ◆ concrete examples
- ◆ eye contact
- ◆ organization
- ◆ solid conclusion

The Demands of Frederick Douglass

Originator: Leatrice Pearson, teacher, Lenoir, North Carolina.

Age/Grade Level or Audience: High school and college debate teams; community forums; civic clubs; newspaper editors.

Description: Discuss the merits of Frederick Douglass's speech in Washington, D.C., April, 1883.

Procedure: Read aloud Douglass's call to action:

> If we find, we shall have to seek. If we succeed in the race of life, it must be by our own energies and our own exertions. Others may clear the road, but we must go forward or be left behind ... What Abraham Lincoln said in respect of the United States is as true of the colored people as of the relations of those states. They cannot remain half slave and half free. You must give them all or take from them all. Until this half-and half condition is ended, there will be just ground of complaint.

Debate with a small group whether African Americans have reached the state of progress and acceptance to which Frederick Douglass addressed his remarks.

Budget: Under $25

Sources:
Asante, Molefi K., and Mark T. Mattson, *Historical and Cultural Atlas of African Americans,* Macmillan, 1992.

Douglass, Frederick, *Autobiographies,* Library of America, 1994.

———, "I Hear the Mournful Wail of Millions," *A Treasury of the World's Great Speeches,* Houston Peterson, ed., Simon & Schuster, 1965.

———. *Narrative of the Life of Frederick Douglass, an American Slave, Written by Himself,* New American Library, 1968.

———, "Speech to the American Anti-Slavery Society" and "What to the Slave Is the Fourth of July?," *The American Reader: Words That Moved a Nation,* HarperCollins, 1990.

"Frederick Douglass," http://www.webcom.com/~bright/source/ fdougla.htm.

"Frederick Douglass and John Brown," http://jefferson.village.virginia.ed/jbrown/douglass.html.

Rice, Alan, "Portrait of Frederick Douglass," http://www.keele.ac.uk/depts/as/Portraits/ rice.douglass.html.

Thomas, Velma Maia, *Lest We Forget: The Passage from Africa to Slavery and Emancipation,* Crown, 1997.

Alternative Applications: Assign small groups to discuss or debate other statements by Douglass and their applicability to current racial tensions. For example:

> ◆ Go where you may, search where you will, roam through all the monarchies and despotisms of the Old World, travel through South America, search out every abuse, and when you have found the last, lay your facts by the side of the everyday practices of this nation, and you will say with

me that for revolting barbarity and shameless hypocrisy, America reigns without a rival. (Independence Day Speech, Rochester, New York, 1852)

◆ Slavery has been fruitful in giving itself names. It has been called "the peculiar institution," "the social system," and the "impediment," as it was called by the General Conference of the Methodist Episcopal Church. It has been called by a great many names, and it will call itself by yet another name; and you and I and all of us had better wait and see what new form this old monster will assume, in what new skin this old snake will come forth. (Speech to the American Anti-Slavery Society, Boston, Massachusetts, May 10, 1865)

◆ We hold it to be self-evident that no class or color should be the exclusive rulers of this country. If there is such a ruling class, there must of course be a subject class, and when this condition is once established this Government of the people, by the people and for the people, will have perished from the earth. (Speech at the National Convention of Colored Men, Louisville, Kentucky, September 24, 1883)

Dramatizing the Black Experience

Age/Grade Level or Audience: High school and college drama classes; community and church theater groups.

Description: Have participants rewrite famous scripts of dramatic, comic, musical, and history plays from the black point of view.

Procedure: Have students view videotapes or read the scripts of stage and Hollywood classics, such as these:

You Can't Take It With You	*1776*
The Music Man	*Jesus Christ Superstar*
I Remember Mama	*Cat on a Hot Tin Roof*
Les Misérables	*A Streetcar Named Desire*
The King and I	*Oklahoma*
Citizen Kane	*Fiddler on the Roof*
Harvey	*South Pacific*
Camelot	*Romeo and Juliet*
Midsummer Night's Dream	*The Sound of Music*
Spartacus	*Ben Hur*
Cyrano	*Lassie*
It's a Wonderful Life	*Cinderella*
Snow White	

Organize a group of volunteer scriptwriters to reset and recast the production to feature black people, themes, and settings. Put on skits or a full production of the script. Advertise the shift in point of view through posters, radio and television spots, e-mail, websites, and handbills. Videotape the performance.

Budget: $25-$50

Sources:

Tapes from video rental services.

Asante, Molefi K., and Mark T. Mattson, *Historical and Cultural Atlas of African Americans*, Macmillan, 1992.

Rubin, Janet E., and Margaret Merrion, *Creative Drama and Music Methods,* Linnet Books, 1996.

Straub, Deborah Gillan, ed., *African American Voices,* U•X•L/Gale, 1996.

Taylor, Kimbelry H., *Black Civil Rights Champions,* Oliver Press, 1995.

"This Person in Black History," http://www.ai.mit.edu/~isbell/Hfh/black/events_and_people.

Alternative Applications: Have a student group brainstorm ways of increasing black roles in television and movie production, news gathering and reporting, sportscasting, and newspaper and magazine production. For example:

- ◆ encourage debating societies that feature questions of black welfare and culture
- ◆ establish black reading theaters
- ◆ organize Toastmaster's Clubs in black areas
- ◆ establish a multicultural storytelling club
- ◆ create black history pages for children's magazines such as *Cricket, Cobblestone, National Geographic World, Ranger Rick,* and *Hopscotch*
- ◆ deliver television and radio editorials and political commentary from the black perspective
- ◆ comment on high school sports events for local radio and television stations

 Experiencing the Underground Railroad

Age/Grade Level or Audience: High school or college language and drama classes; religious schools.

Description: Pantomime slaves escaping to the North.

Procedure: Explain to the group that a network of 3,200 people formed the Underground Railroad, which, from 1830 to 1860, led 2,500 slaves per year toward safety. Many died along the way from hunger, cold, wounds, falls, despair, or drowning; some were recaptured and returned to slavery. Many more built new lives for themselves in free states or Canada. Let students select a role from the numerous possibilities of this movement, including bystander, reporter, traveler, farmer, doctor, minister, leader, parent, aged slave, child, patroller, slave catcher, sheriff, Quaker or Mennonite abolitionist, station master, conductor, overseer, and plantation owner. Include the following scenes:

- ◆ intolerable slave conditions, such as the separation of families, hard labor, dangerous jobs, disease, and inadequate clothing, food, and shelter
- ◆ planning an escape
- ◆ gathering information from knowledgeable and trustworthy sources
- ◆ storing food and supplies for the journey
- ◆ making a getaway
- ◆ moving through forests and swamps or over rivers
- ◆ hopping trains or wagons
- ◆ locating roots, nuts, berries, grain, fruit, and mushrooms for food
- ◆ quietly snaring animals and birds
- ◆ staying warm, dry, and well
- ◆ treating wounds, illness, or crying infants
- ◆ hiding while sleeping
- ◆ getting directions and following the North Star
- ◆ avoiding patrollers, dogs, and slave catchers
- ◆ wearing a disguise
- ◆ locating a conductor and station house
- ◆ acquiring a fake pass or papers of manumission
- ◆ establishing a new home
- ◆ learning to read
- ◆ finding work
- ◆ reuniting with lost relatives and friends

Budget: Under $25

Sources:

"Abolition, " http:/rs7.Ioc.gov/exhibits/african/abol.html.

Badt, Karin L., *Underground Railroad: A Play in Three Acts,* Discovery Enterprises Limited, 1995.

Coil, Suzanne M., *Slavery and Abolitionists,* TFC Books, 1995.

Hornsby, Alton, *Chronology of African-American History,* 2nd edition Gale, 1997.

"The Influence of Prominent Abolitionists," http://www.loc.gov/exhibits/african/ influ.html.

"The North Star: Trading the Underground Railroad," http://www.ugar.Org/.

Rogers, James *T., The Antislavery Movement,* Facts on File, 1994.

"The Underground Railroad in Iowa," http://www.sos.state.ia.us/register/r7/r7undrr.thm.

West, Jessamyn, *Except for Me and Thee,* Harcourt Brace, 1969.

Windley, Lathan A., *Runaway Slave Advertisements: A Documentary History from the 1730s to 1790,* Greenwood Press, 1983.

Yellin, Jean F., and John C. Van Home, *The Abolitionist Sisterhood: Women's Political Culture in Antebellum America,* Cornell University Press, 1994.

Alternative Applications: Have students compose dialogue to accompany emotional moments such as these:

- ◆ parting from old friends and family
- ◆ risking whippings and brandings for trying to escape
- ◆ hiding stores of food, blankets, and utensils
- ◆ trusting an agent of the Underground Railroad
- ◆ memorizing directions
- ◆ reaching a safe house
- ◆ hearing dogs approach
- ◆ fighting off snakes, insects, alligators, and other predators
- ◆ getting lost
- ◆ reaching a free state
- ◆ searching for missing family members

 First Day at School

Age/Grade Level or Audience: Elementary and middle school cross-curricular workshops.

Description: Reenact classes for former slaves.

Procedure: Have students divide into groups to create lessons they would teach former slaves of all ages and backgrounds. Suggest that they concentrate on the most essential information first, for example:

- ◆ American history and constitutional rights
- ◆ anatomy and health
- ◆ days of the week and months of the year
- ◆ fractions and decimals
- ◆ maps of the United States and world
- ◆ multiplication tables
- ◆ numbers
- ◆ printing and writing the alphabet

- ◆ simple addition and subtraction of sums of money
- ◆ standard English conversation
- ◆ weights and measures

Remind students to show sensitivity to the former slaves' heritage from Africa or the Caribbean. Videotape the teaching of each lesson.

Budget: Under $25

Sources:

First grade textbooks; homeschooling and literacy materials; lessons from magazines such as *Instructor.*

Gadsden, Vivian L., and Daniel A. Wagner, *Literacy among Afro-American Youth: Issues in Learning, Teaching and Schooling,* Hampton Press, 1995.

"Homeschooling Education Press-Links," http://www.home-ed-press.com/LNKGS/lnkgs.heml.

"Homeschooling Resources, " http://alumni.caltech.edu/~casner/homeschl.html.

Lande, Nancy, *Homeschooling: A Patchwork of Days: Share a Day with 30 Homeschooling Families,* Windy Creek, 1996.

Molinsky, *Literacy Workbook,* Prentice-Hall, 1995.

"Pointing You to the Homeschooler Top 5%!," http://www.ssnet.com/~hsguide/online.html.

Weinberger, Jo, *Literacy Goes to School: The Parents' Role in Young Children's Literacy Learning,* Taylor & Francis, 1996.

Alternative Applications: Create a big book primer of basic lessons to use in post-slavery schools. Illustrate with large, simple line drawings, such as pictures of currency, calendar pages, anatomical drawings, the solar system, and maps.

Getting to the Heart of Matters

Age/Grade Level or Audience: Middle school or high school writing, history, literature, or speech classes.

Description: Summarize the most significant speeches by African Americans.

Procedure: Establish an open database or school website on significant African American speakers. Videotape speeches from political conventions and campaigns, processions, and historic events, such as the Million Woman March. Cite time, place, purpose, and speaker along with a summary and citations from each speech.

Budget: Under $25

Sources:

News programs and Internet sources.

Halliburton, Warren J., *Historic Speeches of African Americans*, Franklin Watts, 1993.

Alternative Applications: Work with a group to audiotape an introduction to a famous black platform speaker, actor, entertainer, or sports figure. Include information about the speaker's education, achievements, and purpose.

Haiti Seeks Help

Age/Grade Level or Audience: High school or college debate teams.

Description: Have a debate team consider the question of political asylum and/or humanitarian aid for Haitian refugees.

Procedure: Determine whether the United States policy during the Clinton administration of barring Haitians from seeking political asylum is racist. Weigh the alternatives to sending boatloads of political exiles back to their native island and the consequences of jail, torture, or death with accepting them into United States society and subjecting taxpayers to a massive influx of people requiring welfare, medical assistance, homes, jobs, literacy training, and further education.

Budget: Under $25

Sources:

Consult *Newsbank, Infotrac, Silver Platter,* and Internet; *Time, Newsweek, U.S. News and World Report,* and other compendia of world events.

Greenberg, Keith Elliot, *A Haitian Family,* Lerner Group, 1997.

"Haiti," http://www.nt.net/~russell/Haiti/htm.

"Haiti Online: petition," http://www.haitionline.com/petition.htm.

"Human Rights Brief," http://www.wcl.american.edu/pub/JOURNALS/HRB/Vol2N2/mateen.htm.

Reding, Andrew A., ed, *Haiti: An Agenda for Democracy,* World Policy, 1996.

Alternative Applications: Hold an informal consortium to contrast the United States exclusion policy toward Haitians seeking asylum with treatment of these groups:

♦ slaves migrating north on the Underground Railroad

- ◆ Cuban, Vietnamese, Cambodian, and Laotian boat people escaping Communism
- ◆ Russians escaping anti-Semitic communist leaders
- ◆ immigrant victims of AIDS
- ◆ Jews fleeing Hitler's death camps
- ◆ Muslims avoiding Serbian concentration camps
- ◆ Central Americans escaping persecution by slipping through immigration nets to North American safe houses
- ◆ Kurds escaping Iraqi persecution
- ◆ starving Somali sailing toward famine relief

Joseph Cinqué vs the Slave Trade

Age/Grade Level or Audience: High school or college drama, creative writing, or speech classes.

Description: Have students evolve a speech by Joseph Cinque, the kidnapped Mendi tribesman from Sierra Leone who, in 1839, led a mutiny aboard the slave ship *Amistad*. In an attempt to return to Africa, he escaped from Puerto Principe, Cuba, to the Long Island Sound, where he was arrested. Supported by Connecticut abolitionists, he successfully pleaded his case in court and returned to his homeland.

Procedure: Include a logical argument for why Joseph Cinque deserved freedom. Stress the values U.S. judges would be most cognizant of, for example the universal right to personal freedom as epitomized by the concept of habeas corpus. Include consideration of precedent or class action suits as well as humanitarian concerns. Include information derived from the Dred Scott Decision.

Budget: Under $25

Sources:

"The Amistad Trial," http://leap.yale.edu/lcic/projects/ur/amistad.html.

Burrows, Vinie, "The Amistad Revolt: 'All We Want Is Make Us Free'" (video), Linnet Books, 1995.

Chambers, Veronica, and Paul A. Lee, *Amistad,* Harcourt Brace, 1998.

"Democracy NOW October 14, 1997," http://www.pacifica.org/democracy/rundowns/d971014.html.

Jones, Howard, *Mutiny on the Amistad: The Saga of a Slave Revolt and Its Impact on American Abolition, Law and Diplomacy,* Oxford University Press, 1988.

Jurmain, Suzanne, *Freedom's Sons: The True Story of the Amistad Mutiny,* Lothrop Lee and Shepard, 1998.

"OUPUSA: Mutiny on the Amistad," http://www.oup-usa.org/gcdocs/gc_0195038290. html.

Owens, William A., *Black Mutiny: The Revolt of the Schooner Amistad,* Plum, 1997.

Pesci, David, *Amistad,* Marlowe & Co., 1997.

"Spielburg Accused of Theft," http://www.mrshowbiz.com/news/todays_stries/971017/ spielberg1017.html.

Zeinert, Karen, *The Amistad Slave Revolt and American Abolition,* Linnet Books, 1997.

Alternative Applications: Invite a panel of volunteers to rebut Cinque's speech with the pro-slavery point of view and an equally compelling case against the return of his crew to Africa. Stress differing points of view, including economic, legal, ethical, and historical. Include a definition of piracy in international waters.

Market Day

Age/Grade Level or Audience: Kindergarten and elementary social studies classes; church schools; scout troops.

Description: Have students pantomime a market day in an African community.

Procedure: Provide pictures of life in Africa, featuring weekly outdoor market days, where coffee, tea, fruit, vegetables, grains, and meats are sold alongside woven goods, baskets, carvings, leather belts, bags, and sandals, religious carvings, and musical instruments. Have students make booths of their own and sell these and other simulated products made of clay, cardboard, beads, sticks, soap, styrofoam, and other recycled materials:

- dishes and utensils
- belts cut from cardboard
- clothing
- jewelry
- musical instruments
- whistles
- baskets
- bags
- religious items
- lanyards

Include professional letter writers and entertainers, for instance puppeteers and storytellers, snake charmers, dancers, acrobats, and magicians. Create a sense of verisimilitude by providing stacks of imitation African currency. Videotape a day at the African market.

Budget: $25-$50

Sources:

Videos *Out of Africa* (1985), *Gorillas in the Mist* (1988), *The Power of One* (1991), *Mister Johnson* (1991), and *Sarafina!* (1992).

Hamilton, Robyn, ed, *Africa Activity Book: Arts, Crafts, Cooking and Historical Aids,* Edupress, 1996.

Hartmann, Wendy, *One Sun Rises: An African Wildlife Counting Book,* Dutton Child Books, 1994.

Isadora, Rachel, *Over the Green Hills,* Greenwillow Books, 1992.

Margolies, Barbara A., *Olbalbal: A Day in Massailand,* Macmillan Children's Group, 1994.

"Serengeti," http://www.cyberatl.net/~young/.

"Tanzania," http://www.africa.com/~venture/wildfron/wildanz.htm.

Theroux, Paul, "Down the Zambezi," *National Geographic,* October 1997, 231.

"Uganda," http://imul.com/uganda/

Williams, Wendy, "Of Elephants and Men," *Animals,* November/December 1997, 24-30.

"Zimbabwe, " http://www.mother.com/~zimweb/History.html.

Alternative Applications: Have students draw a mural of an African market day and make an audiotape introducing aspects of trade. Provide contrast by showing visitors from North and South America, Europe, Asia, Australia, and other African cultures, who come to trade for foreign goods. Include the shouts of food vendors, trading in varied currencies, native transportation, and dogs and children playing African games in the street. Depict the arrival of an important chief, midwife, or shaman.

Mule Bone

Age/Grade Level or Audience: College drama classes; literary societies.

Description: Research critical responses to *Mule Bone*, a Broadway hit by Zora Neale Hurston and Langston Hughes.

Procedure: Analyze critiques of *Mule Bone*, a three-act folk comedy that opened on Broadway in February 1991, over sixty years after it was written. Determine how Zora Neale Hurston and Langston Hughes depict black dialect and slang and why the work failed to find an audience during the Harlem Renaissance, when it was first published. Study these facts:

♦ Hurston and Hughes collaborated on *Mule Bone*.
♦ They adapted the plot from Hurston's "The Bone of Contention," a tale derived from her life in Eatonville, Florida.

◆ The duo completed only the third act and ended their friendship and work because he accused her of reissuing *Mule Bone* under her name under the title *De Turkey and De Law.*

◆ A resurgence of interest in Hurston's role in the Harlem Renaissance brought *Mule Bone* to the stage at Lincoln Center in New York.

Budget: Under $25

Sources:

Hemenway, Robert, *Zora Neale Hurston: A Literary Biography*, University of Illinois Press, 1977.

Hurston, Zora Neale, *Mule Bone: A Comedy of Negro Life*, Harper Perennial, 1991.

Lyons, Mary E., *Sorrow's Kitchen: The Life and Folklore of Zora Neale Hurston*, Macmillan, 1990.

"People," *U.S. News and World Report*, February 25, 1991, 18.

Pierpont, Claudie Roth, "A Society of One: Zora Neale Hurston, American Contrarian," *New Yorker*, February 17, 1997, 80-91.

Porter, A. P., *Jump at de Sun: The Story of Zora Neale Hurston*, Carolrhoda, 1992.

Sheffey, Ruthe T., ed., *Zora Neale Hurston Forum*, Morgan, 1992.

Walker, Alice, ed., I *Love Myself When I Am Laughing: A Zora Neale Hurston Reader*, Feminist Press, 1979.

Witcover, Paul, *Zora Neale Hurston*, Chelsea House, 1991.

Yates, Janelle, *Zora Neale Hurston: A Storyteller's Life*, Ward Hill, 1991.

"Zora Neale Hurston," http://www.ceth.rutgers.edu/projects/hercproj/hurston/front.htm.

"Zora Neale Hurston," http://www.detroit.freenet.org/gdfn/sigs/l-cornerworld/hurston/html, February 12, 1997.

Alternative Applications: Organize a reading of important scenes from Mule Bone. Select a panel to discuss the significance of the play to black drama and the Harlem Renaissance. Note the authors' compassion for oppressed people, particularly women and children.

 Music, Stars, Action

Age/Grade Level or Audience: High school drama and humanities classes; community theater groups.

Description: Post a boulevard review of shows and plays that feature black singers, dancers, and actors.

Procedure: Organize a mural, frieze, or series of posters that recap the starring roles of black people in Broadway shows and plays. Feature these contributions:

♦ musical drama in *The Green Pastures*
♦ musical comedy in *Cabin in the* Sky and *Running Wild*
♦ operatic drama in *Emperor Jones*
♦ troupe in *Tropical Revue*
♦ choreography in *Show Boat*
♦ dance-drama in *Carib Song* and *Purlie*
♦ drama in *Raisin in the Sun*
♦ solo work of Carmen de Lavallade and Alvin Ailey in *Carmen Jones*
♦ dancers in *The Wiz*
♦ participants in the production numbers in *Bring in Da Noise, Bring in Da Funk*
♦ puppeteers in *The Lion King*

Budget: Under $25

Sources:

Canby, Vincent, "'The Lion King' Earns Its Roars of Approval," *New York Times,* November 23, 1997, 5, 20.
Kroll, Jack, "A Magic Kingdom," *Newsweek,* November 24, 1997, 70-72.
Long, Richard A, *The Black Tradition in American Dance,* Prion, 1995.
Zoglin, Richard, "Stand Up and Roar," *Time,* November 24, 1997, 103.

Oral Interpretation

Originator: Leatrice Pearson, teacher, Lenoir, North Carolina.

Age/Grade Level or Audience: High school and college drama classes; community and church theater groups.

Description: Organize a reading theater.

Procedure: Have participants select poems, essays, short stories, song and hymn lyrics, plays, stories, and parts of novels and biographies to read aloud, taking turns with parts and emulating with intonation, gesture, and cadence the significance of the piece. Some worthy titles for excerpting for oral interpretation include these:

♦ African American stories as told by Rex Ellis
♦ Anna Ruth Henriques, *The Book of Mechtilde*
♦ William Armstrong, *Sounder*

- ◆ Maya Angelou, *I Know Why the Caged Bird Sings* or *Sheba Sings the Song*
- ◆ Ernest T Gaines, *The Autobiography of Miss Jane Pittman*
- ◆ James Weldon Johnson, *The Creation*
- ◆ Charlie Smalls, *The Wiz*
- ◆ Ossie Davis, *Purlie Victorious*
- ◆ Richard Wright, *Black Boy,* "Almos' a Man," or *Native Son*
- ◆ Langston Hughes, *Don't You Want to Be Free*
- ◆ James Baldwin, *The Fire Next Time*
- ◆ Alice Walker, *The Color Purple*
- ◆ Zora Neale Hurston, *Mule Bone*
- ◆ Alex Haley, *Queen*
- ◆ Ralph Ellison, *Invisible Man*
- ◆ Walter Dean Myers, *Scorpions*
- ◆ Jean Toomer, *Cane*
- ◆ Toni Morrison, *The Bluest Eye, Beloved,* or *Jazz*
- ◆ Ann Petry, *Tituba*
- ◆ Margaret Walker, *Jubilee*

Budget: Under $25

Sources:

Hatch, James V, and Ted Shine, Black Theatre U. S. A.: *Plays by African Americans from 1847 to Today,* Free Press, 1996.

Turner, Darwin T., intro., *Black Drama in America: An Anthology,* Howard University Press, 1993.

Alternative Applications: Add drama to oral interpretation by organizing these and other tableaus:

- ◆ an interview with a delinquent youth in *A Hero Ain't Nothin' But a Sandwich*
- ◆ the arrest of the father in *Sounder*
- ◆ Maya Angelou's application for a job as streetcar conductor in *I Know Why the Caged Bird Sings*
- ◆ Richard Wright's baptism in *Black Boy*
- ◆ Sethe's attendance at Baby Suggs's religious meetings in *Beloved*
- ◆ Tituba's interaction with teenage girls in *Tituba*
- ◆ the meeting between Celie and her grown children in *The Color Purple*
- ◆ a prison counseling session in *A Lesson Before Dying*
- ◆ a recitation of the alphabet in *Nightjohn*

Collect presentations in a video encyclopedia of African American creativity.

Playing the Part

Originator: Leatrice Pearson, teacher, Lenoir, North Carolina.

Age/Grade Level or Audience: High school or college drama classes.

Description: Act out skits or plays about black experience.

Procedure: Have students select a significant scene or dialogue from *A Raisin in the Sun, The Learning Tree, The Book of Mechtilde, Wide Sargasso Sea, The Creation, And Still I Rise, Tituba, Beloved, The Bluest Eye, Jazz, I Know Why the Caged Bird Sings, A Lesson Before Dying, The Autobiography of Miss Jane Pittman,* or *Sounder,* or an original story to write in play form. Present the rewritten work to a school or church assembly, community arts festival, or local theater. Videotape the performance and place the tape in a public or school library for public use.

Budget: $50-$75

Sources:
Various issues of the magazine Plays.
Angelou, Maya, *And Still I Rise,* Random House, 1978.
Armstrong, William Howard, *Sounder,* Harper Trophy Books, 1969.
Gaines, Ernest J., *The Autobiography of Miss Jane Pittman,* Dial, 1971.
Hansberry, Lorraine, *A Raisin in the Sun: A Drama in Three Acts,* Random House, 1959.
Henriques, Anna Ruth, *The Book of Mechtilde,* Knopf, 1997.
Johnson, James Weldon, *The Creation,* Little, Brown, 1993.
Morrison, Toni, *The Bluest Eye,* Holt, 1969.
———, *Beloved,* Knopf, 1987.
———, *Jazz,* Knopf, 1992.
Parks, Gordon, *The Learning Tree,* Harper, 1963.
Petry, Ann, *Tituba of Salem Village,* Crowell, 1964.
Rhys, Jean, *Wide Sargasso Sea,* Norton, 1992.
Turner, Glennette Tilley, *Take a Walk in Their Shoes,* Dutton Children's Books, 1989.

Alternative Applications: Have students trade roles, with non-whites playing black parts and vice versa. Then lead a discussion of student perceptions of the change. Conclude with readings from Studs Terkel's *Race,* Stephen L. Carter's *Reflections of an Affirmative Action Baby,* Anne Moody's *Coming of Age in Mississippi,* or Dinesh D'Souza's *Illiberal Education: The Politics of Race and Sex on Campus.*

Quoting Black Voices

Age/Grade Level or Audience: High school or college English, journalism, drama, or speech classes; Toastmaster's Club.

Description: Hold an annual declamation contest in which contestants present readings from great black writers.

Procedure: Publicize a recitation contest through schools, churches, libraries, civic clubs, and the news media Organize a panel to score the performances of entrants on three levels: children, teens, and adults. Require participants to select pieces from a standard list. Some suggested pieces include the following:

- ◆ William Wells Brown, *Clotel*
- ◆ Richard Wright, "Between the World and Me"
- ◆ excerpts from James Baldwin, *The Fire Next Time*
- ◆ Martin Luther King, Jr., "I Have a Dream" or *Letter from a Birmingham Jail*
- ◆ W. E. B. DuBois, speech to the 1919 Pan-African Conference in Paris
- ◆ Dudley Randall, "Booker T. and W. E. B. DuBois"
- ◆ excerpts from Toni Morrison, *The Bluest Eye*
- ◆ Margaret Burroughs, "What Should I Tell My Children Who Are Black"
- ◆ Arna Bontemps, "Golgotha Is a Mountain"
- ◆ excerpts from Ann Petry's *The Street*
- ◆ Frederick Douglass, "What to the Slaves Is the Fourth of July?"
- ◆ Maya Angelou, *Now Sheba Sings the Song*
- ◆ Sojourner Truth, address to the New York legislature
- ◆ Paul Laurence Dunbar, "When de C'on Pone's Hot"
- ◆ Claude McKay, "America"
- ◆ Countee Cullen, "Yet Do I Marvel"
- ◆ Barbara Jordan's speech to the 1992 National Democratic Convention
- ◆ Langston Hughes, "The Negro Speaks of Rivers" and "Epilogue"
- ◆ Zora Neale Hurston, "Sweat"
- ◆ excerpts from Julius Lester, *To Be a Slave*

Budget: $25-$50

Sources:

Fitch, Suzanne Pullon, and Roseann M. Mandziuk, *Sojourner Truth As Orator: Wit, Story, and Song,* Greenwood, 1997.

Kunjufu, Jawanza, *Lessons from History: A Celebration in Blackness,* African American Images, 1987.

Lester, Julius, *To Be a Slave,* Dial, 1969.

Mullane, Deirdre, ed., *Crossing the Danger Water: Three Hundred Years of African-American Writing,* Anchor Books, 1993.

Ravitch, Diane, *The American Reader: Words That Moved a Nation,* HarperCollins, 1990.

Alternative Applications: Videotape a series of public recitations by influential black speakers to use as classroom aids and models. Have students study the presentations to learn speaking techniques, audience awareness, eye contact, gesture, tone, and emphasis. Consider demonstrations by these speakers:

Maya Angelou	Bill Cosby	Marian Wright Edelman
Morgan Freeman	James Earl Jones	Barbara Jordan
Coretta Scott King	Jesse Jackson	Spike Lee
Colin Powell	Cicely Tyson	Oprah Winfrey
Faye Wattleton		

Speaker's Bureau

Age/Grade Level or Audience: All ages.

Description: Create a card file or database of speakers.

Procedure: Organize a school list or library or museum database of speakers and experts on specific subjects. Include these possibilities:

♦ people who have worked in Africa
♦ travelers to Africa and the Caribbean
♦ specialists in such black religions as Santeria or Islam
♦ retired military personnel
♦ health experts on sickle cell anemia
♦ drug awareness experts
♦ dramatists and actors
♦ members of black fraternal organizations
♦ civil rights leaders
♦ politicians who display an interest in promoting racial harmony
♦ union organizers and business leaders
♦ judges and police officers
♦ social workers and counselors
♦ musicians
♦ puppeteers
♦ gymnasts and athletes
♦ storytellers
♦ dancers and artists
♦ weavers
♦ cooks
♦ clothing and furniture designers
♦ architects

Keep this list up to date by adding and deleting information, clipping articles from local media sources, and collecting programs, outlines, speeches, and other useful material. Advertise the speaker's bureau to surrounding areas. Videotape presentations for later showings.

Budget: $50-$75

Sources:

Library lists, volunteer organizations, teachers, League of Women Voters, Business and Professional Women's League, Chamber of Commerce, job counselors, military recruiters, ministerial councils, fraternal and religious organizations, and citizens who know the community well.

Alternative Applications: Collect speeches and sermons delivered by local experts on black culture, black history, Africa, the Caribbean, or race relations. Mount a website database or maintain a vertical file of speeches at a school or county library for use by researchers, students, or teachers.

 Talk to Me

Age/Grade Level or Audience: High school and college speech and writing classes; adult radio audiences.

Description: Organize a black history month talk show.

Procedure: Create a format for a radio talk show. Include segments such as these:

- ♦ African American news of the day
- ♦ news from black people around the world
- ♦ black history briefs, for example "Twenty-Five, Fifty, and a Hundred Years Ago Today"
- ♦ a variety of black music, from rap, hip hop, gospel, and rock to reggae, soul, new age, jazz, opera, choral, show tunes, and calypso
- ♦ the topic of the day, such as ways to counter violent street gangs, health and safety problems in the black community, support for black leaders, or assistance for elderly, sick, or handicapped people living in poverty
- ♦ call-in commentary

Set up a mock run-through by having participants write the script and volunteers call in questions and comments. Tape four weekly segments to run throughout black history month. Vary the types of voices during a single program to include youthful, older, male, and female speakers.

Budget: $25-$50

Sources:

Current news sources from *USA Today, Infotrac, Newsbank;* also *Africa Watch, Newsweek, Time, U.S. News and World Report, Biography, Discover, National Geographic, Ebony, Jet,* and *Emerge.*

Bennett, Lerone, Jr., *Before the Mayflower: A History of Black America,* 6th edition, Penguin Books, 1993.

"Black History, " http://www.slip.net/~rigged/history.html.

"Black History Month: Let's Get Started," http://www.netnoir.com/spotlight/bhm/ jbhm.html.

Dennis, Denise, *Black History for Beginners,* Highsmith, 1992.

Grun, Bernard, *The Timetables of History: A Horizontal Linkage of People and Events,* Simon & Schuster, 1991.

Hornsby, Alton, *Chronology of African-American History,* 2nd edition Gale, 1997.

Mabunda, L. Mpho, ed., *The African American Almanac,* 7th edition, Gale, 1997.

Saari, Peggy, and Daniel B. Baker, *Explorers and Discoverers: From Alexander the Great to Sally Ride,* U•X•L/Gale, 1995.

Alternative Applications: Find fifteen to thirty minutes of air time on local or campus radio broadcasts for a black history program. Spice your format with guest spots, which can be taped or presented live. Include a variety of commentators: fashion designers, storytellers, film makers, athletes, entertainers, judges, entrepreneurs, and activists as well as news about black people in Africa, the Caribbean, and other parts of the world. If your area responds well to the format, encourage a local station to adopt the program as a regular weekly feature.

This Ol' Hat

Age/Grade Level or Audience: Elementary and middle school students.

Description: Present an informal skit entitled "This Ol' Hat."

Procedure: Pass one of a series of hats to the first participant, who will put it on and describe a significant black person who might have worn it.

Have each participant compose a three- or four-sentence explanation of why the hat is significant, then perform or read it aloud. For example:

♦ This ol' hat protected my granddaddy's head along the Mississippi Delta, where he hoed cotton from sunup to sundown. When he died, the hat passed on to my father, then to me. I wore it the day that freedom came to the slaves on the plantation and threw it into the air as church bells rang. All my relatives cried "Jubilee! Freedom!"

◆ I wore this hat as I led runaways along a dark path to the river bank and waited for clouds to part so I could follow the Big Dipper. I held tight to my hat as the wind and snow blew, but I didn't let go of the hand I grasped. When Lincoln proclaimed all slaves free, I retired my hat.

◆ I wore this hat on the day that Rosa Parks refused to take a back seat to anybody. Proudly, I joined the groups that lined the streets of Montgomery to express their unity in the bus boycott. I removed my hat in honor of Dr. Martin Luther King, a brave and good man who did his best to stop violence.

◆ On the day that I was captured and bound by a neck chain, I was wearing this skullcap, which stayed with me across the Atlantic to the auction block at Annapolis, Maryland. During the crossing, I saw my brother leap to his death among hungry sharks and heard my aunt cry as her sickly infant was ripped from her arms and flung into the waves. I will pass my hat to my son in hopes that he might return to Africa and reunite with his grandparents.

◆ I wore this sun hat on the day that Dr. Mae Jemison became the first black woman to blast off into space. As I tilted my head to watch the rocket climb on its way to outer space, I wondered if this voyage would be the one to bring back vital information on pollution or propose an answer to the energy crisis. Whatever its scientific worth, I was sure that it represented great strides for black women.

◆ I wore this hat on the day that Marian Anderson sang in the Washington mall. My hat reminded me to hold up my head to acknowledge a world famous singer who refused to be humiliated by the Daughters of the American Revolution. As a woman among great women, I felt privileged to be in the company of Mrs. Eleanor Roosevelt, a First Lady with the courage to face down bigotry.

◆ My hat is battered from the months I slogged through the jungles of Vietnam, fighting a war that many Americans called unjust. Despite my own feelings against violence, I followed my country's orders and brought my hat safely home to my family. I wore my hat to the dedication of Maya Lin's Vietnam Memorial in Washington, D. C., then passed my hat to my daughter, who served in the nursing corps in the Persian Gulf War.

◆ My sun hat shaded my eyes the day that Hitler snubbed the efforts of black athletes at the 1936 Olympics. When the athletes returned to the United States in victory, I removed my hat out of respect for Jesse Owens and Ralph Metcalfe and tossed it high in the air the day that Hitler was defeated. In the scramble, I recovered my hat and wore it down Pennsylvania Avenue in the victory parade for returning troops. Videotape this presentation, then show it at a PTA supper, retirement home, Scout or 4-H banquet, or church assembly.

Budget: $25-$50

Sources:

Bennett, Lerone, Jr., *Before the Mayflower: A History of Black America,* 6th edition, Penguin Books, 1993.

"Black History," http://www.slip.net,~rigged/history.html.

"Black History Month: Let's Get Started," http://www.netnoir.com/spotlight/bhm/jbhm. html.

Dennis, Denise, *Black History for Beginners,* Highsmith, 1992.

Grun, Bernard, *The Timetables of History: A Horizontal Linkage of People and Events,* Simon & Schuster, 1991.

Hornsby, Alton, *Chronology of African-American History,* 2nd edition Gale, 1997.

Jurmain, Suzanne, *Freedom's Sons: The True Story of the Amistad Mutiny,* Lothrop Lee and Shepard, 1998.

Mabunda, L. Mpho, ed., *The African American Almanac,* 7th edition, Gale, 1997.

Saari, Peggy, and Daniel B. Baker, *Explorers and Discoverers: From Alexander the Great to Sally Ride,* U•X•L/Gale, 1995.

Alternative Applications: Have students select an inanimate object to epitomize a moment in black history, for instance a belt, shoe, scarf, cup, saddle, sack, photo, newspaper clipping, runaway poster, chain, bottle, toy, knife, or stone. Organize a small group to compose a scenario depicting the importance of the object. Produce on website or by desktop publishing a series of dramatic moments for classes or homeschoolers to read or act out.

Thomas Jefferson and Slavery

Age/Grade Level or Audience: High school or college speech, history, or writing classes.

Description: Debate the anti-slavery paragraph removed from the Declaration of Independence in 1776.

Procedure: Read aloud the following paragraph which Thomas Jefferson intended for his declaration to England's King George III:

> He [King George Iil] has waged cruel war against human nature itself, violating its most sacred rights to life and liberty in the persons of a distant people who never offended him, captivating and carrying them into slavery in another hemisphere, or to incur miserable death in their transportation thither. This piratical warfare, the opprobrium of infidel powers, is the warfare of the Christian King of Great Britain. Determined to keep open a market where men should be bought and

sold, he has prostituted his negative for suppressing every legislative attempt to prohibit or restrain this execrable commerce.

Lead a discussion of how the inclusion of this paragraph would have changed United States history.

Budget: Under $25

Sources:

The video *Thomas Jefferson.*

Auchincloss, Louis, "The Jefferson Enigma," *Newsweek,* February 24, 1997, 61.

Burns, Ken, "What Thomas Jefferson Means Today," *USA Weekend,* February 14-16, 1997, 4-6.

Ellis, Joseph J., *American Sphinx: The Character of Thomas Jefferson,* Alfred A. Knopf, 1997.

Lively, Donald E., *Constitution and Race,* Greenwood, 1992.

Alternative Applications: Organize a small group to rewrite this paragraph in more modern English so that it reflects current attitudes toward human rights. Compare the finished product to statements about civil liberties published by the United Nations Human Rights Commission, American Civil Liberties Union, and Amnesty International.

Sports

African American Sports Maze

Age/Grade Level or Audience: High school students; YMCA and YWCA groups; booster clubs.

Description: Have students answer questions on famous black athletes.

Procedure: Distribute game and question sheets to each student, then have students begin at START, draw a line either vertically, horizontally, or diagonally to the block containing the answer to each question, and proceed to the end block. Use this matrix:

1. The first black American to compete in the Olympic Games (George Poage)
2. The black athlete who won four gold medals at the 1936 Berlin Olympics (Jesse Owens)
3. Black Olympic runner who was crippled until the age of nine (Wilma Rudolph)
4. Female athlete who set a world record for the heptathlon in the 1988 Seoul Olympics (Jackie Joyner-Kersee)
5. Boxer who was originally named Cassius Clay (Muhammad Ali)
6. Middleweight boxer who won a gold medal in 1952 (Floyd Patterson)
7. Female runner who set an Olympic record in the 100-meter dash in 1984 in the Los Angeles games (Evelyn Ashford)
8. Sprinter who raised a fist in Mexico City in 1968 during the playing of the national anthem (John Carlos)
9. Heavyweight boxer who defeated Muhammad Ali in 1971 (Joe Frazier)
10. Track and football star who later headed the surgery department at Howard University (Charles Drew)
11. First black to manage a major league baseball team (Frank Robinson)

12. Black golfer who joined the top professionals in 1968 (Lee Elder)

13. First black NBA player (Nathaniel Clifton)

14. Boxer who won the middleweight title five times (Ray Robinson)

15. Batter who broke Babe Ruth's record in 1974 (Hank Aaron)

16. First black Heisman trophy winner (Ernie Davis)

17. Star of the Milwaukee Bucks who became a sportscaster (Oscar Robertson)

18. 1968 Olympic 400-meter runner who works as a trainer in Cameroon, Africa (Lee Evans)

19. First track and field star to jump seven feet (Charles Dumas)

20. First American black to play major league baseball (Jackie Robinson)

START	George Poage	Jesse Owens	Carol Lewis	Guion Bluford
Carl Lewis	Smokey Robinson	Wilma Rudolph	Jackie Joyner-Kersee	Ed Bradley
Malcolm X	Diahann Carroll	Bernard Shaw	Muhammad Ali	Floyd Patterson
Tony Dorsett	Jamaica Kincaid	Clara Hale	William Warfield	Evelyn Ashford
Rosey Grier	Toussaint L'Ouverture	Patrice Lamumba	Bryant Gumbel	John Carlos
Lewis Latimer	Billy Dee Williams	Maya Angelou	Lee Elder	Joe Frazier
Hank Aaron	Ray Robinson	Nathaniel Clifton	Frank Robinson	Charles Drew
Ernie Davis	LeVar Burton	Kevin Hooks	Andrew Young	Edmonia Lewis
Oscar Robertson	Lee Evans	Charles Dumas	Jackie Robinson	FINISH

Budget: Under $25

Sources:

Barrett, Warrick Lee, and Scott Michaels, *Johnny Bright, Champion*, Commonwealth Publications, 1997.

Coffey, Wayne, "Tiger's Roar," *Scholastic Action*, September 8, 1997 2-3.

Margolies, Jacob, *The Negro League: The Story of Black Baseball*, Franklin Watts, 1993.

"Muhammad Ali In the Biggest Fight of His Life," *Scholastic Scope*, October 20, 1997, 5.

Smith, Vern E., and Mark Starr, "Junior's League," *Newsweek*, September 1997, 60-61.

Stravinsky, John, "The Long Reach of Muhammad Ali Still the Greatest," *Biography*, December 1997, 50-56, 94.

———, *Muhammad Ali*, Park Lane Press, 1997.

START ANSWERS	George Poage (1)	Jesse Owens (2)		
		Wilma Rudolph (3)	Jackie Joyner-Kersee (4)	
			Muhammad Ali (5)	Floyd Patterson (6)
				Evelyn Ashford (7)
				John Carlos (8)
	Ray Robinson (14)	Nathaniel Clifton (13)	Lee Elder (12)	Joe Frazier (9)
Hank Aaron (15)			Frank Robinson (11)	Charles Drew (10)
Ernie Davis (16)				
Oscar Robertson (17)	Lee Evans (18)	Charles Dumas (19)	Jackie Robinson (20)	FINISH

Alternative Applications: Extend the game by having students name the achievements of the unused entries. For example, Joseph Cinqué, the slave from Sierra Leone who led a revolt on the schooner *Amistad* in 1839, fought for his freedom in court, and was returned to Africa.

The Black Olympian

Age/Grade Level or Audience: Community and church groups; scout troops.

Description: Lead a study of African American contributions to current Olympic teams.

Procedure: Have participants read current newspapers and magazines for information about important Olympic contenders, particularly these:

baseball Calvin Murray, Jaque Jones

basketball Teresa Edwards, David Robinson, Magic Johnson, Patrick Ewing, Charles Barkley, Cynthia Cooper, Daedra Charles, Karl Malone, Pam McGee, Lynette Woodard, Cheryl Miller, Clyde Drexler, Clarissa Davis, Medina Dixon, Michael Jordan, Anfernee Hardaway, Grant Hill, Reggie Miller, Hakeem Olajuwon, Shaquille O'Neal, Gary Payton, Scottie Pippen, Mitch Richmond, David Robinson, Ruthie Bolton, Teresa Edwards, Venue Lacey, Lisa Leslie, Katrina McClain, Nikki McCray, Carla McGhee, Dawn Staley, Sheryl Swoopes

boxing Eric Griffin, Montell Griffin, Danell Nicholson, Tim Austin, Terrance Cauthen, Lawrence Clay-Bey, Nate Jones, Floyd Mayweather, Eric Morel, Zahir Raheem, David Reid, Antonio Tarver, Roshii Wells, Chris Byrd

coaching Bob Kersee, Chris Martin, and Joe Byrd

figure skating Debi Thomas

gymnastics Dominique Dawes, Betty Okino, Jair Lynch, Chainey Umphrey

handball Derek Brown, Darrick Heath, Chryssandra Hires, Jennifer Horton, Toni Jameson, Sharon Cain, Tami Jameson

hurdling Edwin Moses

ice hockey Val James, Grant Fuhr, Tony McKegney, Ray Neufeld, Eldon Reddick

rowing Anita DeFrantz

soccer Edison Nascimento, Clint Peay, Eddie Pope, Damian Silvera, Brianna Scurry, Thori Staples, Staci Wilson

swimming Bob Murray, Rick White, Charles Chapman

tennis MaliVai Washington, Chanda Rubin

track Jackie Joyner-Kersee, Gwen Torrence, Merlene Ottey, Carl Lewis, Carol Lewis, Cornelius Johnson, Dennis Mitchell, Danny Everett, Alice Coachman, John Tillman, Lawrence Johnson, Michael Johnson, Michael Marsh, Dennis Mitchell, Dan O'Brien, Mike Powell, Butrch Reynolds, Eugene Swift, Anthony Washington, Jeff Williams, Kim Batten, Kelly Blair, Tonya Buford-Bailey, Nicole Carroll, Joetta Clark, Gail Devers, Cheryl Dickey, Cameron Wright, Gail Devers, Juliet Cuthbert, Kevin Young, Linford Christie, Frankie Fredericks, Kirk Baptiste, Thomas Jefferson, Florence Griffith Joyner, Ben Johnson, Robert Howard, Chris Huffins, C. J. Hunter, Allen Johnson, Derek Redmond, Mark Witherspoon, Daley Thompson, Quincy Watts, Steve Lewis, Bob Beamon, Wilma Rudolph, Charles Simpkins, Carlette Guidry, Evelyn Ashford, Esther Jones, Leroy Burrell, Dennis Mitchell, Mike Marsh, Sandra Farmer-Patrick, Kim Graham, Carlette Guidry, Aretha Hill, Joe Greene, Mike Conley, Mark Crear, Calvin Davis, Marc Davis, Jon Drummond, Johnny Gray, Joe Greene, Ronnie Harris, Alvin Harrison, Kenny Harrison, Mike Powell, D'Andre Hill, Shelia Hudson, Regina Jacobs, Lynn Jennings, Maicel Malone, Jearl Miles, Inger Miller, Diana Orrange, Meredith Rainey, Cynthia Rhodes, Connie Teaberry, Lynda Tolbert, Tisha Waller, Shana Williams, Danette Young

volleyball Tonya Williams, Tara Cross-Battle, Beverly Oden, Elaine Oden, Bev Danielle Scott, Elaine Oden

weightlifting Marc Henry, Wes Barnett

wrestling Travis West, Rodney Smith, Kenny Monday, Melvin Douglas, Townsend Saunders, Chris Campbell, Mujashid Mayanrd, Derrick Waldroup

Olympic Committee Anita DeFrantz, Dr. LeRoy Walker, president of the U.S. Olympic Committee.

Create a bulletin board of candid shots of Olympian contenders in action. Indicate the countries they represent.

Budget: $25-$50

Sources:

Consult the *Infotrac, Facts on File, Newsbank, Silver Platter*, the Internet, and other online databases; *Sports Illustrated, Jet, Essence, Time, U.S. News and World Report, Biography, Discover, Ebony, People, Newsweek*, and other news magazines; sports pages of local newspapers, particularly *USA Today*; almanacs.

"Black 1996 U. S. Olympians," *Jet*, July 22, 1996.

"Olympic Black Women," http//www.com-stock.com/dave/plowden.htm.

Plowden, Martha, *Famous Firsts of Black Women*, Pelican, 1993.

"Skating," http//www.sportscelebritiesfestival.ca/pages/skate.html.

Alternative Applications: Have students create a fight song, poster, uniform, TV spot announcement, website, or monument to honor black Olympic stars. Suggest appropriate inscriptions and commentary to include male and female athletes.

The Harlem Globetrotters

Age/Grade Level or Audience: All ages.

Description: Have a local team imitate the style of the Harlem Globetrotters.

Procedure: Invite a team to study films, videos, and newspaper descriptions of the Harlem Globetrotters' unique comic style of basketball. Then have players volunteer to imitate the world famous team's warm-up and court strategies. Accompany the event with their theme song, "Sweet Georgia Brown."

Budget: Under $25

Sources:

The film *Harlem Globetrotters* (1951).

"Black Information Network World Wide Web," http//www.bin.commusicent/ sports/trotters/trotpix.htm.

"Globetrotters," http//cw.csc.edu/STUDINFO/eagleonline/mar397/globetrotters.html.

"The Harlem Globetrotters," http//home.cc.utexas.edu/admin/erwinapplause/de9 6ap/trotters.html.

Wilker, Josh, *The Harlem Globetrotters*, Chelsea House, 1996.

Alternative Applications: Show videos of past performances of the Harlem Globetrotters. Have students comment on the team's combination of wit, agility, humor, and skill. Ask a volunteer to conclude why the Harlem Globetrotters have been called "American Clown Prince Ambassadors."

Hero to Hero

Age/Grade Level or Audience: Middle school or high school writing or journalism class.

Description: Compare two famous black athletes.

Procedure: Have students select two athletes from different eras or fields of endeavor and write a comparison of their careers. For example, consider these pairings:

◆ Jackie Robinson and Muhammad Ali
◆ Mark Mathabane and Tiger Woods
◆ Tiger Woods and Dominique Dawes
◆ Joe Frazier and Hank Aaron
◆ Jesse Owens and Rosey Grier
◆ Carl Lewis and Joe Louis
◆ Arthur Ashe and Wilma Rudolph
◆ Debi Thomas and Kareem Abdul Jabbar
◆ Jackie Joyner-Kersee and Althea Gibson

Budget: Under $25

Sources:
Consult *Infotrac, Facts on File, Newsbank*, the Internet, and other online databases; *Sports Illustrated, Jet, Essence, Time, U.S. News and World Report, Ebony, People, Newsweek*, and other news magazines; sports pages of local newspapers, particularly *USA Today*; almanacs.

"Black Information Network World Wide Web," http//www.bin.commusicent/sports/ trotters/trotpix.htm.

"Black 1996 U.S. Olympians," *Jet*, July 22, 1996.

Margolies, Jacob, *The Negro League: The Story of Black Baseball*, Franklin Watts, 1993.

"Olympic Black Women," http//www.com-stock.com/dave/plowden.htm.

Plowden, Martha, *Famous Firsts of Black Women*, Pelican, 1993.

"Skating," http//www.sportscelebritiesfestival.ca/pages/skate.html.

Stravinsky, John, "The Long Reach of Muhammad Ali Still the Greatest," *Biography*, December 1997, 50-56. 94.

————, *Muhammad Ali*, Park Lane Press, 1997.

Alternative Applications: Discuss the growth of one sport through the contributions of black athletes. For example, place the following boxers in time order and explain how each made strides for the black athlete Sugar Ray Leonard, George Dixon, Muhammad Ali, Ezzard Charles, Floyd Patterson, Joe Frazier, Henry Armstrong, Joe Louis, Sugar Ray Robinson, Thomas Hearns, Riddick Bowe, and Evander Holyfield.

The Professional Black Athlete

Age/Grade Level or Audience: Community and church groups; scout troops.

Description: Lead a study of African American contributions to American sports.

Procedure: Have participants read reference books, newspapers, and magazines for information about important sports figures, particularly these:

baseball Moses Fleetwood Walker, Jackie Robinson, Hank Aaron, Lyle Stone, Reggie Jackson, Satchel Paige, Willie Mays, Rickey Henderson

basketball Wilmeth Sidat-Singh, Magic Johnson, Michael Jordan, Kareem Abdul Jabbar, Cheryl Miller

boxing George Dixon, Muhammad Ali, Ezzard Charles, Floyd Patterson, Joe Frazier, Henry Armstrong, Joe Louis, Sugar Ray Robinson, Thomas Hearns, Riddick Bowe, Evander Holyfield

football Paul Robeson, Fritz Pollard, Joe Lillard, Kenny Washington, Woody Strode, Bill Willis, Marion Motley, Tony Dorsett, Refrigerator Perry, Jim Brown, Walter Payton, Joe Green, Doug Williams

golf Tiger Woods, Charlie Sifford, Lee Elder, Althea Gibson, Calvin Peete

horse racing Jimmy Lee, William Sims

lacrosse Tina Sloan

sailing Art Price, Marty Stephan, Willian Pinkney, Teddy Seymour

tennis Arthur Ashe, Zina Garrison, Althea Gibson, MaliVal Washington, Chanda Rubin, Venus Williams

track Charles Dumas, Carol Lewis

coaching and management Cito Gaston, Dennis Green, Peter C. B. Bynoe, Hal McRae, Lenny Wilkens, Wes Unseld, Frank Robinson.

Organize a game of Twenty Questions in which students pose as famous sports figures. Have class members guess their identities.

Budget: $25-$50

Sources:

Consult *Infotrac, Facts on File, Current Biography, Newsbank,* the Internet, and other online databases; *Sports Illustrated, Jet, Essence, Time, U.S. News and World Report, People, Newsweek, Biography, Discover,* and other news magazines; sports pages of local newspapers, particularly *USA Today* and almanacs.

Alternative Applications: Have students create an oversized mobile featuring branches for each sport and individual pendants marked with names from that sport.

Sports Clinic

Age/Grade Level or Audience: Community and school athletic teams and gym classes.

Description: Locate black athletes to staff a sports clinic.

Procedure: Invite black athletes to instruct students in the fundamentals of gymnastics, skating, volleyball, football, soccer, wrestling, swimming, tennis, and other sports. Provide the workshop free to assist indigent, elderly, and handicapped community members in improving their skills. Extend sports clinics to include boosters, coaches, team managers, cheerleaders, majorettes, and marching band members.

Budget: $50-$75

Sources:

Consult local school, college, and university athletics departments for suggested personnel to staff sports workshops.

Alternative Applications: Hold similar clinics to assist artists, particularly guitarists, pianists, drummers, singers, painters, muralists, potters, sculptors, carvers, cooks, storytellers, and weavers.

Sports Debate

Age/Grade Level or Audience: High school or college black studies, journalism, gym, debate, or speech class.

Description: Debate the actions of Tommie Smith and John Carlos at the 1968 Olympics.

Procedure: Decide whether Tommie Smith and John Carlos were justified in raising the Black Power salute at the Mexico City Olympics or whether their actions constituted an insult to their nation as a whole. As you debate the issue, consider the following points:

♦ An oppressed people have a right to demonstrate their disenfranchisement.
♦ Athletes and entertainers bear the burden of representing not only their talents but also the needs and demands of their race.
♦ No athlete representing the United States has a right to embarrass the whole country by displaying militant or unsporting behavior before the world.

Budget: $25-$50

Sources:

Connors, Martin, Diane L. Dupuis, and Brad Morgan, *The Olympics Factbook*, Visible Ink Press, 1992.

Alternative Applications: Direct this assignment toward a journalism or writing class and use it as an example of point/counterpoint editorial writing.

Sports on Film

Age/Grade Level or Audience: All ages.

Description: Celebrate the success of Wilma Rudolph, Olympic gold medalist who overcame prejudice and polio to become an unprecedented track success.

Procedure: Show the biographical film *Wilma* starring Cicely Tyson and Denzel Washington. Invite a local black athlete to introduce or comment on the values demonstrated by Rudolph as well as the personal strengths and family and community support that buoyed her to victory. Contrast and compare her with these athletes: Earvin "Magic" Johnson, Arthur Ashe, Dominique Dawes, Michael Jordan,

Debi Thomas, Muhammad Ali, Kareem Abdul Jabbar, Carol Lewis, and Tiger Woods. Extend the range with these and other film offerings:

- ◆ *Champions Forever*
- ◆ *Clay vs. Liston*
- ◆ *Fighter of the Century: Muhammad Ali*
- ◆ *Harlem Globetrotters: Six Decades of Magic*
- ◆ *The History of Great Black Baseball Players*
- ◆ *Jackie Robinson*
- ◆ *Jesse Owens Returns to Berlin*
- ◆ *Magic Johnson: Put Magic in Your Game*
- ◆ *Michael Jordan: Above and Beyond*
- ◆ *Michael Jordan's Playground*
- ◆ *Michael Jordan: Come Fly with Me*
- ◆ *Muhammad Ali*
- ◆ *Muhammad Ali vs. Zora*
- ◆ *Ringside with Mike Tyson*
- ◆ *Sugar Ray Leonard*
- ◆ *Sugar Ray Robinson: Pound for Pound*

Budget: $25-$50

Sources:
Video rental stores and public library collections.

Alternative Applications: Organize a writing contest open in three categories: children, teens, and adults. Use Rudolph's perseverance as a theme. Have entrants apply her example to problems such as gangs, random violence, AIDS, poverty, homelessness, and workplace discrimination.

Storytelling

An Aesop Recitation

Age/Grade Level or Audience: Middle school or high school literature, speech, or Latin class.

Description: Have students create an illustrated display of homilies from Aesop's fables.

Procedure: Introduce the background of Aesop (c. 620-560 B.C.), the black Lydian slave who served a Greek owner and earned a reputation as a teller of witty, illustrative fables, most of which focused on animal characters. Published by Demetrius Phalereus, a Roman teller, two and a half centuries after Aesop's death, the fables, succinct and ironic, end in pointed aphorisms, such as:

- The greedy who demand more lose all.
- Danger often comes from where we least expect.
- To change place is not to change one's nature.
- There is always someone worse off than you.
- The lamb follows the wolf in sheep's clothing.
- Appearances are often deceiving.
- Don't count your chickens before they are hatched.
- No act of kindness, no matter how small, is ever wasted.
- Slow and steady wins the race.
- Familiarity breeds contempt.
- A crust eaten in peace is better than banquets consumed in fear.
- It is not fine feathers that make fine birds.
- In union we have strength.
- Be content with your life; one cannot be first in everything.
- People often grudge others what they cannot enjoy themselves.

◆ Self-conceit often leads to self-destruction.

◆ Any excuse serves the tyrant.

◆ Prepare today for tomorrow's needs.

◆ Put a shoulder to the wheel.

◆ The gods help those who help themselves.

◆ We often give the enemy the means to destroy us.

◆ We often see others' vices while ignoring our own.

◆ One person's meat is another's poison.

◆ Necessity is our best weapon.

◆ The smaller the mind, the greater the conceit.

◆ He who pleads with the most pitiful voice does not always suffer the greatest injury.

◆ He who laughs last laughs best.

◆ He who deserts old friends for new deserves to lose both.

◆ One good deed deserves another.

Budget: Under $25

Sources:

Aesop, *Aesop & Company*, Houghton Mifflin, 1991.

———, *Aesop's Fables*, Penguin, 1996.

———, *Aesop's Fables*, University of Kentucky Press, 1993.

Aesop's Fables Coloring Book, Dover.

Snodgrass, Mary Ellen, *The Encyclopedia of Satirical Literature*, ABC-Clio, 1997.

Alternative Applications: Have students work in pairs to create their own beast fables, each ending with a wise saying. Collect these classroom beast fables and publish them in a single collection, add to a database or website, or display in poster form on a hall bulletin board or civic display of student celebration of Black History Month.

African Story Swap

Age/Grade Level or Audience: All ages.

Description: Hold an informal storytelling session.

Procedure: Arrange a story swap featuring African folk tales such as *Mufaro's Beautiful Daughters, Fortune Tellers, The People Could Fly, Who's in Rabbit's House,* or *Why Mosquitoes Buzz in People's Ears.* Have volunteers act out key parts as the storyteller narrates the plot. Offer a prize to enhance participation, such as a book,

CD, or tape of stories by storytellers Linda Goss, Ellaraino, Brother Blue, Diane Ferlatte, Ron and Natalie Blaise, Grace Hallworth, Paul Keens-Douglas, Mary Carter Smith, Ken Corsbie, Shanta, Jackie Torrence, Rex Ellis, Doug and Frankie Quimby, Bobby Norfolk, Carlie Towne, or Chinua Achebe.

Budget: $25-$50

Sources:

Alexander, Lloyd, *The Fortune-Tellers*, Dutton Children's Books, 1992.

Barchers, Suzanne I., *Storybook Stew*, Fulcrum, 1996.

Geisler, Harlynne, *Storytelling Professionally: The Nuts and Bolts of a Working Performer*, Libraries Unlimited, 1997.

Miller, Corki, and Mary Ellen Snodgrass, *Storytellers: A Biographical Directory of 120 English-Speaking Storytellers Worldwide*, McFarland, 1998.

Mooney, Bill, and David Holt, *The Storyteller's Guide*, August House, 1996.

Spalding, Henry D., compl. and ed., *Encyclopedia of Black Folklore and Humor*, J. David Publishers, 1990.

Stotter, Ruth, *About Story: Writings on Story and Storytelling*, Stotter Press, 1996.

Tales as Tools: The Power of Story in the Classroom, National Storytelling Press, 1994.

Torrence, Jackie, *African-American Stories* (video), Curriculum Associates.

———, *Jackie Torrence Shares Stories from Her Family Album,* (video), Curriculum Associates.

Wolkstein, Diane, *The Magic Orange Tree and Other Haitian Folktales*, Schocken, 1997.

Alternative Applications: Hold an evening of stories as a part of TELLABRATION! The Worldwide Evening of Storytelling for Grownups, which takes place each Saturday preceding Thanksgiving. As a part of the story swap, photocopy each story and collate in a booklet. Staple inside covers decorated with drawings of Anansi the spider, Aesop's fables, or Uncle Remus stories. Distribute to participants as a take-home holiday favor.

Around the World with the Trickster

Age/Grade Level or Audience: All ages.

Description: Collect original tellings of trickster lore.

Procedure: Explore different examples of the trickster motif, which is common in African beast fables and African American folklore. Other subgroups of trickster folk tales include these motifs:

◆ beast fables	◆ bondage and emancipation
◆ conjuring, potions, and magic spells	◆ ethnic jokes
◆ exploits of Stagolee	◆ ghost stories
◆ heaven and hell	◆ High John the Conqueror
◆ Mr. Charlie or the white overseer	◆ nature lore
◆ parables	◆ self-denigration
◆ sexual escapades	◆ superstition

Assign individuals to refine the telling of a story. Collect stories on audio or videotape or organize a storytelling troupe to visit schools, community centers, retirement homes, book clubs, and malls.

Budget: Under $25

Sources:

A useful source is the collection of six posters, tales, and whole language activities packaged by Gerald McGermott's *Adventures in Folklore: Trickster Tales*, Jenson Publications.

Aardema, Verna, *Anansi Does the Impossible*, Atheneum, 1997.

Alston, Charlotte Blake, "Introducing African Storytelling" in *Tales as Tools: The Power of Story in the Classroom*, National Storytelling Press, 1994, 174-175.

Bankole, Adisa, "Afrika's Melanin Melody," *National Black Storytellers Newsletter*, Fall, 1996, 3.

Cabral, Len, *Anansi's Narrow Waist* (easy reader in English and Spanish), Addison-Wesley, 1994.

Coggswell, Gladys, *Well Shut My Mouth* (audiocassette), Coggswell Communications, 1995.

Goss, Linda, "Anansi and the Wisdom Tree," *World & I*, February 1995, 272-273.

———, et al., *Jump Up and Say: Anthology of African-American Storytelling*, Simon & Schuster 1995.

Hallworth, Grace, et al., *Our Favourite Stories From Around the World*, Longman, 1994.

Hamilton, Virginia, "The Animals Share," *Scholastic Storyworks*, October 1997, 20-23.

———, *The People Could Fly*, Knopf, 1985.

Harrington, Janice, *Janice N. Harrington, Storyteller* (audiocassette), PogoStudio, 1996.

Miller, Corki, and Mary Ellen Snodgrass, *Storytellers: A Biographical Directory of 120 English-Speaking Storytellers Worldwide*, McFarland, 1998.

Norfolk, Bobby, "Anansi the Spider and His Six Sons" in *We Like Kids*, GoodYear Books, 1995.

Ogunleye, Tolagbe, "Afro-American Folklore," *Journal of Black Studies*, March 1997, 435-456.

"Tricksters from Around the World," *Scholastic Storyworks*, October 1997, 24-25.

Weiss, Jim, *Animal Tales* (audiocassette and CD), Greathall Productions, 1990.

Alternative Applications: Organize a discussion group to determine why black storytellers prize verbal prowess and trickery, as demonstrated in storytelling, jump stories, testifying, the dozens, toasting, dissing or dishing, group participation, call and response, and rap. Comment on the difference between white society's economic or physical power and the disenfranchised black community's psychological power.

Buddies and Pals

Age/Grade Level or Audience: Middle school and high school literature and drama classes.

Description: Tell the stories of biracial friendships.

Procedure: Assign a pair of students to summarize the friendship between a black and a white person. Choose from these works:

The Adventures of Huckleberry Finn	*Aida*
The Autobiography of Miss Jane Pittman	*Brian's Song*
Driving Miss Daisy	*Ellen Foster*
Fallen Angels	*Kaffir Boy*
The Miss Firecracker Contest	*A Patch of Blue*
Queen	*Roots*
Summer of My German Soldier	*To Sir with Love*

Have students tell the story of the friendship from opposite points of view to express character traits, behaviors, and attitudes that strengthen the relationship. Videotape the storytelling session.

Budget: Under $25

Sources:
A variety of stories, novels, plays, biographies, histories, and poems about black-white friendship.

Alternative Applications: Form a character web or Venn diagram demonstrating unifying traits in a black-white friendship. Use the finished diagram as the springboard for impromptu storytelling, for example, a description of the shared travels of Huck and Jim in *The Adventures of Huckleberry Finn* or a summary of the athletic achievements of Brian and Gale in *Brian's Song*.

Encouraging the Storyteller

Age/Grade Level or Audience: Teenage and adult volunteers.

Description: Form a volunteer group to serve as migrant griots.

Procedure: Organize a local griot group to visit libraries, schools, storytelling festivals, malls, retirement homes, and centers for the handicapped. Conduct workshops demonstrating method and delivery styles. Provide the following information about the importance of the storyteller in society:

- ◆ Storytelling is the oldest literary art.
- ◆ It demonstrates the uniqueness of the griot's outlook.
- ◆ It has influenced every nation as a form of expression.
- ◆ Traditional tales grow and develop as outgrowths of the griot's creativity.
- ◆ Imaginative stories demonstrate the power of ideas.
- ◆ Characters can be animals and inanimate objects as well as people.
- ◆ Human themes remain constant from country to country.
- ◆ People naturally love stories.
- ◆ Oral stories pass naturally to the written page.
- ◆ The inspiration of stories often leads to other forms of expression singing, dancing, drawing, making shadow pictures, creating string art, writing, pantomiming, acting, joke-telling, reading, conversing, debating, and worship.
- ◆ In whatever form they exist, they emphasize an important truth—that people everywhere have much in common.

Conclude with examples of the value of storytelling drawn from the life of Alex Haley, the African American author who located a Mandingo griot in Gambia who recalled the episodes of Haley's ancestors.

Budget: Under $25

Sources:

Gonzales, Doreen, *Alex Haley: Author of "Roots,"* Enslow Publications, 1995.
Haley, Alex, and David Stevens, *Alex Haley's Queen*, Avon, 1994.
Ki-Zerbo, Joseph, "Oral Tradition as a Historical Source," *UNESCO Courier*, April 1990, 43-46.
Shirley, David, *Alex Haley, Author*, Chelsea House, 1994.
Williams, Sylvia B., *Alex Haley, Story Teller*, Abdo and Daughters, 1996.

Alternative Applications: Have storytellers invite listeners to develop their own oral skills by embellishing or retelling stories in different settings. For example, try these alterations:

◆ Reset "Zomo the Rabbit" in a country with a different climate and terrain from its native West Africa.

◆ Tell the story of "Tim O'Toole and the Wee Folk" from a southern black point of view.

◆ Create a trickster story about an African animal, such as a crocodile, gnu, dik-dik, ostrich, cobra, wildebeest, or hippopotamus.

Griot for a Day

Age/Grade Level or Audience: Middle school literature, language, drama, or speech classes.

Description: Have students assume the role of griot.

Procedure: Assign students to compile a family history dating back as far as they can put together. Have them speak their family's story into a tape recorder or camcorder in the style of the African griot, who is the repository of African genealogical lore.

Budget: Under $25

Sources:

Interviews with elderly family members or family historians, albums, written histories, genealogies, church records, letters, diaries, family Bibles, or other sources of family data.

"African American Genealogy," http//ourworld.compuserve.com/homepages/ Cliff_m.

"Black Family Heritage," http//www.afrinet.net/~hallhafrotalk/afroaug95/1894.hml.

"Black Pioneers," http//www.localnet.com/~adonis2/pioall.htm.

Carlberg, Nancy E., *Getting a Quick Start Up Your Family Tree*, Carlberg Press, 1993.

"CLP Pennsylvania Department Resources in African American Genealogy," http//www.clpgh.org/CLP/Pennsylvaniaoak_penna.32.html.

Croom, Emily, *The Genealogist's Companion and Sourcebook*, Betterway Books, 1994.

Florman, Kurt, *Take Your Place in History: A Personal Chronology*, Heritage Books, 1993.

Helmbold, F. Wilbur, *Tracing Your Ancestry: A Step-by-Step Guide to Researching Your Family History* and *Tracing Your Ancestry Logbook*, Oxmoor House, 1976.

Ki-Zerbo, Joseph, "Oral Tradition as a Historical Source," *UNESCO Courier*, April 1990, 43-46.

Ramazani, Mwanvuwa A., *African Names: Claiming Your True Heritage*, Montecom Publishing, 1995.

Alternative Applications: Appoint a person to serve as family griot to collect materials for a scrapbook, written history, database, website, or audio genealogy. Encourage the griot to refine and add to the history by performing at family gatherings, such as holiday feasts, reunions, neighborhood parties, or church festivals. Pair the griot with a family photographer, who records events in snapshots, group portraits, or videotape. Link up with other families with the same surname.

Rabbit Ears

Age/Grade Level or Audience: Local library or college storytelling festival; civic festivals; literary societies.

Description: Hold a Rabbit Ears festival.

Procedure: Open a storytelling festival with videotapes of African folk tales such as *Rabbit Ears Anansi,* featuring actor Denzel Washington as narrator, or *Rabbit Ears Koi and the Kola Nuts,* featuring storyteller and actress Whoopi Goldberg. Emphasize the role of the trickster hare, tortoise, chevrotain, or spider by comparing their function and significance to Native American folk tales, such as *Spider Woman's Granddaughter* and *The Way to Rainy Mountain,* or to Joel Chandler Harris's Uncle Remus tales, which derived from African slaves.

Budget: $25-$50

Sources:
The video "Rabbit Ears Koi and the Kola Nuts."
Abraham, Roger D., *African Folktales*, Pantheon Books, 1983.
Alexander, Lloyd, *The Fortune-Tellers*, Dutton Children's Books, 1992.
Miller, Corki, and Mary Ellen Snodgrass, *Storytellers: A Biographical Directory of 120 English-Speaking Storytellers Worldwide*, McFarland, 1998.
"National Storytelling Association," http//users.aol.com/storypagensa.htm.
Spalding, Henry D., compl. and ed., *Encyclopedia of Black Folklore and Humor*, J. David Publishers, 1990.
Wolkstein, Diane, *The Magic Orange Tree and Other Haitian Folktales*, Schocken 1997.

Alternative Applications: Conduct a summer reading program featuring African folk tales, myths, riddles, proverbs, dramas, and tongue twisters. Provide a variety of hands-on activities, such as puppet shows, coloring contests, sidewalk chalk art, and taped retellings in the children's words. Offer prizes of books, tapes, and records by storytellers such as Jackie Torrance and Chinua Achebe.

Round Robin African Adventure

Age/Grade Level or Audience: Kindergarten or elementary language classes; church school, scout troops.

Description: Have students contribute to an African adventure story.

Procedure: Begin a story by introducing a black protagonist, an African setting, and conflict. For example:

♦ On a hot summer morning, Dano rode over the wavy savannah and along the Niger River into the village. On the back of Jako, his faithful gray donkey, Dano was going to buy supplies for the grain harvesters. When he slid down from Jako and reached for the leather coin bag that the chief had tied to his belt, he discovered that the money was missing ...

♦ Miriam stood at the top of the bluff and looked far out over the Serengeti toward a great black cloud. "Could be a herd of wildebeest," she mused. Waiting to see them gallop past, she sat in the tall grass and absentmindedly wove a grass crown spiked with blue tickweed and daisies. Suddenly, a black locust plopped on her lap, followed by three on her head and a fourth on her ear. Before she could jump up, the air filled with swarming locusts ...

Have students take turns explaining what the protagonist does next. As the story passes from one participant to the other, ask questions about the purpose of the character's actions and the likely outcomes. Stop the story before the conclusion and assign each student to end the adventure on paper. Read aloud the varied responses.

Budget: Under $25

Sources:

Baker, Augusta, *Storytelling: Art and Technique*, 2nd edition, R. R. Bowker, 1987.

"ITV Net-Live Webcast-Storytellers," http//mail.itv.net/livestorytellers.htm.

Ki-Zerbo, Joseph, "Oral Tradition as a Historical Source," *UNESCO Courier*, April 1990, 43-46.

Lester, Julian, *How Many Spots Does a Leopard Have?*, Scholastic, Incl, 1989.

"National Storytelling Association," http//users.aol.com/storypagensa.htm.

Alternative Applications: Circulate a group of story beginnings featuring African American characters and/or animals. Have students respond to what has been written on each. As the stories grow, continue passing them around until everyone has had a part in the telling. Select a separate group to illustrate some of the stories. Place typed copies alongside the artwork in a class scrapbook or add to a website or database.

Tell-It-Yourself

Age/Grade Level or Audience: Kindergarten and elementary classes; library story hours; local storytelling festival; literary societies.

Description: Encourage children to make up their own versions of famous stories.

Procedure: Conclude a storytelling session with a prompt that leaves room for children to tell or write their own version of a similar story. For example, finish a telling of Br'er Rabbit stories with these openers:

- One day, Br'er Rabbit was just cranking the bucket up to the top of the well when he looked over his shoulder and saw ...
- On a snowy January morning, Br'er Fox and Br'er Bear got so hungry that they ...
- During the spring, all of the Kenyan animals, big and small, got together in the grassland to ...
- Even though the sun was shining and the grass green, baby zebra was worried because ...
- Around the Yoruba village, there was a lot of talk about the elephant's child ...

Let children take turns audiotaping their conclusions to a story. Type up the finished tales for them to illustrate and bind into a storybook for later story hours or present copies to parents.

Budget: Under $25

Sources:

Baker, Augusta, *Storytelling: Art and Technique*, 2nd edition, R. R. Bowker, 1987.

Henrich, Steve and Jean, *Story Starters on Ancient Africa*, Charlesbridge, 1991.

"ITV Net-Live Webcast-Storytellers," http//mail.itv.net/livestorytellers.htm.

Ki-Zerbo, Joseph, "Oral Tradition as a Historical Source," *UNESCO Courier*, April 1990, 43-46.

Lester, Julian, *How Many Spots Does a Leopard Have?*, Scholastic, Incl, 1989.

"National Storytelling Association," http//users.aol.com/storypagensa.htm.

Alternative Applications: Have students retell or draw European favorites from an African point of view. Reset these and other favorites:

"Cinderella"	"Goldilocks and the Three Bears"
"Jack and the Beanstalk"	"The Little Mermaid"
"Little Red Riding Hood"	"Pinocchio"
"Rapunzel"	"Rumplestiltskin"
"Snow White"	"The Three Billy Goats Gruff"

Uncle Remus

Age/Grade Level or Audience: Kindergarten and elementary school students; religious schools.

Description: Hold a daily reading of an Uncle Remus story.

Procedure: Play recordings or read aloud from a compendium of Uncle Remus stories. Ask volunteers to explain how the weaker animal is able to evade the stronger. Organize groups of students to illustrate or act out key moments in each drama.

Budget: $25-$50

Sources:
The film *Song of the South* (1946) or the filmstrip "Uncle Remus and the Tarbaby Story" from Walt Disney Productions.
Harris, Joel Chandler, *Uncle Remus: Tales*, Beehive Georgia, 1992.
———, *Uncle Remus, His Songs and His Sayings,* Penguin, 1982.

Alternative Applications: Screen a copy of the film or video *Song of the South* or show the Walt Disney Productions sound filmstrip "Uncle Remus and the Tarbaby Story." Have students learn the songs "Laughing Place" and "Zippity Doo Dah." Ask volunteers to add gestures and mimicry as the class sings the songs.

Using the Storyboard

Age/Grade Level or Audience: Kindergarten and elementary students; church school classes; Cub and Brownie scouts.

Description: Arrange storyboard pictures into a workable order, then form a group to compose a single story to fit the pictures.

Procedure: Have students draw pictures of African life, then post their creations in any order on a storyboard. With the group leader's help, have volunteers suggest ways of ordering the stories to comprise a single plot or several variations of a plot. Tape stories or place on a database alongside drawings.

Budget: Under $25

Sources:

Adlerman, Dan, *Africa Calling*, Coyote Press, 1996.

"Africa Online," http//www.africaonline.com.

Alexander, Lloyd, *The Fortune-Teller*, Dutton, 1992.

Arnold, Caroline, *African Animals*, Morrow Junior Books, 1997.

Binns, Tony, *The People and Environment in Africa*, John Wiley and Sons, 1995.

Chadwick, Douglas H., "A Place for Parks in the New South Africa," *National Geographic*, July 1996, 2-41.

Cobb, Charles E., Jr., "Eritrea Wins the Peace," *National Geographic*, June 1996, 82-105.

Fodor's Kenya, Tanzania, Seychelles, Fodor's Travel Guides, 1997.

Halliburton, Warren J., and Kathilyn Solomon Probosz, *African Landscapes*, Crestwood House, 1993.

"Serengeti," http//www.cyberatl.net/~young/.

"Tanzania, "http//www.africa.com/~venture/wildfron/wildtanz.htm.

Theroux, Paul, "Down the Zambezi," *National Geographic*, October 1997, 2-31.

"Uganda," http//imul.com/uganda/.

"Zimbabwe," http//www.mother.com/~zimweb/History.html.

Alternative Applications: Have the class dictate a completed story into a tape recorder, then select one person to point to each picture as the story is played back or record the pictures in order on videotape. Use art software, such as Illustrator, Freehand, MacDraw, or MacPaint, and desktop publishing to produce finished copies for distribution and free reading. Present this program as the focal point of a church, school, banquet, or PTA parent night program.

Writing

An African American Textbook

Age/Grade Level or Audience: College education course.

Description: Outline a K-12 syllabus of black literature.

Procedure: Select works from varied genres and cultures for a K-12 series of reading, writing, and literature studies on black literature. Divide the table of contents by theme, period, or genre. Choose illustrations, photographs, and icons to accompany literary time lines. Propose a title for the series and covers for individual works, workbooks, peripheral materials, and teacher's editions.

Budget: Under $251

Sources:
State syllabi and overviews of scope and sequence for each grade level.

Abrahams, Roger D., *African Folktales*, Pantheon Books, 1983.

Ashabranner, Brent K., ed., *The Lion's Whiskers and Other Ethiopian Tales*, Linnet Books, 1997.

Brown, Stewart, ed., *Caribbean Poetry Now*, Edward Arnold, 1992.

Courlander, Harold, *A Treasury of African Folklore*, Marlowe & Co., 1996.

Discovering Multicultural America (database), Gale, 1997.

Gale, Steven H., *West African Folktales*, National Textbook, 1995.

Gates, Henry Louis, gen. ed., *The Norton Anthology of African American Literature*, W. W. Norton & Co., 1997.

Halliburton, Warren J., *Historic Speeches of African Americans*, Franklin Watts, 1993.

Mullane, Deirdre, ed., *Crossing the Danger Water: Three Hundred Years of African-American Writing*, Anchor Books, 1993.

Naylor, Gloria, *Children of the Night: The Best Short Stories by Black Writers, 1967 to the Present*, Little, Brown & Co., 1996.

Polette, Nancy, *Multicultural Readers Theatre*, Book Lures, 1994.

Rosenberg, Donna, *Folklore, Myths, and Legends: A World Perspective*, National Textbook Company, 1997.

————, *World Literature*, National Textbook Company, 1992.

Segal, Aaron, Carole Berotte Joseph, and Marie-José N'Zengou-Tayo, *Caribbean Literature: An Anthology*, National Textbook, 1998.

Senanu, K. E., and T. Vincent, eds., *A Selection of African Poetry*, Longman, 1990.

Worley, Demetrice A., and Jesse Perry, Jr., eds. *African-American Literature: An Anthology*, 2nd edition, National Textbook, 1998.

Alternative Applications: Create series of Afrocentric textbooks for science, health, math, business, history, speech, drama, vocational studies, foreign language, music, or art.

Black History Essay Contest

Originator: Atlanta-Fulton Public Library, Atlanta, Georgia.

Age/Grade Level or Audience: All ages.

Description: Entrants compete in a theme competition held annually in mid-February.

Procedure: Participants submit a 1,000-word theme on a particular topic, which changes annually. Winners of first or second place awards in middle school, high school, young adult, and adult categories appear at a televised ceremony in early March.

Budget: Under $251

Sources:
Contests for Students, 2nd edition, Gale, 1996.

Henry, Patrick, "An Emerald King," *Traveler*, November 1997, 31.

Kaeser, Gigi, and Peggy Gillespie, *Of Many Colors: Portraits of Multiracial Families*, University of Massachusetts Press, 1997.

"Teen Contest Page," http//users.aol.com/echoesmag/.

Alternative Applications: Organize your own essay contest as a part of a civic, school, library, museum, or church celebration of black history month. Some likely topics include:

♦ Multiracial Families, Multiracial Communities
♦ Black Women and the Civil Rights Movement
♦ The Future of Race Relations in America
♦ Why We Can't Wait
♦ The Dangers of Racial Stereotyping
♦ Returning to Our Roots
♦ Booker T. Washington's Advice: "Cast down your bucket where you are"
♦ The Example of Rosa McCauley Parks
♦ Black Youth and Violence

Black Mystery

Age/Grade Level or Audience: Middle school and high school creative writing classes; writers' clubs.

Description: Brainstorm a mystery around black themes.

Procedure: Join with a small group and outline the plot of a mystery mininovel set in a black community and featuring a black detective. Divide the writing of chapters evenly among the group. Pass the work from one to the other and add events that lead to a solution to the crime. Publish the finished black mystery in mimeographed form or mount on a library website.

Budget: $25-$50

Sources:
Carey, Gary, and Mary Ellen Snodgrass, *A Multicultural Handbook to Literature*, McFarland, 1998.
Holm, Kirsten, ed., *1998 Writer's Market: Where & How to Sell What You Write*, Writer's Digest Books, 1997.
Lester, Meera, *Writing for the Ethnic Markets*, Writer's Connection, 1991.
Winarski, Diana L, "The Rhythm of Writing and Art," *Teaching K-8,* October 1997, 39-40.
Writing in Multilingual Classrooms, Taylor & Francis, 1995.

Alternative Applications: Give a public reading of the finished mystery or have a group act out the story or perform the dialogue in the style of a reading theater. Submit the finished work to a publisher such as Highsmith or Mysterious Press, or to a mystery magazine, particularly *Inside Detective, New Mystery, World's Best Mystery, Crime and Suspense Stories, Ellery Queen's Mystery Magazine, Mystery Review, Alfred Hitchcock Mystery Magazine, Hardboiled, Whispering Willow's Mystery Magazine, Murderous Intent, Red Herring Mystery Magazine, P.I. Magazine,* or

Detective Files. Consult *Writer's Market* for complete details about manuscript submissions.

 ### Campaign Push

Age/Grade Level or Audience: Teenagers and adults.

Description: Support the campaigns of non-white candidates.

Procedure: Organize a volunteer group to assist the political campaigns of non-white candidates, particularly those entering politics for the first time. Consider the following strategies:

◆ Compose short radio and TV spots emphasizing community issues.
◆ Create handouts, leaflets, and brochures featuring facts about the candidates' background and qualifications for public office.
◆ Distribute material in a variety of neighborhoods, particularly where the candidate has the least name recognition.
◆ Organize a satellite group to create get-out-the-vote literature to encourage first-time voters, working people, homebound, and the elderly to go to the polls to protect their interests by selecting worthy candidates.
◆ List an assortment of catchy phrases to use on banners, bumper stickers, lapel pins, and give-aways, such as key rings, balloons, shopping bags, mugs, and fans.

In addition to assisting candidates, present to city officials a list of likely non-white participants for zoning and library boards, appearance committee, and tourism and commerce commissions.

Budget: $75-$100

Sources:
Consult the League of Women Voters or party headquarters for models used by other candidates.

Hershey, Marjorie R., *Running for Office: The Political Education of Campaigners*, Books Demand, 1997.

Alternative Applications: Organize a letters-to-the-editor campaign to keep positive statements before readers' eyes throughout the election pre-season. Keep the tone upbeat and hopeful that your candidates will make a difference in the quality of people's lives.

The Clothilde

Originator: George Schroeder, genealogist and reference librarian, Mobile, Alabama.

Age/Grade Level or Audience: High school or college drama or literature class; thespian society; civic pageant.

Description: Compose a play about the *Clothilde,* the last slave ship to reach America.

Procedure: Assign participants to create their own roles in a play about the last slave ship, such as these:

- ◆ auctioneer
- ◆ boatswain
- ◆ Captain William Fowler
- ◆ first mate
- ◆ overseer
- ◆ slave

- ◆ boat-builder Timothy Meaher
- ◆ buyer
- ◆ cook
- ◆ legislator
- ◆ procurer
- ◆ slave dealer

Dramatize the following events:

- ◆ end of slave trade in 1807
- ◆ launching of the *Clothilde* in 1859
- ◆ kidnapping of Africans from the Guinea coast
- ◆ arrival of Africans in Mobile Bay, Mobile, Alabama
- ◆ apprehension of the illegal delivery in the Mississippi Sound
- ◆ Captain William Fowler's escape up the Mobile River
- ◆ unloading of the human cargo
- ◆ burning of the *Clothilde*
- ◆ freeing of the Guinea slaves
- ◆ creation of the Plateau community
- ◆ life of the last surviving passenger, Cudjoe Lewis

Budget: Under $251

Sources:
"An African-American Chronology of Important Dates," http//athenaenglish.vt.edu/ L17/BWW/chronology.html.
African American History in the Press, 1851-1899, Gale, 1996.
Asante, Molefi K., *Historical and Cultural Atlas of African Americans*, Macmillan, 1991.
"Black History," http//www.slip.net/~rigged/history.html.

"Black History Month Let's Get Started," http//www.netnoir.comspotlight/bhm/jbhm. html.

Cantor, George, *Historic Landmarks of Black America*, Gale, 1991.

Forge, Alice, and Karen E. Quinones Miller, "The Philadelphia Story," *People*, November 10, 1997, 123-124.

Gillespie, Marcia Ann, "Men on My Mind," *Ms.*, November/December 1997, 1.

Hine, Darlene Clark, Elsa Barkley Brown, and Rosalyn Terborg-Penn, *Black Women in America: An Historical Encyclopedia,* Carlson Publishing, 1993.

Mabunda, L. Mpho, ed. *The African American Almanac*, 7th edition Gale, 1997.

"Slavery," http//www.afu.org/~afu43300/slave.html.

Alternative Applications: Write memoirs of individual passengers aboard the *Clothilde*, particularly the captain, first mate, crew, overseer, and the slaves themselves. Compose letters to relatives in Africa or friends who were previously enslaved. Note the political and social situation of the *Clothilde's* passengers.

Denouncing Slavery

Age/Grade Level or Audience: High school or college writing or journalism classes.

Description: Rewrite the Germantown Mennonite Resolution Against Slavery of 1688.

Procedure: Study the logic, spelling, grammar, and phrasing of the first formal abolitionist protest in colonial America. Rewrite strategic sentences in contemporary language, removing tones of sexism and racism. Focus on human rights. Consider these original statements:

◆ Is there any that would be done or handled at this manner?

◆ Yea, rather it is worse for them, which say they are Christians; for we hear that the most part of such negers are brought hither against their will and consent, and that many of them are stolen.

◆ There is a saying, that we should do to all men like as we will be done ourselves; making no difference of what generation, descent, or colour they are.

◆ This makes an ill report in all those countries of Europe, where they hear of (it), that the Quakers do here handel men as they handel there the cattle.

◆ Pray, what thing in the world can be done worse towards us, than if men should rob and steal us away, and sell us for slaves to strange countries; separating husbands from their wives and children.

Budget: Under $25

Sources:

Boyd, Bill, "Who Are the Mennonites," *Macon Telegraph*, October 5, 1997.

Discovering Multicultural America (database), Galenet, 1997.

Mabunda, L. Mpho, ed., *The African American Almanac*, 7th edition, Gale, 1997.

"Mennonite-Related Information on the Internet," http//www.goshen.com/~paulmr/ Menno.html.

Alternative Applications: Discuss in small groups these and other points expressed in the Germantown Mennonite Resolution:

◆ Here is liberty of conscience, which is right and reasonable; here ought to be likewise liberty of the body, except of evil-doers, which is another case.

◆ How fearful and faint-hearted are many at sea, when they see a strange vessel, being afraid it should be a Turk, and they should be taken, and sold for slaves into Turkey.

◆ ... have these poor negers not as much right to fight for their freedom, as you have to keep them slaves?

◆ Now consider well this thing, if it is good or bad.

E-mailing Black History

Age/Grade Level or Audience: Elementary or middle school writing or computer classes.

Description: Start an e-mail chain letter on the importance of black history.

Procedure: Compose a letter about Black History Month to send to neighboring schools or schools in other states. Attach copies of activities calendars. List and explain what activities the local school supports to honor black heroes and achievements. Inquire what events in other districts celebrate black history.

Budget: Under $25

Alternative Applications: Keep a database of replies to the e-mail chain letter. Print the collection and distribute to state education centers, teacher training centers, and educational organizations, such as PTA, NEA, and AFT.

Emblems of Africa

Age/Grade Level or Audience: Elementary or middle school writing classes; religious school; scout troops.

Description: Teach students to write emblem poems.

Procedure: Have students write an emblem poem about Africa. Have them begin by writing vertically on the page a short word connected with Africa, such as Benin, Nile, Congo, Niger, or Shaka. Begin a line of verse with each letter. For example:

> **A**long way from where I live,
> **F**ar from my town, my school,
> **R**ises the outline of a great black nation.
> **I** can't see Africa from here,
> **C**an't here its music or taste its sweet fruits.
> **A**frica seems so far away.

Budget: Under $25

Sources:

Fischer, Alexandra E., *A to Z Animals Around the World*, Putnam Publishing Group, 1994.

Hamilton, Robyn, ed, *Africa Activity Book: Arts, Crafts, Cooking and Historical Aids*, Edupress, 1996.

Hartmann, Wendy, *One Sun Rises: An African Wildlife Counting Book*, Dutton Child Books, 1994.

Isadora, Rachel, *Over the Green Hills*, Greenwillow Books, 1992.

Alternative Applications: Other types of shaped verse may appeal to stronger writers or students learning to use a computer. Type on a word processor a poem shaped like a coconut, mamba, ostrich, ankh, or banana or fill in the shape of Africa with simple verbal images, such as broad sands, mighty rivers, crinkly ferns, splash of falls, black skin, and smiling faces.

Explaining Black Satire

Age/Grade Level or Audience: High school or college writing or literature class.

Description: Compose an introduction to African American satire.

Procedure: Show how black writers make skillful use of complex types of comedy as a means of expressing racial humor. Using models from famous black satirists, particularly Alice Walker, Toni Morrison, Terri McMillan, Paul Keens-Douglas, Maya Angelou, Zora Neale Hurston, Dick Gregory, Mari Evans, Alice Childress, Bill Cosby, or Nikki Giovanni, define and compile a textbook on humor by illustrating these components of comedy:

aphorism	black humor	camp
caricature	diatribe	didacticism
doggerel	epigram	fable
fabliau	farce	folk tale
folly literature	hyperbole	incidental satire
invective	irony	jingle
lampoon	limerick	political satire
rap	repartee	understatement
wit		

Budget: Under $25

Sources:

Bergman, David, ed., *Camp Grounds: Style and Homosexuality*, University of Massachusetts Press, 1993.

Carey, Gary, and Mary Ellen Snodgrass, *A Multicultural Handbook to Literature*, McFarland, 1998.

DISCovering Authors (CD-ROM), Gale, 1993.

Henry, Laurie, *The Fiction Dictionary*, Story Press, 1995.

Snodgrass, Mary Ellen, *The Encyclopedia of Satirical Literature*, ABC-Clio, 1997.

Stern, Jane, and Michael Stern, *The Encyclopedia of Pop Culture*, HarperPerennial, 1992.

Alternative Applications: Compose a chapter, textbook, web site, or encyclopedia entry on African American humor. Include information about epithets, blues style, dialect, sarcasm, call and response, rap, signifying, dissing or dishing, and the dozens.

A Friend to Write

Age/Grade Level or Audience: Middle school geography and writing classes; church groups: scout troops and 4-H clubs; civic, foreign language, and travel clubs.

Description: Start a black-on-white pen pal society.

Procedure: Acquire names of people willing to be pen pals. Match backgrounds with local writers of the opposite race who are eager to start a correspondence. Exchange photos, maps, and information about school events, government, local landmarks and wildlife, food, activities, and holidays.

Budget: $25-$50

Sources:

Friends Around the World, P. O. Box 10266, Merrillville, Indiana 46411- 0266

International Pen Friends, P. O. Box 290065, Brooklyn, New York 11229

"Pen Pals, Pen Pals, and Even More Pen Pals," http//wwwbarfweb.com/wwboard/
messages/1029.html.

Student Letter Exchange, 630 Third Avenue, New York, New York 10017

"Welcome to Pen Pals ... Make New Friends," http//www.halcyon.com2001/forum/
penpals/messages/970173.html.

World Pen Pals, 1694 Como Avenue, St. Paul, Minnesota 55108

Worldwide Friendship International, 3749 Brice Run Road, Suite A, Randallstown,
Maryland 21133

Alternative Applications: Use pen pals as an extension of a French class by pairing writers with French-speaking Africans or Caribbean natives from Martinique, St. Bart's, Algeria, Morocco, or Guadaloupe.

Holiday Themes and Celebrations

Age/Grade Level or Audience: Middle school or high school writing class.

Description: Compose a theme contrasting late winter holidays.

Procedure: Write an informational paper contrasting four contiguous holidays Christmas, Kwanzaa, Winter Solstice, and Hanukkah. Have writers name historical and legendary aspects of each holiday and contrast decor, symbols, spirit, foods, purpose, ceremonial dress, songs, and lore.

Budget: Under $25

Sources:

Copage, Eric V., *Kwanzaa: An African-American Celebration of Culture and Cooking,*
Morrow, 1993.

Oni, Sauda, *What Kwanzaa Means to Me*, DARE Books, 1996.

Robartson, Linda, *The Complete Kwanzaa Celebration Book*, Creative Acrylic, 1993.

Ross, Kathy, *Crafts for Kwanzaa*, Millbrook Press, 1994.

Rufus, Anneli, *World Holiday Book:Celebrations for Every Day of the Year*, Harper, 1994.

St. James, Synthia, *The Gifts of Kwanzaa*, A Whitman, 1994.

Thompson, Sue E., *Holidays, Festival, and Celebrations of the World Dictionary*, 2nd edition, Omnigraphics Inc., 1996.

——, *Holiday Symbols*, Omnigraphics Inc., 1996.

Alternative Applications: Work with a group to design a multiracial winter or spring celebration to coordinate human relations, children's activities, religious beliefs, seasons, music, dance, family, community, history, and tradition.

A Letter of Application

Age/Grade Level or Audience: Middle school or high school writing class.

Description: Have students compose a letter of application to a self-help organization aiding black people.

Procedure: Have students apply to the Catholic World Mission, Peace Corps, Red Cross, WHO, UNICEF, *Medecins sans Frontieres*, or other relief agencies helping black people in Africa, the Caribbean, or pockets of poverty in American cities or counties. Suggest that each letter state the following information:

- ◆ why the candidate chose that place
- ◆ what social or other problems the applicant hopes to alleviate or eradicate, such as hunger, insufficient knowledge of farming or sanitation, poor health standards, or need of industrialization, religion, or education
- ◆ proof that the applicant is dependable
- ◆ talents or skills the applicant plans to utilize
- ◆ examples of projects, responsibilities, or other demonstrations of capability that establish the applicant's sincerity and preparation

Budget: Under $25

Sources:
Descriptions of major social agencies, their aims and purposes, and their organization's style and outreach.

Furtaw, Julia, C., *Black Americans Information Directory, 1993-1994*, 3rd edition, Gale, 1993.

Alternative Applications: Suggest that applicants make a list of preparations, equipment, materials, and supplies necessary for a one-year stay in the chosen location. For example, for a sojourn in Kenya, list these necessities:

bottled water	bush clothing	camping gear
compass	dehydrated foods	first aid kit
hiking shoes	inoculations	maps
medicines	repair kit	shortwave radio

Letter-Writing Campaign

Age/Grade Level or Audience: All ages.

Description: Organize a letter-writing campaign to encourage businesses, newspapers, television stations, and the entertainment media to include blacks more equally in product design and advertising campaigns, particularly in areas heavily populated by African Americans.

Procedure: Divide into small groups and select an area of American life in which blacks are under-represented, such as fashion ads, toys, greeting cards, luxury items, and makeup. Develop positive statements which stress that black Americans are also consumers and that a fair representation of all races benefits both the buyer and the seller. Propose specific items to be altered or deleted, such as Mother's Day cards that depict only white families or toys and games that exclude the faces of non-white children. Conclude with a leaflet campaign directed at a particular group, such as the citizens of a metropolitan area that offers no transportation to non-white residents or bankers who refuse loans to working class people.

Budget: $25-$50

Sources:
Business registries, local companies, newspapers, and radio and television networks.

Alternative Applications: Organize a citizen watch committee to screen local activities, advertisements, and campaign materials for exclusion of minorities and their concerns and interests. Post on a website or in a civic newsletter the committee's findings.

New Laws for Old

Age/Grade Level or Audience: Middle school history and writing classes.

Description: Rewrite laws to include all races.

Procedure: Work in small groups to study specific segments of the Constitution and Bill of Rights. Select paragraphs to improve by establishing laws against segregation, exclusion, or elitism. Assemble the finished document on an overhead projector to read aloud and refine. Appoint a grammarian to settle questions about agreement, tense, punctuation, and capitalization.

Budget: $25-$50

Sources:
The Constitution (audiocassette), Recorded Books.
Fallon, Shannon L., *The Bill of Rights: What It Is, What It Means and How It's Been Misused*, Dickens Press, 1995.
Prolman, Marilyn, *The Constitution*, Children's Press, 1995.

Alternative Applications: Appoint a group to examine local statutes and school laws to locate racial inequities. Copy each law and distribute to students to determine how such laws come to be written and why they discriminate against everyone.

Poetry Workshop

Originator: James C. Morris, poet.

Age/Grade Level or Audience: All ages.

Description: Present a community, library, or school poetry workshop.

Procedure: Organize a poetry workshop to encourage beginning writers of all ages. Divide participants into groups loosely based on expertise rather than age. Use models of major poets as springboards. For example, discuss as a group the emotive, lyrical power of James C. Morris's "Chanson Petite":

Oh, America!

Oh, *my* America!
How much longer
Do I have to
Remain stronger?
Surely, America,
You must know
Endurance carries
Elastic band
Across the mental land
That can only stretch and stretch ...
And stretch just *so!*
How far yet, how far
Do I have to go?
Oh, America!
Oh, *my* America!

After students have developed their own style, subjects, and voice, select the best of their output for publication in a workshop chapbook, newsletter, bulletin board display, poster, literary magazine, web site, or public reading. Offer prizes, such as anthologies of poetry, essay, short fiction, and drama by black authors.

Budget: $25-$50

Sources:

Bontemps, Arna, ed., *American Negro Poetry*, Hill & Wang, 1974.

Brown, Stewart, ed., *Caribbean Poetry Now*, Edward Arnold, 1992.

Dove, Rita, *Selected Poems*, Vintage Books, 1993.

Hudson, Wade, *Pass It On: African-American Poetry for Children*, Scholastic, Inc., 1993.

Linthwaite, Illona, ed., *Ain't I a Woman?: A Book of Women's Poetry from Around the World*, Wings Books, 1987.

Alternative Applications: Extend the writing workshop to other forms of expression, such as rap, songs, essays, letters, short stories, dialogues, biography, memoir, and history. Divide participants into groups to edit, rewrite, and produce works via desktop publishing or to mount on posters and murals in celebration of Black History Month.

 ## Remember Me, Remember Me

Age/Grade Level or Audience: Elementary or middle school writing classes.

Description: Have students compose epitaphs for notable black people.

Procedure: Organize a writing workshop in which students work in pairs. Have them read a variety of source material, then draw on events in the lives of famous black people and compose suitable epitaphs to adorn a statue, roadside plaque, monument, or tombstone. Choose from these and other worthy candidates:

Dr. Charles Drew	Medgar Evers
Zora Neale Hurston	Dr. Ernest Just
Toussaint L'Ouverture	Garrett Augustus Morgan
Jackie Robinson	Emmett Till
Tituba	Nat Turner
Sojourner Truth	Madame C. J. Walker
Ethel Waters	Malcolm X

Have students print their inscriptions on poster paper. Mount their work in a display entitled "Honor Roll of History."

Budget: $25-$50

Sources:

African American History in the Press, 1851-1899, Gale, 1996.

Asante, Molefi K., *Historical and Cultural Atlas of African Americans*, Macmillan, 1991.

"Black History," http//www.slip.net/~rigged/history.html.

"Black History Month Let's Get Started," http//www.netnoir.comspotlight/bhm/jbhm.html.

Corbin, Raymond M., *1,999 Facts about Blacks: A Sourcebook of African- American Achievement*, 2nd edition, Madison Books, 1997.

Dennis, Denise, *Black History for Beginners*, Highsmith, 1992.

Elliot, Jeffrey M., *Encyclopedia of African-American Politics*, ABC-Clio, 1997.

Hine, Darlene Clark, Elsa Barkley Brown, and Rosalyn Terborg-Penn, *Black Women in America: An Historical Encyclopedia,* Carlson Publishing, 1993.

Mabunda, L. Mpho, ed., *The African American Almanac*, 7th edition, Gale, 1997.

Nelson, Rebecca, and Marie J. MacNee, eds., *The Olympic Factbook: A Spectator's Guide to the Summer Games*, Visible Ink Press, 1996.

Saari, Peggy, and Daniel B. Baker, *Explorers and Discoverers: From Alexander the Great to Sally Ride*, U•X•L/Gale, 1995.

Sarpong-Kumankumah, Jojo, "In Defense of Ethnic Studies," *Essence*, August 1992, 134.

Shapiro, William E., ed., *The Kingfisher Young People's Encyclopedia of the United States*, Larousse Kingfisher Chambers, 1994.

Straub, Deborah Gillan, ed., *African American Voices*, U•X•L/Gale, 1996.

Taylor, Kimbelry H., *Black Civil Rights Champions*, Oliver Press, 1995.

"This Person in Black History Thurgood Marshall," http//www.ai.mitedu/~isbell/Hfh/ black/events_and_people/001.thurgood_marshall.

Alternative Applications: Choose a state and make an honor roll of names and accomplishments for its black notables, both dead and alive. For examples, consult this list:

Alabama
Hurston, Zora Neale [traditionally listed as a Floridian] (1891-1960)
Sanchez, Sonia (1934-)
Walker, Margaret (1915-)

Arkansas
Cleaver, Eldridge (1935-)

Delaware
Cary, Mary Ann Shadd (1823-1893)

Florida
Johnson, John Rosamund (1873-1954)
Johnson, James Weldon (1871-1938)

Georgia
King, Dr. Martin Luther, Jr. (1929-1968)
Walker, Alice (1944-)
Yerby, Frank (1916-)

Illinois
Torrence, Jackie (1944-)

Kentucky
Brown, William Wells (1816-1864)

Louisiana
Bontemps, Arna (1902-1973)
Brown, H. Rap (1943-)
Gaines, Ernest (1933-)
Young, Andrew (1932-)

Maryland
Harper, Frances Ellen Watkins (1825-1911)

Mississippi
Moody, Anne E. (1940-)
Wells-Barnett, Ida Bell (1862-1931)
Wright, Richard (1908-1960)

Missouri
Angelou, Maya (1928-)
Gregory, Dick (1932-)
Lester, Julius (1939-)

North Carolina
Jacobs, Harriet Ann (1813-1897)

New York

Haley, Alex (1921-1992)

Ohio

Chesnutt, Charles Waddell (1858-1932)

Oklahoma

Ellison, Ralph (1914-1994)

South Carolina

Childress, Alice (1920-1994)

Jackson, Reverend Jesse (1941-)

Tennessee

Love, Nat (1854-1921)

Texas

Jordan, Barbara (1936-1996)

Virginia

Washington, Booker T. (ca. 1856-1915)

Washington, D.C.

Brown, Sterling (1901-)

Toomer, Jean (1894-1967)

West Virginia

Myers, Walter Dean (1937-)

Slave Days

Age/Grade Level or Audience: High school or college writing classes.

Description: Keep a journal from the point of view of a slave.

Procedure: Have participants record daily life and labors of either a fictional composite character or else a real person, such as Harriet Jacobs, Frederick Douglass, Nat Turner, Sojourner Truth, Tituba, Joseph Cinque, or Harriet Tubman.

Budget: Under $251

Sources:

Films and videos such as *Band of Angels* (1957), *Roots* (1977), *Queen, Glory* (1989), *The Autobiography of Miss Jane Pittman*, or *Amistad* (1997).

"An African-American Chronology of Important Dates," http//athenaenglish.vt.edu/ L17/BWW/chronology.html.

African American History in the Press, 1851-1899, Gale, 1996.

Asante, Molefi K., *Historical and Cultural Atlas of African Americans*, Macmillan, 1991.

"Black History," http//www.slip.net/~rigged/history.html.

"Black History Month Let's Get Started," http//www.netnoir.comspotlight/bhm/jbhm. html.

Cantor, George, *Historic Landmarks of Black America*, Gale, 1991.

Hine, Darlene Clark, Elsa Barkley Brown, and Rosalyn Terborg-Penn, *Black Women in America: An Historical Encyclopedia,* Carlson Publishing, 1993.

Mabunda, L. Mpho, ed., *The African American Almanac*, 7th edition, Gale, 1997.

Ray, Delia, *A National Town: The Story of How the Civil War Began*, Lodestar Books, 1990.

"Slavery." http//www.afu.org/~afu43300/slave.html.

Alternative Applications: Have students combine characters in an adlibbed exchange, such as these occasions:

◆ announcement of a birth	◆ arrival of a new slave
◆ celebration of a wedding	◆ conversation on market day
◆ end of a work day	◆ harvest celebration
◆ manumission	◆ nationwide emancipation
◆ plot to run away	◆ religious ceremonies
◆ reunion with a relative	◆ revolt against harsh conditions

Speaking for the Slave

Age/Grade Level or Audience: Middle school or high school language, drama, or history classes.

Description: Have students write first-person accounts of a slave auction.

Procedure: After a study of the American slave trade, assign every student writer a position on a Civil War era magazine or newspaper. Include editor, columnist, staff writer, proofreader, and layout editor. Have them interview a sea captain, overseer, attendant, slave auctioneer, African captive, observer, wagoneer, or buyer. Combine first-person texts with columns expressing views on pre-war issues, articles on the first black regiment or features on slaves who have gained prominence in the abolitionist movement. Evolve a composite magazine, newspaper, or television document on slavery, which includes information such as:

- ◆ the direction most fleeing slaves take and whom they contact for help along the way
- ◆ why Union generals initially reject the idea of an all-black regiment
- ◆ how slavesellers mask injuries and disease with paint, tar, mixtures of gunpowder and rust, stimulants and other drugs
- ◆ routine use of shackles, flogging, spiked collars, and thumb screws to quell rebels on road gangs or plantation work crews
- ◆ tying rebellious slaves to millstones, windlasses, wheels, and other moving objects
- ◆ how slavers stop hunger strikes by breaking out teeth, prying jaws apart with surgical instruments, and force-feeding strikers
- ◆ what qualities purchasing agents look for in reliable workers, house servants, and breeders
- ◆ why buyers choose members of different tribes so that new slaves could not communicate with each other or raise a revolt
- ◆ the humiliation of being stripped, pinched, prodded, and examined by interested customers, who sometimes tag their choices with colored ribbons or chalk marks
- ◆ the reasons that buyers brand, scar, scald, or hamstring slaves or amputate earlobes, noses, fingers, and toes
- ◆ the reasons that absentee landlords leave unbroken Africans in the hands of brutal, sadistic overseers so that the new arrivals can be properly trained as submissive laborers
- ◆ how overseers degrade African customs so that slaves will reject their homeland and not try to return
- ◆ the sufferings of newly bought slaves traveling in a coffle, bound hand to hand, neck to neck, or ankle to ankle, starved and dehydrated, and lashed by overseers
- ◆ the creation of wearying and confining devices, such as yokes, bells, horns, gags, metal trusses, neck braces, and stocks to keep slaves from running away
- ◆ the increase of torment through the application of pepper, salt water, turpentine, and vinegar to lash wounds
- ◆ the marking of troublesome slaves by the removal of teeth, ears, eyes, fingers, and noses to make them easily identified by slave catchers or patrollers
- ◆ the purchase of hunting dogs trained to the scent of runaway blacks
- ◆ the teaching methods of abolitionists and ministers, who press Africans to learn about Christianity so that they will abandon native rites and religion

Budget: Under $25

Sources:

Films and videos such as *Band of Angels* (1957), *Roots* (1977), *Queen, Glory* (1989), *The Autobiography of Miss Jane Pittman*, or *Amistad* (1997).

"An African-American Chronology of Important Dates," http//athenaenglish.vt.edu/
  L17/BWW/chronology.html.

African American History in the Press, 1851-1899, Gale, 1996.

"Black History," http//www.slip.net/~rigged/history.html.

"Black History Month Let's Get Started," http//www.netnoir.comspotlight/bhm/jbhm.
  html.

Hine, Darlene Clark, Elsa Barkley Brown, and Rosalyn Terborg-Penn, *Black Women
  in America: An Historical Encyclopedia,* Carlson Publishing, 1993.

Mabunda, L. Mpho, ed., *The African American Almanac,* 7th edition, Gale, 1997.

Ray, Delia, *A National Town: The Story of How the Civil War Began,* Lodestar Books,
  1990.

"Slavery," http//www.afu.org/~afu43300/slave.html.

Alternative Applications: Have students recreate slavery with a multi-media show featuring videos, skits, shadow boxes, puppets, posters, schematic drawings, or murals to demonstrate the introduction of new slaves to the working community of a large plantation. Illustrate the tasks of each slave, whether house servant, driver, blacksmith, tanner, carpenter, laundress, nanny, cook, seamstress, weaver, or field hand. Describe beginning English lessons for slaves who haven't learned the language.

 Thank You to the Past

Age/Grade Level or Audience: Elementary school history and writing classes.

Description: Compose a thank-you note to a figure from black history.

Procedure: Explain the style and purpose of a thank-you note, which students will address to heroes and achievers from black history. Choose from these:

- astronauts Mae Jemison and Guinon Bluford
- champions Carol Lewis and Tiger Woods
- humanitarians Clara Hale and Bill Cosby
- inventors Booker T. Washington and Benjamin Banneker
- leaders Barbara Jordan and Martin Luther King, Jr.
- military heroes Colin Powell and Crispus Attucks
- poets Langston Hughes and Gwendolyn Brooks
- storytellers Rex Ellis and Jackie Torrence
- young adult novelists Walter Dean Myers and Virginia Hamilton

Budget: Under $251

Sources:
Carson and Dellosa, *Writing Letters and Thank-You Notes*, Carson-Dellosa, 1995.

Alternative Applications: Extend letter-writing practice with a letter to a newspaper or television news editor encouraging a city-wide celebration of Black History Month or on the improvement of racial relations in public schools.

Words and Snapshots

Age/Grade Level or Audience: Middle school or high school language classes.

Description: Create a story board to describe black people in your community.

Procedure: Have students assemble candid snapshots to discuss and group the photos by mood. Work together to compose an essay describing the different categories, such as monuments, signs, buildings, families, recreation, entertainment, education, worship, markets, neighbors, and race relations.

Budget: $50-$75

Sources:
Local camera clubs, newspaper photos, and library clipping files.
Myers, Walter Dean, *One More River to Cross: An African American Photograph Album*, Harcourt Brace, 1995.
Parks, Gordon, *Half Past Autumn: A Retrospective*, Bulfinch Press, 1997.

Alternative Applications: Create oversized bulletin board displays of photos and essays by copying the words of each composition onto poster paper and surrounding with a frame of photos.

Writing Genre

Age/Grade Level or Audience: Middle school or high school college creative writing or literature classes.

Description: Have students create a resource notebook of literary genres.

Procedure: Instruct students on these and other forms of written language:

aphorism	ballad	beast fable
character sketch	critique	descriptive essay
dialogue	didactic essay	editorial
haiku	legend	letter
limerick	memoir	myth
oral history	personal essay	persuasive argument
riddle	satire	scene
sermon	short story	skit
slogan	sonnet	tableau
travelogue	vignette	written history

As they master the characteristics of each, apply their knowledge to an African American subject, issue, or setting. For example:

- ◆ beast fable involving dissimilar African animals, such as a hyena and an ostrich or a dik-dik and a mamba
- ◆ critique of a film about the black point of view
- ◆ descriptive essay about an imaginary journey during slave times
- ◆ dialogue set in colonial times between slave and master
- ◆ editorial calling for government aid to black migrant workers
- ◆ fan letter to a historical figure, such as Jackie Robinson, Jesse Owens, Josephine Baker, Judith Jamison, Ethel Waters, Hattie McDaniel, or Lionel Hampton
- ◆ haiku describing the goals of Kwanzaa
- ◆ history of a local event involving black people, for instance, a building project
- ◆ legend about a black cowboy, potter, sculptor, or pioneer
- ◆ myth explaining why the leopard has spots, the cobra has fangs, or the zebra has stripes
- ◆ oral history of how the hymn "Amazing Grace" came to be written
- ◆ personal essay about a favorite black athlete or entertainer
- ◆ persuasive argument encouraging employers to hire black laborers and managers.
- ◆ riddles about African animals
- ◆ series of aphorisms explaining why racism hurts everyone
- ◆ short story about a black family
- ◆ skit advertising a product or service offered by a black-owned company
- ◆ slogans to encourage black voters to involve themselves in local political campaigns or community issues, such as representation on the city council
- ◆ travelogue describing the marketplace in St. Bart's, Ocho Rios Falls in Jamaica, Aruba's World War II relics, skin diving in the Virgin Islands, or sailing around the Antigua harbor

Collect the best of genre examples and produce a handbook or database for future reference.

Budget: $25-$50

Sources:

Carey, Gary, and Mary Ellen Snodgrass, *A Multicultural Handbook to Literature*, McFarland, 1998.

Lester, Meera, *Writing for the Ethnic Markets*, Writer's Connection, 1991.

Writing in Multilingual Classrooms, Taylor & Francis, 1995.

Alternative Applications: Create a series of posters on black themes that illustrate rhetorical devices, for example: metaphor, extended metaphor, apostrophe, simile, parallelism, alliteration, caesura, enjambment, personification, synecdoche, metonomy, masculine and feminine rhyme, euphony, cacophony, rhythm, onomatopoeia, hyperbole, and sense impressions.

Appendix

Anthologies

Abrahams, Roger D., *African Folktales,* Pantheon Books, 1983.

African Americans Who Made a Difference: 15 Plays for the Classroom, Scholastic Books, 1996.

Ashabranner, Brent K., ed., *The Lion's Whiskers and Other Ethiopian Tales,* Linnet Books, 1997.

Bontemps, Arna, ed., *American Negro Poetry,* Hill & Wang, 1974.

Brown, Stewart, ed., *Caribbean Poetry Now,* Edward Arnold, 1992.

Carroll, Rebecca, *I Know What the Red Clay Looks Like: The Voice and Vision of Black Women Writers,* Carol Southern Press, 1995.

———, *Swing Low: Black Men Writing,* Carol Southern Press, 1995.

Courlander, Harold, *A Treasury of African Folklore,* Marlowe & Co., 1996.

Day, Frances Ann, *Multicultural Voices in Contemporary Literature,* Heinemann, 1994.

Draper, James P., *Black Literature Criticism,* Gale, 1992.

Ellis, Roger, *Multicultural Theatre: Scenes and Monologues from New Hispanic, Asian, and African-American Plays,* Meriwether Publications, 1996.

Gale, Steven H., *West African Folktales,* National Textbook, 1995.

Gates, Henry Louis, gen. ed., *The Norton Anthology of African American Literature,* W. W. Norton & Co., 1997.

Halliburton, Warren J., *Historic Speeches of African Americans,* Franklin Watts, 1993.

Killens, John Oliver, and Jerry W., Ward, Jr., eds., *Black Southern Voices: An Anthology of Fiction, Poetry, Drama, Nonfiction, and Critical Essays,* Meridian Books, 1992.

Linthwaite, Illone, ed., *Ain't I a Woman: A Book of Women's Poetry from Around the World,* Wings Books, 1993.

Madhubuti, Haki R., and Maulana Karenga, *Million Man March—Day of Absence: A Commemorative Anthology of Speeches, Commentary, Photography,* Third World Press, 1996.

Mullane, Deirdre, ed., *Crossing the Danger Water: Three Hundred Years of African-American Writing,* Anchor Books, 1993.

Naylor, Gloria, *Children of the Night: The Best Short Stories by Black Writers, 1967 to the Present,* Little, Brown & Co., 1996.

Polette, Nancy, *Multicultural Readers Theatre,* Book Lures, 1994.

Rosenberg, Donna, *Folklore, Myths, and Legends: A World Perspective,* National Textbook Company, 1997.

———, *World Literature,* National Textbook Company, 1992.

Segal, Aaron, Carole Berotte Joseph, and Marie-José N'Zengou-Tayo, *Caribbean Literature: An Anthology,* National Textbook, 1998.

Senanu, K. E., and T. Vincent, eds., *A Selection of African Poetry,* Longman, 1990.

Stetson, Erlene, *Black Sister: Poetry by Black American Women, 1746–1980,* Indiana University Press, 1981.

Turner, Glennette Tilley, *Follow in Their Footsteps: Biographies of Ten Outstanding African Americans* (dramatic skits), Cobblehill Books, 1997.

Wickham, DeWayne, ed., *Thinking Black: Some of the Nation's Most Thoughtful and Provocative Black Columnists Speak Their Mind,* Crown Publishing, 1996.

Worley, Demetrice A., and Jesse Perry, Jr., eds. *African-American Literature: An Anthology,* second ed., National Textbook, 1998.

Current Books

Abdul-Raheem, Tajudeen, ed., *Pan-Africanism: Politics, Economy, and Social Change in the Twenty-First Century,* New York University Press, 1997.

African-American Book of Lists, Putna, 1997.

African-American Network, Penguin, 1996.

African-American Resource Guide, Barricade, 1994.

African-American Yellow Pages, Henry Holt & Co., 1996.

Altman, Susan, and Susan Lechner, *Followers of the North Star,* Children's Press, 1993.

America's Victims, Greenhaven Press, 1996.

Anderson, Jervis, *Bayard Rustin: Troubles I've Seen,* Anti-Defamation League, 1997.

Armour, Jody David, *Negrophobia and Reasonable Racism,* New York University Press, 1997.

Bambara, Toni Cade, *Deep Sightings and Rescue Missions,* Random House, 1996.

Barr, Alwyn, *Black Texans: A History of African Americans in Texas, 1528-1995,* second ed., Oklahoma University Press, 1997.

Bwever, Edward, *Africa,* Oryx Press, 1996.

Bonazzi, Robert, *Man in the Mirror: John Howard Griffin and the Story of "Black Like Me,"* Orbis Books, 1997.

Cohn, Janice, *Raising Compassionate, Courageous Children,* Anti-Defamation League, 1997.

Comer, James P., *Waiting for a Miracle: Why Schools Can't Solve Our Problems and How We Can,* Dutton, 1997.

Dyson, Michael Eric, *Race Rules: Navigating the Color Line,* Addison-Wesley, 1996.

Ekeler, William J., ed., *The Black Student's Guide to High School Success,* Greenwood Press, 1997.

Fair, Bryan K., *Notes of a Racial Caste Baby: Color Blindness and the End of Affirmative-Action,* New York University Press, 1997.

Faryna, Stan, Brad Stetson, and Joseph G. Conti, eds., *Black and Right: The Bold New Voice of Black Conservatives in America,* Greenwood Press, 1997.

Gilyard, Keith, *Let's Flip the Script: An African Discourse on Language, Literature and Identity,* Wayne State University Press, 1996.

Hakim, Joy, *A History of Us,* Oxford University Press, 1995.

Holloway, Karla F. C., *Codes of Conduct: Race, Ethics, and the Color of Our Character,* Rutgers University Press, 1995.

hooks, bell, *Killing Rage: Ending Racism,* Henry Holt & Co., 1995.

Hurston, Zora Neale, *Folklore, Memoirs, and Other Writings,* Library of America, 1995.

Inequality: Opposing Viewpoints in Social Problems, Greenhaven Press, 1998.

Interracial America, Greenhaven Press, 1996.

Karas, Phyllis, *The Hate Crime: Teacher's Discussion Guide,* Anti-Defamation League, 1997.

Kelley, Robin D. G., and Earl Lewis, gen. ed., *The Young Oxford History of African Americans,* 11 vols., Oxford University Press, 1997.

Kitchen, Helen, and J. Coleman Kitchen, *South Africa: Twelve Perspectives on the Transition,* Greenwood, 1994.

Lawrence, Beverly Hall, *Reviving the Spirit: A Generation of African Americans Goes Home to Church,* Grove/Atlantic, Inc., 1996.

Levin, Michael, *Why Race Matters: Race Differences and What They Mean,* Greenwood, 1997.

Lobb, Nancy, *Sixteen Extraordinary African Americans,* Walch, 1995.

Maggio, Rosalie, *Talking About People: A Guide to Fair and Accurate Language,* Oryx Press, 1997.

Miller, Randall M., and John David Smith, *Dictionary of Afro-American Slavery,* Greenwood, 1997.

Moon, Spencer, *Reel Black Talk: A Sourcebook of 50 American Filmmakers,* Greenwood Press, 1997.

Nelson, Jill, *Straight, No Chaser: How I Became a Grown-up Black Woman,* Putnam, 1997.

Oliver, Paul, *Conversation with the Blues,* Cambridge University Press, 1997.

Page, Clarence, *Showing My Color: Impolite Essays on Race and Identity,* HarperCollins, 1996.

Parker, Gwendolyn M., *Trespassing: My Sojourn in the Halls of Privilege,* Houghton Mifflin, 1997.

Payne, Lauren, and Claudia Rohling, *We Can Get Along,* Anti-Defamation League, 1997.

Pinsent, Pat, *Children's Literature and the Politics of Equality,* Teachers College Press, 1997.

Prejean, Helen, *The Death Penalty,* Greenhaven Press, 1997.

Proctor, Samuel Dewitt, *The Substance of Things Hoped For: A Memoir of African-American Faith,* Putnam, 1996.

Race Relations, Greenhaven Press, 1996.

Rampersad, Ranold, *Jackie Robinson,* Knopf, 1997.

Rashad, Phylicia, intro., *The African American Family Album,* Oxford University Press, 1995.

Reid-Merritt, Patricia, *Sister Power: How Phenomenal Black Women Are Rising to the Top,* John Wiley & Sons, 1996.

Rodriguez, Junius P., gen. ed., *The Historical Encyclopedia of World Slavery,* ABC-Clio, 1997.

Senna, Carl, *The Black Press and the Struggle for Civil Rights,* Franklin Watts, 1993.

Severino, Carol, Juan C. Guerra, and Johnnella E. Butler, eds., *Writing in Multicultural Settings,* Modern Language Association, 1997.

Shiman, David, *The Prejudice Book,* Anti-Defamation League, 1994.

Shorris, Earl, *New American Blues: A Journey Through Poverty to Democracy,* W. W. Norton & Co., 1997.

Southern, Eileen, *Music of Black America: A History,* W. W. Norton & Co., 1997.

Spencer, Jon Michael, *Protest and Praise: Sacred Music of Black Religion,* Fortress Press, 1997.

Strickland, Michael R., *African-American Poets: Collective Biographies,* Enslow Publishers, 1996.

Wade-Gayles, Gloria, *My Soul Is a Witness: African American Women's Spirituality,* Beacon Press, 1995.

Welfare, Greenhaven Press, 1997.

Worldmark Encyclopedia of Cultures and Daily Life, Gale, 1997.

Electronic Publications

Africa Inspirer (CD-ROM), Tom Snyder Productions.

The Alan Lomax Collection Sampler (CD), Rounder Records, 1997.

American History Inspirer (CD-ROM), Tom Snyder Productions.

American Journey: Women in America (CD-ROM), Primary Source Media, 1995.

American Leaders (CD-ROM), ABC-Clio, 1998.

Anthology of American Folk Music (six CDs), Smithsonian Folkways, 1997.

Associations Unlimited (database), Gale Research.

The Atlantic Slave Trade (CD-ROM), Cambridge University Press, 1997.

Best of Jazz 'Round Midnight (CD), Verve, 1996.

Discovering Multicultural America (database), Gale Research, 1997.

The Essential Jazz Singers (three CDs), Verve, 1996.

Her Heritage: A Biographical Encyclopedia of Famous American Women (CD-ROM), Pilgrim New Media, 1994.

History in Motion: Milestones of the 20th Century (videodisc), Scholastic, 1997.

Holding Up Half the Sky: Women's Voices from Around the World, (four CDs), Shanachie, 1997.

I Can't Be Satisfied—Early American Women Bleus Singers, (two CDs), Yazoo, 1997.

Kidjo, Angelique, *Music from the African World* (CD), Island Records, 1997.

Malcolm X: By Any Means Necessary (CD-ROM), Scholastic, 1997.

The Multicultural Chronicles: American Women (CD-ROM), MicroMedia, 1994.

Powell, Colin, *My American Journey* (four audiocassettes), Audio Editions.

Sourcebook America 1998 (CD-ROM), Gale, 1997.

Struggles for Justice (videodisc), Scholastic, 1997.

Wade in the Water: African American Sacred (four CDs), Smithsonian Folkways, 1996.

West, Cornel, *Race Matters* (three audiocassettes), Audio Editions.

Women in America (CD-ROM), Research Publications International, 1995.

Films and Videos

Africa: Caravans of Gold/Kings and Cities, Knowledge Unlimited.

Africa: Different But Equal/Mastering a Continent, Knowledge Unlimited.

Africa: The Bible and the Gun/The Magnificent African Cake, Knowledge Unlimited.

Africa: The Rise of Nationalism/The Legacy, Knowledge Unlimited.

Africa Before the Europeans, 100-1500, Landmark Films Inc.

African-American Art: Past and Present, Knowledge Unlimited.

African-American Heritage, Schlessinger Media.

The African American Holiday of Kwanzaa, Highsmith.

African American Life, Schlessinger Media.

African Americans, Schlessinger Media.

The Africa Series, University of Illinois.

Alice Walker, Films for the Humanities and Sciences, 1997.

Amazing Grace: Black Women in Sport, Black Women in Sport Foundation, 1993.

American Women of Achievement (video collection), Schlessinger Media.

Amiri Baraka, Films for the Humanities and Sciences, 1997.

Beyond Hate, Anti-Defamation League.

Black Americans of Achievement (video collection), Schlessinger Media.

Black Women Writers, Films for the Humanities and Sciences, 1989.

Booker T. Washington: The Life and the Legacy, Knowledge Unlimited.

Boy, Landmark Films Inc.

Chinua Achebe (video), Films for the Humanities and Sciences, 1997.

The Civil War, Knowledge Unlimited.

Egypt, Knowledge Unlimited.

Frederick Douglass: An American Life, Knowledge Unlimited.

Gifted Hands: The Ben Carson Story, Highsmith.

A History of Slavery in America, Schlessinger Media.

The Klan: A Legacy of Hate in America, Knowledge Unlimited.

Martin Luther King Commemorative Collection, Knowledge Unlimited.

Martin Luther King: "I Have a Dream," Knowledge Unlimited.

Men of Bronze, Knowledge Unlimited.

Mysteries of the Pyramids, Knowledge Unlimited.

Myths of the Pharaohs, Knowledge Unlimited.

Names Can Really Hurt Us, Anti-Defamation League.

Not in Our Town, Anti-Defamation League.

Race and Prejudice in America Today, Highsmith.

Separate But Equal, Knowledge Unlimited.

Sharpton and Fulani in Babylon, Highsmith.

Skin, Landmark Films Inc.

Toni Morrison, Films for the Humanities and Sciences, 1997.

Tutankhamen: The Immortal Pharaoh, Knowledge Unlimited.

Valuing Diversity, Anti-Defamation League.

We Shall Overcome: A History of the Civil Rights Movement, Highsmith.

William H. Johnson: Art and Life of an African American Artist, Knowledge Unlimited.

A World of Difference, Anti-Defamation League.

Zora Is My Name!, Knowledge Unlimited.

Internet Sources

"Africa Express: The Medical Man," httpww.channel14.co.7k/1QVKjkbi/backup/bss/stuck/xpress/xpconn2/xpmedt2.html.

"African-American Census Schedules Online," http://www.mindspring.com/~smothers/AACensus.htm.

"African-American Civil War Websites," http://ccharity.com/indexes/aacivilwar.htm.

"African American Composer Series," http://cwis.usc.edu/dept/News—Service/chronicle—html/1996.02.

"African-American Periodicals and Periodical Reference Materials," http://www.unc.edu/~bsemonch/blackpress.html.

"African American Genealogy," http://ourworld.compuserve.com/homepages/Cliff_m.

"African American History," http://www.msstate.edu/Archives/History/USA/Afro-Amer/afro.html.

"African Center," http://www.nubacom.com.

"African Diaspora," http://www.pitt.edu/~cedst10/.

"African Documents," http://www.halcyon.com/FWDP/africa.html.

"African Language Sites," http://polyglot.lss.wisc.edu/lss/lang/african.html.

"African Music and Dance," http://www.bmrc.berkeley.edu/people/ladzekpo.

"African Music Sources," http://www.matisse.net/~jplanet/ajmx//sources.htm.

"Africa Online," http://www.africaonline.com.

"African Recipes Home Page," http://www.africanrecipes.com.

"African Travel Gateway," http://africantravel.com/home.html.

"African Web Links: An Annotated Resource List," http://www.sas.upenn.edu/African_Studies/Home_Page.www_Links.html.

"African Wildlife News," http://www.awf.org/nf.ele.numbers.html.

"African Writers," http://www.africaonline.com/AfricaOnline/griotstalk/writers/series.html

"Africa:TourNet," http://wn.apc.org/mediatech/tourism/tn090072.htm.

"Altculture: Afrocentrism," http://www.pathfinder.com/altculture/aentries/a/afrocentrism.html.

"Amazing Grace, the Story of John Newton," http://www.wilsonweb.com/archive/misc/newton.htm.

"The Amistad Trial," http://leap.yale.edu/lclc/projects/ur/amistad.html.

"Arab Net," http://www.arab.net.

"Artists Against Racism," http://aar.vrx.net//.

Battle, Stafford L., and Rey O. Harris, *A Guide to the Internet and Only Services,* McGraw-Hill, 1997.

"Biracial Children," http://www.korealink.com/public/general/messages/2468.htm.

"Black Business Initiative—Black to Business," http://bbi.ns.ca/newsletter/index.html.

"Black Business Network," http://www.ibsa.io.org/bblm.htm.

"Black Enterprise Online," http://www.blackenterprise.com.

"Black Family Heritage," http://www.afrinet.net/~hallh/afrotalk/afroaug95/1894.hml.

"Black History," http://www.slip.net/~rigged/history.html.

"Black History Month: Let's Get Started," http://www.netnoir.com/spotlight/bhm/jbhm. html.

"Black Information Network World Wide Web," http://www.bin.com/musicent/sports/trotters/trotpix.htm.

"Black Periodical Literature Project," http://web-dubois.fas.harvard.edu/DuBois/Research/BPLP/BPLP.H.

"Black Pioneers," http://www.localnet.com/~adonis2/pioall.htm.

"Blackseek," http://www.blackweek.com/index.html.

"BlackSeek Black Business—Afro-Americans," http://www.blackseek.com.

"CLP Pennsylvania Department Resources in African American Genealogy," http://www.clpgh.org/CLP/Pennsylvania/oak_penna.32.html.

"The Complete Kwanzaa Celebration Basket," http://lainet3.lainet.com/~joejones/kwanzaa/htm.

"Conflict of Abolition and Slavery," http://www.loc.gov/exhibits/african/confli.html.

"Connections: Enslavement," http://asu.alasu.edu/academic/advstudies/41.html.

"Country-Specific Pages for Africa," http://www.sas.upenn.edu/African—Studies/Home—Page/Country.html.

"Department of Commerce Bureau of the Census on the African-American Population," http://fr.counterpoint.com8000/fr/1996/0610/ 00042.htm.

"Diaspora Art," http://www.diaspora.com/art.html.

"Documents in the NAACP Story," http://www.wh.org/naacp/visit.htm.

"Ebola Outbreaks," http://www.bocklabs.wics.edu/outbreak.html.

"Ebony/Jet Guide to Black Excellence Series," http://www.specialvideos.com/an/dbpage.pl/3721/yyx4654.116029.

"The Emancipation Proclamation," http://rain.org/~Karpeles/.

"The Emancipation Proclamation," http://www.accusd.edu/~sakkinen/abe10.html.

"The Emancipation Proclamation," http://www.winternet.com/~orion/text/emanproc.txt.

"Empowering Communities," http://www.usc.edu/Library/QF/diversity/communities.html.

"Engage, Empower, Educate," http://www.empower.la.ca.us/.

Erb, Jane, "Porgy and Bess," http://www.classicalnet/ ~music/comp.1st/works/gershwin/porgy&bess.html.

"Extremist Groups: The Ku Klux Klan," http://www.acsp.uic.edu/gangs/kkk/aka.shtml.

"The Faces of Science African Americans in the Sciences," http://www.lib.lsu.edu/lib/chem/display/faces.html.

"Freedom Black Military Experience," http://www.inform.umd.edu/ARHU/depts/History/ Freedom/bmepg.htm.

"Ghetto Education," http://www.sirius.com/~adisa/ ghetto.html.

"The Gullah Connection," http://www.afrinet.net/~ hallh/afrotalk/afrooct95/ 1090.html.

"Gullah People and Culture," http://www.tezcat. com/~ronald/gullah.html.

"The Harlem Renaissance," http://www.usc.edu/ Library/Ref/Ethnic/harlem.html.

"Healing Plants of Africa," http://sdearthtimes.com/ et0496et0496s11.html.

"The History of Apartheid in South Africa," http://xenon.stanford.edu/~cale/cs201/apartheid. hist.html.

"History of Black English," http://www.princeton. edu/~bclewis/blacktalk.html.

"History of Ebonics," http://www2.shore.net/~shai/ origins.html.

"The History of Kente Cloth," http://webusers. anet-chi.com/~midwest/history.html.

"The History of the British Abolition Movement," http://miavxl.muohio.edu/~aronowml/History.HTM.

"Hunger and Poverty," http://www.plattsburgh.edu/ legacy/hunger_thesis.html.

"HungerWeb," http://www.brown.edu/Departments/ World_Hunger_Program/.

"The Influence of Prominent Abolitionists," http:// www.loc.gov/exhibits/african/influ.html.

"Instruments of Apartheid," http://www.unp.ac.za/ UNPDepartments/politics/price4.htm.

"The Interracial Family and Social Alliance," http://www.flash.net/~mata9/ifsa.htm.

"Islam in America," http://www.colostate.edu/Orgs/ MSA/docs.iia.html.

"Jet Online," http://ebonymag.com/jethome.html.

"Johnson Publishing Company," http://ebonymag. com/jpcindex.html.

"Kwanzaa," http://www.dca.net/~areid/kwanzaa.htm.

"Kwanzaa Bazaar," http://shops.net/shops/Kwanzaa/ item-5.html.

"Kwanzaa Links," http://new.melanet.com/kwanzaa/ links.html.

"Marine World Africa USA," http://www.freerun.com/napavalley/outdoor/ marinewo/marinewo.html.

"Motown Home Page," http://motown.com/motown/.

"Multiethnic Presence," http://ils.unc.edu/inls110/ projects/brisj/multieth.html.

"Musical Instruments of Africa," http://www. africaonline.com.

"Musical Instruments of Africa," http://www.eyneer. com/World/Af/Instuments/index.html.

"Northeast Abolitionists," http://www.unl.edu/ tcweb/altc/staffpages/.page3.html.

"The North Star: Tracing the Underground Railroad," http://www.ugar.org/.

"Office of International Criminal Justice," http:// www.acsp.uic.edu/.

"Olympic Black Women," http://www.com-stock. com/dave/plowden.htm.

"OUPUSA: Mutiny on the Amistad," http://www.oup- usa.org/gcdocs/gc_0195038290.html.

"Pygmies: Hunter Gatherers in the Jungle," http:// www.ouottherenews.com/congo/glossary/pygmies. htm.

"R&B, Hip Hop, Rap Music Page," http://www.cs. ucr.edu/~marcus/music.html.

"Rap.Org," http://www.rap.org.

"Religions of the World: African Religions, http://jupiter.rowan.edu/~banner/afrterm.html.

"RRC: Archives," http://www.kaiwan.com/rockrap/archive/index.html.

"Sickle Cell Anemia," http://;www.kumc.edu/gec/support/sickle_c.html.

"Sickle Cell: Questions and Answers," http://www.medaccess.com/h_child/siclde/sa_03.htm.

"Slavery in America," http://ils.unc.edu/ingham/index.html.

"South America's Threatened Wildlife," http://www.infoweb.co.za/enviro/ewtbook/page6.htm.

"The Thinker, National of Islam," http://www-leland.stanford.edu/group/thinker/v2/v2n3/NO/Backg.

"Third Person, First Person: Slave Voices," http://scriptorium,lib.duke.edu/slavery/.

"Tolerance," http://home.fia.net/~kjmoros/index.html.

"Tolerance," http://www.igc.apc.org/iearn/projects/tolerance.html.

"Ujamaa Fashions," http://shops.net/shop/Ujamaa—Fashions/.

"University of Texas at Austin Center for African and African-American Studies," http://www.utexas.edu/depts/cadds/.

"University of Michigan Program on Poverty and Social Welfare Policy," http://www.umich.edu/~socwk/poverty/index.html.

"Voice of Africa," http://www.scry.com/ayer/AFRO-AM/4401185.htm.

"Wave Your Banner Project," http://www.artsednet.getty.edu.

"Webcrawler Guide Travel: Africa Travel Guides," http://webcrawler.com/select/trav.africa.html.

"World History Archives: History of Southern Africa in General," http://www.hartford-hwp.com/archives/37/index-1.html.

"Yoruba Religion and Myth," http://www.stg.brown. edu/projects/hypertext/landow/post/nigeria/yorubarel.html.

"zZounds: African Musical Instruments," http://www.zzounds.com/WorldMusicCenter/Africa/.

Miscellaneous Sources

Abyssinian Vibrations Culture Shop and Gallery
23 West Broughton Street
Savannah, Georgia 31401
912-231-1227

African Fabrics
Bukom Textiles
2680 Godby Road
College Park, Georgia 30349
phone: 404-766-0417
fax: 404-478-5761

African International Market
3 West Fourth Street
Wilmington, Delaware 19801
302-427-2662

African Market Place
4978 Holt Boulevard
Montclair, California 91763
909-399-9310
African Pride

Underground Atlanta
88 Lower Alabama Street, Suite 194
Atlanta, Georgia 30303
404-523-6520

American Photographic Artisans Guild
212 Monroe
P. O. Box 699
Port Clinton, Ohio 43452
phone: 419-732-3290
e-mail: allynn@dcache.net

Apple Book Center
7900 West Outer Drive at Southfield Road
Detroit, Michigan 48235
phone: 313-255-5221
fax: 313-255-5230
e-mail: Apple001@aol.com

Atlanta International Market
Woodruff Park
56 Peachtree Street

Atlanta, Georgia 30303
404-521-3389

Black American Cinema Society
3617 Montclair Street
Los Angeles, California 90018
phone: 213-737-3292
fax: 213-737-2842

Black Photographers of California
107 Santa Barbara Plaza
Los Angeles, California 90008
phone: 213-294-9024

By Word of Mouth Storytelling Guild
P. O. Box 56
Frankford, Missouri 63441
phone: 800-875-9885
fax: 314-784-2364

Detroit Free Press Black History Month Contest
Gregory Huskisson, Assistant Managing Editor
321 West Lafayette Boulevard
Detroit, Michigan 48226
phone: 313-222-5104
fax: 313-222-5981

Journey to the Motherland (trivia board game)
Saba International
231 Peachtree Street N. E.
Atlanta, Georgia
phone: 770-242-9678 or 800-346-4893

National Association of Black Storytellers
P. O. Box 67722
Baltimore, Maryland 21215
phone and fax: 410-947-1117

Oyingbo Market
6580 Ager Road
Hyattsville, Maryland 20782
301-422-2223

Partners Book Distributing Inc.
2325 Jarco Drive
Holt, Michigan 48842
800-336-3137

Rounder (Music)
One Camp Street
North Cambridge, Massachusetts 02140
phone: 800-443-4727
fax: 617-868-8769

e-mail: Info@rounder.com
website: http://www.rounder.com

Periodicals

African American Review
Indiana State University
Department of English
Terre Haute, Indiana 47809
phone: 812-237-2968
fax: 812-237-4382

American Visions
1156 Fifteenth Street NW, Suite 615
Washington , D.C. 20005
phone: 202-496-9593
fax: 202-496-9851

Black Child Magazine
P. O. Box 12048
Atlanta, Georgia 30355
phone: 404-364-9195
fax: 404-364-9965

The Black Collegian
140 Carondelet Street
New Orleans, Louisiana 70130
phone: 504-523-0154
fax: 504-523-0271
e-mail: jim@black-collegian.com
website: http://www.black-collegian.com

Black Diaspora Magazine
298 Fifth Avenue, 7th Floor
New York, New York 10001
phone: 212-268-8348
fax: 212-268-83870

Black Elegance
475 Park Avenue, South
New York, New York 10016
phone: 212-689-2830
fax: 212-889-7933

Black Enterprise
130 Fifth Avenue
New Yori, New York 10011
212-243-8000

Black Theatre Directory
P. O. Box 11502
Fisher Building Station

Detroit, Michigan 48211
phone: 419-372-2350
fax: 419-372-2350

Black Women's Voice
1001 G Street NW, Suite 800
Washington, D.C. 20006
phone: 628-0015
fax: 202-785-8733

Ebony Magazine
820 South Michigan Avenue
Chicago, Illinois 60605
312-322-9200

Emerge
1 BET Plaza
1900 West Place NE
Washington, D.C. 20018
phone: 202-608-2093
fax: 212-608-2598

Homefront, the Family Magazine
P. O. Box 60033
Savannah, Georgia 31420

Journal of Negro History
1407 Fourteenth Street NW
Washington, D.C. 20005
phone: 202-667-2822
fax: 202-387-9802

Journal of the National Council for Black Studies
Ohio State University
208 Mount Hall
1050 Carmack Road
Columbus, Ohio 43210
phone: 614-292-1035
fax: 614-292-7363

On the Issues
97-77 Queens Boulevard
Forest Hills, New York 11374
phone: 718-275-6020
fax: 718-997-1206

Philanthropic Foundations and Charities

Christian Children's Fund
P. O. Box 96005

Washington, D.C 20090-6005
800-776-6767

National Coalition for the Homeless
1612 K Street, NW, #1004
Washington, D.C. 20006
phone: 202-775-1322
fax: 202-775-1316
e-mail: nch@ari.net
http://nch.ari.net/

SELFHELP Crafts U.S. and International
704 Main Street
P.O. Box 500
Akron, Pennsylvania 17501-0500
717-859-4971

Thurgood Marshall Scholarship Fund
P. O. Box 44251
Atlanta, Georgia 30336-1251
800-444-4483

UNICEF
1 Children's Boulevard
P. O. Box 182233
Chattanooga, Tennessee 37422
800-553-1200

United Negro College Fund
8260 Willow Oak Corporation Drive
Fairfax:, Virginia 22031
800-3331-2244

Publishers

African American Images
9204 Commercial, Suite 308
Chicago, Illinois 60617
phone: 800-552-1991
fax: 312-375-9349

African Books Collective Ltd.
The Jam Factory
27 Park End Street
Oxford, OX1 1HU, England
phone: 44-01865-726686
fax: 44-01865-793298
e-mail: abc@dial.pipex.com

Africa World
Princess Road, Suites D-F

Lawrenceville, New Jersey 08648
609-844-9583

Afro Resources, Inc.
P. O. Box 192
Temple Hills, Maryland 20748
301-894-3855

Black Classic Press
P. O. Box 13414
Baltimore, Maryland 21203
410-358-0980

Crabtree Publishing Company
Department 2QQ
350 Fifth Avenue, Suite 3308
New York, New York 10118
phone: 800-387-7650
fax: 800-355-7166

Curriculum Associates, Inc.
5 Esquire Road
P. O. Box 2001
North Billerica, Massachusetts 01862-0901
phone: 800-225-0248
fax: 800-336-1158
e-mail: cainfo@curricassoc.com
website: http://222.curricassoc.com/cainfo/

Discovery Enterprises, Ltd.
31 Laurelwood Drive
Carlisle, Massachusetts 01741
phone: 800-729-1720
fax: 508-287-5402
(curriculum materials, plays, poetry, biographies, monographs)

Dover Publications, Inc.
31 East 2nd Street
Mineola, New York 11501
(art books, coloring books, reprints, craft patterns)

Empak Enterprises
212 East Ohio Street
Chicago, ILlinois 60611
312-642-3434

Facts on File
460 Park Avenue South
New York, New York 10016
(general reference, current affairs, subscription service, CD-ROMs)

Greenwood Publishing Group
88 Post Road West
P. O. Box 5007
Westport, Connecticut 06881
phone: 203-226-3571
fax: 203-222-1502
website: http://www.greenwood.com
(general and scholarly reference, trade books)

Jackdaw Publications
Golden Owl Publishing
P. O. Box 503
Amawalk, New York 10501
phone: 800-789-0022
fax: 914-962-1134
(learning packets, posters, documents)

G. O. G. Enterprises
Natalie and Ron Daise
P. O. Box 2092
Beaufort, South Carolina 29901
803-523-9748
(lectures, videos, books, readings, songs)

HarperAudio Caedman
10 East 53rd Street
New York, New York, 10022
phone: 212-207-7000
fax: 212-207-7559
(audiocassettes)

Just Us Books, Inc.
356 Glenwood Avenue
East Orange, New Jersey 07017
201-676-4345

Kitchen Table Women of Color Press
P. O. Box 404920
Brooklyn, New York 11240
718-935-1082

Knowledge Unlimited
P. O. Box 52
Madison, Wisconsin 53701
phone: 800-356-233
fax: 800-618-1570
e-mail: ku-mail@ku.com
website: http://www.ku.com
(books, posters, videos, maps, curriculum kits)

Ladyslipper Music Catalog
P. O. Box 3124-R
Durham, North Carolina 27715
phone: 800-634-6044

e-mail: orders@ladyslipper.org
website: http://www.ladyslipper.org

McFarland & Co., Inc.
Box 611
Jefferson, North Carolina 28640
phone: 910-246-4460
fax: 910-246-5018
http://www.mcfarlandpub.com
(general reference, trade books)

Millbrook Press
2 Old New Milford Road
Brookfield, Connecticut 06804
phone: 800-462-4703
fax: 203-740-2526
(elementary and middle school reference)

Multicultural Media
RR 3., Box 6655
Granger Road
Barre, Vermont 05641
phone: 802-223-1294
fax: 802-229-1834
e-mail: mcm@multiculturalmedia.com
website: http://www.multiculturalmedia.com
(music videos, CDs, anthologies)

National Archives
Trust Fund Board
Washington, D. C. 20408
(genealogical aids)
National Women's History Project
7738 Bell Road, Deptartment P
Windsor, California 95492
707-838-6000
(posters, videos, books, curriculum units, teacher training, archives)

New Day Press/KARAMU
2355 East 89th Street
Cleveland, Ohio 44106
216-795-7070

Opposing Viewpoints
Greenhaven Press
P. O. Box 289009
San Diego, California 92198
phone: 800-231-5163
(print material on controversial or difficult issues)

Really Good Stuff
Cinema Center
Botsford, Connecticut 06404

phone: 800-366-1920
fax: 203-268-1796
(posters, bookmarks, T-shirts)

Recorded Books
270 Skipjack Road
Prince Frederick, Maryland 20678
phone: 800-638-1304
fax: 410-535-5499
e-mail: recordedbok@aol.com
(full-text audiocassettes of classic and popular titles)

Samuel French, Inc.
45 West 25th Street
New York, New York 10010
phone: 212-206-8990
fax: 212-206-1429
(plays, monologues, scenes, dialect tapes, anthologies, melodramas, posters)

Smithsonian Folkways
955 L'Enfant Plaza, Suite 2600
Washington, D. C. 20560
http://www.si.edu/folkways
(recordings, collections, spoken word, ethnographic videos)

Social Studies School Service
10200 Jefferson Boulevard, Room 19
P. O. Box 802
Culver City, California 90232
phone: 800-421-4246
fax: 310-839-2249
(activity packs, art prints, books, CDs, maps, popsters, reproducible masters, software, sound filmstrips, transparencies, videos, workbooks)

Teacher's Discovery
2741 Paldan Drive
Auburn Hills, Michigan 48326
phone: 800-583-6454
fax: 810-340-7212

Third World Press
P. O. Box 19730
Chicago, Illinois 60619
312-615-0700

William Morrow & Co., Inc.
39 Plymouth Street
Fairfield, New Jersey 07007
phone: 800-843-9389
fax: 201-227-6849

Resource Centers

African-American Historical Association
P. O. Box 115268
Atlanta, Georgia 30310
phone: 404-344-7405
fax: 404-523-4672

African American Museum
1765 Crawford Road
Cleveland, Ohio 44106
phone: 216-791-1700
fax: 216-791-1774

Afro-American Historical and Genealogical Society
P. O. Box 73086
Washington, D.C. 20056
phone: 202-234-5350
fax: 202-829-8970

Afro-American Historical Society Museum
1841 Kennedy Boulevard
Jersey City, New Jersey 07305
phone: 201-547-5262
fax: 201-547-5392

American Craft Museum
40 West 53rd Street
New York, New York 10019
phone: 212-956-3535
fax: 212-459-0926

Bethune Museum and Archives for Black Women's History
1318 Vermont Avenue, NW
Washington, D.C. 20005
phone: 202-332-1233

Black Resources Information Coordinating Services
614 Howard Avenue
Tallahassee, Florida 32304
phone: 904-576-7522

Black Theatre Network
P. O. Box 11502
Fisher building Station
Detroit, Michigan 48211
phone: 419-372-2350
fax: 419-372-2350

Foundation for Research in the Afro-American Creative Arts

P. O. Drawer 1
Cambria Heights, New York 11411

JustCause
P. O. Box 170015
San Francisco, California 94117
http://www.webcom/~justcaus/

Museum of African-American History
315 East Warren Avenue
Detroit, Michigan 48201
phone: 313-494-5800
fax: 313-494-5855

Museum of Afro-American History
46 Joy Street
Boston, Massachusetts 02114
phone: 617-742-1854
fax: 617-742-2589

Museum of Tolerance
9786 West Pico Boulevard
Los Angeles, California 980075
http://www.wiesenthal.com/mot/

National Association of Negro Musicians
11551 South Laflin Street
Chicago, Illinois 60643
phone: 312-568-3818
fax: 312-779-1325

National Council of Negro Women
1001 G Street NW, Suite 800
Washington, D.C. 20006
phone: 628-0015
fax: 202-785-8733

National Museum of Women in the Arts
1250 New York Avenue, NW
Washington, D.C. 20005
phone: 2020-783-5000
fax: 202-393-3235

National Women's History Collection
Museum of American History
Smithsonian Institution
Washington, D.C. 20560
phone: 202-357-2008

Negro Leagues Baseball Museum
Lincoln Building
1601 East 18th Street
Kansas City, Missouri 64108

phone: 816-221-1920
fax: 816-221-8424

Women's Heritage Museum
870 Market Street, #547
San Francisco, California 94102
415-433-3026

Women's Rights National Historical Park
P. O. Box 70
Seneca Falls, New York 13148
315-568-2991

Video Distributors

Films for the Humanities & Sciences
P. O. Box 2053
Princeton, New Jersey 08543
phone: 800-257-5126
fax: 609-275-3767

First Run/Icarus Films
153 Waverly Place
New York, New York 10014
phone: 800-876-1710
fax: 212-989-7649
e-mail: FRIF@echonyc.com
website: http://www.echonyc.com/~frif/

Home Film Festival
P. O. Box 2032

Scranton, Pennsylvania 18501
phone: 800-258-3456

Library Video Company
P. O. Box 580
Wynnewood, Pennsylvania 19096
phone: 800-843-3620
fax: 610-645-4040

Movies Unlimited
3015 Darnell Road
Philadelphia, Pennsylvania 19154
phone: 800-4-MOVIES
fax: 215-637-2350

MPI Educational Video
16101 South 108th Avenue
Orland Pork, Illinois 60462
phone: 708-460-0555
fax: 708-460-0175
(current events, history, speeches, social issues)

PBS Home Video
1320 Braddock Place
Alexandria, Virginia 22314
phone: 800-645-4PBS
fax: 703-739-8131
website: http://www.pbs.org/shop

Women Make Movies, Inc.
462 Broadway, Suite 500
New York, New York 10013
phone: 212-925-0606
fax: 212-925-2052

Entry Index

Age/Group Level Index

Middle School (11-14)

High School (15-18)

Adults

General Audience

Budget Index

$25-$50

$50-$75

$75-$100

More Than $100

Subject Index